THE
RISE AND FALL
OF THE
BRITISH EMPIRE

By the same author

Crimea: The War With Russia in Contemporary Photographs
The Savage Wars: British Campaigns in Africa 1870–1920
Mutiny: Mutinies in British and Commonwealth Forces 1797–1956
Imperial Rearguard: The Last Wars of Empire
The Golden Warrior: The Life and Legend of Lawrence of Arabia
The Iron Duke: A Military Biography of the Duke of Wellington
Imperial Warrior: The Life and Times of Field Marshal Viscount Allenby

THE RISE AND FALL OF THE BRITISH EMPIRE

Lawrence James

LITTLE, BROWN AND COMPANY

A *Little, Brown* Book

First published in Great Britain in 1994
by Little, Brown and Company

10 9 8 7 6 5

A CIP catalogue record for this book
is available from the British Library

ISBN 0 316 90506 2

Typeset by M Rules
Printed and bound in Great Britain by
Clays Ltd, St Ives plc

Little, Brown and Company (UK)
Brettenham House
Lancaster Place
London WC2E 7EN

To the memory of Vivian and Tim Williams

Contents

· Contents ·

· Contents ·

Maps

Acknowledgements

I would first like to thank my wife, Mary, for her encouragement, patience and goodwill during the preparation and writing of this book. Thanks are also due to my sons, Edward and Henry, who rendered much valuable assistance. Help, suggestions and valuable advice were also provided by John Adamson, Dr Ian Bradley, Major Euan Campbell, Professor Fred Crawford, John Dishman, Dr Martin Edmonds, David Elder, Dr Nancy Follett, Professor Ray Furness, R.S.M. Joe Mahady, John Hailwood, Michael Halsey, Michael and Veronica Hodges, Mark Hunter, Linda Silverman (who provided most of the illustrations), Andrew Lownie, Dr John Mackenzie, Sheila McIlwraith, Professor Souleiman Moussa, Professor Alan Paterson, Liz Pert-Davies, Professor Jeffrey Richards, Dr and Mrs Nick Roe, Alan Samson, Alex Sinclair, Dr Martin Stephen, Brian and Kate Waldy, Andrew Williams, the late Vivian Williams, Andrew Wille, and Oswald and Jan Wynd. I am also indebted to Mrs Gascoigne and all the staff at the University of St Andrews Library for services far beyond the call of duty. I would also like to thank the staff at the National Library of Scotland, the Scottish Record Office, the Public Record Office, the Imperial War Museum (in particular the photographic department) and the National Army Museum for their forbearance and help.

Quotations from Crown Copyright records appear by permission of the Controller of Her Majesty's Stationery Office.

Introduction

Some time early in the 1980s I undertook a brief tour of what had once been the commercial powerhouse of the British empire. By then, that complex of wharves and solid brick warehouses which stood along the north shore of the Thames was derelict. Nonetheless, the overall effect was impressive, and the cast-iron street signs (Jamaica Street, Ceylon Street) advertised the sources of past prosperity. The abandoned docks of London and Liverpool and Bristol are among the grander monuments to Britain's moment of empire and world power.

There are others: the shells of Lancashire cotton mills which spun yarns for India; the shipyards of the Clyde and the Tyne which built steamers to carry Britain's trade and the men-o'-war which protected it; and the country houses of the merchants and nabobs-turned-country-squires who raked in the profits. One of the latter, Sir Charles Cockerell, having made a fortune in India at the end of the eighteenth century, had his mansion, Sezincote, built in a style which combines the novelties of the Prince Regent's Brighton Pavilion with Indian motifs, including a dome of the sort which would have been set over a mosque. The Cotswold landscape around the house is enhanced with ornamental gardens with an Indian shrine and a bridge decorated with Brahmin bulls. Bringing India to Gloucestershire was a nice reminder that imperialism was a two-way process.

Human memorials of the empire are abundant. David Livingstone, one hand resting on his revolver and the other clasping a Bible, overlooks

Prince's Street, Edinburgh. Walk up towards the castle and one is confronted by embattled, and, thanks to weathering, gaunt stone Highlanders, who form their countrymen's monument to the Boer War. Churches and cathedrals are draped with dusty, threadbare regimental ensigns embroidered with exotic names such as 'Chillianwala' and 'Tel-el-Kebir', and the men who died in these and other battles are often commemorated nearby in marble and brass. Pub signs celebrate imperial heroes, and street names conquests and conquerors. In the northern suburbs of Southampton I once saw a Khartoum Road and an Omdurman Road, and in the small West Riding town of Crosshills, a Rhodesia Road. All, to judge by the houses built along them, date from the beginning of the century.

The physical impact of the empire on Britain is easy to see, the mental is less obvious. Readers may detect in my chapters on the empire and the people the origins of codes of behaviour and outlook which still hold some sway, though less so than thirty or forty years ago when the empire was still in existence. I have tried to show that possession of an empire profoundly influenced the ways in which the British thought of themselves and the rest of the world. The British character was changed by the empire, and this is important. It encouraged a sense of superiority, which is also a feature of another former imperial power France, that frequently bordered on downright xenophobia. It also fostered racial arrogance. And yet at the same time, deeply-rooted liberal and evangelical ideals produced a powerful sense of imperial duty and mission. The empire existed to civilise and uplift its subjects, or so its champions claimed.

They had to, for the British were never entirely easy with the idea of territorial empire. From the seventeenth century, and with considerable official encouragement, the British were taught to be proud of their laws, individual freedoms, and elected government. But, many asked, were the rights of the British exclusive, or could they be exported and shared by everyone under Britain's rule? This question dogged the empire throughout its history and, given that at crucial moments the answer was 'yes', proved to be its eventual undoing. In looking at the eighty years, roughly from the mid-1880s to the mid-1960s, when the empire reached its zenith and then declined, I have endeavoured to examine a related issue, how the British saw their empire. During this period, Britain became a democracy and so the empire could not have been sustained without the general approval of the British people. This is vital both in explaining imperial growth and imperial decline.

Ideas alone did not make the empire. Its story is the sum of the lives of the men and women who built and ruled it. Some achieved greatness, making headlines and in time finding themselves heroes whose deeds became schoolroom reading. Their characters, carefully sifted of all baser qualities, became models for future generations. The superheroes of empire were a mixed bag. There were the conventional but brilliant commanders and statesmen such as Pitt, Wolfe, Rodney, Nelson and Wellington who did their duty according to lofty principles, and were respected accordingly. There were also the wayward who, shipped to a foreign land, discovered hidden energies and vision. Clive was the first, and then Gordon, who, like so many empire-builders, imagined himself the agent of a Divine Providence which had singled out Britain as the maker of a better world. Britain's imperial destiny was also Rhodes's lodestar, but it was clouded by ambition and ruthlessness. Lastly, for the twentieth century there was Lawrence of Arabia, meretricious but fundamentally decent, adding a dash of lustre to the imperial sunset.

Making an empire and setting one's personal stamp on it were more glamorous activities than dismantling it. No one emerged from imperial disengagement with the romantic allure of a Clive or a Lawrence. Mountbatten came close, but he was a shallow figure who owed more to his royal attachments (between the death of William IV and the late 1980s the royal family enjoyed unprecedented reverence) than any outstanding talent. Rather, it was Attlee, Macleod and Macmillan who were, I believe, the real heroes of imperial retreat which they supervised with considerable political adroitness. Unlike France's, Portugal's or Russia's, Britain's empire did not dissolve in tears.

At every stage in this survey, I have looked at the thoughts and actions of many lesser figures. Most important perhaps are the millions who took part in the British diaspora, that process which took colonists to North America, Australasia and South Africa. On this subject, I have been as careful as possible to sidestep the quagmire of post-imperial guilt, that peculiar *angst* which has troubled the British and American intelligentsia for the past thirty or so years. Wherever possible, I have avoided joining in those battles between armies of the night who contend over the rights and wrongs of empires. History cannot be unwritten or written in the subjunctive, and the wholesale application of late twentieth-century values distorts the past and makes it less comprehensible. I have, therefore, left conquerors and colonists to speak for themselves, aware that their authentic voices may sometimes grate on today's sensibilities.

What matters most today is that the British empire transformed the world. What it has now become is in considerable part the consequence of three hundred years of British overseas expansion. The present day demography, economy and political life of North America and much of Asia, the Middle East, Africa and the Pacific owes much to former British rule and influence. English is the most widely spoken global language, and the governance, everyday lives and habits of mind of hundreds of millions of men and women have been shaped by prolonged contact with Britain and its values. For better or worse, the modern, post-imperial world is the product of that age of empires which extended from the early sixteenth to the early twentieth centuries. Britain got most, in every sense, from this surge of European expansion.

I have tried to explain how, why and with what result, and I hope that I have done so with a certain degree of dispassion. I have written in the knowledge that the complex legacy of the British empire remains. Its physical and psychological impact was enormous everywhere, including in Britain. That this country is now a multi-racial nation is a direct consequence of its having once been an imperial one. For this reason alone, it is worth looking closely at the making and nature of the empire, the more so since its history and that of its creators is being excised from school syllabuses. What I have written will, I hope, make its past more understandable to all those who are its inheritors.

PART ONE

---❖---

EXCELLENT
OPPORTUNITIES
1600–89

1

My New-Found-Land: North America

During the summer of 1605 London's theatregoers were diverted by a new play, *Eastwood Ho*, performed in Blackfriars by a troop of boy actors calling themselves the Children of Her Majesty's Revels. It had been written in some haste by George Chapman, Ben Jonson and John Marston and was a satire rich in topical allusions, some of which were directed against the Scots and earned Jonson the displeasure of the new king, James I. The speed of the play's creation owed much, if not everything, to the authors' desire to exploit the current public excitement generated by the Virginia venture. This project to found a North American colony was a source of intense speculation, both intellectual and financial.

Three of the central characters, Sir Petronel Flash, an impoverished and witless gentleman, Quicksilver, an idle apprentice, and Security, a devious moneylender, have conspired to collect funds for an expedition to Virginia where they expect to find gold. Security, on hearing from Quicksilver that the money has been secreted aboard Flash's ship, is beside himself with excitement:

> Now a frank gale of wind go with him, Master Frank, we have too few such knight adventurers. Who would not sell away competent certainties, to purchase, with any danger, excellent uncertainties? Your true knight venturer ever does it.

Later, when the would-be adventurers gather for a pre-embarkation drinking bout, they are entranced by Captain Seagull's description of the wealth of the Virginian Indians:

> Why, man, all their dripping pans and their chamber pots are pure gold: and all the chains, with which they chain up their streets, are massy gold; all the prisoners they take are fettered in gold; and for rubies and diamonds, they go forth on holidays and gather 'em by the seashore, to hang on their children's coats . . .

This was a parody of the extravagant claims made less than ten years earlier by Sir Walter Raleigh, who had promised England riches and power far in excess of those enjoyed by Spain in return for investment in an expedition to uncover El Dorado, a treasure house of precious metals somewhere deep in the Guianan jungle. Seagull's hyperbole echoed Raleigh's and no doubt amused the audience. There may have been laughter too at Security's praise of 'knight adventurers', bold spirits who were prepared to take high risks. Crossing the seas in search of fortune was a fitting activity for a gentleman and equal in virtue to the pursuit of honour on the battlefield. The point was made by Thomas Drayton in his 'To the Virginian Voyage', written in celebration of the colonists' first voyage in 1607:

> *You brave Heroique Minds,*
> *Worthy your Countries Name,*
> *That Honour still pursue,*
> *Goe, and subdue.*
> *Whilst loyt'ring Hinds*
> *Lurke here at home, with shame.*

Such sentiments, in various forms, had been the staple of a handful of colonial propagandists for the past thirty years. The most persuasive had been Richard Hakluyt, an Oxford graduate, whose purpose had been to awaken his countrymen to what he considered their divinely ordained national duty as colonisers. His *Principal Navigations*, first published in 1598, was an extensive recital of all the voyages undertaken by Englishmen and was intended to demonstrate the existence of a long and noble tradition of overseas enterprise. By revealing what had been achieved in the past, Hakluyt hoped to enkindle in his contemporaries a sense of destiny which would impel them to found colonies and penetrate distant oceans in search of trade.

Hakluyt's vision of an expansionist England accorded with the aggressive policies of an influential group of courtiers and councillors, including the Earl of Leicester, Sir Francis Walsingham and Raleigh, all Hispanophobes and passionate anti-Catholics. They were willing to support colonisation projects as a means of damaging Spain and, in the case of a 1580 scheme for a settlement of Newfoundland, as a way of removing potentially subversive Catholics from England. None of these plans came to anything; the minute and under-funded settlements placed on Roanoke Island and Newfoundland during the 1580s soon withered.

One reason for the collapse of these enterprises was the concentration of national energies and resources on the conflict with Spain. Moreover, the largely private-enterprise seaborne war against Spain satisfied those with a taste for glory and quick profits. It attracted sharks like Sir Francis Drake and plenty of minnows who also fared well. Consider George White, a Dorset mariner and owner of the thirty-five-ton *Catherine of Weymouth* that was valued at £89 and armed with two falcons (three-pounder cannon) and two falconets (two pounders). In 1590–1, the *Catherine* captured three Portuguese Brazilmen which with their cargoes were worth £3,600. Encouraged by his success, White sold the *Catherine* and invested in a larger vessel with which he took another Brazilman valued at £4,200 and an East Indiaman crammed with Chinese silk, gems and cochineal.[1]

White and the other Elizabethan sea dogs had turned a public emergency to private advantage. They belonged to a well-established English tradition that stretched back to the Hundred Years War against France during which aristocratic commanders had fought for royal wages and profits from ransoms and plunder. Soldiers and sailors who went overseas to fight did so in the expectation that they might return richer. A popular life of Drake, published in 1628, urged the youth of 'this Dull or Effeminate Age to follow his noble steps for Gold and Silver'. Many did for the next two hundred or so years; a strong cord whose fibres were greed and fearlessness linked the Elizabethan sea rover, the eighteenth-century naval captain hungry for prize money and the early Victorian soldier, for whom the storming of an Indian city offered the chance of loot.

Men of this temper, and there were plenty of them kicking their heels in England after the end of the Spanish War in 1604, would have been easily seduced by Captain Seagull's image of Virginia as a land of precious minerals. It was not, and those who dreamed of instant fortune were quickly disappointed, like the 'divers gentlemen of fashion' who returned home from the new colony of Bermuda in 1613 in disgust after having been asked to cut down trees and build a wooden fort.[2] Opportunities for such creatures came forty years later with the onset of the intermittent wars against the Netherlands, Spain and France for the control of colonies and oceans.

In *Eastwood Ho* Security had described the proposed plantations in North America as 'excellent uncertainties'. It was an ambiguous expression that may have made investors in the Virginia Company uneasy, bearing in mind the history of previous ventures. There was, however, some comfort to be drawn from the fact that the new enterprise, licensed by James I in 1607, was enthusiastically backed by parliament. More substantial reassurance as to its prospects came from the knowledge that its finances were carefully managed and that its future profitability could be calculated on the basis of sound economic arguments.

A prospectus issued in 1620 promised that the expanding settlements on the Chesapeake Bay would, in time, give Britain a self-sufficiency in materials which had hitherto been imported at a great cost to the country. The North American plantations would replace Scandinavia as a source of tar and timber for ship-building. The colony would also provide the mother country with 'The Wines, Fruit and Salt of France and Spain' and 'the silks of Persia and Italy'. Persuaded by such arguments investors, who included noblemen, courtiers, civil servants, country squires (details of the company's activities were broadcast in the shires by London newssheets) and merchants, subscribed £200,000 in thirteen years.

The Virginia Company's promoters and the early settlers had imagined that the entire coastline of North America from Newfoundland south to the Carolinas lay in a temperate zone that enjoyed 'a moderate equality of heat and cold'.[3] At the same time, since the Chesapeake Bay colony shared a common latitude with Spain it was assumed that it would provide an abundance of Mediterranean crops. Vine dressers were among the first ashore and even as late as 1620 plans were in hand for planting olive groves. By then everyone involved should have known better. It was soon discovered that the region lay within a malarial belt and that new arrivals required 'seasoning' during the hot summer months when, like timber, they sweated profusely. Winters were bitterly cold and during that of

1609–10 the disheartened wished themselves 'in England without their limbs' and begging on the streets rather than in Virginia. Within a dozen years the company was near to bankruptcy and in 1624 its settlements were taken over by the crown.

Tobacco rescued Virginia and made it thrive in a manner that astonished the colonists and the government. The first tentative planting of imported South American tobacco plants had been undertaken in 1617. It was a success and began a revolution that transformed the infant colony and the British economy. At the time, tobacco was still a luxury and smoking the indulgence of the rich, some of whom would pay as much as £2 a pound for the prized Guianan leaf. Mass imports from the Virginian plantations changed this and by mid-century the retail price had plummeted to one shilling (5p) a pound. Smoking became a universal habit embraced by every class in Europe. The opening up of what proved to be an unlimited market for a drug which both calmed and stimulated was the chance result of overproduction in the 1630s. By 1700, Britain imported 13 million pounds of Virginian tobacco for domestic consumption and a further 25 million for re-export to Europe, figures that rose steadily throughout the next century.

The Virginian tobacco boom had a profound impact on Britain and its economy. Viewing the colony's prosperity during the 1620s, one commentator perceptively observed that 'Spain is more damaged by the King's peace than by the Queen's war'.[4] His logic was simple and would be repeated by later advocates of colonial expansion. The wealth which flowed from Virginia contributed to that of Britain and its power grew accordingly. In terms of government revenue the imposts on tobacco raised £421,000 between 1699 and 1701, 20 per cent of all customs duties. By this time, Virginia and its tobacco-producing neighbour Maryland had a population of 92,000 and was a major market for British manufactured goods.

In terms of the generation of wealth, Virginia overshadowed the smaller colonies of Newfoundland, established in 1610, and those under the control of the Massachusetts Bay Company, founded in 1620. In all there was a gap between expectation and reality. A 1611 report of one early settler in Newfoundland, written to drum up further investment, described the tiny colony as 'very honest, peaceful and hopeful, and very likely to be profitable'. A visitor the previous year wrote home that 'this savage country of Newfoundland gives men little content but only cruel hard labour hoping to make the best content they can have with small profit.' The attraction of this bleak land lay in the cod fishing banks offshore which had drawn English fishing fleets since the 1520s. The cod were caught (at first with hook and line) then salted, dried and smoked and, with barrels of their oil, were shipped to the ports of the Iberian Peninsula to be traded for local products. By 1620, 300 ships visited the region annually and, according to a petition for naval protection, employed 10,000 sailors 'thereby relieving 20,000 more people of the western parts of England, who are wholly dependent on them for their existence'.[5]

Further south, the Puritan settlers of the fledgling New England colonies faced an equally unkind land. They had crossed the Atlantic ignorant of the local climate which they imagined to be the same as England's. They were soon disabused and in 1629 one wrote mournfully that 'from the middest of October to the middest of May there is a sad face of winter upon all this land' and noted that many were dying from the 'intolerable cold'.

The death rate was high, but the Puritans were psychologically prepared for it, and for the grinding work of clearing woodlands, ploughing and sowing crops. They were men and women with a profound sense of the working of God's will who had voluntarily withdrawn from England where their Calvinist creed attracted official mistrust and, during the 1620s and 1630s, systematic persecution by the state-sponsored Church of England. Their exodus in the next decade was an escape from a spiritually uncongenial world and a manifestation of that Divine Providence which they believed was actively engaged in the affairs of men, promoting some and hindering others. Their settlements were a mark of God's favour on His chosen people, a view held by the Massachusetts Bay Company's governor, John Winthrop. In 1634, having heard reports of an epidemic among the local Indians, he wrote in his diary that 'they are all dead of the small pox so as the Lord cleareth our title to what we possess'.

By 1660 the largely Puritan New England settlements had a population of about 30,000, many of whom were refugees who had challenged and then fled from the rigid orthodoxy of the first, coastal colonies. Theological wrangling was endemic among Puritans and it caused fragmentation as deviant preachers left communities which found their opinions intolerable. Roger Williams, a young divine who like John Milton had learned his Puritanism at Cambridge, arrived in New England in 1631. His doctrinal radicalism, which led him to deny the legal right of James I and Charles I to give away Indian lands to his fellow settlers, caused his voluntary exile in 1636. With a handful of his adherents he

NEWFOUNDLAND

Gulf of
St Lawrence

MICMACS

ACADIA

Quebec

NOVA SCOTIA

Montreal

Grand
Banks
Fishing
Grounds

Lake
Champlain

Connecticut R.

MAINE c.1635)
(to Massachusetts)

NEW HAMPSHIRE
C. 1635

Penobscot Bay

Bay of Fundy

IROQUOIS

Lake Ontario

Mohawk R.

Hudson R.

Portland

ONEIDA

Albany

Springfield

Connect

Portsmouth
Hampton

C. Ann

Salem
MASS.
1628-9

Boston

Lake
Erie

Hertford 1635

NEW
YORK

Newhaven

CONN.

Plymouth

PLYMOUTH
1620

RHODE ISLAND
C. 1636

1681

PENNSYLVANIA

New York

Long Island
(to New York)

ATLANTIC
OCEAN

Philadelphia

EAST JERSEY
1664

MARY
1634

LAND

PA

WEST JERSEY
1664

Delaware Bay

St Mary

Chesapeake Bay

ALLEGHANY
MOUNTAINS

VIRGINIA

James R.

1607

Jamestown

Norfolk

CHEROKEE

Roanoke I.

NORTH
CAROLINA
1663

C. Hatteras

CREEK

C. Fear R.

Wilmington

Cape Fear

SOUTH
CAROLINA
1670

Charleston

Savannah R.

INDIAN TRIBES

Portsmouth
Hampton

WEST COUNTRY

SCOTCH-IRISH

C. Ann

PURITANS

Boston

C. Cod

Newhaven

Long
Island

Source and types
of immigrant

Miles
0   50 100 150 200

Seventeenth-Century Settlement in North America

founded a new colony, Rhode Island, where he was later joined by other banished heretics.

Plans to rid England of another body of religious dissidents, Catholics, had been considered since the early 1570s. Excluded from Virginia, English Catholics finally gained a colony when Lord Baltimore persuaded a sympathetic Charles I to issue him a charter in 1634. The new settlement was named Maryland, in honour of Charles's queen Henrietta Maria, and its colonists were officially cautioned to hold their masses discreetly for fear that they might antagonise their Protestant neighbours.

Catholics and Puritans were among those whom Hakluyt had characterised as 'superfluous persons' whose removal to overseas settlements would be for the general benefit of society. Beggars and criminals also fell into this category and, in 1615, his proposal was translated into action when a party of convicts was shipped to Virginia which was then suffering a temporary labour shortage. New classes of unwanted people emerged as the century progressed, most notably Irish rebels and prisoners-of-war taken during the civil wars of 1642–52. In 1650, Scottish captives taken at Dunbar were sold for between £15 and £20 a head as indentured labourers bound to undertake a fixed period of work on their masters' plantations. After 1660 this convenient and profitable method of punishment became increasingly popular.

Such largely unwelcome immigrants were the exception rather than the rule in the North American colonies, at least before 1660. Nearly all who emigrated were free men and women who did so to work for a living. The companies which financed the first colonising projects wanted profits from rents and the sale of land, and therefore a greater part of their initial outlay was spent on shipping and equipping a substantial labour force whose efforts were expected to repay the investment.

But why were men and women willing to leave Britain for what was, even by the standards of the age, a hard and uncertain existence? Perhaps the strongest impulse lay in habit: there was an old and deeply rooted tradition for craftsmen, labourers and domestic servants to move around the countryside looking for employment. London enticed most. Its population swelled from 200,000 in 1600 to 350,000 in 1650, an increase entirely made up by incoming workers for this was a time when the city's death rate exceeded the birth. It was therefore not a difficult step for, say, a Devonshire tiler accustomed to wandering from town to town for work, to accept passage from Bristol to Jamestown, Virginia. Specialist skills were keenly sought by the Virginia Company which in 1620 was advertising for 'choice men, born and bred up to labour and industry', especially Sussex ironworkers.

Nearly all those who went to North America went as indentured servants, legally bound to labour on the plantations, or practising their own craft for fixed periods of between four and ten years in return for wages. When their terms of service had expired they were free to enter the local labour market or return home. Between 1654 and 1660 just over 3,000 of these indentured servants were shipped from Bristol, more than half destined for the tobacco colonies of Virginia and Maryland. Former yeomen farmers and farmhands were the biggest group but there was a scattering of skilled artisans such as blacksmiths and coopers. Most came from the counties adjacent to Bristol and South Wales and were between eighteen and twenty-five.[6]

Such young men (and women too) were the sinews of the new colonies. All hoped to flourish in a society where the domestic obstructions to advancement did not exist. In time it was widely imagined that those with talent, application and an injection of good luck would flourish irrespective of birth or connections. At the beginning of the next century, Daniel Defoe used the fictional career of Moll Flanders to illustrate this principle. Moll, born in Newgate gaol, returns there after a sequence of picaresque adventures in which she displays resource and intelligence. Transported as a felon to Virginia she and her highwayman husband eventually overcome their backgrounds and become respected and wealthy planters.

Moll Flanders was not pure fantasy, nor a tract by a writer who believed that a person's place in the world should be determined by ability. In 1755 an officer serving with General Edward Braddock's army in Virginia recalled having supper with a 'rich planter'. His wife, he discovered, 'had passed through the education of the college of Newgate as great numbers from thence arrive here yearly; most being cunning jades, some pick up foolish planters.' But this man was no fool, he had married his wife for her charms and her 'art and skill' in managing his business.

The pursuit of profit remained the most powerful driving force behind Britain's bid for North American colonies. But from the start it was closely linked to a moral imperative founded upon contemporary conceptions of Divine Providence and the nature of the world and its inhabitants.

In a sermon compiled in 1609 by a clerical apologist for the Virginia

Company, America was described as a land which had been 'wrongly usurped by wild beasts and unreasonable creatures' (i.e. native Americans, or Indians as they were then known); according to the author, God intended the land to be redeemed by English settlement. In 1625, Simon Purchas, a churchman and disciple of Hakluyt, insisted that what he called the 'Virgin Portion' of North America had been divinely allocated to his countrymen, 'God in wisdom having enriched the savage countries, that those riches be attractive for Christian suitors'.

The conceit that the American continent was a richly endowed virgin bride awaiting a husband enjoyed considerable usage at this time. It was not just a courtier's knack for flattery that had inspired Raleigh to name the eastern seaboard of North America 'Virginia' in honour of Elizabeth I. A deeper meaning was intended since Raleigh, in his plea for the occupation of Guiana, had described it as 'a country that hath yet her Maidenhead, never sacked, turned, nor wrought, the face of earth hath not been torn, nor the virtue and the salt of the soil spent by manurance'.[7] In coarser vein, Captain Seagull rallied the settlers in *Eastward Ho* with the cry, 'Come boys, Virginia longs till we share the rest of her maidenhead.' Most famously this likeness of America to an unblemished maiden is employed by John Donne (among other things a chaplain to the Virginia Company) in his 'To his Mistris Going to Bed', in which the seducer is both explorer and planter:

> *License my roaving hands, and let them go*
> *Before, behind, between, above, below.*
> *O my America! my new-found-land . . .*

The moral question faced by Englishmen was, by what authority could they claim the fertile, untilled lands of North America? A broad and infallible answer was provided by the prevailing view of the divine ordering of the world and man's place in it. 'God', wrote John Milton in a defence of colonisation, 'having made the world for use of men . . . ordained them to replenish it.' The newly revealed American continent was favoured with abundant natural resources by a benevolent God, but it was peopled by races who had never recognised nor acted upon their good fortune. Their wilful inertia, combined with other moral shortcomings, debarred them from their inheritance which passed to more industrious outsiders. Similar arguments, with variations, would later be applied to Australasia and Africa.

One hundred years of detailed reports from European explorers had created a literature in which, almost without exception, the Amerindians were represented as a degenerate and inferior species of mankind. Sir Martin Frobisher, encountering the Inuits of Northern Canada in the 1580s, described them as 'brute beasts' who 'neither use table, stool or tablecloth for cleanliness' and lived in caves. Fifty years later a French Jesuit missionary, horrified by the cannibalism and public torture of prisoners among the Indians of the St Lawrence basin, called them 'ferocious beasts having nothing human about them save the exterior formation of body'. The standards of Renaissance European civilisation were absolute and, judged by them, the native Americans were found wanting.

The natives of America, when first confronted with Europeans, believed they were in the presence of supernatural beings. In Mexico, the Aztec Emperor Moctezuma imagined that his people's conqueror, Hernán Cortés, was a reincarnation of the god Quetzalcoatl. Sixty years later, in 1569, when Drake landed in California, the Miwok Indians identified him and his party as gods. Sacrifices were immediately offered and, much to their visitors' distress, some Miwoks mutilated themselves, as they did when they fancied themselves in the presence of ghosts. Everywhere Amerindians regarded Europeans as gods whose ships were floating islands, their sails white clouds and their cannon the makers of thunder and lightning. Such naïveté was easily exploited; in 1633 a French sea captain entranced Indians by using a magnetised sword blade to pick up a knife so that, in his words, they would 'imagine some great power in us and for that love and fear us'.

Indian customs dismayed most European observers. They appeared a race without order, that vital ingredient of what Renaissance men considered to be civilisation. They were idolators and, according to Cotton Mather, a Bostonian Puritan, were 'Lazy Drones, and love Idleness Exceedingly'. Indolence was a form of devilment for those of his persuasion and it seemed an inevitable outcome of God's purpose that the Indians should be dispossessed by colonists just as the Israelites had driven out the pagan Canaanites.

Nevertheless, while the Indians, like Caliban in Shakespeare's *The Tempest*, were unfit to occupy their land, they might be put in the way of improvement. The idea of conversion and elevation was given exotic form in the masque *The Virginian Princess*, staged in 1614. The pagan Indian nobility, dressed in fanciful gold-embroidered and feathered costumes designed by Inigo Jones, were addressed in James I's name:

Virginian Princes, ye must now renounce
Your superstitious worships of these suns . . .

And of your sweet devotions turn the events
To this Britain Phoebus.

In the beginning the promoters of the Virginia Company had made much of plans for the conversion and education of Indians, and during the colony's early years relations between settlers and natives had been harmonious. But as the colony grew the settlers clamoured for fresh land which could only be gained at the Indians' expense. War broke out in 1622 and after a massacre in which over 300 colonists were killed, a new and understandably fierce mood prevailed. 'The way of conquering them is more easy than civilising them by fair means,' ran a pamphlet issued by the company, 'for they are a rude, barbarous, and naked people, scattered in small communities, which are helps to Victory, but hindrances to Civility.' In future the native Americans would be brought to heel by the destruction of their camps and crops and 'by pursuing them with our horses, and Blood-Hounds to draw after them, and Mastiffs to tear them, which take these naked, tanned deformed Savages, for no other than wild beasts.'

This mandate for extermination anticipated similar calls for ruthless wars against a dehumanised enemy that would be heard from land-hungry colonists in southern Africa, New Zealand and Australia. It was also a reminder that the first colonisation of North America was contemporaneous with the far larger settlement of Ireland, mainly by Presbyterian Scottish immigrants. Between 1620 and 1642 120,000 colonists arrived to help undertake what Sir Francis Bacon revealingly called 'the reduction to civility' of the Gaelic-speaking, Catholic Irish. On both sides of the Atlantic the settlers faced sporadic but determined resistance and their response was the same, a resort to counter-massacre and the most extreme forms of repression. Half a century of land wars against the Indians calloused the New England settlers' consciences. In 1703, soon after the slaughter of Pequot Indians, a soldier wrote, prompted by a clergyman, 'Sometimes the scripture declareth women and children must perish with their parents.' When founded, the Massachusetts Bay Company had set on its seal a device which showed an Indian with a scroll above his head with the inscription 'Come over and help us'.

Native Americans were not the only people who advanced territorial

claims in North America. In 1494, Spain and Portugal had signed the
Treaty of Tordesillas by which the New World was divided between them,
and their agreement was endorsed by a Papal bull. This accord was naturally disregarded by Protestant Englishmen who undermined its legality
with counter-claims based on John Cabot's 1497 voyage. He had, at Henry
VII's bidding, crossed the Atlantic and made landfall at either Nova Scotia
or Newfoundland, no one is sure which, and formally annexed the region
in the King's name. Furthermore, there was the legendary transatlantic
expedition made by the twelfth-century Welsh prince, Madoc. This insub-
stantial tale assumed, in the hands of Elizabethan expansionists, the force of
historical truth and was cited to override Spanish and Portuguese claims.

Such antiquarian nonsense was superfluous since, by 1600, it was obvious that the Iberian nations lacked the seapower to defend their New
World monopoly. The limitations of their control had been repeatedly and
dramatically exposed by French, Dutch and English privateers from 1560
onwards. Nevertheless, Spain did expel the French from their settlement at
San Augustin in 1565 and for a few years the Virginians feared similar
treatment. It was not meted out by a state which had been at peace with
Britain from 1604 and, after 1609, needed all its resources for a renewed
war with the Netherlands. For the first thirty years or so of their existence,
the North American settlements enjoyed a vital immunity from foreign
interference.

—◆—

Baubles for the Souls of Men: The West and East Indies

Englishmen had first been drawn to the Caribbean, known often as the Spanish Main, in the middle of the sixteenth century. Sir John Hawkins, a Devon shipowner and entrepreneur, led the way having heard, according to Hakluyt, that 'Negroes were very good merchandise in Hispaniola [the Spanish colony of Española, now Haiti], and that the store of negroes might easily be had upon the coast of Guinea'. The Spanish settlers were grateful for Hawkins's cargoes of West African slaves, but their government objected to his infraction of the official monopoly that gave Spaniards alone the right to trade with Spanish possessions. In 1568, Hawkins's tiny flotilla of trading vessels was ambushed at San Juan de Ulúa and driven off with heavy losses. He soon returned with others, including Drake, as a privateer preying on Spanish shipping.

This was a holy war for Protestantism as well as a trawl for profit in ill-defended waters. Drake recited passages from Foxe's *Book of Martyrs* to captive Spanish seamen, and one of his captains, John Oxenham, turned the tables on a captured official of the Inquisition by placing a chamber pot on his head and striking him 'many fisticuffs'.[1] Oxenham himself was later taken and burned by the Inquisition for his combination of heresy and temerity. Piracy may not have done much for the Protestant cause, but many pirates prospered. Memories of their more spectacular coups against

treasure ships remained evergreen and in 1621, when Anglo-Spanish relations were deteriorating, the Puritan Earl of Warwick proposed the
despatch of a massive armada to the Caribbean whose costs, estimated at
£364,000, would be met by public subscription.

This scheme for a profit-making, maritime crusade came to nothing,
but a preliminary reconnaissance of the Caribbean revealed the existence
of Barbados, a fertile, well-watered and uninhabited island that was said to
be highly suitable for tobacco-growing. The vision of a second Virginia
lured investors and in 1627 Charles I granted a charter to the newly
formed Barbados Company. Its settlers were soon in difficulties; Barbadian
tobacco failed to compete with the Virginian product and a hurried switch
to cotton did nothing to revive the island's fortunes.

Sugar saved Barbados. It was first planted in 1643 and within fifty years
sugar plantations covered four-fifths of the island and refined sugar,
molasses and rum made up nine-tenths of its exports. What later historians called the 'sugar revolution' transformed the economy of the West
Indies, opened the way for a subsidiary but equally profitable commerce in
negro slaves and, incidentally, made the region into a war zone where until
1815, Britain, France and Spain struggled for control of the islands and
mastery of the seaways. Sugar enabled some plantation owners to become
millionaires. In 1681 it was calculated, perhaps optimistically, that £5,000
invested in a sugar estate would within a few years yield £1,000 annually.
By this date a mass domestic and European market for cheap sugar was
emerging and British producers were getting the upper hand in a price war
with competitors in Portuguese Brazil. The boom benefited Britain and its
government which levied duties on sugar imports which, between 1699
and 1701, were valued at £280,000.

Barbados's success story accelerated the occupation of other islands by
settlers. By 1660, St Kitts, Antigua, Nevis, Montserrat and Jamaica (seized
from Spain in 1655) had been occupied and planted with sugar cane. In
1638 a small party attempted to settle St Lucia but were soon driven out by
the native Caribs who, showing considerable ingenuity, 'smoked out' the
colonists from their forts with bonfires of dried peppers.

Indigenous diseases, especially the mosquito-borne malaria and yellow
fever, together with the labour-intensive processes by which sugar was cultivated, harvested and refined, presented enormous problems to the early
planters. Contemporary medical wisdom cautioned Englishmen against
leaving their temperate homeland for the tropics. Applying current
Hippocratic principles concerning the balance of internal humours, one

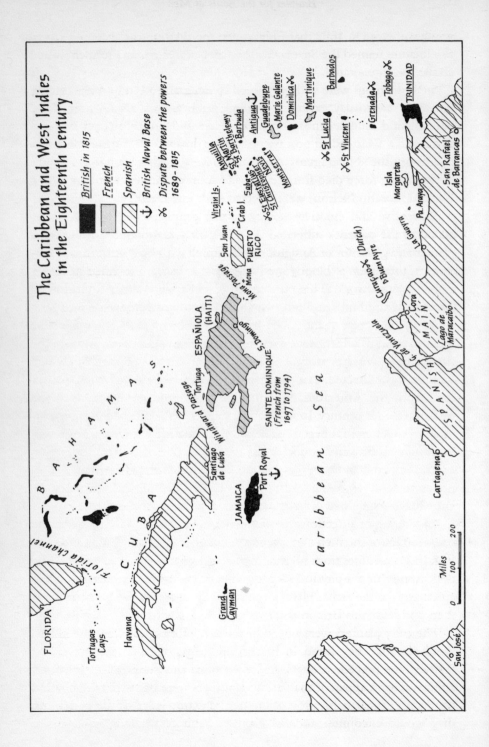

The Caribbean and West Indies
in the Eighteenth Century

■ British in 1815
▨ French
▨ Spanish
⚓ British Naval Base
✕ Dispute between the powers
1689–1815

FLORIDA

Tortugas
Cays

Florida Channel

Havana

CUBA

Santiago
de Cuba

Grand
Cayman

B A H A M A S

Port Royal ⚓
JAMAICA

Windward Passage

Tortuga

ESPAÑIOLA
(HAITI)

S. Domingo

SAINTE DOMINIQUE
(French from
1697 to 1794)

Mona Passage

Mona

San Juan

PUERTO
RICO

Virgin Is.

Crab I.

Saba
St Eustatius
St Christophe

Anguilla
St Martin
St Barthélemy
Barbuda

Montserrat

Nevis

Guadeloupe ⚓
Marie Galante
Dominica ✕

Antigua ⚓

Barbados

Martinique

St Lucia ✕

St Vincent ✕

Grenada ✕

Tobago ✕

TRINIDAD

Isla
Margareta

Pa. Araya

Curaçao ✕ (Dutch)
B. Buen Ayte

La Guayra

Cora

Lago de
Maracaibo

Golfo de Venezuela

S P A N I S H   M A I N

San Rafael
de Barrancas

Cartagena

San José

C a r i b b e a n   S e a

Miles
0   100   200

physician wrote in 1602 that Englishmen should shun the 'burning zones' for, 'Nature framed the Spaniards apt to such places where melancholy and choler were generated.'[2]

Such warnings were widely ignored by emigrants keen to make money, but their day-to-day existence in the Caribbean was always precarious. Soldiers and sailors, whose diet was sparse and unhealthy, suffered the worst and a West Indian posting was always dreaded. During a brief campaign on the Nicaraguan coast in 1778–79, three quarters of an 1,800-strong force died from fevers, and most of the survivors, including Captain Horatio Nelson, were infected with malaria.[3]

Preventive and curative medicine were primitive and in some cases added to the patient's sufferings. In 1704, Sir Christopher Codington, a planter and governor of Antigua, dosed himself with 'vast quantities of laudanum' to assuage a 'bloody flux' (dysentery) that he imagined had been caused by overwork. This nostrum triggered fresh distempers including paralysis of the limbs and internal pains which he treated by sea-bathing and drinking 'great quantities of cold water (which I take to be the West Indian panacea)' which was probably contaminated and contributed to the persistence of his dysentery. The value of the chinchona bark, from which quinine was extracted, as a prophylactic against malaria had been discovered from the Amerindians, but it was not used generally until the mid-nineteenth century. In its absence, victims of malaria had to suffer stoically like General Robert Venables. 'I was but a mere skeleton,' he wrote during the 1655 Jamaican campaign, 'and per times had been in a raving condition about three weeks.' He attributed his own and his army's sicknesses to God who was chastising them for 'the Sins of the Nation', knowledge which may have given them some extra, inner stamina.[4]

Endurance of infections and extremes of heat and humidity was the common lot of the men and women who emigrated to the West Indies to make their fortunes from sugar. But the drive to make money alone could not compensate for physical suffering and, by the end of the century, it was customary for the richer planters to place their estates in the hands of managers and return to Britain and live, often in high style, from the profits.

The early planters were not so fortunately placed, nor were the indentured servants they hired in Britain. To begin with, the sugar estates followed the precedent established in Virginia and imported their labour, but it was soon apparent that British labourers were not up to the physical demands of sugar cultivation in the tropics. Knowledge of the conditions they would encounter and the planters' habit of working new arrivals hard to recoup the cost of their transport deterred men and women from freely committing themselves to indentured service in the West Indies.

Various stopgap measures were adopted to overcome what, by the 1650s, had become a permanent labour shortage. After Oliver Cromwell's Scottish and Irish campaigns of 1650–52, captured rebels were transported for fixed periods to the West Indies, a punitive measure that was revived in 1685 after the suppression of the Duke of Monmouth's uprising. Irish labourers, whether deported for treason or driven by poverty, were the most numerous, but they proved sullen and unwilling workers. 'Scotchmen and Welshmen we esteem the best servants,' the St Kitts planters observed in 1673, 'and the Irish the worst, many of them being good for nothing but mischief.' They were also disloyal; in 1674 Irish workers on Montserrat assisted a French attack on the island and twenty years later their country-men in Jamaica were suspected of being pro-French.[5]

Reluctant to employ Irishmen, the desperate St Kitts planters were bargaining in 1677 to pay £1.11 shillings (£1.55) a head for convicts from English gaols and pay the costs of their passage. This was a private arrangement although, in 1664, the home government contemplated the mass deportation of 'all vagrants, rogues and idle persons that can give no account of themselves, felons who have benefit of clergy . . . gipsies and low persons having resort to unlicensed brothels' to the sugar colonies. Those under twenty were to be bound for seven years, those over for four.

The prospects for those, whether the hopeless poor, the criminal or the rebellious, who found themselves compelled to undertake indentured ser-vice were not entirely bleak. If they survived until the end of their term they received £10 or 400 pounds of sugar with which to better them-selves. Some became overseers, earning as much as £50 a year, and those with such skills as carpentry could make twice as much. Nevertheless, work on the plantations remained intensely unpopular and for many, per-haps the majority, it was a gruelling alternative to the gallows, prison or starvation. 'We had nothing before us but slavery,' wrote the spokesman for a handful of Jacobite rebels transported to the West Indies in 1716 who, in desperation, overcame their gaolers and seized the ship which they steered to Bordeaux and freedom.[6]

It is instructive that these bold men likened their future condition to that of the negro slaves who since the 1650s had taken the place of the increas-ingly scarce white workers. There were many occasions when negroes and

Europeans worked alongside each other in the fields and boiling rooms, an experience that the whites found degrading even though, unlike their black counterparts, they were not their masters' property and there was a period to their servitude.

Given the insoluble problem of finding a willing and hardy workforce, it was inevitable that British plantation owners would adopt the Spanish colonial system of using imported African slave labour. The Spaniards, having through forced labour, overwork, the spread of alien germs and viruses, and systematic massacre exterminated most of the Caribbean Amerindians by the mid-sixteenth century, turned to negro slaves. They were the only means by which the highly labour-intensive Spanish latifundia and mines could be sustained. For economic rather than demographic reasons, British planters followed the Spanish example and, from 1650 onwards, slaves gradually replaced indentured labourers on the plantations. At the same time slave labour was introduced to the Chesapeake basin tobacco estates and, soon after, slaves were imported into Carolina.

Economic necessity was always the first and, for its supporters, the strongest justification for slavery. Their reasoning was simply outlined in a report prepared in 1663 to procure royal backing for the occupation of the Dutch colony of Surinam on the Guianan coast. 'Were the planters supplied with negroes, the sinews and strength of this western world,' it was claimed, 'they would advance their fortunes and His Majesty's customs.'[7] Slavery underpinned the expanding West Indian economy and enriched both planters and the home government which, it went without saying, would direct additional revenues towards the protection and enlargement of this new source of national wealth.

There was, and few would have denied this in a country where much store was set on individual freedom, a moral issue involved in the sale and exploitation of slaves. In his *Reform of Manners* (1702) Daniel Defoe, usually a fervent upholder of British overseas enterprise, expressed doubts about 'the barter of baubles for the *souls of men*', but overcame them by reference to what he imagined to be the 'Natural Temper' of the negro, that is awe of and thraldom to the white man. This view, found in Defoe's novel *Colonel Jack*, was widely and uncritically held throughout Europe during the late seventeenth and eighteenth centuries. It was based upon Old Testament and Graeco-Roman traditions of thought which represented the negro as an inferior creature who, at one and the same time, was the descendant of the accursed Ham and a specimen of that lesser humanity described by Plato and Aristotle.

As with the Native Americans, the negro was measured against the standards of contemporary European civilisation and judged unfavourably. He was, asserted the eighteenth-century philosopher, David Hume, 'naturally inferior' because his race possessed 'No ingenious manufactures . . . no arts, no sciences'. Whenever he displayed what might pass for wit, his behaviour was akin to that of a parrot 'who speaks a few words plainly' but cannot grasp their meaning. Those who travelled to Africa, often in connection with the slave trade, endorsed such conclusions with lurid tales of a dark and chaotic land whose people indulged in fetish cults, cannibalism, massacres and tribal wars.

Although burdened by moral and intellectual disabilities, the negro was part of a divinely ordered world in which the prime justification for a man's existence was his productive usefulness. This principle of the utility of all humankind impelled British governments to deport idlers, vagrants and criminals to the colonies where they would redeem themselves through work, and the French to condemn miscreants to perpetual labour rowing war galleys. Plantation slavery was the means by which negroes could fulfil the role for which God had intended them and add to the general well-being of the world. 'I was shock'd at the first appearance of human flesh exposed for sale,' wrote John Pinney, an absentee Nevis planter in 1764. 'But surely God ordain'd 'em for the use and benefit of us: other his Divine Will would have been manifest by some sign or token.'

Enslavement was not without its advantages. With breathtaking smugness Gilbert Burnet, Bishop of Salisbury, argued in the early 1700s that since the slaves had given so much to Britain it was only proper that they should receive Christianity in return. This exchange was unwelcome to planters who imagined, with good reason as it turned out, that conversion would make their slaves 'more perverse and intractable'. Addressing the Barbadian plantocracy, assembled in the island's parliament in 1681, the governor Sir Richard Dutton remarked that slaves deserved the 'good usage of Christian servants, but as to make negroes Christians, their savage brutishness renders them wholly incapable'.[8] Slave-owning was compatible with the Christian life, at least in the form it was taught by Catholic and Church of England divines. One of the latter, Bishop Fleetwood, preached in 1711 that, 'The laws of God did not forbid the keeping of Christian slaves, nor do the laws of the land. The following year his church's missionary organisation, the Society for the Propagation of the Christian Gospel, was bequeathed a plantation in Barbados. Each of its slaves was branded on the chest with the word 'Society' to denote his new owner; not surprisingly the rate of conversion was disappointing.

Nevertheless, and despite all the clerical humbug that surrounded the subject, the admission that slaves could be converted opened a debate, which intensified as the eighteenth century progressed, as to how, if at all, a religion that claimed the equality of souls before God could reconcile itself to a system founded upon the hereditary inferiority of one part of mankind. Moreover, as the planters predicted, a knowledge of Christian doctrines led many slaves to interpret their own circumstances unfavourably. One who did told a missionary in the 1820s, 'Buckra [the white man] left him God in England, and devil in Jamaica stir him to do all dis wickedness.'[9]

The brandmark that identified the Society for the Propagation of the Christian Gospel's slave was an unmistakable reminder that he or she was, in the eyes of the law, the property of a master. According to the constitution of Carolina that was framed by the philosopher John Locke in 1669 'every free man' was 'to have absolute authority over his negro slaves', a principle which, in different forms, obtained throughout much of North America and the West Indies. Its everyday application gave plantation life a peculiar and often grotesque brutality. Much has been written about this, so one incident set down in the diary of the manager of a Jamaican estate may stand for many others: '(25 May 1756) Derby caught by Port Royal [both slaves] eating canes. Had him well flogged and pickled, then made Henry [another slave] shit in his mouth.'[10]

Eating the young cane shoots was the inevitable outcome of having to undertake heavy physical labour on a sparse diet. A recent forensic examination of 101 skeletons of slaves exhumed from a Barbadian graveyard, in use between 1660 and 1820, revealed an average life expectancy of twenty-nine and a high death rate for children under ten. Evidence of nutrition indicated a diet that was inadequate for the tasks demanded of the slaves, who commonly assuaged their hunger by smoking tobacco in pipes.[11] This high wastage rate was not offset by the slaves' ability to reproduce themselves, despite the active encouragement of concubinage. This phenomenon was explained with some percipience by one planter who noted in his journal that, 'Negresses can produce children at pleasure, and when they are barren, it is just as hens will frequently not lay eggs on shipboard, because they do not like their situation. Low birth rates and high death rates meant that planters had continually to replenish their stock of slaves and so the slave trade was perpetuated.

The mechanics of the transatlantic slave trade were simple. Negroes were obtained by barter with the tribal rulers of the West African seaboard states, confined in compounds attached to trading posts and then shipped for sale in the West Indies. During the second half of the seventeenth century the commonest items of exchange were cowrie shells, bolts of Indian-manufactured cloth (both local units of currency), copper, iron, tobacco and alcohol. After 1700 some British dealers offered muskets which were greatly prized and a form of indirect investment since tribal armies equipped with firearms enjoyed a considerable advantage on the battlefield and could, therefore, capture more prisoners to sell on the coast.

During its early stages, returns from the slave trade were very high. A slave could be exchanged for goods worth between £4 and £5 and the cost of passage was a further £5, including his food and the attendance of a doctor. On a West Indian quayside the slave would be sold for between £15 and £17 or 2,400 pounds of sugar depending on his or her age and health. The high profit margin was in great part a reflection of the losses of slaves during the voyage for as many as one in four perished from sickness or despair, or a mixture of the two.

During the 1650s the trade was already flourishing, with an average of 3,000 slaves being sold annually in Barbados, some for re-export to other islands or Virginia and Maryland. The scope of the trade, with markets in Dutch as well as British colonies, attracted the intervention of the government which hoped to secure a share of the profits. In 1660 a monopoly was granted to the Company of Royal Adventurers (in which Charles II invested £5,000) which gave it the right to sell licences to British slave traders who did business on the West African coast. Reorganised as the Royal African Company in 1672, the corporation controlled a string of fortified and garrisoned trading stations on the shores of what today are Gambia, Senegal, Ghana and Nigeria. The company never enjoyed a total monopoly – enterprising slavers operating out of Boston and New York ignored it and traded with Madagascar. In 1698 it was abolished, allowing hundreds of independent traders to stake a claim in the commerce. Most were based in London, Liverpool and Bristol, but there were many, often small-scale businesses, with vessels of less than a hundred tons, based in Lancaster, Whitehaven and Dumfries.

India

Among the commodities bartered for slaves were cheap textiles imported from India by the East India Company. Indian and Far Eastern markets had first been penetrated by the Portuguese at the beginning of the sixteenth century. The arrival of their heavily-gunned caravels was unwelcomed, but proved unstoppable. In 1501 Vasco da Gama's men-o'-war bombarded Calicut to show its inhabitants the power of European cannon, and a year later his outnumbered flotilla decisively defeated an Arab fleet off the Malabar coast. These victories gave the Portuguese a local supremacy that lasted for nearly a hundred years.

The challenge to Portugal's domination of the trade in spices and Far Eastern textiles came from English and Dutch merchants and shipowners. After a number of preliminary reconnaissances, the London-based East India Company was formed in 1600, the brainchild of Levant Company merchants who were keen to by-pass middlemen in the eastern Mediterranean and deal direct with spice suppliers in the East Indies (modern Indonesia). The company was small, with a capital of £68,000, and at first confined itself to annual expeditions by small fleets. The risks, not least of the journey around the Cape of Good Hope, were great. When the *Globe* and the *Peppercorn* returned in 1617 with full holds and the prospect of a good return, the company's governor called the stockholders to prayer for 'all ought to lift up their hearts unto God to be thankful . . . and to be more thankful for the same; not doubting that the more thankful we be, the more His blessings will increase.'

The blessings and the profits did increase, satisfying the business acumen and piety of investors in an age which believed that God never failed to reward His elect. Those who put their money on the early voyages received, on average, a return of twenty per cent. Moreover, in 1614 two company ships had engaged and driven off four Portuguese vessels by the mouth of the River Tapti, a demonstration of British fighting skill which was watched by the Mughal army on shore. In India at least the company had secured a toehold and, within twenty years, the Portuguese had conceded the East India Company the right to set up factories, as trading posts were known, wherever it chose on the Indian coast.

And yet as the company's name indicated, its founders had pinned their hopes on gaining a share in the spice trade at its source: Malaya, Java and the Molucca Islands. Here the rival Dutch Compagnie van Verre (Company of Far Distant Lands) was already strongly entrenched and ready to resist interlopers. Founded in 1602 with capital of £500,000, the Dutch company quickly established fortified trading posts at Batavia (Jakarta), Amboina Island and Malacca on the Malay coast which they took from the Portuguese in 1641. Tolerance of British intruders was thin and, in 1623, eighteen British merchants were tortured to death on Amboina in an exercise of brutality designed to frighten off others. It did not wholly succeed but it helped turn the minds of British traders towards India where their presence was not opposed.

The Mughal emperors, India's overlords, and their provincial nawabs (governors) were willing to come to terms with the East India Company and allow them to secure a string of trading posts along the western and eastern shores of the subcontinent. A continual flow of ships replaced the earlier annual sailings and by the mid-century a profitable trade was developing. In 1674–5 the Company exported £155,000 worth of British manufactured goods and £410,000 in silver bullion, and imported £860,000 worth of Indian goods, largely textiles. At the same time, and in imitation of the Portuguese and Dutch, the Company was entering the shipping business, carrying goods between India and ports in southern Arabia and the Far East. In 1664 a minute amount of tea, still an exotic luxury, was obtained from China solely for the use of the directors.

As the Company's interests expanded and diversified, its establishments became larger, although the directors insisted that it had no political or territorial ambitions in a country that was enjoying a period of stability under Mughal government. And yet in a land where the outward signs of prestige and power were important, the Company had to maintain an impressive public face. In the 1670s, Thomas Bowrey, a visitor to the Company's factory at Fort St George near Madras, found it 'surrounded by very potent and strong bulwarks, points, and batteries' like any fort in Europe. The governor and his council behaved like local potentates 'for the Honour of an English Nation keeping and maintaining the place in great splendour, civil and good government, entertaining nobly all foreign ambassadors'. The grandees were also merchants and Bowrey saw 'great quantities of muslins, calicoes etc.' stored for export to Britain and ships bound for Arabia, Persia and China with cargoes of British broadcloths, knives and scissors.[12] The Indians were a 'harmless idolatrous people' among whom there were well-established business communities of Parsis, Gujaratis and Moplahs willing to trade with the Company. By this time textiles, produced by weavers who earned an anna (½p) a day, had become the staple of the company's exports. Between 1699 and 1701 imports of these products totalled £522,000 and two thirds were re-exported to Europe and West Africa where they were exchanged for slaves.

3

The Necessary Union
of Plantations:
Crown and Colonies

In 1645 the trading vessel *Dolphin* left London with a cargo of manufactured goods that included glass, castors, shoes, hats, bales of canvas, and pewter, iron and brass utensils, all for sale to the New England colonists. These wares were unloaded at Boston where the hold was filled with local products: wheat and rye, barrels of preserved beef, pork, herrings and mackerel, and 7,000 pounds of tobacco, presumably shipped from Virginia and Maryland. The *Dolphin* then sailed southwards to Barbados where some of its cargo was discharged and replaced with sugar. It then began the haul across the Atlantic, pausing at the Canaries where the pickled fish was removed for sale to those pious Catholics who obeyed the church's rules concerning meatless Fridays.[1]

This round voyage and hundreds like it marked a significant change in the pattern of British trade. Fine woollen cloth, so long Britain's main export, was steadily losing ground to tobacco, sugar, fish and, during the last quarter of the century, Canadian beaver pelts for hat-making. By 1700 the re-export of these commodities made up 30 per cent of Britain's foreign trade. Cloth's share of the export market had fallen dramatically from 90 per cent in 1640 to 47 per cent at the end of the century and continued to decline. At the same time new markets were emerging. Between 1630 and 1700 half a million men and women had emigrated to the colonies, two thirds of them to North America, and all were dependent on home-manufactured goods; during the 1650s 20,000 pairs of boots and shoes and 1,500 horses were imported into Barbados.

The early stages of this economic revolution coincided with a period of domestic political instability which culminated in the outbreak of the Civil War between Charles I and parliament in 1642. The principle source of contention was control over the making of policy, particularly in matters concerning religion and taxation. The waves stirred by the war in Britain sent ripples across the Atlantic. From 1640 onwards, many New England Puritans returned home to fight for parliament and in Virginia, its governor Sir William Berkeley, a former courtier and playwright, welcomed royalist refugees after the collapse of their cause in 1649. The new, republican Commonwealth disapproved and removed him from his post, allowing him to retire to his plantations, from where he emerged to recover his position on Charles II's restoration in 1660.

The establishment of Commonwealth in 1649 may be reckoned as marking a major turning point in the history of the empire. The next eleven years witnessed continuous and dynamic government activity to preserve and enlarge Britain's overseas possessions and their trade. There was legislation to assert the total dominance of Britain over all aspects of colonial commerce; an ambitious programme of naval rearmament; a challenge to Dutch seapower; and a partially successful offensive against Spain in the Caribbean.

One thing was clear to the ministers and civil servants who framed these policies: Britain's colonies and the new transatlantic commerce they were generating were a vital national asset to be coveted, protected and extended, if necessary by aggression. At every turn, the government was influenced by the prevailing economic dogma, mercantilism. This assumed that a limit existed to global trade and measured a nation's wealth in terms of its self-sufficiency. Autarky, especially in raw materials, was also an indicator of a country's international status since it released it from dependence on other powers and allowed it to accumulate a surplus of treasure. For this among other reasons James I and Charles I had been willing to charter colonies which, their promoters hoped, would provide alternative sources for commodities previously imported from Europe. They were largely mistaken, but, unexpectedly the American and Caribbean settlements offered products for which there appeared a growing but finite continental market. If trends already detectable during the 1640s continued, Britain would soon become the focus of a transatlantic commerce based upon tobacco, sugar, fish and the new traffic in slaves.

The future of this commerce was by no means assured. Britain's position in North America was vulnerable: the French had already begun to penetrate the St Lawrence basin, and further south the Dutch had a toe-hold in what is now New York. The Dutch also posed another threat for, temporarily disengaged from European conflicts after 1648, they were free to increase their already vast merchant fleet and become the world's main sea carriers.

In broad terms the government aimed to tighten commercial links with the colonies, which were compelled to conduct all their seaborne trade through Britain and in British-owned ships. This was the objective of the Navigation Acts of 1649 and 1660, the Staple Act of 1663 and the Plantation Act of 1673. Non-British carriers were banned from conveying goods of any kind between Britain and its colonies or between individual colonies. At first, 'British' meant English, Welsh, Irish and Scottish but in 1660, when Scotland and England again became separate kingdoms under one king, Scottish shippers were included in the interdict. As well as being given a monopoly of colonial freightage, British shipowners were given the right to Royal Navy protection by an act of 1649 which was confirmed at the Restoration.

Although keeping the title Royal Navy, the British fleet was now a national force at the disposal of those subjects with foreign and colonial business interests. The act had originally been introduced to suppress roy-alist privateers, but by 1680 warships were regularly escorting British merchantmen in the Mediterranean as a deterrent against Algerine pirates; policing the Yarmouth, Iceland and Newfoundland fisheries; and patrolling in Atlantic and Caribbean waters.[2] Henceforward, the navy would be an instrument of commercial and colonial policy.

Extensive protection to merchant shipping required additional war-ships. From 1650 onwards, the government embarked on a ship-building programme which continued after the Restoration; in 1679 the navy pos-sessed 86 ships and double that number by 1688. Much of the credit for this must go to Samuel Pepys, the diarist and Secretary to the Board of Admiralty, who strove to eliminate corruption within the navy's bureau-cracy and create a formidable fleet that could be swiftly mobilised and manned in the event of war against France, Spain or the Netherlands.

It was the Dutch with their huge merchant marine who were seen as the greatest danger to British commerce, at least before 1680. They were most vulnerable in the English Channel and North Sea through which their vessels had to pass on their way to Amsterdam and it was here that they were challenged by the Royal Navy. The three Anglo-Dutch wars of 1652–4, 1665–7 and 1672–4 were inconclusive. The successes of the first, achieved by Admiral Blake, were offset by the attack on the Medway ports in 1666 when British shipping was seized and burned. This humiliation was outweighed by the occupation and subsequent annexation of New York.

While British broadsides may not have substantially harmed the Dutch, the latter's position of economic strength was deceptive. Unlike their rival, they had few colonies and no single staple such as sugar or tobacco upon which to rely and, as the wars demonstrated, their carrying trade could be disrupted at will by Britain. Moreover, from the mid-1660s the Dutch were driven to divert more and more of their surplus wealth into the fortification of their southern, landward frontier against France.

God, not Admiral Blake's battleships, was given credit for the navy's victories in 1652–4, or so ran the official proclamation which marked the signing of the peace treaty with the Netherlands. It concluded that 'the dispensations of the Lord have been as if he had said, *England* thou art my first-born, my delight among nations.' It is easy to see the hand of the Lord Protector, Oliver Cromwell, behind such sentiments which reflected a new, triumphalist and expansionist mood in the country. Late-Elizabethan ideas of national and Protestant destiny were in the process of resuscitation and translation into action at the hands of Cromwell, who throughout his life had a profound sense of serving a Divine Providence. He also had a vision of a godly, industrious nation whose Protestant faith and commerce qualified it for a pre-eminent position throughout the world.

1654 had not only seen the Dutch humbled, it had witnessed the Portuguese government make far-reaching concessions to British merchants which were tantamount to an admission that Portugal no longer possessed either the will or wherewithal to uphold its old authority in the East or the Americas. Cromwell next considered a blow against Spain in the West Indies. It would simultaneously damage the wealth and prestige of a leading Catholic power, be interpreted as a victory for Protestantism, and expose the emptiness of Spanish pretensions to a commercial monopoly in the region. In preparing what was called the 'Western Design', Cromwell was swayed by Thomas Gage, an apostate Dominican friar whose *England in America* urged the total overthrow of Spanish power in the New World and its replacement by British. He also listened to the more down-to-earth opinions of Sir Thomas Modyford, governor of Barbados, a planter with a knack of extracting private advantage from official policy.

In many ways the Western Design was a forerunner of many later, aggressive imperial enterprises. Commercial advantage, private greed and a sense of divinely directed historic destiny were intermingled and bound together, not quite convincingly, with a high-minded moral cause. To excuse what was a pre-emptive attack on the territory of a friendly power, Cromwell's propagandists presented the expedition as an act of revenge for a hundred and fifty years of Spanish and Catholic atrocities in the Americas. 'We hold our self obliged in Justice to the people of these nations for the Cruelties, Wrongs, and injuries done and exercised upon them by the Spaniards.'[3] Cromwell himself sincerely hoped that the expulsion of the Spaniards and their Inquisition would be followed by the arrival of a new and worthier breed of settlers, 'people who knew the Lord' from New England and Ulster.

On Christmas Day 1654 a fleet of seventeen men-o'-war under Admiral Sir William Penn and twenty transports carrying General Robert Venables's 5,000 strong army, recruited from the Irish garrison, sailed from Spithead. Five weeks later this armada hove to off Barbados. The campaign opened promisingly with the seizure, in the name of the Navigation Laws, of £5,000 worth of Dutch shipping anchored off the island. After picking up some companies of militia from Barbados and the Leeward Islands, the fleet approached its target, Española. The landings were a disaster, with heavy losses among a force already being reduced by malaria and dysentery. In May 1655 an attack was made on what is now Kingston, Jamaica, and succeeded after half-hearted Spanish resistance.

The capture of Jamaica was a major coup. The island was ideal for sugar cultivation (some of the surviving soldiers were given grants of land for plantation) and strategically well-sited to command the shipping lanes that ran eastwards from Spanish Central America, Cuba and Española. A Spanish attempt to retake the island in 1658 failed and, after years of grumbling, Spain formally ceded it to Britain in 1671. By then there were fifty-seven sugar refineries in operation, with cocoa being developed as a secondary crop, and Port Royal had become a regular anchorage for Royal Navy men-o'-war. Its development as a naval base was swift; by 1690 it was guarded by the loyally named Forts Charles, James and Rupert and in 1739 a dockyard with barracks and store-houses had been built.

The seizure of Jamaica was part of a wider plan which embraced the occupation in 1659 of St Helena, an outpost on the Cape route to India, and the projected seizure of either Gibraltar or Minorca as a Mediterranean base. Even without these prizes, Cromwell had demonstrated the effectiveness of a bold, global strategy that would be imitated by successive governments which in varying degrees shared his view of Britain's place in the world.

His Western Design was followed, on a smaller scale, by Modyford, now governor of Jamaica, who on the eve of the outbreak of the second Anglo–Dutch war in 1665, proposed a scheme for 'rooting the Dutch out of the West Indies'. His partners in this private enterprise war were local buccaneers who 'upon my gentleness to them' were ready to 'offer life and fortune to His Majesty's service'.[4] The buccaneers were freelance, seafaring cutthroats who lived by piracy and attracted those on the margins of Caribbean society, including former indentured labourers and runaway slaves. Despite Modyford's assurances, they were a liability when it came to fighting. During a landing on the Dutch island of St Eustatius in July 1665, the volunteers went on strike until the booty had been parcelled out and afterwards, according to an eyewitness, there was 'great confusion as usually attends such parties whose plunder is their pay and obedience guided by their wills.' Nevertheless, with the right leadership and driven by an overwhelming greed, the buccaneers could achieve wonders. In January 1671, commanded by Edward Morgan, a sometime indentured servant on Barbados, they attacked and thoroughly plundered Panama City.

This *coup de main* gave Morgan the means to make himself a Jamaican planter and to secure a knighthood, respectability and the governorship of the colony. It also, like Drake's similar exploits a hundred years before, made a deep impression on the public imagination and reinforced that popular image of distant lands as places where quick fortunes were waiting for the energetic and ruthless.

The belligerent overseas policies of Cromwell and the subsequent piratical war against Spain in the West Indies satisfied nascent British patriotism and, of course, individual cupidity. They were proof, if any was needed, of what could be accomplished by the audacious use of seapower and how it could enrich the country. This idea was not new; it had been first vented in the mid-fifteenth century by mercantilist propagandists who urged the government to 'keep the seas'; that is, forcefully assert English control over the Channel. Maritime superiority, this time extended far beyond home waters, had been advocated by Elizabethan expansionists and their message gained a new force as Britain's foreign trade and overseas possessions increased.

As well as calling for naval supremacy, the early followers of what would later be called the 'Blue Water' school of foreign policy and strategy

warned governments to shun continental entanglements that squandered
the nation's treasure and brought no visible profit. In his pamphlet *The
Conduct of the Allies* (1711), Jonathan Swift contrasted the costly, laborious
and inconclusive campaigns of the Duke of Marlborough in Flanders and
Lord Peterborough in Spain with the dashing enterprise of Bristol-based
privateers. 'Inflamed by a true spirit of our age and industry', they had rav-
aged Spanish shipping and taken the Acapulco treasure ship. Far better,
claimed Swift, to concentrate national resources on the navy and employ
it for a piecemeal conquest of the Spanish Indies rather than pour cash and
men into unwinnable wars in Europe.

In essence, he had put a case that would be repeated by others throughout the eighteenth, nineteenth and early twentieth centuries. Nature had
separated Britain from the continent by the sea and through the ingenuity and perseverance of her people she had become dependent on
seaborne trade and colonies for her wealth. In the event of a continental
war, Britain's first concern was always the preservation of her overseas
resources and the destruction of her adversaries'. The commitment of men
and material to any European theatre of war was a secondary consideration, since gains there did little or nothing to assist maritime security or
commerce.

The conflicts with the Netherlands had given British statesmen and commanders their first taste of waging a global war, although the struggles in
the Caribbean and North America had been peripheral and small in scale.
Even so, it was virtually certain that at some time in the future European
wars were bound to become global contests between empires with each
side seeking to hinder its opponents' commerce and seize their colonies.
To meet such an emergency it was vital that the government asserted its
control over the colonies and took measures for their defence.

It was, argued Charles II's Treasurer, the Earl of Danby in 1664, a matter of urgency that arrangements were made to 'bring about the Necessary
Union of all Plantations in America which will make the King great and
extend his royal empire in those parts.'[5] There was more to Danby's proposal than the assertion of the power of London over distant settlements;
close direction of colonial government would facilitate the raising of local
revenues which would be needed to foot the bill for the colony's defence.

The implementation of this policy was largely left to a man who became
the first imperial civil servant, William Blathwayt. According to the diarist

John Evelyn who met Blathwayt in 1687 when his star was in the ascendant, he was a man who had 'raised himself by his industry, from very moderate circumstances. He is a very proper, handsome person, and very dexterous in business.' A lawyer by training, Blathwayt had been appointed Clerk of the new Privy Council committee for plantations in 1676; four years later he was made Surveyor and Auditor–General of American Revenues; and from 1683 until 1703 he was Secretary-at-War. His assiduity and experience made him invaluable and so, unshaken by political convulsions, he served successively Charles II, James II, William III and Anne.

In the process and in common with other Stuart bureaucrats he made money from bribes and he was lucky enough to marry an heiress. Her house at Dyrham in south Gloucestershire became his country seat, which he had rebuilt from 1687 onwards in the fashionable baroque style under the direction of a refugee French architect. The interior decoration was striking: his study was panelled in black walnut shipped over by the governor of Maryland; stairs and stairwells were cut from cypress and cedar wood from South Carolina; and the gardens were laid out in the modish Dutch manner (William III had become king in 1689) and planted with imported flora from Virginia.

These exotic gifts were tribute from a land where Blathwayt had imposed the King's will and consolidated royal authority, often at the expense of local proprietors and assemblies. The agents of his policies were usually men accustomed to giving orders and expecting obedience – army officers. It was their experience as much as their temper which recommended them since their duties included making arrangements for the colonies' defence.

Until the mid-1670s measures for the safeguard of the settlements in North America and the Caribbean had been haphazard and amateurish. A survey of the military resources of the Leeward Islands, forwarded to London in 1676, revealed their extreme vulnerability. The author, a professional soldier, was dismayed by the tiny garrison of regulars on St Kitts who were 'in the greatest necessity soldiers ever were, in the sight of the French whose soldiers are well paid, well armed and accoutred'. A polyglot militia was not to be trusted since it was suspected that the French and Dutch volunteers would forget their oaths of allegiance in a crisis. On Nevis there were twenty-two regulars, a small cavalry detachment whose horses were 'generally used to carry sugar', and 1,300 militiamen who were 'the worst for arms he had ever seen'.[6] In short, none of the islands could withstand an assault by trained troops.

The need for garrisons of professional soldiers and closer royal supervision of government was evident in North America. In 1676 Virginia was convulsed by an insurrection led by Nathaniel Bacon against the allegedly feeble Indian policy of Governor Berkeley, his corrupt and partial government, and an assembly where, according to the insurgents, 'all the power is got into the hands of the rich'. To restore order, the government in London had to despatch over a thousand troops, artillery and warships.[7] Whilst Virginia faced what was close to a class war, the New England colonies were engaged in interminable frontier wars against the Indians who were getting stronger thanks to French assistance. Indians captured near Fort Pemaquid in New York in 1689 carried French muskets, bayonets, waistbelts, cutlasses. One, speaking in broken English, told an officer that his people 'no care for the New England people; they have all their country by and by.'[8]

The colonists could not face these perils without outside assistance, and this uncomfortable fact of life made them acquiesce to a series of measures which reduced the powers of local assemblies and great landlords. Administrative adjustments were conceded, sometimes grudgingly as in New England, but colonial parliaments still retained considerable law-making powers. These bodies, it must be added, were representative rather than democratic. Like their English and Scottish counterparts, they were the exclusive preserve of men of wealth and property. The North American and West Indian legislatures were filled with planters, estate-owners, merchants and lawyers who were thought to have the best interests of their colony at heart. These men accepted the supremacy of the King's governors, judges and officials as the price for protection.

They were not deferential. In 1700, a member of the Nevis assembly protested to an army officer that, since there was no law that permitted the billeting of soldiers on his estate, they could work in the fields alongside the negroes in return for their keep. As for the officer's orders, he could 'wipe his arse' with them.[9] Such attitudes, coupled with an indifference to the law which was marked in the North American frontier colonies and some Caribbean islands, made the work of governors an uphill struggle and the process of imposing order and inducing submissiveness was often long drawn out. As late as 1775, Colonel Montford Brown, governor of the Bahamas, complained to the government about the prevalence in the islands of crime. The 'inability and laziness' of the Bahamanian made it impossible for him to live other than by smuggling and wrecking; that is, luring ships on to reefs and plundering the wreck. No one, it seemed, understood what was meant by an oath – 'the grand security of the liberty, the property, and the lives of Englishmen' – and so the courts could not function.[10]

The Bahamas may have been exceptionally anarchic. Elsewhere, as colonies developed, their inhabitants became profoundly aware of how their industry contributed to Britain's wealth and power. In 1706 the assemblies of St Kitts and Nevis petitioned parliament for over £100,000 in compensation for losses suffered at the hands of the French. The plantations, it was argued, deserved generous treatment on the grounds of the 'advantage of trade' that flowed from them as well as 'the large Returns they made to the public' from import and export duties. The House of Commons concurred and voted the sum demanded, no doubt seeing it as a valuable investment.

4

———◆—◆———

Dispositions of
Providence:
The Colonists

Britain's overseas colonies would not have happened without large numbers of emigrants who were prepared to abandon their homes, undertake long and hazardous voyages and then submit themselves to a régime of hard labour in an unfamiliar and often unkind environment. Elizabethan expansionists had likened the process to a bodily evacuation, a spewing out of unwanted and harmful matter.[1] This image was invoked by a visitor to Barbados in 1655: 'This island is the Dunghill whereon England doth cast forth its rubbish: Rogues and whores and such like people are those which are generally brought here.'[2]

Up to a point this was true, and some would have added Puritans and Quakers to the indigent, idle and lawless who were coerced into leaving Britain. There were also plenty of so-called voluntary emigrants who had in fact been cozened into crossing the Atlantic. In 1671, a 'spirit' admitted to having kidnapped 500 indentured servants annually, and another calculated one year's haul at 840.[3] Even if these confessions were exaggerated, they indicate that among this, the largest category of emigrant, there were large numbers who travelled unwillingly. Their reluctance was understandable, for their future tribulations were vividly set down in a contemporary popular ballad, 'The Trapann'd [kidnapped] Maid':

> Five years served I, under Master Guy
> In the land of Virginny, O,

Which made me for to know sorrow, grief and woe
When that I was weary, weary, weary, O.

I have played my part, both at the plough and cart,
In the land of Virginny, O;
Billets from Wood upon my back they load,
When that I am weary, weary, weary, O.[4]

This woman was particularly unlucky since female servants were normally allocated domestic work indoors, although in Maryland during the 1650s 'some wenches that are nasty and beastly' were ordered to labour in the fields. The temptation to escape must sometimes have been very great, but so were the dangers of recapture on the island colonies or falling into Indian hands in North America. These risks diminished as the colonial population rose and made it easier for the fugitive to find anonymity. One who tried in the 1760s was described by her owner in a Virginian newspaper advertisement:

Between the Sixth and Seventh Day,
Mary Nowland ran away;
Her age I know not but appears
To be at least full twenty years;
The same religion with the Pope.
Short neck, scarce room to fix a rope:
She's large and round from neck to hips,
Brown hair, red face, short nose, thick lips;
Short, thick and clumsy in her jog
As neat as any fatten'd hog.
Upon her tongue she wears a brogue
And was she man would be a rogue.

Marriage and a household of her own may have been this Irishwoman's motive for leaving her employer, although by this time the old imbalance between men and women settlers in the colonies had been redressed. In 1704 there were 30,000 men and 7,000 women, 85 per cent of them indentured servants, in Maryland.[5] Those free to do so married young; the average age in Maryland was sixteen, twenty-one in Virginia, and brides were frequently pregnant. Indentured servants, who were usually around twenty-four or twenty-five when their terms expired, married later. There was also a high illegitimacy rate despite the humiliating public punishments laid down for unmarried mothers by colonial legislators.

By 1700, a large proportion of colonists were native born. Population growth in the Chesapeake basin colonies had been slower than elsewhere thanks in part to the shortage of women and a high death rate. A twenty-year-old immigrant who survived seasoning might expect to live another twenty years, while a locally born Virginian or Marylander who picked up some immunities would survive a further ten years. Life expectancy in the more astringent climate of New England was sixty.

The lack of women was a handicap in the early phases of colonisation, but it was unavoidable. Clearing forests, breaking ground, tending crops and building houses required a male workforce, a fact of life that was reflected in the occupations of those emigrants who were in most demand by settlement companies and proprietors. The most urgent need was always for skilled artisans. On board the *Increase*, which sailed for New England in 1636, were 116 passengers including a butcher, carpenter, clothier, stonemason, ploughwright, sawyer, surgeon, tailor, two linen weavers, a joiner and a dozen farm labourers. There were also, well down the list, twelve men without trades, twenty-four adult women, twenty-six girls under eighteen and thirty boys.[6] This distribution of occupation, age and sex was typical, although there was no certainty as to whether it would be reproduced in the colony because of losses during the voyage and acclimatisation.

The ideal colonists were described by the Massachusetts Bay Company in the 1630s as 'endowed with grace and furnished with means'. The first quality was essential for the fulfilment of the Puritan vision of a settlement peopled with men and women who knew themselves to be chosen by God and therefore were glad to submit themselves to disciplined labour and regulations based on Old Testament texts.

At the same time an immigrant needed cash and a stock of tools. The transatlantic fare was about £5 a person, to which had to be added the price of food during the voyage, and freightage was £4 a ton. An English yeoman farmer with his family and their farming implements and domestic utensils would expect to pay at least £100 for transit to North America. Given that such a man's annual income might be between £40 and £60, if he wished to emigrate, he would be forced to sell his land. In other words, his decision to leave would have to be final.[7] Of course there were many cases where companies subsidised colonists who were, at least for the Massachusetts Bay Company, carefully screened beforehand to weed out the morally unsuitable. One who passed the test was John Dane who, having considered emigration to one of the Caribbean islands, directly asked God for guidance. 'Utterly forlorn in my spirit' and anxious to be 'free from temptation', he followed current Puritan practice and randomly opened his Bible. He found the text, 'Come out from among them, touch no unclean thing, and I will be your God and you shall be my people.' He immediately left his native Hertfordshire and its temptations and took ship for New England.[8]

There were more direct inducements. In 1667 the potential colonist for the Cape Florida settlement was lured with the promise of a hundred acres for himself and a further hundred for each of his children and musket-armed servants (this was Indian country) at an annual rent of ten shillings for every thousand acres. A further fifty acres would be granted for every female servant or slave in his possession.

On the expiry of his contract, every indentured servant was to be given a hundred acres by his master, together with farming tools and two suits of clothing.[9] This pledge was deliberately framed to attract men who already enjoyed considerable wealth in England, for they would have had to have provided the costs of shipping and sufficient stocks of food to see themselves and their households through the time it took to cultivate, harvest and market cash crops.

To a large extent the existing, but never inflexible, British social hierarchy was transported across the Atlantic and re-erected in North America and the Caribbean. In the colonies gentlemen commanded the same respect as they did in Britain. One gentleman, who died during the early days of Virginia, had a memorial brass imported for his gravestone which showed him in full armour, an anachronism on the battlefield but still the accepted public token of his social standing. It was set in the floor of Jamestown church from where it was later stolen. Looking back on his childhood in the 1690s, a Virginian farmer recalled, 'A periwig, in those days, was a distinguishing badge of gentle-folk.' The same adornment denoted a gentleman in Britain.

As in the home country, property was the ultimate measure of social position for, as one tobacco planter observed, 'If a [man] has Money, Negroes and Land enough he is a complete Gentleman.' Another, who had all three, wrote in 1726:

> I have a large Family of my own, and my Doors are open to
> Every Body, yet I have no Bills to pay, and half-a-crown will

rest undisturbed in my Pocket for many Moons together. Like one of the Patriarchs, I have my Flocks and my Herds, my Bond-men and Bond-women [indentured labourers], and every sort of trade amongst my own servants, so that I live in a kind of Independence on everyone but Providence.[10]

In outlook and circumstances such men were little different from their near-contemporaries, Squires Allworthy and Western in Henry Fielding's novel *Tom Jones*.

The dominance of the rich gave colonial society a cohesion and made it easy for public order to be maintained since humbler immigrants were already conditioned to accept the magistracy of men of substance and property. In the New England settlements public responsibility was confined to the senior and invariably more prosperous members of church congregations. The laws they framed in their assemblies and enforced from the bench combined the Common Law of England with the injunctions for a pure life extensively laid down in the Old Testament. Blasphemers and homosexuals faced execution, as did masturbators, in New Haven, and fornicators were whipped, a punishment from which, revealingly, gentlemen were excluded. Such laws and proscribed penalties poured from the small legislatures of the New England states and reflected, in an extreme manner, a mentality that prevailed in Britain. Wickedness in all its forms was endemic throughout society and was most concentrated among the lower classes, who required constant and often condign reminders of their duty to God and the civil authorities who upheld His and the King's laws.

This need for a harsh and vigorously enforced code of law was most obvious in the slave-owning colonies. There the élite was ultimately defined by the colour of its skin and, from the second half of the seventeenth century onwards, it stood in continual danger of being overwhelmed by the spiralling slave population. In 1628 Barbados contained 14,000 inhabitants, most of them white indentured labourers. There was a rapid influx of negroes after 1650 and by 1673 their total was 33,000 compared with 21,000 whites. As more and more manual work was undertaken by negroes the European population slumped; in 1712 it was 15,000 against 42,000 slaves.

Fears about security were inevitable. The governor of Barbados expressed misgivings in 1692 about the deployment of the local, all-white militia in the island's forts which might encourage a negro insurrection. Soon after, a suspected conspirator revealed, under torture, the existence of a plot to seize one of the island's arsenals in which, interestingly, several disaffected Irishmen were involved.[11] The Barbadian demographic pattern was repeated in Jamaica and caused similar alarms about the racial imbalance in population. In 1690 there was an uprising by 500 slaves on a plantation in the middle of the island in which several whites were killed. After its suppression, a relieved governor informed the royal council, 'The rebellion might have been very bloody considering the number of negroes and the scarcity of white men.' His apprehension was shared by members of the island's assembly which, in 1697, pleaded with the government to recruit 'poor craftsmen' in England for 'white men are so scarce that they will easily find employment'[12]

The reaction of the West Indian and North American legislatures to the presence in their societies of huge numbers of potentially rebellious slaves was paranoid. Deep fears expressed themselves in sheaves of laws which restricted the movements and activities of slaves and inflicted ferocious penalties, including castration and burning alive, for every form of insubordination. According to the 1696 Barbadian code, which was later imitated in South Carolina, the negroes' 'barbarous, wild, savage natures' placed them beyond the bounds of the laws by which white men lived. Instead they had their own regulations specially drafted to 'restrain the disorders, rapines and inhumanity to which they are naturally prone and inclined'.[13] Special prominence was given to bans on sexual relations between negroes and white women. There was also a need to produce a legal definition of slavery, which had not existed in Britain since the early Middle Ages, and the powers exercised by the master over his slave.

The negro's place within colonial society was at the bottom of the pile. Like a pet dog he owed his name to his master; among the more popular were: 'Juno', 'Bacchus', 'Caesar', 'Quashy', 'Monday', 'Cuffy', 'London' and 'Sambo'. He also learned to speak and think in a new language, English. Writing in 1724, a Virginian clergyman noted that 'the languages of the new Negroes are various harsh jargon', but those born in the colony 'talk good English, and affect our language, habits and customs'. Assimilation was limited; African traditions and mythology were perpetuated in what became the slaves' underground culture. A suspect interrogated after the discovery of a plot to seize Antigua in 1736 revealed that a magician or *obeah* man had used his supernatural powers to ensnare conspirators. 'I am afraid of the Obey [Obeah] man now,' he told his inquisitors, 'he is a bloody fellow, I knew him in Cormantee country.'[14] Not surprisingly, colonial lawmakers saw the transmission of African customs as subversive and slaves were forbidden crepuscular drumming, blowing on conch shells and fetish ceremonies.

The submission of the negro, and for that matter the Native American, was the foundation of the colonial order. It is symbolised in Defoe's novel *The Life and Adventures of Robinson Crusoe* (1719) when the Amerindian 'Friday' places Crusoe's foot on his head and acknowledges him as his overlord. Admittedly his life had just been saved, but the gesture would have had a universal significance for Defoe's readers. So too, but for different reasons, would that section of the story in which Crusoe was shipwrecked on an island somewhere off the coast of modern Venezuela and stranded there. The close examination of his state of mind during his exile and the description of his practical response to his situation transformed the novel into a parable of colonial settlement.

In the beginning Crusoe, the son of a Hull merchant, becomes a mariner-entrepreneur with ambitions to make his fortune in the slave trade. He is temporarily frustrated when he is taken prisoner by Arab pirates operating from Salé, a Moroccan port. Mediterranean and Caribbean piracy was an everyday hazard throughout the seventeenth, eighteenth and, in a lesser degree, the early nineteenth centuries. In 1698, as his ship the *Unicorn* neared the Leeward Islands, Colin Campbell recalled how every sail sighted on the horizon immediately triggered fears of pirates among the crew.[15] If their ship was taken, the passengers and crew faced death, enslavement or, if they appeared to have money, ransom. John Darbey, one of the marginally more fortunate victims of piracy, testified to the governor of Jamaica in 1675 how he had been taken from his ship, a New England barque, by Dutch privateers. He was put ashore at the Spanish port of Havana where he soon found himself 'in miserable slavery' building a fort at the orders of the governor. Before his escape he encountered a sadistic Spanish naval captain, Don Philip Fitzgerald (probably an Irish renegade), who shot and stabbed several other captive English seamen in what appears to have been a fit of pique.[16]

To judge from his matter-of-fact account of his adventures, Darbey had a considerable degree of stoicism which enabled him to bear up to his misfortunes. A similar, quietistic spirit is demanded of Crusoe when, after his release by the pirates, he is shipwrecked. The only survivor from the crew, Crusoe is able to salvage a stock of muskets, pistols, gunpowder, knives, clothing, preserved food, alcohol and, perhaps most importantly, tools such as a saw and hatchets from his ship. He is equipped with the basic artefacts of contemporary European technology and therefore in a position similar to that of a more conventional colonist. In November 1610 the settlers at Cupid's Cove, Newfoundland had been supplied with muskets, spades, mattocks, scythes, cheeses, barrels of 'Irish beef' and pork, a Bible and a book on 'the General practise of physick'.

They were more fortunate than Crusoe in that they possessed an imported sow which had farrowed, poultry, six goats and, oddly, a single rabbit. Crusoe is able to make up for deficiencies in this area by shooting game and, in time, taming some local wild goats. Improvisation and the ingenious use of the tools he has to hand enable Crusoe to impose his will on what he discovers is an uninhabited island wilderness. He gradually investigates the island's resources which include lime, lemon and cocoa trees and tobacco plants. Some barley recovered from the wreck and carelessly thrown down takes root. Its shoots astonish Crusoe who, like others who settled in the Americas, was constantly amazed by the fecundity of the region. His reaction was the same as that of those early colonists who later explained the natural abundance of the New World in terms of the heat which, it was assumed, encouraged livestock to grow fat and produce more offspring.

There are drawbacks. It takes Crusoe some years to calculate the correct seasons for planting and harvesting his small crop of barley. Here as in other matters he learns patience and adopts a prudent and rational system of husbanding his resources. At the start he guesses, rightly as it turns out, that he will need to defend himself, and so he constructs what eventually becomes an elaborate network of wooden palisades and hedges around his dwelling and barley field.

The performance of these and other mundane tasks requires mental as well as physical stamina. Crusoe, hitherto not a religious man, finds this through reading his Bible and surrendering himself to what he calls the 'dispositions of Providence'. By accepting Divine Providence, Crusoe discovers he can endure the isolation, uncertainty and all the petty frustrations he has to face. Crusoe's interior development is paralleled by his methodical and largely successful efforts to master his surroundings and make an ordered life for himself.

This life is finally ended with the successive appearances of Carib Indians from whom Friday, his servant companion, is rescued and the landing of a party of Englishmen, the passengers and officers of a ship whose crew has mutinied. With the assistance of Crusoe and Friday, the mutineers are overthrown and their survivors left on the island. Crusoe sails back to England, enriched by coin and bullion he had earlier salvaged from a grounded Spanish ship. The story concludes in the year 1694 when he returns to his island which he now calls 'my new colony'. Divided between the survivors of the Spanish shipwreck and the mutinous English seamen, the colony is prospering and Crusoe, a shrewd investor, makes arrangements to have women, skilled craftsmen, livestock and supplies imported.

What emerges most forcefully from this story is Crusoe's fortitude and willingness to persevere against the odds. He combines an inner spiritual strength that makes it possible for him to accept his fate as the will of God with an ability to overcome his physical environment by the application of reason and hard work. He is the embodiment of all the virtues needed for a colonist.

Defoe's fiction was founded on reality. There were plenty of colonists who showed some if not all of Crusoe's qualities and prospered accordingly. One who showed remarkable tenacity was a north countryman, Anthony Hilton, who was employed as an agent by a group of Barnstaple merchants trading with Virginia. A visit to St Kitts during one of his transatlantic voyages left him convinced that he had found an ideal site for a tobacco plantation. With backers, who included some 'gentlemen of Ireland', he returned to the island, cleared the ground and built wooden houses. His plantation was overrun by local Carib Indians so he moved elsewhere on the island and raised a crop which sold for £1 a pound. Worried by Carib hostility, Hilton hurried back to London and persuaded investors to support a fresh venture on a nearby island, Nevis. The colony was established in 1628 and the following year it was attacked by the Spanish who destroyed crops and buildings and expelled the settlers. Undeterred, Hilton restarted the colony which, in time, flourished.

Hilton's determination was matched by the ruthlessness of Sir Thomas Warner, 'a good soldier and man of extraordinary agility', who also established a plantation on St Kitts in 1624. He made terms with a local Carib chief and prudently built a wooden fort with loopholes for muskets which, he explained to the suspicious Caribs, was an enclosure for chickens. Soon after, he was informed that the Indians were plotting to massacre the settlers. He attacked first when the Caribs were drunk and killed their chief as he lay in his hammock. In its earlier stages colonisation was always a struggle for survival; Crusoe's first priority had been to build a small fort and he always gave careful attention to the conservation of his gunpowder.

The diligent management of resources in which Crusoe excelled was the particular skill of the merchant. He was, according to Thomas Mun, an early seventeenth-century apostle of mercantilism, the 'steward of the Kingdom's Stock, by way of Commerce with other Nations . . . so the Private Gain may ever accompany the public good.' His calling was therefore an elevated one for, 'There is more Honour and Profit in an Industrious Life, than in a great inheritance which wasteth for want of Virtue.'[17] If a merchant flourished he could, with no difficulty, secure himself a substantial inheritance. As Defoe pointed out in his 'The True-Born Englishman' of 1703:

> Wealth, howsoever got, in England makes
> Lords of mechanics, gentlemen of rakes:
> Antiquity and birth are needless here;
> 'Tis impudence and money makes a peer.

And a good thing too, thought the essayist Richard Addison, who wrote that it served a spendthrift aristocrat right if he was forced to sell out and make way for an ex-merchant who 'deserves the estate a great deal better when he has got it by industry'.

Much of the colonial merchant's industry was, like Crusoe's, routine and dull and could only be undertaken with a high degree of self-discipline and dedication. The diary kept by Anthony Beale, 'a very careful, honest man', the governor of the Hudson's Bay Company's River Port trading post during 1706, is a record of what must often have been a tedious existence in an extremely remote region where a very strong sense of duty was essential for men to survive.[18] There was a staff of forty-six at the fortified settlement, nearly all skilled artisans, who were paid annual wages of between £20 and £48.

The highlight of their year in terms of activity was midsummer when the Company's ships arrived to unload supplies and collect the furs and beaver pelts which were brought to the post by local Indians and exchanged for manufactured goods. There followed the frozen winter of the tundra when the only occupations were fishing and shooting and trapping game which seems to have been plentiful. A stock of sheep and goats, cheeses and a garden planted with imported turnips, radishes, spinach, chervil, cress, cabbage and lettuce provided a varied and healthy diet. A tenuous and emotional link with home was the celebration on

23 April of Queen Anne's birthday when the Union flag was hoisted and every man was given 'a bottle of strong beer'.

Governor Beale's daybook also reveals a busy world of commerce with meticulously kept accounts and inventories of supplies and barter stock which included needles, powder horns, fish hooks and, for the vainer Indian, fifty Ostrich feathers, presumably purchased in London from a merchant trading in Africa – a nice example of intercolonial trade. Exchanges were made according to strict rules in which the unit of currency was the beaver pelt; two secured a pair of scissors, a hatchet or an ostrich feather, four a gallon of brandy and between seven and ten a musket. There was another scale of barter for furs: four marten furs equalled one beaver, as did two deerskins, and one bear pelt was worth two beavers.

Like Crusoe, Beale existed in an isolated wilderness. His vegetable garden like Crusoe's barley field was a minor triumph; there were many others wherever colonists overcame even the most inclement environment and made it work to their own advantage. They did so for many complex reasons, not least necessity and nearly all attributed their success to the intervention of a just God who rewarded faith and industry. When Captain Leonard Edgcombe sailed from London to Hudson's Bay in 1691, the Company's directors commanded him to call his crew to prayer every morning and evening 'from which we may hope and expect a Blessing from Almighty God'.[19] Just over forty years later, an anonymous correspondent wrote in the *National Merchant* (January 1736), 'I look upon our Colonies as a charitable Benefaction bestowed on this nation by *God* . . . which if rightly improved, must needs make us a great, happy and flourishing people.'

But God's gifts could only be made fruitful by the application of human labour. Whether or not they possessed the qualities and sense of dedication displayed by Robinson Crusoe – and many indentured servants, transported convicts and slaves certainly did not – those who laboured in the colonies had, by the end of the seventeenth century, created a thriving empire. This word was not in general usage until well into the eighteenth century, when it began to replace 'colonies' or 'plantations'.

Psychologically the change of title was important, carrying with it notions of grandeur and power on a world scale. And yet the period which witnessed the first growth of Britain's colonies also saw the first germination of that aggressive, self-confident patriotism which flowered during the next two hundred years and facilitated further imperial expansion. Seventeenth-century colonial expansion had taught the British how to make money overseas, given impetus to ideas about national destiny and God's mandate to colonists, and produced archetypes like Robinson Crusoe who demonstrated what could be accomplished by men of energy and dedication.

What was achieved fascinated subsequent generations who attempted both to romanticise the founders of empire and invest all of them with qualities they never possessed. During the late-Victorian surge of empire-building, the stories of the sixteenth- and seventeenth-century settlers and seafarers were retold in a form designed to inspire the young to follow their example. Drake, Morgan and the American pioneers were endowed with such contemporary virtues as manly courage, fortitude, comradeship and a love of adventure for its own sake, and the ruthless pursuit of profit was underplayed or left unmentioned. This was a distortion both of the men and their motives, but an attractive one which, during this century, has been given a new lease of life through Hollywood's popular, swashbuckling movies in which dashing pirate captains swing from halyards with merry smiles on their faces.

In a more serious vein, American historians have minutely examined the world of the early colonists to find evidence in support of theories that today's social attitudes and political systems were rooted in the assumptions and behaviour of the Anglo-Saxon settlers rather than the later frontier experience or the ethnic multiplicity that followed mass immigration in the nineteenth century. What has been revealed is, not surprisingly, a rich diversity of outlook and motive among the settlers; if anything bound them together it was a common urge for self-improvement coupled with a determination to master their environment.

PART TWO

PERSIST AND CONQUER
1689–1815

1

Rule of the Main:
The Making of British
Seapower, 1689–1748

On the ceiling above the main staircase of the Commissioner's House at Chatham Dockyard is a large painting set there in about 1705. It is baroque in style and triumphant in mood; Mars receives a crown of shells from Neptune, while, in the foreground, stand symbolic figures of Peace, Plenty, Justice and Charity. The whole piece is an allegory of Britain, a prosperous, just and Christian nation which thrives under the protection of the ruler of the oceans. What would have struck onlookers most forcefully was the majestic figure of Neptune, whom they would have immediately identified as a symbol of the Royal Navy's mastery of the seas. This allusion was understood by Britain's enemies; in 1775 a French official, regretting the growth of British seapower, observed that, 'Neptune's trident has become the sceptre of the world.'[1]

The Chatham painting was executed during the first phase of a sequence of global wars against France which had started in 1689 and would continue until 1783. They were: the Nine Years War (1689–97), the War of the Spanish Succession (1702–14), the War of the Austrian Succession (1739–48), the Seven Years War (1756–63) and the American War of Independence (1775–83) in which the French intervened in 1778. What added up to over forty years of fighting consisted of two parallel struggles, one fought to prevent France from establishing a hegemony in Europe, the other to enlarge Britain's overseas trade and colonies at the expense of France and Spain.

On the surface, Britain and France appeared unequal adversaries. In

1700, the population of France was 19.2 million, and in 1780 it was 25.6 million, while that of Britain rose from 6.9 to 9 million during the same period. Britain's total of foreign trade in 1700 was £9 million, France's £13 million, figures that increased to £22 million and £23 million respectively during the next eighty years. For each country a century of permanent rivalry and intermittent war was also a time of steady economic growth.

These figures are deceptive in terms of resources available for war, particularly public credit. Britain was always the stronger power because, at times of crisis, she could raise huge amounts of money without resort to additional taxation. The British method of paying for wars was an emergency measure introduced in 1692–3 when it seemed that existing arrangements for obtaining credit were on the verge of collapse. Then, the government adopted the expedient of what became known as the national debt. Corporations and individuals were invited to loan money to the government in return for stock which paid an annual dividend. Investors received a reliable source of income and the government found the wherewithal to pay for armies and navies whenever they were needed. Each successive war added to the debt; in 1757 it stood at £57 million, and by 1787 it had risen to £240 million. In that year interest payments cost the Treasury £9.4 million, a large sum for a nation with an annual income from taxes and customs duties of just over £13 million.

Nevertheless, the burden of servicing the national debt was more than offset by the advantages it offered to British statesmen and commanders. It freed them from anxieties about public opinion, which would have inevitably reacted adversely to emergency taxation or extra customs duties that might easily have harmed trade and triggered inflation. Unity among the political classes was vital for any war effort and this was only possible if the king's ministers took account of opinions expressed in parliament and by newspapers and journals.

The deposition of James II in 1688 and the accession of the Dutch *stadtholder* William of Orange and his wife Mary in 1689 had witnessed an irreversible shift in the balance of power between the crown and parliament. The legislation of what was called the Glorious Revolution of 1688–9 placed executive authority in the hands of the king's ministers, who in turn depended upon the support of a majority of members of the House of Commons. The actual process by which ministers assumed their new responsibilities was gradual, and throughout the eighteenth century the crown continued to exert often considerable influence over the shaping of policy.

What mattered was that neither kings nor ministers could ignore the voice of the Commons, an assembly whose members spoke up both for their own interests and what they saw as the country's. The largest sectional interest within the Commons and the Lords was land, but it never enjoyed a complete dominance. Aristocrats and country squires had to share power with merchants, shippers and financiers from the City of London which, since the 1690s, had developed rapidly as a centre for stock-dealing, banking and marine insurance. There was also a strong presence in both houses of men with direct and indirect colonial interests such as plantation owners, former Indian traders, directors of the East India Company and naval and army officers, of whom nearly three hundred served as MPs between 1754 and 1790. Commercial and colonial interests could and did exert a strong pressure on the king's ministers which they ignored at their peril.

By and large, the commercial and colonial lobbies wholeheartedly endorsed aggressive, acquisitive, anti-French and anti-Spanish policies. They did so because they regarded them as serving the national interest; wars that ended with annexations offered fresh opportunities for overseas trade and investment, as George III reminded the Commons in his speech from the throne in 1762. 'My territories are greatly augmented,' he told members, 'and new sources open for trade and manufacture.' Wars also stimulated domestic productivity, particularly ship-building and the expanding metallurgical industries of the Midlands; Birmingham-made muskets and swords armed the troops of the East India Company. Increased trade meant more revenue from customs that satisfied the dominant landed class which was spared increases in land taxes.

During the eighteenth century, there emerged a significant concert of interests among the politically active classes, irrespective of individual attachment to Whig or Tory factions. They believed that it was necessary, even desirable for Britain to go to war in order to become richer and to assert her mastery of the seas. No one ever objected to increases in the annual vote of funds for the navy. More importantly, the national debt meant that a belligerent foreign policy caused no undue distress to taxpayers, businessmen or manufacturers.

France was less fortunately placed when it came to waging war. It was impossible for her governments to harness national resources effectively, thanks to a system of public finance which had become ossified and grossly inefficient. Wholesale tax exemptions were enjoyed by the clergy and aristocracy who resolutely defended their privileges, with the result that, whenever a national emergency occurred, the government had no choice but to borrow from the money markets and pay back loans and interest from increased imposts. These fell heavily on imports, exports and domestic commercial transactions and had the effect of strangling commerce.

In 1697, when France was facing economic exhaustion after a nine-year war effort, an envious Frenchman wondered why Britain, superficially a poorer nation, 'bears a burden of debt larger than ours'. The question was asked again and again throughout the eighteenth century, and in Britain the government took a keen interest in the overdue and abortive efforts of the French to overhaul their fiscal apparatus. Details of the reforms proposed during 1775 were reported, along with other economic intelligence, to London by the Admiralty's Paris spy or 'correspondent' as such creatures were then called.[2]

The imbalance between French and British resources did not guarantee automatic British success; far from it. Throughout this period, France could field a formidable army and, when the occasion demanded, a powerful fleet, as well as large numbers of privateers who harassed British trade. Moreover, and this was a permanent headache for the élite of ministers who devised British strategy, if France allied with Spain then their combined fleets could overturn the maritime balance. In this situation, Britain could not be strong everywhere and the government would face uncomfortable choices as to where to concentrate its ships and where to allow its enemies superiority.

This dilemma was first encountered in 1689, when Louis XIV's first objective was to overthrow William III and restore James II and thereby fracture the Anglo–Dutch front which stood in the way of his expansionist policies in Europe. In terms of numbers of ships, France was capable of challenging both powers in the Channel for, since the early 1660s, Louis's minister, Jean-Baptiste Colbert, had masterminded an ambitious policy of naval rearmament. A mercantilist, he had a vision of France's future as a colonial, commercial power which, like Britain, would draw its strength from international trade. His master was more conventional; Louis preferred to channel his nation's energies into the piecemeal creation of an extended France whose frontiers would enclose the Low Countries and the Rhine Valley.

The French attempt to dethrone William and detach Britain from its alliance with the Netherlands was marked by missed opportunities and mismanagement. The Catholic James II's strongest support was among the Gaelic-speaking Catholic Irish, but campaigns in Ireland required regular transfusions of French men and equipment. Between 1689 and 1690 there were two French expeditions to Ireland, neither of which were seriously impeded by the Royal Navy. The initial Anglo–Dutch response to this threat was fumbling and, after the defeat of a British fleet at Beachy Head in June 1690, control of the Channel was temporarily lost.

No attempt was made by the French to follow up this advantage, and in 1691 the French navy lost the initiative. There were no further convoys to Ireland where James II's cause soon withered. 1692 saw the Anglo–Dutch fleet secure the upper hand with twin victories at Barfleur and La Hogue in May, when a French fleet, outnumbered two to one, lost twelve battleships, a quarter of its strength. The French navy had not brought Britain to its knees and Louis, realising that further expenditure on ships would bring few returns, cut the naval budget by two-thirds. His fleet was already under strain because of a permanent shortage of skilled sailors, which was wholly the consequence of his foolish revocation of the Edict of Nantes in 1685 by which he withdrew religious toleration from Protestants. Thousands of seamen from France's Atlantic ports, where Protestantism had been strong, chose exile, many coming to England. For many years to come, the French navy had to draw on a comparatively small pool of trained sailors for its crews.[3] Matters were made worse after 1692, and again in the 1700s, by the official policy of keeping fleets in harbour which preserved fighting ships but deprived their crews of valuable experience at sea.

After 1692 the French wisely shunned fleet actions and turned instead to a war of commerce raiding intended to undermine Anglo–Dutch trade. Despite a handful of audacious commanders, like Jean Bart, this war of attrition in the end failed to produce the expected result. There was, however, one nasty shock for the Allies. Between 1689 and 1691, French pressure in home waters had forced the Royal Navy to withdraw its presence from the Mediterranean, which damaged Britain's trade with Italy and the Levant. An attempt to reassert British naval power in the Mediterranean was made in 1693 and ended in calamity when a heavily escorted convoy of 400 merchantmen was attacked in Lagos Bay in southern Portugal. A hundred ships were lost, but the French again chose not to exploit their success. During 1694–95, the French Mediterranean fleet remained bottled up in Toulon harbour and its adversaries resumed their command of that sea.

Outside Europe, naval operations were limited. At this time, French overseas trade was not great, although this did not stop hundreds of British privateers, including the infamous Captain Kidd, from seeking official letters of marque to attack French merchant ships. In 1694, an eight-strong squadron of warships sailed for the West Indies with orders to interrupt French seaborne trade, raid French islands and burn plantations. Much damage was done, but a 'violent and uncommon distemper' struck down the crews of this flotilla and brought the campaign to a premature end. So many seamen died on one ship that there were not enough left to man it properly and it ran aground on the Florida shoals.[4]

Neither side gained a decisive advantage at sea between 1689 and 1697, although the Allies could claim some satisfaction at having seen off the French challenge in the Channel and the Mediterranean. On land the story was similar, and both sides, exhausted and war-weary, made peace. It was in fact only a truce since Louis, through diplomatic manipulation, secured, by 1700, what amounted to an amalgamation of France with Spain.

It was unthinkable that Britain could stand by and allow France to take possession of Spain, its Italian territories, and, most importantly, its transatlantic empire. From the start, Louis was determined to engross all Spanish commerce, from which the British and Dutch were to be excluded. This was a disaster for Britain; markets would be lost and command of the seas pass to the Franco–Spanish fleet. War began in 1702 with Britain as the lynchpin and paymaster of the Grand Alliance whose other members included the Netherlands, Austria and Prussia, all of whom wanted to resist French domination in Europe.

The decisive battles of the War of the Spanish Succession were fought on land by the armies directed by John Churchill, the Duke of Marlborough. Most of the men he commanded, whether British, Dutch or German, were paid for by Britain which, in 1711, had 171,000 men on its payroll. British seapower alone paid a peripheral part in this conflict which was marked by no decisive, full-scale fleet actions. Nevertheless, in terms of the future use of the navy, the war provided useful lessons and experience.

From the beginning, British strategy aimed at the elimination of Franco–Spanish power in the Mediterranean. This required the acquisition of a naval base in the region so that men-o'-war could be armed, victualled and overhauled without having to sail back to ports in Britain. To this end, Gibraltar was occupied and held in the teeth of a Franco–Spanish counter-attack (1702–04) and Minorca, with its deep-water harbour at Port Mahon, was seized in 1708. Both acquisitions were of tremendous importance, for British fleets could now be permanently stationed in the Mediterranean and British political influence exerted over its small maritime states.

As a token of Britain's new position in this area, Admiral Sir Clowdisley Shovell's fleet cruised in the western Mediterranean in 1703 to demonstrate to local rulers that Britain was now a force to be reckoned with. One, the Duke of Savoy, was so impressed that he changed sides and joined the Grand Alliance.[5] The intimidatory value of a fleet was quickly appreciated. In 1708 the Duke of Manchester, Queen Anne's ambassador to Venice, commenting on the uncooperative attitude of the Pope, observed, 'I wish our fleet would make him a visit, that he may know what a Queen of Great Britain is.' Such a show was hardly needed; in 1705 Barcelona was occupied after an amphibious landing, and three years later a similar attack on Toulon did severe damage to the French fleet anchored there.

These enterprises were part of a larger strategy, warmly endorsed by Marlborough, by which France was driven to split her land forces to counter threats in southern Europe, including an invasion of Spain itself by an army under Lord Peterborough. His campaign, like Wellington's a century later, could not have been sustained without the Royal Navy's domination of the Atlantic and Mediterranean.

Beyond European waters, the Royal Navy undertook a number of small-scale operations against French and Spanish shipping and colonies with mixed results. A small squadron, under the command of Vice-Admiral John Benbow, a determined and courageous officer, cruised in the West Indies and severely mauled a French flotilla in a six-day engagement off Santa Marta in April 1702. Following what would become Nelson's dictum that an officer who attacked his adversary without hesitation could do no wrong, Benbow took the offensive, but was deserted by four of his seven subordinate commanders. Towards the end of the action, his right leg was shattered by chain shot, but he remained on his quarterdeck in a hastily constructed cradle and continued to direct the fighting. He died some months later from fever, having had his leg amputated. Two of his cowardly officers were subsequently court-martialled and shot, while Benbow lived on in a popular ballad as a golden example of the tenacity, sense of duty and fighting spirit that Britain expected from its sailors:

> *Brave Benbow lost his legs by chain shot, by chain shot,*
> *Brave Benbow lost his legs by chain shot.*
> *Brave Benbow lost his legs,*
> *But on his stumps he begs,*
> *'Fight on, my English lads, 'tis our lot, 'tis our lot.'*

Benbow's virtues were also displayed by Rear-Admiral Sir Charles Wager, who encountered a Spanish treasure fleet off Porto Bello in May 1708. Abandoned by two timorous commanders, he went straight for the enemy and, firing broadsides at close range, sank one battleship that was stuffed with bullion and crippled another. A representation of the battle, carved in marble, was later set on his flamboyant tomb in Westminster Abbey.

Wager's destruction of the bullion ships, like the seizure of another treasure fleet at Vigo on the Portuguese coast in 1703 (some of the captured silver was used to mint coins which were stamped 'Vigo'), hampered the Franco-Spanish war effort. What was too easily forgotten by the Allies, who naturally celebrated such coups, was that nearly all the convoys of precious metals from Spanish America did reach their destination. Even so, it was clear by 1710 that the two sides were evenly matched on land and that France, thrown back on the defensive and close to bankruptcy, had been fought to a standstill.

In Britain a new, Tory ministry adopted a strategy which, it was imagined, would bring the country advantages in the form of conquered French colonies. Successful amphibious attacks were made on French settlements in Nova Scotia and Newfoundland. A more ambitious project to capture Quebec in 1711 went awry because of careless planning and ignorance of the fogs and shoals of the St Lawrence River.

Peace was made in 1714 at Utrecht where France recognised continued Spanish independence. Britain was rewarded with Gibraltar and Minorca, confirming her ascendancy in the Mediterranean, and Nova Scotia and the grant of the *asiento,* an official licence that permitted one ship a year to trade with the Spanish American colonies. The war had marked Britain's coming of age as a European and a global power, a status which owed everything to her fleet of 124 ships, nearly twice the strength of the combined Franco–Spanish navies. While her adversaries and the Dutch had been debilitated by twelve years of conflict, British overseas trade had actually increased. This achievement had been in large part the result of the 1708 Cruisers and Convoys Act which bound the navy to allocate warships to protect merchantmen against privateers and commerce raiders, a duty which, by the close of the war, occupied two-thirds of the navy's strength.

From 1714 to 1739 Britain and its colonies enjoyed a period of peace, domestic tranquillity and economic growth. Relations with France were outwardly cordial, but many Frenchmen were deeply apprehensive about the scope of Britain's global ambitions. 'The financial power of the English . . . gets every day larger and more ambitious,' observed a French official in 1733, seemed poised to extinguish his country's own expanding trade. Commercial competition between the two nations was therefore keen, in particular in North America, the Caribbean and on the east coast of India, where France was extending its network of trading posts, much to the alarm of the East India Company.

It was Spanish high-handedness rather than fears of French enterprise which led to war in November 1739. For the past five years, the Spanish authorities in America had been cracking down on what, with good reason, they considered abuses of the *asiento* contract by British merchants. The attempts of the *guada-costas* (customs officers) to stem the flow of contraband led to violent incidents when British ships were boarded, searched and, in many cases, their captains and cargoes arrested. Most famously, one zealous *guarda-costa* sliced off the ear of Captain Jenkins of the *Rebecca* and suggested that he took the organ to George II in language that was too coarse to be repeated in the Commons. When MPs debated this and other outrages in March 1739, the mercantile interest clamoured for war. They claimed that Britain's entire transatlantic commerce would be ruined unless Spain was taught a sharp lesson.

National pride had been bruised and one member contrasted 'The mean Submission of Great Britain' with 'the triumphant pride, and stubborn Haughtiness of Spain'.

There was a broad principle at stake according to William Pitt, the future prime minister. 'It is vain to negotiate and make treaties', he argued, 'if there is not Dignity and Vigour to enforce the observance of them.'[6] It was clear, at least from the perspective of the Commons chamber, that Spain had failed to uphold her obligations to Britain and therefore needed to be reminded of them in a way that would deter any future backsliding. The navy was the obvious means of bringing home to Spain the folly of meddling with British trade. The doctrine of the corrective use of seapower which later, and after many applications, would be known as gunboat diplomacy was born. Most of the war party were unconcerned with the surgical use of seapower to punish Spain; they wanted a rerun of the campaigns of Drake and Morgan with warships returning to British ports crammed with the silver and gold of the Spanish Indies. Drawing attention to the presence of large numbers of army and naval officers among those calling for war, Henry Pelham, the MP for Sussex who

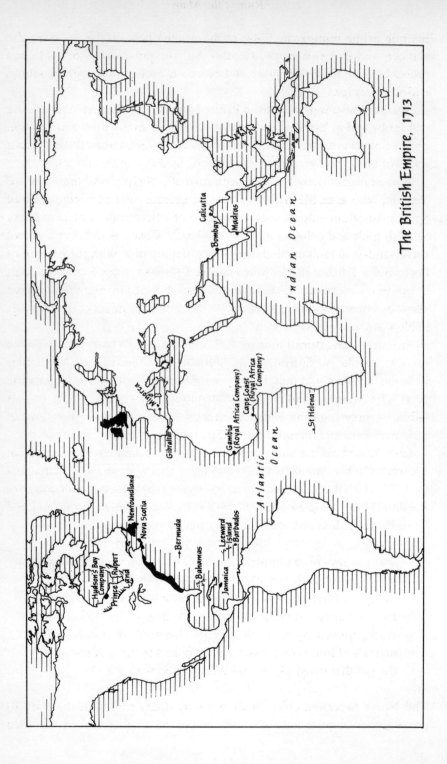

The British Empire, 1713

became prime minister in 1744, tartly recalled how, in the last war, 'the Officers and Sailors were the Gainers, but the public was not'.[7] He was probably right; the lure of prize money was as strong as the urge to uphold national prestige.

Despite the misgivings of the Prime Minister, Sir Robert Walpole, the war lobby and its extra-parliamentary supporters in the press and London coffee houses got their way. A war, begun in anger, resolved itself into a series of blows delivered randomly against Spain's empire and trade.

Almost immediately war had been formally declared, Admiral Edward Vernon, who as an MP had called for the overrunning and occupation of Spain's American empire, took command of a fleet under orders to harry Spanish trade and colonies in the Caribbean. What was in effect a war of smash-and-grab raids opened on an encouraging note with the capture of Porto Bello. Further attacks were launched against Cartagena (on the coast of modern Colombia, Havana and Santiago de Cuba during the next two years, but were bloodily repelled. By the end of 1742 hopes of quick, profitable victories had evaporated.

From the start, British strategy had been flawed. To have any chance of success, assaults on Spanish strongholds in the Americas required their isolation, which could only be achieved by a blockade of Spain's Atlantic ports. Operational difficulties, most notably the inadequate base facilities at Gibraltar, prevented the Mediterranean fleet from stopping the flow of reinforcements and munitions from Spain to its colonies.

Climate and disease also played their part in frustrating the Caribbean adventure. Tobias Smollett, a surgeon's mate during the siege of Cartagena in 1741, described the action in his novel *The Adventures of Roderick Random* (1748). He drew a brutally realistic picture of the miseries suffered by ordinary soldiers and seamen, in particular their diet:

> . . . our provision of putrid salt beef, to which the sailors gave the name of Irish horse; salt pork of New England, which, though neither flesh nor fish, savoured of both; bread from the same country, every biscuit whereof, like a piece of clockwork, moved by its own internal impulse, occasioned by myriads of insects that dwelt within it; and butter served out by the gill that tasted like train-oil thickened with salt.

The North American colonies were clearly doing well from the war. To noisome victuals were added the torments of the weather, and what proved to be the final blow for the ill-fed sailors came with the onset of the West Indian rainy season which:

> . . . conspired with the stench that surrounded us, the heat of the climate, our own constitutions impoverished by bad provisions, and our despair to introduce bilious fever among us, which raged with such violence, that three-fourths of those whom it invaded died in a deplorable manner.

Fatal illnesses, of which scurvy was the commonest, killed the same proportion of the crews of Admiral Sir George Anson's flotilla during its four-year cruise around the world between 1740 and 1744. Anson, an extremely able and intelligent commander, had been ordered to intercept Spanish shipping off the western shores of South and Central America. He returned in his one surviving ship, HMS *Centurion*, with £1,250,000 worth of plunder, nearly half of it taken from the Manila galleon which had been captured off the Philippines.

By the time that Anson reached Portsmouth, the war against Spain had become a general European conflict in which Britain, the Netherlands and Austria were fighting Spain, France and Prussia. The perilous military situation in Flanders and the need to defend George II's province of Hanover demanded a large commitment of British troops to the continent. There was a further call on manpower in 1745, when Prince Charles Edward (the 'Young Pretender'), backed by French troops and cash, landed in Scotland. The last Jacobite insurrection was a desperate gamble from start to end; the Prince's only substantial support lay in the Highlands of Scotland, where, after an excursion as far south as Derby, his army was cornered and overcome at Culloden in April 1746. Throughout the campaign he had been denied further French assistance by the Royal Navy.

The Jacobite uprising, which caused some temporary and highly exaggerated alarm in England and the Lowlands of Scotland, was a distraction from a war where France was now identified as the main enemy. A methodical strategy was evolved, aimed at the extinction of her overseas trade and the occupation of her settlements in North America. A squadron of men-o'-war was also despatched to assist the East India Company in its miniature campaign against French enclaves on the Coromandel coast and to interrupt France's Asian commerce.

In February 1745. two ships of the line, the *Deptford* and *Preston*, fell in with and took three French vessels returning from China as they sailed through the Sunda Straits. There was general rejoicing on both men-o'-war at the prospect of prize money beyond the dreams of even the most avaricious naval officer. One, Henry Clerk of the *Preston*, spoke for all in a hurried letter to his parents in Scotland, which was delivered to a passing Dutch East Indiaman for the first stage of its journey. He also gave them an uncomfortable reminder that the pursuit of easy wealth in the tropics had its drawbacks too:

> We have had very good luck since we came to this country, having taken three French China ships at one time Richly laden, but alas I wish I could say so much for my Health for I have been sick since I came round the Cape [of Good Hope]. I hope the three prizes will be able to support me for some time . . . or God grant me my health. I believe my Prize money will amount to 3 × 4,000 Pounds sterling and a little more luck will be sufficient to buy a little estate somewhere near Cramond.[8]

In America, the war opened with a successful attack on Cape Breton Island at the mouth of the St Lawrence and the capture of Fort Louisbourg in 1745 by a force which included a 4,000-strong New England volunteer contingent. Within a few months, preparations were in hand to establish a naval base at Fort Louisbourg which would serve as a springboard for amphibious operations against Quebec.[9] These had to be abandoned when a French relief force arrived the following year.

The setback in Canada, like those in the Caribbean, exposed the need for a global naval strategy. Before any offensive could be mounted in America it was essential that the French or, for that matter, the Spanish were in no position to send reinforcements to their colonies. To guarantee this quarantine, the Royal Navy would either have to bottle up its adversaries' fleets in their home ports or engage them as soon as they emerged. A blockade required constant patrols, an activity that caused enormous wear and tear to hulls, masts, spars and sails, not to mention crews. By 1745, a system had been adopted by which a ship undertook a fixed period of duty with the blockading squadron and then returned for refitting, while its place was taken by another which had just been refurbished. This method of maintaining a continual presence in the western Atlantic worked, so long as the Royal Navy could call upon superior numbers of warships and efficiently managed dockyards.

The results of this strategy were highly encouraging. In May 1747, a French squadron attempted to break the blockade and was caught off Cape Finisterre by a larger force under Anson's command. He had used the past months of watching and waiting to exercise his captains and men in a new battle tactic, known as the general chase. It was a simple manoeuvre which required expert seamanship, discipline and skilled gunnery. The British line-of-battle ships (that is, 1st, 2nd, 3rd and 4th rates armed with sixty or more cannon) approached their adversaries in line astern. As the leading British battleship came alongside the rearmost French, it fired a broadside and then sailed on, firing in turn at each opposing vessel as it passed along the line. This pattern was repeated by each of the succeeding ships.

This technique worked; six French battleships were sunk or taken by Anson's squadron. Further proof of the new tactic's efficacy came in October when Rear-Admiral Sir Edward Hawke engaged a West Indies-bound French squadron, again off Cape Finisterre. Six of the eight French battleships were sunk or taken and the convoy of 250 merchantmen they were escorting was scattered. Many of these were later captured, for Hawke had had the foresight to send a sloop to Port Royal to warn the naval authorities there that a French convoy was heading in their direction.

These two victories vindicated the new strategic formula for isolating France, and the general chase as a battle winner. They were also a sign of the emergence at the top of the navy's hierarchy of a new breed of senior commander. Anson and Hawke were admirals who were prepared to snatch at whatever opportunity came their way to force a battle, even if this meant taking risks. Both understood that British naval supremacy could only be maintained if individual commanders were willing to get to grips with the enemy's battlefleets whenever they left port. It was, of course, never possible to predict the outcome of a battle, but both Anson and Hawke rightly believed that the better training, experience, discipline and stamina of their crews would always give them a vital edge over the French.

1747 saw British maritime supremacy preserved. Elsewhere the war had become a stalemate for, while unable to defend their colonies, the French had occupied most of the Austrian Netherlands (modern Belgium). The following year, the exhausted combatants agreed the Peace of Aix-la-Chapelle which did little more than restore the pre-war *status quo*, although Britain had to sacrifice Louisbourg in order to secure the removal of French forces from the Low Countries. Aix-la-Chapelle was, in fact, an armistice and, justifying it to the Commons in 1749, Henry Pelham predicted further conflict with France. Like Rome and Carthage, the two powers were irreconcilable rivals and only the navy could save Britain from the latter's fate. 'I am afraid', he told MPs, 'we may be taught by experience, that our navy is not invincible; and if that should ever happen our navigation, our commerce, our independency, will be at an end.'[9]

The Prime Minister was unduly pessimistic, but correct in his view of Britain's total dependence on her navy for survival as a great power. Nearly sixty years of intermittent war against France had shown both the advantages and limitations of maritime supremacy; alone, it had not been the key to victory, but it had been the means of preventing defeat. Moreover, the general strategy which had been devised after 1745 showed that, properly used, command of the world's seas offered Britain the means of expelling the French from North America and possibly India, endeavours that had been forestalled by events in Europe and the peace. Nevertheless, what had been achieved during the war bred a new and aggressive self-confidence within the navy which was spreading to the country at large despite the disappointments in the Caribbean. Anson and Hawke emerged from the war as heroes and their audacious fighting spirit enthused their subordinate captains, men like George Rodney and Edward Boscawen who succeeded them in high command during the next twenty years. The two admirals came to embody the superior qualities of the navy, which were celebrated in a popular patriotic ballad, written in the late 1770s to commemorate the commissioning of ships named after them:

> *These two noble heroes, whose names our ships bear,*
> *Make the Spaniards to tremble, the Frenchmen to fear,*
> *Secure of success, then, your fortune ne'er balk,*
> *But enter on board the Lord Anson and Hawke.*
>
> *Let the wise politicians of France and of Spain*
> *Threat to take from Great Britain her rule of the main,*
> *Their plate ships shall pay for such arrogant talk*
> *If they come in sight of the Lord Anson and Hawke.*

2

Tis to Glory we Steer: Gains and Losses, 1749–83

The peace of Aix-la-Chapelle settled nothing: Anglo-French commercial and colonial rivalry persisted and deepened after 1748. The French remained convinced that their antagonist's long-term aim was to stifle their trade and expropriate their colonies. Britain continued to fear a concert between the Bourbon Louis XV and his Spanish cousin which would bring their fleets into a dangerous conjunction. Despite the late war, Britain was becoming richer and more and more dependent on trade with her colonies. Exports to North America rose from a yearly average of £524,000 in the late 1720s to just over £1 million twenty years later. During the same period the annual total of exports to the West Indies increased from £473,000 to £732,000 and to India from £112,000 to £522,000.

And yet as exports to the colonies spiralled, Britain's economic future remained uncertain. The chief threat came from France and was most menacing in India and North America where fighting had hitherto been limited and inconclusive. The danger was greatest in North America where, by 1754, violent clashes had increased as the advance guards of British and French settlers collided in the Ohio valley. The French and their Indian allies had been penetrating the Ohio River for some years, moving southwards from Quebec. Far to the south, parties of Frenchmen were simultaneously edging north from their coastal settlements on the Gulf of Mexico along the Mississippi River. If uninterrupted, France would, in the near future, establish a title to the entire region around the

Mississippi and its tributaries and so occupy a broad swathe of territory from New Orleans in the south to Quebec in the north, blocking the westwards expansion of Britain's colonies.

Skirmishes between French and Virginian frontiersmen along the upper Ohio, the demolition of a wooden fortalice and its replacement by Fort Duquesne, named in honour of the energetic and able governor of Quebec, set the alarm bells ringing in London during the summer of 1754. National prestige was at stake and possibly the future of British North America. Measures were immediately taken to draft regular troops to Virginia and additional warships to North American waters, and the French followed suit.

Having struck a belligerent posture, the Duke of Newcastle's government was beset by misgivings. It feared, with good reason, that a localised war in the North American backwoods would inevitably spread to Europe. Here, France, with its enormous resources of manpower, had two attractive options; the invasion of George II's province of Hanover, or an amphibious cross-Channel attack on Britain. In either event, Britain would be compelled to detain soldiers and ships for home defence or detach them for service in northern Germany. The King naturally insisted that everything possible should be done to protect his territory, but for many of his subjects, including Pitt, its defence was an incubus. The country gained nothing from the possession of Hanover, which soaked up resources which should have been more advantageously deployed to secure colonies and new markets. Nevertheless, since 1714 Britain had been ruled according to the principles laid down by the Revolutionary Settlement of 1688-9, by the Hanoverian dynasty, and the dominant Whig party felt obliged to assist its kings to keep their German possessions, wherever possible at the smallest charge to the country. This goal was achieved in January 1756 with an alliance with Frederick II of Prussia which, in turn, led to the creation of a Franco-Austrian-Russian axis. Hemmed in, the Prussian king struck first, invading Saxony in September.

Britain was now engaged in a general war on the Continent and obliged to dilute the forces she had originally intended to concentrate in America. With free use of the Austrian Netherlands, France could muster men along the Channel coast and force her opponent to divert men and material to counter an invasion threat. Moreover, subsidies to Prussia deprived Britain of cash that was needed elsewhere.

★★★

It was not the burden of Britain's Continental commitment, but unpreparedness, ill-luck and operational problems which led to a dismal sequence of reverse during 1756 and 1757. The worst was the loss of Minorca after Admiral John Byng refused to risk a general engagement with the French Mediterranean fleet, and withdrew to Gibraltar. His prudence, based upon the fear that it was better to preserve his fleet rather than hazard a battle, was almost universally interpreted as cowardice by an indignant public. Byng was recalled in disgrace, court-martialled and executed in March 1757, according to the famous remark of Voltaire, 'pour encourager les autres'. He was as much a scapegoat for a discredited ministry as a warning to faltering admirals who failed to manifest the expected pugnacious spirit whenever the French appeared.

Elsewhere, the navy was in more difficulties. There had been a quick mobilisation, thanks to the direction of Anson, First Lord of the Admiralty, who revealed himself as capable an administrator as he had been a seaman. But it took time to build new ships and refit old and the naval dockyards and victualling services needed to adjust to the new, and often overwhelming, demands placed upon them. At the same time as support systems were moving into gear, the navy had to find and retain sailors to serve in its ships, many of which were forced to go to sea partially manned. The biggest problem was wastage; out of 70,000 men recruited between 1756 and 1759, 12,700 deserted and a slightly larger number died from disease. By contrast, 143 died as a result of enemy action between 1755 and 1757.[1]

The immediate solution was the widespread use of the press gang, which was unpopular with its victims, their kinsfolk and with merchants and shipowners, who lost skilled seamen to the navy. In 1757, a highly efficient and probably ruthless press in New York rounded up 3,000 men, a quarter of the adult male population, of whom about 400 were later released.[2] In the long term, the answer to wastage lay in the preservation of sailors on ship and shore. In this field, and contrary to the commonplace historical view of everyday life in the Georgian navy, considerable and often highly successful efforts were made to keep sailors in good health. Each man received daily a pound of biscuit, a gallon of beer, three-quarters of a pound of cheese or six pounds of preserved beef or pork a week. Whenever possible, crews were given rations of fresh meat and vegetables, the last as a preventative against scurvy, which still decimated crews despite the knowledge that regular eating of lemons or marmalade reduced the chances of catching it.[3]

Naval pay in the 1750s compared well with that of sailors in the merchant service and was from time to time augmented with prize money, although allocations to ordinary seamen were never more than a few pounds. A sailor could, therefore, find some satisfaction in his lot which compared favourably with that of the soldier. The difference was celebrated in a song sung by the girls of Gosport in 1780:

> Sailors, they get all the money,
> Soldiers they get none but brass;
> I do love a jolly sailor,
> Soldiers they may kiss my arse.

There was little cash jingling in sailors' pockets during the first three years of the Seven Years War. At first, hopes of swift victories and prize money had been high. As he sailed in pursuit of a French squadron bound for North America in May 1756, Boscawen was in optimistic mood when he wrote to his wife: 'If these French gentry do not escape me this time, they will pay for the house and furniture too, beside something to save for our children.'[4] Fanny Boscawen was disappointed; her husband took no prizes and the French reached their destination, as did another squadron of eighteen battleships and five frigates the following year.

The blockade continued and measures were taken to construct new facilities at Halifax, Nova Scotia, including a careening dock where warships were rolled on their sides to caulk leaky seams and scrape off the seaweed and barnacles that clung to hulls and reduced speed. This was not ready until 1759, after which it was possible to keep a squadron of at least eight battleships in American waters without the need to send them back to Britain for repairs. Such preparations ultimately paid dividends, but they took time.

In retrospect, the years 1756 and 1757 were a period of slow, methodical mobilisation for later offensives. Contemporaries, dismayed by the retirement from the Mediterranean, fears of invasion, the temporary loss of control over the Atlantic, reverses in Canada and India and the poor performance of the Prussians which opened the way for an invasion of Hanover, blamed a government which appeared confused and faltering. The war effort was subject to critical scrutiny inside parliament and outside by journalists and pamphleteers on the look out for evidence of ministerial incompetence.

The most trenchant and influential attacks on Newcastle's ministry came from William Pitt, who ascribed the government's failures to its squandering cash on Prussian subsidies. America was the theatre of war where Britain's real interests were at stake, not Europe, and resources needed to be distributed accordingly. Unable to survive without Pitt who, his allies claimed, enjoyed widespread popular support, Newcastle brought him into a coalition in June 1757. Pitt was given responsibility for the affairs of the army, navy and colonies, which made him to all intents and purposes the minister in charge of the war effort on all fronts.

William Pitt's father and grandfather had made their money in India. He was forty-nine in 1757, a victim to prolonged and excruciating attacks of gout which at times forced him to address the Commons seated, an indulgence seldom granted. To the world, he was a figure who, for all his private ambition, had always stood apart from the factional wrangling and heaving and shoving for government patronage which consumed so much of the energies of other politicians. To the public he was a man untainted by party, a patriot who wished to unite the country in the pursuit of national interests. Pitt was a compelling and unequalled parliamentary orator at a time when MPs' minds were often decided by an individual speaker's eloquence.

Pitt the politician attracted adherents, largely Tory in sympathies, from the country gentry and a powerful and vociferous lobby from the City, led by Alderman Sir William Beckford, whose wealth from Jamaican plantations and sugar gave him the wherewithal to finance two Pittite journals. Around Beckford clustered a coterie of London merchants and financiers with overseas interests for whom the war could only be justified in terms of conquered colonies and foreign markets taken from France.

For his supporters and later generations of patriots and imperialists, Pitt was a national saviour who, singlehanded, took over a flagging war effort and secured a series of spectacular victories on land and sea, which renewed British mastery of the seas and enlarged the empire. Such is the Pitt who stands, firm-visaged and robed as a Roman senator, above a seated, self-assured Britannia and proud lion on a statue erected by admirers in London's Guildhall. Underneath, a fulsome inscription catalogues the virtues of a statesman who had been 'the means by which Providence raises a Nation to Greatness'. This is, perhaps, somewhat overblown. Pitt inherited a war-machine and strategy that had been created by others, most notably Anson who continued to do valuable work as First Lord of the Admiralty. What Pitt did provide was a sense of vision, a steady nerve and iron willpower.

Once in office, Pitt repudiated his former views. The policy of paying

Frederick II to fight the French became the cornerstone of his strategy. 'While we had France for an enemy,' he told the Commons in August 1762, 'Germany was the scene to employ and baffle her arms.'[5] The flow of money continued and, at Frederick's urging, a series of amphibious raids was undertaken against French ports during 1758. These expensive operations were mocked as breaking windows with guineas, but they forced the French to hold back men from the German front. Here, the tide was turning in Prussia's favour. In November 1757 a Franco-Austrian army was resoundingly beaten at Rossbach; a month later Frederick defeated an Austrian army at Leuthen and, the following spring, won a victory over the Russians at Zorndorf. There was also heartening news from India where, in June 1757, Robert Clive had routed Siraj-ud-Daula's army at Plassey and restored British power in Bengal.

At sea, the French suffered two dire misfortunes. An epidemic of typhus broke out among the crews of the squadron which had protected Louisbourg and was carried back to Brest when the ships returned at the close of the year. Early in 1758 the Toulon squadron, under orders to sail to the West Indies and North America, were driven back to port by a combination of operational muddles, bad weather and a brief engagement with a British force off eastern Spain. In one fight, between the *Monmouth* and the more heavily-armed *Foudroyant*, the French gunners deserted their cannon, scared by the weight of the British broadsides. Morale throughout the French navy was sagging; low pay and thin rations drove men to desert in large numbers from ships which were unseaworthy thanks to inefficient dockyards.[6] Meanwhile, the Royal Navy was steadily growing in strength. In 1757 there were ninety ships of line in commission and a further 149 frigates, sloops and bomb ketches. Two years later the fleet had grown to 300 ships of all kinds.

Britain's naval supremacy made possible Pitt's grand strategy of the piecemeal conquest of France's stranded colonies. In May and December 1758, the fortified slaving stations of Fort Louis and Gorée on the coast of Senegal were taken at little cost. The latter surrendered after a brief exchange of fire between warships and shore batteries in which the British casualties were dead and 68 wounded.[7]

The heaviest blow was delivered in North America. Louisbourg was captured in 1758, and the following year a three-pronged land and sea offensive was launched against Quebec which was finally taken in September. In the West Indies, the reduction of the French sugar islands began with the capture of Guadeloupe in February 1759. As the year progressed and Pitt's strategy unfolded, it seemed only a matter of time before the whole of France's empire would be swallowed and her overseas trade extinguished. Unable to match the Royal Navy in North American, Indian and West Indian waters, France had no chance of reinforcing her outnumbered colonial garrisons. Her only hope lay in an invasion of Britain, a project advanced by Louis XV's chief minister, Etienne-François, Duc de Choiseul, who believed it would force Pitt to pull back men and ships to defend his country's shores.

The first prerequisite of the 1759 invasion scheme was the amalgamation of France's Brest and Toulon fleets. This was frustrated by Boscawen who intercepted and scattered the Mediterranean fleet off Lagos Bay in June. The 21-strong Brest fleet under the command of Hubert de Brienne, Baron Conflans, was discovered off Quiberon Bay in November by Hawke. The French admiral ordered his ships to run to port as Hawke's slightly larger force bore down on him. A storm was blowing up and both fleets were heading towards treacherous waters broken by reefs and rocky islets.

Hawke was unperturbed by these hazards. After being warned about them by the master of his flagship, the *Royal George*, he calmly replied, 'You have now done your duty in apprising me of the danger; let us see how well you can comply with my orders. I say, lay me alongside the French admiral.' Given the sailing conditions and failing light, he was taking a desperate gamble, but the harsh calculus of seapower demanded that he snatch at any opportunity to sink or capture French men-o'-war. A general chase followed through rough seas which dramatically illustrated the superiority of British seamanship and gunnery. Two broadsides from the *Royal George*, aimed low into the waterline, were sufficient to sink the *Superbe*. Pummelled by the broadsides of each ship that passed her, the *Formidable* lowered her colours; *Héros* was driven ashore, and *Thésée* foundered after her captain foolishly ordered the opening of her lower gun ports in a heavy sea. By dusk, the French had been scattered and Hawke commanded his ships to cast anchor. Dawn revealed the French flagship, the *Soleil Royal,* in the middle of the British fleet. After slipping her cable, she was attacked, forced inshore and wrecked, the seventh French battleship to be lost.

Quiberon Bay was a classic naval victory and elevated Hawke to the status of a national hero, possessed of all the virtues appropriate for a British naval commander. According to Smollett's popular history of England, Hawke delivered his order to attack, 'Steeled with the integrity and fortitude of his own land, animated by a warm love for his country, and well acquainted with the importance of the stake'.[8] The battle that followed was the last in a gratifying tally of victories on land and sea during 1759. It joined Lagos Bay, Quebec, the fall of Guadeloupe and Minden, in which an Anglo-Hanoverian army defeated the French and guaranteed Hanover's security. Together these triumphs were celebrated by the song 'Hearts of Oak', written by David Garrick for his impromptu entertainment *Harlequin's Invasion*, first performed on the last day of the year.

> Come cheer up, my lads, 'tis to Glory we steer,
> To add something new to this wonderful year;
> To honour we call you, not press you like slaves,
> For who are so free as we sons of the waves?

Pitt was the man of the hour, widely acclaimed as the architect of these victories. As the year closed, his admirer, Smollett, wrote, 'The people here are in high spirits on account of our successes, and Mr Pitt is so popular that I may venture to say that all party is extinguished in Great Britain.'[9] The poet William Cowper recalled how the events of 1759 had made him, 'the son of a staunch Whig and a man that loved his country . . . glow with that patriotic Enthusiasm which is apt to break forth in poetry.'

Poets were kept busy as the next three years yielded fresh victories. Their spoils were listed by Cowper's friend, John Duncombe, in a mock-Horatian ode to the new king, George III:

> And lakes and seas before unknown,
> Exulting commerce calls her own,
> The lakes that swell, the seas that roll,
> From Mississippi to the Pole,
> Who drink, Quebec, they stream profound,
> By Britain's righteous laws are bound;
> The faithless Cherokee obeys,
> Rich Senegal her tribute pays,
> And Ganges' tyrant shakes with fear,
> For vengeance whispers, 'Clive is near.'

Comparisons between Britain and the empires of Greece and Rome were plentiful in an age which sought aesthetic and literary inspiration in the Classical past. Horace Walpole was so impressed with Britain's imperial conquests that he dismissed the Greeks and Romans as 'little people' when compared to his countrymen.[10] A correspondent to the *Gentleman's Magazine* felt sure that the siege of Quebec deserved to be set alongside that of Troy as an epic of courage.[11] Others, less learned, simply wanted an excuse for a drunken rout:

> *Come all ye brave* Britons, *let no one complain*
> Britannia, Britannia! *once more rules the main:*
> *With bumpers o'erflowing we'll jovially sing,*
> *And tell the high deeds of the year Fifty-nine.*[12]

Keen to exploit the public mood, David Garrick followed up his *Harlequin's Invasion* with two similar pieces, *The English Sailors in America* and a pantomime, *The Siege of Quebec*, which appeared in the spring of 1760.

The exuberance of the festivities which marked the victories of 1759 and the unparalleled imperial expansion they made possible deserves close attention. They owed much of their intensity to the mood of introspective gloom which had characterised the previous three years. 'We are rolling to the Brink of a Precipice that must destroy us,' wrote John Brown, a north country cleric, whose *An Estimate of the Manners and Principles of the Times* (1757) was widely read and commented on. It was more than a jeremiad against current behaviour and tastes, because Brown directly attributed the nation's misfortunes to interior moral weaknesses, in particular among the ruling classes.

'The Conduct and Fate of Fleets and Armies depend on the capacity of those that lead them,' argued Brown. These men, the gentlemen of Britain, had become contaminated by what he called 'effeminacy', whose symptoms were a preference for such comforts as sedan chairs – gentlemen worth their salt rode – warm rooms and gluttony. Young men 'whose Talk is of *Dress* and *Wagers, Cards* and *Borough-jobbing, Horses, Women,* and *Dice*' were lacking in what he called '*public spirit* or *Love of our Country*'. No such degeneracy marred the ordinary soldier or sailor for, 'It is well known there are no better Fighting Men upon Earth. They seldom turn their Backs upon their Enemy, unless their Officers shew the way.'[13]

There was an equation between the collective moral worth of the nation's upper class and its achievements. This proposition, like Britain's current performance on the battlefield for which it was part explanation, was disturbing. If, as was commonly believed, human development passed through phases of growth, fruition and decay, then Britain might be approaching the last state.

The contrary was proved by the successes of 1759. National self-esteem and self-assertion grew stronger, as did that already deep-rooted sense that Britain was specially favoured by Providence. It was a nation which was moving forwards and the inexorable expansion of trade and empire was striking evidence of this progress. Innovations in the arts, science and industry added to this popular impression of the overall advance of British society. The 1760s and 70s witnessed the introduction of labour-saving machinery in the manufacture of cotton, iron, steel and pottery, as well as the first practical applications of James Watt's and Matthew Boulton's steam engines. A national genius could be detected behind this quickening pace of advancement in every field of human activity. Furthermore, it was agreed that the growth of empire and industry had been achieved because of Britain's felicitous political system which was neatly summarised by Isaac Watts, the contemporary hymn-writer:

> *The crowns of British princes shine*
> *With rays above the rest,*
> *When laws and liberties combine*
> *To make the nation bless'd.*[14]

And yet, as John Brown had shown, national prosperity, the overthrow of Britain's foes and the enlargement of its power in the world depended upon the determination, sense of duty and courage of its leaders. Their greatness of spirit was the vital ingredient for national greatness. Writing of empire-building, Cowper, with Pitt in mind, observed that 'Great men are necessary for such a purpose.' Cowper and others, excited by the victories of 1759, felt themselves part of an empire whose size was a measure of their country's virtues. The war had and would continue to create a belligerent, over-confident patriotism which extended to all classes, a fact which made Smollett, among others, uneasy. Popular – that is, mob – patriotism was, he thought, dangerous among a people who were 'naturally fierce, impatient, and clamorous'.[15]

The noise of celebrations of victory reached a crescendo in 1762. Martinique and a scattering of French sugar islands were taken by Admiral Sir George Rodney. Profit-seekers followed the landing parties for his victories and the admiral was struck by the speed with which planters from British islands flocked to Martinique to stake out claims to land.

Greater prizes were now available, since Spain had taken the plunge and joined France. Almost immediately, she suffered two stunning blows.

Manila surrendered to an expeditionary force from India, and Havana was surprised by a fleet commanded by Admiral Sir George Pocock which had, at considerable risk, approached its target by the Old Bahama Channel, a seaway normally shunned because of its reefs and cays. The gamble paid off; thirteen Spanish battleships were taken in Havana harbour and Pocock and Lord Albemarle, who commanded the landing force, each received £123,000 in prize money. Rank-and-file soldiers and sailors got about £4.

At the moment when optimistic patriots believed that the Spanish as well as the French empires might pass into Britain's hands, the government was negotiating a peace. Pitt had resigned in October 1761 after falling out with his colleagues over the terms that could be extracted from France. Negotiations were continued by the new ministry under the Marquess of Bute, a well-meaning mediocrity who enjoyed the confidence of George III. Although both France and Spain were prostrate, there was a fear among some that what the Whig Duke of Bedford called Britain's 'monopoly' of seapower would 'excite all the naval powers of Europe to enter into a confederacy against us', a pusillanimous view which ignored the fact that these other nations did not possess enough ships to challenge the Royal Navy. In fact, it was the rising cost of the war and resort to additional taxation, including increased duties on beer, which encouraged the government to reach a settlement.

The Treaty of Paris, signed early in 1763, was controversial. Britain retained the slaving forts on the Senegal coast; the West Indian islands of Grenada, St Vincent, Dominica and Tobago; Canada and all the lands to the west of the Mississippi, Minorca and Florida, which the Spanish conceded in return for the evacuation of Havana. France withdrew its forces from Germany and was allowed to keep Gorée Island, St Lucia, Martinique, Guadeloupe, a share in the Newfoundland fisheries and all the possessions she had held in India before 1749, so long as they were demilitarised. Manila was returned to Spain in return for a ransom (which was never paid) and given title to all lands west of the Mississippi.

These terms excited much public indignation, on the grounds that too much had been surrendered merely to provide for the security of Hanover. This criticism was handled clumsily by the government which revived antique laws to punish one of its opponents, John Wilkes, for an article in his journal *The North Briton*. Ineptitude of one kind or another marked the performance of all the ministries between 1763 and 1775, a period dominated by politicians of limited talents and narrow horizons. Matters were not helped by the frequent interventions of George III. Emotionally a paternalistic patriot and directed by an urge to do what he considered best for his people as a whole, the King, who was also interested in farming, did little more than reveal himself a better judge of livestock than of men.

Politics after the Treaty of Paris revolved around relations with the North American colonies and these, together with the war which broke out in 1775, will be examined in a later chapter. Of equal importance, from the point of view of the overall development of the empire, was the massive programme of naval rearmament begun by the French in 1762. The impetus behind this attempt to rebuild the French fleet was Choiseul, who was determined to avenge the defeats of 1759–62 and restore his country's former position as an imperial, global power. Within eight years, the total of French battleships had risen from 40 to 64, and frigates from 10 to 50.

This development was closely watched by the Admiralty, which had a well-organised network of agents in France and Spain, managed, until his death in 1770, by Richard Wolters, the British consul in Rotterdam. During the Seven Years War, Wolters controlled spies in Versailles, Brest, Toulon, Le Havre, Rochefort and Madrid who reported to him on the movements of French warships. During the winter of 1759–60, he was able to send to London information about the arrival home of the Comte D'Achée's East Indies squadron and plans for its return to Pondicherry.[16] Although still little-known even today, the Admiralty's intelligence-gathering system was extremely valuable in giving advance warning of the deployment of the French navy. Additional details were given by British consuls elsewhere who regularly sent the Admiralty information they considered useful. They often employed their own spies, like the 'intelligent person who knows the country well', paid by the consul in Oporto to reconnoitre the positions of the Spanish army which had invaded Portugal in August 1762. The consul at Ligorno questioned the skippers of neutral merchantmen to discover the whereabouts of French warships in the Mediterranean, and his colleague at Helsingör recorded details of Russian men-o'-war as they sailed through the Skaggerak.[17]

This excellent service was continued in peacetime and enabled the Admiralty to keep an accurate and up-to-date breakdown of the numbers and condition of ships in the French and Spanish navies. By 1770, the picture emerging from intelligence sources indicated that the gap between the Royal Navy and the combined fleets of its former antagonists was narrowing. Between them, France and Spain had a total of 121 ships of the line against Britain's 126. Pitt had estimated that 125 of this type of vessel was the minimum needed for security everywhere, a figure that had been kept to in spite of a post-war reduction in the naval budget.[18]

For the moment, however, British naval paramountcy seemed unassailable. In 1764–5 the naval big stick had been wielded to good effect against France and Spain. The threat of naval action alone had upheld British claims to the Turks Islands, defended British loggers' rights to cut mahogany on the Honduran coast and ensured the expulsion of the French from slaving posts in the Gambia. In 1769–70, the fleet had been mobilised in defence of British interests in the Falkland Islands and, rather than risk war, the Spanish gave way.

These successful exercises in gunboat diplomacy may have encouraged official complacency, but they did not excuse the government's shortsightedness after the first outbreak of rebellion in North America in 1775. Lord North's administration assumed that the insurgents would be easily and swiftly overcome, and that no other power would consider intervention. Both judgements were mistaken; after two years of fighting it was clear that the Americans would survive and the surrender of General Burgoyne's army at Saratoga in 1777 finally convinced the French that the moment had come to launch a war of revenge against Britain. France therefore entered the war in February 1778 and was followed by Spain in June 1779 and the Netherlands soon afterwards. The remaining powers of Europe were malevolent neutrals.

Between 1778 and 1783 the British empire faced a crisis which remained without equal in seriousness until the summer of 1940. Britain had no allies in Europe; her main line of defence, the navy, was outnumbered; and no outstanding statesman or commander came forward to match the time. Fortunately, as it turned out, there was a similar lack of imaginative leadership among Britain's enemies and, while the French navy had been physically transformed, it had yet to produce a breed of aggressive commanders prepared to adopt bold, if risky, tactics. Time and time again, when presented with a tactical advantage, French admirals allowed it to slip from their grasp.

At the beginning of the war, France had three major strategic objectives. The first was to transfer troops to North America and assist the rebels there; the second was to attack and occupy British sugar islands in the West Indies, and the third, and most ambitious, was an invasion of the southern coast of England.

The early phases of each campaign were disappointing. The Comte d'Estaing's North American squadron disembarked troops on the shores of Delaware Bay, but discovered that a smaller British squadron had escaped. Unable to establish local superiority in North American waters, d'Estaing sailed southwards to begin the conquest of the British West Indies. This required complete dominance of the Caribbean, which eluded him after he allowed a badly mauled British force to withdraw after an engagement off Grenada in July 1779.

The French record in home waters looked more promising and, by August 1779, Britain faced the ominous prospect of losing control of the Channel. The combined Franco-Spanish fleet mustered 63 battleships and 16 frigates, more than enough to escort the 500 transports which had assembled to carry the 30,000-strong invasion army to the Isle of Wight and Portsmouth. Against this force, the Channel squadron could raise 42 ships of the line. Not surprisingly, when Lord North hurriedly proposed a massive increase in militia numbers, he was faced with charges of having neglected the navy.

French preparations were meticulously monitored by Admiralty spies, one of whom reported the presence of Irish dissidents in Paris, which raised fears that the attack on the south coast might be combined with an insurrection in Ireland. There was, however, consolation in the knowledge that the Franco- Spanish armada was bedevilled by vacillating leadership, half-hearted commitment by the Spanish, rough weather, delays in the deliveries of rations and a savage epidemic of scurvy which put over 8,000 sailors out of action. In mid-September, as the equinoctial gales were approaching, Admiralty agents reported that the invasion had been postponed. At the same time, intelligence from Cadiz suggested that enormous efforts were in hand to step up the siege of Gibraltar, which had begun in June.[19]

Having shelved the invasion plan, and with it the chance of a quick end to the war, France shifted her resources to the siege of Gibraltar and the North American and West Indian theatres. She now faced what she was least able to sustain, a war of attrition against a power with a longer purse. Moreover, released from the threat of invasion, the British were able to divert more ships to other fronts.

Admiral Sir George Rodney had been appointed to take command in the West Indies in October 1779. He was a gallant, resolute officer who wrote, '*Persist and Conquer* is a maxim that I hold good in a War, even against the elements.' And yet for all his tenacity, he was short-tempered, dogged by ill-health and quarrelsome. His prickliness contributed considerably to the lack of coordination between senior commanders in the West Indies and North America, and helped prevent the evolution of a grand strategy for the entire area. Nevertheless, his men were in good heart when they set sail from Spithead in the spring of 1780. William Home, a young marine officer aboard HMS *Intrepid*, wrote enthusiastically to his parents how he was bound 'on an expedition to Puerto Rico or some place on the Spanish Main, which I hope will enable us to come home with our pockets full of Dollars'.[20]

His tour of duty during the summer of 1780 brought him no rewards, nor did his commander obtain the decisive victory needed to re-establish British dominance of the Caribbean. Instead, Rodney discovered that his subordinate commanders were disobedient, slack and cautious to the point of cowardice. After a desultory engagement off Martinique in May 1780, he complained that 'the British Flag was not properly supported' since several captains had refused to commit their ships to the action. His remedy was sharp; henceforward all refractory officers were promised dismissal and possibly the fate of Byng. 'My eye on them had more dread than the enemy's fire,' he told his wife, and they knew it would be fatal. No regard was paid to rank: admirals as well as captains, if out of their station, were instantly reprimanded by signals, or messages sent by frigates: and, 'in spite of themselves, I taught them to be, what they had never been before – *officers*.' The key to this transformation was, according to Rodney, acceptance of his principle, 'Yours to obey. The painful task of *thinking* is mine.'[21]

In terms of results, Rodney's lessons in discipline took time to bear fruit. He returned to the Caribbean in 1781 when his fleet attacked and took the Dutch island of St Eustatius, which yielded £3.5 million in prize money. *Intrepid* was not present, and so Lieutenant Home had to be satisfied with twenty-three guineas – 'no small sum for a subaltern' – his share from the attack on another Dutch island. Gratifying as such windfalls may have been, their obtainment did not do much material harm to the French fleet, which still sailed unchallenged in West Indian and North American waters.

While matters hung in the balance in the Caribbean, the tide of war swung irreversibly against Britain in North America after the surrender of Major-General Sir Charles Cornwallis's army at Yorktown in October 1781. France and Spain gained nothing from this victory and, after three years of fighting, both powers were feeling the pinch. In what turned out to be a final attempt to secure a substantial return for their outlay, the

French and Spanish decided to launch a seaborne attack on Jamaica in the spring of 1782.

Rodney was again ordered to the West Indies, warned by Lord Sandwich, the First Lord of the Admiralty, that, 'The fate of the empire is in your hands.' His captains now responsive to his commands, Rodney, with thirty-six ships of the line, encountered Admiral de Grasse's slightly smaller squadron off Les Saintes in the channel between Guadeloupe and Dominica in April. What followed was described by Rodney as 'the most important victory I believe ever gained against our perfidious enemies, the French.' The battle was long, bloody, and decisive, obstinately fought as if the fate of both nations depended upon the event. Success attended the British flag, and the French admiral with the *Ville de Paris* and four other ships remained as trophies of our victory.'[22]

The battle of the Saintes not only saved the British West Indies, it demonstrated the awesome firepower of the carronade, a short-barrelled cannon nicknamed the 'smasher' from the ability of its 32- and 68 pound shot to tear into ships' hulls. Introduced to the navy in 1779, the new guns were manufactured by the Carron ironworks at Falkirk in sufficiently large numbers to be widely distributed throughout the fleet by 1782. At the Saintes, the effect was devastating; for the first time in this war, French gunners flinched and ran from their pieces, terrified by British broadsides. Another recent innovation, copper sheafing for the lower hulls of ships, improved the speed and manoeuvrability of British men-o'-war. After his five-week, stormy crossing of the Atlantic before the battle, Rodney had remarked, 'None but an English squadron and copper-bottomed could have forced their way to the West Indies.' The new technology of the Industrial Revolution had rescued the empire.

Checkmated in the Caribbean, the Franco-Spanish war effort wilted. Soon after the Saintes. a small Spanish squadron turned tail and withdrew from the West Indies rather than face Rodney. In October 1782, the combined fleet blockading Gibraltar failed to intercept a relief squadron under Admiral Sir Richard Howe, and the siege was ended.

The exhaustion of France and Spain and their failure to exploit their early advantages at sea were reflected in the Peace of Versailles, which was signed in 1783. The North American colonies apart, Britain's losses were confined to Minorca and Florida, which were delivered to Spain; Senegal, St Lucia and Tobago. which were returned to France, and Ceylon, which was handed over to the Netherlands. Considering what had been taken from her adversaries during the past hundred years, Britain had come out of the war remarkably well. She had survived largely thanks to her wealth; the government had borrowed £94.5 million during the war and some of this money had been spent on laying down thirty-two additional battle-ships. Maritime supremacy had been preserved, but only just.

Even so, the British had suffered a psychological shock. A limit appeared to have been set on national greatness and the vulnerability of the empire exposed. Those who had cheered so loudly in 1759 were in a soberer mood in 1783, and one of them, Cowper, struck a pessimistic note when he surveyed Britain's future in his poem 'The Task' (1785):

> England, with all thy faults, I love thee still!
> Time was when it was praise and boast enough
> In every clime, and travel where we might,
> That we were born her children. Praise enough
> To fill the ambition of a private man,
> That Chatham's language was his mother-tongue,
> And Wolfe's great name compatriot with his own.
> Farewell these honours, and farewell with them
> The hope of such hereafter!

3

———— ◆ ————

The Empire of America:
Settlement and War,
1689–1775

Hail Pennsylvania! hail! thou happy land,
Where Plenty scatters with a lavish Hand:
Amidst the Woods we view the Friendly Vine,
With Purple Pride, spontaneously entwine;
Where various Cates arise without the Toil
Of labouring Hind, to cleave the stubborn Soil.

This picture of a fecund Eden, set down by an anonymous poet and published in the *Pennsylvania Gazette* in January 1729, owed more to the
author's acquaintance with Virgil and Milton than experience of everyday
frontier life. Nevertheless, these lines reflected a commonplace, if unrealistic view of the fertility of a region which was gradually being penetrated
by pioneers. Throughout the first half of the eighteenth century they
moved inland along the banks of the Hudson, Delaware and Potomac
rivers and their tributaries. Woodlands were razed, land ploughed, and
small settlements appeared in the wilderness. Between 1710 and 1730 the
population of Pennsylvania alone grew from 24,500 to 85,700, an increase
largely made up of incomers, mostly Scots-Irish from Northern Ireland.

A new phase in the development of the North American colonies was
underway, with expansion westwards across the Appalachians and northwards towards the St Lawrence basin. The new migration aroused
misgivings among the Indian tribes, whose lands lay in its path, and alarm
among the French, whose underpopulated colony of New France seemed

in danger of being overwhelmed. Both reacted with defensive measures, but neither the Indians nor the French possessed resources adequate for the task. They could temporarily deflect, but never stem the advance of the colonists who, when the going got tough, could summon up assistance from Britain.

The Indian tribes were sadly ill-equipped to understand, let alone take action to prevent what was happening to them. They could never wholly grasp the alien, European principle of land-ownership and all the legal paraphernalia of deeds of sale and titles that went with it. Nor could Europeans appreciate the Indian concept of the land, which was simply expressed many years later by a Sauk chieftain: 'The Great Spirit gave it to his children to live upon, and cultivate, as far as is necessary for their subsistence; and so long as they cultivate it, they have a right to the soil.'[1]

It was therefore possible for a tribe to sell large tracts of land in the belief that they retained the right to cultivate it or hunt its game. When they discovered that this was not so, and were excluded by settlers from what they still considered their property, Indians were puzzled and angry. Often tribes were unclear as to what they had relinquished since they knew nothing of European measurements, delineating boundaries by reference to natural features rather than lines drawn on maps.

The agents of the land speculators, who were the forerunners of the colonists, commonly used every form of chicanery to dupe a people only dimly aware of what was being asked of them. One negotiator was identified by an Oneida *sachem* (supreme chief) during a meeting between representatives of the Iroquois Confederation and the colonies at Albany in 1754. He fingered the man and described his methods:

> That man is a Devil and has stole our lands, he takes Indians slyly by the Blanket one at a time, and when they are drunk, puts some money in their Bosoms, and persuades them to sign deeds for our lands upon the Susquehana which we wlll not suffer to be settled by other means.[2]

Alcohol was the lubricant which eased many Indians off their lands. Ever since the arrival of the first settlers, Indians had been tempted and undermined by spirits, which were made freely available by unscrupulous traders. 'Rum ruins us,' an Oneida *sachem* complained to officials in Pennsylvania in 1753. He pleaded with them to ban the 'Wicked Whiskey Traders', who bartered alcohol for beaver pelts and furs, and took all the money which the Indians had saved to pay their debts for cloth and utensils bought from 'Fair Traders'. This appeal ended on a bathetic note, which underlined how strongly the Indians had become addicted. Requesting a ritual exchange of presents, the chief concluded, 'Our Women and Young People present you with this bundle of skins, desiring some Spirits to make them cheerful in their own Country; not to drink here.'[3]

The harsh truth was that the frontier tribes had long ago abandoned a culture based upon stone, animal skins and bone and become dependent on the goods offered by the colonists. Warning the Creek Indians against making war in April 1774, Sir James Wright, the Governor of Georgia, brutally outlined their predicament. 'And what can you do?' he asked. 'Can you make guns, gunpowder, bullets, glasses, paint and clothing, etc.? You know you cannot make these things, and where can you get them if you quarrel with the white people and how will your women and children get supplied with clothes, beads, glasses and scissors and all other things that they now use and cannot do without?'[4]

In return, the Indians could offer beaver pelts and furs. The beaver pelt, carefully trimmed to leave a thin covering of fur, was a tough, waterproof material that had been used for hat-making in Europe since the mid-seventeenth century. The familiar tricorn hat, a mark of social respectability and universally worn throughout most of the eighteenth century (Governor Wright no doubt wore his when he addressed the Creek Indians), had its origins in the rivers and streams of North America. Europe's millinery fashions provided the staple trade of the North American frontier; by the 1750s, the annual value of beaver pelts exported from New York and the Hudson's Bay Company posts in northern Canada was £250,000.[5] Further south, in Pennsylvania, the trade in beaver pelts and furs was worth £40,000 a year.

From its start in the mid-seventeenth century, the commerce in furs and beaver skins had been intensely competitive. The French had tried, vainly, to evict the Hudson's Bay Company traders from their bases and had taken systematic steps to secure a monopoly of fur and beaver-pelt trading with all the tribes along the St Lawrence basin and the shores of the Great Lakes. During the last quarter of the seventeenth century, French governors in Quebec had negotiated treaties with the Indians that allowed them to build a chain of fortified posts which ran west from Montreal to the north-ern tip of Lake Michigan. Each was strategically sited to seal the narrow waterways between the lakes and so control the routes taken by fur-traders.

Forts Frontenac, Niagara, Detroit and Mackinac were more than guard-posts, they marked the southern limits of New France and laid a tenuous claim to a wilderness that would shortly be entered by British settlers.

French domination of this area was challenged in 1727, when New York established a fort at Oswego on the south-eastern shore of Lake Ontario. Four years later, the French countered by erecting a stronghold at Crown Point on the southern extremity of Lake Champlain. It served both to defend the approaches to Montreal and as a barrier against New York colonists advancing along the Hudson.

Fort-building and efforts to win over the six tribes of the Iroquois Confederacy, who occupied the region south of Lake Ontario, were part of a cold war between the British colonists and the French. The strengths and weaknesses of both sides were exposed in 1744 when Britain and France declared war. There was a series of minor actions at various points along the frontier, the most serious of which were a sequence of Franco-Indian raids which devastated isolated settlements on the upper Hudson and Mohawk rivers. In the struggle for the hearts and minds of the Indians, the French had the upper hand, largely because both parties were appre-hensive about the scope of British expansion.

The British colonists' war effort was fragmented and therefore ineffec-tual. The colonies were disunited and without an apparatus to prepare and execute a common defensive strategy. Nevertheless, in 1745, the New Englanders had responded enthusiastically to a summons to send volunteers to the siege of Louisbourg. There were widespread festivities when the fort was taken and many who celebrated were already looking ahead to the col-lapse of New France and, with it, opportunities to move into and settle the empty lands of Lower Canada. The land-hungry were disappointed; the peace of 1748 restored the situation in North America to what it had been at the start of the war.

There was no peace in the disputed territory between New France and British North America. After 1748, the focus for contention shifted to the upper Ohio, where the Ohio Company was in the process of buying 200,000 acres from the local Indians. The French reaction was swift and designed to stem the inevitable flow of pioneers into the region. The Marquis Duquesne, governor of Quebec, ordered an armed reconnaissance of the Ohio valley in 1749. This expedition was followed by further shows of force and, by the end of 1752, a string of outposts had been con-structed which linked the southern shores of Lake Erie with Fort Duquesne, placed at the confluence of the Ohio, Monagahela and

Allegheny rivers. British settlers and fur-traders who ventured too close to the new centres of French power were warned off.

Duquesne's bold move in the frontier chess game stunned the British colonists. Pennsylvania, the colony immediately threatened, was in a state of disarray since the Quaker minority, which dominated political life, had for years refused to contemplate any measures to defend the colony. Still without any machinery with which to plan and coordinate a common defence policy, the response of the other colonies was fumbling. An attempt by a detachment of the Virginia militia, commanded by a young landowner, George Washington, to keep a toehold in the Ohio region came unstuck in April 1754 when he was driven to abandon Fort Necessity.

This setback panicked the colonies into action. Representatives from each assembled at Albany in the spring of 1755 in an effort to create a common front against the French and the Iroquois. Seen from the perspective of a small town in New York, the colonists' position appeared extremely perilous. They were confronted by what seemed the overwhelming strength of New France, an offshoot of Europe's greatest military power. Recent events indicated that France was now intent on pursuing an aggressive frontier policy which, if it succeeded, would confine the British to a coastal strip of North America. Moreover, France was a Catholic nation, which aroused deep fears among the colonists, a large proportion of whom were Presbyterians. Their anxiety was not solely based upon an ancestral loathing of Popery; Catholic priests and missionaries were abroad among the Iroquois and, with official approval, were warning them that the British intended to seize all Indian lands.[6]

The outcome of the Albany assembly was an appeal to the British government for help. Alone, the colonists could not hope to beat regular French troops and their Indian auxiliaries. The desperation implicit in the request convinced Newcastle's cabinet that recent French encroachments would, if unchecked, 'endanger all the Northern colonies, and tend to the total Destruction thereof and their Trade'. Britain would not allow the colonies and their wealth to slip from her grasp, even if this meant a war with France, although, during the summer of 1754, the government hoped that the conflict would remain localised.

The decision to send troops to North America had far-reaching consequences. It was a recognition of how vital the colonies were for Britain and, in a short time, it transformed North America into a war zone in which British forces were fighting for complete dominance of the region.

Furthermore, and this was not fully appreciated by all those involved, the colonists had been placed under an obligation to the home government which would have to be redeemed. For their part, the colonists had for the first time found the will to shed their particularism and join together.

The first priority in 1754 was the reassertion of British authority in the Ohio valley. In September, General Edward Braddock was sent to Virginia with two regiments of foot, an artillery battery and orders to expel the French from Fort Duquesne. He was a competent officer who had learned his trade on the battlefields of Europe where warfare had become an exact art. Firepower – that is concentrated, synchronised, close-range musketry – was the key to victory. Therefore soldiers, elegantly uniformed and drilled, manoeuvred in rigid lines to take positions from where they could most effectively fire the volleys which won battles. It would be very different in the backwoods of North America as Braddock soon discovered.

In May 1755, Braddock set up his forward base at Fort Cumberland, a hundred or so miles from Fort Duquesne. His regulars had been augmented by some Virginian militiamen, who resembled Falstaff's ragged regiment and were rated by Braddock 'very indifferent men'.[7] Equally unpromising, at least in the eyes of a professional soldier, were the droves of Indians who congregated around the fort and offered their services. All these men, and in many cases their wives, doxies and children, needed rations and these were carried by packhorses and horse-drawn wagons which were obtained, with much difficulty, from colonial governors. The horses came from local copers whose tendency to sell the army worn-out and sickly beasts provoked much irritable comment about dishonest colonials.

Transport problems had to be put on one side after Braddock received intelligence that 3,000 French regulars, under the command of Johann Herman von Dieskau, were expected in Quebec by mid-summer. Von Dieskau was a specialist in what was then the novel art of partisan warfare in rough country, a subject about which Braddock knew next to nothing. Nevertheless, he had with him men like Washington who knew the rudiments of a type of fighting in which concealment, ambushes and rapid withdrawals were all important.

If Braddock received any advice on this subject it was ill-heeded, since he took no precautions against sudden attack nor sent men ahead to spy out the land. His column, with its cumbersome tail of horses and wagons, trundled through the forests, watched at every turn by unseen Indian scouts in the French service. Soon after it forded the Monagahela River,

Miles
0   100   200   300

Gulf of
St Lawrence

Louisbourg
(1758)

R. St Lawrence

1759
Quebec

NEW
FRANCE

Montreal

MAINE

Halifax
Port Royal

Bay of Fundy

NOVA SCOTIA

Lake Superior

Lake Huron

Lake Michigan

Fort Frontenac

Crown
Points
X Fort
Ticonderoga
Fort Oswego

Lake Ontario

Lake
Champlain

NEW
HAMP-
SHIRE

Portland

Portsmouth
Boston

Cape Cod

Albany

Fort
Niagara

Detroit

Lake Erie

NEW
YORK

RHODE ISLAND

New York

Long
Island

PENN

RESERVED

Fort Duquesne
(Fort Pitt)
Braddock X
1754

Fort Cumberland
R. Potomac

Philadelphia

Atlantic

Ocean

Chesapeake Bay

FOR

Ohio River

ALLEGHANY MTS

Jamestown
VIRGINIA

Norfolk

BLUE RIDGE MTS

INDIANS

NORTH
CAROLINA

Mississippi River

SOUTH
CAROLINA

Savannah R.

Wilmington

Charleston

San Agustin

FLORIDA

New Orleans

Gulf of Mexico

Area of settlement
British offensives
French offensives
Boundary for settlement
proclaimed in 1763
Area of French settlement

North America 1755-75

the vanguard was ambushed by a Franco-Indian detachment who drove it in confusion back into the centre of the column. Panic followed; a third of Braddock's army was lost and he was fatally wounded. Prisoners were tortured to death by the Indians, a practice which was tolerated by the French, and for which the British would later take condign revenge. The detritus of Braddock's army retired to Fort Cumberland, leaving the French masters of the region.

The disaster on the Monagahela shook the colonists and bruised British prestige, but it did not alter the balance of power in North America. The French army there was scattered across the mid-west in penny packets and was nowhere strong enough to deliver a sustained offensive. It did, however, give its opponents some nasty surprises; in August 1756 Fort Oswego was captured and, during the following year, there were raids against settlements in the Mohawk valley.

In the meantime, the colonial authorities and the British army took stock of the situation. The Quakers were ousted in Pennsylvania and the colony placed on a proper war footing. Most significantly Braddock's successor, John Campbell, Earl of Loudoun began a programme of training soldiers to fight a bush war. Loudoun was well-qualified for the task since he had had experience of guerrilla fighting during and after the 1745-6 Jacobite rebellion. Undistinguished as a field-commander, he had the good sense to realise that a new form of warfare required a new type of soldier. They were the Ranger, an American huntsman or trapper, and the light infantryman, a British regular chosen for his stamina, agility and quick-wittedness. They were given practical uniforms, often dark green or dun-coloured, which allowed them to pass unnoticed through woodland and bush.

The Ranger and light infantryman learned the arts of woodcraft, marksmanship and rapid movement across rough terrain, accomplishments which enabled the British army to fight a partisan war on equal terms with the French and Indians. Such troops, deployed as scouts and skirmishers ahead of a column, were also an insurance against the sort of disaster that had overtaken Braddock.

Flexible and imaginative commanders were needed if soldiers adept in frontier warfare were to be used to the best effect. These were provided by Pitt, who sent to North America two outstanding and energetic young officers, Major-General Jeffrey Amherst and Brigadier James Wolfe. Amherst was thirty and Wolfe two years older and each took his profession seriously, an uncommon virtue among George II's officers.

The new high command in North America in 1758 was the instrument of Pitt's grand strategy for the invasion and conquest of Canada. The cabinet was convinced that nothing short of the complete extinction of French power in North America would guarantee the future security of Britain's colonies there. Such an ambitious undertaking required a massive concentration of sea and land forces and, it went without saying, a tight sea blockade that would deny succour and reinforcements to the French commander, Louis-Joseph, Marquis de Montcalm.

Three armies invaded New France in 1758. General Lord Abercromby, the commander-in-chief, with 11,000 regulars, advanced on Forts William, Henry and Ticonderoga. Brigadier John Forbes, with nearly 7,000, mostly colonial militia, followed in Braddock's tracks to take Fort Duquesne. The third and largest army of 30,000 was led by Amherst, who was directed to make a seaborne attack on Louisbourg and then, if time permitted, proceed down the St Lawrence to assault Quebec. His transports were escorted by a squadron of twenty-three battleships and nineteen frigates commanded by Boscawen.

What was the largest imperial campaign yet undertaken met with mixed fortunes. Abercromby was thrown back from Ticonderoga by Montcalm and Forbes occupied Fort Duquesne unopposed.

The Louisbourg operation was the most complicated of all. Amphibious attacks always needed methodical preparation and precise execution. Troops, landing-craft, ammunition and stores had to be systematically stowed aboard transports for a swift and smooth disembarkation. Getting the soldiers ashore was always a dangerous and complex business; first the beaches had to be surveyed and then an operational plan concocted to secure them and any inland defences as quickly as possible. At Louisbourg, Amherst and his subordinate, Wolfe, took responsibility for the crucial reconnaissance and, after they had closely examined the Cape Breton Island beaches, Wolfe drafted a plan of attack.

It was several days before the sea was calm enough for the landing-craft to be rowed ashore. These were shallow-draught, flat-bottomed boats, which carried between 40 and 60 soldiers each and were propelled by 20 oarsmen.[8] The first wave, as usual, were the most reliable troops, in this instance light infantrymen led by Wolfe.

On the beach and in the charge to storm the French shore positions, Wolfe behaved with that aloof indifference to danger and cool-headedness which were regarded as the distinguishing marks of a gentleman officer. These qualities of leadership were, he believed, only found among gentlemen. 'I never can recommend', he once wrote, 'any but a gentle-man to serve with gentlemen. There is little prospect of a low dog doing any shining act.'[9] Before Louisbourg, Wolfe conducted himself in the manner expected of a gentleman of fine breeding, even pausing during the action to give a guinea each to the two Highland soldiers who had been the first ashore. Such gestures, like his courage under fire, won his soldiers' hearts.

Wolfe's advance guard cleared the way for the disembarkation of the rest of the army and its siege-train. The siege dragged on through June and well into July before the French, worn down by continual bombardment and without hope of relief, surrendered. Many, Wolfe among them, were keen to press on to Quebec, but Boscawen was uneasy about taking his ships into the hazardous waters of the St Lawrence. Furthermore, if oper-ations extended into November, the armada would be stranded when the river froze.

Pitt's masterplan had whittled down, not destroyed, French power in North America. The following year it was the chance of new generals. The dud Abercromby was replaced by Amherst, who conducted a renewed offensive against Ticonderoga. Wolfe was chosen by Pitt to com-mand the St Lawrence expedition, partly on the recommendation of those officers who had served with him at Louisbourg, and partly because the war minister had been deeply impressed by his commitment to the cam-paign's objective. He nearly had second thoughts after a private dinner during which Wolfe delivered a histrionic exhibition of his martial ardour. Whether this sword-waving outburst of patriotism was a consequence of his vanity, which was considerable, or of over-drinking, is not known. Newcastle, on hearing of the incident, is alleged to have warned George II that Wolfe was mad. 'Mad is he?' remarked the King. 'Then I hope he will bite some of my other generals.'

The Quebec campaign, which began in June 1759, proceeded smoothly at first. Wolfe's transports were protected by a squadron of twenty-two battleships under an able and brave officer, Admiral Sir Charles Saunders, whose valuable contribution to the operation has often been overlooked. Much depended on him; his light craft sailed ahead of the main force with officers skilled in navigation aboard, including the future explorer James Cook, who charted a course through what was still a little-known waterway.

Progress was therefore methodical and slow in a campaign where time mattered. Outnumbered, and unlikely to get assistance from France, Montcalm's only chance of avoiding defeat lay in delaying his adversary until the beginning of winter. For a time it appeared that he might succeed. After occupying the Ile d'Orléans at the beginning of July, Wolfe found himself bogged down, his way impeded by the French batteries on the bluffs downstream from Quebec. A landing by the Montmorency Falls, intended to dislodge these cannon, went awry when the assault force of grenadiers and light infantrymen from the recently raised Royal American Regiment were driven back to their boats by the volleys of French-Canadian militiamen.

Wolfe was disheartened by this reverse, which was made more galling by the fact that his finest troops had been routed by amateurs. He considered colonial militiamen as no more than an armed rabble. At Louisbourg, he had described the American militia as: 'the dirtiest, most contemptible cowardly dogs that you can conceive. There is no depending upon 'em in action. They fall down in their dirt and desert by battalions.'[10] As the war progressed, it revealed a deep social gulf between aristocratic British officers and colonials, whom they believed to be without moral fibre. This disdain was shared by French officers, one of whom sourly observed that French-Canadian militiamen were 'very brave behind a tree and very timid when not covered'.[11]

Other tensions emerged during Britain's first large-scale imperial war of conquest. British officers were appalled to discover that European laws of war, devised to restrain its worst excesses, went unrecognised on the frontier. Wolfe, like many of his fellow officers, was shocked by the promiscuous brutality of colonial warfare, in particular the murder of prisoners and civilians by Indians. Wolfe blamed Montcalm personally for the Indian outrages and pledged himself to repay in kind.[12] A year before he set off for Quebec, he had given notice of the sort of punishment he had in mind in a letter to his friend, Lord George Germain. 'I am neither inhuman or rapacious yet I own it would give me pleasure to see the Canadian vermin sack'd and pillaged.'[13] He kept his word; during the summer of 1759, parties of Rangers and other light troops harried the villages along the shores of the St Lawrence, burning houses and crops and carrying off what they could. Those French-Canadians who refused to swear allegiance to George II were evicted from their homesteads.[14]

A pattern was set for future colonial wars. Ideals of humanity held by often highly urbane and well-read officers were very soon shed when they were confronted by the primitive struggle for survival which lay at the heart of frontier conflicts. Wolfe, who recited Thomas Gray's *Elegy in a Country Churchyard* to his officers and, according to legend, accounted its composition an accomplishment equal to the taking of Quebec, could at the same time order the firing and pillage of French-Canadian settlements.

The deadlock at Quebec ended early in September. Wolfe, faced with the onset of winter in two months' time, agreed to a plan proposed by some of his senior officers. It involved a risky nocturnal dash past Quebec and a dawn landing upstream from the city. With British troops between Montcalm and his supply base, Montreal, he would be forced to emerge and offer battle on the Plains of Abraham. Everything went as predicted; the British were able to disembark undetected and form up in time to meet Montcalm's attack.

The battle for the control of North America was fought in an orthodox manner with columns and lines marching to the beat of the drum. The French manoeuvred clumsily, partly because the militiamen misunderstood what was expected of them in an unfamiliar kind of battle, and the entire French line crumpled under British volley fire. Montcalm was killed in the confusion as was Wolfe. Both had a reputation for gallantry and their deaths gave the entire campaign the quality of an epic contest between two worthy adversaries. Wolfe was quickly transformed into an imperial hero, the first of a breed that would proliferate over the next century and a half, whose patriotism, courage, attachment to duty and perseverance were set up as examples to be followed by their countrymen.

The fall of Quebec did not mark the end of the campaign. Disturbed by Amherst's presence at Ticonderoga, Montcalm had detached a substantial force, under the Chevalier de Lévis, to protect Montreal. These troops tried to retake Quebec in the spring of 1760 and were beaten in a hard-fought battle at Sainte-Foy, in which both sides suffered casualties four times as great as on the Plains of Abraham.

The capture of Quebec and its less well-known sequel at Sainte-Foy marked the end of French power in Canada. There were suggestions during the peace negotiations in 1762-3 that part of New France might be restored to France in return for keeping Guadeloupe, but in the end the long-term security of British North America counted for more than quick profits from sugar.

The British government, having acquired complete control over North America, was immediately faced with a dilemma. Stability, which had been the war's principle objective, proved elusive. Having removed the external threat to the colonies' security, the government had to cope with new, unexpected threats to local tranquillity, all indirect consequences of the fall of Quebec. First, policies had to be devised to satisfy the aspirations of 70,000 French Canadians, and to reassure an unknown but larger number of Indians, who were scattered across Britain's new territories in America's mid-West. At the same time as attending to the needs of its new subjects, the government had to heed the demands of the old; thousands of colonists were impatient to exploit the fruits of victory and move westwards.

Land speculation boomed between 1763 and 1774. A new empire was in the offing, which would be carved from the territories now open beyond the Appalachians, and speculators swarmed into the region to stake their claims. On both sides of the Atlantic investors were quick to respond, and land companies found no difficulty in attracting capital. Greed, and a faith in the ability of the new lands to pay their way, bound together American men of substance, like the scientist and political philosopher Benjamin Franklin, and British aristocrats, like his future antagonist, Lord Dartmouth. The land fever also infected men of humbler means; in 1771–2, Clydesdale farmers and artisans combined to form their own company which, they hoped, would purchase land in America for settlement by Scots.

Immigrants poured into North America at an unprecedented rate to people the vast tracts of wilderness being purchased by the speculators' agents. Between 1760 and 1775, 30,000 English, 55,000 Irish and 40,000 Scots crossed the Atlantic; many, perhaps the biggest proportion, hoped to settle on the frontier. Two thousand pioneers passed annually down the Shenandoah Valley in western Virginia on the way towards the backlands of Carolina. The appeal of the West was always the strongest; during the early 1770s plans were in hand to create two new inland colonies, named, in a wonderful flight of fancy, Transylvania, roughly modern Kentucky, and Vandalia, which lay between the Ohio and Allegheny rivers.

Reports of abundant and cheap land in America were naturally most enticing to those who faced a bleak future in Britain. A recession during 1773–4 in the woollen, cotton and silk-weaving industries forced men and women to leave the West Country, Yorkshire, Spitalfields in London, and Paisley; Paisley silk weavers, on strike for higher wages in 1773, bluntly told their employers that they would 'go off in a body to America' if they were not satisfied.[15] There were plenty of others discontented with their lot. In the Scottish Highlands and Western Isles there was a mass flight from grinding lairds who demanded high rents for poor land. It was the same in Ireland, where rack-renting had reached a peak in the early 1770s. Crofters and smallholders were joined by indentured servants, who were naturally in demand to undertake the donkey work of breaking new lands. By 1770, the old underworld of kidnappers and cozeners of indentured servants was back in action

The government, landlords and employers were dismayed by the scale of emigration and in Scotland, where it was believed that three per cent of the population had shifted to America in less than ten years, an attempt was made to stem the flow. This was legally impossible since no authority could remove a British subject's traditional liberty to go where he or she wished. Some pondered where it would all end and foretold that Britain, like Greece and Rome, would eventually lose the sources of its wealth and power which would pass to America. In 1774, a futuristic story appeared in which visitors from 'the empire of America' tour London in 1974. They discover a ruined metropolis very like the Rome depicted in Piranesi's engravings. The explanation for this desolation was the exodus of Britain's merchants who 'are now scattered over the whole world, and more especially have they settled in America, whither they were followed by most of our artisans and mechanics'.[16]

Britain was not the only loser from this wave of immigration. Many were destined for lands which had been appropriated from Indian tribes who, during the early 1760s. fought a number of unsuccessful campaigns to expel the intruders. The familiar pattern of frontier warfare repeated itself with neither side showing pity. In the 1760–61 Carolina war, one volunteer soldier reported to the governor: 'We have now the pleasure to fatten our Dogs with their carcasses, and to Display their Scalps, neatly ornamented on the Tops of our Bastions.'[17]

And yet, in the eyes of the British government, such creatures were subjects of George III and, as long as they kept his laws, had the right to expect his protection. From 1763 onwards, the king's ministers and their officials in North America endeavoured to fulfil this obligation, in particular protecting the Indians from the legal chicanery practised by speculators. Everywhere the government faced obstruction. As Sir William Johnson, a Superintendent of Indian Affairs, observed, equitable treatment for the Indians 'strikes at the Interest of some the most leading men in this Province'. The colonial merchants and proprietors with investments in land speculation hindered the government's efforts to secure fair play for the Indians and made sure that the local sheriffs and justices of the peace did likewise.[18]

Johnson's own position was ambivalent, for he was both a government official entrusted with the affairs of the Six Nations and the owner of an extensive estate in upper New York, where he lived in rollicking style with successive mistresses, one a runaway indentured servant, the other a Mohawk squaw. Johnson also speculated in land and encouraged emigrants, most from his native Scotland, to settle on it. And yet he retained his strong sense of natural justice and honestly tried to balance Indian and settler interests.

These were irreconcilable and a source of increasing frustration to British governments who wanted a stable frontier. Every solution to the problem proved unsatisfactory or created new difficulties. Bans on settlement, which pleased the Indians, were unenforceable, and contemporary reverence for the rights of property was so strong that ministers were reluctant to take too firm a line with speculators who, for all their underhand methods, often possessed legally defensible claims to Indian lands.

A means to cut through the tangle of conflicting rights and claims was finally devised in the summer of 1774; the Quebec Act. It defined the frontiers of Canada, which were extended as far south as the Ohio and Allegheny basins. Henceforward this region, so long a magnet for speculators and settlers, would be detached from the North American colonies and governed from Quebec according to a peculiar mixture of old French and English laws. The Quebec Act not only split British North America, it ended over fifty years of expansion by the North American colonists and barred them from those western lands to which they had long believed themselves entitled. It was widely and bitterly resented and the British government, having apparently sorted out the frontier imbroglio, soon found itself faced with an infinitely greater problem, a colonial rebellion.

4

The Descendants
of Britons:
North America Rebels,
1765–75

The influx of immigrants into North America coincided with an intense and increasingly passionate debate about the nature of the empire and the identity of its inhabitants. These issues were first raised in the summer of 1765 when Lord Grenville's ministry passed the Stamp Act, a measure which imposed a levy on all legal documents throughout the empire. It provoked an outcry in the West Indies and North America, where the colonists resurrected the precedent of the 1754 crisis and called a Continental Congress, which agreed to place an embargo on British imports. Simultaneously, and throughout the colonies, there were rowdy demonstrations in which gruesome threats were uttered against those officials whose job it was to collect the stamp duty.

This spontaneous and violent reaction took the government completely by surprise. Grenville's successor, the Marquess of Rockingham, decided to temporise and withdraw what was obviously a detested and, given the mood of the colonists, an unenforceable law. The parliamentary exchanges which marked the repeal of the Stamp Act revealed two conflicting views about the relationship between Britain and its colonies and the political rights of the colonists.

George III, Grenville and defenders of the Stamp Act asserted that the British parliament had an unquestioned right to make laws for the colonies. They clung to the old orthodoxy that the colonies were economic satellites of Britain, and existed solely to generate wealth for the mother country. This dogma was deeply rooted in official thinking and was expressed, no doubt with an eye to his minister's approval, by Governor Patterson of Prince Edward Island in his annual report for 1770. 'This island,' he wrote, 'with proper Encouragement in its infantile state, may be made extremely plentiful and useful to the Mother-Country.'[1] The use of the word 'infantile' is instructive, since it reflected the widely-held contemporary view that the colonies were Britain's offspring and, like children, needed firm but kindly guidance from their parent.

The patriarchal view of empire was explained during the Stamp Act debate by Grenville who likened the Americans to children, placed in their lands by a generous father, who had subsequently made every provision for their welfare. Implicit in this statement was the assumption that the colonists would continue to look to their parent for assistance and security. Evidence for this lay easily to hand; in the recent war British troops and warships had removed the threat posed by France, and redcoats continued to man the forts which held the frontier against Indians. These benefits were expensive and it was reasonable that part of the bill should be paid by the grateful colonists.

Variations of the familial metaphor were used frequently by both sides at every phase of the dispute. In 1775, representatives of the American Congress warned the Iroquois to keep out of a 'family quarrel' and, a year later, a British officer described the colonists collectively as a 'spoilt child' in need of chastisement.[2] Another, less severe perhaps, opened his diary for the year 1777 with the impromptu verse:

> *May peace and plenty crown the land*
> *And civil discord cease,*
> *When Britain stretches forth her hand*
> *To give her children peace.*[3]

As late as 1780, General James Robertson, the governor of New York, appealed to Americans as wayward children whom their patient father, Britain, 'wishes to include in one comprehensive System of Felicity, all Branches of a Stock, intimately connected by Ties of Language, Manners, Laws, Customs, Habits, Interests, Religion, and Blood.'[4]

Behind these sentiments lay the fear that imperial unity was in danger. The historian Edward Gibbon, then beginning his account of the decline and fall of the Roman empire, was convinced that a rupture between

Britain and its North American colonies would be the first stage of a general collapse of British commerce and power. Likewise, George III and his ministers were thoroughly alarmed by the temper of the colonists whose defiance, if unchecked, could fragment the empire and ruin Britain. Not surprisingly, the King and his supporters regarded the repeal of the Stamp Act as a surrender to organised sedition and an encouragement to further mischief.

Dissident Americans and their supporters in Britain agreed that the empire was an extended family, but differed in their intepretation of the ties of kinship. Rhode Islanders, who assembled in 1765 to burn the effigies of revenue officers, declared themselves the heirs in spirit of those Englishmen whose defiance of the Stuarts in the last century had secured the constitution and liberty of the subject:

> *Those blessings our Fathers obtain'd by their blood,*
> *We are justly oblig'd as their sons to make good:*
> *All internal Taxes let us then nobly spurn,*
> *These effigies first – next the Stamp Paper burn.*

Their claims were echoed in parliament during the Stamp Act debate, when William Pitt, now Earl of Chatham, argued that, 'The Americans are the sons, not the bastards of England.' It was therefore proper that they should share all the legal and political rights of their siblings in Britain.

This concept of a common inheritance of freedom was the mainstay of the American argument against governments which asserted parliamentary supremacy over all colonists and offered no representation in return. In 1775, Governor Jonathan Trumbull of Connecticut demanded to know why Americans were disbarred from 'the constitutional rights and liberties delivered to us as men and Englishmen, as the descendants of Britons and members of an empire whose fundamental principle is liberty and security of the subject'.[5] The question had been continually asked by Americans over the past ten years and they had been given no answer. Instead, they had been told to accept that they were unequal members of a family and that their individual rights had been suspended or diluted for no other reason than that they or their ancestors had crossed the Atlantic.

What was perhaps most perplexing to Americans, faced with what was an arbitrary view of their status, was that they were excessively proud of their Britishness. Benjamin Franklin assured readers of the *London Chronicle* in November 1770 that Americans 'love and honour the name of

Englishmen; they are fond of English manners, fashions and manufactures; they have no desire of breaking the connection.' It was, he said, a measure of their patriotism that they insisted that 'the Parliament of Britain hath no right to raise revenue from them without their consent'.[6]

There was much truth in Franklin's view of the pervasive Britishness of America. Over nine-tenths of the colonists were of British descent and many lived in towns and villages which had been deliberately given British names; in southern New York there were a Stamford, Rye, Gravesend and two Bedfords. Here and elsewhere, settlers had built homes in the vernacular style of the British countryside and had preserved the popular culture of their homeland by passing down folk tales and folk songs. Educated Americans saw themselves not as provincials, but as part of the mainstream of British intellectual and political life. In 1764, a Maryland landowner requested a London merchant to send him 'the best political and other pamphlets, especially any that relate to the colonies'. Later, when a political break with Britain seemed unavoidable, Franklin was distressed by its possible cultural repercussions for him and his countrymen. Would they be cut off for ever from Shakespeare?

Away from the frontier, American life had developed a social sophistication which struck some observers as unexpected and remarkable. An encounter in a Rhode Island town in December 1776 caused Captain John Peebles to comment drolly in his diary:

> Met with a Lady in the Street well dress'd and had a very genteel appearance, and came afterwards into a Shop when, upon enquiring, I found this was Miss Sal Leake, whom I had often heard mention since we came here. She keeps a house of Pleasure, has done for a good many years past in a more decent and respectable manner than is common, and is spoke of by everybody in Town in a favourable manner for one of her Profession, a well-look'd Girl about 30. This place has arrived to a degree of modern luxury, when houses of that kind were publicly allowed of, and the manners of the people by no means rigid when subjects of that sort become family conversation.[7]

American morals may have earned the approval of an urbane gentleman, but they were the product of a society in which men of his kind and outlook did not enjoy the same automatic respect and monopoly of power as they did in Britain. American society was pyramidal, but it lacked an aristocracy, so those at the top were the equivalent of the British middle class. Moreover, Americans followed that essentially bourgeois notion that men rose in the world as a result of talent and exertion rather than birth.

This is not to say that America was democratic. Personal wealth was the yardstick of social position, as it was in Britain, and men of property played a key part in the daily ordering of their communities by serving as magistrates and county sheriffs. They could and did sometimes demand the kind of deference which was found in Britain. When a Baptist interrupted an Anglican service in a Virginian church with impromptu psalm-singing in 1771, he was ejected and whipped by the vicar for his impertinence, and later given a further flogging by the local sheriff, a 'gentleman'.[8] And yet the Church of England, the spiritual backbone of British Toryism, had made little headway in North America where Nonconformists predominated. As a result, a New York Anglican parson regretted that few Americans upheld 'the principles of submission and obedience to lawful authority' which lay at the heart of his church's doctrine.[9]

In general, the American temperament was egalitarian and obstreperous and men from all backgrounds did not submit unquestioningly to authority as a matter of habit. In April 1775, Sir James Wright, the governor of Georgia, detected 'a levelling spirit and contempt for government' abroad in his colony. The cure was a permanent garrison because British troops would 'keep up some little show of dignity and command respect, and the officers mixing in with the gentlemen of the towns, the young people would hear the king and government spoken of with that veneration which is proper and due.'[10] What had particularly upset Wright was the emergence of a loose alliance between men of substance and what in Britain was called the mob. Whenever the government had been challenged, the reasoned remonstrances of the patricians had been paralleled by popular, disorderly protests. These were most virulent in Boston where, in 1770, Thomas Hutchinson, the assistant-governor, complained that the local magistrates were hand-in-glove with the disaffected and refused to take action against them.[11]

By this time, the government was becoming exasperated by the waves of protests and demonstrations which had greeted each of its attempts to raise money from America. After the repeal of the Stamp Act early in 1766, ministerial face had been saved by a Declaratory Act which insisted that parliament had full powers to make laws for the North American

colonies. This gesture had had little impact since the colonists, having discovered their political muscle and encouraged by the overturning of the
Stamp Act, continued to resist new taxes and soon scored further successes.

The 1767 Townshend duties on tea and manufactured imports proved
uncollectable because of a campaign of mass intimidation, and were withdrawn after two years. The chief problem was that the day-to-day
administration of the colonies, like that of Britain, depended upon the
goodwill of unpaid officials drawn from the ranks of property-owners
and, in the towns, the richer merchants. By 1770, this group had become
divided, and many of its members were no longer willing to cooperate
with a government whose policies they disagreed with. Royal governors
and excisemen therefore found themselves isolated figures without the
wherewithal to enforce the king's laws.

Faced with continual assaults on its authority, the government turned in
1770 to that most foolhardy of all policies, selective and limited coercion.
A small garrison was stationed in Boston to uphold a hard-pressed administration, and keep the peace in what was the most intractable town in
America. The force deployed proved not enough to cow the Bostonians,
but more than enough to stiffen their resolve and swell the numbers of the
rest of the dissident colonists. The shooting of some civilians after a scuf-
fle at the end of December, known as the 'Boston Massacre', gave the
Americans their first martyrs and a propaganda coup. There was further
violence in 1772 when a revenue cutter, the *Gaspée*, was set alight after it
had been beached on Rhode Island. The Tea Act of 1773, contrived to
assist the monopoly of the East India Company, was challenged by a party
of Bostonians who, masquerading as Indians, came aboard a merchantman
and tipped its cargo of tea into the harbour. Boston had clearly not been
overawed, and fresh astringents were applied in the form of regulations
devised to stifle its commerce.

This new stern line on America was taken by Frederick North who had
become prime minister in 1770. Lord North's strength lay in his skills as a
parliamentary manipulator and dispenser of patronage rather than his vision
or intellect. He remained in power until early 1782, relying on the steadfast support of a parliamentary mountain of Tory backbenchers who were
happy to let ministers do their thinking for them. What bound North's
adherents together was common hostility towards anyone who rocked the
boat, whether in Britain or America.

There existed within the inner recesses of the contemporary Tory mind
a suspicion that a democratic spirit was infecting Britain and America. At

home, it was fomented by John Wilkes who, having survived prosecution for criticising the government in 1763, had emerged as a focus for popular, extra-parliamentary opposition to the king and his ministers. The demonstrations which followed his election as an MP in 1768, and ham-fisted government attempts to unseat him, ran parallel to and mirrored the current unrest in America. Furthermore, and this thoroughly alarmed the Tories, both Wilkes and the colonists were willing to fight their political battles in concert with the mob. Disturbed by what seemed to be an upsurge in disloyalty and popular insolence, both at home and in North America, North's supporters reacted by closing ranks and minds against any form of censure of the king and his ministers.

What might otherwise have appeared bone-headed reaction could be defended, up to a point, on the grounds that concessions to American opinion threatened the integrity of the empire. Firmness, always commendable in a father, would quickly silence the tumult that had been stirred up by a minority of Americans, who had been allowed to become intoxicated by libertarian ideas. Once the government's resolution had been demonstrated, their countrymen would return to their senses and allegiance.

This simple diagnosis of complaint and remedy was rejected by a small group within parliament who pressed for a compromise. Chatham, Rockingham and, later, Edmund Burke, passionately believed that British and American subjects were morally and legally entitled to the same rights and freedoms. Moreover, the sixteenth-century precedent of returning MPs from Calais and Tournai was cited as evidence that Britain's overseas possessions had the right to a voice in parliament. If this was withheld, and their judgement of the mood of the Americans correct, North's opponents argued that his uncompromising line would create the rupture he was striving to avoid. The King, his ministers and the mass of backbenchers were unmoved and pointed out that the Americans, by the very reckless-ness of their actions, showed themselves strangers to reasoned compromise.

In the end, it was the Quebec Act of 1774 that impelled Americans to adopt a course of action which transformed civil protests into an armed rebellion. There was much anger against those provisions which closed the frontier and attached to Canada a great swathe of territory south and west of the Great Lakes which Americans had hitherto believed would be open to them for settlement. The official recognition of Catholicism in Canada provoked an outburst of Protestant hysteria. The lurid imagery of ancient sectarian nightmares was revived among a population which was overwhelmingly Protestant, and among whom memories of the persecutions and wars of the past century were evergreen. Early in 1775, the New England backwoods buzzed with rumours that Popery was about to be imposed and that the King was sending Anglican bishops to harass American Presbyterians.[12] In Massachusetts. a congregation heard the apocalyptic vision of their pastor, who predicted that 'the Scarlet Whore would soon get mounted on Her Horned Beast in America, and, with the Cup of Abominations in her hand, ride triumphant over the heads of true Protestants, making multitudes Drunk with the Wine of Her Fornications.'[13]

This was absurd, but by now many Americans were ready to believe any calumny against George III and his ministers. New England farmers, already fearful of the imminent arrival of Popery, were further agitated by tales that the government intended to reduce them to abject tenantry under English lords. Apprehensions of this kind, skilfully manipulated by the anti-government press and individual agitators, helped convince many waverers that American freedoms were in danger of being swept away by a ruthless king, whose government would stop at nothing in its efforts to assert its authority over the colonies. As paranoia gripped much of America, it was easy for propagandists to convince the credulous that they would soon find themselves enslaved. This American dread of slavery struck Samuel Johnson as ironic; 'How is it', he asked, 'that we hear the loudest *yelps* for liberty among the drivers of slaves?'

The American political response to the Quebec Act and the measures taken against Boston was rapid, and followed a pattern which had proved efficacious during previous crises. A Continental Congress was convened at Philadelphia at the beginning of September 1774 to devise a programme of retaliatory measures which, it was hoped, would make the British government think again. The delegates proceeded cautiously for, while they were united in their rejection of parliamentary sovereignty, they did not want to precipitate a complete break with Britain. First, they repeated their legal position as subjects of a government which denied the existence of what they knew to be their inalienable rights. Then, they brandished the sword of American economic power with a call for a boycott of all trade with Britain and its other colonies. The Congressional apologist, Alexander Hamilton, claimed that this would soon 'introduce beggary and wretchedness in an eminent degree both in England and Ireland; and as to the West-India plantations, they could not subsist without us.'[14]

Representatives at the Congress were careful not to discuss military preparations publicly even though, while they debated, the British government banned the import of arms and gunpowder into North America. In what was a spontaneous reaction, many Congress supporters began to stockpile weapons and make arrangements for the swift mobilisation of militiamen in case the government used force to disarm them. The headstrong went further and seized colonial arsenals and forts; in December a body of men, in which the 'Sons of Liberty' were prominent, occupied Fort William and Mary at Portsmouth and carried off cannon, muskets and gunpowder.

5

The World Turned Upside Down: The American War of Independence, 1775–83

At the close of 1774 the British empire faced a crisis of unprecedented seriousness. During the past six months British power in North America had evaporated. Colonial governors had become stranded symbols of an authority they lacked the means to assert, and were reduced to writing dismal accounts of their impotence to Lord Dartmouth, the Colonial Secretary. Cadwallader Colden of New York was marginally luckier than his colleagues since the sloop HMS *Kingfisher* had cast anchor in the harbour in December, and he had a garrison of a hundred men from the Royal Irish Regiment. Nonetheless, he was anxious, since the 'moderate inhabitants' needed the reassurance of 'a formidable power in the place to awe the licentious and encourage the friends of the government'.[1]

Real power was passing into the hands of hard-line supporters of Congress. By April 1775, local committees of these men had superseded the governors of New Jersey, Pennsylvania, Maryland, Virginia and South Carolina. There was nothing which the government could have done to halt this process, beyond issuing minatory proclamations which were largely ignored. What troops and warships were available were concentrated at Boston, the colonial militia could not be relied upon, and the customary instruments of coercion, the sheriffs and magistrates, either sided with Congress or were scared into neutrality. Even without partial or disinterested law officers, Americans in 1774 enjoyed considerable political

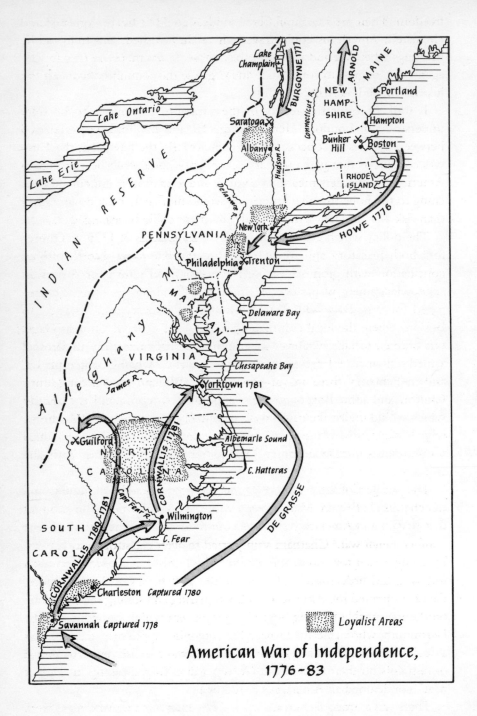

Lake Champlain
BURGOYNE 1777
MAINE
ARNOLD
NEW HAMP-SHIRE
Portland
Lake Ontario
Connecticut R.
Hampton
Saratoga
Bunker Hill
Boston
Lake Erie
Albany
Hudson R.
RHODE ISLAND
INDIAN RESERVE
Delaware R.
HOWE 1776
PENNSYLVANIA
New York
Philadelphia
Trenton
MARYLAND
Delaware Bay
Alleghany
VIRGINIA
James R.
Chesapeake Bay
Yorktown 1781
CORNWALLIS 1781
Albemarle Sound
Guilford
NORTH CAROLINA
C. Hatteras
DE GRASSE
Cape Fear R.
CORNWALLIS 1780-1781
Wilmington
SOUTH CAROLINA
C. Fear
CORNWALLIS 1780
Charleston Captured 1780
Savannah Captured 1778
Loyalist Areas

American War of Independence,
1776~83

freedom. Their <u>press</u> was unfettered so ideas could be freely expressed and circulated; Americans could <u>travel</u> where they wished, and hold <u>public meetings</u> whenever and wherever they chose. It was therefore easy for the agents of Congress to consolidate and organise the committed, convert the lukewarm, and bully the Loyalists.

It took time for the reality of the situation in America to be fully understood in London. Here, George III and his ministers vacillated between policies of concession and coercion. By the new year, the King was convinced that parliamentary sovereignty could only be restored in America by condign measures. North and Dartmouth concurred, but clung to the hope that the Americans would ultimately back down rather than risk war, and that a negotiated settlement could be arranged.

The policy which evolved during the early months of <u>1775</u> was therefore both placatory and threatening. On the one hand, North offered conciliation with promises of fiscal concessions in return for American acknowledgement of parliament's supremacy, and on the other, he prepared for war. Four additional regiments of infantry were drafted to Boston, where the local commander, Lieutenant-General Thomas Gage, was ordered to take whatever measures he thought necessary to forestall armed resistance. A large-scale campaign was already being contemplated, and in February three major-generals, Sir William Howe, Sir Henry Clinton and John Burgoyne were appointed to command the armies which would undertake it. All were second choices since Jeffrey Amherst, who had extensive American experience and was a better general, had refused the supreme command because his sympathies lay with the colonists.

<u>The prospect of a war with the Americans was</u> greeted with dismay and <u>disbelief inside Britain.</u> Many agreed with the poet Cowper, who thought that Britain and America were 'one country', which made the imminent conflict a civil war.[2] Chatham vainly tried to avert catastrophe in January by laying a plan for compromise before the Lords, but the debate which followed did little more than expose the gulf between the two sides. Chatham praised the Americans as 'men prizing and setting the just value on the inestimable blessing liberty', a judgement which was contested by Dartmouth, who cynically dismissed the colonists' appeals to conscience as a device to obscure their real motive, which was a selfish desire to be rid of restraints on their trade. Lord Gower, a dim Tory speaking 'in a great heat', condemned all Americans as traitors.

There was a strong feeling among military men that the Americans were bluffing and that, when put to the test of arms, they and their cause would quickly fall apart. In a report prepared for Lord Sandwich, the First Lord of the Admiralty, early in March 1775, Major John Pitcairn was confident that 'one active campaign, a smart action, and burning two or three of their towns, will set everything to rights.'[3] His commanding officer, Gage, was less sanguine and feared that precipitate action would provoke 'irregular and incessant' resistance, which might prove too much for the troops at his disposal.'[4]

His misgivings were confirmed on 19 April when, acting on Dartmouth's instructions, he sent a column of his best men to secure the arsenals at Worcester and Concord. Alerted by spies inside Boston, the Massachusetts militia mobilised. A small section was scattered after a brief exchange of fire at Lexington, but a larger body forced the British column to abandon Concord. As it retreated to Boston, it endured a sequence of guerrilla attacks in which it suffered 300 casualties, nearly three times as many as its adversaries. Within a few days, an American force, commanded by the impetuous and highly talented Benedict Arnold, occupied Forts Ticonderoga and Crown Point, opening the way for an invasion of Canada.

The slide to war was now irreversible. News of the skirmishes in Massachusetts left the cabinet with no choice but to apply *force majeure* to all the colonies. This move was welcomed by George III, who had always been impatient with appeasement, and by those amateur and professional strategists who imagined that well-trained soldiers would easily disperse what was commonly seen as a rabble in arms.

Foremost among the advocates of a short, sharp war was Lord George Germain, who, in August, replaced the more flexible Dartmouth as Secretary for the Colonies with a mandate to mastermind operations throughout North America. It was a task he relished and, if resilience and singlemindedness counted for something in the exercise of high command, Germain was well qualified. Despite having been cashiered from the army in 1760 for cowardice during the Battle of Minden, he inspired considerable confidence among the troops in North America who were looking to him for rigorous measures.[5]

Germain's formula for victory was based upon a variety of American intelligence sources which agreed that the colonists' will to fight was fragile and would never survive a major defeat. He therefore proposed to deploy a large force in America which would seek out, engage and overcome the rebel army in a single, decisive action. It was confidently imagined that a victory of this nature would not only destroy the rebels, but would give encouragement to Loyalists and those who had remained aloof from the contest. Again, intelligence reports from America had described the existence of a substantial Loyalist element, temporarily driven underground by the intimidation of Congress supporters, which would reveal its sympathies when it was safe to do so. The forthcoming war would be a struggle for hearts and minds, and the British generals knew that one of their most important tasks was to assure the Loyalists that they would be protected for, as Clinton later observed, they would never declare themselves 'before there is the strongest certainty of his army being in a condition to support them'.[6]

Manpower was the key ingredient in Germain's battleplan. From the start of the war there were difficulties in procuring sufficient troops for operations of the scale he had in mind. During 1775–6 garrisons in Ireland, Gibraltar and Minorca were pared to the bone and, as the war progressed, an intense recruiting campaign was undertaken in Britain.

It was never an easy job to tempt men to enter a world where they could expect a flogging for a trifling misdemeanour, low pay, thin rations, capricious officers, exposure to danger and the contempt of so-called respectable society. Patriotism, that is soldiering, was regarded by Samuel Johnson as the last resort of the scoundrel; in other words, a man without the ability or inclination to live honestly. It was a harsh judgement, but supported by current practice; many desperate recruiting officers scoured prisons to fill out the ranks. In 1776, Lieutenant Ridout of the 46th Regiment discovered some 'very fine lads' in Shrewsbury gaol for 'petty offences' and obtained their pardon and enlistment into his regiment. One, grateful for this chance of redemption, rose to the rank of sergeant during the American War.[7]

There were recidivists and others for whom the war was an opportunity for rape and plunder, and their conduct gave American propagandists a stock of stories about British brutality. Even experienced men of good character joined in the looting, which some believed was the reward for victory, or just vengeance against civilians who insulted them and secretly favoured their adversaries. This may have been why officers encouraged their men to steal during the campaign around Boston in April 1775.[8] The more audacious even robbed their own officers. Captain Peebles of the Black Watch found some linen and six or seven bottles of rum and wine taken from his tent, and observed that 'there are some sad rascals in this Batallion who are wicked enough to do anything, and have cunning enough to escape.'[9] No doubt these spoils were consumed, but there were plenty of enterprising American fences willing to buy stolen goods from soldiers and resell them.[10]

The supply of rogues was not enough to meet the demands of Germain's strategy and so a stopgap measure of the Seven Years War was revived and mercenaries were purchased. An approach made to Tsaritsa Catherine for 20,000 Russians failed and so the government turned to the Landgraf of Hessen-Kassel who proved more obliging. In all, 19,000 Germans, two-thirds of the Hessians, served with the British army in North America, of whom approximately 3,000 deserted, 500 were killed as a result of enemy action and 4,500 died from diseases.[11]

On the whole, the Hessians proved good value for money and well-motivated, brave soldiers. Schooled in the habits of submission as the subjects of German autocrats, they were willing to fight for the rights of monarchy against an enemy whom British propaganda depicted as inhuman fiends. Two Hessians, captured in November 1776, revealed to an American army surgeon that they had been told that their opponents were 'savages and barbarians' who tortured their prisoners in the Indian manner.

For the greater part, British soldiers fought out of a sense of duty and loyalty, first to their comrades and then to their country. Officers of aristocratic background, and most were, had little but contempt for adversaries who were their social inferiors. 'I hope that we shall soon have done with these scoundrels for one dirties one's fingers by meddling with them,' wrote Major Lord Rawdon, Clinton's adjutant. An Anglican, brought up to associate religious dissent with political radicalism, Rawdon was also disgusted by the 'godly twang' of the rebel 'psalm singers'.[12] Captain Peebles was enraged by being overcharged by his landlady who was 'greedy and cunning like the rest of the Yankees', but he also felt pity for those unwillingly drawn into the war. After the court martial of a rapist, saved from the gallows by the intercession of his victim, he wrote in his journal, 'hard is the fate of many who suffer indiscriminately in a civil war'.[13] A humane man, Peebles like many others, was distressed by the sight of abandoned or burned farmsteads and the fate of families driven from their homes.

Derision of the Americans' fighting stamina quickly gave way to grudging respect. A year's campaigning taught Clinton that 'the Americans were trained to stratagem and enterprise' and 'they knew every trick of chicane'.[14] They were also capable of fighting in the conventional manner, which was proved in June 1775 during the struggles for Breed's and

Bunker's Hills overlooking Boston. Further north, Benedict Arnold and General Richard Montgomery had taken the initiative and launched an invasion of Canada which they advertised as a war of liberation.

As the Americans advanced towards Quebec, they called on the French-Canadians to free themselves from tyranny, and for a time it was expected they might. 'The Canadians talk of that damned absurd word liberty,' complained one British officer, and General Guy Carleton, the governor of Quebec and veteran of Wolfe's campaigns, feared defections from his militia.[15] In fact, most Canadians remained prudently neutral and waited to see what, if any, success the Americans would achieve. The arrival of winter, Montgomery's foolish decision to besiege Quebec with an outnumbered force, and Carleton's brilliantly improvised defence combined to frustrate the Americans. The city was relieved in May 1776 by a British flotilla, by which time Arnold had withdrawn with the remnants of his army.

It was impossible to hold Boston. Relations between townsfolk and soldiers were sulphurous and the Americans controlled the immediate hinterland. In March 1776, the commander-in-chief, Howe, ordered the city's evacuation. 'It is not possible to describe to you the confusion everything is in here,' Lieutenant Charles Cochrane of the King's Regiment told his uncle. 'To embark (under the guns of those Rascals) the above remaining stores with the heavy baggage of Women and Children, friends of the Government, which last, I believe, might be put in a canoe, is such an operation as probably never happened before.' It was the climax to a year of humiliation, and Cochrane added ruefully that 'an uncommon bad fate has attended our Affairs here from first to last; after scrambling through this disagreeable winter with so little assistance from any quarter that we must make a *moon light flit* is most irksome.'[16] Nevertheless, Cochrane found grounds for optimism and believed that the army's fortunes would soon revive once Germain's grand strategy was implemented.

Cochrane's confidence was misplaced. The North American battlefield encompassed a million square miles, most of them covered with mountains, woodland and scrub. Armies were easily swallowed up in this wilderness, through which they often marched blindly; Clinton, traversing New Jersey in 1778, had only the vaguest idea of Washington's whereabouts until he was attacked at Monmouth.[17] The possession of major towns counted for less than it did in Europe because economic resources, such as iron foundries, were scattered. Boston, New York, Philadelphia and Charleston were all under British control at various times, but their occupation did little to hamper the American war effort.

Bold and imaginative generals might have overcome these difficulties, but the thinking of the British high command was uninventive and often timid. Moreover, and this became painfully apparent as the war proceeded, the British command structure was shaky. Germain in London retained overall direction of strategy, but his instructions to the commanders in America were often delayed by as much as eight to ten weeks because the ships carrying them faced contrary winds. Misunderstandings between him and his subordinates remained uncorrected, and in some instances the generals in the field had no choice but to follow their own judgement. There was also, at least in 1775–6, confusion over objectives. Germain favoured an all-out effort while North still held out hope for a negotiated settlement.

It took time for these flaws to reveal themselves. Howe's operations in the summer of 1776 had started slowly, thanks to delayed reinforcements, but they showed every sign of prospering. He had decided to concentrate his forces on New York in the centre of an area where Loyalism was believed to be strong. The landing on Staten Island went off smoothly and, in mid-August, Howe launched his 23,000-strong army against the outer defences of New York City. A solid, painstaking commander, Howe proceeded cautiously and in doing so missed the opportunity to fight a decisive engagement. For a time, Washington had been prepared to risk the bulk of the rebel army to save the city, but Howe did not offer battle. Instead he attacked the enemy's earthworks piecemeal and, when it was clear that New York would fall, shrank from a pursuit of the badly mauled and demoralised American army.

There now seemed no need for the hammer-blow which Germain had imagined would end the war. Howe's successes around New York during the autumn of 1776 indicated that the British army was unbeatable, and at the end of November he felt strong enough to issue a proclamation which offered an unconditional pardon to all rebels who surrendered and reaffirmed their allegiance to George III. Many Americans, well aware of the pitiful state of Washington's army, were glad to accept Howe's clemency. The temper of the colonists seemed to be changing and Howe, several victories to his credit and with a base at New York, felt he could safely alter his strategy. Henceforward he would aim to occupy territory rather than coaxing Washington into a full-scale engagement. This shift offered tempting political dividends; wavering rebels would be further disheartened and the presence of British troops in an area would rally the local Loyalists.

Detachments of British and Hessian troops fanned out across Delaware and New Jersey. At first this subsidiary campaign went well, but Washington, for psychological as much as military reasons, took the offensive and overcame a Hessian unit at Trenton on Christmas Day. This coup was followed by another at Princeton a fortnight later.

The battles of Trenton and Princeton were small-scale affairs which had a disproportionate effect on American opinion. In July 1776, the radicals inside Congress had pushed for and obtained a Declaration of Independence which severed all links with Britain, and ruled out any future compromise based on British sovereignty over America. It is impossible to assess precisely how many Americans supported this move; John Adams, one of the signatories to the declaration, calculated that about a third of the colonists were wholeheartedly behind independence and that the rest were either Loyalists or neutral. To judge by the numbers who took advantage of Howe's amnesty, the balance was in danger of swinging against supporters of independence. Trenton and Princeton reversed this trend by demonstrating that the British army was not invincible and that there was plenty of fight left in the Americans.

A blow had been struck against Loyalism, which soon began to wither in Delaware and New Jersey. The Loyalist predicament then and throughout the war was summed up by William Smith, the Chief Justice of New York. 'How unfavourable the Prospects of the Americans who have joined the British Army! They can be safe by Nothing but Conquest of their own Country – If America prevails by the Sword or obtains Concessions to her Contentment, the Tories are ruined. In either Case they must finally abandon the Continent – In the Interim they must borrow Subsistence, which will be to many of them immediate Ruin.'[18] The British were losing the war for hearts and minds.

The year 1777 marked the turning point of the war. After over a year's fighting, the British army had made little headway; there had been no signal victory over the Americans, inroads into territory held by Congress had been limited and Loyalist support had proved disappointing. Howe was pessimistic, and early in July he told Clinton that he expected the war to drag on for at least another year. Clinton, who had just returned from leave in Britain, observed that the government wanted victory by winter. Howe replied, 'If the ministers would not carry it on another year, they had better give it up now.'[19]

Germain's strategy for 1777 was an invasion of Pennsylvania by units of Howe's army. Simultaneously, a mixed force of 8,000 British, Hessians, Canadians and Indians, commanded by Burgoyne, would advance southwards along the Hudson towards Albany, where he would be joined by reinforcements sent by Howe from New York. If everything went to plan, a wedge would have been driven between the militant New England colonies and the rest of America. This was what Germain intended, and it was made clear in a despatch written on 18 May which Howe received on 16 August, when he was bogged down in Pennsylvania and in no position to assist Burgoyne.

The blame for this blunder lay with Howe. In March, he had read the general outline of Germain's strategy, but believed that he could safely disregard his obligation to Burgoyne. He felt that the advance on Albany was a peripheral affair and that the attack on Pennsylvania, which had been his brainchild, needed most of his resources and all his energies. These had been noticeably flagging during the spring, and preparations for the Pennsylvania campaign were only completed at the very end of July. By then, a majority of Howe's senior officers were pressing him to help Burgoyne, but they were overridden and the invasion of Pennsylvania went ahead.[20] A totally inadequate force was left behind in New York under Clinton, who was ordered to do what he could to support Burgoyne.

What followed was a débâcle. Burgoyne's lines of communication were cut and his path was blocked by superior forces. Rather than squander the lives of his men in a battle he had no chance of winning, Burgoyne surrendered his army to General Horatio Gates at Saratoga on 16 October. There were no compensations in Pennsylvania where Howe had nothing but bad luck. At Brandywine he gave Washington's army a severe shaking, but the Americans made their escape in the nick of time. Philadelphia was taken, but it could not be held since the British had failed to secure control of the Delaware River.

The events of the autumn of 1777 confirmed the Declaration of Independence and the survival of the American republic. Germain's grand strategy was in ruins and hopes of restoring British sovereignty over all the colonies had been shattered. France, hitherto a benevolent neutral, threw in its lot with the colonists in February 1778 and the American struggle became part of the global war.

Germain's new strategy reflected the changed political situation and Britain's weakness. Outright victory was beyond the grasp of the British army so all efforts were directed towards a salvage operation designed to conquer and retain Georgia and the Carolinas, where Loyalism was report-edly still strong. The campaign of conquest and conciliation was directed by Clinton, who had replaced Howe as commander-in-chief, and it opened promisingly. Savannah was captured in December 1778 and Charleston in May 1780. The mood of the army was now buoyant, and some sensed that a swift and triumphant end to the war was imminent. On hearing the news of Charleston's fall, General Robertson wrote to Germain that, 'Britain will recover her former grandeur and the Question you will leave posterity to discuss will be, whether bravery or humanity had the greatest share in reducing America to obedience.'[21]

As the campaign in the Carolinas progressed, the old problem of Loyalism re-emerged. There were, as predicted, plenty of Loyalists, but they would only cooperate if their safety was guaranteed by the British army. Some of those who did, found themselves embroiled in a subsidiary war of terror and counter-terror that was waged with enormous ferocity in remoter parts of South Carolina. There was also, in 1779, an attempt by the British to enlist the help of the slaves. An appeal to them had been made in November 1775 by Lord Dunmore, the fire-eating and energetic governor of Virginia, who eventually mustered 300 runaways in his 'Ethiopian Regiment', whose uniforms carried the slogan, 'Liberty to Slaves'.[22] The local plantocracy had been horrified and Dunmore's daring move was ultimately self-defeating since it drove scared whites into the arms of Congress.

Between 1779 and 1781 thousands of negroes made their way to the British army, drawn by Clinton's offer of freedom to any slave of a rebel. Most found themselves employed as labourers, digging earthworks or looking after the army's massive transport train. By the end of the war, large numbers had been carried to New York from where some were sold back into servitude.[23]

Neither the white Loyalists nor black slaves who flocked to the British army as it proceeded through the Carolinas made any impact on the cam-paign. General Sir Charles Cornwallis, who had charge of the operations, won two victories, at Camden in August 1780 and Guilford Court House the following March, but lacked the men to maintain a permanent occu-pation of the territory which fell into his hands.

The end of the war in the South came, unexpectedly, in October 1781 at Yorktown. The events which led up to this battle were in many respects a rerun of those of 1777. The British high command was again beset by misfortune and muddle, which were made worse by ill-feeling between

Clinton and Cornwallis, who later accused his commander-in-chief of starving him of men. This was debatable, but what was certain early in 1781 was that neither general had any clear idea of how best to deploy their forces.

Cornwallis favoured an attack on Virginia, launched a half-hearted invasion and then settled down at Williamsburg to await Clinton's instructions. Clinton, who had built up a formidable intelligence network, feared an attack on New York, but hoped that he might forestall it by diversionary operations undertaken in Pennsylvania or Rhode Island in conjunction with Cornwallis. Much to his annoyance, Cornwallis was therefore ordered to hold himself in readiness for a seaborne evacuation, and to this end he placed his army within a fortified encampment at Yorktown on the estuary of the York River in southern Virginia. In the meantime, the Franco-American attack on New York had materialised.

At this point the key to the campaign was seapower. So long as supplies and reinforcements could pass by sea between Yorktown and New York, Cornwallis and Clinton were relatively secure. This was not the case after late August when Admiral de Grasse's fleet arrived from the West Indies and took up positions in the Chesapeake Bay. After a brief, inconclusive action the British North American squadron retired to New York, and with it went Cornwallis's chances of reinforcement or escape. As the balance of naval power swung against Britain, Washington, forewarned of de Grasse's intentions, broke camp and began a 450-mile dash from New York to Yorktown. The upshot was that Cornwallis, outnumbered, isolated and under bombardment, surrendered his army on 17 October. As his men marched out and laid down their arms, the band played a popular song, 'The World Turned Upside Down'.

The disaster at Yorktown was a profound shock for the British. An army had been lost and hopes of holding on to the southern colonies had evaporated. For a time both sides had been showing signs of war-weariness: there had been serious mutinies by American troops, dissatisfied with their pay and conditions, in 1780–1, and there were signs that the discipline of some British regiments was cracking. In February 1781 Captain Peebles, then stationed in New York, noticed that he and his brother officers were drinking more heavily than usual. Morals too relaxed during the twilight of British rule in New York. At a grand ball given by the military governor in March 1781 there were country dances until one in the morning, when supper was eaten. The ladies left at three, after which 'the Gentlemen closed their files and drank and sang till past 8 o'clock when the remaining few retired to another room and got breakfast after which some went to bed, some to visit their partners, and some to the bawdy house.'[24]

For six months George III had pig-headedly refused to acknowledge the verdict of Yorktown, and a few other diehards, including Cornwallis, wished to fight on. North was not one of them, and in March 1782 the King finally accepted his resignation. The new prime minister, Rockingham, was a moderate who opened negotiations with the Americans. The successful defence of Gibraltar and the restoration of British seapower in the Caribbean strengthened the hand of British diplomats and the Americans proved willing to forgo claims to Canada on the grounds that a British presence in North America was an insurance against possible French and Spanish expansion in the region. Nevertheless, Britain was obliged to cede those lands to the west of the Mississippi which had been incorporated in Canada under the terms of the Quebec Act.

Pre-war predictions that the British empire would not survive the loss of the American colonies proved false. Naturally there were alarms about the commercial consequences of a break between Britain and America, and in January 1781 a frantic attempt was made to retain the American market with the American Intercourse Bill. But this measure, designed to give American traders exemptions from the navigation laws, was unnecessary for, as the bill's critics pointed out, the new republic could not survive economically without Britain.

This was true; the volume of Anglo-American trade actually increased after 1783, in particular exports of raw cotton, which rose from an annual average of 15.5 million pounds in the late 1780s to 28.6 million by 1800. Only the American, slave-worked and partly-mechanised cotton plantations could provide the output needed to satisfy the demands of the new, machine-operated Lancashire mills. By 1840, 80 per cent of Lancashire's supplies of raw cotton came from America. The harvest failures of 1799–1800 led British grain importers to buy up American surpluses which, between 1810 and 1812, helped feed the British army in Spain and Portugal.

The continuance and growth of Anglo-American commerce after 1783 gave the lie to the old mercantilist justification of colonies as exclusive markets, protected and controlled in the economic interests of the mother country. The intellectual props which supported this contention had been knocked away in 1776 with the publication of Adam Smith's *The Wealth of Nations*, which went through five editions before the author's death in

1790. Smith's purpose in this and his other economic tracts had been to measure human progress and employ his calculations to formulate natural laws which governed economic activity. The result was his concept of the Free Market, a product of natural human competition, which, if unfettered by official rules and unhindered by monopolies, provided the most efficient distribution of resources and the greatest benefits to the consumer.

According to Smith, colonies were redundant. The apparatus of state control over their trade was an encumbrance to commerce which interfered with natural market forces and raised prices. Indirect proof of the futility of regulations had been provided by the market's response to the official trade embargoes imposed during the American War, when the annual value of smuggled goods was calculated as at least £2 million. A sophisticated trading nation like Britain could flourish in an expanding international free market. This was proved beyond question by the growth of non-colonial trade during the 1790s, in particular with America and Europe.

Smith's theories and the post-war pattern of British trade undermined the economic arguments which had hitherto justified the empire. Moreover, the events of the American War strongly suggested that Britain, having enlarged its territories by the victories of 1759–62, had overstretched its naval and military resources to a point where contraction was inevitable, even desirable. French operational difficulties and not the strength of the home fleet had prevented the invasion attempt of 1779. The strain had been too great and it only needed a temporary loss of seapower in North American waters during the autumn of 1781 to demonstrate that the defence of a global empire required Britain to be equally strong everywhere. Cornwallis's capitulation at Yorktown may have been a psychological shock, but it was not a surprise.

No distinctly imperialist political ideology had emerged after the spectacular conquests of the Seven Years War. Then and later, the ownership of a vast overseas empire was generally seen as a source of wealth and a monument to national virtues, in particular those displayed on the battlefield. In 1778, a despairing American Loyalist wrote from England; 'I fear this nation has sunk into too selfish, degenerate, luxurious a sloth, to rise into such manly, noble exertions as her critical situation seems to demand.' The question as to whether moral decadence contributed appreciably to slipshod planning and poor generalship was left unasked.

The crisis in 1774–76 had, however, prompted some examination of the political nature of the empire and a discussion about its future. Some

British Whigs and Radicals accepted that there were no moral or political reasons to prevent the Americans from choosing to go their own way, even if this meant independence. In practical terms, it was ridiculous to spend large sums of money in holding down the colonies and, at the same time, allege that they were a vital source of national wealth. The abandonment of rigid control by London and its replacement by some form of American self-government would not automatically dissolve the economic connection between Britain and North America. If there were any imperial bonds between Britain and the colonists they were, as many Americans pointed out, those of shared beliefs in personal liberty and representative institutions.

Thinking along these lines influenced post-war official policy towards the Canadian provinces. After 1783 their population had been swelled by thousands of Loyalist refugees and former soldiers in the Loyalist corps who had been rewarded with land grants. There were also schemes to give financial help to the new settlers who ended the demographic imbalance between French and British colonists. The political future of Canada was given consideration with plans for representative assemblies which would enjoy powers and rights similar to those of the British parliament. In taking such a line, the British government showed that it had learned something from the recent upheavals in America, but it was hoped that an 'aristocracy' of wealth and talent would emerge in Canada which would naturally attach itself to the British crown rather than lead a movement for complete self-government.

Elsewhere it was impossible to proceed with policies of the kind proposed for Canada which, conceivably, would lead to its eventual independence. The Caribbean colonies, vulnerable to France and with vast populations of slaves, needed British protection, as did the West African outposts who were the source of labour for the West Indies. As for India, successive governments faced the problem of how to assert their authority over a process of territorial expansion which appeared to have run out of control.

6

The Terror of
Our Arms:
Conquest and Trade in
India, 1689–1815

One of the panels carved between 1728 and 1730 by the fashionable sculptor Michael Rysbrack for a chimney piece in East India House showed Britannia receiving the riches of the East in the form of a half-clothed native woman proffering a small treasure chest. The same theme was rendered almost identically on a ceiling painting executed fifty years later by an Italian, Spiridione Roma. Britannia, a lion at her feet, examines a string of pearls she has taken from a cushion held up by an Indian woman. Another woman grasps a large, Chinese-style urn, presumably filled with tea, while, commanded by Mercury the god of commerce, a third figure approaches with a bundle, perhaps filled with calico or muslin. In the foreground of both carving and painting is a representation of Father Thames, a reminder that London was the principle beneficiary of this outpouring of oriental wealth.

While the decorations of East India House symbolised pure commerce, there was a distinctly imperial look to the triumphal arch erected in front of the new Government House at Calcutta in the early 1800s. Roman in scale and grandeur, the great central arch was crowned by a stone lion, its pose both commanding and vigilant. Behind this imposing gateway lay Government House, a palace in the Georgian Palladian manner faced with tall marble columns. These public buildings were erected at the orders of Richard Wellesley, Earl of Mornington and later Marquess Wellesley, who served as governor-general of India between 1798 and 1805. They reflected his own aristocratic addiction to the pomp and trappings of power, and the new self-confident, imperious spirit which was abroad among his countrymen in India. They were no longer men of business; they were the masters of an empire who required the architectural style of Rome and the permanence of marble to give substance to their authority.

The official buildings of Calcutta and their equally grandiose counterparts in Madras were a striking witness to the revolution which had occurred in India during the past sixty years. In 1740 the East India Company was purely a commercial enterprise, which imported and exported goods from its factories at Bombay, Madras and Calcutta, unbothered by the internal politics of India. By 1815, the Company owned the most powerful army in India and governed, directly and indirectly, Bengal, much of the upper Ganges basin and extensive areas of eastern and southern India. Independent native princes feared its power and many sought its friendship and protection. Most important of all, the Company was flexing its muscles as a major Asian power; during the past twenty years its army and navy had seen action in Arabia, Mauritius, Malacca and Java.

Trade still mattered, but less than before. Since 1793 the Company's monopoly had been whittled away by the British government, which was falling under the spell of Adam Smith's economic theories. The Company lost out; by 1810 interlopers had captured a quarter of the Indian market and were selling goods worth £2 million a year. Changing patterns of trade rescued the Company, in particular the mass importation of cheap Lancashire cottonware which was underway by the early 1800s and which, incidentally, swamped and extinguished India's village-based cotton industry. There was also a burgeoning and lucrative two-way trade with China which imported Bengali opium and exported tea for the British market. Opium exports were worth a million rupees in 1802–3 (about £250,000), a total which rose by 20 per cent in the next ten years. And yet, despite new opportunities for trade, the Company was, by 1800, principally dependent on land taxes collected from the provinces it ruled.

The metamorphosis of the Company was accomplished without any plan and according to no general principle. It was largely undertaken by a handful of ambitious officials and generals, who sincerely believed that they could enrich themselves while at the same time advancing the interests of their country and their employer. Their predatory and private-enterprise imperialism was ideally suited to conditions in eighteenth-century India where the central authority of the Mughal emperors was dissolving. Of course, opportunism and greed were already endemic among the Company's servants, all of whom were in India to accumulate enough capital to return to Britain and a life of ease. 'I may be made Governor, if not that I may make a fortune which will make me live like a gentleman,' Stair Dalrymple told his elder brother in 1752. He was seeking a Company post and needed £500 to cover a bond for his good behaviour and a further £200 for his kit and passage out.[1] This investment would soon be recovered once Dalrymple exercised his right to trade on his own account, although, like other fortune-seekers, he faced exposure to diseases and a climate which reduced his chances of returning home.

At the time when Dalrymple was importuning his brother, new and unlooked for ways of self-enrichment were presenting themselves to the Company's employees. In 1742 Joseph-François, Marquis Dupleix, had taken up the post of governor of the French Compagnie des Indes. In many ways he was very similar to the belligerent, greedy and overreaching British proconsuls with whom he and his successors contended for the next twenty years. During the final year of the War of the Austrian Succession, the principal French trading port of Pondicherry had been threatened by a Company army operating from Madras. Worried about its safety and knowing that a further Anglo-French war was extremely likely, Dupleix decided that Pondicherry needed a defensive *glacis*. To this end, he set about making the Compagnie des Indes the power-broker of the Carnatic.

Dupleix excused this meddling in local affairs by promising his employers rich returns from the land taxes levied on those areas which passed into French control.[2] There were also, although this was omitted from his despatches to Paris, vast opportunities for him and his staff to divert some of these revenues into their own pockets, along with gifts from Indian princes who sought France's friendship. Dupleix began his excursion into the complex, uncertain and violent world of Indian dynastic politics in 1749 when he engineered the installation of his stooge, Chandra Sahib, as nawab (governor) of the Carnatic.

The East India Company's governor and council at Madras could not stand by and allow the Carnatic to slip into French hands and they were soon sponsoring a rival nawab, Muhammad Ali Khan. Both companies supported their puppets with troops, and a proxy war for control of the region was underway by 1750.

Among the British officers engaged was Robert Clive. He had come to India, aged nineteen, in 1744 as a clerk and had drifted into soldiering four years later. In England he had been an idle misfit whose despairing family (Shropshire gentry) arranged his shipment to India. There he might have remained in obscurity, but for a French sally against Madras in 1748 which released in him remarkable talents. He swiftly absorbed all that was needed to master the art of war as it was waged in India, and revealed a knack for commanding the Company's Indian troops, or sepoys. He was physically brave at a time when, like their British counterparts, Indian soldiers responded to daring and courageous officers. Clive was also highly ambitious: he craved what his age called 'glory', that public lustre which attached to victorious generals, and once his career was underway he used his fortune to propel himself into the British ruling class.

As a soldier and later as an administrator, Clive came in close contact with Indians and he later believed himself the possessor of that arcane branch of human knowledge, an understanding of the inner working of the Indian mind. All Indians, he imagined, were accustomed to that form of arbitrary government which his liberal-minded countrymen called 'despotism'; were mesmerised by temerity, and awed by 'prestige', an abstraction which blended military prowess and moral authority in roughly equal proportions.

The siege of Arcot in 1751 gave Clive the chance to display his flair as a commander. He held off a superior Franco-Indian detachment and his leadership was, allegedly, so charismatic that a battalion of French-trained sepoys later deserted and demanded to serve under him. The small-scale operations which characterised the struggle for the Carnatic dragged on for three more years, by when it was clear that Dupleix had bitten off more than he could chew. Nonetheless, he had every reason to persevere and so did the British; Robert Orme, an officer serving with the Company's army, heard that in 1753 the Compagnie des Indes had extracted £535,000 in land tax from the territory it occupied.

The stakes were high and, as Orme observed, winning presented few difficulties for Europeans or European-armed and trained troops. 'The actions of a single platoon in India may have the same influence on the general success, as the conduct of a whole regiment in Europe.' The key to victory lay in what he called the 'superiority of European arms' and Clive

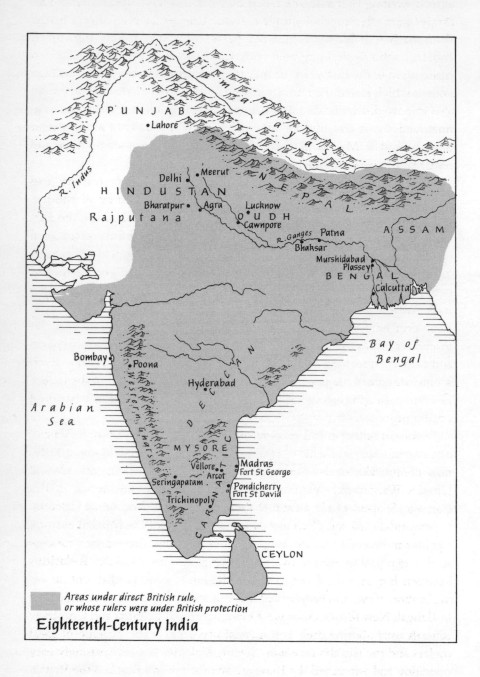

PUNJAB

• Lahore

R. Indus

HINDUSTAN

Rajputana

Delhi • • Meerut

Bharatpur • • Agra

Lucknow
• OUDH
Cawnpore

R. Ganges Patna
Bhaksar

NEPAL

ASSAM

Murshidabad
Plassey
BENGAL
Calcutta

Bay of
Bengal

Arabian
Sea

Bombay
• Poona

Hyderabad

Western Ghats

DECCAN

MYSORE

Vellore •
• Arcot
Seringapatam •

Trichinopoly

CARNATIC

Madras
Fort St George

Pondicherry
Fort St David

CEYLON

Areas under direct British rule,
or whose rulers were under British protection

Eighteenth-Century India

agreed, writing later that 'the terror of our arms' was so great that Indian armies were often psychologically defeated before they even offered battle. Both the British and the French companies stepped up the recruitment of Indians, who were equipped with flintlock muskets, and drilled to manoeuvre in the European manner to deliver the devastating, close-range volleys which scared their adversaries and won battles. White troops were also imported, which was not an easy task since soldiering in India was as unattractive as it was elsewhere; Orme, surveying a body of recruits who disembarked at Madras in 1752, noted that they were all 'as usual the refuse of the vilest employments in London'.[3]

The French too were learning the lessons of Indian warfare and Dupleix, faced with a stalemate in 1753, resolved to end it by an infusion of French professional troops. To even the local balance of power, the East India Company asked the British government for reinforcements, and received the 39th Regiment and four warships. The French and British governments' decision to intervene in what hitherto had been a contest between rival commercial interests had momentous consequences for India. Backed by the military and naval resources of Britain and France, the two companies were now a formidable political force in India. For the moment they were roughly equal in terms of manpower and equipment, and their energies were wholly consumed by the war in the Carnatic. Even if one side gained the upper hand there it was quite likely, given the nature of Franco-British diplomacy, that gains made in India might be bartered during peace negotiations.

European power in India was tested not in the Carnatic, but in Bengal, in an unexpected war which broke out in June 1756. While Robert Clive, now commander of the Madras army, the Madras Council, and Admiral Charles Watson were planning an offensive against the French in the Carnatic, Siraj-ud-Daula, nawab of Bengal, attacked and occupied Calcutta.

Siraj-ud-Daula was a product of the dissolution of the Mughal empire, a prince in his early twenties who had inherited an independent state created a generation earlier by the sword of his great-uncle. Relations between him and the Company had previously been cordial, but, as his declaration of war showed, he was nervous about the spread of its influence in Bengal. New fortifications were being set round Calcutta and Company officials were abusing their commercial privileges at the expense of local traders and the nawab's revenues. Seizing Calcutta was a surprisingly easy operation and astonished the Bengalis, who afterwards mocked the British as 'banchots' (cowards).

It was the damage inflicted on the Company's prestige as much as the loss of revenues from Calcutta, now needed to boost the war effort in the Carnatic, which convinced Clive that the city's recapture had to be given priority over operations against the French. Calcutta was retaken in January 1757 by Clive and Watson and war was declared against Siraj-ud-Daula. It was masterminded by Clive who proceeded by diplomatic stealth and cunning against an adversary whose weak character, capriciousness and predatory sexuality made him an Indian Caligula. Like the Roman emperor, Siraj was encircled by courtiers and soldiers of brittle loyalty who were easily seduced into a conspiracy against him. Mir Jafir, the commander of Siraj's army, needed little coaxing to accept Clive's bribes and the promise of the Bengal throne, and Siraj's financial props, the Seth banking clan, were also enticed into Clive's web. Politically undermined by Company cash, Siraj was finally destroyed by the Company's firepower at Plassey on 23 June 1757.

Plassey was a spectacular demonstration of the Company's military muscle and one which made a deep and lasting impression on the Indian mind. Outwardly, the two armies were unequally matched: Clive commanded 1,000 European troops, 2,000 sepoys and eight small-calibre cannon and a howitzer, while Siraj mustered a host of at least 50,000 cavalry and infantry and a large train of massive, bullock-drawn cannon. This vast, sprawling and loosely-commanded horde was driven by internal dissension.(Mir Jafir's contingent deliberately stayed aloof from the fighting) and was soon unnerved by the unfamiliar tactics of its adversaries. Those who retained some will to fight soon lost it when faced with volleys of musketry and close-range bombardment. Clive's gunners knew from experience how to create havoc by aiming at artillery bullocks and the elephants which carried Indian commanders. The wounded beasts stampeded and careered wildly through the ranks of infantry and cavalry. What tipped the balance was Clive's overwhelming self-confidence and offensive spirit which made his army like a tiger, who 'never charges if he can scatter his enemies with a roar'.[4] The roar proved too much for Siraj's army; it fell apart and fled. Shortly after, he was taken and murdered by Mir Jafir's servants. The Company's losses were seventy-three killed and wounded.

Plassey proved, crudely but effectively, that the Company was a force to be reckoned with in India. For the next fifty years, the rulers of Mysore, Hyderabad, the Mahratha states and the Punjab scrambled to acquire the new military technology and the specialists, usually Europeans, who would train their soldiers to use it. Other Indian princes chose to preserve their independence by seeking an accommodation with the Company through unequal treaties, in which they agreed to surrender revenues and some of their authority in return for the Company's protection in the form of a permanent garrison.

The pattern of expansion by coercion and treaty was first seen after Plassey when Clive played kingmaker and installed Mir Jafir as nawab of Bengal, Orissa and Bihar. All the customary land taxes of these provinces passed to the Company and Mir Jafir was left responsible for justice and policing, functions that were taken over by the Company in 1772. All Frenchmen were expelled from Bengal, and soon some of its taxes were flowing into the Carnatic to subsidise the war effort against France. After some awkward moments, including an amphibious assault on Madras, the war in the Carnatic went in the Company's favour. Pondicherry fell in 1761 and its fortifications were levelled. French pretensions in southern India were in shreds, even though Pondicherry was returned to them in 1763 under the terms of the Treaty of Paris.

Bengal gave the Company the wherewithal to sustain its new position as a major military power within India. The circumstances of its acquisition gave impetus to further wars of conquest and pacification as civilians and soldiers discovered that the profits of war far exceeded those of trade. Looking back on twenty years of intermittent campaigns, Edmund Burke told the Commons in 1785 that, 'The great fortunes made in India at the beginnings of the conquest, naturally excited emulation in all parts, and through the whole succession of the Company's servants.'

This was true. Those who played the game of high politics and war in India found themselves tantalisingly close to huge sources of wealth which could be easily tapped. It was, Clive correctly stated, 'the known and usual custom of Eastern Princes' to make generous gifts to those who helped them. Mir Jafir followed tradition and between 1757 and 1766 gave Clive a total of £234,000 and, during the same period, extended his largesse to other officials in Calcutta, who individually received sums of between £5,000 and £117,000. The goodwill and influence of powerful men were purchasable commodities in Indian political life, as they were in eighteenth-century Britain, and the Company's agents saw no reason why they should not benefit from the accepted practices of a country where they were now power-brokers. Corruption was also endemic in the day-to-day administration of India, and officials who were placed in charge of the tax-collection in Bengal and elsewhere soon 'went native', channelling revenues into their own pockets.

These were all the fruits of conquest. War also generated profits, most of which found their way into the hands of soldiers, which was why so many of them always favoured aggressive policies. Clive made £40,000 between 1744 and 1753 during which time he held relatively junior posts, while the more scrupulous Arthur Wellesley (younger brother of the Marquess and later Field-Marshal, the Duke of Wellington), who held more senior commands between 1798 and 1805, returned home £43,000 better off.[5] Junior officers were always itching for action, especially if it offered chances of promotion, campaign allowances and, most welcome of all, loot and prize money. In September 1797, young officers in Madras were plunged into despair when they heard that an expedition against Manila had been cancelled. One wrote to his parents, 'Judge of the gloom, the disappointment, and vexation which overspread the faces which a few moments before had exhibited the highest symptoms of hope, and ardour for distinction.'[6]

No doubt there were some fire-eaters genuinely dismayed that they had missed a chance to show their prowess in the field, but there were many, perhaps the majority, who had been dreaming of plunder. The official, and therefore suspect, total of loot taken from Nagpur in 1758 was £25,000. The actual value of the booty was probably far greater, since much of what had been stolen would never find its way on to the Company's reckoning sheets. This was understandable since the procedures for prize-money allocation were slow and heavily weighted in favour of senior officers. Participants in the 1817–19 Mahratha War had to wait eight years for the pay-out of the £2 million owed them, so it was inevitable that many soldiers grabbed what they could and never declared it.

Acquisitiveness at the top was transmitted downwards. An unknown private of the 11th Dragoons recalled the wave of excitement which animated British and Indian other ranks in 1825 after they heard the news that they were about to besiege Bharatpur. When the city fell in January 1826, he watched seven cartloads of gold and silver auctioned, and a soldier offer two gold moidores (about £3.50p) for a bottle of spirits, which would normally have been sold for a tenth of that amount. He also noticed soldiers carrying off gold necklaces, jewellery and camel-hair shawls, while others dug up the floors of houses in search of cash buried by their owners, a common precaution against looters and tax-collectors.[7] This kind of behaviour had attended every war in India during the past eighty years and was beyond the control of officers. When Lieutenant Robert Blakiston apprehended some British plunderers after the capture of Gawilghur in 1803, he was threatened with a bayonet and called a 'meddling rascal' for having dared to prevent them from exercising what they regarded as a natural right.[8]

Over and above the often considerable windfalls which came their way on campaign, officers could expect to earn enough from their pay and maintenance subventions either to provide a nest egg for retirement or to provide an annuity for their families at home. John Malcolm, in many ways a model of administrative probity, who entered the Company's service in 1781, had accumulated £13,000 twenty-three years later and was still able to send home £400 annually to support his parents and sisters. He calculated that when he retired in 1806 his pension and savings would yield him £1,500 a year, enough to place him firmly in the ranks of the gentry.[9] In the 1790s the poet Samuel Coleridge's family was sustained by his elder brother, a junior officer in the Company's army. Colin Mackenzie, an engineer attached to the Madras army in 1790, was willing to risk contracting local diseases working in the interior as a surveyor of forests (he knew nothing of botany) in order to qualify for higher rates of pay, some of which he sent back to his family on the Isle of Lewis.[10]

By the end of the century, placing a son in the Company's army had become a valuable source of additional income to many middle-class families in Britain. Lacking the means to buy a commission in the regular army and provide a private income to supplement the low pay of junior officers, they had the satisfaction of seeing their offspring established in a gentlemanly occupation. Perhaps for this reason, officers of the king's army looked down their noses at their Indian counterparts.

Late eighteenth-century India was a bustling society, peopled by men on the make whose judgements in Company matters were always swayed by self-interest. The free-for-all which followed Plassey encouraged others to promote thrusting, acquisitive policies from which they had everything to gain. Moreover, as the Company annexed land and infiltrated the princely states, the demand grew for administrators, collectors of revenue, surveyors and residents. All these posts were well-paid and many were filled by ambitious young army officers. The dynamic of expansion generated bellicosity; Robert Blakiston thought there was something in the air of India which made British soldiers more 'blood thirsty and ferocious' than usual.

Even some of the Company's directors, who were uneasy about the process of conquest and war, found themselves intoxicated with the new spirit. One, interviewing the twelve-year-old John Malcolm in 1781, asked, 'Why, my little man, what would *you* do if you were to meet Hyder Ali?' 'Do, Sir, I would out with my sword and cut off his head,' was his answer and it qualified Malcolm for a commission in the Company's army.[11]

Hyder Ali Khan, Sultan of Mysore, was the most persistent of the Company's enemies after Plassey. He had invaded the Carnatic in the 1760s, and in harness with the French made war on the Company and its allies in southern India in the late 1770s and 1780s. His son, Tipu (the Tiger) Sultan, continued the duel and was only narrowly beaten by Lord Cornwallis of Yorktown fame in 1793. Tipu, like the other independent princes of southern and central India, knew that survival depended on beating the Company at its own game, warfare in the European manner. During 1791 his agents in Paris were procuring arms from dealers in the Netherlands and, according to Admiralty intelligence sources, had purchased 50 cannon, 80 gun carriages, 100,000 cannon balls, 10,000 muskets and 20,000 'best tempered sabres'.[12] The nizam of Hyderabad had acquired a 14,000-strong corps, armed with muskets and instructed in European methods by French mercenaries, and the princes of the Mahratha Confederacy possessed an estimated 30,000 troops, drilled and organised by freelance European officers.

The late eighteenth-century arms race presented a challenge to the Company, which was accepted with relish by the Marquess Wellesley when he took up the governor-generalship in 1798. Britain had been at war with Revolutionary France since 1793, and the Company's intelligence officers made much of the fact that French mercenaries in India were all left-wing Jacobin Republicans, and that Tipu, who obligingly called himself 'Citizen Tipu', was begging for French assistance. Invoking the bogey of French Revolutionary subversion made sense in 1798, the year of Napoleon's invasion of Egypt, which was seen in London and Calcutta as a prelude to an overland attack on India. Wellesley, a passionate opponent of the French Revolution, did not wait on events; he struck. Hyderabad was neutralised and neutered by coercive diplomacy, and in 1799 the Company's army overran and conquered Mysore.

Tipu died fighting in his capital, Seringapatam, and the nocturnal scene in which Company officers discovered his body became a favourite with British genre painters. His famous mechanical tiger was brought to London in 1808 and displayed as a trophy in the Oriental Repository, a museum attached to the East India Company's headquarters in Leadenhall Street. This contraption immediately aroused enormous curiosity and made a deep and lasting impression on all who came to see it. They stared at a brightly painted, life-sized tiger mauling a uniformed Company officer and heard one emit roars and the other shrieks which subsided as he succumbed; sounds created by a crank-operated barrel organ within the beast.[13] This was the 'Man-Tiger-Organ' that entertained the Indian emperor in John Keats's fairytale, 'The Cap and Bells', an exotic toy which, in the original, seemed a fitting plaything for an oriental despot. In fact Tipu had been nothing of the kind, but this did not stop the wars between him and the Company from being publicly presented as a contest between fickle tyranny and civilising order. The point was graphically made by contemporary prints and paintings of Tipu's sons surrendering themselves to the trustworthy and benevolent Company officers. Indians saw things differently; Muslims venerated Tipu as a martyr for Islam, whose name was being used thirty years later to encourage resistance against the British.[14]

After the conquest of Mysore, it was the turn of the Mahratha states. The initiative came from Wellesley who, by a mixture of force and diplomacy, secured the impoverished and weak Mahratha overlord, the Peshwa, as a Company ally. The result was the Mahratha War of 1803 against the armies of Sindia Daulat Rao of Gwalior and Raghugi Bhonsle of Nagpur. After a whirlwind campaign, their armies were defeated by Arthur Wellesley at the battles of Assaye and Argaon, while in the north, General Sir Gerard Lake occupied Aligarh, Delhi and Agra. With two of the leading Mahratha princes on their knees, the Marquess snatched at the chance to eliminate the third and declared war on Jaswant Rao Holkar in 1805. The second phase of the war went badly; a Company column was roughly handled near Agra and Lake found Bharatpur too tough a nut to crack. The Marquess Wellesley had overreached himself and in 1806 he was recalled to London.

The Marquess had come unstuck because of over-confidence and temerity. He had not gone to India to enrich himself, but to prove his worth as a dynamic and visionary administrator (he founded a college for Company civil servants at Madras), and hoped that his achievements would qualify him for high office in Britain. He was the first of a breed of high-handed, patrician proconsuls who relished the exercise of absolute power; when he visited Cawnpore in 1802, he rode on a magnificently bedecked elephant and 'in the true style of Eastern pomp, distributed his [the Company's] rupees with a liberal hand' just like an Indian potentate.[15] A man of such temperament had nothing but disdain for balance sheets and the Company's directors who were, he wrote confidentially in 1799, 'held in universal contempt and ridicule in every branch of the service in India'.

The businessmen in London had profound misgivings about the Marquess Wellesley and those men of similar stamp who, over the past forty years, had engineered a revolution in the Company's affairs. This apprehension was well founded since the policies of these wilful and some-times venal servants had thrown the Company's accounts into chaos, and given it responsibilities it did not want and for which it was unfitted. In 1744 the Company had loaned the government £1 million; twenty-eight years and various wars later, it was in the red and seeking to borrow £1.4 million from the Treasury. By 1815 the Company's debt was £40 million and just over three-quarters of its annual budget was consumed by the expenses of its army, which was now 150,000 strong. There had been brief signs of financial resurgence in the mid-1760s as the land taxes from Bengal began to pour in, but these quickly vanished and the Company lurched from crisis to crisis. In order to stay afloat, it had fallen back on the dubi-ous expedient of raising capital by regular share issues, and had created what in effect was a private version of the national debt.

Where would it all end? A considerable body of opinion, stronger in London than in India, feared that the Company was becoming dangerously overstretched. In 1779, when it was locked in combat with Hyder Ali and his French sponsors, Major-General James Stuart, the resident in Tanjore (Thangayu), voiced the widely-held anxiety that the Company 'already possesses more Territory and Influence than they well know how to make good use of'.[16] Twenty-five years later, the naturally cautious Arthur Wellesley was convinced that his brother had overstepped himself in his efforts to subdue the Mahrathas. He also believed that there were great risks in making treaties with native princes which left them with the façade of their former power, while real authority was exerted by the Company with the result that they lost respect and their puppet-master gained none.

Critics of expansionism were also uneasy about the swiftness with which senior Company officials resorted to war as an instrument of policy. A quick and unexpectedly arduous foray into Nepal in 1814–15 troubled the Duke of York, the commander-in-chief of the British Army, who won-dered why 'it was ever necessary'.[17] There was, of course, little that he or anyone else in London could do about it, for the men who made the deci-sions were thousands of miles away. If challenged, they fell back on a stock explanation which involved local prestige and the refusal of the Company's strategists to tolerate a powerful or obstreperous independent state on their borders. The government and the directors were not always convinced; in 1816 there was some reluctance to allow the Nepal campaign's hero, Major-General Sir David Ochterlony, a £1,000 annuity, which was understandable given the Company's debts.[18]

Behind the debates that had flared up in Britain whenever the men-on-the-spot in India adopted aggressive policies, lay a deep unease. Altogether the events of the fifty years after Plassey suggested that those who held power in India considered themselves beyond the restraint of either the Company or the British government. The growing Indian empire was becoming a state within a state. At the same time, it appeared that those responsible for India underwent a moral transformation, abandoning British habits of mind and codes of public behaviour and embracing those of the subcontinent.

Clive had recognised the temptations, to which he had earlier succumbed, when he returned to Bengal as governor-general in 1765 with a mandate to establish honest and fair government. 'In a country where money is plenty, where fear is the principle of government, and when your arms are ever victorious,' he observed, 'I say it is no wonder that corruption should find its way to a spot so well prepared to receive it.' For the next two years he did what he could to stamp out the worst abuses and the task was taken up by two of his successors, Warren Hastings (1772–85) and Lord Cornwallis (1785–92); but in a country where highly-paid posts proliferated, and the opportunities for graft were still plentiful, old attitudes died hard. In 1791, when a storming party at the siege of Cuddadur had been halted by fears of a mine, an officer rallied them with the cry, 'If there is a mine, it is a mine of gold!'[19]

Efforts to cleanse an administration which, among other things, tolerated torture as a means of extracting taxes, were regarded sceptically by many in Britain who felt that there was something disturbingly un-English about the Indian empire. Hitherto, imperial conquest and annexation had been confined to America and accompanied by emigration from Britain. Along with the emigrants had gone Christianity, British political values and systems of government which had been reproduced in the colonies. In India things had been different. In the space of sixty years the Company had acquired provinces that possessed their own machinery of government, which had evolved along autocratic lines and sophisticated, well-organised societies with their own deeply-rooted religions and customs.

There was no reason for the Company's officials to upset the established order in India, a course of action which they lacked the means to under-take and which would have caused untold havoc. Instead, the Company behaved as an inheritor, accepting what it found, and making changes only when practical necessity demanded. This pragmatism involved compromises; religious practices repugnant to Christians were tolerated, and wherever possible Hindu and Muslim legal traditions were accommodated. The prevalent attitude was summed up by an incident in 1814 at Jaganath, when the acting magistrate encountered a widow about to commit sati, that is the Hindu custom of throwing herself on the funeral pyre of her husband. He tried to dissuade her, but 'she said that she loved her husband, and was determined to burn with him', so the magistrate departed and the ceremony went ahead.[20] Elsewhere, officers of the Company's army would attend Hindu rituals with their men and allow Hindu priests to bless regimental colours.

There were limits to toleration which were invariably defined by the need to maintain public order. Small-scale campaigns were fought to suppress organised banditry, which was an integral part of the Indian social order, but which interfered with trade and represented a challenge to the Company's authority. Drastic measures such as executions without trial were commonly adopted by officers, who claimed that they were a medicine which both doctor and patient understood. Arthur Wellesley, who never had any qualms about hanging bandits whenever he found them, later commented that the 'liberal' ideals which held sway in Britain were utterly unsuited to a country whose people were conditioned to authoritarian government and expected their rulers to act with a firm hand.

The nature of Indian society and the conditions which Company administrators faced ruled out any importation into India of the freedoms and political rights taken for granted in Britain. And yet, as liberal thinkers in Britain argued, despotic forms of government were corrupting, and the Company was growing into an institution so powerful that it might subvert the British state. Edmund Burke, the most persistent and trenchant critic of the Company and its officials' behaviour, claimed in 1783 that 'a corrupt, private interest' had come into existence 'in direct opposition to the necessity of the state'. This was hyperbole, but it highlighted contemporary misgivings about an institution which seemed outside the control of parliament. Brakes, not always effective, were placed on the Company by the 1772 and 1784 India Acts which imposed parliamentary control over the board of directors, the latter setting up a board of control chaired by the Secretary of State for India, who was also a cabinet member. Gradually a private interest came under public control.

Of probably greater importance than the extension of parliamentary control over the Indian empire was a fundamental change in attitude of that generation of young Company servants who were taking up their posts at the turn of the century. They arrived having been exposed to evangelicalism, a creed which was making considerable headway among the British middle and upper classes during the 1780s and 1790s. Evangelicalism was a form of Protestantism which emphasised personal spiritual regeneration through the acceptance of Providence, and useful service to mankind, undertaken in accordance with Christian humanitarian principles. Cornwallis seems to have been one of the first to have been swayed by evangelical ideals for, on his appointment as governor-general, he listed his priorities as: 'Try to be of some use; serve your country and your friends [and] take the means which God is willing to place in your hands.'[21]

Personal moral uprightness was essential if the evangelical was to perform his duties to the rest of the world. John Malcolm, whose Indian career began in the early 1780s, believed that British power there rested on the gallantry of British troops and the high moral standards of its administrators, in particular their truthfulness and integrity. 'When they condescend to meet the smooth-tongued Mohammedan, or the crafty Hindoo, with the weapons of flattery, dissimulation, and cunning,' he remarked, 'they will to a certainty be vanquished.'[22] In other words, if the British continued to adopt what were taken to be the values of the people they governed, they would be undone. Arthur Wellesley concurred, telling Malcolm in 1804, 'I would rather sacrifice Gwalior or every frontier in India ten times over, in order to preserve our credit for scrupulous good faith.'[23]

Arthur Wellesley spoke with the voice of the British aristocracy, a class that considered the right to rule others as its birthright, and which enjoyed a monopoly of political power at home. The India Act extended this monopoly to India, where high offices were soon occupied by men such as Cornwallis, the Marquess Wellesley, and in the next century, Lord Hastings and the Earl of Minto. They applied, in varying degrees, the traditional principles of aristocratic government to the people of India, mingling firmness with benevolent paternalism, and endeavoured to keep a high standard of personal probity.

They and the home government accepted that Britain's Indian empire was a national asset although its acquisition had never followed any predetermined plan. By 1800, British domination of India was an accepted political fact of life despite parliamentary misgivings about the activities of grandee governor-generals who were just as pugnacious as their predecessors when it came to securing frontiers and enforcing Britain's will on recalcitrant native rulers.

The momentum to acquire more and more power could not be allowed to slacken. India had become a base from which Britain could dominate southern Asia and the Indian Ocean and promote its commercial interests which were beginning to reach out towards China. The Indian army gave Britain the power with which to protect these interests, and enforce its will throughout a region which extended from the Red Sea to the Malay Peninsula. The potential of the Indian army was first revealed during the wars against Revolutionary and Napoleonic France when a combination of Indian manpower and local naval supremacy enabled the British to wage war in Egypt and conquer Mauritius and Java. After 1807, when it was clear that the French were supreme in Europe, British strategists began to lay plans for the conquest of Spanish America which involved conveying Indian troops across the Pacific to Mexico and Chile.

These schemes were laid in the knowledge that British-trained Indian units were more than up to the task; during the siege of Cuddadur in 1783 Madras sepoys overcame French troops who had previously repelled a European assault party, and, at Bharatpur in 1805, Indians had advanced into action when the British 76th Regiment had flinched.[24] Nonetheless, those who ruled India had no illusions about the real source of their power, the legend of British invincibility. 'Every European soldier', wrote Cornwallis, 'should be carried in a *dooly* to the scene of action, when, like a panther or a blood hound, he might be let slip against the enemy.'[25] A wave of unrest among native troops during 1809 was an uncomfortable reminder that stability throughout the subcontinent ultimately rested on British troops alone.[26] This fact would never be forgotten, even by those who dreamed of bringing European enlightenment to the people of India.

7

The Desert of Waters: The Pacific and Australasia

The Pacific Ocean appeared as a huge void on eighteenth-century world maps. In the past two hundred years a handful of sailors had crossed its waters and returned with tantalising but fragmentary reports of islands and one, possibly two continents far to the south. Questions about the region had to remain unanswered. Sailing to and then traversing the Pacific was an extremely perilous enterprise; sailors cooped up for long periods and living on a stodgy diet contracted scurvy, and inexact methods of reckoning longitude sometimes forced captains to sail blindly. In 1741 Anson's officers miscalculated their fleet's position by 300 miles when rounding Cape Horn.

The technical impediments to Pacific reconnaissance were removed by 1765 with the publication of the *Nautical Almanac* and the almost simultaneous invention of an accurate maritime chronometer which together made it possible to measure longitude precisely. Regular rations of lime and lemon juice, laced with rum, reduced but did not eliminate scurvy epidemics. And yet, while these innovations made systematic exploration of the Pacific easier, the voyages undertaken by Captain James Cook and others from the late 1760s onwards remained tests of nervous stamina and physical endurance. Sailors jumped ship before each of Cook's three expeditions, and in 1790 a sixth of the crew of the *Discovery* deserted rather than face an 18,000-mile voyage to the north-west coast of America.[1] What lay ahead of them was described by Captain Sir Henry Byam Martin in a melancholy note added to his ship's log in July 1846. 'The Pacific is the desert of waters – we seem to have sailed out of the inhabited world, and the *Grampus* to have become the Frankenstein of the Ocean.'[2]

Isolation, the tensions generated by unchanging companions, the monotony of shipboard routine in an unfamiliar, sometimes frightening seascape were the common lot of the officers and men who first sailed the Pacific. What they experienced was shared with the public whose curiosity about an unknown ocean, its islands and their exotic inhabitants ensured that first-hand accounts of the early voyages became best-sellers. One avid reader of this travel literature, Coleridge, considered writing a poem on the 1787–88 cruise of the *Bounty* which had ended in the famous mutiny and the remarkable trans-Pacific voyage of its commander, William Bligh, and the loyal crewmen. What particularly fascinated Coleridge and many others was contemplation of how those who undertook these epic voyages, and encountered new and completely different societies, might be inwardly transformed by their experiences. The poem was never composed, but Coleridge later drew upon Cook's vivid descriptions of the Antarctic seas for his 'Rime of the Ancient Mariner'.

The intelligence brought back from the Pacific generated enormous public excitement and assured the early navigator-explorers popular heroic status. Cook towered over all. When he set sail for his first voyage in 1768, he was probably the most skilled navigator of his age. He was a patient, highly professional technician who had risen in the Royal Navy through the sheer force of his talent, since he was the son of a Whitby labourer and largely self-educated. Within ten years he had achieved, through his discoveries, international respect. When, in 1778, France declared war on Britain, French naval commanders were ordered not to interfere with his ships for to do so would hinder the advance of human knowledge. After his death in 1779, Cook entered the pantheon of British imperial heroes. His elevation was advertised in the frontispiece to Thomas Banke's *New System of Geography* published in 1787. Cook stands in the centre of the engraving, presented by Neptune to Clio, who is about to record his deeds, while above hover a cherub bearing a laurel crown and an angel blowing a trumpet. Below, as a reminder that Cook's exploits had benefited British trade, Britannia receives the tribute of four kneeling figures who symbolise the four continents. In the distance Cook's ships, *Resolution* and *Adventure*, head out to sea and new discoveries.

Cook had no need of a muse to exalt his deeds; he had published his own journals which entranced armchair travellers anxious to know every detail of a world completely different from their own. By his fireside in rural north Buckinghamshire, Cowper was able to travel in his mind to the South Seas and see them through Cook's eyes. His debt to the explorer was acknowledged in 'The Task':

> *[Man] travels and expatiates, as the bee*
> *From flower to flower, so he from land to land;*
> *The manners, customs, policy of all*
> *Pay contribution to the store he gleans;*
> *He sucks intelligence in every clime,*
> *And spreads the honey of his deep research*
> *At his return, a rich repast for me.*
> *He travels, and I too.*

Cook's three voyages between 1768 and 1779 were undertaken, as Cowper suggests, to add to universal (i.e. European) enlightenment by the accumulation of geographical, scientific and anthropological observations of a hitherto secret world. But the acquisition of knowledge for its own sake had not been Cook's principle objective. While the eighteenth-century mind prized abstract knowledge, it placed a higher value on that kind which could be used to accelerate human progress. Properly interpreted, the data and specimens which Cook's ships carried back to Britain could be employed to his nation's advantage. He fully understood this, once admitting that he was no more than 'a plain man exerting himself in the service of his country'. There was a purely utilitarian purpose to exploration, chart-making, the measurement of winds and currents and the collection and cataloguing of rocks, fish, birds, animals and plants.

Over two hundred years of overseas expansion had taught Europeans that new worlds contained products desired by the old. Some, like potatoes, tomatoes and spinach, were found to flourish in Europe while others, such as cotton and tobacco, had to be cultivated in the tropics. With Cook sailed teams of experts who, as they discovered and recorded new species of plants, were encouraged to find out whether they might be the cash crops of the future. Since Cook's expeditions served as models for future reconnaissances, subsequent investigations of natural phenomena were always undertaken with an eye to possible profit. In 1790 Captain George Vancouver, bound for Hawaii and the Pacific coast of America, was ordered by the Admiralty to look for evidence of minerals and coal; to record 'what sort of Beasts, Birds, and Fishes' he found; and investigate whether they might 'prove useful, either for food or commerce'. He was also to look out for seals and whales and undertake industrial espionage by probing the secrets of how the natives dyed cloth.[3]

Details about the breadfruit plants of Tahiti, collected during Cook's visits there, provided the impetus for Bligh's voyage to the island in 1787. These edible plants had been identified as potential money-spinners by Sir Joseph Banks, Cook's companion, who saw his own speciality, botany, as the handmaiden of British trade. It was Banks who urged the government to secure breadfruit plants which could solve the current economic problems of the West Indian planters who, deprived of American food imports, were looking for a cheap staple with which to feed their slaves. Bligh was ordered to take his breadfruit plants to the botanic gardens at St Vincent, where they were to be replanted and used as a breeding stock. During his outward passage, Bligh was also asked to make a botanic raid on the eastern coast of the Dutch island of Java and carry off cuttings from trees and plants, including rice, which might flourish in the soil of a British tropical colony.[4]

Cook was a pathfinder for British commerce. He was also the representative of British seapower. It was essential if Britain was to remain paramount on *all* the world's oceans that the Admiralty possessed accurate maps of the Pacific, its islands and their anchorages. Furthermore, the appearance in the area of the French navigator, Louis-Anthoine de Bougainville, in 1766 made it an urgent matter that the British flag was seen there and that the Pacific islanders were apprised of the existence and power of Britain. It was also vital, as international interest in the ocean increased, for Britain to find out more about the mysterious southern continents and possibly lay claim to them.

When Cook left England in 1768 he was seeking to do more than satisfy his own natural inquisitiveness and push back the frontiers of knowledge. He was an instrument of national commercial and strategic ambitions, and his most distinguished passenger, the gentleman naturalist and botanic pirate Banks, viewed their destination as a secret garden whose fruits might be harvested to Britain's advantage. During the next three years their ship, the *Endeavour*, visited Tahiti and then turned southwards to New Zealand and the eastern seaboard of Australia, which Cook named New South Wales. He then proceeded northwards, steering along the Great Barrier Reef and through the Torres Strait to prove that Australia was an island.

Cook carried with him a mandate to declare British sovereignty over any territory which he found to be unpopulated or whose inhabitants were manifestly making no use of their land. His right to do so had the backing of the law, at least as it was interpreted by Chief Justice Blackstone, for whom anyone who owned but did not exploit land forfeited his claim to it. So, with a clear conscience, Cook declared Australia *terra nullus* (land of no one) and annexed it. What Banks saw of George III's latest dominion convinced him that its climate and soil made it suitable for future colonisation. Its natives, the aborigines, could be discounted. They were nomads who did not till the ground and lacked any discernible form of social organisation or religion. Cook characterised them as 'the most wretched people' in the world, although well contented in their condition.

His second expedition to the Pacific (1772–5) was dominated by the search for the second southern continent. He skirted the edge of the Antartic ice pack, got as far as latitude 71° 10', exclaimed 'Ne Plus Ultra', and steered towards New Zealand and Australia. His final voyage, begun in 1776, was intended as a reconnaissance of the coastline of north-west America and Alaska, where, it was hoped, he might discover the outlet of the North-West Passage. Ever since the late sixteenth century navigators had pursued this geographic will-o'-the-wisp, a channel around the edge of northern Canada which linked the Atlantic and Pacific oceans. Like his predecessors Cook was unsuccessful, although, while charting Nootka Sound, his sailors accidentally came across large numbers of sea otters, whose pelts fetched a high price in China.

This was Cook's last discovery; he was killed in a brawl with Hawaiian natives in February 1779 while his ships were wintering by the island. His greatest achievements were the breaking of psychological barriers that had hitherto prevented Pacific exploration and filling in large areas of the map of the ocean. The commercial results of his discoveries were disappointing, but British entrepreneurs were grateful for any new markets, however small. Within a few years the East India Company was developing the sea otter fur trade with China and, sixty years after Cook's death, Hawaii was importing British manufactured goods worth between £30,000 and £50,000 a year.

It was the people of the Pacific rather than prospects for trade there which captivated the imagination of Cook's contemporaries. Revelation of their existence and way of life coincided with a period of intellectual ferment in which questions were being asked about the basic assumptions of the European moral and social order. Since the late seventeenth century thinkers had contemplated a semi-abstract creature called the 'noble savage'. He existed in a state of nature beyond the boundaries of Europe, where he lived without its elaborate social codes and, most importantly of all, that system of rewards and punishments laid down by the Christian religion. In this condition he was imagined a happier man than his European counterpart.

The account of Tahiti by de Bougainville and his surgeon, Philibert Commerson, which appeared in 1772, presented Europe with the living version of the noble savage. Tahiti, the Frenchmen insisted, was an Edenic world in which men and women thrived and found unparalleled happiness by living according to their own reason and consciences rather than following the injunctions of revealed religion. Nature, in the form of abundant fruits and wild creatures, provided for their needs and so the greater part of their time was spent in pleasure, mostly uninhibited sex. The existence of this Utopia (the word was used by de Bougainville) appeared to challenge the entire social-religious order of Europe.

The level-headed Cook was sceptical of de Bougainville's claims, which bordered on fantasy. The Tahitians were not without vices, and during Cook's visit were actually in the middle of a long-drawn-out civil war. As for the free and open sexuality of their women, of which the rakish Banks took advantage, Cook drily observed that the Tahitian beauties who tempted his men were not so different from their equivalents who enticed sailors on the quaysides of Chatham or Plymouth, save that the former took payment in iron nails rather than cash. Cook was, however, dismayed that the Tahitians called venereal disease 'Apa no Britannia' or, an unfortunate pun, 'Brit-tanne' (British disease) and, as a point of national honour, he insisted that it had been introduced to the islands by French sailors.[5]

While Cook noticed that the peoples he encountered appeared happy, he never subscribed to the notion of the noble savage. Nonetheless, what he and others had reported provided ammunition for the increasingly powerful humanitarian and evangelical lobby which demanded the abolition of slavery throughout the British empire. Those evangelicals opposed to slavery took on board the evidence of the existence of noble savages to strengthen their case that the negro was not a morally inferior man. There was also some concern for the protection of vulnerable societies from outside oppression and abuse, but this weighed less with the evangelicals than the fear that their Christian countrymen might become contaminated by alien vices. Cook and Bligh were accused of having compromised themselves by the 'complacency with which they assisted at idolatrous ceremonies' on Tahiti.[6] Their corruption had parallels with that of slavers, slave-owners and venal and despotic officials in India.

Virginian Gold: a Dutchman enjoys a pipeful of tobacco, a commodity which would soon enrich the new colony of Virginia and Britain, 1623. *Mary Evans Picture Library*

West Indian wealth creation: a plantation owner discusses productivity with an overseer while his slaves harvest sugar cane, 1830s. *Mary Evans Picture Library*

A toehold in America: the fort at
Charleston, South Carolina keeps
Indians at bay while merchant ships
are loaded with cargoes of local
cotton. *Mary Evans Picture Library*

'Benbow was his name': Queen
Anne's fighting admiral prepares to
face the French again as a figurehead
for a man-o'-war. *Peter Newark's
Historical Pictures*

An empire lost: General Burgoyne surrenders his army and Britain's chances of crushing the American colonists, Saratoga, 1777. *Hulton Deutsch*

An empire won: Robert Clive accepts the submission of Mir Jaffir after the battle of Plassey, Bengal, 1757. *Topham Picture Source*

Pathfinder of empire: James Cook. *Hulton Deutsch*

Into the pirates' lair: R.N. paddle steamers and landing parties attack a pirates' village, North Borneo, 1845. *Author's own collection*

Emigrant life: a would-be gold digger and his family prepare to find a new life and possibly a fortune, the Melbourne gold fields, 1853. *Author's own collection*

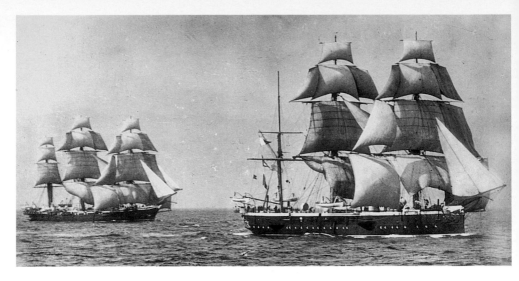

COMMAND THE FAR SEAS!

H.M.S *Calypso* and another cruiser unfurl their sails, c.1880: Ironclads relying on steam and sail, scattered across the world watching over Britain's interests, were visible evidence that Britannia ruled the waves. *Imperial War Museum*

H.M.S *Camperdown*, c.1900: a preponderance of such powerful, armoured battleships upheld Britain's pretensions as a world power, but building enough to keep ahead of rivals was becoming a burden. *Imperial War Museum*

HEROES OF EMPIRE

Charles Gordon, the warrior martyr of Khartoum, in the uniform of an Egyptian general. *Hulton Deutsch*

The survivors of Rorke's Drift stand down after their epic battle against the Zulus, 1879. *Foreign and Commonwealth Office*

Images of Conquest: the reverse of the 1879 Afghan War medal shows a cannon carried by elephants and guarded by turbaned lancers. That of the 1899 Boer War Medal shows Britannia handing the laurels of victory to the empire's fighting men. *Author's own collection*

The Spirit of Empire: a whisky distiller cashes in on the recent victory at Omdurman, 1898. *Author's own collection*

Christian consciences were appalled by reports of what one missionary apologist called the 'lasciviousness which degrades the Tahitians even below brute beasts'.[7] The evangelical imperative demanded the moral reformation of the South Sea islands and their conversion. The first missionary came ashore in Tahiti early in 1797, bringing with him the Mosaic and Pauline 'thou-shall-nots' and a determination to enforce the Protestant work ethic. Within the next ten years others fanned out among the Polynesian islands and were soon sending back reports of tribal wars, torture and cannibalism, which gave the lie to the concept of the noble savage, and appeals for additional missions. Reassuringly, the inhabitants of Tongatabu were found to have a patriarchy, no priests and a legal code which treated adultery as a crime, all factors which made conversion easy.

Missionary activity in the Pacific, well underway by 1815, was an extension of colonisation. By exposure to Western Christianity, the Pacific islanders were made aware of their own apparent deficiencies and the superior culture of their instructors. The process was outlined in a review of an account of New South Wales published in 1803. 'The savage no sooner becomes ashamed of his nakedness, than the loom is ready to clothe him; the forge prepares for him more perfect tools' and so on until he is dependent on the artefacts and techniques of Europe.[8] Cook had been disheartened when Omai, a Tahitian whom he had taken to Britain, returned to the island without any wish to apply what he had seen and learned to his homeland. The missionaries changed this for ever; through their efforts the Pacific islanders were integrated into the British commercial system. They supplied coconut oil, arrowroot and fresh pork and in return received guns, metalwares and cloth. It is one of the ironies of history that Cook's Hawaiian assailants may have been armed with blades manufactured in Matthew Boulton's Birmingham steelworks, which had been given them as examples of the products of Britain's new industrial technology.

Cook had not been given a warrant to annex those islands whose natives cultivated their land, but, as trade with them developed, Britain's naval presence in the Pacific increased. From 1790 onwards warships regularly cruised among the islands and their captains assured chiefs of George III's goodwill, gave some medals showing his features (a thousand were specially minted for Vancouver's 1790 voyage), and warned them not to harm European sailors and missionaries. This naval activity provoked the Spanish government to claim prior rights to the Pacific under the terms of the 1494 Treaty of Tordesillas, a scrap of paper which meant nothing to

Britain. A Spanish threat to enforce sovereignty over Nootka Sound in 1787 was answered by a partial mobilisation of the fleet which was enough to bring about a sullen but prudent climb-down. It was an admission of weakness by a fading imperial power all too aware of Britain's proven ability to hurt her trade and colonies.

By 1800 the Pacific had become a British lake. French interest in the region dwindled after 1789 and American interest had yet to be awakened. The outbreak of the Anglo-American War of 1812 led to a foray into the ocean by the commerce raider, USS *Essex*, but, outgunned, it was forced to surrender after an encounter with a small British squadron.

It is possible that if the *Essex* had not been intercepted it would have headed for Britain's new colony of New South Wales. Banks had spotted New South Wales's economic potential in 1769, and ten years later urged the government to use one of its harbours, Botany Bay, as a penal settlement. His suggestion was well-timed: the American War had halted the flow of convicts to the tobacco colonies and the early 1780s witnessed a crime wave which swamped the inadequate and often privately-owned prisons. Official thinking favoured transportation as the only way out of the problem, but there was no agreement as to where best to ship the felons. Gambia was the first alternative, but its climate and indigenous diseases meant that sending criminals there would be the equivalent of a delayed death sentence. The healthier alternative was a port on the deserted shores of south-west Africa, but this too was dismissed. Finally, in August 1786, the cabinet plumped for New South Wales.

The choice had been dictated by Banks's description of local conditions; the need to have even a small settlement in Australia as a token of British ownership; and the possible strategic value of a base which might serve as a launching pad for a seaborne invasion of the undefended western coast of Spanish America. This was not as far-fetched as it seemed. At the time, conflicting Anglo-Spanish claims in the Pacific were unresolved, and there was a chance that the two powers might fight a naval war in the region. The scheme was revived in 1806–7, when an influential circle of strategists and businessmen laid plans for a naval descent on Mexico and Chile, Spain then being an ally of France. Among the suggestions was one which proposed shipping Indian troops to New South Wales on the first leg of their journey to Chile.

A further consideration was the convicts. They were to provide the sinews of a new colony that, in time, would profit Britain, which was preferable to having them idling in prison cells or the hulks (dismasted battleships anchored in the Thames) at considerable cost to the government. Transportation was a utilitarian and, according to its supporters, humane form of punishment which offered the criminal the chance of redemption and a return to society. Although today transportation may appear harsh, and conditions on board ship and in New South Wales were harsh, the men who ruled Britain in the late eighteenth century sincerely believed it was both an effective check on crime and a device by which criminals could be reformed. Everyone in society was expected to perform some useful function, which was beneficial to himself and contributed to the general good. The law-breaker sought to live by other means and had to be shown his error. This was the view of Governor Lachlan Macquarie who, in 1817, described New South Wales as a 'Penetentiary Asylum on a Grand Scale' in which the 'Children of Misfortune' learned through submission and hard work to become honest and industrious subjects of George III.

The first flotilla of ships with their cargoes of male and female convicts, soldiers, free settlers and officials sailed from England in May 1787 and cast anchor off Botany Bay in January 1788. Its commander and the first governor, Captain Arthur Phillip, found the harbour unsatisfactory and shifted his ships to a better one nearby, which was named Sydney in honour of the Colonial Secretary. Landfall appears to have been marked by a night-long bout of drinking and sexual excess by the convicts and those sent to guard them. Later, a clergymen regretted that the long ocean voyage encouraged torpor and a taste for wine and spirits which immigrants found hard to lose once they were in Australia.[9]

The making of early Australia was an extremely complex process. It had been officially assumed that convict muscle would carve out an agrarian colony which would be self-supporting and possibly profitable. Australian society would be pyramidal and paternalist. Executive and judicial power would be in the hands of former officers, whose service experience had presumably prepared them for exercising authority over men from the lower classes who were easily led astray. From the beginning there were three kinds of Australians: officials and guards, free settlers and convicts. The last made up the bulk of the population and were there unwillingly. Analyses of the backgrounds of the criminals who found themselves in Australia after 1788 indicate that the typical convict was an urban recidivist, aged under twenty-five, who had existed on the margins of society, and lived by theft of one kind or another. In their new environment, such creatures had to sink or swim; or, as Phillip put it, 'Men able to support themselves, if able and industrious, I think cannot fail,' while those without the 'spur to industry' will starve.[10]

Phillip and his successors hoped that one spur to hard work might be the presence of female convicts. In 1794, the arrival of sixty women, all under forty, was welcomed by Lieutenant-Governor Francis Grose who told the Colonial Secretary that 'there can be no doubt, but that they will be the means by intermarriage of rendering the men more diligent *and* laborious.'[11] This may have been over-optimistic; one passenger on a convict ship was horrified by the 'shamefully indecent' behaviour and 'abundantly gross' language of the women convicts which drove the respectable to shun the decks whenever they took their daily exercise.[12]

After disembarkation, the convicts were allotted to various duties. The canny never revealed any particular skill when asked their trade, for this might mean detachment to onerous labour up-country.[13] For this reason, perhaps, rather than truthfulness, many gave their occupation as 'thief', which was rendered as 'labourer' in the official register. Labour, skilled or unskilled, was undertaken for the government or the handful of free settlers. Discipline was rigorously enforced; flogging was the common corrective for most offences, and on Norfolk Island in 1790 three runaways were warned that they would be shot as outlaws if they did not surrender.[14]

Escape was perilous and rarely attempted, although the geographically ignorant imagined that by plunging inland into the bush they would, eventually, reach China. In 1791, the government made it plain that every hurdle was to be placed in the way of those convicts who wished to return home after the end of their sentences. Instead, they were to be offered grants of land in the hope that they might become self-supporting farmers, and in 1794 men still serving their sentences were allowed to earn 10d (5p) an hour for work done in their spare time. On Norfolk Island, convicts and their marine guards were each given twenty-four acres and some pigs, with the intention that the settlement would become a self-supporting community.[15]

Among the Australian labour force were a small group of men who had been sentenced for subversion. Among the first of this category of political prisoners were the three so-called Scottish Martyrs who had been found guilty of disseminating French Revolutionary doctrines. The lieutenant-governor was ordered to keep a 'watchful eye over their conduct' in case they began to preach Jacobinism. One, Thomas Palmer, a Unitarian minister, had been allowed a servant during his passage out, who, once his master's sentence began, was given the privileges of a free settler.[16] The late 1790s and early 1800s saw an influx of a new type of political offender, Irish nationalists. They had been sentenced for joining underground societies, participating in the 1798 rebellion or mutiny and were considered extremely dangerous by the New South Wales authorities. Crossing the seas did not purge the Irish of their rebelliousness; in 1804 some planned an insurrection which was swiftly crushed.

In the same year, a book was published which reviewed the development of New South Wales. Its anonymous author listed many encouraging signs of future prosperity: the settlement's growth rate seemed to surpass that of the former American colonies and one recent innovation, a local newspaper (the *Sydney Gazette and New South Wales Advertiser*), was seen as a milestone on the road to maturity. The Australians, he noted approvingly, were trying to find a 'national character' though nothing was said about its ingredients.[17] This silence is understandable, for there appeared to be little cohesion among the 8,000 or so colonists, many, perhaps the majority of whom had no wish to be there. They represented what their descendants would call the 'us' who were watched over, controlled and judged by the 'them', that smaller body of administrators, soldiers and free landowners. Unlike America, where common bonds of religion or an urge for self-advancement had given a sense of purpose to the first colonists, early Australia was a divided society. In any case, it would have been hard for religion to have had much impact on men and women with a proven immunity to sermons. Moreover, the fact that during the early days colonial chaplains were Anglicans, who preached obedience to the secular authorities, which they often served as magistrates, made it well nigh impossible for them to have any moral influence over the convicts. There were, as elsewhere in the empire, public displays of loyalty to Britain, celebrated by the rituals of toasts to the king and balls on royal anniversaries. But this attachment to a country which oppressed their homeland and sent them into exile meant nothing to the growing body of Irish convicts, who would bequeath their ancestral grudges to their children and grandchildren.

The 'them' of early Australian society was an open élite into which former convicts who had taken advantage of land grants (there were forty-four in 1791) were allowed once they had made their fortunes. Its most powerful members, outside the senior government officials, were the officers of the New South Wales Corps, which had been formed in 1791 as part garrison and part police force. It was manned by rogues of various sorts, including deserters from the regular army under sentence of transportation, and was commanded by scoundrels.[18]

The Corps's officers were a flock of raptors who used their privileges to fill their pockets through the accumulation of land grants and liquor licences. Captain Bligh, who became governor in 1806, attempted to challenge the vested interests of the Corps and its greediest officer, John Macarthur, by authorising the distribution of government stores to poor settlers, many former convicts. 'Them were the days, sir, for the poor settler,' one, an ex-smuggler, recalled, 'he had only to go tell the Governor what he wanted, and he was sure to get from the stores.'[19] This enlightened system of state investment was overthrown by private enterprise when Macarthur, fearing the loss of profits, engineered a Corps mutiny against Bligh. Bligh, whose unhappy fate it was to have his authority affronted by malcontents (he had also been on the receiving end of the 1797 Nore Mutiny), was unseated by the plotters and recalled in 1810.

His successor, Macquarie, a strong-willed army officer, presided over the disbandment of the Corps and, up to a point, continued Bligh's policy of assistance to the small settlers. Free immigrants continued to be scarce and Macquarie realised that many of the yeoman farmers, whom he saw as the future backbone of Australia, would have to be ex-convicts. He left his office in 1821 by when it was clear that the colony was flourishing; its population had risen to 38,000 and its economy was sound. Burgeoning prosperity owed much to Macarthur's entrepreneurial shrewdness for he had been among the first to recognise that sheep would thrive in New South Wales. He also had a measure of good luck for, in 1807, when the first Australian wool was unloaded in Britain, the increasingly mechanised Yorkshire cloth industry had just been deprived of Saxon and Spanish imports. New South Wales merino was judged finer than its former rivals and the demand soared. By 1821 there were 290,000 sheep in Australia and within twenty years raw wool exports topped 10 million pounds annually. Sheep had been to the colony what tobacco had been to Virginia and sugar to the West Indies.

8

Wealth and Victory:
The Struggle against
France, 1793–1815

Until 1914 the war against Revolutionary and Napoleonic France was sometimes called the Great War. It began in February 1793 and lasted until June 1815 with a thirteen-month break, which was little more than an armed truce, between April 1802 and May 1803. Historically, this war appeared to be an extension of the Franco-British conflict which had started in 1689, but it was markedly different from its predecessors, not least in the scale of the fighting and the aims of the contestants.

First, it was seen by both antagonists as a struggle for survival, a Roman–Carthaginian duel that could only end with one side stripped of its overseas empire, commerce and independence. The French had learned from previous struggles that Britain's greatest strength was its system of government credit which rested on public confidence. This confidence could be eroded to the point of collapse if, as both Revolutionary governments and Napoleon believed, Britain lost her Continental trade, which was the chief source of her wealth. With nothing to sell, the 'nation of shopkeepers' would have no surplus money to advance their government.

From 1795 to 1805 Britain was threatened by invasion, and with it the prospect of occupation by a power bent on remodelling every nation it conquered according to Revolutionary principles. The monarchy would have been removed, the constitution dissolved, and a republic established. The pattern changed somewhat after 1803, when Napoleon crowned himself emperor. States under his control were transformed into military dictatorships governed by puppet princes, whose main task was to supply men and cash for the French war machine. Individual freedom would have vanished had Britain become a Napoleonic satrapy, a point based on the experience of other countries in Europe, and repeatedly made by government propagandists. One, the author of *The Dangers to the Country* (1807), warned the Englishman that he would have to endure the bullying of the 'ruffian familiars of the police' on the streets, and have his domestic peace disturbed by 'some insolent young officers, who have stepped in unasked to relieve their tedium while on guard, by the conversation of our wives and daughters.'

This, unlike previous Franco-British wars, was a contest of ideologies. The French, at least during the 1790s, were animated by an urge to emancipate the people of Europe, and share with them the blessings of the new Revolutionary order based on equal rights for all men and government by the general will. The ideals of the Revolution appealed to many in Britain, particularly those excluded from power, who saw them as the blueprint for a new political order in their own country. Jacobin theories of equality also won converts, but they and more moderate apostles of the Revolution were soon driven underground. In 1794–5, the government, desperate to secure national unity and fearing the existence of what later would be called a fifth column, began the legal persecution of anyone suspected of Revolutionary sympathies. Their numbers and powers of persuasion were exaggerated, but nevertheless they became, like their French counterparts, bogey men intoxicated by wild fancies:

> *I am a hearty Jacobin,*
> *Who owns no God, and dreads no Sin,*
> *Ready to dash through thick and thin for Freedom:*
>
> *Our boasted Laws I hate and curse,*
> *Bad from the first, by age grown worse,*
> *I pant and sigh for Universe-*
> *al Suffrage.*[1]

And yet, in the political climate of the late 1790s, such a figure had a potential for mischief-making. War-weariness, food and anti-militia riots, the naval mutinies of 1797 and their successors, and the 1798 insurrection in Ireland were reminders that, at times, British political unity was brittle.

Political propaganda which emphasised national solidarity was vital in what quickly became a total war in a modern sense. Sustained and effective resistance to France required the greatest ever mobilisation of Britain's manpower and financial resources. Just over a tenth of Britain's adult males were drafted into the armed services during the war, and even then there were continual complaints from commanders of shortages of men. By 1810 there were 145,000 sailors and 31,000 marines, 300,000 regular soldiers and militiamen and 189,000 volunteers, an early version of the Home Guard.

The total cost of the war was just over £1000 million of which £830 million was consumed by the army and navy. Part of this sum came from increased customs and excise duties, which was why it was so important to maintain the flow of British trade, and from new imposts, including income tax which was first introduced in 1798 and had yielded £142 million by the end of the war.[2] Government borrowing spiralled, and by 1815 the national debt stood at £834 million. It was not surprising that the rich were willing to invest so much of their money in government stock for it was, in a way, an insurance against imported, levelling Jacobinism.

Britain clearly possessed the capacity to wage total war and at every stage outmatched her antagonist when it came to raising cash. This meant that when the going got bad, as it did in 1797 and again after 1806, Britain could continue fighting, even without allies. This ability to hang on counted for a lot, since the Franco–British conflict was essentially a war of attrition. Wearing down France, through weakening its economy, had been central to British strategy since the outbreak of the war. Remembering the triumphs of 1759–63, the government in 1793 looked to the sea as the means of bringing about the breakdown of France and, incidentally, the strengthening of Britain. The process was explained to the Commons in March 1801 by Henry Dundas, the Secretary of State for War, who had been one of its stoutest advocates:

> . . . the primary object of our attention ought to be, by what means we can most effectively increase those resources upon which depend our naval superiority, and at the same time diminish or appropriate to ourselves those which might otherwise enable the enemy to contend with us in this respect.

It was, he continued, therefore imperative to 'cut off the commercial resources of our enemy, as by doing so we infallibly weaken and destroy their naval resources.'[3]

Dundas's war was an imperial contest, waged in the manner of the elder Pitt, in which Britain picked off her opponent's colonies and swept her merchantmen from the seas at the same time as preserving, even enlarging, her own commerce. Some of the loot would be kept and the rest bartered for a European settlement designed to restrain France. As in 1763, Britain would emerge richer and stronger than ever, or, in the words of a pro-government versifier of 1798:

> *Matchless Heroes still we own;*
> *Crown'd with honourable spoils*
> *From the leagued Nations won*
> *On their high prows they proudly stand*
> *The God-like Guardians of their native Land*
> *Lords of the mighty Deep triumphant ride,*
> *Wealth and Victory at their side.*[4]

The results of the naval war were up to expectations. In 1793 the French fleet was bottled up in its harbours, and a blockade imposed on its Atlantic and Mediterranean seaboards. There followed a series of seaborne offensives against the French West Indian colonies and, after 1795, when Holland surrendered, the Dutch. As supporters of these operations predicted, they were highly profitable; the prize money from Demerara and Essequibo (now part of Guyana) was £200,000 and the invasion forces were followed by British planters keen to buy up sugar estates at knock-down prices.[5] The cost in lives was enormous with a death rate of 70 per cent among sailors and soldiers, nearly all of them victims of malaria and yellow fever exacerbated by alcoholism.[6] As the wastage rate among fighting men rose, local commanders decided to recruit free negroes, despite the protests of planters horrified by the idea of any black men trained in arms. In 1798 a new expedient was tried to increase the numbers of the West India Regiment and the army began buying slaves to fill its ranks; within nine years just over 6,800 had been purchased at a cost to the Treasury of £484,000.[7]

The fruits of this campaign fought by slave-soldiers and fever-ridden redcoats were listed by Dundas in 1801. In eight years, Britain had acquired Tobago, Martinique, Guadeloupe, St Lucia and the Saintes from the French, Curaçao, Demerara and Essequibo from Holland, and Trinidad from Spain, which had entered into an alliance with France in 1795. Further overseas gains were Malta, Minorca, and the Dutch colonies in the East Indies,

Trincomalee on the coast of Ceylon (Sri-Lanka) and Cape Town. It was, by the standards of any previous war, an impressive haul and deeply satisfying to the commercial community who welcomed new markets.

These were desperately needed in 1801. On the Continent the war had gone the French way, despite early prophecies that the makeshift Revolutionary armies would quickly fall apart when they encountered regular troops. The reverse had happened, with Austrian, Prussian and Russian armies coming off worse in nearly every engagement. What was more, the French had discovered how to compensate for their financial weakness by making war pay for itself; as they fanned out into the Low Countries, the Rhineland, Switzerland and northern Italy, French armies lived off the land, and topped up their war-chests with forced contributions from the people they had liberated. At the same time French soldiers, learning as they fought, developed a tough professionalism and the Revolutionary principle of making talent the sole criterion for promotion encouraged the emergence of a cadre of highly able and intelligent commanders.

Britain's contribution to the land war in Europe had been negligible. Following earlier precedents, the younger Pitt had despatched expeditionary forces to the Low Countries but, undermanned and mismanaged, they were quickly sent packing. Another old expedient had to be reluctantly revived in 1794–5, when Pitt was forced to offer subsidies and loans to Austria and Prussia for whom the financial strain of the war had been too great. British credit kept Austrian, Prussian and, in 1799, Russian armies in the fight, but it did not improve their performance on the battlefield. France's armies remained unbeatable, and by 1801 it had absorbed the Austrian Netherlands (Belgium) and the Rhineland and established satellite republics in Holland, Switzerland and northern Italy.

The fortunes of the land war in western Europe affected the naval balance of power in the Atlantic and Mediterranean. In 1793 this had strongly favoured the Royal Navy, which mustered 115 line-of-battle ships against France's 76. The conquest of the Netherlands in 1795 added 59 battleships to the French total, and the Spanish alliance a further 76. The risk of an overwhelming Franco-Dutch-Spanish concentration in home waters was so great that, early in 1797, the Mediterranean fleet withdrew to deploy off Spain's Atlantic coastline. The alarm proved premature; in February 1797 Admiral Sir John Jervis led his heavily outnumbered fleet in an attack on the Spanish off Cape St Vincent and took four battleships, and in October, Admiral Lord Duncan severely mauled the Dutch at Camperdown.

The pressure was off for the time being, although the nerves of the Admiralty and fleet commanders had been severely jolted by the waves of disaffection that had run through the Channel and Mediterranean fleets during the early summer. There were further mutinies, mostly by pressed Irish sailors infected with the nationalist virus, and a spate of unrest on foreign stations which lasted well into 1798. The hidden hand of Jacobin agitators was feared and some were uncovered, but for the greater part the sailors' grievances were limited to their working conditions, wages and treatment, matters on which the government was willing to offer concessions.

The victories of 1797 confirmed British paramountcy in the Channel and Atlantic, but the French held the initiative in the Mediterranean. By the beginning of 1798, the Toulon fleet had been refurbished and transports were assembling in the harbour to take on board a 17,000-strong army, commanded by Napoleon. Its purpose was to strike a knock-out blow against Britain, but a question mark hung over its destination. There were two alternatives; an invasion of Ireland, where the French landfall would be a signal for a mass uprising by the Gaelic, Catholic Irish, or Egypt. Egypt was chosen on strategic grounds since its occupation would jeopardise Britain's considerable commercial interests in the Middle East, and place a French army within striking distance of India.

The sheer boldness of Napoleon's plan still astonishes. Yet it was taken seriously by Dundas, whose specialist advisers agreed that an attack on India, either overland across Syria and Iraq or through the Red Sea, was perfectly feasible, and that Napoleon might expect assistance from the Shah of Persia (Iran) and the Amir of Afghanistan. Moreover, it was imagined that even a small force of European troops could easily tilt the Indian balance of power against Britain. All this was a nasty shock for the cabinet, and Dundas, who was certain that the loss of India would prove 'fatal' to Britain, ordered reinforcements to be rushed there.

They were not needed. Napoleon's master-stroke was frustrated when his fleet and transports were destroyed by Admiral Sir Horatio, later Lord, Nelson at Abukir Bay in August. The French army, abandoned by its General who hurried back to Paris to further his political career, was left isolated in Egypt. It was finally evicted by a British expeditionary force sent for the purpose in 1801. In India the Marquess Wellesley moved quickly to eliminate France's potential ally, Tipu Sultan, and prepared to do like-wise to the Mahrathas who employed French mercenaries.

The episode had been nerve-wracking for British ministers, who had

been given an object lesson in the vulnerability of India and its communications. Even if Napoleon had simply stayed put in Egypt, he would have
severed the so-called 'overland route' to India. This stretched from Port
Said across the Suez isthmus to Alexandria and provided the fastest means
of communication between Britain and India. It was clear from the events
of 1798 that the future security of India required British control of the
Mediterranean and political domination of the Ottoman empire, whose
territories now became a vast *glacis* defending India's western frontiers.
Furthermore, the possibility that the rulers of Persia and Afghanistan might
have connived with Napoleon made it imperative that both countries
were drawn into Britain's orbit. Napoleon's Egyptian adventure had laid
the foundations of British policy in the Mediterranean and Middle East for
the next hundred and fifty years. It had also opened up a new region for
Franco-British imperial rivalry which gathered pace after 1815.

For the moment, France's war aims were confined to Europe. Here there
had been a brief peace, signed at Amiens in the spring of 1802, which was
no more than a breathing space during which Britain and France bickered
and recovered their strength. When the war reopened just over a year later,
Napoleon set his mind on the conquest of Britain, which he recognised as
his most formidable and implacable enemy. His invasion plans demanded
mastery of the Channel by the Franco-Spanish fleet based at Toulon. This
broke through the blockade in May 1805, made a feint towards the West
Indies, but was intercepted by Nelson off Cape Trafalgar in October and
destroyed. Eighteen battleships were taken or sunk and with them went all
hopes of France ever again challenging Britain at sea. Stringent measures
were taken to hinder the rebuilding of the French navy, including a pre-
emptive attack on Copenhagen and the seizure of the Danish fleet in
1807. Fears of an invasion receded, France's overseas trade was choked and
Britain was free to continue engorging itself on her enemies' colonies,
including some which had been returned at Amiens.

On land, Napoleon was triumphant. His Grande Armée, originally
earmarked for the invasion of Britain, turned against her allies, Austria,
Prussia and Russia. Between 1805 and 1807 he chalked up an amazing
sequence of victories: Ulm, Austerlitz, Jena-Auerstädt, Eylau and
Friedland. As a result, Austria, Prussia and Russia were impelled, literally
at gunpoint, to accept a new European order devised by Napoleon. The
Continent was now dominated by an enlarged France and its satellites, the

Kingdoms of Italy and Westphalia, the Confederation of the Rhine and the Grand Duchy of Warsaw. Whether or not directly under Napoleon's heel, all the states of Europe were forced to adopt his 1806 Berlin Decrees which forbade all commerce with Britain.

Britain answered with an embargo of its own, enforced by the Royal Navy, which brought Europe's overseas trade to a virtual standstill. Europeans were denied such products as tobacco and sugar, which had been re-exported by Britain, and British manufactured goods such as cotton. France could not make up the shortfall since her industry lacked the capacity to satisfy Europe's markets, and her import trade had been all but extinguished by the blockade. While Europe's trade stagnated, Britain's actually expanded as merchants penetrated new markets in the United States (until the war of 1812), Asia, the Middle East and, despite resistance, Spanish South America. Fresh outlets for British goods obviously offset the loss of older markets, but they did not entirely replace them. By the winter of 1811–12 a recession seemed likely as exports were in the doldrums and manufacturing output was falling.

The search for new commercial advantage was carried on with great vigour. After the reoccupation of Cape Town in 1806, the local commander, Admiral Sir Home Popham, off his own bat delivered a *coup de main* against Buenos Aires in May of that year. News of his exploit aroused enormous excitement in London, where senior army and naval officers combined with business interests to promote a profitable war of conquest against the whole of Spanish America. Dreams of a new American empire with vast markets proved illusory; nerveless command and mismanagement led to an ignominious evacuation of the River Plate by midsummer 1807.

By this time events in Europe were taking a new turn. Napoleon's attempts to browbeat Portugal and set his featherbrained brother, Joseph, on the throne of Spain dragged him into an unfamiliar type of war. The Spanish insurrection of May 1808 was a spontaneous, popular uprising, which took the French by surprise, and forced their generals to fight a guerrilla war in a countryside where food and fodder was scarce. The Portuguese and Spanish appealed to Britain, and the government immediately pledged cash, arms and an army. Pitt had been dead for two years, but his ideas still formed the framework of British policy, which was to offer unqualified help to anyone who promised to fight France.

The resulting Anglo-Spanish-Portuguese alliance was one of convenience rather than conviction. Portugal was transformed into a British dependency for the next six years, and the Spanish, suspecting that Britain coveted their American possessions and commerce, steadfastly resisted demands to open their markets to British merchants. Old hatreds died hard; in 1814 British merchants in Buenos Aires complained that local officials were 'arbitrary, insulting and vexatious', and that they suffered the 'bigotted Zeal and vindictive rage of the soldiery', and in the same year a British sloop was fired on by the guns of the fort at Cartagena.[8] Nevertheless the alliance held, thanks to the tact and firmness of the British commander-in-chief, Arthur Wellesley. He was a consummate strategist who saw from the first that he was about to conduct a war of attrition in which the winning army would be that which was well-fed and supplied. The navy escorted convoys of merchantmen to Lisbon, where cargoes of grain and fodder were unloaded for distribution up country. There were many nail-biting moments, but on the whole Wellesley's troops did not starve. The French, living off the land, did.

Moreover, Wellesley repeatedly beat French armies. His string of victories between 1808 and 1812 made the Iberian peninsula the graveyard of French marshals' reputations, and dispelled for ever the myth of French invincibility. Disengagement from an unwinnable war was unthinkable for Napoleon, since it would be a confession of weakness which was bound to encourage resistance elsewhere. He was politically bankrupt, with nothing to offer Europe but economic stagnation, heavy taxes and conscription, the last two necessary to preserve the war machine with which he menaced anyone who opposed his will. His confidence, one could almost say hubris, remained high, and at the beginning of 1812 he was preparing to solve his problems in the only way he knew how, by war. He intended to overawe Russia, which was showing disconcerting signs of independence, and then, in person, take charge of affairs in Spain.

The invasion of Russia, designed as an exercise in intimidation, went awry. French muddle, miscalculation and over-confidence combined with Russian doggedness to cause first the disintegration, and then the destruction of the Grande Armée during the autumn and winter of 1812–13. Prussia broke ranks and joined Russia, and so too did Austria after a little hesitation. Britain was swift to rebuild a new coalition delivering its members just over £26 million in subsidies and loan guarantees as well as cannon and muskets from her foundries and workshops.

Napoleon's European *imperium* fell apart quickly. Founded on victories, it could not survive the defeats inflicted on its master's armies in the autumn and winter of 1813–14. Joseph Bonaparte was finally turned out of Spain, and in January 1814 Wellesley, now Duke of Wellington, led an

Anglo-Portuguese army into southern France. Squeezed between Wellington and the Austrians, Prussians and Russians who were striking deep into eastern France, Napoleon abdicated in April. A year later he returned from Elba, convinced that he could again mesmerise his countrymen with fresh dreams of martial glory. The end came at Waterloo where he suffered a decisive defeat at the hands of Wellington and Blücher's Prussians. At the end of June, Napoleon surrendered to the British, and was sent in exile to their remotest colony, St Helena where, unchastened, he brooded on his mistakes.

Winning the war against France had been a Herculean effort. The conventional wisdom, then and later, attributed final victory to seapower because, above all, it ensured that Britain stayed in the ring. The ships of the Royal Navy had prevented invasion; they had confined French power to Europe and allowed Britain to occupy nearly all the overseas possessions of her adversaries; they had guarded the convoys which sustained Wellington's army in the peninsula; and they had guaranteed the survival of Britain's global commerce, which generated the wealth needed to pay for her war effort, and underwrite those of the three big European powers with armies large enough to engage Napoleon on equal terms.

There were many reasons for the navy's success. The determination, self- confidence and professionalism of its officers and crews owed much to traditions established in the previous hundred years. Nelson was outstanding as a leader and tactician, but Duncan, Jervis and Collingwood also deserve high praise. All understood their country's predicament and how much depended on them, which was why, whenever the chance came for battle, they grabbed at it, regardless of the odds. In the decisive battles of Cape St Vincent, Camperdown, Abukir Bay and Trafalgar the British fleets were outnumbered but, trusting to superior seamanship and gunnery, their admirals took the offensive. An aggressive, gambling spirit paid off. As Nelson famously observed, an officer who laid his ship alongside the enemy could never be in the wrong.

Much depended on the individual naval officer's instinctively correct response to an emergency, something which Nelson cultivated among his subordinates to the point where they knew without being told what he expected of them. This quality filtered downwards. During an engagement with the French frigate *Topaze* off Guadeloupe in January 1809, Captain William Maude of the *Jason* saw no need to inform the commander of his consort, the *Cleopatra*, of his intentions. 'I considered it unnecessary to make any signals to him, and he most fully anticipated my wishes by bringing his ship to anchor on the frigate's starboard bow and opening a heavy fire,' Maude wrote afterwards.[9] The action lasted forty minutes and was decided by superior broadsides aimed against the French ship's hull.

Adroitness and accuracy in manning of guns and agility in reefing or unfurling sails, so vital for quick manoeuvres, required careful and intense training of crews, nearly all of whom were pressed or conscripted lands-men. Many, perhaps the majority of officers ruled their ships as the squire did his village, with a strong but fatherly hand. This pattern of leadership, which reflected the values of the ruling class and the hierarchy of con-temporary civilian life, also extended to the army where it was encouraged by Wellington who insisted that a gentleman's sense of personal honour included an active concern for the welfare of those beneath him. In 1783, a naval officer reprimanded for spending money to provide treatment for his sick, responded with a classic statement of service paternalism:

> As a British officer I always consider myself accountable to my King and Country for the lives of the Seamen under my com-mand and more particularly in the present instance, as they are returning to their Native Country after having endured great hardships and fatigues in His Majesty's Service, and had so gal-lantly distinguished themselves in several actions in India.[10]

Not all officers shared such sentiments, especially during the Revolutionary and Napoleonic wars. The desperate need to transform civilians into skilled seamen as quickly as possible, and fears that some might be infected with Jacobin opinions, led many officers to rely on intimidation as the sole means of preserving discipline. According to the crew of HMS *Magnificent*, Lieutenant Marshall was one of this kind.

> His tyranny is not bearable, we are able and willing to loose the last drop of Blood in Defence of our Gracious King and coun-try, but to fight under him will hurt us very much, for the least fault he makes the Boatswain's mates thrash us most unmerci-ful . . . He threatens to make us all jump over board. Indeed part of his threats is already taking place as two unfortunate fel-lows in attempting to swim on shore is drowned.[11]

Abuse of this kind was made worse by the fact that ships remained at sea for longer periods than before. The hulls of copper-bottomed men-o'-war did not need regular scraping in dockyards, and the squadrons in distant waters were now provided with bases with repair facilities and stores. Wartime commitments had created additional naval establishments at Malta, Alexandria, Bermuda, Barbados, Martinique, Rio de Janeiro, Mauritius, Cape Town, Madras, Bombay and Penang. Intelligence services had also expanded with the enlistment in 1793 of the world-wide network of Lloyds shipping insurance agents. They provided much that was useful; in November 1813, Brown Lindsay, Lloyds's agents in Pernambuco, informed London of the movements of three American privateers which were preparing to intercept homebound East Indiamen off Brazil.[12]

The war which had enhanced the reputation of the navy also rescued that of the army which had been blemished by its performance in the American War, and the series of catastrophic forays into northern Europe between 1794 and 1809. Credit for the army's rehabilitation deservedly went to Wellington and those hand-picked senior officers who ran the peninsular campaigns. As he freely admitted, his achievements in Europe owed everything to lessons he had learned in India. He had shown that imperial soldiering, hitherto a despised and arcane branch of warfare, was an ideal apprenticeship for ambitious officers.

The deeds of soldiers and sailors were widely celebrated in Britain. Church bells were rung and services of thanksgiving held as news of a victory spread across the country, and the print shops were quickly filled with portraits of admirals and generals or representations of battles on land and sea. No previous war had excited such enormous public interest and generated so much patriotic enthusiasm, or, on occasions, anxiety. On hearing the news of Waterloo, the Countess of Jersey exclaimed, '*For glory* we had enough before, and this battle only confirms what one always felt – the English are the best soldiers in the world.'[13]

Self-assuredness of this kind had been commonplace throughout the eighteenth century, and had grown stronger after the victories of 1759–62. Britain 'is the best in the world' a Yorkshireman assured a French émigré in 1794. He and his fellow refugees had been greeted in London by shouts of 'God damn the French dogs' from some bargemen, who then showered them with lumps of charcoal. It was equally bad in Edinburgh, where the visitor was stared at by a girl, who then remarked, 'Mother, he is certainly not French for he is fat and not black.'[14] At the outbreak of war British arrogance and xenophobia were as strong as ever.

Hostility and contempt towards a traditional foe were not enough to bind the nation together in a long-drawn-out war against France. A more positive patriotism was needed by Pitt's government, fearful of the persuasiveness of Revolutionary political propaganda, which naturally concentrated on the inequalities in British society. Moreover, popular patriotism in the early 1790s laid great stress on individual freedom and the merits of the constitution so that reformers could and did claim to be true patriots. A subtle but important change was needed to the nature of British patriotism. National unity, prosperity, opportunities for self-advancement, social harmony and the charity shown by the rich to the poor were emphasised as vital sources of national pride. Most important of all was loyalty to the crown; George III was the keystone of the state and the guarantor of its tranquillity. France had killed its king and thereby had thrown itself into chaos.

This vision of British nationhood was universally promoted by the government, ministers of the Churches of England and Scotland, mainstream Methodists and private associations, of patriots.[15] Always the appeal was to bonds of allegiance and unity:

> *Thus Britons guard their ancient Fame,*
> *Assert their Empire o'er the sea,*
> *And to the envying world proclaim*
> *ONE NATION still is Brave and Free –*
>
> *Resolv'd to conquer or to die*
> *True to their King, their LAWS, their LIBERTY:*
> Un-ransom'd *ENGLAND spurns all Foreign Sway.*[16]

As for the French, they were depicted by cartoonists as brainsick, skeletal starvelings eating grass or frogs for want of anything else. After the advent of Bonaparte, they appeared posturing in comic-opera uniforms. Louis Simond, who toured Britain during 1814, found his countrymen everywhere portrayed as simian pygmies 'strutting about in huge hats' and brandishing sabres.[17] By now the image of England was John Bull, a rubicund, overweight farmer who carried a cudgel and had no time for anything foreign. This stereotype, complete with early nineteenth-century clothes, would endure for a further hundred and fifty years, reappearing in cartoons of the two twentieth-century world wars.

The French wars had reinvigorated British patriotism and laid the foundations of that assertive superiority which was manifest throughout the nineteenth century and beyond. The popular, belligerent, jingoist imperialism which emerged in the 1880s and 1890s had its roots in the nationalism of the Napoleonic era.

Inseparable from aggressive patriotism was a sense of moral rectitude. The war had been an ordeal which had tested the nation's inner strengths and from which it had emerged with its values vindicated and enhanced. An obituary of George III, who died in 1820, idealised him and the younger Pitt as national saviours at a time of extreme peril:

> Together they walked in noble sincerity and purpose, and heroic energy of resolution, throughout the darkest periods of our modern history – struggling to defend the ark of the British constitution, and the majesty of the British name, against the storms by which they were assailed – maintaining the native hue of courage and constancy amid the wreck of empire and desolation of the civilised world.[18]

There were other heroes. Nelson and Wellington were elevated as models of all that was outstanding in the British national character. Their quiet, manly courage, love of the country, selflessness and high sense of duty would be continually set before youth as examples worthy of imitation. The moral disciplines of the great were understood and adopted by many of those whom they led. A cavalry trooper who served under Wellington and then in India, summed up his memoir of twenty-six years' service with a statement of his private creed. 'I only did the duty of a soldier, the task that was put before me I managed with God's assistance to acquit myself with faults, blame or shame.'[19]

The war against France had been a testing ground for another virtue which was now thought to be peculiarly British; self-sacrifice in a just cause. 'England lamented but did not grudge the carnage of Waterloo,' wrote Lord Denman in an appeal for renewed efforts against the slave trade. 'Many a British mother bewailed a son fallen on that fatal field, but no British mother repented of the sacrifice. England felt, we all felt, that that field was worthy of the sacrifice.'[20] The debt was passed to future generations, and was acknowledged by Robert Browning in his 'Home Thoughts from the Sea' written in the heyday of mid-Victorian prosperity:

Nobly, nobly Cape Saint Vincent to the north-west died away;
Sunset ran, one glorious blood-red, reeking into Cadiz Bay;

Bluish mid the burning water, full in the face Trafalgar lay;
In the dimmest north-east distance, dawned Gibraltar grand and gray;
'Here and here did England help me: how can I help England?' – say,
Whoso turns as I, this evening, turn to God to praise and pray,
While Jove's planet rises yonder, silent over Africa.

After 1815 the British saw themselves, as they had always done, as a nation favoured by Providence, but now the fine metal of their special virtues had been assayed and found to be pure and infinitely superior to baser, foreign alloys. Victory bred arrogance and a feeling that Britain represented, in its system of government and the industry of its people, the highest state yet reached by civilisation.

The possession of overseas territories contributed little as yet to this national pride. The peace treaties of 1814–15 had added to British possessions with confirmation of ownership of Malta, the Ionian Islands, Trinidad, Tobago, St Lucia, what is now Guyana, Cape Colony and Mauritius. With the exception of the West Indian islands, the chief fruits of conquest were naval bases sited to secure future control over the Mediterranean and Indian Ocean. Significantly, Britain was prepared to hand back some of her spoils, all of commercial value. Guadeloupe and Réunion were returned to France, and Java and Surinam to the Netherlands, which helped bring about concessions on the Continent which favoured British interests.

The post-war bargaining over colonies is instructive. Britain was a maritime power which lived by international trade. Her by now rapidly expanding manufacturing industries and her older commerce in re-exported tropical commodities found their largest markets in Europe. European peace and stability were therefore essential for British commerce; as for the rest of the world, all that was required was a permanent naval presence which would safeguard the sea-lanes and, on occasions, assert the rights of British businessmen. In 1815 captive, colonial markets and sources of raw materials were a bonus to the country which dominated every area of world trade. The war had helped Britain achieve this ascendancy and it had fostered a belligerent, often self-righteous outlook which made it relatively easy for the British to exploit their advantages at the same time as representing themselves as mankind's benefactors.

PART THREE

WIDER STILL
AND WIDER
1815–1914

1

Power and Greatness:
Commerce, Seapower
and Strategy, 1815–70

For the first three-quarters of the nineteenth century Britain appeared as a colossus astride the world. Britain dominated every field of human activity and its people seemed to possess an almost demonic energy. On seeing the thriving port of Sydney in January 1836, Charles Darwin wrote, 'My first feeling was to congratulate myself that I was born an Englishman.'[1] The city's buildings and bustle were evidence of 'the power of the British nation' and a contrast to the lassitude of the Spanish and Portuguese, whose former colonies he had just visited and where, he concluded, little progress had been made over the past three hundred years. Likewise the missionary-explorer David Livingstone, on passing through the Portuguese colony of Angola in 1855, observed that 'had it been in the possession of England' it would have become a mass-producer of cotton and its interior been opened up by a railway.[2]

Men of Darwin's and Livingstone's generation recognised three sources of that peculiarly British power which was currently transforming the world. The first was the native inventiveness and application of its people which had been the moving force behind the second, the growth of Britain's manufacturing industry. Finally, there was naval supremacy, which made it possible for Britain to penetrate new markets and to count for something in the affairs of the world.

There was also, and this was continually announced from the pulpit and set down in tracts and editorials, that inner strength and purposefulness that individuals derived from a Christian faith which set a high store on personal integrity, hard work and a dedication to the general welfare of all mankind. Something of these qualities and their effect on the mind and conduct of a man active in the promotion of British interests abroad can be found in the musings of Edward Pine, a surgeon with the 58th Regiment. In 1842 he had served in the China War and two years later, having failed to find a practice in Britain, he was bound with his regiment for New South Wales. Crossing the Pacific and in melancholic mood, he analysed his faith, whose ingredients were:

> A piety which refers every event to the providence of God; every action to his will; a love which counts no service hard, and a penitence which esteems no judgement severe; a grati-tude which offers praise even in adversity; a holy trust unbroken by protracted suffering, and a hope triumphant over death.

Reassured by these thoughts, Pine later wrote, 'the greatest satisfaction results from the strict performance of one's duty – I pray God that my best efforts may be directed to that end.'[3] This and similar private creeds col-lectively strengthened what was to become a national conviction: Britain had been chosen by Providence as an instrument of universal progress.

Progress was inseparable from the Industrial Revolution. It had pro-ceeded slowly and unevenly from the middle of the eighteenth century and would be more or less complete by 1860. The growth of large-scale man-ufacturing industry had coincided with a population explosion: in 1801 there were roughly ten million people in Britain, a total which had risen to over twenty-two million by 1871 despite emigration and the Irish famine of 1845–7. Had Britain remained a largely agrarian country, the inevitable outcome of growth on this scale would have been famines of the kind seen today in parts of Africa. The Industrial Revolution proved Britain's salvation for it absorbed its surplus population.

This process solved one problem, but created others. In the thirty years after Waterloo the new workforce faced a precarious existence, since its only hope of survival lay in an ever-increasing market for manufactured goods. This could only be achieved as long as products remained cheap, and so wages were depressed. Here industrialists were assisted by the 1834 Poor Law, which was deliberately contrived to make conditions for the unemployed so unbearable that they were driven to seek work or emigrate. Sometimes there was no work available even for the willing. Recessions, which occurred regularly between 1815 and the mid-1840s, were accompanied by mass lay-offs, public disorders and outbursts of often violent political radicalism. Matters were made worse by the fact that by 1840 Britain could no longer produce enough food to sustain its population.

Free trade offered an escape from these difficulties. Its partisans argued that the abolition of all duties would lower the costs of imported raw materials and make exports more affordable, and therefore more competitive. At the same time, food prices would fall thanks to the opening of the British market to American and European grain. Steps towards free trade had been taken, tentatively, in the 1820s when the Tory government had removed the Navigation Acts and reduced tariffs. The slump of the early 1840s saw a revival of demands for free trade, largely from Northern and Midland industrialists who were keen to stimulate business and reduce unemployment through an export drive.[4] The Tory government of Sir Robert Peel responded encouragingly, but the stumbling block was the Corn Laws which protected home-grown grain against foreign competition. The hitherto dominant landed interest resisted what it saw as an erosion of its source of wealth, but its claims were ultimately overridden by the fact that domestic agriculture could no longer satisfy national demand. This failure was horrifyingly demonstrated by the Irish famine, and in 1846 the Corn Laws were jettisoned.

Britain's conversion to free trade in the 1840s coincided with a determined effort to open up new markets. The volume of Britain's overseas trade had expanded steadily since 1815. The largest outlets were Europe and the United States, which together accounted for two-thirds of the £50 million earned by exports in 1827. This pattern continued for the next forty years. In 1867, when Britain's exports totalled £181 million, goods sold in countries outside the empire accounted for £131 million. There had been expansion everywhere, most spectacularly in South America where, in 1867, Argentina, Brazil, Chile and Peru imported products worth just over £12 million.

For a time it had been imagined that free trade would irreparably damage those colonial economies which relied on preferential treatment for their raw materials. The West Indian sugar producers suffered worst. They were the victims of a breathtaking example of contemporary humbug, for they had been forced to emancipate their slaves in 1833 and then, by the 1846 Sugar Duties Act, had to compete in a free market with sugar imported from the slave-operated plantations of Cuba and Brazil. Not surprisingly, the economy of the British West Indies collapsed. An estate in

British Guiana, which had been purchased for £24,000 in 1840, was sold for £2,700 nine years later, and then parcelled into small-holdings for former slaves, who became subsistence farmers. The annual value of Britain's exports to her West Indian colonies plummeted from an average of £4 million in the 1820s to less than half that amount by the 1860s.

Other colonial economies survived the loss of their old commercial privileges, a phenomenon which puzzled some observers who believed them incapable of surviving in a free market. Indeed, during the 1850s and early 1860s there had been a lobby of free-traders who had called for the cutting of political links with the colonies, whose government and defence were an unwelcome charge on Britain's budget for which there was no obvious return. In fact the empire was a valuable outlet for British products. In 1867, India imported goods worth £21 million, which made it a market equal to Britain's largest foreign customer, the United States. The other totals were impressive; exports to Australia totalled £8 million, Canada £5.8 million, Hong Kong £2.5 million, Singapore £2 million, and New Zealand £1.6 million. Of course given that Britain possessed just under half the world's industrial capacity at the time, her colonies, like everyone else, had little choice but to import British manufactures.

The expression 'workshop of the world' is now a cliché, but it still best describes Britain's international trading position from 1815 to 1870. There were some free trade enthusiasts in the 1840s who looked forward to a time in the near future when all Britain's energies would be devoted to industry, whose workforce would live off cheap imported food from America and Europe. As in the seventeenth and eighteenth centuries, Britain's commercial success rested on the export of inexpensive staple goods. Machine-produced cotton dominated; during the 1830s cotton-ware from the Lancashire mills made up more than half of Britain's exports. In 1867 the value of all kinds of cotton, including yarn for weaving elsewhere, was £55.9 million. Next in importance came woollen cloth (£18 million), coal (£5.4 million), railway track (£4.8 million) and steam engines (£1.9 million). The last items indicate that by this time Britain was exporting her technology to other countries to assist their programmes of industrialisation.

Britain also exported capital. The accumulated private wealth of the country, drawn from both industrial and agricultural profits, was channelled into foreign and imperial investments. What turned out to be a massive diffusion of British capital was already well underway in the 1830s, when income from overseas dividends averaged about £5 million yearly.

This figure rose to £50 million by the 1870s, and continued to soar as more and more British capital flowed abroad. By and large, middle-class and aristocratic investors prudently chose to put their money in stocks which offered a fixed annual return, rather than speculative ventures. Raising capital for foreign governments and commercial enterprises, along with banking, marine insurance and stockbroking were the work of the City of London. These specialisms, experience and the sheer volume of money available in Britain for overseas investment assured London pre-eminence among the world's financial centres.

London lay at the hub of an unseen empire of money. The Industrial Revolution had made possible a financial revolution, well advanced by 1870, in which Britain became the world's major exporter of capital. Money-lending complemented manufacturing. By injecting large sums of money into undeveloped and developing economies, British investors were stimulating new demands. British-funded enterprises such as cattle ranches in Uruguay, railroads in America and Indian cotton plantations drew new countries into her global network of trade. At the same time, although this was not immediately apparent, British investment was also creating industries which would, in time, compete with her own.

The export of goods and money led to the creation of what had been called an 'unofficial' or 'informal' empire. In the scramble for new markets it was inevitable that British merchants faced local opposition or found themselves in countries where governments were either too feeble or lazy to take measures to protect them or their goods. This was the case in Buenos Aires in the spring of 1815, when the city was caught between the two sides in the Argentinian revolt against Spain. Fearing local anarchy once street-fighting began, British merchants appealed to the naval commander in Rio de Janeiro to safeguard them and their property. They reminded him that they were 'in pursuit of those objects of Mercantile Enterprise to which Great Britain owes so much of her power and Greatness'.[5]

Nineteenth-century consuls, admirals and foreign secretaries were naturally well aware of this, and of the prevalent feeling among those who created the nation's wealth that they were entitled to their government's support. The world was full of areas of chronic instability, like the River Plate republics, and countries where the authorities were hostile to British business, or whose officials were obstructive or corrupt. In such places, British lives and property were perpetually endangered unless there was the assurance of some kind of protection or, if the worst occurred, retribution.

Bond-holders expected their dividends and, if they were withheld for reasons which appeared frivolous or dishonest, they looked to the government for redress. Free trade required the uninterrupted passage of goods and services through nations and local legal systems that offered justice to the businessman who had suffered losses.

These conditions did not exist in the states on the shores of the Mediterranean, the Ottoman empire, the coastal states of Africa, the Latin American republics, and China. It was necessary for the British government to teach the rulers of such nations where their duty lay, and when they refused to heed the lesson, to make them see sense through the application of naval force. For instance, in 1821, during the war between Spain and its former colonies, Spanish privateers had seized a British merchantman, the *Lord Collingwood*, in the Caribbean. No compensation was offered by the government in Madrid so, in 1823, a squadron was ordered to Puerto Rico to confront the governor and recover the captured vessel. If he proved intractable, then men-o'-war flying the Spanish flag were to be attacked and Spanish ships arrested.[6]

As usual, forceful measures were a last resort. There were, successive British governments realised, recidivists who needed frequent chastisement, as the Foreign Secretary Lord Palmerston explained to the Commons in September 1850:

> These half-civilized Governments such as those of China, Portugal, Spanish America, all require a dressing down every eight or ten years to keep them in order. Their minds are too shallow to receive an impression that will last longer than some such period and warning is of little use. They care little for words and they must not only see the stick but actually feel it on their shoulders before they yield to that argument which brings conviction.[7]

This was a typically candid explanation of the principles of unofficial empire.

Palmerston was also speaking in defence of his decision to send seven battleships and five steamers to Salamis Bay in January after the Greek government had refused to consider compensation for losses suffered by various British subjects, including Don Pacifico, a Gibraltarian moneylender. Palmerston ordered the local admiral to take 'measures' designed to impress the Greek government with Britain's determination to have its

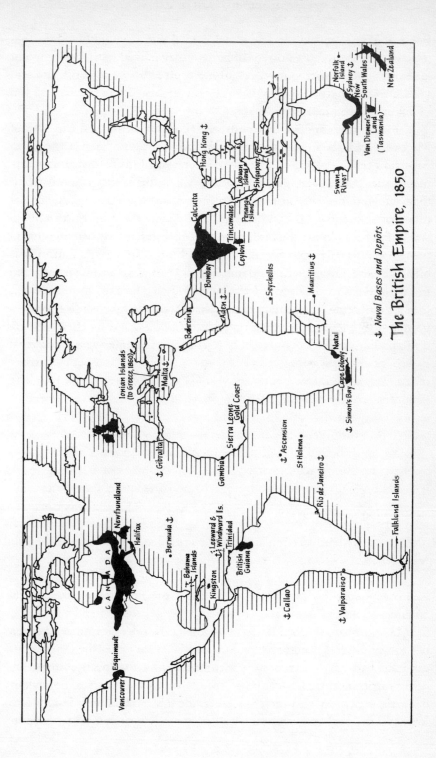

The British Empire, 1850

‡ Naval Bases and Depôts

Vancouver
Esquimault
C A N A D A
Newfoundland
Halifax
Bermuda ‡
Bahama Islands
Kingston
Leeward & Windward Is.
Trinidad
British Guiana
Callao ‡
Valparaiso ‡
Falkland Islands
Rio de Janeiro ‡
St Helena •
Ascension •
Gambia
Sierra Leone
Gold Coast
Gibraltar ‡
Ionian Islands (to Greece, 1860)
Malta ‡
Bahrein
Aden ‡
Bombay
Calcutta
Ceylon
Trincomalee
Penang Island
Labuan Island
Singapore
Hong Kong ‡
Seychelles
Mauritius ‡
Natal
Cape Colony
Simon's Bay ‡
Swan River
Van Diemen's Land (Tasmania)
New South Wales
Sydney ‡
Norfolk Island
New Zealand

subjects' claims honoured. The Greek navy was seized without a struggle; Greek merchantmen were arrested at the Piraeus, Spezia and Patras; and an embargo was imposed on Greek shipping.[8] This was what Palmerston meant by feeling the stick.

More commonly, persuasion backed by the threat of force worked. In a bizarre but revealing incident in 1845, the consul-general in Beirut, Colonel Hugh Rose, was able to secure the sacking of the Turkish governor, whom he described as an 'infamous man' and 'fountainhead of corruption'. It appears that three men had committed an outrage of 'a revolting and unnatural nature' at the consulate and Rose had demanded that one be punished by bastinado (flogging on the sole of the feet), to be carried out in front of the consulate, while the other two swept the street there. The homosexual governor connived at the trio's escape, and a furious Rose passed the case to the embassy in Constantinople. In the meantime HMS *Warspite* was summoned to Beirut as a token of how seriously the British government took what Rose thought was a calculated insult to its dignity.[9] It was not really needed, since by this time the Ottoman government desperately needed to accommodate Britain, its potential ally against Russia.

Another form of coercion was to remind local rulers that they would be held personally responsible for any harm that befell British subjects or crimes committed within their jurisdiction. When two dhows were taken by pirates in the Persian Gulf in 1855, a naval officer ordered the local sheik to find the culprits. If he failed, he would be made to pay blood money and compensation or face the bombardment of his village.[10] As Palmerston appreciated, pressure had to be constantly exerted. Noting a resurgence of piracy in the waters around Malaya in 1852, the commander of a man-o'-war regretted 'the inherent propensity a Malay has to return to his lawless traffic when unrestrained by personal fear of immediate punishment.[11]

The campaigns against piracy in Far Eastern waters and against slavers in the Atlantic and Indian oceans were uphill struggles, undertaken in the complementary causes of the advancement of civilisation and the protection of commerce. Once slaving and piracy had been eliminated, those who had profited from them would turn to what was called 'legitimate' trade. Even so, there were some parliamentary protests against what seemed brutal methods. In 1849 Richard Cobden, a free-trade radical and manufacturer, expressed disgust at the awarding sailors 'head money' of £20 each for dead or captured pirates. He was rebuked by a Tory, Colonel

Charles Sibthorp, who asked whether his humanitarian concern for Borneo pirates extended to his own factory workers.[12]

Anti-piracy operations were part of a wider effort to break into Far Eastern markets during the 1840s and 1850s. Siam (Thailand) and Japan signed favourable commercial treaties and informal control was tightened over Malaya, Borneo and Sarawak, but China remained adamant in her refusal to accept any more trade with Britain than was necessary. The result was three wars, in 1839, 1856 and 1859, all fought to force the Chinese government to concede markets and naval bases. There was disquiet at home about this ruthless aggression, especially from those Liberal free-traders who believed that, correctly applied, their doctrines would bring about universal peace. They objected strongly to the vigorous measures adopted by the authorities in Hong Kong after a British-registered junk had been seized by Cantonese officials in 1856. Palmerston, then Prime Minister, backed the men-on-the-spot and asked MPs whether they wished to 'abandon a large community of British subjects at the extreme end of the globe to a set of barbarians – a set of kidnapping, murdering, poisoning barbarians'.[13] The Commons vote went against him, and so he took the unusual step of calling a general election over an issue of foreign policy. The largely middle-class electorate responded with John-Bullish patriotism, and enthusiastically endorsed Palmerston's iron fist policy towards China. His principal opponents, Cobden and the pacifist John Bright, lost their seats. Informal empire, even if it meant waging wars against countries which obstinately refused the blessings of free trade, was almost universally supported by the business community.

Palmerston's minatory policies were known as gunboat diplomacy. Small, shallow draft, heavily-armed gunboats were an innovation of the 1850s and were soon distributed across the world as the workhorses of informal empire. Each new class of gunboat was equipped with the most up-to-date technology; by 1890 they had searchlights, quick-firing breech-loaders, and machine-guns, which gave them a firepower far beyond that of their potential adversaries. Some were given names that combined belligerence with jaunty arrogance: *Bouncer*, *Cracker*, *Frolic*, *Grappler*, *Insolence*, *Staunch* and *Surly*.

Arrogance and resolution were needed by consuls (often ex-naval and army officers) and the men who commanded the ships which provided the cutting edge of unofficial empire. Consider Commander Sir Lambton Loraine, a thirty-five-year-old baronet who commanded the modern iron-clad *Niobe* based at Kingston, Jamaica in 1873. In May of that year he was summoned to Puerto Plata on the coast of the Dominican Republic, where the local governor had broken into the British consulate and arrested three asylum-seekers. For this violation of British prestige, Loraine made the governor personally unshackle his prisoners before they were sent on board the *Niobe*. Then Dominican troops were ordered to hoist the Union Jack over the consulate and honour it with a twenty-one gun salute.

Disturbances in Honduras and Guatemala in June 1874 brought the *Niobe* to Puerto Cortéz. Her primary purpose was to safeguard the property and staff of a railway construction company which, with British finance, was laying track for a line between the Caribbean and the Pacific. The engineers and their workers had been threatened by a local commander, Colonel Streber, who added to his infractions of British rights by later kidnapping refugees from British-owned islands off Belize. So far, Loraine had confined his actions to cruising off the troubled coast, and once bringing on board a Honduran general, who was treated to a display of British sailors' cutlass and rifle drill. (Had he been a day earlier he would have witnessed the flogging of a boy sailor.) Shows of force were not enough; and Loraine, having demanded the return of British property from Streber, bombarded his fortress at Omoa with war-rockets and seven-inch shells. Within a few hours the colonel capitulated and handed over his loot.

Loraine and the *Niobe* were in action again in November 1874 at Santiago de Cuba. Less than a week before, a Spanish warship had captured an American steamer, the *Virginius*, which was carrying Cuban rebels and arms. The *Virginius* was carried back to Santiago, where the governor began shooting not only the rebels but the crew. Thirty-seven British subjects had been murdered by the time *Niobe* entered Santiago harbour, and the governor was preparing to kill more. Loraine, accompanied by the British consul, went ashore and told the Spaniard that if another execution occurred he would immediately sink a Spanish warship. There were six in the harbour, but so great was the fear of the Royal Navy that the governor immediately stepped down. In Britain, France and the United States Loraine was hailed as a hero, and the Spanish government was forced to grovel and pay compensation to the families of the men killed.[14]

The activity of the *Niobe* during 1873–4 was exceptional, but it illustrates well the mechanics and purpose of unofficial empire. The Dominican government was too weak to control one of its officials, anarchy in Honduras endangered British investment, and the lives of British subjects were being taken by the brutal agent of a decayed empire. Each situation demanded prompt action, which was undertaken by a naval officer with formidable self-assurance and, importantly, the knowledge that his conduct would be endorsed by his government. More usually ships like the *Niobe* cruised the seas, putting into port from time to time to remind Latin Americans, Chinese, Arabs and Africans of the power of Britain. Whenever a crisis occurred a warship would be summoned by the local consul or ambassador, acting on Foreign Office instructions where practical, and its commander would keep watch. Direct engagement, save in an emergency as at Santiago de Cuba, was discouraged since the British government preferred to persuade the local authorities to do their duty. It was the Sultan of Pahang's police who rounded up the murderers of some British tin-mining engineers in 1892, prompted by the appearance of two gunboats off his coast.[15]

By 1870 the apparatus of informal empire was in place in every quarter of the world. Asian and African princes were bound by treaties in which they pledged themselves not to molest missionaries and merchants, and to suppress slave-trading and piracy; Latin America was safe for business and investment; and it was possible to speak of Britain's 'practical protectorate' over the Turkish empire.[16] Even though the primary purpose of informal empire was to make the world a safe place for the British to trade in, it was also the imposition of a higher morality. Slavery and piracy were wrong, and, when they moved abroad, the British expected to find the same standards of official honesty and detachment as obtained at home.

Informal empire depended on British maritime supremacy. In 1815 the Royal Navy possessed 214 battleships and nearly 800 smaller vessels. There were considerable post-war cuts, but in 1817 the Foreign Secretary, Viscount Castlereagh, insisted that Britain's security required her to maintain 'a navy equal to the navies of any two powers that can be brought against us'.[17] This principle was more or less upheld for the rest of the century, despite regular calls for cheeseparing from lobbies who held that it was the government's first duty to keep down expenditure and taxation. Invasion scares, which occurred frequently throughout Victoria's reign, silenced demands for a reduced naval budget and usually triggered a crash programme of ship-building.

Behind fears of invasion lay suspicions of Britain's old rival, France. Between 1815 and 1870 Anglo-French relations swung between extremes of friendship and hostility. Outright war seemed possible in 1840, in 1844–5, when an aged Wellington anxiously toured the south coast looking for possible French landing sites, and in 1859. Old misgivings about French militarism and what was believed to be a national addiction to *la Gloire* died hard. On the other hand, Britain was largely tolerant of French efforts to rebuild their territorial empire by conquest in North Africa. Likewise, no action was taken when France sought to acquire Diégo Suarez as a naval base in the Indian Ocean, and made treaties with the rulers of West African states, which, unlike the agreements of British informal empire, insisted that France had sovereign rights.

This indifference vanished in 1840 when France gave its backing to Muhammad Ali, the khedive of Egypt, who was endeavouring to carve a personal empire out of Ottoman provinces in the Middle East. Memories of Napoleon's Egyptian adventure were still fresh, and so the Mediterranean fleet was ordered to intervene. France backed down rather than risk a one-sided naval war in the Mediterranean, and British warships were free to bombard Muhammad Ali's coastal fortresses in Syria and the Lebanon. The shells which fell on Acre were a forceful reminder that Britain would employ her seapower whenever she believed a vital interest was at stake.

There were, however, limitations to seapower. Could it, many wondered, protect Britain from her other rival, Russia? Throughout this period, Anglo-Russian relations were severely strained; what was in effect a cold war lasted from the late 1820s until the beginning of the next century. This cold war became a hot one in 1854, and very nearly did again in 1877 and 1885. Russophobia infected the minds of nearly every nineteenth-century British statesman, diplomat and strategist, and was strongly felt among all classes and shades of political opinion. It was commonly agreed that Czarist Russia was the antithesis of Britain. The personal, political and legal freedoms which characterised Britain and, according to many, gave it its strength and greatness, were totally absent in Russia. Its Czar was a tyrant and its masses a servile horde ready to respond unthinkingly to their master's whim. 'As the power of Russia has grown, the individuality of its subjects has disappeared,' claimed one Russophobe in 1835. It was a state 'irretrievably bent on acquisition', enlarging itself to provide living space for its growing population.[18] And yet for all its obvious political, social and economic backwardness, Russia had the means, an 800,000-strong army, with which to hurt Britain.

Behind this apprehension, which at times approached hysteria, was the fear that Russia would launch an overland invasion of India. The possibility of such an attack had been discussed in political, military and naval circles since the beginning of the century, when Napoleon had shown the way. Speculation and anxiety reached a new pitch after the Russo-Persian War of 1826–28 and the Russo-Turkish War of 1828-29. In the first, a Russian army, based on the Caucasus, had beaten a Persian one, and in the second, the Russians had come within striking distance of Constantinople. What emerged was that Russia had demonstrated the weakness of two Asian powers and revealed that it had the will and wherewithal to challenge Britain in a sensitive area.

India was more directly threatened by Russia's thrust eastwards towards the Caspian. Her empire-building plans were plain and, according to the logic of the Russophobes, it was inevitable that once the khanates of central Asia had been overcome, Russia would turn its attention to India. An Indian civil servant, writing in 1838, predicted that the people of India would be 'overwhelmed by the sea of Russian despotism'. He added, significantly, that the forthcoming contest would be between benevolent and oppressive imperialisms. If Russia won, the Indians would be made 'the serfs of a government which, though calling itself civilised, is in truth barbarian'.[19]

Everyone agreed that Russia had the advantage of manpower, and much was made of the legendary endurance and ferocity of the Cossacks. Against such an adversary, the fleet would be of marginal value, although in 1832 a naval officer observed that 'if the Russians think of going to Calcutta, we may think of visiting St Petersburg'.[20] Two years later, Wellington, who was as fearful as anyone of the threat to India, put his faith in the training and courage of the Indian army. There were, however, a few isolated voices who asked the pertinent question as to how the torpid and hidebound Russian military bureaucracy would cope with the management of supply lines stretching across the Himalayas to the Caspian.[21] Nevertheless, there were some Russian generals who imagined that the campaign was practical and talked airily of an expedition to India.

Their boasts, and Russian activities in Persia and on the fringes of the Turkish empire, were taken very seriously in London and Calcutta. Somehow the Russians had to be checked and it became axiomatic that Britain's foreign policy should be directed towards this end. The Czar's fleet had to be kept out of the Mediterranean; the integrity of Turkey, and particularly its Middle Eastern provinces, had to be preserved; and the rulers of Persia and Afghanistan had to be taught to fear Britain more than Russia.

The 1830s and 1840s witnessed all the activities which marked a cold war: diplomatic manoeuvre, intrigue, subversion and, in 1838, a British invasion of Afghanistan which went horribly awry. A Russian invasion of the Turkish Balkans in 1853 also went wrong, and led to a direct clash between Britain and France and Russia. Although the Russian army got bogged down, its navy sank the Turkish fleet near Constantinople, and Britain immediately responded by sending its Mediterranean fleet into the Bosphorus. Russia, its bluff called, tried to evade a confrontation and withdrew its ships into Sevastopol harbour, where they were later scuttled. Under pressure from the Admiralty, the British cabinet approved a seaborne expedition to the Crimea with orders to capture Sevastopol and demolish its dockyards and storehouses.

The Crimean War (1854–6) was an imperial war, the only one fought by Britain against a European power during the nineteenth century, although some would have regarded Russia as essentially an Asiatic power. No territory was at stake; the war was undertaken solely to guarantee British naval supremacy in the Mediterranean and, indirectly, to forestall any threat to India which might have followed Russia replacing Britain as the dominant power in the Middle East.

The war's outcome was a crushing defeat for Russia. Her armies were beaten four times and Sevastopol was abandoned. Now chiefly remembered in Britain for the blunders of the British high command and the War Office's and the Treasury's mismanagement of the army's logistics (which was quickly rectified), the war exposed the emptiness of Russia's military pretensions. Its army was poorly led, armed with antiquated weaponry, supported by systems that fell apart under the slightest pressure and which could not be repaired. As British, French and some intelligent Russian observers concluded, two 'modern' nations had beaten one which was hopelessly backward in terms of its government, society and economy.

The *status quo* had been maintained in Britain's favour. In November 1856 a British army landed in Persia to persuade the Shah Nasr-ud-Din to abandon his claim to Herat. This fortress on the Afghan-Persian frontier was one of those distant places which had achieved an immense symbolic and strategic importance during the Anglo-Russian cold war. The Russians had urged the Shah to hold on to it in defiance of Britain, but faced with an Anglo-Indian army, Nasr-ud-Din gave way. India's security had been preserved, although Russia continued her advance eastwards beyond the Caspian towards the northern border of Afghanistan. Between 1864 and 1868 Russian forces occupied Khiva, Tashkent, and Samarkand.

While Russian armies were tramping towards the foothills of the Himalayas, Europe was being dramatically changed. The Crimean War had destroyed the harmony between the big powers which had prevailed since 1815. The immediate beneficiaries were the Italian and German national-ists. Between 1859 and 1870 Italy was united, with French and Prussian assistance and British approval. In three successive wars, Prussia defeated Denmark, Austria and the South German States and, supported by the rest of Germany, France. The final victory was marked by the declaration of the German empire in Louis XIV's former palace at Versailles. Britain's influence over the reshaping of Europe had been slight, since her strategic and commercial interests were not endangered. Indeed, the latter were advanced by the 1870–71 Franco-Prussian War during which 300 million pounds of woollen cloth were exported to make uniforms for both armies.

Some of the deals for this cloth may well have been settled in the Bradford Exchange, an imposing building finished in 1867. Its Gothic exterior was ornamented with medallions showing the features of the men who had contributed to Britain's present wealth and greatness. Palmerston, who had died in 1865, represented firmness in dealing with anyone who interfered with Britain's right to do business everywhere; Cobden appeared as the champion of free trade; James Watt, Richard Arkwright and the railway engineer George Stephenson were reminders of the inventive genius of the Industrial Revolution; and the features of Drake, Raleigh, Anson and Cook proclaimed the triumphs of seapower. The spirit behind this choice of images was caught by Charles Dickens in his *Dombey and Son*, which had first appeared in 1848:

> The earth was made for Dombey and Son to trade in, the sun
> and the moon were made to give them light. Rivers and seas
> were formed to float their ships; rainbows to give them the
> promise of fair weather; winds blew for or against their enter-
> prises; stars and planets circled in their orbits, to preserve
> inviolate a system of which they were the centre.

———————

2

We are Going as Civilisers: Empire and Public Opinion, 1815–80

What did the empire mean to the British public? This question became a vital one as the nineteenth century proceeded. The thoughts and feelings of the people on this and other subjects of national concern mattered more and more as the country moved towards democracy. The 1832 Parliamentary Reform Act created a middle-class electorate, and the Reform and Redistribution Acts of 1867 and 1884–5 extended the vote to most urban and rural working men. Contemporaries sensed that they were living in an age of political progress, in which reasoned debate between educated men was being proved as the most perfect means of solving all human problems. Simultaneously, there was a growth in the numbers and readership of daily newspapers and weekly journals which disseminated information and fostered discussion of national issues. The London press took advantage of the extension of the railway network between 1840 and 1860 to build up a national circulation, and with it the ability to influence opinion throughout the country.

Views on the empire differed enormously during this period, and there was much passionate debate about how it should be managed, the best treatment for its subjects, and whether or not it should be extended. There was, on the whole, general agreement that the empire was a powerful force for the spread of civilisation through trade and the imposition of superior codes of behaviour on its 'savage' inhabitants. Few would have disagreed with an editorial in the *Sun*, which welcomed the announcement of the form of government chosen for Britain's newest colony, New Zealand, in January 1847. 'So speedy an attainment of the choicest fruits of civilisation, in a country where, a few years since, a hardy race of savages alone ranged free, ignorant of their better nature, is without parallel in history.'[1]

There were, however, profound differences of opinion as to whether the Maoris and other races possessed a 'better nature', and how it could be cultivated. On one side there were the pragmatists, who were for the most part soldiers, sailors and administrators (often former servicemen), colonists and their adherents in Britain who were sceptical about the capacity of native peoples for advancement. On the other hand there was a powerful body of Christian philanthropists who believed that these races could be raised to standards of education and conduct which would place them alongside Europeans. Members of this group tended to be Nonconformists, middle-class, and Liberal or Radical in their politics. Their opponents were largely Anglicans with aristocratic or gentry backgrounds and Whig or Tory sympathies, although this was a period when party labels mattered far less than they did later.

At the beginning of the century the great imperial issue was slavery. The movement for its abolition had gained impetus during the 1770s and won considerable support from all classes. Evangelicals, with their strong belief in salvation through saving others, were naturally attracted towards a campaign which was pledged to release the slaves from bondage and convert them. Much anti-slavery propaganda was emotional, highlighting the callous treatment of slaves and their inner suffering, and this appealed to those under the influence of the Romantic Movement. Reason might, and did argue that slavery was vital to the country's economy, but sentiment replied that the misery it inflicted alone justified its abolition.

The power of the anti-slavery movement owed much to the energy and singlemindedness of its leaders, William Wilberforce and Thomas Clarkson. To demonstrate their faith in the ability of the negro to regenerate himself, they joined the sponsors of an experimental colony, Sierra Leone, founded in 1787. The Sierra Leone Company's object was to 'introduce civilisation among the natives and to cultivate the soil by means of free labour' and to educate them to a level which proved them the equals of Europeans in accomplishments and civilisation. Sierra Leone flourished and, in 1808, became a crown colony and its capital, Freetown, one of the bases for the new Royal Navy anti-slaving squadron.

Britain's abolition of the slave trade in 1807 was the movement's first triumph. Thereafter, British statesmen and diplomats did their utmost to induce other governments to follow Britain's example. Squadrons of warships were deployed to pursue and arrest slavers, first off the West African and Congo coasts, and later in the Indian Ocean and Persian Gulf to suppress the Arab slave trade.

What, at first, was Britain's singlehanded war against the slave trade aroused considerable fervour and was universally regarded as a source of national pride. During the annual meeting of the Society for the Extinction of the Slave-Trade and for the Civilisation of Africa, held in Exeter Hall in June 1840, Prince Albert opened the proceedings with a speech which praised the nobility of the cause. He was wildly cheered and there were cheers too for Sir Robert Peel, the Tory leader and future prime minister. Speaking impromptu, he asserted that Britain 'never would be able to convince the black population of Africa of the superiority of their European fellow men' until slave trading had been eradicated from the continent.[2] Eight years later, one who shared Peel's sentiments expressed the view that his prediction was being fulfilled:

> The name of *Englishman* is already, through the African continent, becoming a simple passport of safety. If a white missionary visits a black tribe, they ask only one question, does he belong to the people who liberated our children from slavery?[3]

In 1855, when David Livingstone took some Africans on board British men-o'-war anchored off Luanda, he introduced the sailors with the words, 'Now these are all my countrymen, sent by our Queen for the purpose of putting down the trade of those that buy and sell black men.'[4]

Britain's moral uprightness and its will to enforce justice were themes in the play *Freedom*, first staged in 1883, in which a young naval officer, Ernest Gascoigne, rescues some Egyptian girls from slavery. Confronted by the local authorities, he proclaims, 'These girls were slaves, they are free! England has decreed it, and in England's name I speak. Touch them at your peril! I defy you!'[5] His speech brings loud hurrahs from his sailors, and no doubt cheers from audiences, delighted by a stirring reminder that their nation was the banner-bearer of liberty and civilisation.

The global war against the slave trade was advertised as the most glowing example of Britain's humanity and enlightenment. The concept of slavery had become abhorrent to a people which, thanks to the propaganda of the French wars, was increasingly aware that personal freedom was their birthright. Reginald Heber, the hymn-writer and Bishop of Calcutta, felt an inner chill whenever, as was customary, an Indian servant used the expression, 'I am your slave.'[6]

It proved easier to outlaw the traffic in slaves than it did to abolish the institution of slavery in the British empire. There was unremitting resistance from the West Indian plantocracy and its allies in parliament. Some of their apologists sniffed hypocrisy, and asked why those who made so much fuss about the slaves did so little about the sufferings of their destitute countrymen. According to one pro-slavery pamphlet of the early 1800s, 'Many a Gentleman's gelding, or high-mettled racer, and many a Lady's pad, in England, is looked after and tended with kinder treatment than some of our own poor.'[7] Moreover, as the Tory *Anti-Jacobin* claimed in 1807, the 'Crying, methodistical philanthropists' were mistaken in their assumption that every planter maltreated his slaves.[8] Plantation owners went to some lengths to present themselves as humane men; in 1816 those of Barbados pointed out that pregnant women were excused field work and added, with unintentional irony, that when they gave birth they received a payment.[9] Such generosity seems to have made little impression for there were slave uprisings in Barbados in 1816, in Jamaica in 1823, 1824 and 1830, and in British Guiana in 1823. The last was a nuisance to the Colonial Office which was hard pressed to find additional troops to put it down.[10]

A reformed Commons, in which Whigs and Radicals dominated, abolished slavery in 1833, allowing several years for the transition from unpaid to paid labour on the plantations. Throughout the debate over slavery the issue of what would happen to the slaves after emancipation had been central. Supporters of slavery had repeatedly argued that the slaves would 'soon sink into miserable penury, and languishingly pine away in their old African laziness, inaction and want'.[11] As a result, the local economy would dissolve.

Abolitionists had always held that the end of slavery was the first stage in the elevation of the West Indians. Released from servitude, they would be free to make their own future and raise themselves by their own efforts. An abolitionist who visited Antigua in 1839–40 found encouraging signs that this was happening. Seven thousand children were attending schools, where there was regular Bible-reading, and the Methodist meeting house at St John's was filled with a congregation of 'respectable-looking' worshippers drawn from a community of busy smallholders. Equally grat-ifying was the evidence of a long overdue sexual reformation. 'Even the overseers are ceasing, one after another, from the sinful mode of life, and are forming reputable connexions and marriages.'[12]

The view from the top was less sanguine. Giving evidence to a Commons committee in 1849, Sir James Light, the governor of British Guiana, feared that many ex-slaves had imagined that emancipation meant equality with the white man. He lamented the decay of deference within his colony, where he and other men of substance were now exposed to the 'jeering and impertinent remarks of loungers' as they rode through the capital, Georgetown.[13] What was worse was that former slaves shunned plantation work, forcing the owners to look elsewhere for labour. An early seventeenth-century precedent was resurrected and indentured ser-vants were imported. In what was one of the first internal migrations within the empire, poor Indians and Chinese were hired and shipped to the West Indies. By 1857 well over a half of the 14,000-strong workforce on the Trinidadian plantations were from China and India. The number would have been larger, but many immigrants died during the six-month voyage in insanitary and ill-ventilated ships.[14]

The campaign to end slavery within the British empire coincided with the growth of organisations devoted to Christian missions throughout the world. Conversion was one of the highest forms of Christian service: 'And a vision appeared to Paul in the night: There stood a man of Macedonia, and prayed him, saying, Come over into Macedonia and help us' (*Acts*, XVI, 9). This injunction had a powerful appeal to evangelicals, many of whom experienced that form of personal conversion in which they sensed God's grace come alive inside them. The 'soul of a poor hea-then was as valuable as his own to God' claimed Thomas Kendall, who, from the moment of his salvation, was determined to bring others to that grace he had found within himself. He began missionary work among the Maoris of New Zealand in 1817.[15]

The Christian missions of the nineteenth century not only redeemed souls, they regenerated whole races. An account of Cape Colony written in 1819 praised the work there of the Moravian missionaries, who 'have converted the indolent degraded Hottentot into an active moral member of society'.[16] 'We were going as civilisers as well as preachers,' wrote James Stewart in 1874. He was one of a new generation of evangelists, having studied medicine as well as theology, who set off into Central Africa with a party of practically qualified men to carry on the work of his mentor, Livingstone. He had taken artisans to teach new crafts to his flock and to build a new, self-sufficient, ordered Christian society where there had once been chaos. What he helped to achieve was revealed to him some years later when a tribesman told him, 'Give me a Gospel for an assegai as the love of war has been taken out of my heart.'[17]

As well as preaching the Gospel, missionaries were also responsible for bringing their congregations into contact with the values of the West. George Brown, a stouthearted Methodist missionary who began his work on the island of New Britain, west of Papua, in 1875 was more than a saver of souls. Within three years he 'succeeded in opening up a large extent of the coast of New Britain and New Ireland to the influence of Civilisation and Christianity so that Traders were allowed to land and live on the islands in comparative safety.'[18] This praise came from a naval officer who warmly endorsed his methods. On one occasion, when inland tribal chiefs had threatened to kill him, his flock and every European they could find, Brown attacked and defeated them with a small force of Fijian converts armed with two fowling pieces and a revolver. Such men were useful; writing about his experiences in Sarawak in the 1860s Charles Brooke believed that missionaries would help make the head-hunting Dyaks more tractable.[19]

Missionaries were not only pathfinders of empire, and even, at times, pacifiers. Through their connections with British churches they linked the empire with the ordinary men, women and children who collected money for and promoted their activities. One of these helpers, Mrs Jellyby, was caricatured by Dickens in *Bleak House* (1851) as a creature who 'could see nothing nearer than Africa' and neglected her family duties in favour of work for the mission settlement of 'Borrioboola-Gha' on the banks of the Niger. But then Dickens had no time for the noble savage – 'His virtues are a fable; his happiness is a delusion; his nobility, nonsense.'[20] Nonetheless, thousands of Dickens's countrymen went to considerable effort to provide for the metamorphosis of such creatures into useful Christians.

Subscribers to missions were encouraged to donate money, Bibles and material by sheaves of tracts which outlined the wretchedness and depravity of the heathen. Lurid accounts were presented of Indian infanticide, sati, idolatry and superstitions. From the Pacific and Africa came stories of tribal warfare, cannibalism, domestic slavery and thinly veiled details of sexual promiscuity. There were in central Africa vices which 'cannot be explained or named for shame'. According to one exasperated missionary, 'The imagination of the Kaffir runs to seed after puberty. It would be safer to say it runs to sex,' which explained why, after the age of fifteen, white pupils surpassed blacks![21] Church- and chapel-goers in Britain were all conscious of the vastness of the task which faced the missionaries, and knew too well what lay behind the words of Bishop Heber's popular hymn for foreign missions:

> *What though the spicy breezes*
> *Blow soft o'er Ceylon's isle,*
> *Though every prospect pleases*
> *And only man is vile . . .*

Interestingly, these lines were written in a Shropshire parsonage, *before* their author set foot in India.

The soldier, like the missionary, was also seen as a civiliser. This was a period of almost continual imperial warfare. Between 1817 and 1878 there were intermittent campaigns against the tribes of the eastern Cape, known indiscriminately as Kaffirs, and in 1879 a British army invaded Zululand. An expedition entered Abyssinia in 1867 to rescue hostages held by the Emperor Theodore, and in 1873–4 there was a large-scale punitive war against the Asante of the Gold Coast. The army in India fought campaigns in Burma (1824 and 1853), Afghanistan (1838–42 and 1878–80), conquered the Sind (1843) and the Punjab (1845–6 and 1848–9), and suppressed the Mutiny (1857–8).

From time to time large columns penetrated the North-West Frontier punishing its notoriously recalcitrant tribesmen. There were also campaigns in New Zealand fought on behalf of the colonists against the Maoris between 1846 and 1870. A rebellion was put down in Canada in 1837, China was attacked three times between 1839 and 1860, Persia once in 1856.

The British press gave extensive coverage to the earlier campaigns, usually reproducing stories from local papers, official despatches and letters from men serving at the front. On 10 January 1840 *The Standard* reprinted the *Bengal Gazette*'s account of operations in Afghanistan together with despatches from senior officers there. The same paper also came by some servicemen's letters, including one with an eyewitness account of the drowning of men and horses of the 16th Lancers during the march to Kabul.[22] Similar sources were used by the *Sun* during 1847 for its pieces on the frontier campaigns in New Zealand and Cape Colony.

Within the next ten years there was a revolution in journalism which completely transformed the treatment of imperial news. The nearness of the Crimea had allowed pressmen, the first war correspondents, to follow the army, compile reports, and send them back by fast steamer and train for publication ten to fourteen days later. The time lapse was reduced to forty-eight hours in May 1855, when a telegraph office was established at Balaklava, the army's base. Henceforward, the wars of empire were covered first-hand. War correspondents accompanied British forces during the Indian Mutiny, the 1859–60 China War, and the Abyssinian, Asante, Afghan and Zulu campaigns. Each of these wars gained a further immediacy through the reproduction as engravings of on-the-spot sketches and photographs in the *Illustrated London News*, which had been founded in 1842. Ten years later it was running pictures of scenes from the fighting in Cape Colony, including a lively and realistic drawing of the 76th Highlanders skirmishing in the bush, which was accompanied by a description of the action by the officer-artist.[23] The popularity of these illustrations was so great that by the 1870s specially commissioned war artists were being sent to the front alongside reporters.

Amateur journalists and artists held their own for many years. Some families who received letters from soldiers passed them to the local newspaper for publication. These descriptions of campaign life often had a striking verisimilitude. One, written by an unknown 78th Highlander after the Cawnpore massacre and published in the *Aberdeen Chronicle* in October 1857, may stand for many others:

> It [the massacre] made our blood boil with rage, and I could later hear the men of the 78th saying one among another, 'I will never spare a man with a black face' . . . I have seen some terrible sights. Oh dear! it would make you sick if I were to tell you all I have witnessed during the short time I have been in Bengal. I am sick tired of it, as we have much to do. There is only a handful of us and we have to encounter about nineteen to one of us, and sometimes more. I have had some narrow escapes lately, and I am in danger of my life every moment: but I still live in hopes that I will be spared to see this affair finished

and return home to Scotland again. He will be a lucky dog, however, who gets through it safe . . . We have hard marching and hard fighting, with very little to eat; and as our clothes and shoes are nearly worn out, we are just like so many ragga-muffins. However we are keeping our spunk up in the hopes of the 'good time' coming.

Those who pored over this must have felt a thrill of admiration for the sta-mina and bravery of their countrymen. No other imperial war had been reported in Britain in such detail or with such a wealth of eyewitness detail. Most of it was horrific; the *News of the World* promised its readers the 'fullest and exclusive details of Indian atrocities' in November 1857. Its pages and those of the other papers were full of blood-chilling accounts of the random slaughter of men, women and children and hints of darker, unprintable outrages by the mutinous sepoys. Assailed by these hideous tales, there was a universal demand for retribution. Thus a speaker in the usually sedate Cambridge Union: 'When the rebellion has been crushed from the Himalayas to Comorin; when every gibbet is red with blood; when every bayonet creaks beneath its ghastly burden; when the ground in front of every cannon is strewn with rags, and flesh, and shattered bone – then talk of mercy.'[24] Similar bloodthirsty rhetoric poured from editorials and pulpits.

What happened in India during 1857 and 1858 had a profound impact on British thinking about the empire and its peoples. According to their masters, the Indians had for many years been the beneficiaries of a humane system of government, deliberately contrived to uplift them and modernise their country. In the light of this, the Mutiny was both an act of betrayal and a wilful rejection of progress. Had the British failed to penetrate into the interior of the Indian mind? The *National Review* thought so: 'The CHILD and the SAVAGE lie very deep at the foundations of their [the Indians'] being. The varnish of civilisation is very thin, and is put off as promptly as a garment.'[25] If this were so, and the events in India strongly suggested it, then much humanitarian endeavour had been in vain. Furthermore, the premises on which it had been based were false. Reclamation of the 'savage' through exposure to European religion and knowledge might not be possible because of indelible flaws within his character.

The Indian Mutiny strengthened British racism and threw doubt on the gospel of the philanthropists. The gulf that was emerging between the two approaches to empire was dramatically revealed during the repercussions that followed the Morant Bay insurrection in Jamaica at the end of 1865. Unrest and unemployment among the black population had been causing tension throughout the island for some time. A riot at Morant Bay, in which several white officials and militiamen were killed, was interpreted by the governor, Edward Eyre, as a signal for a rebellion, equal in scale and ferocity to the Indian Mutiny. Immediately, and in some ignorance as to what exactly was happening, he declared martial law and launched a reign of terror in the Blue Mountains of western Jamaica. Something of its flavour, and the state of mind of those ordered to enforce it, is revealed by a message sent by Colonel Thomas Hobbs of the 6th Regiment describing the execution of suspected rebels: 'I . . . adopted a plan which struck *immense* terror into these wretched men, FAR more than death, which is, I caused them to hang each other. They entreat to be shot to avoid this.'[26] It is highly likely that many who died this way were unconnected with the disturbances. Hundreds were hanged, including the Reverend G.W. Gordon, a black Baptist minister, and many more flogged. Where trials were held they were short and summary.

When reports of the uprising first reached Britain, Eyre was congratulated for having taken swift and vigorous measures which had prevented a massacre of the colony's 15,000 whites by half a million blacks. A satirical magazine, *Fun*, printed a cartoon in which a manic negro, wielding a firebrand and a machete, cavorts over the corpses of white women and children, an unmistakeable reminder of the Mutiny. Underneath is the caption, '*Am* I a man and a brother?' a sneering reference to the anti-slavery campaign's motto, 'I am a man and a brother'.

Once the grim details of Eyre's operations had filtered back to Britain, there was a unanimous cry from every humanitarian lobby for his prosecution for murder. In response to this clamour, a committee was hastily organised for Eyre's defence as the saviour of Jamaica. Intellectual and literary heavyweights attached themselves to both camps: Thomas Carlyle, Charles Kingsley and Dickens stood by Eyre, John Stuart Mill and Darwin against him. Much of the debate was emotional and focussed on the victims, the Jamaican blacks, who, claimed Eyre's partisans, had brought their misfortunes on themselves through laziness. Edward Cardwell, the Whig Colonial Secretary, considered the youth of Jamaica 'idle, vicious and profligate', an opinion quoted approvingly by the *Quarterly Review*, which feared that the entire negro population of the West Indies was being 'driven back to its ancestral barbarism'.[27] The controversy spluttered on for the rest of 1866; Eyre was sacked by the Whig-Liberal ministry, but, like its Tory successor it refused to indict him. He was not re-employed and died in 1900.

The significance of the Eyre scandal lay in the fact that it revealed a substantial body of intellectually respectable opinion which believed that a large proportion of the empire's subjects were impervious to improvement and needed a firm hand to keep them in order. Humanitarians had misjudged the 'savage': he was a fickle creature whose capacity for moral and intellectual elevation was limited. For some, his role within the empire was that of a permanent underdog. Nevertheless, the fuss that had been made about Eyre acted as a brake on others of like mind. In 1879, General Sir Garnet Wolseley, commander-in-chief in South Africa, had reluctantly to abandon a plan to unleash the Swazis against the Zulus. He wrote:

> I have to think of the howling Societies at home who have sympathy with all black men whilst they care nothing for the miseries inflicted on their own kith and kin who have the misfortune to be located near these interesting niggers.[28]

The Eyre debate coincided with a wider political controversy over the empire's future. There existed in Liberal, Nonconformist and free trade circles a fear that the empire engendered belligerent nationalism and militarism, which undermined what they saw as Britain's real national virtues, thrift and industriousness. John Bright took a characteristically extreme standpoint when he claimed that, 'Inasmuch as supremacy of the seas means arrogance and the assumption of dictatorial power on the part of this country, the sooner it becomes obsolete the better.' Waving cudgels had no justification in a world where free trade was increasing the interdependence of nations and reducing the friction which had formerly been the source of wars. As for the colonies, they had no economic value and the bill for their defence and administration was an expensive luxury.

Canada, Australia, New Zealand and Cape Colony were all moving towards self-government and there seemed no reason why, in the near future, they should not detach themselves from Britain as America had done. *The Times* rejected this argument and, in an editorial of 4 February 1862, asserted that the white colonies were 'uniformly prosperous, and desirous of maintaining their connexion with the mother country and each other', and that their present felicitous state was 'a triumph of civilisation' of which Britain ought to be proud. Many colonists agreed. A New

Zealand settler predicted that his colony would 'rise as a community to the enviable status of their forefathers, and then they would form the stoutest of all bulwarks to guard our noblest of privileges, civil and religious liberty.'[29] Potential colonists were anxious that Britain kept its empire. The working-class journal, the *Bee Hive*, believed that the colonies belonged to the whole nation and collected 100,000 signatures for a petition which asked the Queen to promote state-funded emigration schemes for the unemployed.

The nearest the government came to taking imperial disengagement seriously was in 1865, when a parliamentary committee recommended the evacuation of tiny stations on the West African coast. Nothing came of the proposal, largely because of the practical difficulties and uncertainty about what would replace British rule. The anti-imperialists had always been a small lobby making a great deal of noise about an issue which aroused little public interest. Moreover, predictions that the world was about to enter a golden age of harmony and free trade were dramatically disproved by the Franco-Austrian war of 1859, the Danish war of 1863, and the Austro-Prussian war of 1866. Nor did it make much political sense to contemplate disbandment of empire when Britain's rivals were engaged in empire-building: Russia was advancing into central Asia and France had completed the subjugation of Algeria in 1860 and Cochin China (Viet Nam) in 1867.

Benjamin Disraeli viewed the mutable world of the 1860s with misgivings. He was the most striking and influential figure within the Conservative party, which he led after 1868. His advancement within a party in which cleverness was mistrusted had not been easy. Flamboyant, Jewish, a novelist by profession and frequently strapped for cash, Disraeli once likened his career to the ascent of a 'greasy pole'. But he was, as he would have been the first to admit, the most talented figure in a party which had not won a general election since 1841, and whose only taste of power in the intervening years had been as partners in a couple of coalitions. It entered office again in July 1866 with Lord Derby as Prime Minister and Disraeli as Chancellor of the Exchequer and the power behind the throne.

Disraeli had been angered by every turn of Liberal foreign and imperial policy, which he considered fainthearted. As a pragmatist, he realised that Britain had to maintain its standing as a global power actively, and if necessary forcefully, pursuing its interests. This could only be done if Britain maintained and strengthened her overseas empire for it was these possessions, particularly India, which made Britain strong and respected. The empire was an asset to be cherished. Disraeli the politician detected a reservoir of imperial and patriotic sentiment among the electorate, and he intended to tap it in the interests of his party. Within a year of taking office, and with Disraeli's encouragement, the government demonstrated that Britain was still a power to be reckoned with. In the summer of 1867 an Anglo–Indian army landed on the Abyssinian coast, marched inland, and stormed Magdala. where the Emperor Theodore had been holding a number of European prisoners, including British officials. The Abyssinian expedition was a minor triumph and proved that the spirit of Palmerston was alive and his mantle had fallen on Disraeli.

Success in Africa did not bring Disraeli an election victory. In 1868 the Liberals under Gladstone were returned and with them a foreign and imperial policy based upon high-minded abstract principles. Disraeli continued to beat the patriotic drum, defending the monarchy from the assaults of Liberal republicans, and exposing his opponents' failure to uphold British interests abroad. Much of what he had to say was contrived to arouse the national pride of the new working-class electorate. They were the target of a seminal speech, delivered at the Crystal Palace in June 1872:

> When I say 'Conservative', I use the word in its purest and loftiest sense. I mean that the people of England, and especially the working classes of England, are proud of belonging to a great country, and wish to maintain its greatness – that they are proud of belonging to an Imperial country.

He went on to pledge himself and his party to maintain all those institutions, particularly the empire. Henceforward, the Conservative party was closely identified with patriotism, the monarchy and the empire.

In 1874 the Conservatives were returned to power, not so much because of their John Bullishness, but because the Liberals had run out of steam and the electorate was keen for a change. The next six years revealed the nature of Disraeli's populist imperialism. In practice it followed lines laid down by Palmerston: Ottoman integrity and Indian security had to be upheld at all costs and informal empire enforced with vigour. The completion of the Franco-Egyptian-financed Suez Canal in 1869 had increased the need for Britain to remain the dominant power in the Middle East, since it was now India's lifeline. By a feat of legerdemain, Disraeli secured a controlling interest in the Suez Canal Company in 1875 and added the Canal to Britain's unofficial empire.

It was fears for the Canal as well as an urge to fracture the recent unity between Russia, Germany and Austria-Hungary which drove Disraeli to intervene in the affairs of Turkey. A rebellion of its Balkan subjects in 1875 had led to a war of massacre and counter-massacre, which the European powers and the Liberals in Britain blamed on the Turkish government. British moral outrage at Turkish atrocities in what today is Bulgaria was orchestrated by the Liberals, with Gladstone leading the denunciation and calling on the government to abandon its support for the decrepit and callous régime in Constantinople. The interests of humanity outweighed those of India's safety. Fortunately for Disraeli, Russia invaded the Balkans and by the end of 1877 its army was within sight of the Straits.

Public opinion began to swing behind Disraeli. A British fleet, led by the most up-to-date battleship in the world, the splendidly named HMS *Devastation*, anchored in the Dardanelles and, just to make sure that no one forgot that India's security was at stake, Indian troops were shipped to Malta. The empire was mobilising for war, and music hall audiences, infected with war fever, bellowed out the song of the moment:

> *We don't want to fight, but, by Jingo if we do,*
> *We've got the ships; we've got the men; we've got the money too!*

Thereafter the word 'jingoism' came to stand for every form of clamorous, pugnacious and intestinally inspired patriotism. Neither it nor its manifestations were novel; there had been 'jingoes' in 1759 and throughout the Napoleonic and Crimean wars. The 1877 crisis was solved by diplomacy and not war. Russia, severely debilitated by its war effort, withdrew from the Straits, and Britain received Cyprus, a potential sentry post for the Suez Canal.

What had been demonstrated by the war scare during 1877 was the fickleness of public opinion, which had swung between the emotional poles of extreme moral indignation against Turkey and an equally passionate urge to fight on its behalf against Russia. The pendulum swung again in 1879, this time against Disraeli.

He was not by instinct an annexationist, preferring policies which affirmed and consolidated British power where it was already established, rather than those that enlarged it. For instance, in 1877 he had Queen

Victoria proclaimed Empress of India, a gesture designed to link the monarchy with the empire, to bind India more closely to Britain and to serve as an earnest of the permanence of British government there. It was, therefore, very much against Disraeli's wishes that his ministry became embroiled in the takeover of the Transvaal in 1877, the invasion of Afghanistan in 1878, and the war against the Zulu kingdom which began in January 1879. All had their roots in the responses to local crises by individual officials who believed, mistakenly, that the home government would support belligerent policies. Matters were made worse by the near annihilation of a British column at Isandlwana in Zululand in the first month of the war, and there were some near-run things in Afghanistan.

This rash of aggressive wars was a signal to Gladstone to abandon semi-retirement and the study of theology and to arouse the conscience of the nation against the iniquities of what he called 'Beaconsfieldism' – Disraeli having taken the title Earl of Beaconsfield in 1877. Beaconsfieldism was an unwholesome political cocktail whose main ingredients were amoral opportunism, military adventures, and a disregard for the rights of others. During the winter of 1879–80 Gladstone, brimming with energy and moral indignation, traversed southern Scotland and denounced the policies which were destroying Britain's reputation for fair play and justice. Ten thousand Zulus had died, he told a Glaswegian audience, for 'no other offence than their attempt to defend against your artillery their homes and families'. Villages had been razed in Afghanistan and their inhabitants left to starve, victims of a government bent on conquest.

Some of those who listened may have been among the crowds which had gathered in Edinburgh in February 1879 to watch three dozen volunteers from the 50th Regiment march from the castle to Waverley Station, the first stage of their journey to Zululand. Thousands cheered, handkerchiefs were waved from windows and the bands played 'Cheer Boys! Cheer!', 'Who will care for Mother now?' and 'The Union Jack of Old England'. Those seeking an explanation of this brave show would have found it in the *Scotsman*, which defined the Zulu as 'a savage pure and simple, abjectly submissive to the loathsome superstitions of the witch finder and rain doctor, and with his life and belongings entirely at the will of a brutal tyrant.'

Patriotic euphoria was a transient thing, and some who had succumbed to it thought again, and voted for Gladstone. The Liberal victory in the 1880 general election was, for him, a sign that the nation had turned its back on flag-waving jingoism and lost whatever taste it may have had for conquest. Under the new Liberal government the country would return to its old ways; through free trade and self-help its people would gain in prosperity and moral strength, and Britain, through example, would continue to reshape the world in its own image.

3

— ◆ —

The Mission of
Our Race:
Britain and the
'New Imperialism',
1880–1902

In 1880 the British could still regard the world as their oyster, but with marginally less confidence than twenty or thirty years earlier. Britain was still the world's only global power and much, perhaps the greater part, of its international strength lay in its ability to influence weaker, less developed states rather than in the possession of a territorial empire. India was, of course, a priceless asset. During the past twenty years, Indian troops had undertaken the coercive work of unofficial empire in China, Malaya and Abyssinia and had been summoned by Disraeli to defend Turkey from Russian aggression.

In some areas the need for the old-style informal empire was disappearing. In 1886 the commander of the Cape Squadron told the Admiralty that it was no longer necessary for warships to police the waters off the Plate. The days of violent revolutions and civil wars had passed and the slave trade had been ended. Now governments kept order and, even during the tensions of presidential elections, British lives and property were respected. He added that the navy's ships in this part of the world were obsolete and 'objects of ridicule', unlike the modern men-o'-war which guarded local French and Italian interests.[1] This observation was a reminder that other European powers were following Britain's example and providing world-wide naval protection for their businesses and investments. German and French warships now cruised regularly in the Atlantic, Indian and Pacific oceans.

The appearance of foreign warships in areas which had been almost wholly under British surveillance was a token of a greater change that was occurring throughout the world. Contemporaries called it the 'new imperialism', a phrase that was subsequently taken up by historians to describe the sudden surge of annexations by the great powers, chiefly in Africa, the Far East and the Pacific. In fact, there was little that was novel about this phenomenon save its frenzied pace and the participation of Germany, Italy, the United States and Japan, states which had previously avoided overseas expansion.

The reasons for this outbreak of conquest and occupation of underdeveloped and militarily weak countries by the industrial nations were complex. Everywhere, there was plenty of heady talk about the progress of mankind and the spread of civilisation. After America's annexation of the Philippines in 1899, Senator A.J. Beveridge proclaimed his faith in 'the mission of our race, trustees under God, of the civilisation of the world'. The same sentiments were expressed by German, French and Italian imperialists, and in Britain they had been uttered repeatedly over the past sixty years. Vaunting one's own civilisation usually involved decrying someone else's, a common indulgence whenever powers clashed over who should have what. In 1885, when a British army was fighting its way down the Nile to rescue General Charles Gordon from Khartoum, *La France* scornfully observed:

> England, who would have done nothing to save civilisation, or Khartoum, its citadel in the Sudan, has only undertaken her costly and adventurous expedition in order to deliver one of this arrogant race which considers itself superior to the rest of humanity.

Behind the bombast of late nineteenth-century imperialism lay economic uncertainties and self-doubts which troubled both old and new imperial powers. From 1872 the patterns of world trade were changing in ways which hurt all countries, particularly Britain. From then until 1896 there was a world-wide recession whose effect was tempered by sporadic, short-lived booms. The French, German, Italian, Russian and United States governments reacted by dropping free trade in favour of protection.

As the tariff barriers went up, British exports to these countries tumbled. And yet in Britain the old faith in free trade remained as strong as ever, especially in the Liberal party. There were objections from the fainthearted and realists, like the Liberal-Radical Joseph Chamberlain, but they never overrode the simple belief that the golden age of free trade would somehow return and with it Britain's dominance of world trade.

So, in 1880, the new Liberal government was stuck with free trade, faced with slackening exports (they fell from an annual average of £234 million in the first half of the decade to £226 million in the second), rising imports, a growing population and an increase in urban deprivation. Furthermore, Britain was no longer the world's only industrial power and her rivals were gradually catching up and overtaking her. Between 1880 and 1910 Britain's portion of the world's trade shrank from 23 to 17 per cent, and by the latter date her share of the world's industrial capacity was 15 per cent, compared to the United States's 35 per cent and Germany's 16 per cent.

These figures reflected industrial stagnation, the decline of the entrepreneurial spirit, and the lack of that inventiveness which had marked the early phases of the Industrial Revolution. Britain lagged behind in the development of new industrial technologies and production methods, leaving the United States and Germany to make the pace in chemicals, oil, electrical engineering and motor cars. It was paradoxical that during the 1870s and 1880s those vital accessories for Britain's imperial campaigns, Gatling and Nordenfelt machine-guns, were manufactured in America. Those two innovations of the early 1880s, telephones and electric lighting, were both promoted in Britain by American-owned companies. Nevertheless, Britain was cushioned against the effects of diminishing exports and backward production methods by the 'invisible' earnings from banking, shipping, insurance and investments. By 1913 these last totalled £3,780 million.

Britain had to come to terms with cutthroat competition in a contracting world market. As the 1880s proceeded, export outlets were further reduced as her protectionist rivals began to stake out stretches of the world, occupy them, and then declare them exclusively reserved for their own traders and investors. Britain attempted to deflect this process, but with limited success. Diplomatic pressure ensured that in 1884 the markets of the privately-owned Congo Free State were open for all comers. Again, in 1898, the British government protested when Germany and Russia were negotiating with China for concessions in Shantung and Manchuria which would give each power a monopoly of trade and investment in its province.[2]

Disapproving diplomatic noises were not enough. While adhering to the dogma of free trade, Britain had to keep abreast of her rivals. Businessmen, often acting through their local chambers of commerce, began urging a policy of annexation on the government to prevent existing or potential markets from being lost to competitors. Colonial lobbying became a growth industry during the last years of the nineteenth century with well-organised and funded expansionist pressure groups springing up in Germany and France. In these countries and in Britain the imperialists made alliances with the owners of the new, cheap, mass-circulation press which had the power to sway lower-middle- and working-class opinion.

The popular press invited the public to participate in the international bargaining for territory and occasional head-on collisions which marked the period of the new imperialism. It was soon found that the masses could be whipped into a belligerent frenzy whenever it appeared that their country was being flouted. Consider the fictional Mr Madison in Henry Williamson's *Donkey Boy*, a City insurance clerk who was proud to be 'the father of a son and daughter in the greatest nation on earth'. He read one of the new, tabloid papers, *The Daily Trident* which:

> . . . with its reiterated, almost pronged policy of fidelity to
> King, Country, and Empire through the triple virtues of Faith,
> Hope, and Vigilance, was the bedfellow of his mind. Let the
> radicals call it the Yellow Press; he knew the truth when he saw
> it: he had a mind of his own in such matters.[3]

The proprietors of the new papers understood what the Mr Madisons wanted; Lord Harmsworth, owner of the *Daily Mail* (founded 1896), once remarked that his readers relished a 'good hate'. There were plenty of opportunities for this pleasure as the 1880s and 1890s unfolded and imperial rivalries intensified.

How could Britain adjust to and survive in a world which was rapidly changing and where the dice were no longer loaded in its favour? It could, as many Liberals believed, rely on the old formula of free trade and unofficial empire. But the latter was no longer practical in an age when other countries were establishing their own, jealously guarded spheres of influence across the world, and in many instances taking control of so-called 'empty' areas in Africa and the Pacific. The practical response was to jettison old shibboleths and join in the rush to acquire territory, if only to forestall rivals.

When unofficial empire collapsed in Egypt in 1882, Gladstone's government substituted direct control, occupying the country by force. Likewise when, in 1884, it seemed that German settlers in South-West Africa (Namibia) might join forces with the Boers of the Transvaal and take over Bechuanaland (Botswana), hitherto loosely controlled through British missionaries, the government stepped in and declared a protectorate. It was all very galling for Gladstone who had so firmly set his face against imperial filibustering, but he could not allow power to slip from Britain's grasp. Moreover, he could not ignore strategic arguments put forward by imperialists within his own cabinet or public opinion.

In broad terms, Britain was committed to hanging on to its old influence, even if this meant replacing informal with direct control. There was no imperial masterplan beyond a determination to ensure the absolute security of India. 'As long as we rule India we are the greatest power in the world,' claimed Lord Curzon in 1901. 'If we lose it we shall drop straight away to a third rate power.' No one would have seriously challenged this assertion nor the policies designed to protect the subcontinent. They were pursued ruthlessly to the point when, during the winter of 1898–9, Britain was willing to go to war to prevent France from keeping a toehold in the Nile valley. Less than a year later, in October 1899, Britain did go to war against the Transvaal and the Orange Free State to defend its paramountcy in South Africa. Loss of control over the Nile valley would have jeopardised Egypt and weakened Britain's grip on India's lifeline, the Suez Canal. Similarly, the dilution of British power in southern Africa would have imperilled the Cape and with it British naval supremacy in the South Atlantic and Indian oceans.

Elsewhere Britain could afford to compromise. The partition of East and West Africa, the sharing out of Pacific islands, and the balancing of the great powers' interests in China were managed diplomatically, if not always cordially.

The enlargement of the empire and the wars which accompanied it attracted enormous public interest in Britain. The process coincided with a widespread revision of ideas about the empire and its future. Rethinking the empire had been stimulated by two speculative books, Sir Charles Dilke's *Greater Britain* (1869) and the best-selling *The Expansion of England*

(1882) by Sir John Seeley. Both offered consolation for those who were apprehensive about Britain's future. For Seeley the empire was the main source of British strength and its expansion and unity were vital for the nation's survival as a great power. In the modern world size equalled strength and vitality; both America and Germany had grown in area and population during the past twenty years and had accordingly increased in strength. The sinews of British power were its colonies, particularly the white dominions, which were an extension of Britain. If, as Seeley hoped, they continued to expand then Britain could hold her own in the world and eventually outdistance her new rivals.

The British empire was an expression of what Seeley considered to be the special genius of the Anglo-Saxon race, that is the British. Social Darwinism was now fashionable and its theories, a rough and ready transfer of Darwin's principles from the world of plants and animals to that of men, suggested that certain races were better fitted to survive and flourish than others. Leaving on one side the pertinent question as to who exactly were the Anglo-Saxons, and late nineteenth-century imperialists usually did, there was a common agreement that their assumed progeny, the British, represented a super-race. This conclusion could be justified in terms of material, scientific and intellectual progress and adaptability. The fact that the Anglo-Saxons had dispersed across the globe and mastered their environment added to the general feeling that they were ideally qualified to rule.

Notions of racial superiority blended with arguments for imperial unity to produce an ideology for the new imperialism. It suited the times, since it offered Britain a chance to reverse the decline of its international power and revive a torpid economy. After all, in 1884 three million Australians consumed £23 million pounds' worth of British goods. Here was not only a valuable market, but a country whose ties of kinship, language and institutions were with Britain. Striking proof of this was provided the following year when New South Wales sent troops to serve alongside British and Indian units in the Sudan.

The most significant convert to the imperial creed of Dilke and Seeley was Joseph Chamberlain. He was probably the most able politician of his time and certainly the most restless and difficult to label. In appearance he looked like an archetypal aristocrat with elegant features, a monocle and a fresh orchid in his buttonhole. Chamberlain was in fact a Birmingham businessman who progressed from a Radical Lord Mayor with fierce republican views to a Liberal minister under Gladstone, and, in 1895,

Colonial Secretary in a Conservative government. During the course of his political perambulations he split two parties, the Liberals in 1886 and the Conservatives in 1904, a unique achievement which says much for his influence.

Of all the causes which Chamberlain embraced, that of the empire was the most deeply felt and longest lasting. Attachment to the ideal of imperial unity, as well as frustration with Gladstone's indifference towards social reform, drove Chamberlain to desert the Liberals over Irish Home Rule in 1886. Thereafter, he led his splinter Unionists towards a coalition with the Conservatives, reserving for himself what had hitherto been a minor cabinet office, Colonial Secretary. His brand of imperialism was an amalgam of older notions of disseminating civilisation and modern concepts of race. In 1893, when Britain had accepted a protectorate over Uganda, he told the Commons that the country welcomed the new addition to the empire. The people, he continued, were well matched to the tasks of spreading civilisation since they were animated by the traditions of the past, and by what he called 'that spirit . . . of adventure and enterprise distinguishing the Anglo-Saxon race [which] has made us peculiarly fit to carry out the working of colonisation.'[4]

It was essential that the Anglo-Saxon race should understand the qualities that it needed to foster if it was to fulfil its historic destiny. Most importantly, the young had to be given models of how the Anglo-Saxon should behave and which of his innate virtues he should cultivate and how. A generation of university teachers, schoolmasters, clergymen, poets, journalists and boys' fiction writers concentrated their minds and energies on popularising the cult of the new imperialism. At its heart lay the concept of 'Anglo-Saxon manhood', an abstraction compounded in equal parts of patriotism, physical toughness, skill at team games, a sense of fair play (sometimes called 'sportsmanship'), self-discipline, selflessness, bravery and daring.

The ground had been well prepared for the apostles of the Anglo-Saxon ideal. Since the 1840s the public schools had undergone a revolution, started by Dr Thomas Arnold of Rugby, which transformed the habits of mind of the middle and upper classes. Arnold and his acolytes sought to instil Christian altruism into their pupils and direct their ambition and aggression towards the playing field. The public schoolboy, educated according to the Arnoldian code, also learned how to control himself and control others through the prefectorial system, a perfect preparation for ruling and chastising the empire's 'lesser breeds'. Intelligence mattered less than the acquisition of 'character', and intellectual activity was largely restricted to otiose and repetitive exercises in the languages of two former imperial powers, Greece and Rome. The end product was a Christian gentleman with a stunted imagination, who played by the rules and whose highest aim was to serve others. If he had to earn his living, he elected to become an army or navy officer, a senior civil servant, a clergyman, a barrister, or joined a branch of the Indian or Colonial administration.

By 1880 a generation had passed into manhood with an outlook which made them ideally suited to govern the empire and fight its wars. Incidentally, the late-Victorian public schoolboy shunned trade and industry, even if one had been the occupation of his father. Both activities were consequently starved of talent, which has been seen as one of the causes of the paralysis which was spreading through British manufacturing and commerce during this period.

The qualities cherished by public schools were those which marked out the banner-bearers of Anglo-Saxon civilisation. By the turn of the century the obsession with games had become a mania. It was the belief of J.E.C. Welldon, headmaster of Harrow (1881–95) and later Bishop of Calcutta, that, 'If there is in the British race, as I think there is, a special aptitude for "taking up the white man's burden" . . . it may be ascribed, above all other causes, to the spirit of organised games.' These fostered team spirit from which sprang self-sacrifice. The highest examples of this were represented in a stained-glass window in the chapel of Sedbergh School which showed three Christian heroes of empire: Sir Henry Lawrence, a warrior proconsul in India, and two martyrs, General Gordon and Bishop Patteson, a South Seas missionary. The ideals of Arnoldian Christian manliness merged easily with those of the new imperialism.

Throughout the 1890s schoolboys were bombarded by popular magazines written specially for them and steeped in the ideas of the new imperialism. They interwove thrilling adventure yarns with patriotism and reminders of imperial duty. The older, evangelical *Boys' Own Paper* was joined by *Chums*, *Pluck* and *Union Jack*, the last two both of 1894 and from the Harmsworth stable, whose titles reflected their contents. *Chums* was packed with tales of imperial derring-do and coloured illustrations, including 'Storming the Heights of Dargai', which showed an incident in the 1897 North-West Frontier campaign in which Highlanders rushed a Pathan position, spurred on by the playing of a wounded piper who was later awarded the Victoria Cross. The cover of the *Young England* annual for 1902 symbolised its own and its competitors' values; alongside a cavalryman dressed to fight the Boers were rowing oars, cricket bats, stumps, tennis racquets and a fisherman's basket.[5]

Those who read *Young England* would also have enjoyed the many full-length tales of derring-do which poured relentlessly from publishers during the 1890s. Of these, the best were the yarns of G.A. Henty, a dyed-in-the-wool imperialist who had served as a war correspondent during the 1873–4 Asante War. Henty turned out on average three boys' stories a year, which appeared in time for the Christmas market and cost five or six shillings (25–30p) each. In his earlier works, Henty addressed his readers as 'My dear lads' and confessed that he found it painful to write of any campaign in which the British were defeated.[6] Mercifully, there were plenty of victories for him to choose from and work into straightforward narratives in which a resourceful young man finds himself caught up in the events of history. Henty ranged from Pharaohic Egypt to his own times, but his commonest subjects were the wars of empire.

His purpose was to excite his readers. A reviewer of *On the Irrawady* (based on the 1824 Burma War) described his hero as a lad whose 'pluck is even greater than his luck, and he is precisely the boy to hearten with emulation the boys who read this stirring story.'[7] Just how his younger readers should behave was laid down by Henty in *Through the Sikh War*, in a passage where the hero is told what would be expected of him when he joined the East India Company's army:

> Think it over yourself, Percy. Can you thrash most fellows your own age? Can you run as far and as fast as most of them? Can you take a caning without whimpering over it? Do you feel, in fact, that you are able to go through fully as much as any of your companions? Are you good at planning a piece of mischief, and ready to take the lead in carrying it out? . . . It is pluck and endurance and the downright love of adventure and danger, that have made us the masters of the great part of India, and ere long makes us the rulers of the whole of it.

The values of the 1890s empire-builder have been transferred back to the 1840s.

Henty's ideal *beau sabreur* of empire was portrayed in embryo in Rudyard Kipling's *Stalky & Co.* This public school tale revolved around the pranks of Stalky and his cronies, a reckless, and at times ruthless band who cocked a snook at authority. They were just the fellows to run the empire, as one of them, Beetle, explained: 'India's full of Stalkies, Cheltenham and Haileybury and Marlborough chaps – that we don't know anything about, and the surprises will begin when there is a really big row on.' The point was taken up by a reviewer who claimed that Stalky and his cronies were 'the very men the Empire wants'.[8] Paradoxically, the figure on whom Stalky was modelled, Major-General Lionel Dunsterville, led a force that made an audacious attempt to seize the Baku oilfields in 1918; just the sort of exploit on which Henty would have hung a story.

The huge public fascination with the early stages of the Boer War was a godsend to Henty and his imitators. Christmas 1900 saw a cascade of boys' tales set in South Africa, including Henty's *With Buller in Natal*. The politics of these books was crude; Henty represented Britain as the 'greatest civilised power on earth' fighting against one 'without even the elements of civilisation, ignorant and brutal beyond any existing white community'.[9] An example of Boer depravity was revealed in Fox Russell's *The Boer's Blunder* (1900) in which the villain abducts an English girl and promises her sister to an African chief. Readers of Captain F.S. Brereton's *One of Our Fighting Scouts* (1903) were urged, at the end of the story, to follow the hero's example: 'If it is your fortune to take a rifle and go forth to fight for your king and country – may you keep your face to the enemy, and ride as boldly as did George Ransome, one of the Fighting Scouts.' Many had not needed such bidding. In the winter of 1899–1900 thousands came forward to volunteer for service in South Africa as imperial yeomanrymen like the 'large limbed Anglo-Saxon heroes' who sailed for the Cape with the future novelist and Irish patriot, Erskine Childers.[10]

Imperial propaganda of the gripping kind produced by Henty and his fellow wordsmiths was deliberately spread to all classes. Henty's publishers encouraged state and Sunday-school teachers to present his books as prizes, and thousands were duly presented. Working-class children could share in the adventures of their social superiors, learn about the deeds which shaped the empire, and absorb some of the imperial ideas. The new imperial ideology was already penetrating the elementary-school classrooms through the curriculum. Nearly all the geography learned by trainee teachers at Cavendish College, Cambridge in 1896 consisted of lists of colonies, details of how they were obtained, their products and accounts of their native inhabitants, all of which were passed on for their pupils to memorise. In the same year the recommended outlines of a lesson on South Africa drew attention to the primitive Calvinism of the Boers and their reluctance to wash frequently. As for the blacks, they 'have become reconciled to the inevitable supremacy of the whites' and had been taught to be 'useful servants'.[11]

Even the nursery was not closed to imperialism. *An ABC for Baby Patriots* published in 1899 included:

> *C is for Colonies*
> *Rightly we boast,*
> *That of all the great nations*
> *Great Britain has the most.*

While the infant mouthed this, its elder brothers and sisters battled with the brightly-painted lead soldiers which became so popular after 1890. There were plenty of imperial units: red-coated British infantrymen, sailors in straw hats, Sudanese in fezes, Bengal cavalry in turbans, and colonial horsemen in khaki and broad hats with turned-up brims. The fighting men came complete with the paraphernalia of modern war: cannon, machine-guns, heliographs and field ambulances.

There were plenty of real soldiers in exotic uniforms marching through London to celebrate Queen Victoria's Diamond Jubilee in 1897. Troops from every part of the empire took part in the festivities, which also included a review of the fleet at Spithead. The Jubilee was more than a display of imperial muscle; the Queen was at the heart of the empire and it was loyalty to her which helped give it a sense of cohesion. There was no other obvious bond to hold together white settlers from Canada or Australia who were now managing their own affairs; Indians governed from Delhi; Nigerians ruled by the privately-owned Royal Niger Company; and the subjects of protectorates and colonies ruled from Whitehall through local officials with the cooperation of their own chiefs. The Queen whose head appeared on their stamps and coins symbolised the unity of the empire. Her genuine, maternal care for her subjects (she had deliberately chosen Indian attendants for her household) was widely publicised.

There was plenty of entertaining imperial pageantry, though not on the same scale, before and after the 1897 Jubilee. Bands played and crowds cheered as the Grenadier Guards, dressed in the new khaki, marched through London in February 1885 on the first leg of their journey to the Sudan. As their train steamed out of Waterloo Station plate-layers waved their shovels, and there were hurrahs from workers in factories along the track. Guardsmen who stayed behind were hired out to take part in 'Lord' George Sanger's show *Khartoum*, which was performed at the Grand National Amphitheatre in London during March and included tableaux entitled 'The British Square at Abu Klea' and 'Gordon's Last Appeal to England'. Some of the audience may have been moved to buy an oleograph print of Gordon priced at sixpence (2.5p) and available at all stationers, or a superior version, together with a ballad 'A Song of Gallant Gordon', for three shillings (15p). Perhaps this was the portrait of Gordon which hung in Sherlock Holmes's Baker Street rooms.

Prints and pageants of battles had been popular for over a hundred years and would remain so. At the Crystal Palace in July 1898 a 'striking and well-executed' re-enactment of the recent fighting on the North-West Frontier was produced by soldiers from the Royal West Surrey Regiment, some dressed up as Pathans. This type of show was already being superseded; that year an enterprising journalist had taken a film camera to the Sudan, but his footage was destroyed or lost. Preparations were made to film the return to London in October of troops from the Sudan.[12] Such material, like sequences from the Boer War, was shown at fairgrounds and in the new cinemas.

Newsreels from the front, including shots of the battle of Spion Kop in January 1900, were the inevitable outcome of the intense public interest in imperial campaigns. The new cheap press offered extensive coverage by war correspondents whose style was vivid and punchy. Moreover, the spread of the telegraph network meant that details from even the most far-flung battlefields could reach Britain within twenty-four hours, the time it took for news of the Ndebele rebellion in Rhodesia (Zimbabwe) to appear in the London newspapers in June 1896.

Thrilling front-line reports in mass circulation newspapers, like the popular boys' magazines and stories, coloured the public's view of the empire. Photographs and sketches in the *Daily Graphic* during the 1896–8 Sudan War showed various battle scenes, British and Egyptian medical orderlies treating wounded Dervishes and, by way of a contrast to this humanity, skeletons of tribesmen massacred at the orders of the Khalifah Abdullah. Further confirmation that Britain was fighting for civilisation came with an illustration in June 1896 of Muslim chiefs in northern Nigeria, swearing on the *Quran* to renounce slavery.

Imperial themes and images were hijacked by advertising artists and copywriters. The results were often remarkably durable: a bearded sailor

WIDER STILL AND WIDER

and an ironclad of the 1890s still appear on the Players Navy Cut cigarette packet, and another Victorian warship is the trademark of England's Glory matches. It was the Boer War which gave advertisers their chance, and the public was soon swamped with cheery soldiers and sailors endorsing beef extracts, patent cure-alls and Colman's mustard. Manly, firm-jawed and moustachioed fighting men in khaki bestowed *machismo* on various brands of tobacco and cigarettes. Bovril led the field in patriotic puffs, offering a print of the relief of Ladysmith to buyers of a product which, if the testimonials from men at the front were to be believed, more or less kept alive the entire army in South Africa. One ingenious copywriter alleged that the letters BOVRIL traced out the lines of Lord Roberts's march through the Orange Free State.

The Boer War saw an unprecedented boom in the manufacture of every kind of patriotic souvenir. There were buttons with portraits of the leading commanders, whose features also stared from all kinds of commemorative pottery and cigarette cards. There were songs for music-hall patriots ranging from the sentimental 'The Boers have got my Daddy' to the swaggering 'Soldiers of the Queen'. What was an explosion of mass patriotism came to a hysterical climax in May 1900 when news came through that the town of Mafeking had been relieved. Everywhere the announcement prompted spontaneous and often abandoned celebrations, a nationwide street party which produced, hangovers apart, the word 'mafficking'.

Those who 'mafficked' were celebrating something more than the rescue of a comparatively insignificant garrison. The high jinks that May night were a mass release of tensions and a momentary dispersal of fears that had been deepened by the war. During the winter of 1899–1900 the army had suffered a series of unexpected and humiliating reverses, and the British people discovered that they were no longer invincible. Furthermore they were friendless, for all the great powers were hostile, particularly France and Germany. There had been a recovery on the battlefield in the spring of 1900, which raised national morale to the point where uninhibited festivities were in order, but their clamour did not drive away self-doubt.

To a large extent those who proclaimed the triumphs of empire were whistling in the dark. A nation which had been so full of self-confidence forty to fifty years earlier, when it had appeared the supreme force for mankind's improvement, was now tormented by apprehension. It was true that between 1890 and 1900 the empire had grown at an unprecedented rate; in Africa Britain had secured control over the Sudan, Uganda, Kenya, Nyasaland, Nigeria, Rhodesia, the Transvaal and the Orange Free State, making it the largest imperial power on the continent. And yet the newspapers and journals which chronicled these acquisitions were also filled with baleful analyses of what was wrong with the country.

The psychological roots of this critical introspection stretched back well into the century. Invasion scares were a regular occurrence and were usually accompanied by hair-raising tales of how Britain, for all its outward strength, could be overrun by a daring enemy. For instance, in 1871, a best-seller, Sir George Chesney's *The Battle of Dorking*, described a Prussian invasion and a whirlwind campaign that ended with the occupation of London. Soon after the end of the Boer War, Erskine Childers's thriller *The Riddle of the Sands* cleverly showed how a German fleet could steal across the North Sea undetected and support landings on the British coast. These were fantasies, usually written to shock the country into demanding extra cash for the army and navy's budget. But there were also plenty of sober appraisals of underlying weaknesses in Britain's economy and unfavourable comparisons of its performance with those of its rivals. There was, for instance, much heart-searching during the 1890s about the shortcomings in Britain's educational system which seemed to be pro-ducing a workforce inferior in aptitude to those of Germany and the United States.

As ever, the strength of the navy became the ultimate yardstick for Britain's relative power in the world. From 1878 France, Russia and Italy had adopted ambitious programmes of naval rearmament that soon had alarm bells ringing in Britain. The result was the 1889 Naval Defence Act, that confirmed the traditional two-power standard by which the Royal Navy's total of battleships equalled that of its two closest rivals. A naval race was now on, with Britain vying against France and Russia in build-ing battleships. The margin was always tight; in 1898 Britain possessed 52 battleships with 12 under construction, France and Russia 39, but with a further 18 on the stocks. Within six years, naval intelligence estimated, Britain's two rivals would have overtaken her. These disturbing figures took no account of Germany, which had 17 battleships and 5 being built.[13]

As the pace of the naval race gathered momentum, British strategists realised that their country no longer had enough ships to be strong everywhere. The shortfall was most apparent and dangerous in the

Mediterranean. In 1892 a Russian squadron had sailed through the Bosphorus and joined the French Mediterranean fleet at its Toulon base, a gesture designed to advertise the new alliance between the two powers and unnerve Britain. It did; the Admiralty was forced to admit that, given a war against France and Russia, the British fleet could not seize the Bosphorus, and so the Russian fleet was free to join their ally's whenever an emergency occurred. A year later Chamberlain declared to the Commons that the Royal Navy had ceased to control the Mediterranean.

The shifting balance of power in the Mediterranean endangered the Suez Canal and therefore threatened India. Here the appearance of Russian troops on the Afghan border in 1885 had re-awakened fears of an invasion. This was now more feasible than ever since railway construction in Central Asia directly linked the region with the Russian heartlands to the north. Most menacing of all, from an Indian standpoint, was the Orenburg to Tashkent line which was started in 1901. Within three years it was within 240 miles of its terminus, bringing the Russian rail network to within striking distance of the Afghan frontier. As Russia acquired the means to transport and supply a mass army for an attack on India, strategic planners in Delhi and London wrestled with the problems of defending the sub-continent. They came to no definite conclusions save that if local Anglo-Indian forces were to hold the Afghan passes, they would need substantial reinforcements from Britain, which would have to be carried by sea by way of the Suez Canal or the Cape. Additional forces would also be needed to keep order in India where, it was predicted, a Russian invasion would trigger mass disturbances.

There remained the uncomfortable fact that, in the event of an assault on India, Russia could mobilise 300,000 men within three months and launch them against an Anglo-Indian army of 95,000 holding a line between Kabul and Kandahar. Prestige demanded an aggressive stance in Afghanistan, but there was no way of knowing how the volatile Afghans would react to the intrusion. The outbreak of the Boer War further exposed India's vulnerability, since by the end of operations in South Africa Britain had had to commit 295,000 regular, reservist and volunteer troops to that theatre. The presence of thousands of Canadians, New Zealanders and Australians helped, but they could not disguise the fact that the imperial battleline was stretched to breaking point. There was a bad, but not unexpected attack of jitters when, in February 1900, the War Office received intelligence of Russian concentrations near the Afghan border.[14] The attack did not materialise, but the lesson was clear; had the

Russians moved against India there would not have been enough troops to counter them.

Britain entered the twentieth century as the world's greatest imperial power at least in terms of territory and population. The fact was widely trumpeted by politicians and journalists, along with platitudes about dispensing civilisation to those who lacked it. There was also a steady stream of reassuring propaganda which emphasised national greatness and the innate strengths of the Anglo-Saxon character. What effect all this had is difficult to measure precisely. Certainly, many exposed to the writings of Henty and his fellows emerged convinced that brawn mattered more than brains, and large numbers of them acted in a manner of which their boyhood heroes would have approved when they volunteered for war in 1914 and 1915.

Some, mostly on the left, were distressed by the brashness and belligerence of the new imperialism which, they believed, had made militarism fashionable and undermined national moral values. One critic regretted that the businessman of the 1890s asked the question, 'is it expedient and profitable?' unlike his mid-Victorian predecessor, who asked, 'is it right?' It is extremely doubtful whether the latter was ever so high-minded, but the middle years of the century had already become a golden age in the eyes of old-style, free trade Liberals. Among other faults of the new age was a middle class that indulged in 'speculation which necessitates new conquests of territories and constant acts of aggression' and 'that modern monstrosity and anachronism, the Conservative Working Man', who had 'exchanged his birthright of freedom and free thought for a pat on the head from any rump-fed lord that steps his way and spouts the platitudes of Cockney patriotism.'[15]

'Cockney patriotism' could drown the voices of those who believed they spoke with reason, but it quickly fell silent when there was nothing to celebrate. There was no mafficking during the tedious anti-guerrilla campaign in South Africa, which dragged on during 1901 and half of 1902. Indeed, politicians sometimes wondered whether the capriciousness of public opinion would prevent them from ever following through the long-term policies which were needed to renovate the country and consolidate the empire. Both were urgently required as the new century opened for, despite all the jingoes' rhetoric, Britain's former global pre-eminence could no longer be taken for granted. Kipling, who had become the poet of empire, sensed the new mood and struck a sombre note of warning in his *Recessional* of 1897:

God of our fathers, known of old,
Lord of our far-flung battle-line,
Beneath whose awful Hand we hold
Dominion over palm and pine —
Lord God of Hosts, be with us yet,
Lest we forget — lest we forget !

The tumult and the shouting dies;
The Captains and the Kings depart;
Still stands Thine ancient sacrifice,
An humble and a contrite heart.
Lord of Hosts, be with us yet,
Lest we forget — lest we forget!

Far-called, our navies melt away;
On dune and headland sinks the fire:
Lo, all our pomp of yesterday
Is one with Nineveh and Tyre!
Judge of the Nations, spare us yet,
Lest we forget — lest we forget!

If, drunk with sight of power, we loose
Wild tongues that have not Thee in awe,
Such boastings as the Gentiles use,
Or lesser breeds without the Law —
Lord of Hosts, be with us yet,
Lest we forget — lest we forget!

For heathen heart that puts her trust
In reeking tube and iron shard,
All valiant dust that builds on dust,
And guarding, calls not Thee to guard.
For frantic boast and foolish word —
Thy mercy on Thy People, Lord!

4

The Miracle
of the World:
India, 1815–1905

The Empire of India Exhibition, which opened at Earl's Court in 1895, captivated Londoners. It was a colourful imperial extravaganza, which suited the mood of the times and both educated and entertained. Indian scenery was reproduced and there were displays which reflected the country's past and present states. The overall theme was clear: modern India was the product of British patience and genius. This truth was spectacularly illustrated by 'India', a pageant performed daily in the adjacent Empress Theatre. The climax of the show was a glittering tableau entitled 'Grand Apotheosis: The Glorification of Victoria, the Empress Queen'. The Queen-Empress appeared in 'an allegorical car', drawn by white horses and accompanied by the symbolic figures of Love, Mercy, Wisdom, Science, Art, Commerce, Prosperity, and Happiness.[1] Dazzled, the audience would have left to stroll through the Indian gardens or eat at the curry house where, no doubt, they would have felt a thrill of pride in their country's achievements. British India was nothing less than 'the miracle of the world' according to the Marquess Curzon, who was appointed Viceroy in 1898.[2]

There was indeed something miraculous about the way in which less than a hundred thousand soldiers and administrators held in thrall two hundred and fifty million Indians. India also possessed elements of glamour and mystery which entranced the Victorians, and everyone sensed that ruling it gave Britain power and prestige. Furthermore, and this was made clear in the Earl's Court displays, everything that was good in India derived from Britain's influence. What had happened there during the past

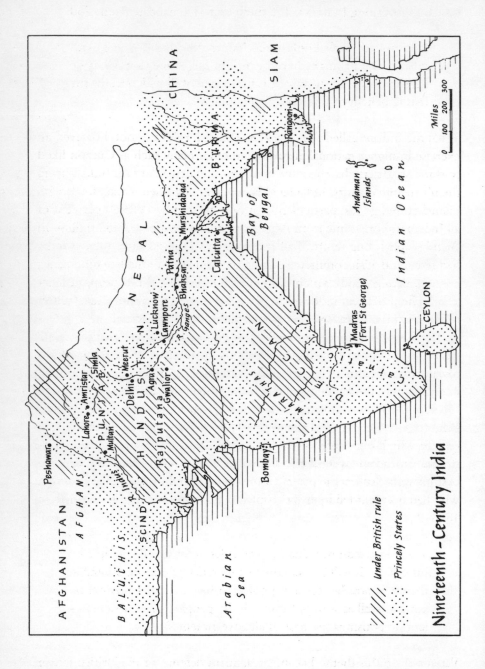

Nineteenth-Century India

Under British rule

Princely States

AFGHANISTAN

CHINA

SIAM

Arabian Sea

Indian Ocean

Bay of Bengal

CEYLON

BURMA

NEPAL

HINDUSTAN

Rajputana

PUNJAB

SCIND

BALUCHIS.

AFGHANS

DECCAN

Carnatic

Gujarat

MARATHAS

Peshawar

Lahore

Amritsar

Simla

Multan

Delhi

Meerut

Agra

Gwalior

Cawnpore

Lucknow

Patna

Bhaksat

Murshidabad

Calcutta

Bombay

Madras (Fort St George)

Rangoon

Andaman Islands

R. Indus

Ganges

Miles

0 100 200 300

hundred years was inspiring evidence of Britain's civilising mission. For Curzon, governing India was the fulfilment of a mandate from God:

> I do not see how Englishmen, contrasting India as it is with what it was or might have been, can fail to see that we came here in obedience to what I call a decree of Providence, for the lasting benefit of millions of the human race.[3]

What the Indians called the *angrezi raj* (English rule) was not, however, an exercise in higher national altruism, although many such as Curzon liked to think so. Britain had become economically dependent on India during the nineteenth century. India had become an unequalled market for British manufactured goods, particularly cottonware, and by 1913 60 per cent of all Indian imports came from Britain and it had absorbed £380 million in British capital, one tenth of all the country's overseas investments. India had rescued British commerce during the lean years of the late nineteenth century, taking goods which had previously been sold in European markets.[4] The process of modernising India, which gave so much satisfaction to the Victorians, was vital for balancing the books at home.

The history of India since 1815, as chronicled by the British, was a steady ascent from the depths of chaos, ignorance and backwardness towards the heights of peace, order and material progress. And yet, in many quarters, doubts lingered about the ambiguity of Britain's position in the country. How was it that a nation with liberal traditions and deeply-held convictions about personal liberty could maintain an authoritarian empire which ultimately rested on force? The answer was that the constraints on Indians were applied humanely by a régime devoted to their best interests. Autocratic paternalism was defended by Herbert Edwardes, who had been guided by its principles as a commissioner in the Punjab in 1848–9:

> There laws exist not, and he who rules, must rule the people by his *will*. If his will be evil, the people will be far more miserable than it is possible for any people to be . . . but if his will be good as well as strong, happy are the people . . . for a benevolent despotism is the best of all governments.[5]

Variations on this theme became a standard defence of the British raj for the next hundred years. The framework of Indian government meant the concentration of power in the hands of a few men, but their sense of duty and standards of honesty were such that they never acted capriciously or oppressed their subjects. This self-image of the men who ruled India was tirelessly promoted both in Britain and the subcontinent, and it contained much truth. And yet in the application of enlightenment, the administrators of India found themselves confronted with resistance from subjects who did not see things in the same way, and were deeply devoted to customs which their masters despised. A collision between rulers and ruled became inevitable as the Indian government turned its attention towards what it imagined to be the emancipation of India from its past.

After 1815 the old Company live-and-let-live approach to the governing of India was replaced by one which set great store by remoulding the country along Western lines. India became a sort of laboratory for current British liberal, evangelical and utilitarian theorists who sought, in various ways, to regenerate all mankind. John Stuart Mill, historian, pamphleteer, philosopher and, from 1823, a Company bureaucrat based in London, wanted above all to liberate the Indian mind. Native religions were the chief obstacle to this process:

> By a system of priestcraft, built upon the most enormous and tormenting superstition that ever harnessed and degraded any portion of mankind, their [the Indians'] minds were enchained more intolerably than their bodies; in short; despotism and priestcraft taken together, the Hindus, in mind and body, were the most enslaved portion of the human race.[6]

Using their dictatorial powers, humane British officials would sweep away these supernatural encumbrances on Indian thought. The poet and historian Thomas Macaulay, who was chairman of a committee formed in 1833 to consider future educational policy in India, predicted that Hinduism would wither away as Western learning spread across the country.[7] To accelerate this process, he insisted that all teaching was in English and based on English texts. With remarkable foresight, he claimed that exposure to British ideas and patterns of thinking would, in time, create an Indian élite which would demand self-government. Some years later, the Governor-General, Lord Ellenborough, remarked to a babu (an English-speaking Indian clerk), 'You know, if these gentlemen succeed in educating the natives of India, to the utmost extent of their desire, we should not remain in the country three months.' 'Not three weeks,' was the reply.[8]

British-style schools, run by missionaries, had been established in India by the mid-1820s. Evangelical pressure from, among others, Wilberforce, had persuaded the Company to allow missions in its territories despite fears of a Muslim backlash. Nevertheless, the directors allowed themselves to be overwhelmed by the familiar missionary lobby arguments that conversion would advance civilisation and create new customers for British products.

There was much that was crass in the thinking of those who imagined that they could remake India in the British mould. High-mindedness and an urge to improve often appeared like meddlesome arrogance, and this was all too apparent in the almost universal contempt shown towards India's existing culture and religions. Hinduism and its caste system were singled out for the worst abuse; one exasperated champion of progress declared that its polytheist followers displayed 'an ignorance and a credulity almost approaching idiocy'.[9] What was worse was that some Hindus stuck resolutely to their faith despite Western instruction. In 1824 Bishop Heber sensed divided loyalties after an Indian pupil at a mission school had shown him a shrine of Shiva, and explained the legends of different Hindu gods and goddesses. The enthusiasm of his discourse perturbed the cleric, who afterwards wondered whether Indian boys might become 'accomplished hypocrites, playing the part of Christian with us, and with their own people of zealous followers of Brahma'.[10]

The agitation of British political and religious theorists did push the Company in the direction of benevolent, paternalist policies which, by their nature, disturbed Indian society. Non-interference with native customs was abandoned and campaigns undertaken against religious rituals which offended European sensibilities. Under Lord William Bentinck, governor-general from 1828 to 1835, systematic measures were adopted to eradicate thagi (the Hindu cult of assassin-priests who preyed on travellers) and sati. The Thugs, as they were called, were all but eliminated by condign methods, as was sati, although there were still isolated cases being uncovered in the 1920s.[11] At the same time Company employees were encouraged to dissociate themselves from Hindu ceremonies and involvement in the administration of temples.

Nonetheless, passive tolerance had to be shown publicly to native religions. A handbook of advice for young officers, published in 1833, suggested that they would have to show forebearance towards their men's religions even though they were unwholesome. This had obviously been hard for the author, who later commented disparagingly about the 'self-venerating Hindu' and 'the bigotted Mussulman [Muslim]'. Such expressions became commoner in British works on India in the 1820s and 1830s, and provide hints of a growing gulf between the British and the Indians.

One indicator of shifting racial attitudes was a reduction of sexual con-tacts between British men and Indian women, which had been extremely frequent throughout the eighteenth century. On one level such behaviour was seen as condoning an indigenous morality and therefore unfitting for men whose duty was to serve as detached administrators and commanders. Indian sensuality revolted British churchmen who saw it as debilitating and potentially subversive. In 1816 one complained that young Christian men were morally undermined by India, succumbing to all its temptations even to the point of letting their faith lapse.[12] Eight years later Bishop Heber was glad to notice that keeping native mistresses was no longer 'a fashionable vice' among younger officials in Calcutta, although laxity of this and other kinds was thriving in remote districts.[13] The high-principled Metcalf, despite prizing that 'pure love which exists between man and man', had three sons by his native mistress, and General Ochterlony, the Resident in Delhi from 1803 to 1825, had a harem of thirteen concubines.[14]

There were plenty of busybodies who did what they could to stamp out such indulgences, but old habits proved resilient; a young officer who first arrived in India in 1834 recalled how he 'commenced a regular course of fucking' with delightfully uninhibited native girls who understood 'in perfection all the arts and wiles of love'. His example was later followed by among others, the explorer and anthropologist Sir Richard Burton, and the future field-marshals, Lords Roberts and Wolseley.[15]

These officers' conduct could be justified by the fact that they needed to know the languages of those they commanded, and a concubine could also serve as a schoolmistress. The sepoy army was, even in the era of reform, the chief prop of the British raj, as many of its officers were quick to point out. In 1837, one dismissed as nonsense any suggestion that the empire was one 'of opinion', that is, resting on native goodwill, rather than armed force.[16]

The era of tentative internal reform inside India was also one in which the Company consolidated and extended its authority. In 1818 the Mahrathas had been forced to submit, and in 1824 a part of the independent kingdom of Burma was annexed after a short war. By the 1830s attention was turn-ing towards India's northern borders, the powerful Sikh state of the Punjab, and the possibility of a Russian invasion. The question was whether the Indian frontier should lie on the Indus or be pushed forward into the Himalayan foothills, where the passes from Afghanistan debouched.

It was generally agreed in Calcutta that India's safety required a *cordon sanitaire* which encompassed Afghanistan. An attempt in 1838 to transform that country into an Indian dependency ended in catastrophe three years later, when the Kabul garrison was evicted and all but wiped out during a harrowing winter retreat down the Khyber Pass. It was a humiliating reverse which tarnished British prestige. The Governor-General, Lord Ellenborough, ordered General Sir George Pollock to restore its lustre through a series of raids deep into Afghan territory where villages, crops and livestock were destroyed.

The Afghan débâcle provided a pressing reason for the government to flex its muscles against the Baluchi amirs of Sind and the Sikhs. The latter were the most menacing, since they possessed the Khalsa, a well-disciplined and equipped modern army trained by imported European specialists, which astonished those who encountered it. General Sir Harry Smith reckoned the rapidity of fire and accuracy of the Sikh gunners equal to those of their French counterparts during the Peninsular War.[17] Another officer, present during the siege of Multan in 1848–9, paid the Sikh infantry the highest compliment possible by saying that they charged into battle 'like Britons'.[18]

The taming of the Baluchi tribesmen and the emasculation of Sikh power required three hard-fought campaigns: one against the Sind in 1843, and two against the Sikhs in 1845–6 and 1848–9. All were undertaken by commanders brimming with a self-confidence and an offensive spirit as strong as those of their eighteenth-century predecessors. 'Never give way to barbarians' was the motto of General Sir Charles Napier when his 2,400-strong army was faced with 35,000 Baluchis at the battle of Meanee. He placed his men behind barricades of straw bales and kneeling baggage camels, and put his faith in the Irishmen of his only British regiment, the 22nd. They were 'strong of body, high-blooded, fierce, impetuous soldiers' who, as he expected, terrified their adversaries with volleys of musketry and bayonet charges.[19] Beaten, the amirs submitted and Napier sent his famous punning message to Calcutta, 'Peccavi' (I have sinned).

The victory at Meanee confirmed the by now unshakeable belief that British power in India rested on the stamina and courage of the British soldier. Both qualities were tested to extremes during operations against the

Sikhs, largely because of the bungling of the commander-in-chief, Lord Gough. He was, according to Sir Harry Smith, 'a very stupid and obstinate old man', addicted to head-on charges with what he called, in his Irish brogue, 'could steel'. Smith feared that his men were not up to rushing the cannon's mouth since soldiers, like imported dogs and horses, 'deteriorate from John Bulls after a long residence in the ennervating plains of this relaxing climate'.[20]

His fears were well-grounded; after a victory at Aliwal, British troops had to pull back from the Punjab because of the hot season. Nevertheless self-assurance was at a high pitch during the second Sikh campaign; on the eve of the battle of Chillianwala in January 1849 an officer overheard British soldiers discussing the approaching fight 'in a tone of vaunting superiority'.[21] During the contemporary skirmishes in the siege-lines at Multan, Herbert Edwardes was struck by the ferocity of the British soldier in hand-to-hand combat. 'How like the deadly conflict of the lion and the tiger in a forest den was the grapple of the pale English soldier with the swarthy Sikh.'

The British soldiers in the Punjab owed some of their strength to the fact that they had been carried some of the distance to the battlefield, in some cases in barges pulled by shallow-draft paddlesteamers. The Indus squadron of steamers, employed in the Sind and Punjab campaigns, was a token of the quickness of the Company to utilise the new technology of the Industrial Revolution. A steamer had been used during the 1824 Burma War to great practical and psychological effect:

> The inhabitants observing the smoke, and hearing the noise, which they had never seen before, fancied we were bringing some infernal engine to destroy them, and ran in all directions towards the plains, carrying with them such light things as they valued.[22]

Puzzlement, alarm and dismay were common reactions of many Indians to the many less obvious changes to their lives being introduced by a determined and energetic government. A few tried to avert the new order. Early in 1832, a frightening conspiracy to massacre Europeans had been discovered at Bangalore. The ringleaders had exploited fears that the government was preparing for the mass conversion of Muslims to Christianity. Jolted by this unpleasant reminder of the fragility of British power, the local authorities turned the punishment of the chief culprits into a sombre public display of retribution. Four condemned men, all sepoys, were escorted to the place of execution by military bands playing the 'Dead March' from Handel's *Saul* and were tied to cannon barrels and blown to pieces. According to the superintendent of police, this spectacle 'struck much terror into all Classes, Civil and Military', and he felt certain that it would be a long time before further signs of resistance manifested themselves.[23]

This incident was quickly dismissed as an example of the waywardness of the native character and the particular naïveté of Muslims, who readily swallowed any rumour, however preposterous. The method of execution, traditional in India, also dramatically illustrated the internal contradictions of a 'despotism' which simultaneously boasted its humanity and enlightenment.

By this time, the spread of Western enlightenment was becoming one of the chief purposes of the government. It was a task for which it was not well-fitted. There was no uniform administration throughout the subcontinent: in the old Company presidencies of Bengal, Madras, and Bombay and their dependencies authority was exercised by district judges and collectors, while in other regions, native princes ruled under the guidance of British residents. A considerable part of administrative energy was consumed by the collection of land revenue from the rural peasantry. At the lowest level this was undertaken by local proprietors, the zamindars and taluqdars. Their powers had been confirmed and enhanced during the late eighteenth century when the government wanted to enlist the support of men of substance and influence. Reformers, including Mill, questioned this system, comparing the tax-collectors to leeches. But there was no alternative; in the fiscal year 1856–7, the Indian government's income was approximately £30 million, of which £16.7 million came from land revenues and nearly £7 million from salt and opium monopolies.

The raj therefore rested on the ability of its servants to extract the small surpluses made by peasant farmers, who at best lived a hand-to-mouth existence. Their cash provided the wherewithal for schemes designed to transform and regenerate their country. Land taxes funded the schools, and the metalled roads which from 1836 onwards radiated out from and connected the large centres of commerce and administration. Twenty years later, the government's investment programme included a railway network 3,000 miles in length and linking Calcutta with Delhi, Delhi with Peshawar, and Bombay with Nagpur. By the beginning of 1857 nearly three hundred miles of track had been laid and, in advance of the railway gangs, engineers had criss-crossed the country with 4,000 miles of tele-graph lines.

Roads, railways and telegraph wires symbolised the irreversible march of progress, probably more than the schools, colleges and teaching hospitals which were springing up in provincial capitals. For Indians who tried to fathom their meaning, these novelties were a source of unease. As the tempo of change quickened and the results began to affect new areas of everyday life, the old, persistent fear of forced conversion became stronger. When, in January 1857, a mob burned down the new telegraph office at Barrackpore, it did so because the building symbolised change imposed from above by an alien power.

During the winter of 1856–7 two new twists were given to the famil-iar tale of impending conversion. There was one widely credited report that the cartridges for the new Enfield rifle were greased with a blend of pork and beef fat, and another which alleged that the powdered bones of pigs and cows had been surreptitiously added to ration flour issued to the sepoys of the Bengal army. Both rumours were false, but what mattered was that they gave substance to hitherto vague fears that Christianity was about to be imposed.

Muslims and high-caste Hindus of the Bengal army were particularly susceptible to misgivings. Their elevated self-esteem had been eroded by new military regulations designed to promote efficiency, and they were perturbed by the new policy of recruitment of the 'traditional' warrior races of the Sind and Punjab. Sepoys born in Oude, where soldiering had long been regarded as an honourable occupation for Brahmins, for whom no other source of dignified labour existed, had an additional grievance. In 1853 the province had been peremptorily annexed by the Governor-General, Lord Dalhousie, who had ridden roughshod over Indian customary law by ignoring the rights of the nawab's adopted heir, Nana Sahib. This offered further proof that the government would stop at noth-ing to get its way.

These undercurrents of apprehension and anger broke surface at Meerut in the last week of May 1857 after sepoys had been publicly humiliated and punished for refusing to touch the by now infamous cartridges. One cav-alry and three infantry regiments spontaneously rebelled, ransacked the European cantonment and murdered several officers and their families. The insurgents fled to Delhi, seized the city and proclaimed the aged Badahur Shah, a descendant of the Mughals, Emperor of India. Then the mutineers paused to await the reactions of their countrymen and their rulers.

The raj had been challenged by its own soldiers with a suddenness which left everyone momentarily dazed. Prestige was at stake and the classic British response would have been a counter-attack, whatever the risks. But no hammer-blow struck Delhi until the second week of June, when a scratch force of 4,000 men, hastily assembled in the Punjab, arrived outside the city walls and began a blockade. Elsewhere administrators and generals decided to sit tight and, like the first mutineers, wait on events. Their pusillanimity was later condemned, but there was little else they could have done given the vast local disparity in numbers between British and Indian troops. In all there were 45,000 white and 232,000 Indian soldiers dispersed across the subcontinent. Of the 23,000 British and 136,000 Indians in Bengal and northern India, nearly all the British were concentrated in the newly annexed Punjab. There were only four white battalions scattered across the potentially disaffected districts, and no local commander was willing to relinquish his only insurance against a sepoy mutiny to attack Delhi.

So, at Agra, Cawnpore (Kanpur) and Lucknow the British withdrew behind makeshift defences, having wherever possible disarmed any sepoys whose loyalty looked shaky. The spirit of insurrection slowly spread out from Delhi, and by early July there had been uprisings in Aligahr, Benares, Jhansi, Gwalior and Indore. Sepoys attacked and murdered their officers and their wives and children, and they were joined by civilians who had in various ways been losers as a result of recent government changes. The dispossessed, like Nana Sahib and the Rani of Jhansi, were augmented by peasants whose marginal lands were overtaxed, soldiers from the disbanded army of Oude, Muslim holy men, and petty criminals and bandits for whom any collapse of authority was a chance to make a profit. One group, the Gujars, a caste of pastoral nomads living in the neighbourhood of Meerut and Delhi, stole from both sides.[24] Everywhere there prevailed a feeling that the raj, like the defenders of the three cities, was at bay.

It took roughly six weeks for British authority to dissolve throughout the upper Ganges and in the northern areas of central India. Then the Mutiny appeared to lose direction and run out of steam. This was probably inevitable since from the beginning it had lacked both overall leadership and a sense of purpose. Those who revolted were united only in what they hated and, for this reason, converged on the three beleaguered outposts of Agra, Cawnpore and Lucknow. These cities acted like magnets and embroiled the greater number of the rebels in prolonged sieges. At the same time, a large body of mutineers allowed itself to be trapped inside

Delhi by a smaller British army. The insurgents' advantages of surprise and numbers were therefore thrown away. There were two possible explanations for this inertia, the first the fact that perhaps the majority of rebels wanted loot, of which the greatest quantities lay within the cities, and the other was the nature of their movement. It was essentially a *jacquerie*, whose supporters were hitting back randomly against the figures and symbols of an authority they believed was changing their lives for the worse. They possessed no ideology, beyond Muslim appeals for an anti-British jihad, and from what is known had no alternative system of government for the districts they had temporarily liberated.

Attempts to enlist allies among magnates outside the immediate area of the outbreak made little headway since they were reluctant to declare themselves until they knew which way the war would go. This depended on the outcome of the sieges. These in turn consumed men who might have been better employed in guerrilla operations against the enemy's extended and fragile lines of communication to Calcutta. These were left alone and the British were given a breathing space in which to improvise armies and transport them and their supplies to the front in Oude.

From the end of July British troops began to pour into India. The government had asked for 39,000 from Britain, but these were not expected until the end of the year. In the meantime there were reinforcements from Burma, Mauritius and the China Expeditionary Force, which was diverted to Calcutta. The nature of the revolt made it obvious that white soldiers would restore a white man's raj, but there was invaluable assistance from Ghurkas and Sikhs, of whom there were 23,000 in arms by the end of the revolt.

Manpower shortages and innumerable transport hitches made life difficult for the commanders of field armies during the first counter-offensives in June, July and August. It was the hot season and when bullock carts, palanquins, river-boats and elephants were unavailable, men marched. Lieutenant George Barker of the 78th Highlanders, attached to General Sir Henry Havelock's column between Allahad and Cawnpore, estimated that more men died from sunstroke than mutineers' fire. Casualties from all causes, but mainly heat exhaustion and dysentery, were exceptionally high during the siege of Delhi, where in four weeks the 52nd Light Infantry were reduced from 600 to 242.

Only a superhuman will kept men in the field during these and later phases of the campaign. This was fuelled by a universal desire to take revenge on an inhuman foe who had murdered women and children.

Worst of all was the mass murder of civilians in Cawnpore, after they had been promised safe conduct by Nana Sahib at the end of June. Prisoners and anyone suspected of sympathising with or assisting the rebels were executed randomly, and at Cawnpore all those implicated in the massacre were defiled or stripped of their caste before being hanged. In the eyes of their captors the rebels were less than wild beasts and many eyewitness accounts of operations used hunting metaphors to describe the fighting. A gunner officer approvingly recorded the actions of a colleague who, on the march near Bareilly, suspected some mutineers of taking refuge in a field of corn. 'Forming his line precisely as he would have beaten a field of turnips for game, a scene commences which baffles all description: pea fowl, partridges, and Pandie [mutineers] rose together: the latter giving the best sport.'[25]

Through ruthlessness and iron stamina the British were getting the upper hand by early autumn. The turning point was the capture of Delhi on 19 September, a psychological blow which 30,000 or more rebels had anticipated when they deserted the city in the four weeks before the final assault. Further south, Havelock and General Sir James Outram cut their way through to Cawnpore and relieved Lucknow, but were trapped there by superior numbers of the mutineers. In October, the siege of Agra was raised by a column from Delhi and a month later the garrison and civilian population of Lucknow was evacuated. The war of containment was ending, and as the new year approached preparations were in hand for the campaign of pacification under the new commander-in-chief, General Sir Colin Campbell, a grizzled Glaswegian veteran who had first seen action as a fifteen-year-old ensign in Portugal in 1808.

1858 saw the crushing of almost all the remaining resistance. Campbell with 20,000 men advanced on Lucknow, which was retaken in March, and smaller-scale subsidiary operations pacified the outlying centres of the revolt, Rohilkhand, Gwalior and Jhansi, whose Amazonian rani was killed in a cavalry skirmish.

Participants in the war had no doubt as to why the raj had triumphed. One evening during the campaign in Oude, Garnet Wolseley, then a junior officer, had watched some Sikhs exercising with clubs and had been impressed by their physiques and dexterity. He turned to the strongest British soldier in his company and asked if he could match them. 'No sir,' was the reply. 'But I'll fight any three of those fellows.' Remembering the episode over forty years later, Wolseley concluded, 'It is that belief in the superior pluck and fighting qualities of our race that won us India and still enables us to hold it. Had our men no such confidence in themselves we should never have relieved Lucknow nor retaken Delhi.'[26] And yet, as his anecdote suggests, there were plenty of Indians willing to stand by the raj.

The Indian Mutiny was a civil war. Thousands of Indians fought alongside the British, including traditionally militant Pathans from the North-West Frontier, who defied calls to fight for Islam against the infidels. Dost Muhammad, the Afghan amir and no friend of Britain, made no hostile move. Others who had suffered at the hands of the British also refused to commit themselves; Judge George Edmondson, a fugitive in June 1857, found one prince willing to assist him even though the government 'had reduced his army and taken away his guns'.[27] Like many other benevolent neutrals, this magnate recognised that the Mutiny was primarily a soldiers' rebellion, which had temporarily got out of hand because the government lacked the forces to contain it. It was localised, negative in its objectives, destructive in nature and therefore limited in appeal.

The Mutiny pushed India into the forefront of British political life and there was much heart-searching as to what had gone wrong and why. The immediate result was the dissolution of the East India Company in 1858. Henceforward, a secretary of state and ultimately parliament were responsible for the government of India, with local law and policy-making in the hands of a viceroy and provincial governor-generals, assisted by councils composed of bureaucrats and a handful of Indian princes. Admission to a reconstituted Indian civil service was through an examination and was, theoretically, open to educated Indians.

In the year of the Mutiny twelve Indian doctors had graduated from the newly-founded medical school at Agra, a fact which would have more long-term significance for India's future than the battles in the Oude. These doctors would join a steadily growing élite of educated Indians who had undergone instruction in English in government schools, colleges and universities. By the mid-1880s it was estimated that there were 8,000 Indians with degrees and a further half a million who had graduated from secondary schools. All had been taught in English and had been exposed to British political ideas.

The experience of one Western-trained Indian, Romesh Chunder Dutt, is instructive, not only about the type of education available to Indians but its effect on their thinking about themselves and their country. Dutt was born in Calcutta in 1848, the son of a middle-ranking administrator, whose family had become westernised through several generations of service to the Company. Dutt attended school until he was sixteen, developing a fondness for English literature, in particular the historical romances of Sir Walter Scott. He proceeded to University College, Calcutta, then highly popular with the sons of priests, government clerks, merchants and zamindars, and set his sights on entry to the Indian civil service. To this end he travelled to London to cram for an exam geared for English entrants – Latin and Greek carried higher marks than Arabic and Sanskrit.[28] He passed, well up the list, and entered the Middle Temple.

Dutt was fascinated by British life. He travelled widely while studying, once touring Scotland to view scenes familiar from his reading of Scott, and took an intense interest in British political life. He witnessed the 1868 general election, parliament in action, and had discussed Indian affairs with British Radicals and Liberals, including John Bright who had championed Indian causes in the Commons. Then and later, Indian students gravitated towards those British progressive circles which were anti-imperialist in sentiment.

When Dutt returned to take up his administrative duties in Bengal in 1871, he was keen to apply the liberal principles of self help and enlightened self-interest which he had absorbed in Britain. Furthermore, he hoped that he could show the British that an educated Indian was equally adept as them in the arts of government, and that India could be changed from *within* by Indians as well as from above. What he had observed in Britain gave him a powerful sense of what could be achieved by the middle class and he had returned home convinced that its Indian equivalent deserved the same political power. Dutt's intellectual development and the conclusions he reached were similar to those of many other educated Indians, who believed that what they had learned gave them equality with the British.

This was certainly not a view shared by the majority of the British in India. There were widespread protests in 1883 at a government proposal to extend the jurisdiction of Indian local magistrates to Europeans, and the Viceroy, Lord Ripon, was forced to withdraw the measure. Educated Indians felt affronted at what was an assertion of racial superiority. This slight led indirectly to the formation in 1885 of the Indian National Congress, an association of educated Indians from all professions, which met annually to discuss issues relating to their country. In its early days it was compared to an earnest public-school debating club, but its membership soon grew and by the end of the century it had become an influential forum for Indian opinion.

The emergence of what was essentially a highly respectable and respectful assembly of Indians imbued with British political ideas caused some alarm. Ripon's successor, Lord Dufferin, a Liberal appointee, had no time for the 'Bengali Babu', whom he found 'a most irritating and troublesome gentleman'. He also detected a 'Celtic perverseness, vivacity and cunning' among educated Indians, qualities which he believed they shared with contemporary Irish nationalists. Certainly there was much in common between the proto-Indian nationalists and their Irish counterparts: both lobbied sympathisers in Britain and knew how to manipulate public opinion through the press and public meetings. The Indians did not, however, go as far as the Irish in their demands, which were largely confined to the assimilation of more and more of their educated countrymen into the middle and higher ranks of the government.

Of course, this was rightly seen as the prelude to Indian self-government, which was why Curzon (viceroy from 1898 to 1905) steadfastly refused to consider greater Indian participation in government. He rejected in forthright terms the request made by Dutt, Congress president in 1901, for the appointment of Indians to the viceregal council. The Marquess's adamantine position on the advancement of Indians to senior posts, and his well-known view that the Congress was an unrepresentative and disruptive body, had the effect of beginning its metamorphosis into a focus for active political opposition to the raj.

A collision between westernised Indians and the government had been predicted at the onset of the government's educational reforms in the 1830s. Although in many ways a despotism, British India had never been a totalitarian state in which the government proscribed books, newspapers and foreign travel and banned political debate. If Indians were allowed free access to British political and philosophical writers, it was inevitable that they would apply what they read to their own country, and ask why they were excluded from those political rights which were their rulers' birthright. It was a tricky question which Curzon and those of like mind could only answer with reference to the peculiar conditions of India. Divisions of religion, wealth, caste and clan were so profound and a source of so much fission that only a disinterested and fairminded British government could command the loyalty of all Indians, protect them and secure internal order. Reference was frequently made to the state of India before British rule when life had been precarious and anarchy was endemic. Above all was the fear that democracy and moves towards self-determination would, in the words of Sir Michael O'Dwyer, a rigorous and plain-dealing administrator who served in India from 1885 to 1919, release 'the demon of discord' so that the country would be convulsed by 'all the latent feuds and hatreds' hitherto reined in by men of his stamp.[29]

On another and all-too-common level, Indian aspirations towards self-determination were countered on racial grounds. These were candidly expressed by Major-General Sir Francis Younghusband, who served with the Indian army intermittently between 1878 and 1918:

It is never wise to stand studied impertinence, or even the semblance of it, from any Oriental. Politeness, and courtesy, by all means, and even camaraderie, as long as these are reciprocated, and all is fair, and square, and above board. But the moment there is a sign of revolt, mutiny, or treachery, of which the symptoms not unusually are a swollen head, and a tendency to incivility, it is wise to hit the Oriental straight between the eyes, and to keep on hitting him thus, till he appreciates exactly what he is, and who is who.[30]

Younghusband spent some time putting this doctrine into practice on the northern frontiers of India in the endless small wars of punishment and pacification. Their common purpose was summed up by one of Younghusband's colleagues after a bout with the Chins of the Assam frontier when he had taught them 'that the only thing that mattered was the Great White Queen across the waters'.[31] Resistance was toughest and most persistent among the tribes along the North-West Frontier, a remote, mountainous region where British control was always precarious.

There was a special romance about the North-West Frontier campaigns largely because they were contests in which the British usually managed to overcome brave, resourceful and daring warriors on their home ground. Of course technology mattered and probably tipped the balance, but there were plenty of close shaves, since the tribesmen were adept at ambushes. Two campaigns were needed in 1888 and 1890 against the recidivists of the Hazara district, who defiantly refused to pay fines for raiding and sniped at patrols. On the first occasion 14,000 men were sent against them, and on the second, 8,000, of whom at least a quarter were British, a custom established after the Mutiny.

This was a highly specialised form of warfare in which every use was made of up-to-date technology. The two Hazara forces used the field telegraph for communication between commanders and columns, and were armed with Gatling machine-guns, breech-loading rifles with a range of up to 1,000 yards, and small, collapsible mountain guns (the 'screw guns' of Kipling's poem) which were carried by mules. Despite the weight of firepower, charging tribesmen armed with swords and knives sometimes careered into British lines and caused havoc. This occurred during a skirmish during the 1890 Hazara campaign, when, according to the official report, a British officer 'engaged in combat with two fanatics, one of whom he killed, but was wounded by a second, a big powerful man, who almost overpowered him'.[32] In 1895, seasoned frontier fighters were perturbed by the allegations that the new .303 rifle bullet lacked the stopping power of the old .457. Secret forensic tests were therefore carried out on the corpses of Pathan mullahs, who had been executed by firing squads using the two types of ammunition, to discover their relative merits.[33]

Grisly details like this were deliberately kept from the public in Britain, who were also kept in the dark about the full extent of the systematic burning of villages, crops and granaries, and the slaughter of livestock which marked every frontier operation. Instead, newspaper reports and eyewitness accounts like Winston Churchill's popular *Malakand Field Force* (1897) presented the wars as tales of derring-do and adventure. When justification was offered it was in familiar terms of quite literally pushing back the frontiers of civilisation. The North-West Frontier wars (there were nearly twenty between 1863 and 1901) were a glamorous and headline-catching feature of a grander, often more mundane business, the government and regeneration of India.

5

They Little Know Our Strength: The Far East and the Pacific

Claydon House in Buckinghamshire contains a Chinese room embellished in a style which brings together Chinese and rococo motifs. It was created in the 1760s when men of discrimination looked on China with awe and wonderment. It was an ancient, orderly civilisation whose artefacts, particularly porcelain, were prized by collectors and imitated by craftsmen like those employed at Claydon. China tea, imported by the East India Company, was well on the way to becoming a daily palliative for all classes. Within eighty years attitudes to China had changed radically. A popular encyclopaedia published in 1842 said little on Chinese civilisation, but instead described China as 'an unbounded mart' with a population clamouring for British goods. These were denied them by their rulers, who refused to recognise the benefits of free trade and had gone as far as to exclude British commerce.[1]

Opium rather than manufactured goods was what the Chinese people demanded. The felicitous combination of the British taste for tea and the Chinese for opium had been exploited by the East India Company which, since 1773, had enjoyed a monopoly over the drug's production. The rise of the opium trade coincided with a period of Chinese decline. By 1800 China had become a static, introverted society governed by an intensely conservative and ossified bureaucracy. The Ching dynasty of emperors were Manchus, outsiders who found it hard to rally their Chinese subjects at moments of crisis. But rulers and ruled were united by a common mistrust of all foreigners, whom they designated 'barbarians' and treated with condescension. This had been amply demonstrated in 1793 and 1816 when two British missions, headed by Lords Macartney and Amherst, had travelled to Peking in an attempt to establish formal diplomatic relations between Britain and China. Both embassies were politely cold-shouldered, and departed in no doubt that they had been regarded as representatives of some distant, tributary state.

Given Chinese insularity and apprehension of all things alien, it was inevitable that a clash would occur with Britain, which believed it had a right to conduct unrestricted trade throughout the world. The first collision occurred in the spring of 1839 at Canton, the main port open to foreign commerce. The Chinese imperial government, disturbed by the harmful social and economic consequences of opium addiction, decided to curtail the trade and instructed Commissioner Lin Tse-hsü to cut it off at its source, Canton. His measures provoked an angry response from Captain Charles Elliot, the Superintendent of Trade, and when news of them reached London, the government came under pressure from companies with Chinese interests. Lin's behaviour was represented as another example of Chinese obstructiveness and a direct challenge to the principles of free trade. The Foreign Secretary, Lord Palmerston, therefore authorised the despatch of a seaborne expeditionary force to the mouth of the Canton River.

Today the First Opium War (1839–42) is commonly portrayed as a shameful act of aggression contrived to promote a trade which was immoral, and to which the Chinese government had rightly taken exception. Contemporaries regarded the war and its successors as highly praiseworthy enterprises undertaken as a final resort. The fault lay with the Chinese who had formerly connived at the trade at the same time as treating Britain and its merchants in a high-handed manner. The war was therefore seen as a showdown in which Britain, its patience exhausted, revealed its muscle in the hope that, thereafter, a chastened Chinese government would prove more amenable to perfectly reasonable demands.

The war was a severe shock to the Chinese who knew nothing of the technology of their adversaries. In every engagement the Chinese were, in the words of an eyewitness, 'unable to contend against the fearful weapons of their determined foe'. He had been astonished when, during the early fighting, a Congreve war rocket struck a junk which then caught fire and exploded, killing all its crew.[2] When the British landed at Amoy in

September 1841 they suffered no losses, but their musket volleys killed at least a hundred Chinese who were armed with matchlocks and bladed weapons.[3]

At the start of the war operations were confined to the Canton River. Hong Kong island was seized and annexed as a future naval base and commercial centre. There followed a sustained demonstration of firepower on the Yangtze River, devised to show the imperial government the hopelessness of further resistance. During June and July 1842 Woosung, Shanghai and Chinkiang were shelled and taken by landing forces. It was a tough campaign, fought in the hot season, and there were heavy British losses from sunstroke, malaria, dysentery and cholera. Of the thirty-four men killed during the capture of Chinkiang, sixteen died from heat exhaustion.[4]

The Yangtze campaign paid off politically. A stunned Chinese government signed the Treaty of Nanking which confirmed British possession of Hong Kong and opened Canton, Amoy, Foochow, Shanghai and Ningpo to British commerce. The apparatus of unofficial empire was soon in place: consulates were established; British subjects were allowed exemption from Chinese jurisdiction; a naval base with coaling facilities was set up at Shanghai; and British men-o'-war were permitted to patrol Chinese rivers and coastal waters. France and the United States quickly followed Britain's example and were granted similar privileges.

The Opium War had far-reaching consequences for the history of the Far East. China's technical backwardness and vulnerability had been exposed and Britain had made itself the major commercial and military power in the region. In 1853, when the American Admiral Perry visited Japan to persuade its rulers to open their country to Western trade, he warned them if they did not, then the British would appear and treat Japan as they had China. The Japanese wisely conceded, and within a few years had made commercial agreements with the Western powers, including Britain.

Having dragged China into the informal empire, Britain turned its attention to making it safe for trade by the suppression of riverine and coastal piracy. This was exciting and rewarding work; in 1849 one squadron of warships earned £42,000 in head-money which was calculated at £20 for each dead or captured pirate and £5 for each of those who escaped. Actions were brief and brisk and their flavour is captured in an official report of an engagement between the steamer HMS *Hermes* and five junks near Hong Kong in March 1853. Proceeding under sail, the

Hermes lured the pirates towards her until, realising their mistake, they scattered and three got away. The remaining two:

> Finding they could not escape, closed and lashed themselves together, prepared to fight, and sent men aloft to throw stink pots [primitive hand-grenades which emitted a noisome smoke] as we ranged up alongside them, firing musketry; as we closed they put their helms hard over and got under our bows, and commenced throwing stink pots most furiously, when we backed off and opened fire on them . . . offering to cease if they would yield, but they would not. Finally, having driven them below with Grape, Canister and Musketry, Lieutenant Burton boarded and got possession.

Twenty-eight pirates had been shot or drowned and a further fifty-seven, all in red turbans and red-trimmed robes, were taken prisoner. Forty-five pirates were estimated to have escaped and so, in all, the *Hermes*'s crew were entitled to £1,755. Save for a few sailors scalded by the stink pots, there were no British casualties.[5]

This incident in the war against piracy occurred at a time when Sino-British relations were deteriorating. The flashpoint came in 1856 when Cantonese soldiers, searching for a pirate, boarded the British-registered *Arrow* and hauled down its flag. The legal grounds for claiming the *Arrow* as British were flimsy, but this did not deter John Bowring, the consul in Canton, from using the affair to provoke a trial of strength with the local Chinese commissioner, Yeh Ming-chin. Yeh had never hidden his disdain for all foreigners, and for some time had done everything in his power to exclude them and their goods from Canton. Bowring was equally stiff-necked and summoned a flotilla which shelled the city to show Yeh and its inhabitants the folly of interrupting trade.

Like its predecessor, the Second Opium War of 1856–8 was an exercise in intimidation. This time, however, the French collaborated, using as their excuse the murder of a missionary, a ploy they adopted to justify simultaneous aggression in Annam and Cambodia. While Anglo-French forces battered ports along the Canton River, Lord Elgin was ordered to China with powers to settle outstanding differences between Britain and its government. The result was the Treaty of Tientsin of 1858 which granted fresh concessions to foreign business interests and legalised the opium trade.

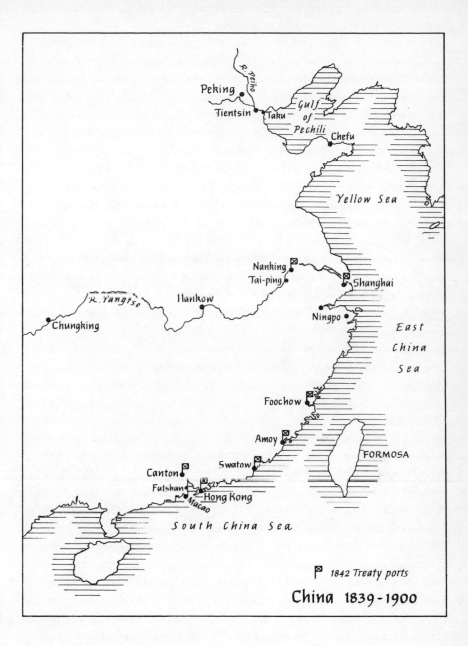

Peking

R. Peiho

Tientsin

Taku

Gulf
of
Pechili

Chefu

Yellow Sea

Nanking

Tai-ping

Shanghai

Harkow

R. Yangtse

Ningpo

East
China
Sea

Chungking

Foochow

Amoy

FORMOSA

Canton

Swatow

Fuishan

Hong Kong

Macao

South China Sea

⚑   1842 Treaty ports

China 1839-1900

What the British and French interpreted as Chinese stone-walling and prevarication over enforcing various clauses in this treaty led to a final application of *force majeure* in 1859–60. An Anglo-Indian and French army landed in north China and marched on Peking. Again modern weaponry triumphed over mediaeval: Robert Swinhoe, an interpreter, was impressed by the unflinching fortitude of the Tartar cavalry who refused to retire under close-range shellfire. 'Poor heathens!' he wrote later. 'They little know our strength although they have shown themselves brave fellows.' Another 'brave fellow', Private Moyes of the Buffs, won undying fame after he had been beheaded for refusing to kow-tow to the Mongol general, Prince Seng-ko-lin-chin. Moyes's defiant courage made him an ideal model for imperial manhood and was celebrated in Sir Francis Doyle's stirring poem, 'A Private of the Buffs':

> Last night among his fellow roughs
> He jested, quaffed and swore,
> A drunken private of the Buffs
> Who never looked before.
> Today beneath the foeman's frown
> He stands in Elgin's place,
> Ambassador from England's crown,
> And type for all her race.[6]

Other, less worthy examples of soldierly conduct marked the advance on Peking. Looting became endemic and Swinhoe was amused to see provost-sergeants joining in. The big prizes lay inside the imperial palaces in Peking which were precipitately abandoned by the Emperor Hsien-feng and his court in October 1860. According to Swinhoe, the French were first off the mark in what soon became a general free-for-all. On entering the Emperor's throne room he found 'the floor covered with the choicest curios' which were being sifted through by General de Montauban, who was making piles of presents for Queen Victoria and Napoleon III.[7] Shortly after, the summer palace was burned down at the instructions of Elgin as a reprisal for the torture and murder of several emissaries and their escort.

The plundering of Peking and the destruction of the summer palace symbolised the prostration of China. She had been hammered in three wars and driven to submit to forces which few of her people or rulers could comprehend. As the country with most to gain from a pliant China, Britain had taken the lead in this process of humiliation, although by 1860 she had been joined by France, which was already infiltrating Indo-China, and Russia, which had its eyes on Korea and territory along China's northern boundaries. Britain had no interest in annexation, save for Hong Kong and the adjacent Kowloon peninsula; all she had ever wanted was unrestricted access to China's trade.

For forty years after 1860 Britain dominated China's commerce. In 1895 Britain enjoyed two-thirds of all China's foreign trade, which then totalled £53.2 million. Opium remained at the head of the list of China's imports, accounting for an average of £10 million a year during the 1880s, with Lancashire cottonware in second place with an annual value of about £3 million. As well as having a near-monopoly of China's markets, Britain had a stranglehold on the Chinese customs. These had passed under foreign control in 1853 as an emergency measure when Taiping insurgents threatened Shanghai. Twenty years later the entire Chinese customs service was managed by Sir Robert Hart, who had a staff of eighty-nine Europeans of whom more than half were British. This supervision guaranteed the government a reliable source of revenue and was also a safeguard for foreign capitalists. In a passage which gives an insight into the mind of British investors, the *Economist* of 15 January 1898 commented that, 'The Customs Houses of China are within reach of British shells', which presumably might be fired if its government defaulted on its loans.

British political paramountcy in China ended in 1895. The sudden and complete collapse of China in the 1894–5 Sino-Japanese War signalled the country's weakness, to the rest of the world. Japan was the first to take advantage, with demands for sovereignty over Formosa (Taiwan), a £35-million indemnity and the Liaotung Peninsula. This last was withdrawn after protests from France, Russia and Germany, who had combined in a cynical conspiracy to protect China. In return, a grateful Chinese government granted France mineral rights in Yunnan, Kwangsi and Kwantung and Hankow was delivered to Germany. Russia, already dreaming of an empire in Manchuria, was allowed a controlling stake (paid for by the Czar's treasury) in the Chinese Eastern Railway which, when finished, would connect northern China with the eastern terminus of the projected Trans-Siberian Railway.

In 1897 Germany put in a bid for more territory, using the by now well-worn excuse of murdered missionaries, this time in Shantung. Their deaths opened the way for the German occupation of Kiachow, which was turned into a naval base, and a monopoly of investment in mines and railways in Shantung. Russia, sensing that the 'scramble for China' had begun, slipped into Port Arthur in March 1898, two years after she had helped shift the Japanese out.

These brutal manifestations of the new imperialism caused dismay in Britain. Hitherto British governments, confident in the knowledge that their businessmen enjoyed supremacy in China, had supported a free-trade-for-all-comers policy, and turned a blind eye to French and Russian efforts to lop off China's outlying tributary provinces, Indo-China and Korea. The events of 1897–8 suggested that China, like Africa, would be partitioned with the result that Britain would lose markets. The encroachments of protectionist Russia posed the most serious threat; the Trans-Siberian railway would facilitate mass emigration to underpopulated eastern Russia and, once its branch lines to the south had been laid, would serve as a conduit for China's trade with Europe, which had previously been carried by British ships.

After statements that it had no territorial claims to China, the Marquess of Salisbury's government announced in April 1898 that it had leased Wei-heiwei on the coast of north China as a naval base. At the same time a promise that no other power would be allowed concessions in the Yangtze basin had been extracted from Peking. Not that this counted for much, since soon afterwards China approved the Russian-funded Hankow-Peking railway which infringed Britain's local investment monopoly. Fears of further confrontations led to the reinforcement of the Far Eastern squadron, which was increased to three battleships and ten cruisers, making it equal to combined Franco-Russian fleets in the area.

Salisbury feared that defending Britain's informal, commercial empire in China would stretch the country's resources to breaking point.[8] Britain was currently embroiled in the conquest of the Sudan, was preparing for a showdown with France on the upper Nile, and was on a collision course with the Boer republics in South Africa. The transfer of warships to the China station depleted the home and Mediterranean fleets, but Britain could not afford to let Germany, Russia and France do as they wished in China.

The quickening pace of foreign penetration provoked popular resistance inside China. There had been spasms of violent xenophobia, largely directed against missionaries in 1891–2, and by the end of 1898 a new anti-foreigner movement had emerged, the I-ho chüan (Righteous and Harmonious Fists), or Boxers. Its members hated all Europeans, Chinese Christians and anyone who used alien manufactures. The Boxers boasted magical powers which made them immune to bullets, and possessed what turned out to be a suicidal addiction to fighting with traditional swords and spears. They were, initially, anti-Manchu, but their obscurantist ideology won them friends among the ultra-conservatives at court and in the government. The sympathetic governor of Shansi, Yü-hsien, incorporated the Boxers in the local militia and then unleashed them on foreign missionaries and their converts.

By the beginning of 1900 the Dowager Empress, Tzu-hsi, had cobbled together an alliance with the Boxers in order to deflect popular anger away from the dynasty and towards the foreigners. It was a shortsighted and self-defeating policy since the Chinese government's ambivalence towards the Boxers was already serving to draw more and more British, French, German, Russian and American warships to the Gulf of Chihli. Fearing an allied advance on Peking, Tzu-hsi finally took the plunge on 18 June and committed imperial troops to join 30,000 Boxers in an attack on the walled legation quarter of Peking.

This was madness and the Empress's pro-Boxer policy was swiftly repudiated by the more realistic provincial mandarins. More importantly, from the viewpoint of the few hundred defenders of the legations, General Jung-lu refused to lend the defenders his modern artillery. On 14 August an international army, 18,000-strong, entered Peking and relieved the legations.

The Boxer troubles were a godsend for Russia. They provided the excuse to pour 200,000 troops into Manchuria and to transfer warships from the Baltic to Vladivostok and Port Arthur. Mutual distrust between Britain and Russia was as strong as ever, but there were strategic restraints on how far the British government could go to frustrate the annexation of Manchuria and preserve the *status quo* in China. During 1900 and 1901 the Admiralty just managed to maintain naval parity with France and Russia, but at the cost of reducing the numbers of the home and Mediterranean fleets. The only answer lay in reaching an accommodation with Japan, which was forcefully contesting Russian claims to Manchuria and Korea.

The Anglo-Japanese alliance of January 1902 allowed Britain to withdraw from the Far Eastern naval race. Each power promised to assist its partner if it was attacked by two or more countries, an arrangement which left Japan free to go to war with Russia without fear of French intervention. In terms of the history of the British empire, the accord with Japan was a turning point. Britain had been forced to admit that she could no longer maintain her paramountcy in China singlehandedly, and henceforward her informal empire there would depend upon the goodwill and cooperation of Japan.

Nevertheless, the short-term results of the alliance were invaluable. In February 1904 Japanese warships made a pre-emptive strike against the Russian squadron at Port Arthur, the first of an amazing sequence of land and sea actions which shattered Russia's dreams of a Far Eastern empire and overturned the local balance of power. Russia's humiliation was greeted with undisguised pleasure throughout Britain and the alliance with Japan, now a vital prop to British pretensions in the Far East, was renewed in 1911. For the people of this region, and for that matter the rest of Asia, Japan's victory had a far greater significance. Japan, an Asiatic power, had proved that European armies and navies were not invincible; the trend of over a hundred years had been reversed.

Elsewhere in the Far East and in the Pacific the nineteenth century witnessed the gradual replacement of informal by formal empire. In the early 1800s Malaya and the islands of the East Indies had attracted a handful of energetic, ambitious young opportunists: Sir Stamford Raffles, John Clunies-Ross, Alexander Hare and Sir James Brooke. All were animated by the spirit and vision of Clive and, like him, had a peculiar knack of turning local circumstances to their own and their country's advantage. Dutch power was in eclipse and the small independent states of Malaya and Borneo were fragile and therefore keen to obtain British friendship and armed assistance.

Raffles, frustrated of the chance of starting an empire for the East India Company in Java, laid the foundations of another in Malaya by acquiring Singapore island in 1819. Placed athwart trade routes between India and China, Singapore soon became a major free trade *entrepôt* for South-East Asia and the East Indies. Hare tried to establish himself as an independent prince in southern Borneo, but failed, while his partner, Clunies-Ross, finally ended up as 'king' of the Cocos-Keeling islands in the Indian Ocean. Their enterprise inspired another romantic swashbuckler, James Brooke. Something of a misfit in England, Brooke had sought service with the East India Company's army and had been invalided out as a result of wounds received leading a charge of irregular horse in the Burma War.

Brooke's lucky break came in 1833, when he inherited £10,000 which provided him with the wherewithal to launch a venture designed to acquire territory and open trade on the coasts of northern Borneo. There was something distinctly Elizabethan about Brooke and his scheme, but it had the passive support of the East India Company and the Admiralty.

Brooke's greatest assets were his audacity, singlemindedness and the well-armed, 142-ton schooner, appropriately named *Royalist*, which made him a power to be reckoned with in regional politics. Between his first reconnaissance of the shores and creeks of northern Borneo in 1839 and 1841, Brooke had made himself indispensable to Hasim Jeal, the regent of Brunei, who was attempting to bring the province of Sarawak to heel. When Hasim feared that Brooke might desert him, he installed him as Rajah of Sarawak.

Appointed as a strong man to rule what beforehand had proved an ungovernable territory, Brooke set about restoring peace and laying the foundations of a stable government and economy. The suppression of coastal piracy was his hardest task, despite regular assistance from British men-o'-war based at Singapore. The Malay and Borneo pirates were persistent and elusive, although their light craft were no match for modern ships' guns. During one riverine engagement in 1843 Brooke recorded how a single round of grapeshot 'swept all the men from paddles on one side' and forced the rest of the crew to jump into the water, where they were shot.[9]

The British government approved Brooke's position as Rajah of Sarawak, although he had many enemies among humanitarians, who deplored his vigorous methods of handling pirates. He and his tiny state were a useful addition to Britain's local unofficial empire. Territorial ambitions in the area were confined to the occupation of islands and small strips of land for naval bases and commercial centres from which influence was exerted over Malaya, Siam and the East Indies. To this end, Penang Island, Port Wellesley, Singapore and Malacca had been secured between 1785 and 1824, toeholds known collectively as the Straits Settlements.

Informal empire in Malaya depended on the cooperation of the local hereditary princes who were expected to keep the peace and safeguard British lives, property and investment. After 1870 these duties proved beyond the capacities of the Malay rulers as the region slid into a period of violent political and economic upheavals. Since the mid-1850s, Selangor and Perak had enjoyed a tin-mining boom, which had brought a mass influx of Chinese immigrants. There were 40,000 in Perak by 1870, and they, like their countrymen in Selangor, were passionately attached to various, mutually hostile secret societies. The Chinese faction struggle in Selangor had deteriorated into a civil war by 1870, and a year later a succession contest broke out in Perak.

Successive governors of the Straits were faced with a dilemma: they had

Nineteenth-Century Malaya

to do all in their power to restore stability inside Malaya while, in the best traditions of informal empire, staying neutral. It proved practically impossible for the British to keep out of Malaya's internecine conflicts, not least because they had triggered a revival of piracy. In 1870 gunboats had been driven to shell the stockades of a contender to the throne of Selangor after his adherents had impeded the arrest of some Chinese pirates. Such incidents multiplied until, by 1873, the Straits' authorities had become completely entangled in Malayan politics. Long before, the men–on–the–spot had concluded that the apparatus of informal empire was inadequate to settle the crisis, which could only be resolved by direct intervention.

A tug–of–war consequently developed between British officials and the Liberal Colonial Secretary, Lord Kimberley, who was determined to stop the drift towards Britain taking full responsibility for Malaya. In the end he gave up when the annexationists warned that inactivity would invite German or Dutch intervention. Then and later, even outwardly anti-imperialist governments like Gladstone's would not dare take the political risk of allowing Britain's informal power to be superseded by that of another country. The colonial officials got their way; Britain threw its weight behind one of the pretenders in Selangor and Anglo-Indian forces were ordered to pacify Perak and Sungei-Ujong in 1875.

The result of the 1873–4 crisis was Britain's assumption of formal protection over Perak, Selangor, Negri Sembilan and Pahang. Existing political structures remained in place with the local princes, like their Indian counterparts, submitting to guidance by British residents. In time, under British direction, debt and domestic slavery were abolished and the princes were actively encouraged to become improving, paternalist rulers. As part of this process of enlightenment, a college was established at Kuala Kangsor in 1905 where the prince's sons underwent a British public-school régime which, it was believed, would teach them how to govern responsibly.

Events in Malaya were paralleled by those in Fiji, where informal empire also disintegrated under the pressure of changes brought about by economic development and contact with Europeans. The complex and serpentine politics of Fiji had, by 1871, given rise to a bizarre situation in which King Thakombau was ruling as a constitutional monarch advised by a cabinet of European cotton-planters and merchants (including a bankrupt Sydney auctioneer on the run from his creditors) and two native chiefs. The government's many internal problems were made worse by the existence of a local lobby which claimed that the only solution to Fiji's difficulties was British rule.

The annexationists had allies in New Zealand, New South Wales and Britain. In the former two, Fiji was represented as a country ripe for colonisation, an argument which Australian expansionists extended to Papua and New Guinea. In Britain, Gladstone's ministry had to contend with pressure from humanitarian and missionary groups. Between 1835 and 1860 the Fijian missions had made 60,000 converts, but it was believed that only British rule would extirpate cannibalism and ritual sacrifice from among the islands' remaining animists. There was also concern about the spread of 'blackbirding', a form of slave trading in which Pacific islanders were cajoled or forced aboard ships, and then transported as indentured labourers to the Peruvian guano fields or the Queensland sugar plantations. The Royal Navy had tried to interrupt this traffic during the 1860s, but had been hampered by the refusal of Australian juries to convict kidnappers.

A combination of commercial and philanthropic arguments persuaded an unwilling British government to investigate the alleged collapse of central authority in Fiji. The men-on-the-spot, naval officers, were easily convinced that the islands would slide into anarchy if the British flag was not hoisted, and so in 1874 the government approved annexation. There was a strong and understandable feeling in anti-imperialist Liberal circles that ministers had been outmanoeuvred by a determined coalition of interest groups.

After 1874 British policy in the Pacific reverted to the old pattern of policing the islands by warships and careful avoidance of any action that might lead to permanent occupation. Australian adventurers, keen to do a Rajah Brooke in Papua and New Guinea, were frowned on by the Colonial Office which, however, made it clear that steps to acquire these regions would be taken if there were signs that another power was considering their annexation.

The coming of the new imperialism in the 1880s saw Germany and France preparing to stake out claims to various South Sea islands. German interest in the region went back thirty years, and during the 1860s the Hamburg-based Goddeffroy and Son had outstripped all its rivals as general traders in the Pacific. The firm collapsed in 1879, but Bismarck was happy to subsidise its successors, the New Guinea Colonial Company, and the Deutsche-See-Handels-Gesellschaft, in order to win political favours from the business community and the colonial lobby. He also approved a series of annexations of islands between 1883 and 1886.

There was something surreal about the German procedure of establishing sovereignty. In 1886 a German gunboat hove to off one of the

Solomon Islands and sent a landing party ashore. Local chiefs were given trading flags and a proclamation in a presentation box, while a board inscribed 'German Imperial Protectorate' was set up. A German flag was then raised and lowered, and the officials and sailors returned to the ship.[10] Whether or not they understood exactly what was happening to them, the Solomon Islanders were deeply impressed by this display, for they related its every detail to a British naval officer fourteen years later. As they sailed through the islands the Germans also renamed them: New Britain became New Pommern, and so on.

The island names were changed again when Britain, Germany, France and the United States haggled over a final settlement of who kept what. Britain got Papua, the Solomon and Gilbert and Ellice Islands, while the Germans were satisfied with Samoa, New Guinea, the Bismarck Archipelago and the Caroline and Marianna Islands. The Chancellor, Prince von Bülow, was delighted and predicted that this sprinkling of islands and atolls would become 'milestones along the road . . . to *Weltpolitik*'. Global power of this kind was an expensive luxury for, in 1913, Germany had to pay a 1.8 million mark subsidy to sustain its Pacific empire.[11]

But in the heyday of the new imperialism economic value took second place to prestige, which bestowed an exaggerated importance on even the tiniest island. In August 1900 French officials boasted to New Hebridean tribesmen that, 'This land belongs to the French Company and you are not to work it any more . . . We will drive you and the British, too, from the island and have it for ourselves.'[12] As so often was the case, such bluster meant very little, although it must have been frightening for those on the receiving end. Six years later the British and French governments agreed to govern the New Hebrides as a condominium.

Britain's scattering of Pacific islands remained for many years the most backward and forgotten of her colonies. None had any great economic potential and all were afflicted by falling population levels; Fiji's dropped by 30,000 between 1860 and 1873 and the decline only ceased in 1921. Imported diseases, against which the islanders possessed no effective immune systems, were largely responsible for these losses. Efforts were made to reverse this process with some success. The death rate of indentured labourers on the Solomons was cut from five to three per hundred between 1906 and 1921, thanks to the work of a colonial medical officer and the building of a hospital.

The new colonial administrations were also concerned with the moral welfare of the Pacific islanders, but attempts to eradicate such disruptive customs as inter-tribal warfare met with resistance. Feuding continued on the Solomons well into the 1920s, despite frequent hangings of warriors found guilty of murder. The Malaita fighting men, or ramos, were proud of their warlike traditions, and when they were challenged by a local district officer, who styled himself 'super ramo', the result was a skirmish in which he and thirteen native policemen were killed in October 1929. Another source of irritation to the authorities was the islanders' unwillingness to integrate into the newly introduced market economy. A 1932 official account of the Solomons' development regretted that the Gela islanders were still refusing to grow more than was needed for themselves and the purchase of tobacco and a few other necessities.[13] Nevertheless nearly 7,000 islanders had become part of the new economy by taking work as indentured labourers on the European-owned copra plantations. Conditions appear to have been severe: in 1922 three native overseers were charged with murdering a worker, but were acquitted, as was a Mr C.V. Maxwell, a plantation manager who had been accused of beating to death a servant boy. There were some very dark and unpleasant corners in the remotest parts of the empire.

6

A Great
English–Speaking
Country:
South Africa

'The true value of this colony is its being considered an outpost sub-servient to the protecting and security of our East Indian possessions,' wrote Lord Caledon, governor of Cape Colony in 1809.[1] This view of what otherwise was an unprofitable and turbulent backwater explained why the British had occupied the Cape three years before, and why they insisted on its retention at the end of the French wars. The strategic value of the Cape remained unaltered for the next hundred years. In the early 1900s, Admiral Lord Fisher, the First Sea Lord, designated Cape Town, along with Singapore, Alexandria, Gibraltar and Dover as one of the 'Five strategic keys [which] lock up the world'.[2] In 1887, nearly twenty years after the opening of the Suez Canal, Cape Town was chosen as the prin-ciple staging post for reinforcements bound for India in the event of a war with Russia.[3] At that time the Cape was guarded by 4,200 regular troops, supported by 3,000 local volunteers.[4]

If Britannia was to rule the waves, Britain had to keep the Cape. This was neither an easy nor rewarding task since the Cape lay in a region where racial tensions were acute and, for the first seventy years of the nine-teenth century, economic growth was sluggish. Britain had inherited a dispersed population of whites of Dutch and French ancestry, who called themselves Boers or Afrikaners, 25,000 black slaves who worked for them, and 15,000 Khoikhois (Hottentots). On the colony's eastern borders lived

17,000 Xhosa, whose lands the Europeans coveted, and who had been at war to defend them since 1779.

The Boers were the dominant race. They had first come to the Cape in 1652 and saw their past, present and future in terms of an unending struggle to subdue the land and its black inhabitants. Both had been willed to the Boers by God who, according to their primitive Calvinist theology, had chosen them, as He had the Israelites of the Old Testament, to be the masters of a new Canaan. Like the British, the Boers imagined themselves the blessed instruments of Providence, a belief which gave them extraordinary resilience and reserves of inner strength.

Under the minimalist administration of the Dutch East India Company, the Boers had been largely left to their own devices and were allowed a free hand with the natives. This state of affairs ended with the installation of British colonial administration, which felt morally obliged to deal even-handedly with all its subjects, and extend basic legal rights to those who were black or of mixed race. Therefore no partnership emerged between the Boers and a régime which attempted to apply liberal and humanitarian principles, which the former found incomprehensible. There were further sources of misunderstanding and friction between rulers and ruled. The governors of the Cape were patricians, some, like Sir Benjamin D'Urban and Sir Harry Smith, with illustrious records of service in the French wars, and they and their equally well-connected staffs could distinguish no marks of civilisation among Boers, who appeared uncouth, obstructive and extremely touchy. Missionaries were horrified by the practice of slavery, and by the raiding parties who preyed on native communities whenever the need occurred to replenish the Boer labour force.

Relations between the colonial authorities and the Boers deteriorated rapidly after 1815 to the point in 1834 when thousands of Boers decided to withdraw into the South African hinterland. What subsequent Boer mythology called 'the Great Trek' was a slow and uneven process which lasted several years. In part it was a reaction to the British parliament's abolition of slavery in 1833, although pressure on the land in the Cape forced many Boers to emigrate. At first, the Cape government feared that the mass exodus would lead to a widespread war once the Boers collided with the expanding Ndebele and Zulu states which lay in their path, and in 1842 the new Boer republic of Natalia was annexed as a precautionary measure. In fact, the well-armed Boers were able to take care of themselves, and their spectacular victories over the Ndebele and Zulus in the late 1830s assured them occupation of what became the Transvaal and Orange Free State republics.

[R H O D E S I A]
MASHONALAND
• Salisbury

1893
Campaign • Fort Charter

Shangani
Bulawayo • • Fort Victoria

M A T A B E L E L A N D

SOUTH
WEST
AFRICA

B E C H U A N A L A N D
P R O T E C T O R A T E
(1864-5)

British South Africa Column 1890

Pietersburg •
S O U T H   A F R I C A N
× Seh uk unis Fighting
Kopje 1879
R E P U B L I C
• Pretoria

Angra-Pequeña
• (Luderitz)

1885
GOSCHEN

Mafeking
Pitsani •

Doorn Kop
1896
Jameson's × • Johannesburg
Raid [T R A N S V A A L]

Delagoa
Bay •

Vryburg •

BRITISH
BECHUANALAND

R. Vaal

ORANGE FREE STATE

Harrismith •
Colenso
1899

× Ladysmith
Newcastle
1899-1900

R. Moder

1846-
54

BASUTOLAND
(1884)

N A

• Durban

R. Orange

De Aar •
R. Orange

Kaffir Wars
1815-53

C A P E   C O L O N Y
GAIKA

Kingwilliamstown •

Gt. Fish R.

1878 Campaign
East London

Cape Town •
Simon's Bay

• Port Elizabeth

Miles
0   100   200

Southern Africa 1815-1902

Given that the overriding aim of British policy in southern Africa was the achievement of local stability, the government saw no useful purpose in attempting to coerce the Boer republics. In 1854 Britain officially recognised their independence, with the proviso that they acknowledged British sovereignty, which made them, on paper at least, part of Britain's informal empire.

One persistent Boer complaint had been that the British had failed to deal firmly with the Xhosa on the Cape's volatile eastern frontier. The recent history of the Xhosa, or Kaffirs as they and other South African blacks were indiscriminately and contemptuously called, was one of inter-mittent wars to protect their land from settler encroachment. This conflict continued and intensified after the arrival of the British; there were major campaigns in 1811–12, 1819, 1834–5, 1846–7 and 1850–53. The Xhosa were in the same position as the Red Indians of North America and, if the colonists had their way, were destined for the same fate. This was brutally outlined in a letter written to the War Office by a commander during the 1846 campaign: 'The Kaffir must be driven across the Kei; he must be made your subject; he is wanted to till the Colonists' land.' Another offi-cer went further, and predicted the elimination of the Xhosa as the only outcome of the contest for land. 'They must recede before the white man – all attempts at civilisation are futile. The great want here is a body of energetic colonists to follow in the back of the troops.'[5] Irksome fron-tier wars against an elusive enemy always hardened consciences, but these remarks make it clear that some British were beginning to think in the Boer fashion. South Africa belonged to the white man and the black had a stark choice between submission or extinction.

The business of grinding down the Xhosa was fraught with difficulties since they were ingenious guerrillas, fighting in rough country which they knew intimately. Explaining this to his superiors in London, a British commander in the 1846 campaign characterised the Xhosa warrior as 'a greasy savage, whose full dress consists of a feather in his head and a sheaf for his organ of generation, who runs about as quick as a horse'.[6] Getting to grips with such an opponent was hard and frustrating work. Nevertheless, bush-fighting came as a relief from tedious garrison duties. 'I can scarcely keep myself from jumping out of joy at the idea of really being a soldier,' Lieutenant Fleming of the 45th Regiment told his fam-ily as he prepared for action in July 1846. Six months later he was suffering from dysentery, loss of appetite and a hacking cough and was keeping himself alive with doses of quinine and port.[7] When the war ended, he had had his fill of excitement and returned to England to take holy orders.

As in so many imperial frontier wars, there were natives who were willing to place their local knowledge and skills at their conquerors' disposal. Khoikhoi were widely employed as scouts and skirmishers, although large numbers deserted during the 1850–53 operations against the Ngquika Xhosa. Gradually, and by a scorched earth policy which starved out their opponents, the British soldiers, known as 'amarwexu' (small-pox Satans), got the upper hand, but the spirit of resistance remained strong. In 1855 the Xhosa were heartened by rumours that Britain had been beaten in the Crimea, and that Russian troops would shortly appear and drive all the British from the Cape.[8] Soldiers did in fact arrive from the Crimea, but they were former German mercenaries who had been employed to make up the wartime shortfall of British recruits. The War Office, sick of costly frontier campaigns in the Cape, had resurrected a precedent which had been used by the Romans to keep order on chaotic frontiers. The mercenaries, like ex-legionaries, were given farms in return for defending fortified villages in districts recently seized from the Xhosa.[9]

Seen from the perspective of London, the Cape and its tiny offshoot, Natal, were Cinderella colonies, continually disturbed by internal and external ructions. Both were unrewarding as markets for British manufactures; in 1855 South Africa imported British goods worth £922,000, which put it on the same level as Peru and well behind the Argentine and Chile. The political development of the two colonies followed the same course as that of the Canadian provinces and Australian states: under Colonial Office guidance, elected parliaments were established in the Cape in 1854 and Natal two years later. Pressure from British and local liberals devised a franchise which included richer black and mixed-race voters. This was done in the hope that a non–white middle class would eventually emerge and join with the white to form a stable, responsible electorate like that in contemporary Britain.

The late 1860s witnessed an economic revolution in the Cape whose repercussions soon affected every part of southern Africa. The discovery of diamonds in Griqualand, which was swiftly annexed as a crown colony in 1871, attracted investment and immigrants on an unprecedented scale. British imports into the Cape soared from £2 million in 1871 to £7.7 million twenty years later, when the total of the Cape's exports stood at £9.5 million, a third of which came from diamonds. Between 1871 and 1875, the Cape government inaugurated an ambitious programme of railway construction that, by 1890, gave the colony a network which extended for over 2,000 miles.

Digging for diamonds and laying railway tracks were both labour-intensive activities requiring a vast, unskilled workforce, which could only be found among the black population. If industrialisation was to proceed, the blacks of southern Africa had to be completely pacified and brought under white control. The need for a final assertion of white supremacy was becoming urgent by the mid-1870s as black migrant workers, particularly Pedi from the Transvaal, and Basotho, were using the wages they earned on the diamond fields to buy guns. Obsolete muskets and modern breech-loaders, some imported through Natal, were becoming widely available, and for some years the Zulu kings had been building up an arsenal of firearms.[10]

A passive black population was also necessary in order to implement the Colonial Secretary Lord Carnarvon's plan for a South African federation, comprising the Cape, Natal and the two Boer republics. This appeared an ideal solution to regional problems since it would create a stable unit which, thanks to the Cape's mineral revenues, would be self-supporting. Cautiously welcomed in the two British colonies, the scheme found little favour with the Boers, who saw it as a stratagem by which Britain could dominate the entire region.

Progress towards a federation was halted in 1876–8 by a sequence of native rebellions and wars, which were, as it turned out, the last major effort by South Africa's blacks to stem the advance of white power. There was unrest among the Griquas in the northern Cape, the Pedi and Basotho in the Transvaal, and the Ngquika and Gcaleka Xhosas in the eastern Cape. Local British and troops, bluejackets and marines were able to handle the unrest in the Cape, employing the latest military technology, including the new Martini-Henry breech-loading rifle and Gatling machine-guns. The Boer campaign against Sekhukhuni's Pedi soon ran out of steam and into trouble when a kommando (unit of mounted volunteer riflemen) was beaten. This reverse exposed the fragility of the Transvaal, and gave Carnarvon a welcome pretext to order its annexation in January 1877. The Boers were grateful for British intervention which, for the time being, guaranteed their safety.

The coup against the Transvaal was delivered by Sir Theophilus Shepstone, a singleminded colonial bureaucrat with a flair for native languages and a taste for intrigue. While the Boers may have seen him as a saviour, Shepstone saw the occupation of their republic as the prelude to its incorporation into the proposed South African federation. An enthusiast for the federation, Shepstone had convinced himself that measures for its creation could not proceed until the Zulu state had been emasculated. The overthrow of the Zulu kingdom was also the objective of Sir Bartle Frere, the new governor of the Cape, whose Indian experience had taught him that it was dangerous to tolerate the existence of any independent and well-organised native state on an imperial frontier.

During 1878, Frere and Shepstone conspired to engineer a war with the Zulu King Cetshwayo, ignoring the fact that he showed no hostility towards his southern neighbour, Natal. The two proconsuls doctored their reports to the Colonial Office to make Cetshwayo appear a warlike tyrant, and exaggerated the size of his army, which they falsely alleged was a standing force, rather than a body of men who were only mobilised in an emergency. Behind their cynical machinations was the hope that once Cetshwayo's kingdom had been dismantled, his subjects would become a subservient labour force at the disposal of Natal's white farmers and the mining companies.[11]

Having manoeuvred Cetshwayo into a corner, Frere and Shepstone got the war they wanted in January 1879. It started badly thanks to ill-luck and the slipshod generalship of the commander-in-chief, Lord Chelmsford. At the end of the month, a 1,200-strong column of British troops and native auxiliaries was all but wiped out at Isandlwana. Immediately after, and in defiance of Cetshwayo's orders, an impi of between three and four thousand warriors crossed into Natal and attacked the mission station at Rorke's Drift, which was defended by 139 men from the 24th Regiment, many of them invalids. In the epic battle which lasted for over twenty-four hours the attackers were repelled with losses of over 500 dead. The Zulus were exhausted and had not eaten for two days, and British fire-power more than compensated for the imbalance in numbers. One survivor, Colour-Sergeant, later Colonel Bourne, remembered how a few Zulus had managed to reach the improvised defences. Those who did, 'to show their fearlessness and their contempt for red coats and small numbers . . . tried to leap the parapet, and at times seized our bayonets, only to be shot down.'[12] Nonetheless the defenders showed extraordinary steadiness and eleven were awarded the Victoria Cross.

The trouble for the Zulus was that their indunas (generals) were fatally addicted to the traditional headlong charge of assegai-armed warriors. It had succeeded, just, at Isandlwana, but at a cost of 5,000 casualties. Nevertheless, similar tactics were repeated throughout the war, although

Cetshwayo urged his commanders to adopt a guerrilla strategy and attack the extended and vulnerable British lines of communication.[13] The British government was also disappointed by its servants' performance and sacked Shepstone, Frere and Chelmsford, who was replaced by the abler and more methodical Sir Garnet Wolseley. He arrived in Zululand too late for the final destruction of the Zulu army at the battle of Ulundi in July. By this time everyone involved knew what to expect; the British deployed in a Napoleonic-style square, the better to concentrate their fire-power, and the Zulus, who had been progressively disheartened, launched their usual charge, but, observers noticed, without much conviction. The overthrow of the Zulu kingdom had required a tremendous effort, which indicated the importance the government attached to the achievement of paramountcy in southern Africa. 17,000 reinforcements had been rushed to Natal and the two invasions of Zululand had required 27,000 oxen, 5,500 mules and 30,000 native porters and labourers.[14] The final bill was £4.9 million.[15]

With Zululand prostrate, Wolseley turned his attention to Sekhukhuni, whose Pedi were defeated by a mixed force of Highlanders and Swazis. The Basotho, who copied the Boers and fought as rifle-armed mounted infantry, proved a harder nut to crack. The result was that Basutoland became a British protectorate governed through local native chiefs. Experiments of a similar kind in Zululand failed and it was finally absorbed by Natal. The campaigns of 1877–9 had achieved their purpose: large-scale black resistance had been extinguished and white supremacy, which would last for just over a hundred years, was confirmed.

The pacification of South Africa's black population by the British army marked the start of a new power struggle between the British and the Boers. Once it became clear that Britain's occupation of the Transvaal was not a stopgap measure, but a preparation for its amalgamation into a South African federation, the Boers rebelled. The Transvaal's war of independence of 1880–81 ended with the defeat of a small British force, which had been trapped on the summit of Majuba Hill in northern Natal. Rapid, long-range rifle fire had done for the British infantrymen, but the Boers celebrated their victory as the judgement of God in favour of His elect and against a race commonly considered impious. The newly-elected Liberal ministry saw the battle as the outcome of an amoral policy, which Gladstone had campaigned against during the general election. Plans for a federation, which the Boers had so forcefully rejected, were dropped and the Transvaal's independence was restored. And yet, during negotiations at Pretoria in 1881 and London three years later, the government clung to pretensions of sovereignty over the Boer republics, and with it the right to interfere in the shaping of their domestic and foreign policies.

What at the time was no more than an academic legal point assumed enormous significance during the next twenty years. It was a period which witnessed tentative Boer expansion northwards and eastwards, and, after the discovery of gold on the Witwatersrand in 1886, the transformation of the Transvaal's economy. Once in production, the Rand mines provided a quarter of the world's supply of gold and ensured that the centre of economic power in southern Africa shifted away from the Cape to the Transvaal. By 1896 the Transvaal government was the richest in Africa with annual revenues of over £8 million from minerals. British credit underwrote this economic revolution: in 1899 British investment in the Transvaal totalled £350 million, and two-thirds of the Rand's mines were owned by British stockholders.

The questions which hung over southern Africa during the last two decades of the nineteenth century were, how would the Transvaal's new wealth be used, and what effect would it have on Britain's position in the area. This last was very much the concern of Cecil Rhodes, who, while still in his early thirties, had made himself a multi-millionaire by an accumulation of diamond-mining concessions. A shrewd manipulator, he had by 1891 secured a monopoly over the Kimberley diamond fields for his Rhodes De Beers Consolidated Company and had extensive investments on the Rand.

Rhodes became the most famous, many would have said notorious imperialist of his age. He was amoral, instinctively acquisitive (sleeping in the open during the 1884 Bechuanaland campaign, he had contrived to get for himself a blanket he was sharing with a British officer) and a brilliant businessman. His fortune was the servant of his dreams. These were inspired by contemporary Social-Darwinism and the new imperialism, which convinced him that it was the destiny of the Anglo-Saxon races to civilise the world. Nothing could withstand the force of this destiny, certainly not the rights of those who stood in its way. In a revealing episode, he listened to Kaiser Wilhelm II's complaint that Germany had entered the race for empire too late and that there was nothing worthwhile left for her anywhere. 'Yes, your Majesty there is,' Rhodes responded. 'There is Asia Minor and Mesopotamia.' That these belonged to Turkey did not trouble Rhodes. The compass of Rhodes's temerity and ambitions startled contemporaries. Viscount Milner observed, 'Men are ruled by foibles and Rhodes's foible is *size.*'

Like other mavericks, such as Clive, Brooke and, later, T.E. Lawrence, who came to empire-building by chance, Rhodes's imagination and talents were not apparent in his earlier life. He also shared the former trio's good luck by being the right man in the right place at the right time and, of course, had the singular advantage of a private fortune with which to fulfil his dreams. He also had, at every turn, the assistance of successive British governments which, while many of their members did not share Rhodes's breadth of vision, saw him as an extremely useful instrument for the preservation and extension of Britain's influence in southern Africa at a time when it was in jeopardy.

Rhodes's first coup, achieved with the cooperation of Gladstone's ministry, was the annexation of Bechuanaland in 1884–5. During the past five or so years, parties of Boer settlers had been penetrating this region, where they established the miniature republics of Goschen and Stellaland. Simultaneously, German colonists were moving inland from the embryo settlement of Angra Pequeña, and there were fears in Cape Town and London that they would eventually link up with the Boers. The result would be the blocking of the 'Missionaries Road', which ran northwards towards what was then known as Zambesia (roughly modern Zimbabwe and Zambia), a region widely believed to be rich in minerals. There was also, and this caused the greatest anxiety to the British government, the possibility of the emergence of a German-Transvaal axis. In April 1884, when Paul Kruger, the Transvaal's president, had visited Berlin he had spoken publicly of his people's affinity with Germany. 'Just as a child seeks support from his parents so shall the young Transvaal state seek, and hopefully find, protection from its strong and mighty motherland, Germany, and its glorious dynasty.[16]

This was enough to arouse the British government, already uneasy about the appearance of German settlements in South-West Africa (Namibia), and under pressure from an alliance of Rhodes and the missionary lobby, which feared for the future of the Tswana of Bechuanaland under Boer rule. In December 1884 a small, well-armed force was ordered into the area to evict the Boers and declare a protectorate over Bechuanaland, which it did without resistance.

Rhodes was the ultimate beneficiary from the acquisition of Bechuanaland, a colony of little economic value, which was costing Britain £100,000 a year in subsidies during the 1890s. Bechuanaland was the springboard for Rhodes's incursion into Zambesia, an undertaking that would be accomplished by his British South Africa Company, which was officially chartered in 1889. This company, like its contemporaries the Royal Niger Company, the British Imperial East Africa Company and the North Borneo Company, represented a revival of seventeenth-century, private enterprise colonisation and trading. The government gained overlordship of new territories on the cheap since their day-to-day administration and policing were in the hands of the company's staff. The British South Africa Company's mandate was for farming and mining in Mashonaland, where mineral and settlement rights had been granted by the Ndebele king, Lobengula, in return for a company pension, 1,000 now obsolescent Martini-Henry rifles and a gunboat for the Zambesi River, which was never delivered.

At the end of 1890, the first column of settlers, less than 400 in number but heavily armed with machine-guns and artillery, entered Lobengula's kingdom. The events of the next ten years paralleled those which had been played out in North America during the previous two centuries. Lobengula gradually realised that by making concessions to the company he had weakened his own authority, which he attempted to reassert in the autumn of 1893 by ordering his impis to raid Shona villages close to British settlements. He played straight into the hands of the company's chief magistrate, an extremely foxy and belligerent former physician, Dr Leander Starr Jameson. Jameson had long believed that two sources of power could not co-exist in the region, and that the company's future would never be assured until the formidable Ndebele war machine was dismantled. The raids were therefore just what Jameson wanted and gave him the excuse for a war against Lobengula.

The first Matabele War of 1893–4 was a one-sided affair, for Ndebele generals, like their Zulu counterparts, stuck to traditional frontal attacks. These were suicidal against the company's Maxim machine-guns, the latest and most deadly of their kind, which fired six hundred rounds of .45 ammunition a minute. The Maxims terrified the Ndebele, who saw them as some awesome kind of magic; a native baby, born at this time and alive in the 1970s, explained his unusual name, Zigga-Zigga, as being based on the sound made by the machine-guns, and therefore believed by his parents as having some supernatural power.[17] Ndebele resistance did not end with the overthrow of Lobengula's state, for there was a further uprising in the spring of 1896, in which settlers and their families were attacked and murdered.

The killing of the colonists generated bitter racial passions in Britain and Rhodesia (Zimbabwe), as the company's territories were now generally known. 'Permanent peace there cannot be in countries like Mashona and Matabeleland until the blacks are either exterminated or driven back into the centre of Africa,' proclaimed the *Saturday Review*.[18] Its forthrightness echoed the views of settlers, like the big-game hunter Sir Frederick Selous, who thought that armchair imperialists were mistaken if they expected gratitude from natives who had been freed from oppressive rulers and the powers of the witch-doctors. Only condign chastisement repeatedly applied would teach the Ndebele 'the uselessness of rebelling against the white man'.[19] Delivering these lessons in quietism was a horrifying business. Rifleman John Rose, one of the 1,200 British soldiers hurried to Rhodesia from the Cape, described the storming of a kraal during mopping-up operations in August 1896:

> . . . all over the place it was nothing but dead or dying niggers. We burnt all the huts and a lot of niggers that could not come out were burnt to death, you could hear them screaming, but it served them right. We took about 5 women prisoners, but let them go again; one woman was holding a baby and some one shot the baby through the leg and through the woman's side, but it was nothing [and] our doctor bandaged the wounds up.[20]

Details of this nature shocked Liberals and Radicals at home, and there were some sharp exchanges in the Commons between Chamberlain and the company's critics. Henry Labouchere questioned him on Rhodes's stated intention of 'thoroughly thrashing the natives and giving them an everlasting lesson', executions without trial and village-burning. The last, Chamberlain insisted, was 'according to the usages of South African warfare', which must have puzzled those who believed that the advance of Anglo-Saxon civilisation in Africa would bring an end to such practices.[21] Parliamentary protests did little to change the nature or the course of the war, which dragged on into 1897, when the last guerrilla groups were finally hunted down.

A secondary, equally bloody campaign of pacification was being fought to the north-west of Rhodesia on the eastern shores of Lake Nyasa. British penetration of this region had followed Livingstone, whose early missions had been superseded by the Scottish Presbyterian African Lakes Company. It received government patronage in its armed struggle against Arab slave-traders, who operated from Zanzibar and supplied slaves to the tribal potentates of Arabia and the Persian Gulf. A British protectorate was declared over the area in 1891 to forestall acquisition by the Portuguese, who were, with good reason, suspected of not pulling their weight in the international effort to suppress Arab slaving. There followed four years of small-scale wars, subsidised by Rhodes, and fought by Sikh troops, commanded by Sir Harry Johnston, and a flotilla of tiny gunboats. Arab slavers and those tribal chiefs who had refused to accept Britain's paramountcy were successively defeated; the latter were characterised by Johnston as slavers, which made it easier for him to justify his rigorous measures to the Foreign Office.[22]

Those who took part in the small wars waged across southern Africa during the 1890s believed they were the pathfinders of the vast new British dominion with its own iron racial order. 'Africa south of the Zambezi must be settled by the white and whitish races,' claimed Johnston in 1893, 'and that Africa which is well within the tropics must be ruled by whites, developed by Indians, and worked by blacks.'[23] William Brown, an American naturalist-turned-colonist who had been captivated by Rhodes's dreams and helped to make them reality, believed the process of conquest and settlement was inexorable since it was an expression of 'the spirit of the age'. This, he insisted, 'decrees that South and Central Africa shall become a great English-speaking country', perhaps another United States, which in time would fulfil 'the destiny for which Providence seems to have chosen the Anglo-Saxon race'.[24]

By 1914 the process seemed well underway. Southern Rhodesia had a white population of 34,000, who had their own elected legislative council which lorded it over the 732,000 blacks, half of whom lived in reservations. Many of the whites were Boers, who brought with them the racial prejudices of South Africa. In 1903 a law was made which punished a black man found guilty of raping a white woman with death; a protection not available to black women.[25] In Northern Rhodesia (Zambia), where white settlement was sparse, British law obtained under a separate and, by and large, a more humane form of government which owed its form to British rather than South African influence. In 1924 it was taken over by the Colonial Office.

The period that saw the establishment of British supremacy in Rhodesia and Nyasaland was one during which it was under assault in South Africa. The British government continued to regard South Africa as its exclusive sphere of influence, and clung to the hope that its constituent parts would eventually merge in a federation which would, of course, be within the empire. Rhodes was of the same opinion and, on becoming prime minister of the Cape in 1891, he endeavoured by charm and cheque book to convince its Boer population to accept the permanence and value of the British connection. There was, however, an alternative future for South Africa as part of a predominantly Boer federation in which the Transvaal would be paramount.

Such an arrangement was wormwood to Britain. Neither Rosebery's Liberal ministry (1893–5) nor its Conservative successor under Salisbury could allow a strategically vital region to slip from Britain's grasp into Germany's. It was argued that a United States of South Africa under the Transvaal would be too weak to resist German encroachments, and might easily become a German satellite. Much to Britain's irritation, the Transvaal had now become a pawn in the game of international imperial power politics, which was being played by Germany in order to extract concessions elsewhere. German political interest and investment strengthened the Transvaal's sense of independence and, seen from both London and Cape Town, were evidence of the urgent need for measures to reassert British prestige and authority.

Developments during 1894 and 1895 heightened tension. The completion of the Delagoa Railway gave the Transvaal free access to the sea (German warships attended the opening celebrations at Lourenço Marques) and was followed by a brief trade war in which hindrances were officially placed in the way of British businessmen in the Transvaal. This petulant display of independence helped concentrate the mind of the British government on how to bring the Transvaal to heel. Rhodes's answer was a *coup de main* delivered by mounted forces of the Rhodesian and Bechuanaland *gendarmerie*, who would descend on Johannesburg in support of an uprising there. The rebels were drawn from the largely British Uitlander (outsider) community of miners, engineers and entrepreneurs, who outnumbered the Boers and, for this reason, had been denied political rights.

What became known as the Jameson Raid was botched from the start. Rhodes's private army began assembling at Pitsani on the frontier with Transvaal in November 1895 amid conflicting rumours that it would attack either the Transvaal or a local native chief. There was no security here, nor in Johannesburg, which meant that the Transvaal authorities had warning of what was in hand.[26] Spurred on by abundant supplies of whisky and promises of high wages, the troopers launched their attack at the very end of December, were intercepted, and forced to surrender early in January 1896. President Kruger had the ringleaders sent back to Britain for trial, and Rhodes, his political integrity compromised, withdrew from public life.

Just how much Chamberlain, the new Colonial Secretary, knew of Rhodes's plans is not known for certain, although there can be no doubt that he would have warmly applauded the coup had it succeeded. Inside South Africa, the raid raised the political temperature and was widely seen as the first round in a contest between Britain and the Transvaal. Lewis Michael, manager of the Standard Chartered Bank in Cape Town, believed that the issue could now only be resolved by war. 'The ambition of the Transvaal to become the rising power in the land is beyond doubt,' he wrote in April 1896, 'and I don't think we shall all quiet down again until the question is settled one way or another. The whole school is looking at the "two big boys" who aspire to be "cock of the school", and I fear there is only one way of settling the dispute; viz. the old school way.'[27]

Chamberlain agreed, but he knew that if war came it would have to have the wholehearted support of the British electorate. He had been a populist politician, and was therefore more aware than his aristocratic colleagues of the need to proceed with the backing of public opinion, particularly in the provinces. What was needed to prepare the ground for a war against the Transvaal was a moral cause which would win wide support. One was available: Kruger's steadfast refusal to allow the vote to the Uitlanders was presented as an affront to those democratic principles which were now the basis of Britain's government, Chamberlain's efforts to swing British opinion behind a strong line with the Transvaal were helped by an ill-judged telegram of congratulations and a pledge of support sent to Kruger by the Kaiser after the Jameson Raid. From 1896 until the outbreak of the Boer War in October 1899, Chamberlain was able to pose both as a champion of democratic rights and the defender of Britain's historic influence in southern Africa against Germany, which was already being publicly identified as an international rival. But it was the Uitlanders who always held centre stage; in May 1899, when the drift to war seemed unstoppable, Lord Selbourne, the Under-Secretary of State for the Colonies, summed up Britain's moral case:

> We take our stand on . . . the duty and right of every civilised government to protect its subjects resident in foreign countries when they are oppressed and our own especial interest in everything South African as the Paramount power there.[28]

Ironically, both British and Boers imagined themselves specially chosen races whose right to govern rested on the dispensation of Providence. Boer preachers and newspapers constantly reiterated claims that the British were an ungodly people, while British propagandists dismissed the Boers as a backward, semi-barbaric race. Viscount Milner, High Commissioner in South Africa since February 1897 and a fervent apostle of Britain's imperial destiny, perceptively summed up the Transvaal's government as a 'mediaeval race oligarchy', which existed solely to perpetuate Boer dominance. Bernard Shaw, playwright and Fabian Socialist, concurred and added pointedly that 'small communities of frontiersmen' were totally unfitted to control the assets of South Africa, especially its minerals.[29] During the war British soldiers were struck by Boer naïveté (which included the acceptance of elaborately printed biscuit-box labels as five-pound notes), callousness towards the blacks ('Johnny Boer, he used to shoot niggers like you'd shoot a dog') and coarseness.

War broke out in October 1899 after the breakdown of negotiations between Kruger and Milner over the Uitlanders' franchise. The only strategy open to the Boers was the seizure of railway lines in the Cape and Natal and the occupation of Durban and Cape Town, which would frustrate the landing and dispersal of British reinforcements. Successful at first, the Boer offensive soon ran out of momentum, and by the end of the year the Boer armies were bogged down besieging Ladysmith, Kimberley and Mafeking. British attempts to relieve the former two were beaten back at the battles of Stormberg, Magersfontein and Colenso during the second week of December.

The loss of ground and the three defeats stunned the British public, which had grown used to its army winning spectacular victories over poorly-armed natives. In South Africa it faced opponents who were mobile, adept in bushcraft and armed with modern rifles and artillery. It was fortunate that during the winter of 1899–1900 the Boer high command threw away these advantages and chose static warfare, giving their opponents a breathing space in which to collect armies and develop a strategy. This was the responsibility of a new commander, Field Marshal Lord Roberts and his chief-of-staff, General Lord Kitchener.

It was Roberts who masterminded the downfall of the Transvaal and the Orange Free State by adapting Boer principles of mobility. Using massed cavalry, he swiftly outflanked his enemies, occupying Kimberley and trapping Piet Cronjé's army at Paardeberg, where it surrendered on 28 February 1900, Majuba Day. A cavalcade followed in which Roberts's forces successively took Pretoria and Johannesburg. Further east, in Natal,

General Sir Redvers Buller, a courageous but intellectually limited soldier, relieved Ladysmith, and then advanced to the Transvaal frontier.

By midsummer 1900 many fighting men believed the war was over, won by superior manpower and matériel. It was not; a younger generation of Boer commanders came to the fore with a new, war-winning strategy of attrition. Kommandos, disencumbered from their wagon trains, would maintain a continual pressure on the British by lightning raids on camps and lines of communication. Ceaseless guerrilla warfare would make South Africa ungovernable and force the war-weary British to restore the Boer republics' indepedence.

During the next two years the nature of the war changed radically. Kitchener, who replaced Roberts as commander-in-chief, devised a counter-strategy, which was also based on attrition, but designed to make life unbearable for those who continued to resist. Disaffected areas were criss-crossed with barbed wire and blockhouses; carefully coordinated mounted columns rode to and fro in search of kommandos; and Boer farms and livestock, which provided sustenance for the partisans, were destroyed. Boer women and children and their black servants were coralled into internment camps.

In the early days of the war, British public opinion had rallied to the government with an upsurge of patriotic clamour. Domestic jingoism did not reach the front line, where the 'soldiers' songs of the death and glory quality' which pleased music-hall audiences were actively discouraged around campfires.[30] The tedium of garrison duties, long hours in the saddle, thin and irregular rations, extremes of heat and cold, and disease quickly disenchanted even the most zealous patriot. In a book kept in Cape Town, the ardent young men who volunteered as Imperial Yeomanrymen during the winter of 1899–1900 were asked to fill in their reasons for their arrival in and departure from South Africa. One, who must have spoken for thousands, wrote 'Patriotic Fever' and 'Enteric Fever'.[31]

Kitchener's campaign inspired no patriotic fever in Britain, rather unease about what the war's critics described as 'methods of barbarism'. The phrase rang true as Britain heard reports of epidemics sweeping through the internment camps, killing women and children. Contrary to Boer legend, these were not a consequence of deliberate British policy, but the result of contemporary medical and sanitary ignorance. The same distempers which decimated the inmates of the camps also laid low over 16,000 British soldiers, nearly three times as many as died from enemy action. Nonetheless, there was mounting concern at home among humanitarians, left-wing Liberals and Socialists who refused to believe that the ends justified the means.

They did, at least for Kitchener, and in the spring of 1902, when both sides were approaching exhaustion, peace negotiations began. The Treaty of Vereeniging, signed at the end of May, gave the British what they had always wanted, political supremacy. The Boers got £3 million, which they needed to rebuild and restock their farms, and the promise that self-government would eventually be restored to the Transvaal and the Orange Free State. The Boer *volk* was also assured that Britain would not make an issue of legal rights for blacks when it came to framing a constitutional settlement for the region.

Britain's largest imperial war had cost £200 million and had witnessed the mobilisation of 295,000 soldiers, which was evidence of the lengths the government was prepared to go to to uphold paramountcy in South Africa. In a sense, Britain had been defending the imperial *status quo*, which from 1895 onwards appeared imperilled by the Transvaal's bid for independence and German meddling. To have ignored both would have been to admit weakness, which would have been unthinkable at a time when Britain was under pressure from France, Germany and Russia, who were challenging her position elsewhere in Africa and the Far East. The war was, in international terms, a demonstration of Britain's imperial will and determination to retain global power, whatever the cost.

Practitioners of the conspiracy school of history, mostly on the left, believed that the war had been secretly engineered by a handful of capitalists, some Jewish, to advance their interests on the Rand. This theory was superficially attractive, but failed to show exactly how the plotters had benefited, something which did not prevent it from becoming widely accepted by those already convinced that capitalism was wicked. In one sense, however, the war assisted business interests by perpetuating the system which relegated the black population to the role of a passive labour force. When the British army rode into Pretoria and Johannesburg, black workers burned their passes, the hated symbol of Boer oppression. They had acted prematurely, as the documents would be needed under the new order. Hundreds of thousands of blacks had been employed by the British during the war, often for wages higher than those commonly on offer. Smaller numbers had been used as armed scouts by column commanders, much to the fury of the Boers who naturally insisted that the war, like the future of South Africa, was the white man's affair.

7

That Heroic Soul:
The Struggle for
the Nile

In 1882 Egypt appeared on the way to becoming a thriving, modern state. Its improvement owed much to the ambition and energy of Khedive Muhammad Ali and his successors who, for the past sixty years, had run the country as a private estate. They had encouraged investment in irrigation, railways, ship-building, cotton plantations, schools and universities. Two-fifths of Egypt's cultivated land was given over to the growing of cotton, most of which was exported to Britain, Egypt's major trading partner. The remaking of Egypt had been paid for by British and French capital, and by 1880 its total debt topped £100 million, a huge amount for a country whose annual exports averaged £13 million.

In spite of Khedive Ismail's sale of his 44 per cent holding in the Suez Canal to Britain for £4 million in 1875, Egypt was sliding into insolvency. Various expedients were adopted by the great powers to keep her afloat: in 1876 an international commission was imposed on the government with a mandate to enforce financial stringency, and three years later the new Khedive Tawfiq was persuaded to accept Anglo-French control of his treasury, customs, post offices, telegraphs, railways, ports and even museums. What added up to the gradual erosion of Egyptian sovereignty and the commandeering of its government by foreigners was bound to provoke a nationalist backlash. It first manifested itself in February 1881 with a protest by unpaid army officers, led by Urabi Pasha who, the following September, carried out a *coup d'état* and made himself Minister for War with full control of the army. Urabi was a nationalist who united the

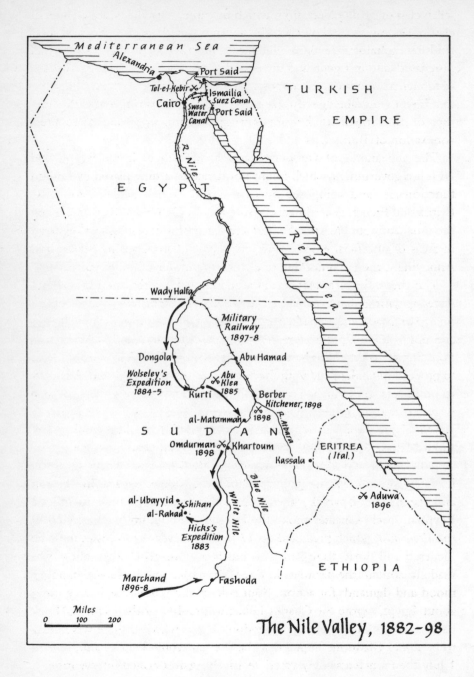

Mediterranean Sea

Alexandria

Port Said

Tel-el-Kebir

Ismailia
Suez Canal

Cairo

Sweet
Water
Canal

Port Said

R. Nile

TURKISH

EMPIRE

EGYPT

Red Sea

Wady Halfa

Military
Railway
1897-8

Dongola

Abu Hamad

Wolseley's
Expedition
1884-5

Abu
Klea
1885

Kurti

Berber
Kitchener, 1898

R. Atbara

al-Matammah

1898

S U D A N

Omdurman
1898

Khartoum

ERITREA
(Ital.)

Kassala

al-Ubayyid

Shikan

al-Rahad

White Nile

Blue Nile

Aduwa
1896

Hicks's
Expedition
1883

ETHIOPIA

Marchand
1896-8

Fashoda

Miles

0   100   200

The Nile Valley, 1882–98

fellah class of smallholders, from which he came, with the educated effendi class of landowners and officials. The fellahin were being squeezed off their lands by capitalist agriculture, much of it practised by foreigners who had purchased land in Egypt, and the effendiya were alarmed by the irruption of foreigners into government posts. There were also fears, natural enough, that Egypt would be directly taken over; during the spring and early summer of 1881 the French were putting the finishing touches to their annexation of Tunis.

The appearance of a popular national movement inside Egypt, and with it a government which might not dance to a tune played by foreign functionaries and composed by British and French bankers, took the British and French governments by surprise. In October 1881 they applied the usual antidote prescribed whenever symptoms of restlessness appeared in areas of unofficial empire, and sent a pair of ironclads to Alexandria. Annoyingly, these did nothing to change the minds of the Egyptians.

The British government was in a quandary. Gladstone and his cabinet were operating under considerable constraints since, two years before, their party had campaigned against the amoral adventurism of the Tories and in favour of a pacific foreign policy based on international cooperation. For this to work in the case of Egypt, Britain and France would have to proceed in tandem and with the backing of the rest of Europe. Attempts to produce a joint Anglo-French policy aimed at restoring the *status quo* were, however, overtaken by events in Egypt.

On 11 June 1882 a row over a fare between an Egyptian donkey boy and a Maltese led to a riot in Alexandria in which nearly fifty foreigners were murdered and their property plundered. What was interpreted as the first step towards anarchy in Egypt shook the money markets in London and Paris, where panicky French investors were beginning to offload Egyptian stock. Unease among the business community was reflected in the *Economist*, which predicted on 17 June that 'very great losses must be incurred and great disturbances to business must arise' if no effort was made to contain the disorders in Egypt. In parliament there was an angry mood and demands for action. 'Our side in the Commons is very jingo about Egypt,' wrote Sir Charles Dilke, a member of the cabinet. 'They badly want to kill somebody. They don't know who.'[1] If there was killing to be done, Gladstone hoped that the French would lend a hand, but on 1 July the French assembly voted decisively against armed intervention.

Britain was now alone and facing further defiance from Urabi. After his troops had restored order in Alexandria, he ordered the strengthening of the port's defences with modern Krupp cannon. By now, a substantial British squadron was lying in the roads, and on 3 July its commander, Admiral Sir Beauchamp Seymour, demanded the dismounting of the new batteries. Urabi refused, and eight days later the cabinet approved the bombardment of the gun emplacements. On 13 July landing parties of sailors and marines entered Alexandria, where law and order had collapsed after the departure of Urabi's soldiers.

Defending the attack on the fortifications, Gladstone claimed that Egypt was 'in a state of military violence, without any law whatsoever'.[2] This being so, his government was prepared to send an expeditionary force which would restore order and install a new administration. During August two armies, one 24,000-strong from Britain and the other 7,000-strong from India, converged on Egypt under the command of Wolseley. Warships occupied the canal unopposed and the British landed at Ismailia on 18 August. Four weeks later, Urabi's fortified camp at Tel-el-Kebir (al-Tall al-Kabir) was stormed and overrun, opening the way for a triumphal march on Cairo. Urabi was taken prisoner, court-martialled and banished to Ceylon.

Gladstone's government was deeply embarrassed by what had happened, and argued that it had no other choice but to rescue Egypt from self-destruction. Having done so, Britain would, in the same spirit of high-minded altruism, supervise the regeneration of Egypt. This would be accomplished by a cadre of British bureaucrats who would oversee the country's administration under the direction of Sir Evelyn Baring, later Lord Cromer. At the same time, the Egyptian army would be revitalised by a body of senior British officers, assisted by a corps of drill-sergeants. At its inception, it was claimed that this system of control was a temporary measure which would last as long as Egypt required tutelage.

What had been created in Egypt was an imperial hybrid. It was neither a colony nor an official protectorate, and outwardly it remained an independent country ruled by a khedive, whose overlord was, in purely legal terms, the Sultan of Turkey. In reality Egypt was, after 1882, a state where power rested in the hands of a higher civil service staffed by British officials, whose first priority was to bring the country to solvency. Two, Cromer and Milner, later produced extensive books which explained Britain's mission to Egypt and listed what had been accomplished to promote the well-being of the Egyptians.[3]

This orthodox view of the occupation of Egypt as a service to its people was challenged by those who saw the Anglo-Egyptian War of 1882 as having been foisted on the government by a clique of investors. Sir William Gregory, a former Tory MP and governor of Ceylon, argued that, 'We are the only nation which had an honest sympathy with the unfortunate peasants of the Nile Valley, and yet we are forced to be the nigger-drivers, the administrators of the lash to exact the last piastre from these poor wretches for the benefit of bondholders.'[4] This line was taken up and expanded by Wilfrid Scawen Blunt, a Tory squire with an instinctive mistrust of the machinations of all financiers, whom he cast in the same mould as the pushy and dishonest Augustus Melmotte in Anthony Trollope's *The Way We Live Now*.[5] Interestingly, traditionalist Tories and left-wing Radicals both identified the manifestations of the new imperialism of the 1880s and 1890s with the backstairs influence of capital.

Inside Egypt, British occupation provoked sullen resentment. Cromer, while publicly boasting that the fellahin were thankful for even-handed British government, confessed to the Committee of Imperial Defence in 1902 that little loyalty could be expected from Egyptians if their country was invaded by France or Russia. During the winter of 1914–15, the Turko-German high command felt confident that an attack on Egypt would immediately trigger an anti-British rebellion. Such conclusions were not surprising; Britain had entered Egypt to suppress a national movement, and the sentiments behind it did not just evaporate after the battle of Tel-el-Kebir, where, incidentally, the fellah soldiers had fought stubbornly. Nationalism remained a strong emotional force among all Egyptians, especially the educated class, who had the added grievance of finding themselves largely excluded from the highest ranks of the civil service, judiciary and army. Despite an energetic and highly competent police intelligence service, run by the British, nationalist agitation continued during the 1880s and 1890s and was covertly fomented by Tawfiq's successor, Abbas II. In January 1900 Egyptian officers stationed at Khartoum, heartened by the news of British defeats in South Africa and rumours of a Russian advance on India, encouraged their Sudanese askaris to mutiny in the hope that the rebellion might lead to the expulsion of the British from Egypt.[6]

What then kept the British in Egypt? Free passage through the Suez Canal appeared a compelling reason, since most of its traffic was British-registered shipping; of the 2,727 vessels which used the Canal in 1881, 2,250 were British. And yet at no time did Urabi indicate that he would interfere with the running of the Canal, and it was the British administration in Egypt which terminated the Canal's status as an international waterway at the outbreak of war in August 1914. Of course, in 1882 there was no way of knowing what Urabi might do in the future, and, most important of all, if Britain did nothing, another power could step in.

In the end, as in so many other areas where the machinery of informal empire broke down, formal, and in this case extremely swift occupation by Britain was the only alternative to annexation by another country. Moreover, there was no way of knowing whether the mood of the French deputies would change and a majority would emerge in favour of intervention, with or without British assistance. Subsequent international developments added weight to this argument. The growth of Anglo-French colonial jealousies after 1885, the Franco-Russian alliance of 1892, and with it the prospect that the Mediterranean might become 'le lac français' of French imperialist dreams, justified the decisions taken in 1882 and ruled out any withdrawal from Egypt. A firm grip on Egypt could also be defended when it became clear, as it did in the late 1880s, that Turkey could no longer be relied on to stop the Russian navy from passing through the Bosphorus. The cost of Egypt was high in terms of Britain's international influence. In order to obtain support for her position there, Britain was compelled to make compromises and offer concessions to Germany and France which, had the circumstances been different, she might have refused.

Possession of Egypt gave Britain responsibility for the Egyptian empire in the Sudan. After sixty years of gradual conquest and pacification, the Sudan was still a turbulent province where Egyptian authority was fragile. Forty thousand soldiers and officials struggled to hold the lid down on unrest and gather the taxes needed to sustain the khedive's credit. Most recently the Egyptian administration had been engaged in the suppression of slave trading, a duty undertaken by foreign governors, including the famous General Charles Gordon.

In 1881 the Egyptian authorities faced a new rebellion, led by Muhammad Ahmad, a thirty-seven-year-old messianic holy man, who called himself the Mahdi. As a chosen servant of Muhammad, it was his mission to purify Islam and chastise those whose faith had lapsed or become contaminated. His simple piety, powerful faith and message of spiritual rebirth won him thousands of converts, the ansars (servants), with whom he attacked and took the town of El Obeid. With the permission of Cromer, a well-equipped Egyptian army commanded by Colonel William Hicks was sent south to crush the insurrection. Led on a desert wild goose chase, Hicks was ambushed at Shaykan in November 1883, where his army was overwhelmed and its rifles, machine-guns and modern artillery captured. During the winter of 1883–4, one of the Mahdi's adherents, Uthman Diqna, started a new front in the vicinity of the Red Sea port of Suakin with attacks on local Egyptian garrisons.

It was now obvious that the Egyptian army could not contain let alone suppress the Mahdist movement, and that Egyptian administration in the Sudan was falling apart. Rather than waste treasure and men fighting a desert war to put it together again, the cabinet agreed in January 1884 to the evacuation of all Egyptian garrisons and personnel. Imperial disengagement proved as complex and vexatious an undertaking as imperial conquest. Forces rushed to Suakin in February 1884 soon found themselves drawn into a trial of strength with Uthman Diqna, and were consequently forced to make a series of limited offensives to uphold British prestige. This was preserved by victories at El Teb and Tamai, where the British soldier had his first and unnerving experiences of the tenacity and courage of the ansars, or Dervishes as they were usually called.

Overall supervision of the withdrawal from the Sudan was given to General Charles ('Chinese') Gordon. It was a controversial appointment, ostensibly made because of his previous local experience, but in fact engineered by the press. Gordon was already a popular hero, whose combination of bravery and intense evangelical fervour was bound to appeal to the Victorian public. Wilful and confident of his own charisma, Gordon saw himself as an agent of Providence, and, like Gladstone, answered to God for his decisions. He also had a peculiar talent for inspiring non-European soldiers: in the 1860s he commanded the 'Ever Victorious Army', which crushed the Taiping rebellion on behalf of the Chinese emperor, and in the 1870s he led Egyptian troops against Sudanese slave-traders. He spoke hardly any Arabic, but, despite his Christian zeal, believed that he had the hearts of the Sudanese. Their devotion to him was apparently confirmed by the enthusiastic reception he was given when he arrived in Khartoum in February. What he failed to understand was that the city's population imagined that he had the power to summon British soldiers who, as events around Suakin had shown, could beat the Mahdi's ansars. Not that Gordon was unduly worried by Mahdism, which he mistakenly believed was shallow-rooted and unlikely to make much headway.[7] He therefore jettisoned his orders to evacuate the Sudan, and instead prepared to defend Khartoum and resist the Mahdi.

Gordon singlehandedly reversed the government's policy. From Khartoum he issued a series of highly emotional but powerful appeals to the public conscience in which he called upon his countrymen to shoulder the burden of civilisation, and save the Sudan from being overwhelmed by what he considered the forces of darkness. His pleas and predicament captured the public imagination; he was an embattled warrior in a remote land who had placed Christian duty and service to humanity before expediency. Public opinion swung behind Gordon and, early in August, impelled a reluctant government to send an army to rescue him.

Gordon's position was becoming more and more precarious. Mahdist forces had been concentrating near Khartoum since May, which made evacuation of the city impossible. The main Mahdist army converged on the city in September and a month later the Mahdi took command of the siege. In the meantime, a 10,500- strong expeditionary force, commanded by Wolseley, had mustered and was beginning a cautious advance down the Nile. The press and the public saw the campaign as a race, but Wolseley, as ever, proceeded with care, in the knowledge that the desert had already swallowed up Hicks's army.

By early January 1885, the advance guard of the army had reached Kurti, from where the Desert Column would move across the Bayuda desert to al Matamma. Here, a token detachment would embark on three steamers sent from Khartoum. At Gordon's instructions, it was to contain some men in the traditional scarlet jackets rather than khaki in order to convince the Sudanese that the British really had arrived. The Mahdi, alarmed by the nearness of the relief force, ordered his generals to intercept the Desert Column at the wells of Abu Klea (Abu Tulayh).

What followed was a classic imperial battle. The British force of just over 1,000 men, many cavalrymen mounted on camels, had been told by the intelligence department not to expect serious resistance and was unaware of its opponent's numbers and dedication. Its first sight of the enemy was the appearance of green, red and black banners, inscribed with Quranic texts, waving above a hidden ravine.

All of a sudden the banners were in motion towards us at a

rapid pace led by spearmen on horseback. The enemy advanced against our square at a very rapid pace and in a dense black mass, keeping capital order.[8]

Skirmishers ran back to the square, which opened to receive them, making a gap through which some Dervishes surged. Infantrymen were unable to discern their attackers until the last moment, and sand and mechanical faults jammed machine-guns and rifles. Where the square had fractured there was 'a mass of yelling men and camels – alive, dead and dying'.[9] What saved the day was the presence of mind of men on an unengaged side of the square, who turned about and fired volleys into the mêlée. The breach was then sealed and the attackers driven off. It was all over in less than twenty minutes, but casualties had been high and all involved were stunned by the ferocity and daring of the ansars.

Among the dead was Colonel Frederick Burnaby of the Blues, whose famous portrait by Tissot represents him as the embodiment of the elegant and devil-may-care insouciance which was the distinguishing mark of a perfect British officer. He would doubtless have approved of colleagues who remarked after the battle that it would have been awful to have been killed without knowing the results of the Derby.[10] Burnaby had taken part in the fighting near Suakin a year before, when newspaper reports of his 'potting' Dervishes as if they had been partridges shocked left-wing Liberals and humanitarians. That Burnaby was also a Tory candidate for parliament probably added to their indignation.

Abu Klea aroused the imperial muse. In his 'Vitaï Lampada', Sir Henry Newbolt saw the battlefield as a testing ground for the virtues fostered on the public-school playing field:

> The sand of the desert is sodden red, –
> Red with the wreck of a square that broke; –
> The Gatling's jammed and the Colonel dead,
> And the regiment blind with dust and smoke.
> The river of death had brimmed his banks,
> And England's far, and Honour a name,
> But the voice of a schoolboy rallies the ranks:
> 'Play up! play up! and play the game!'

Kipling turned to the defeated. In his 'Fuzzy Wuzzy' (the soldiers' nickname for Dervishes taken from the Hadanduwa tribesmen's characteristic bushy hairstyle), he produced an imaginary Cockney soldier's tribute to their reckless courage:

> 'E rushes at the smoke when we let drive,
> An' before we know, 'e's 'ackin' at our 'ead;
> 'E's all 'ot sand an' ginger when alive,
> An' 'e's generally shammin' when 'e's dead.
> 'E's a daisy, 'e's a ducky, 'e's a lamb!
> 'E's a injia-rubber idiot on the spree,
> 'E's the on'y thing that doesn't give a damn
> For a Regiment o' British infantree!
> So 'ere's to you, Fuzzy-Wuzzy, at your 'ome in the Soudan;
> You're a pore benighted 'eathen but a first-class fightin' man;
> An 'ere's to you, Fuzzy-Wuzzy, with your 'ayrick 'ead of 'air —
> You big black boundin' beggar — for you broke a British square!

After Abu Klea, the Desert Column moved on to al Matamma, which was reached two days later. Further Dervish attacks forced the commander to take defensive measures, and it was only on 24 January that the steamers sailed for Khartoum. The ululations of the women whose husbands had been killed at Abu Klea were heard in Khartoum, now in its last extremity, and the news of the battle drove the Mahdi to risk storming the city. The assault succeeded and on 28 January, as the steamers closed on Khartoum, it was obvious that it had fallen.

What had become of Gordon? The Mahdi, who admired his steadfastness and courage, had wanted him taken alive. Forty years after, ansar eyewitnesses to his last moments testified that he had been killed fighting, one claiming that he had shot several adversaries with his revolver before being shot himself. This evidence bore out the account of Karl Neufeld, who was taken prisoner in Khartoum, and described Gordon as displaying 'superhuman strength' during the fighting.[11] Information along these lines reached Wolseley's intelligence department during February, but it was contradicted later by unreliable sources which offered an altogether more dramatic story. These described how Gordon had stood, aloof, unarmed and in full dress, on the steps of the Khartoum residency, and stared contemptuously at a mass of ansars. Turning disdainfully away, he had been speared and killed.

This version of Gordon's death was promulgated by Sir Reginald Wingate of the intelligence department, who realised that it was the only fitting end for a Christian hero. He knew that the 'martyrdom' of Gordon would inspire his countrymen to reconquer the Sudan as an act of vengeance. So emerged the familiar icon of Gordon facing his enemies and making the ultimate self-sacrifice for the cause of civilisation. This was how his death was seen in Britain; 'a grave misfortune has fallen on civilisation', announced the *Spectator* on 7 February 1885 as a wave of dismay and anger swept the country. Gladstone took the brunt of the blame, and was left with no choice but to pledge a full-scale campaign to recover Khartoum and punish the Sudanese.

Gladstone was let off the hook in March, when a Russian incursion across the Afghan border led to a general mobilisation. Troops were withdrawn from Sudan for shipment to India, leaving only a garrison at Suakin. In June the Mahdi died, probably from typhus, and the government of the Sudan passed to the Khalifah (successor) Abdullah bin Muhammad. His militant Islamic state posed no threat to Egypt after 1889, when an invasion force was decisively routed at the battle of Toski (Tushki).

Late-Victorian statesmen and strategists were haunted by a fear that the flow of the Nile could be artificially stopped with the result that Egypt's agriculture would be destroyed and the country ruined. It was agreed that blocking the Nile was well beyond the capabilities of the Khalifah's Sudan, but it could be managed by European engineers. This was the opinion of Victor Prompt, a French hydrologist who, in January 1893, published a technical paper that described how a dam could be constructed on the Upper Nile which would effectively cut off Egypt's lifeline.[12] It was, in fact, an unworkable plan, but its possibilities fascinated Théophile Delcassé, the French Under-Secretary for the Colonies. Prompt's scheme, and French official interest in it, caused consternation in Britain which had for some time been endeavouring to secure international recognition of an exclusive sphere of influence which extended down the Nile Valley. There were also simultaneous attempts to secure control over the northern shores of the White Nile's headwaters, Lake Victoria.

Between 1888 and 1898 the headwaters of the Nile were the prize in an extended and at times convoluted game of chess played by the governments of Britain, Germany, Italy and France and King Leopold II of the Belgians, the owner of what was, in effect, a private estate known as the Congo Free State.

As virtual ruler of Egypt, Britain claimed to have inherited that country's historic claims to the Nile Valley as far as Lake Victoria, and was anxious to secure its shores. This region, modern Uganda, had already been penetrated by British missionaries, and in 1888 one of their sponsors, a self-made Scottish businessman, Sir William Mackinnon, founded the British Imperial East Africa Company. Chartered by the government, this firm was empowered to develop trade and extend British influence. Hitherto, the dominant power in East Africa had been Germany. Its interests were represented by an energetic explorer, Carl Peters, who in 1884–5 had gathered a sheaf of treaties with native rulers in the hinterland of Dar-es-Salaam, which provided the legal foundation for what would become German East Africa (Tanganyika). Italy, keen to acquire the prestige which went with overseas possessions, concentrated its efforts on Ethiopia and the horn of Africa. France was, to start with at least, on the periphery of the contest since her ambitions lay in the Western Sahara, although in 1885 she had acquired the French Congo, a small colony on the north bank of the Congo River. The southern shores of that river and its vast, inland basin were the personal property of Leopold II. His ownership was the result of a compromise made by the European powers in 1885 at the Berlin Conference, but there was no way of knowing whether the company he formed to exploit the area would flourish. If it failed, then France hoped to step in.

1888 saw the first moves in the contest for central Africa. Each of the players was concerned to rescue Eduard Schnitzer, a Silesian Jew who had taken the title Emin Pasha when he had been appointed one of the khedive's governors in the Sudan. After the fall of Khartoum, he had led the detritus of his staff and army southwards into Equatoria, where he was stranded. Mackinnon and Peters planned armed expeditions to extricate him in the name of humanity, and at the same time plant their national flags close to the headwaters of the Nile. They were overtaken by Sir Henry Stanley, the Welsh workhouse boy who had become successively war correspondent, explorer, discoverer of Livingstone and, from 1885, administrator of the Congo Free State. Stanley brought back the none-too-willing Emin, and, by his brief presence in Equatoria, established his royal master's claim to the region.

This episode jolted Lord Salisbury's government into action. Through a series of determined diplomatic gambits, it obtained a bundle of agreements with Italy, Germany and Leopold II which, on paper at least, affirmed British supremacy over the Nile Valley. The Anglo-German agreement of 1890 affirmed British claims to Uganda and what is now

Kenya, and German to Tanganyika, an arrangement made possible by Britain's willingness to barter the North Sea island of Heligoland for Zanzibar. Next, an accommodation was reached with Italy. Since 1885 Britain had encouraged her ambitions in Ethiopia, and had even delivered her the Egyptian Red Sea port of Massawa to facilitate operations in Eritrea. In gratitude, the Italians promised in 1891 to keep clear of the Nile Valley. Three years later, Lord Rosebery's Liberal government agreed, after considerable internal debate, to declare a protectorate over Uganda, where the financial collapse of the British Imperial East Africa Company had coincided with the spread of tribal war. Soon after, King Leopold pledged not to push his estate's boundaries to the Upper Nile. So, by 1894, the state of play was in Britain's favour. At this stage France entered the game.

France's bid for territory on the shores of the White Nile was intended to overturn the new political order in Egypt. Once it was clear that Britain was not going to abandon her position there in the foreseeable future, France became increasingly embittered and resentful. Hostility towards Britain was orchestrated by a powerful lobby of predominantly right-wing, ultra-nationalist politicians, officials, soldiers and newspaper editors, who claimed that France had been deliberately tricked by her rapacious neighbour. The only way for France to regain her rightful influence in Egypt was by an aggressive challenge to Britain somewhere on the Upper Nile. If successful, this would either compel Britain to evacuate Egypt or concede the sharing of power there. Such an outcome would immeasurably raise France's international prestige and tilt the balance of power in the Mediterranean in her favour. Not everyone in French political circles was convinced; it was argued that if Britain was somehow forced out of Egypt then the entire Near and Middle East would be destabilised, which would hurt French interests.

Nevertheless, the anglophobe faction within the government, army and colonial service were determined to play their hand. Towards the end of 1894, Victor Liotard, the administrator of Upper Ubangi, was instructed to make his way to the Upper Nile, but a change of ministry led to his orders being countermanded. A second expedition was under consideration during the summer of 1895 which was to be commanded by Captain Jean-Baptiste Marchand. He was an officer of immense resolution and an experienced colonial soldier of that breed which, for the past decade, had been busy planting the *tricolore* across the Western Sahara, often in defiance of the wishes of Paris. Marchand was the man for the job, and in March 1897 he set off from Gabon with 163 officers and askaris and orders to negotiate '*alliances sérieuses et des titres indiscutables*' with whomever he encountered on his trek to the Upper Nile. He was engaged upon what he and his sponsors knew to be a gamble, and which some of the latter revealingly compared to the Jameson Raid.[13]

In July 1898 Marchand's party arrived at Fashoda (Kokok) on the shores of the Upper Nile after an epic journey during which, on occasions, he had ridden on a solid-wheeled bicycle, now preserved in the museum of St Cyr Military Academy. While he was pedalling across the southern Sahara, the governor of French Somaliland was making clandestine offers of protection and friendship to the Ethiopian Emperor, Menelik II.

The possibility of French intrusion in an area which was nominally a British sphere of influence was one of the reasons why the government sanctioned the first stage of the reconquest of the Sudan in March 1896. Another was the recent defeat of an Italian army by Menelik at Aduwa, which had changed the balance of power in the Upper Nile basin and gravely damaged European prestige. The advance southwards towards Khartoum was undertaken in the name of Egypt by a largely Egyptian and Sudanese army under the command of Sir Herbert Kitchener. From Protestant Ulster stock, Kitchener was a soldier of considerable energies, most of which were channelled into the furtherance of his career. He was a dedicated imperialist who believed that he was waging war in the Sudan in the name of civilisation, a consideration which did not prevent him from treating his enemies with extreme ruthlessness.

Kitchener's war was, of necessity, a slow, piecemeal advance down the Nile. It was also a model of logistic efficiency with a single-track railway following the fighting line, which impressed the host of war correspondents who accompanied the army and sent back enthusiastic reports for the public. Press versions of the war contrasted the modern technology of the conquerors with the barbarism of their opponents and continually emphasised the loftiness of Britain's motives. The invasion of the Sudan was a crusade for civilisation and vengeance for the death of Gordon.

Public interest in the war intensified during the winter of 1897–8 as more British troops were sent out at Kitchener's request in readiness for a final, decisive battle with the Khalifah's main army, believed to be 60,000-strong. The government expected a victory and was already contemplating the future political settlement of the Sudan. Salisbury put aside his reservations about the burden of governing a vast and profitless province, and accepted that British occupation of the entire Sudan was inevitable. And there was Marchand to be considered. A counterstroke to his expedition was approved by Salisbury at the end of 1897 when Major J.R.L. Macdonald was instructed to advance northwards along the White Nile from Uganda with a force of Sudanese askaris. His purpose was to forestall a meeting between Marchand and another French detachment, which was wrongly imagined to be travelling from Ethiopia to the river. There was no collision between Marchand and Macdonald; at the outset of the latter's expedition most of the Sudanese mutinied and the campaign was abandoned.

Further north, Kitchener was making steady progress with an army of 7,500 British and 12,500 Egyptian troops, supported by a flotilla of river gunboats. The climax of the war came on 2 September 1898 on a plain near Omdurman where the Khalifah's army delivered a sequence of frontal attacks. All were repelled by long-range rifle, machine-gun and artillery fire which killed 11,000 ansars and wounded a further 16,000. It was tantamount to a massacre which, more than any other encounter between European and native armies, illustrated the gulf between the technology of the industrialised powers and that of their opponents in Africa and Asia. The difference was summed up by Winston Churchill, then a young sub-altern, and combining the duties of a staff officer with those of war correspondent. On first seeing the ansar host with its banners, mailed cavalry and masses of spear- and swordsmen, he immediately recalled pictures he had seen of twelfth-century Crusader armies.

The day after Omdurman, the British and Egyptian flags were ceremonially raised over the ruins of the governor-general's palace in Khartoum, and a memorial service was held for its last occupant, Gordon. A Catholic chaplain prayed that God might 'look down . . . with eyes of pity and compassion on this land so loved by that heroic soul', words which moved Kitchener and other officers to tears.[14] There was no sign of divine mercy on the battlefield where, much to Churchill's disgust, Kitchener had left the wounded ansars to die. Inside Khartoum there was looting with Kitchener leading the way.[15] At the same time, many of the Khalifah's leading followers were summarily shot, some at the orders of Major, later General Sir John Maxwell, who commented afterwards that he regarded 'a dead fanatic as the only one to extend any sympathy to'.[16] As commander-in-chief in Ireland in 1916, he applied the same principle to Irish nationalists after the Easter Rising.

Accounts of the outrages at Omdurman and Khartoum provoked a group of MPs to take the unprecedented step of opposing the payment of a £30,000 reward to Kitchener for his work in the Sudan. There were acerbic exchanges over his exhumation of the Mahdi's bones, which he had had thrown into the Nile, after having briefly considered having the skull mounted as a cup. One Tory MP, a former officer, pooh-poohed the allegations of inhumanity, and reminded the House that 'we are bringing into the Dark Continent Civilisation' and it was 'a fatal thing to get in the way of a nation that is fulfilling its destiny'. 'Murder, rapine, whisky and – the Bible' were the ingredients of this civilisation, retorted an Irish Nationalist, Michael Dillon, while a Liberal asserted that 'imperialism is nothing but organised selfishness'.[17] The debate, like others of its kind, may have served as a warning to commanders not to jettison the rules of civilised conduct whenever they waged the wars of civilisation, but the vote went Kitchener's way and he got his cash.

He contributed some of it to the Gordon Memorial College at Khartoum, his brainchild and a visible symbol of Britain's civilising mission. Among the other subscribers to this institution were the machine-gun manufacturers, Vickers Son and Maxim, who had done as much as anyone to facilitate the triumph of civilisation in the Sudan.

The political future of the Sudan was sealed shortly after the capture of Khartoum; henceforward the province would be governed jointly by Britain and Egypt through a British governor-general. There remained the problem of Marchand, whose presence at Fashoda had been revealed to Kitchener by Mahdist prisoners. The commander-in-chief had been given secret orders on how to proceed if he encountered French intruders in the southern Sudan. They were to be evicted, but without the direct use of force.[18] Privately, Kitchener thought that Marchand's escapade was 'Opera Bouffe', not to be taken seriously, but when he met the Frenchman he treated him courteously, and, tactfully, had the Egyptian rather than the British flag hoisted over Fashoda. Faced with firmness and overwhelming force, Marchand withdrew, believing that he had upheld his own and his country's honour.

An international row followed between Britain and France with plenty of warlike noises on both sides. Checkmated and humiliated at Fashoda, the French government accused Britain of flouting its rights in the southern Sudan and bullying its representative there. Britain rejected these charges and insisted that France possessed no claim whatsoever to any portion of the Upper Nile. The public, which was both elated by the victory at Omdurman and displeased by recent concessions in the Far East, backed the government's unbending policy. A stand had to be made over Fashoda because Britain's rivals would certainly interpret any compromise as evidence of irresolution and would, therefore, be encouraged to challenge British power elsewhere.

Britain's imperial will appeared unshakeable and France stepped down. She had little choice, for her people were divided by the Dreyfus scandal and her ally, Russia, refused to become entangled in a dispute over a stretch of sand in the middle of Africa. Moreover, as the French Foreign Minister Delcassé appreciated, British naval superiority would make any war an unequal contest, with France's overseas trade suffering damage similar to that which had been inflicted by Britain during the eighteenth century. He also had the wisdom to realise that by turning Britain into an enemy, perhaps even an ally of Germany, France's power in Europe would be fatally undermined.

Having emerged the winner of the struggle for the Nile, Britain and its partner, Egypt, had to confront the task of pacifying and ruling a huge and still largely unexplored region, inhabited by people who had hitherto known little or no outside government. There was also the Khalifah who, with a force of about 10,000 ansars, had fled south after Omdurman. He was finally run to earth in November 1899 and defeated at the battle of Umm Diwaykarat. Apparently having learnt nothing from Omdurman, the ansars again threw themselves into the killing zone created by rifle and machine-gun fire and were cut down in hundreds. It would not be too far-fetched to see this engagement, like its forerunner at Omdurman, as a form of mass suicide by men who preferred death to submission to the new, infidel order. The Khalifah certainly possessed the means partly to redress the military imbalance, since he had carefully preserved the modern weaponry captured during the 1884–5 campaigns. Equally extraordinary was the failure of British commanders to understand the significance of what they had witnessed during the Sudan campaign. Major, later Field Marshal Lord Haig saw for himself the devastating effects of modern fire-power at Omdurman and yet, as commander-in-chief on the Western Front between 1915 and 1918, he sanctioned offensives in which British troops faced the same odds as the Khalifah's Dervishes.

There were sporadic Mahdist and pan-Islamic insurrections for nearly twenty years after Omdurman. The most threatening was in 1916 and led by Ali Dinar, the semi-autonomous Sultan of Darfur, who hoped for but did not receive Turko-German assistance. British propaganda dismissed him as insane, a diagnosis that was extended to nearly every Muslim who rejected British rule in Africa and Asia. Muhammad Abdille Hassan, who persistently resisted the British in Somaliland between 1898 and 1920, was called the 'Mad Mullah', and there were other 'mad' faquirs and mullahs on the North-West Frontier. Their excesses do not appear to have matched those of Ali Dinar who, Sir Reginald Wingate confided to an American newsman, had once forced a mother to eat her own baby.[19] It is not known whether the journalist asked why the British had tolerated the presence of this monster in Darfur for the past eighteen years.

It took over thirty years to subdue the animist tribes of the southern Sudan who objected to the naturally unwelcome novelty of taxation, and refused to renounce such customs as stock rustling and inter-tribal feuds. Thirty-three punitive expeditions were needed to persuade the tribesmen of the remote Nuba Mountains to accept the new order. No newspapermen accompanied the small detachments, and so the public remained ignorant about what occurred during these campaigns, which was just as well for the authorities in Khartoum and Cairo. 'The less attention is drawn to these matters the better,' observed Lord Cromer after he had read a report of the summary public hangings that had followed the suppression of a small uprising in the Sudan in 1908.[20] Another form of deterrent was applied in 1928 when a party of Dinka and Guer chiefs were treated to an exhibition of machine-gun and artillery fire during a visit to Khartoum.[21]

Impatient and exasperated officials often resorted to more forceful methods of coercion. During the 1917–18 operations in the Nuba Mountains, villages and crops were burned, and tribesmen and their families driven into the bush to die of thirst.[22] At Wingate's suggestion, aircraft had been brought from Egypt to bomb and strafe Ali Dinar's army, and thereafter they were frequently deployed against tribes in the deep south of the Sudan. The results were horrendous; in February 1920 incendiary bombs were dropped to start bush fires and flush out Nuer warriors, and they and their herds of cattle were regularly bombed and machine-gunned. [23] Casualties were often high (in one sortie against the Bahr-al-Jabal islands in January 1928, 200 tribesmen were killed), but the victims, like their counterparts in Europe during the Second World War, were not easily cowed.[24]

The official justification for these harsh measures was that they brought stability to remote and turbulent districts. And yet there was something profoundly incongruous and distasteful about the employment of aircraft to intimidate people whom Britain claimed she wished to regenerate. Administrators, who had been taught to believe in their country's civilising mission and who dedicated their lives to its fulfilment, were ashamed of what was euphemistically called 'air control'. It was suspended after 1930, although flights continued over potentially disaffected areas as a reminder of what lay in store for the insubordinate. The brief resort to air power as a means of punishment revealed, as did the episodes that followed the fall of Khartoum, the gulf which separated the lofty, humanitarian ideals of British imperialism and the methods of its agents.

8

The Greatest Blessing that Africa has Known: East and West Africa

There were two 'scrambles' for Africa during the 1880s and 1890s. The first was a sedate, although sometimes acrimonious, diplomatic game in which statesmen pored over maps and drew lines across them. The second was a more robust business in which individuals ventured into largely unknown hostile regions and cajoled or coerced their inhabitants into accepting new masters and new laws. This activity was confined to a handful of men whose fixity of purpose gave them the strength to endure extremes of discomfort and danger. One described Africa as 'a training ground for young men' with a taste for reckless adventure for, 'once started on *safari* – i.e. the line of march in Africa, one never knows where it may lead to, nor does one very much care.'[1] Of course some did; for Kitchener and his equally ambitious French counterparts, Joseph Simon Gallieni and Joseph Jacques Joffre (the conqueror of Timbuktu), the byways of Africa led to the highest commands in the First World War. Others, like Louis Hubert Lyautey, Wingate and Frederick, later Lord Lugard, stepped sideways and became senior proconsuls.

Lugard set his stamp on East and West Africa. He was a tough, lean officer with a straggling walrus moustache, which was exceptionally extravagant at a time when no self-respecting fighting man went bare-lipped in the tropics. Kitchener's growth may have been more famous, but Lugard's was more striking. It helped give him, and for that matter other bristly officers, a fearsome appearance, which may have been advantageous whenever he had to overawe natives. In 1887 Lugard, with three campaigns under his belt, was at a loose end. Having been diagnosed by his physician as exhausted, he immediately decided that, 'What I needed was active hard work – rather than rest.' Africa would provide his cure, and, after an unsuccessful attempt to offer his services to the Italian army in Eritrea, his sword was accepted by the missionary Lakes Company. During 1888 and 1889 Lugard commanded their levies in a war against slavers around the shores of Lake Nyasa.

He liked the way the Scottish missionaries ran their affairs and he learned much from them. The neat, clean mission houses and the schools with their tidy, well-dressed pupils were an 'object lesson' in European civilisation. White men in Africa, Lugard concluded, should always stick to a separate way of life that was an 'assertion of superiority which commands the respect and excites the emulation of the savage'. 'Insolent familiarity' by blacks was never to be tolerated and would be rebuffed automatically by a 'gentleman'. Like the British lower classes, the African instinctively recognised and respected a 'gentleman' and followed his lead.[2]

This opinion was widely shared by British officers and administrators. The gallant, public-school educated British officer, who commanded by force of character and innate self-confidence, could secure the loyalty of simpleminded black men who recognised him as a true warrior. Sporting prowess, particularly the singlehanded stalking of big game, added to the appeal of the British officer. In an intelligence report of 1906 on German East Africa a British official noted that, 'The Germans never move off the roads, they don't care for sport, and have no idea of the word as used by the British.' Moreover, they hunted in a distinctly ungentlemanly manner, ordering askaris to fire volleys at elephants, rhinoceroses and buffalo.[3] French colonial officers, like the British, imagined they had an interior quality which won them the hearts of natives. This was baraka, an inner spiritual charisma possessed by Muslim holy men which brought luck. The officer with baraka had, quite literally, a charmed life and appeared mirac-ulously preserved in battle; it was General Franco's baraka which saved his life in battles in Morocco in the 1920s and won him the loyalty of Moroccan troops.

Survival in Africa needed physical as well as moral stamina. Lugard devised his own eccentric, but, as events turned out, effective regimen for daily life in the tropics. He wore a broad-brimmed hat and drank large amounts of weak tea or water, often indifferent as to the latter's source. For Lugard the vital organs were the stomach, spleen and liver, which he kept covered with a flannel cummerbund at all times since their chilling was the cause of 'most of the fever, dysentery, diarrhoea and cholera' which laid men low in Africa. A substantial breakfast, taken just after sunrise, prevented fever which could arise from the sun overheating an empty stomach. When this precaution failed and he contracted fever, Lugard took doses of quinine and buried himself under a pile of clothing to sweat it out.[4] These rough and ready nostrums appear to have worked successfully.

Healthy exercise further reinforced the white man's constitution. Lieutenant Richard Meinertzhagen, posted to the King's African Rifles in Kenya in 1902, recommended 'vigorous hunting', which not only tested 'manliness', but developed bushcraft and marksmanship. Not everyone was so dedicated; he observed disapprovingly that while he stretched nerves and muscles 'many of my brother officers were drinking rot-gut or running about with somebody else's wife'. But this was to be expected in a mess which contained homosexuals and men who boasted about their native mistresses.[5]

Self-discipline and a stringent régime kept Lugard fit and enabled him to play a crucial part in the remaking of East and West Africa. Between 1889 and 1893, he was employed by the British Imperial East Africa Company, first to establish a military presence in its territory by building stockades and making treaties with native rulers, with whom he sometimes made pacts of blood brotherhood. Later he was a peace-keeper, suppressing slavery and intervening for the Protestants in a civil war between them and Catholic converts in Uganda.

Lugard was profoundly affected by what he saw as he traversed East Africa. The region was collapsing into anarchy from which it could only be rescued by Britain:

> The African knows no peace. One day you may see peace and plenty, well-tilled fields, and children playing in the sun; on the next you may find the corpses of the men, the bodies of the children half burnt in the flames which consumed the village, while the women are captives of the victorious raiders. Not against the slave-trade alone are our efforts needed . . . The *Pax Britannica* which shall stop this lawless raiding and this constant inter-tribal war will be the greatest blessing that Africa has known since the Flood.[6]

Such descriptions of the uncertainty and violence of African life were the stock-in-trade of the first-hand accounts of the continent which appeared

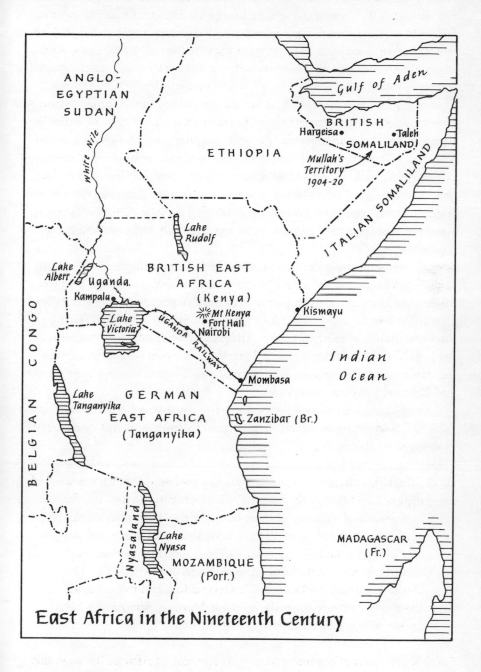

ANGLO-
EGYPTIAN
SUDAN

White Nile

Gulf of Aden

ETHIOPIA

BRITISH
Hargeisa ● SOMALILAND ● Taleh

*Mullah's
Territory
1904-20*

ITALIAN SOMALILAND

*Lake
Rudolf*

*Lake
Albert*
Uganda.
Kampala ●

BRITISH EAST
AFRICA
(Kenya)

※ Mt Kenya
● Fort Hall
Nairobi ●

● Kismayu

*Lake
Victoria*

UGANDA RAILWAY

*Indian
Ocean*

BELGIAN CONGO

*Lake
Tanganyika*

GERMAN
EAST AFRICA
(Tanganyika)

● Mombasa

Zanzibar (Br.)

Nyasaland

*Lake
Nyasa*

MOZAMBIQUE
(Port.)

MADAGASCAR
(Fr.)

East Africa in the Nineteenth Century

in late-Victorian Britain. Readers were introduced to a land of contrasts in which all that was good was of European origin and all that was bad was of African. For instance, two eyewitness descriptions of Nigeria, published in the 1890s, refer to 'vile pagan customs', 'wild lawless people' and a 'kingdom of darkness'.[7] One author was struck by the coastal town of Bonny where the cleanness and order of the missionary settlement highlighted the grossness and depravity of the native township, where, ironically, the streets were littered with discarded bottles of 'trader gin'.[8] Like the mission tracts of an earlier generation, such material provided a call to duty; the British people had to give their wholehearted support to men like Lugard, who had shouldered what Kipling called 'the white man's burden'. It was appropriate that his employer, the British Imperial East Africa Company, set its device of a lightbulb on their postage stamps: it symbolised modernity and bringing light to a benighted region.

Lugard had developed his own views on how enlightenment should be spread in Africa, based on his experiences there and as a soldier in India. He wanted government along the lines that had evolved in India in which the administration would be impartial, firm, and respect local institutions and conventions. 'An arbitrary and despotic rule, which takes no account of native customs, traditions and prejudices,' he wrote, 'is not suited to the successful development of infant civilisation nor, in my view, in accordance with the spirit of British colonial rule.'[9] He had in mind the Indian practice of indirect rule by which Britain had adopted and sometimes adjusted existing political structures and cooperated with established rulers. It was an attractive alternative to the infinitely more expensive and wearisome process of creating an entirely new system of government, which was bound to provoke upheavals and resentment.

This theory was not of course new but, as applied by Lugard to Africa, proved very influential. There as elsewhere, Britain entered into an alliance of convenience with local rulers who, in return for concessions such as the extirpation of slavery, were allowed to continue in positions of authority so long as they exercised their power in a manner approved by British advisers. By the early 1920s schools had been set up in East Africa where chiefs' sons were educated for future responsibility. At these and other government schools, boys and girls wore a uniform based upon African rather than European dress, which had been once *de rigueur* for an African seeking a European-style education. In some areas, missionaries were adapting pagan initiation rites so that the traditional period of preparation for circumcision became one in which the youth learned the virtues of Christian 'manliness'.[10]

Money-making as well as civilising had been a function of the British Imperial East Africa Company. The two were not as compatible as they had once been in India, and by 1891 the company was tottering on the verge of bankruptcy. The upshot was that Uganda and British East Africa (Kenya), which had fallen to Britain's lot after the 1890 agreement with Germany, passed into Foreign and then Colonial Office control. The misfortunes of the company were evidence that claims that Africa offered an unlimited outlet for British manufactures were overblown. They had, however, helped provide the original impetus for African colonisation and had given hope to British businessmen trapped in a recession. The *Leeds Mercury* of 28 February 1885 had predicted that Africa would become a 'vast market' for 'cotton goods, blankets, crockery, muskets [this was true enough], hardware of all kinds, and cheap finery of every description'. But how were the Africans to pay for all these goods?

This irritating question was ignored during the optimistic period when Africa was being opened up, but it returned to trouble governments and businessmen at the turn of the century, by which time everyone was wiser about the actual conditions on the continent. Outside South Africa there were no King Solomon's mines. An economic revolution was clearly needed to create customers and, given that nearly all of them were under foreign government, the change would have to be imposed from above. A favourite metaphor of the 1890s, and one used by Chamberlain, was that the colonies were outlying 'estates' which, through careful management and investment, could be made profitable both to their owner and their inhabitants. This process was, however, complicated by the fact that the Colonial Office had inherited and cherished the old liberal tradition that it and its agents were trustees for gullible and child-like native populations, who needed protection from the unscrupulous and from each other.

At the same time, current economic orthodoxy insisted that capital investment in any enterprise was the task of individuals, not governments. There had been considerable opposition to demands by the British Imperial East Africa Company for a subsidy to help fund a railway from Mombasa to the shores of the Indian Ocean, which would both serve as a conduit for trade and tighten Britain's grip on the source of the White

Nile. In 1896, Chamberlain recognised the line's potential and agreed to underwrite some of its costs. By 1913, when the arrangement ended, the British government had paid £2.8 million in grants for the development of East Africa.

The railway was completed in 1903 and five years later was making a respectable annual profit of £60,000. By this time the economic development of Kenya was well underway, the local authorities having, in 1903, agreed to set aside a huge upland region of temperate climate and fertile soil for white settlement. Agriculture, practised by Europeans using modern methods, offered the only means of making the region self-supporting and, incidentally, of helping make the railway pay. As in Southern Rhodesia, land on either side of the track was reserved for Europeans who therefore had easy access to transport and outside markets.

Richard Meinertzhagen encountered one of the first white pioneers in Nairobi in 1902, and heard from him that in Kenya 'the white man is the master race and that the black man must forever remain cheap labour and slaves'.[11] It was a view which, in various and often less trenchant forms, was held by successive settlers. In 1916 they numbered 8,000 and included a sprinkling of Boers who had trekked up from South Africa, bringing with them the racial attitudes of their homeland. Matters were further complicated in East Africa by another consequence of economic changes, the presence of Indians. They had been shipped there as indentured labourers to help build the railway, and afterwards settled as shopkeepers and clerks; they were also undertaking skilled work for which there were no qualified Africans. By 1920, there were 23,000 Indians in Kenya squeezed between 10,000 whites, mostly settlers and their families, and nearly three million Africans.

The colonial government faced a dilemma. Although no money-spinning staple such as cotton, sugar or tobacco had emerged to provide an early boost for the Kenyan economy, coffee- and maize-growing and ranching were flourishing and the 1914–19 war in East Africa had provided a welcomed impetus for growth. In the latter year there were two million acres earmarked for white farmers, and the government was extensively advertising a scheme to attract British ex-officers to invest their gratuities in Kenyan farms. Private capital was essential for the Kenyan settler, as it had been for his North American predecessor (£2,000 was considered the minimum in 1919), and he needed abundant, cheap labour.

Since the start of white colonisation, the colonial authorities had had to concoct ways in which to push sections of the black population towards regular wage-earning and the market economy. The annual Hut Tax of three rupees (20p) a hut, with a further three rupees per wife for hut-owners with more than one, and a poll tax of three rupees for every adult non-householder, forced Africans to seek cash. Kenya also adopted in 1918 a measure that had its origins in South Africa, and which had been copied in Southern Rhodesia and Nyasaland, by which blacks were banned from living in areas set aside for Europeans unless they undertook to work for the owner.

Unskilled labour for Europeans was at this period highly unpopular for understandable reasons. For years the prevailing wisdom had been that the reason why most Africans kept out of the western economy was ingrained laziness. Hard work for regular hours appeared not to come naturally to them, nor did they appreciate its moral value. An explorer who had crossed East Africa in 1884 with a party of unwilling porters, congratulated himself on his return for having driven them forcefully, for they had come back 'as men, with their moral and physical defects cast off'.[12] Lugard, faced with malingerers among his porters, dosed them with a mixture of water, salt and mustard, which one, who was cured, pronounced 'a very fierce medicine'.[13] A more common astringent was the sjambok, a rhino-hide whip which was commonly used on black miners at the Wankie colliery in Southern Rhodesia during the early 1900s.[14] It had been a frequent form of punishment for insubordinate black labourers during the Boer War, and in November 1914 the commander of HMS *Dartmouth* at Cape Town asked Admiralty permission to flog striking Arab and Indian lascars, on the grounds that no other correction would have any effect.[15]

Lord Cranworth, in his guidebook for would-be farmers in Kenya published in 1919, warned against too many beatings; but for offences such as lying, petty pilfering, cruelty to children and animals, 'the whip is the best and kindest preventive and cure'.[16] Lady Cranworth, counselling the new settler's wife, strongly recommended regular inspections of the kitchen, a disagreeable chore which invariably ended with 'a feeling of soreness on the part, the posterior part, of the cook'.[17] It appears that Swahili (part African, part Arab) and native cooks were never fastidious about washing utensils.

Not surprisingly, given their needs, a substantial minority of Kenyan settlers favoured a union with South Africa, whose government would, they believed, treat them more sympathetically than the Colonial Office.[18] Despite regular polo and soccer matches between teams of officials and farmers, tension remained high. It reached breaking point in 1921 after the announcement that Indian representatives were to be added to the governor's council. This measure was interpreted as a step towards a multi-racial Kenya in which the outnumbered settlers might soon find their interests overridden.

A resistance movement sprang up and there was heady talk of rebellion. The man of the moment was Brigadier-General Philip Wheatley, an ex-officer in the Indian army with a hearty dislike of Indian nationalism, whose blustering, extreme right-wing views made him a living prototype of David Low's cartoon figure, Colonel Blimp. Kenya was a natural sanctuary for Blimps, and they rallied round Wheatley and concocted a hare-brained plan for settlers' *coup d'état* with the slogan 'For King and Kenya'. What in many respects was a trailer for the unilateral declaration of independence by Rhodesia in 1964, turned out to be a damp squib with the settlers pulling back at the last moment. The episode did provoke the Colonial Office to issue a white paper in 1922 that set out official policy in an unambiguous manner: 'Primarily Kenya is an African territory' in which 'the interests of the African natives must be paramount'.[19]

West Africa was also a black man's country. It was an inhospitable region where a combination of humidity, heat, and a febriferous coastline combined to give it the notorious reputation of 'the white man's grave'. In the late eighteenth century convicted criminals were sentenced to undertake garrison duty there as a form of delayed death sentence, and during most of the nineteenth, the mortality rate among troops in Sierra Leone was the highest in the empire. Advances in medical knowledge increased a European's chances of survival, but in the years immediately before the First World War, officials in the Gold Coast were expected to spend no more than twelve months there before being sent on leave. Their colleagues in Northern Nigeria did eighteen-month stints and, one observed, they counted themselves unlucky if they had more than three bouts of fever in a year.[20]

For most of the nineteenth century, Britain's West African colonies were derelict outposts. The Gambia and Gold Coast settlements were relics of the slave-trading era, no longer of economic value. Sierra Leone served as a glowing example of what could be achieved by black men and women with a Christian education, and was also a major coaling station for the Royal Navy. A visitor in 1898 found it a 'most terrifically civilised place', even though the sight of black people going to church in European

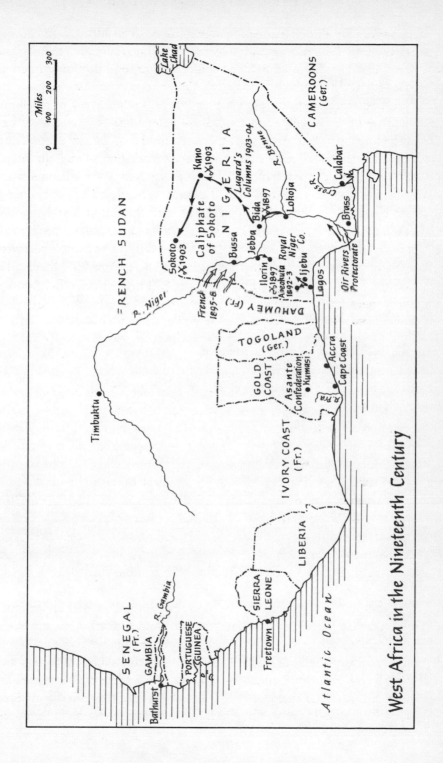

West Africa in the Nineteenth Century

clothes, which would have so pleased an earlier generation of philanthropists, struck him as 'grotesque'.[21] Lagos, acquired in 1861 as a base for anti-slaving operations, was a toehold in Nigeria, the only part of this region which attracted British commerce.

The magnet here was palm oil, a vital commodity for British industry which used it as a lubricant and the basis for making soap and candles. The profitable trade in palm oil was dominated by Liverpool entrepreneurs whose interests were guarded by a network of consuls, backed by intermittent naval patrols, some of which penetrated the Niger and Benue rivers. The natives here and elsewhere in West Africa were enthusiastic consumers of 'trader gin', a noxious but potent narcotic; in 1889 1.35 million gallons were imported into Nigeria and, despite protests from temperance and missionary groups in Britain, the flow steadily increased. In 1908 the total West African gin trade was worth £1.2 million, with nearly 90 per cent going to Nigeria.

So long as palm oil poured out of Nigeria and gin poured in, Britain had no interest whatsoever in acquiring additional territory there or elsewhere in West Africa. Until the early 1880s, it was a region where the machinery of informal empire functioned more or less effectively. If a local ruler proved obstructive, as did Kofi, Asantehene of the Asante ('King Coffee'), in 1873, a small but well-armed military force delivered a rap over the knuckles.

This local equilibrium was upset by France. From the mid-1870s a small, highly motivated clique of French soldiers and politicians became entranced by the idea of creating a sprawling empire, which would stretch from West Africa across the western Sahara. This province might prove another India, enriching France and enhancing its status in the world, which had been diminished by the humiliations of the Franco-Prussian War. The key to the region's economic exploitation was thought to be a railway that would cross from West Africa to the Red Sea, never leaving French soil, and which would serve as a conduit for the entire trade of Africa north of the Sahara. The inspiration for this trans-continental railway was the American Union Pacific Railroad, which had been completed in 1869 and was currently opening up the West. Rhodes had also recognised the potential of a railway bisecting Africa and, from the 1890s, planned a Cape to Cairo line which would, needless to say, run across British territory.

The French took their first steps towards a West African empire in the late 1870s. The impetus came from two highly-placed imperialists,

Admiral Jean de Jauréguiberry, the Minister for Marine, and Charles de Freycinet, a railway enthusiast, who was Minister for Public Works. They approved probes inland from Senegal, while the gunboat *Voltigeur* was ordered into Nigerian waters to make contact with and extract treaties from local chiefs. Simultaneously the explorer, Savorgnan de Brazza, was making agreements with rulers in the Congo basin. Confronted with trespassers in regions hitherto under the loose control of Britain, British consuls started to collect treaties.

These pledges were ammunition for British and French statesmen and diplomats to whom fell the task of haggling over who had what. Britain's main fear was that the protectionist French would obtain swathes of the West African hinterland, which would leave the Gambia, Sierra Leone and the Gold Coast as stranded coastal colonies without any inland trade. Furthermore, France might secure the Upper Niger and so strangle the trade that passed down the river from northern Nigeria and the western Sudan. British commercial interests got some safeguards from the settlement made at Berlin during 1885: Britain was allowed a sphere of influence which stretched up the Niger and inland from the Gold Coast.

As elsewhere in Africa, the British government now faced the problem of giving substance to its authority over paper protectorates. It was, as in southern and eastern Africa, lucky to find a private corporation that was willing to undertake what otherwise was a tiresome and costly business. The Royal Niger Company was chartered in 1886 to trade and govern along the lower and mid-Niger. The company was the creation of George Taubman Goldie, a Manxman who had, until 1877, led a directionless life as an extremely diffident professional soldier and wanderer. In that year he visited the Niger coast and saw the chance to make his mark on the world. A childhood worshipper of Rajah Brooke, Goldie later claimed that, 'My dream as a child was to colour the map red,' and there is no reason to disbelieve him. In Nigeria he found a convenient blank, and like Brooke, he had the cash to fulfil his ambitions. Within a few years he had organised the local merchants and laid the foundations for his own company.

During the late 1880s and early 1890s, there were plenty of Goldies, and for that matter Lugards among the young French officers who were pursuing promotion and medals in West Africa. Their collective motto was '*Prenez l'initiative*', even if that meant, and it often did, ignoring orders from hesitant bureaucrats in Paris. By the early 1890s, the French conquest of West Africa and the western Sahara had entered a decisive phase, with the momentum sustained by soldiers convinced that they knew better than their masters, one of whom once remarked that colonial commanders constituted what was in effect an independent state, answerable to no one. Perhaps so, but politicians were wary of asserting authority over the French army which, in right-wing, ultra-nationalist circles was seen as the embodiment of the country's honour.

French aggression in West Africa had never unduly troubled Salisbury, who once sardonically questioned the ultimate value of vast areas of 'light soil', his euphemism for sand. This view was quietly held by many in France, and was reflected in the failure of the projected trans-Saharan railway to attract any investment. It was less easy, however, for British ministers to dismiss out of hand France's West African adventures after 1894, when it had become plain that they might end with the seizure of the Upper Niger. Goldie had been among the first to sense the danger, and in July 1894 he hired Lugard to lead a small expedition deep into northern Nigeria and negotiate treaties which would bring its rulers into Britain's orbit. Almost simultaneously, Captain Decouer had been commissioned to proceed from Dahomey into the same area and for the same purpose. There was also a rumour that the Germans were preparing an expedition for this end.[22]

Lugard's treaty-gathering trek through Borgu during the autumn and early winter of 1894 was a superhuman feat of perseverance. He and his party endured extremes of temperature (his dog died of heat exhaustion), torrential rain, an ambush and bouts of fever. Lugard overcame the latter by self-medication in the form of a course of antipyrin and a thirteen-mile march in the blazing sun, which produced a curative sweat. Native medicines, whose ingredients he did not investigate too closely, provided an apparent antidote to poison from an arrowhead which had pierced his skull. Lugard deserved and got what he wanted, an agreement in which the aged and decrepit King of Nikki accepted the protection and friendship of Britain and its agent, the Royal Niger Company. The trouble was that just over a fortnight later Decoeur arrived at Nikki and went away, like Lugard, with a treaty.

The Upper Niger now became a focus for Anglo-French rivalry. The chief protagonists were Chamberlain, who became Colonial Secretary in June 1895, and Gabriel Hanotaux, who took over France's Foreign Ministry in April 1896. Chamberlain refused on principle to relinquish an inch of African territory to which Britain had a legal claim, while Hanotaux sought to prevent Africa from becoming another India in which French ambitions were checked by a combination of British guile and bullying. The British, he believed, used their language as a cover for deception ('*elle affirme, elle n'explique pas*') and therefore France would have to resort to action to get her way rather than waste time on otiose negotiations over the validity of treaties. Only Marchand on the banks of the Nile and Senegalese *tirailleurs* on the banks of the Niger would stop Britain in her tracks.

It was Britain which was first off the mark in the confrontation on the Niger. With Chamberlain's blessing, Goldie launched a war against Bida and Ilorin, whose rulers had refused to fulfil their promises to abandon slave-raiding. The campaign of January 1897 was not just a humanitarian crusade, it was a fearsome demonstration of the military power of the company and, by association, Britain. A twelve-pounder gun was manhandled, with considerable difficulty, through the bush to hurl shells against the walls of Bida at a range of two miles. But what really struck terror into the spearmen and mailed cavalry of the two states were the company's six Maxim guns, the 'bindigat ruiva' (water guns) or 'piss guns'. They enabled an army of 500 men, mostly Hausa constabulary, to beat a mediaeval horde, believed to outnumber them by thirty to one.

Goldie's little war alerted the French to British intentions, and during 1896–7 advance parties of their colonial forces filtered into Borgu, where *tricolores* were hoisted over native villages and old treaties waved about as proof that they were now French property. Chamberlain foresaw a collision, and began taking precautions. In June 1897 he proposed the immediate formation of a 2,000-strong black army, the West Africa Frontier Force, and appointed Lugard its commander and Britain's special commissioner for northern Nigeria. Obviously Lugard's experience counted, but Chamberlain was also making a gesture designed to show the French that Britain was going to take a tough line. In France, Lugard was detested on account of his alleged massacre of Catholic converts in Uganda and, more recently, his coup at Nikki. When Lugard arrived in Nigeria in the spring of 1898, *The Times* reported that for Frenchmen he 'symbolised . . . the fierce and grasping spirit of perfidious Albion. He is for them the stuff of which legends are made.'[23]

A comedy of manners rather than a legend emerged from the Anglo-French stand-off in Borgu during the summer of 1898. Lugard had officered the West Africa Frontier Force with men of his own kidney, all of whom could have stepped from the pages of a G.A. Henty yarn. They were young, ex-public-school boys with a love of sport and taste for adventure. Field command was in the hands of Colonel James Willcocks, another sportsman and veteran of several Indian campaigns. It was he who set out from Jebba into Borgu where, at Lugard's instructions, he was to hoist the Union Jack wherever he thought fit, taking care to avoid villages over which the *tricolore* was already flying. There followed a bizarre charade in which British units sidestepped French villages and occasionally collided with French detachments. There were some wrangles, usually about such niceties of protocol as saluting flags, but the prevailing mood on both sides was one of nervous good humour. International rivalries were forgotten as professional empire-builders discovered, over drinks and cigarettes by a campfire, that they had much in common as soldiers and gentlemen.[24] As Captain George Abadie observed of one French officer he encountered, he was 'a gentleman . . . and one knows how to deal with him.'[25]

There were a few fire-eaters on both sides, including some of the native troops, who yearned for a fight. The French position was, in fact, precarious, since their rule was still being resisted in other parts of West Africa. During the confrontation on the Niger, troops had had to be hurried to the Ivory Coast to deal with Samory Touré, France's most tenacious adversary in West Africa, and to suppress an uprising in Soudan (Mali). Furthermore, as Lugard appreciated, a shooting war on the Niger would leave the French isolated throughout the region since the navy would blockade their West African ports.

Throughout the crisis, Chamberlain remained in full control as the telegraph line had been extended from Lagos to Jebba so that the men-on-the-spot could not take matters into their own hands. It was diplomatic camel-trading that finally ended the confrontation and Britain, who got the best of the deal, secured Borgu and with it all the territory which now lies within the boundaries of modern Nigeria. All that remained was for Chamberlain to tie up the administrative loose ends. Lagos and the coastal Oil Rivers Protectorate were amalgamated in 1900 as Southern Nigeria, the company was abolished, and its territories passed into the government of the new colony of Northern Nigeria, whose first governor was Lugard.

Similar consolidation occurred in Sierra Leone and the Gold Coast where, boundaries having been fixed with the French, pacification followed. Regions where British control had hitherto been fitful or non-existent were brought to heel. In 1887, at the conclusion of a campaign against the Yonni of Sierra Leone, the British commander told their chiefs, 'The Queen has shown you her power by sending her force and taking the country, which now belongs to me and the governor.' The message was punched home with a demonstration of Maxim-gun fire which 'much surprised' them.[26] It took two expeditions, in 1895 and 1900, to convince the Asante of the strength and permanence of the new order in the Gold Coast. The last was a particularly brutal affair in which British officers had the utmost difficulty in restraining their native troops who seemed to have regarded the campaign as a licence to plunder and rape.[27]

As the terrifying lessons of conquest sank in, the conquerors often found it easy to overawe their new subjects. When Captain Abadie arrived in Ilorin a year after Goldie's campaign, he found its people submissive. Commandeering lodgings was an easy business, and afterwards Abadie remarked on the drollery of 'two very hot and dirty, begrimed, badly clothed Englishmen dictating to a crowd of about six hundred Muhammadans, all big swells, and kicking them out.'[28] A clue to their reaction was revealed soon after; when Abadie set up his camera to photograph the local prince all his attendants fled at the sight of the tripod which reminded them of the mounting for a machine-gun.

The two men's overbearing behaviour was an extreme example of the self-confidence of their class. British social attitudes were exported to Africa, where the orthodoxy that the government of naïve native peoples was best entrusted to gentlemen was already taking root. Surveying the employees of the trading companies in Lagos in 1898, Lieutenant Archibald Eden was appalled by what he saw:

> The type of Englishman, in the shape of the trader, whom we meet in these parts, is too awful for words to describe; they are all more-or-less counter-jumpers of the worst type and biggest bounders into the bargain.[29]

Lieutenant Ladislaus Pope-Hennessey, who arrived at the same time, took an instant dislike to the colonial government officials, who were all 'bounders' and 'cads' addicted to 'cocktails', a novelty which the young officer found distasteful. Lugard shared these prejudices and feared that the conduct of men who were not gentlemen lowered respect for all white men.

He and Goldie had separately discovered 'gentlemen' among the Fulani Muslim princes of central and northern Nigeria and were impressed by their sophistication, bearing and the orderly procedures of their law courts and administration. Here were men with whom the British could cooperate, and Islamic institutions could be adopted to suit British needs. The first preliminary was the by now ritual trial of strength which occurred between 1902 and 1904, when the states of Sokoto and Kano were invaded and their armies defeated by Lugard.

Resistance from the ruling élite ceased, but there was a sudden upsurge of popular opposition to the British in February 1905 under the banner of Mahdist millennialism. The followers of this movement, including many slaves and ex-slaves, identified the British and French armies which had entered their country during the past decade with Baggal, an anti-Christ figure who, in Islamic eschatology, would appear before the coming of the Mahdi. The rebels surprised and overcame a British column at Satiru, capturing a slightly damaged Maxim gun, rifles and ammunition. No use was made of these spoils. Like its counterpart in the Sudan, the Nigerian Mahdist movement was backward-looking, and so the insurgents disdained to use the implements of modern, infidel war, relying instead on faith and traditional weaponry. In their next engagement, they adopted a mass charge and were defeated with over 2,000 dead.[30]

The Fulani aristocracy cooperated with the British in the suppression of this uprising, which threatened their own as well as their conqueror's authority. The two were now working in tandem as Lugard had introduced the system known either as 'indirect rule' or 'dual control'. He wanted above all to maintain a continuity of government and assure Britain's new subjects that, with the exception of slavery, Islamic practices were to be preserved and respected. Once this was clear, Muslim princes and clergy rallied behind the new order and the old courts and civil service continued to function, but under the eye of a British resident. This form of government suited the circumstances of Northern Nigeria for it was inexpensive and required limited manpower. Moreover, an instinctive *rapport* developed between the princes and the conservative, public-school and university educated administrators who were filling the ranks of the Nigerian civil service during the 1900s. Interestingly, the Colonial Office recruiters preferred sportsmen, who were presumably fitter and, most importantly, knew how to play by the rules.

The day-to-day running of indirect rule is vividly described in Joyce Cary's *Aissa Saved* (1932), which is set in the fictional province of Yanrin in 1921. Cary, who served in the Nigerian civil service, was aware of the tensions created by the new order. Alongside the emir and his Muslim staff, all of whom followed the paths of tradition, was a new élite which had been created over the past forty years by British educators in Sierra Leone and southern Nigeria. Early colonial government depended on this body

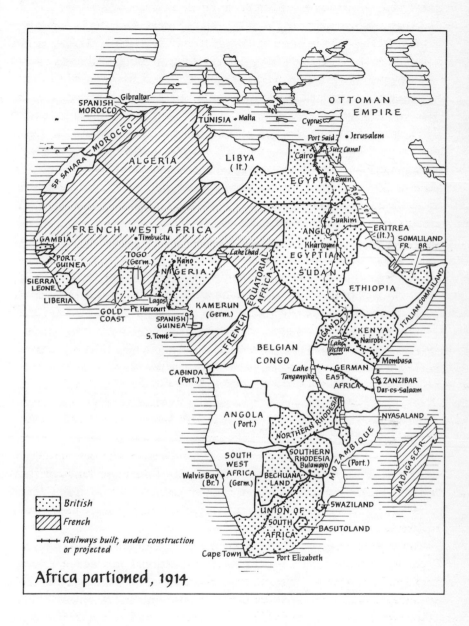

SPANISH
MOROCCO
Gibraltar

TUNISIA • Malta

Cyprus

OTTOMAN
EMPIRE

SP. SAHARA
MOROCCO

ALGERIA

LIBYA
(It.)

Port Said • Jerusalem
Cairo
Suez Canal
EGYPT Aswan

FRENCH WEST AFRICA

• Timbuctu

GAMBIA
PORT.
GUINEA

SIERRA
LEONE
LIBERIA

TOGO
(Germ.)

Lake Chad

• Kano
NIGERIA

GOLD
COAST

Lagos
Pt. Harcourt

SPANISH
GUINEA
S. Tomé •

KAMERUN
(Germ.)

FRENCH EQUATORIAL AFRICA

ANGLO-
EGYPTIAN
SUDAN

• Suakim
Khartoum

Red Sea

ERITREA
(It.)
SOMALILAND
FR. BR.

ETHIOPIA

ITALIAN SOMALILAND

BELGIAN
CONGO

UGANDA
Lake
Victoria

KENYA
Nairobi •

Lake
Tanganyika
GERMAN
EAST
AFRICA

Mombasa

ZANZIBAR
Dar-es-Salaam

CABINDA
(Port.)

ANGOLA
(Port.)

NORTHERN RHODESIA

SOUTHERN
RHODESIA
Bulawayo

NYASALAND

MOZAMBIQUE
(Port.)

MADAGASCAR

Walvis Bay
(Br.)

SOUTH
WEST
AFRICA
(Germ.)

BECHUANA-
LAND

SWAZILAND

UNION OF
SOUTH
AFRICA

Cape Town

Port Elizabeth

BASUTOLAND

British

French

Railways built, under construction
or projected

Africa partioned, 1914

of literate blacks, one of whom, a graduate from a Sierra Leone mission school and a Royal Niger Company agent at Ekow, was described by a British officer who met him in 1892. The clerk was 'sleek and polite' and, 'a great man in the eyes of the local aborigines' with whom he exchanged palm oil for 'gaudy Manchester cottons'. In the evening he 'played selections from *Hymns Ancient and Modern* on a harmonium in the drawing room of a hut, hung with portraits of the royal family.'[31]

Lugard admitted the value of such men, but insisted that they should never usurp or interfere with the functions of men whose power derived from tradition. No African clerk or constable could override the judgement of, say, a village headman. This was the rule in Cary's Yanrin, where Jacob, an educated Christian from the coast, considered himself one of the three 'civilised persons' in the region. He wore white man's clothing, was less deferential than the local natives, and had absorbed some politics. On hearing that a massacre of Christian converts was imminent in a nearby town, he urges Bradgate, the British resident, to take immediate action. 'I run for you, sah, because I say, if dem Christians done get killed someone go write paper in England, write praps parliament member, den ma frien Mister Bradgate catch big trouble.' As in India, the British faced the dilemma of how to handle a class of educated natives who were vital for everyday administration, but who knew something of the outside world and the political values which obtained in it. They were not always compliant collaborators, as Jacob's remarks suggest, and it is not surprising that British administrators preferred the old hierarchies of Africa.

9

Ye Sons of the Southern Cross: The White Dominions

In his patriotic vision, *The Poets' Pilgrimage to Waterloo*, Robert Southey wrote of 'those distant lands, where Britain blest with her redundant life the East and West'. He was thinking of Canada and Australia, which, like many of his countrymen, he saw as repositories for superfluous men and women, unwanted by reason of their poverty or criminality. This was the age of Robert Malthus, the parson-schoolmaster who devoted his life to studying the calculus of population growth, and concluded that a spiralling birth rate could only be checked by cyclical famines. This bleak prognosis was widely accepted and appeared confirmed by the starvation that followed bad harvests during the 1810s.

Emigration to Canada, Australia, South Africa and, after 1840, New Zealand offered salvation for those who might otherwise have languished and died in a homeland which could not provide for them. The government concurred and, between 1819 and 1825, allocated £95,000 in subsidies for pauper emigration. Local authorities followed suit; in 1826 the Board of Guardians of Benenden in Kent paid £14.10 shillings (£14.50p) each to twenty-seven men, women and children for their passage to New York. This was a large outlay, but it was a once and for all measure which relieved ratepayers of people who would have been a burden for many years to come. For this reason, the 1834 Poor Law included provisions for assisting poor emigrants. The 1891 Reformatory and Industrial Schools Act gave their governors the power to send delinquent children to the colonies. Private charities did likewise: the Salvation Army and Dr Barnado's paid for the passage of orphans to the colonies and, in the sixty years after 1870, 100,000 were settled in Canada alone.[1] As in previous centuries, enforced emigration provided a solution to domestic social problems.

Most nineteenth-century emigrants were not state-funded. When they did receive help, it came from voluntary charities set up for the purpose and based upon the principles of self-help. Typical of this sort of body was the Highlands and Islands Emigration Society which assisted crofters from an economically moribund region to settle on farms in Australia during the 1850s. It was axiomatic that anyone who was industrious and thrifty would prosper in the colonies. A prospectus for the Canadian province of New Brunswick, issued in 1842, claimed that a workman there, drawing wages of between twenty and thirty pounds annually, could in a few years accumulate enough capital to buy his own farm since average land prices were about three shillings (15p) an acre. 'Were young persons of either sex to engage themselves in this way,' the author concluded, 'they would be certain of succeeding to comfort and independence – would become useful members of society – and would strengthen those ties by which this colony is attached to the parent state.'[2]

Many underwent this process of regeneration, and some who did wrote home letters which were circulated to encourage other emigrants. Typical was that sent by James Dobbie of Lanark, Canada, to his father and friends in 1826:

> I really bless God every day I rise, that He was ever pleased in the course of his providence to send me and my family to this place. We are not without difficulties here, but they are nothing to your wants in Glasgow; we have always plenty to eat and drink, and have always a little to spare . . . I wish you would try and do all you can to come out: you will find plenty of work, and hard work, but be assured it will pay well. My stock of cattle consists of one yoke of oxen, three milk cows and three young ones. I have got up a very handsome new house, with the assistance of fifteen young men, it was raised in one day; it is 24 feet in length and 15 in breadth.[3]

This must have been very tempting since Clydeside was suffering badly from a trade recession. In January 1827, when handloom weavers' wages had dropped to four shillings (20p) a week, reports that five times that amount were being paid in America persuaded 800 heads of families to ask the local authorities for assisted passage. High wages, as much as the chance to become a self-sufficient farmer, always acted as a magnet for immigrants. William Lang, an ex-waiter and ward room steward of HMS *Lark*, jumped ship in Sydney in April 1885. His defence was poverty, for he could only send home twenty-five shillings [£1.25p] a month to his wife and six children in England. 'The thought of this drove me wild,' he pleaded, 'and the temptation of employment on shore at good wages, at a Hotel in the Blue Mountains, enabling me to provide for my little ones proved too great, and I ran.'[4] A stony-hearted court martial gave him eighteen months' hard labour since there had been a rash of similar desertions.

The conventional immigrant paid the cost of his passage. In 1834 transatlantic fares from Liverpool and Glasgow were as little as twenty-seven shillings (£1.35), for which the passenger endured the misery of sleeping on the deck, and cabins were between £14 and £35. The 12,000-mile journey to Australia and New Zealand cost £23 steerage and £50 with a cabin and, as on all other voyages, passengers had to provide their own food. Those who paid the lowest fares suffered much discomfort. A well-to-do passenger crossing the Atlantic in 1834 peeped into the steerage-class quarters and saw 'children crying, women screaming, and all tossing about from side to side as the vessel pitched: butter, biscuit, treacle, beef and potatoes all lying higgledy-piggledy or rolling from side to side.'[5] Conditions improved and fares fell after 1840 when steamships superseded sailing vessels: in 1898 a single ticket to Australia could cost as little as thirteen guineas (£13.65p).

It is estimated that 16 million emigrants sailed from Britain between 1815 and 1914, of whom about one in four went to the United States, the rest to the colonies. Periods of recession witnessed the largest exoduses; 1.8 million left Britain between 1901 and 1910, half settling in the white dominions, whose popularity rose steadily during the next sixty years. Ireland provided a large proportion of these immigrants; about 800,000 between 1815 and the 1845–6 famine and an astonishing one million in the seven years after, most of whom were destined for the United States.

There were also smaller flows of immigration within the empire. When Scots left Clydeside in the 1820s, they were replaced by Gaelic, Catholic Irish (there were 27,000 in Glasgow in 1827), who were willing to take lower wages and so contributed to further emigration from Scotland. A combination of overpopulation, chronic poverty and demands for cheap unskilled labour lay behind the Irish migration as it did that of Indians and

Chinese. Indian labourers were recruited for plantation work in the West Indies from the 1850s onwards and Fiji from the 1880s, where they balanced the fall in the native birth rate. The agricultural, mining and railroad boom on the west coast of the United States and Canada drew Chinese, Japanese and, by the turn of the century, Sikhs. In 1852 there were 52,000 Hong Kong Chinese alone in California, and by 1900 15 per cent of the population of British Columbia was Asian.

The influx of Chinese and Japanese into Canada stirred up racial tensions and official efforts were made to ban Asians.[6] This was possible because since the mid-1890s the government had been encouraging mass immigration from central Europe and Russia, where there were plenty of destitute men and women who were glad to accept low wages in the expanding lumber, construction and mining industries of Canada's midwest. There was racial friction in Australia following the import of Chinese labourers after the gold rush of 1852. For the next forty or so years the Australian trade union movement and later the Labour party agitated against further Chinese immigration on the grounds that it would drive down wages. The result of this campaign was the 1901 Immigration Restriction Act which codified what became known as the 'White Australia' policy.

Non-white labour was required for work which was shunned by British immigrants. Most emigrants had been enticed to the colonies by official promises of cheap land and with it the chance to achieve financial independence. It was universally accepted in Australia and New Zealand, as it had been in North America, that the original occupants of the land had forfeited their rights of possession by their failure to use it productively. Landing in New Zealand in 1845, Surgeon Pine was dismayed to find, 'Its fields are uncultivated . . . its mines unworked; its rivers unnavigated.' He automatically concluded that the country should become the property of 'intelligent people of the old world.'[7] They were already there, introduced by the New Zealand Company, whose guiding spirit was Colonel Edward Gibbon Wakefield. He was a singleminded enthusiast for emigration which, he believed, had to be practised with scientific precision so that the fledgling colony would have a proper balance of men and women, landowners and labourers. Gibbon had an elastic conscience (he had once allegedly abducted an heiress) which made it easy for him to persuade the Maoris to forsake their lands in return for such cheapjack trifles as razors, ribbons, looking-glasses and Jew's harps.

These and other British manufactures were among the loot British soldiers carried off from the pah (fortified camp) of Paramatta in 1845.[8] Paramatta had refused to accept the new order and his resistance started twenty-six years of intermittent wars between the Maoris and the settlers, backed until the mid-1860s by the British army. The Maoris could not hope to win and, like other South Sea Islanders, their population fell as they came into contact with alien diseases, but they held their own with a courage and skill which impressed their adversaries. They were not, like the Australian aborigines, driven into the wastelands and hunted like kangaroos, but allowed to become integrated into New Zealand. Maoris who passed the property-owning hurdle were given the vote when New Zealand received its constitution in 1852, and British soldiers paid them a unique tribute by erecting a war memorial to their dead in Christ Church Cathedral.

Men and women contemplating emigration to Canada in the 1820s were assured that on arrival they would enjoy the same rights there as they had in Britain, whatever this may have meant to the poor of that time. In a similar vein, an invitation to immigrants issued by the Queensland government in 1908 offered them the chance to help 'lay the foundation of a nation of brave, diligent, and liberty-loving men'.[9]

Between these two dates the internal government of the white colonies had been transformed. The process had started in 1839 with the publication of a report by Lord Durham of an investigation he had conducted in Canada after small-scale disturbance there two years before. The Whig peer's recommendations for local self-determination were the basis for a policy which his party implemented between 1847 and 1867. The Canadian provinces, the Australian states, New Zealand and Cape Colony were each given constitutions that provided them with elected governments with powers to make laws and distribute land. From the early 1840s there had been a flow of former Chartists to Australia and New Zealand and their radical ideas provided a leaven for political life in both colonies. Without an aristocracy to act as a brake on reform and with a large population drawn from the British working class, it was inevitable that the colonies soon had a wider franchise than Britain and governments willing to undertake novel and far-reaching social reforms.

Local autonomy led the way to the voluntary creation of nation states: in 1867 Canada became a confederation, Australia a federation in 1901, and South Africa in 1910, including the Transvaal and the Orange Free State, which had been granted self-government in 1906. Here there were no liberal franchises, for the British government had been forced, for the sake of obtaining political peace, to accept the exclusion of black and mixed-race voters from the Transvaal and Orange Free State electorate. Non-white voters made up 1 per cent of Natal's voters and 15 per cent of Cape Colony's. The price paid by Britain for a stable and tractable dominion in South Africa was toleration of what, in 1910, was a customary apartheid, a system of discrimination and segregation that would, in thirty-eight years' time, be given the force of law.

The compromise in South Africa was a reminder that political expediency as well as liberal principles had shaped Britain's policies towards her white colonies. The Whig dogmas of *laissez faire* and public economy, as well as the belief that British political rights should be enjoyed by all British subjects, wherever they lived, had dictated the first moves towards colonial self-determination. Self-governing colonists could raise their own taxes and pay for their own administration and, most importantly, protection; in 1858 the Canadian garrison had cost the Treasury £261,000. By 1871, the redcoats had been recalled from all the colonies save the volatile Cape, and the colonists had to raise and fund their own militias.

As administrative bonds were severed, the question was raised as to the future relationship between Britain and her colonies. Despite predictions that home rule was the first step along a road that led towards complete independence, there were few signs that any of the colonies wished to break their remaining political ties with Britain. Queen Victoria remained the head of state in each dominion, as the self-governing colonies were called, and her features appeared on their postage stamps and coins. Canada and Newfoundland, more royalist perhaps than the king, produced issues which showed Prince Albert, the Prince of Wales and obscurer members of the royal family.

Alongside such advertisements of attachment to Britain, there were indications that the colonies were developing a distinctive identity and culture of their own. These were most pronounced in Australia. A prospector who arrived at the Victoria gold diggings in 1853 found himself in the middle of 'an American type of society'. 'All aristocratic feelings and associations of the old country are at once annihilated,' he observed. 'Plebianism of the rankest, and, in many instances, of the lowest kind, at present dwells in Australia, and riches are now becoming the test of a man's position.'[10] Digger egalitarianism soon became part of the Australian consciousness. The ANZAC (Australia and New Zealand Army Corps) soldier 'is no lover of privilege of class. He does not understand it,' proudly announced the Queensland *School Paper* in November 1917.[11] According to the official Australian history of the war, the classless Australian fighting men were also independent-minded, refusing 'to take for granted the pre-scribed opinions' and were ready always to take the 'vigorous and unfettered initiative'. Individualism was balanced by a powerful sense of brotherhood which lay at the heart of the Australian male psyche. It was known as 'mateship' and its only rule was that 'a man should at all times and at any cost stand by his mate'.[12] None of these qualities endeared Australians to that stick-necked breed of Englishmen, often army com-manders, who believed in an orderly, disciplined society in which everyone stuck to the rules. A gentleman cricketer, writing in 1888, regretted that players in Australian touring XIs tended to contest umpires' decisions.[13]

There was a small but clamorous group of Australians who rejected British standards. The Sydney *Bulletin* regularly poured scorn on what it called 'colonial cringe', a mass inferiority complex which accepted the innate superiority of all things British. The *Bulletin* also denounced attempts to promote imperial consciousness in Australia as a ploy to further Britain's selfish interests, and accordingly renamed Empire Day as 'Vampire Day'.[14] The *Bulletin*'s carping did not seriously weaken Australian imper-ial sentiment nor convince Australians that Britain's interests were not necessarily their own.

The *Bulletin*'s anti-British shafts were being launched at a time when Australia and the other dominions were becoming increasingly aware of the political and strategic value of the imperial connection. So too was Britain which, since the mid-1870s, was endeavouring to survive in a mutable and none too friendly world. As she entered into competition with hostile powers whose strength matched her own, it became impera-tive for Britain to cultivate colonial goodwill. The colonies were becoming valuable assets, since their assistance might prove vital in the event of con-flict with France and Russia. Shifts in the global balance of power generated anxieties within the dominions, which had for the first time to come to terms with their own isolation and vulnerability. The possibility of an Anglo-Russian war in 1877–8, and with it seaborne raids by Russian warships on the Pacific coastlines of Canada, Australia and New Zealand, made the governments of each appreciate the extent of their dependence upon the Royal Navy.

One immediate consequence of this scare was the purchase of warships by Victoria and Queensland in 1882–3 and a greater willingness on behalf of these and other dominion governments to contribute to Britain's naval budget. A sense of common purpose and shared responsibilities prompted the New South Wales government to send 700 volunteers, all in red coats, to join the British army in the Sudan in May 1885. These soldiers, and offers of help from South Australia, Victoria and New Zealand, impressed Wolseley. He wrote warmly to Lord Loch, the governor of Victoria, and said that he had welcomed the Australians 'not only as comrades, but as countrymen'. Their disembarkation at Suakin was an event of tremendous significance for Britain, which was far beyond the blinkered 'vestry who ruled in Downing Street and there pose as the successors of Pitt, Palmerston and Beaconsfield.' For Wolseley, the common ministerial failing was that lack of imperial imagination which made it impossible for them to appreciate the power of the empire. Nor could they see its future potential as Britain's partner. And yet he predicted, 'When war with Russia comes, as come it must before many years pass away, we shall have help from all our Colonies.'[15]

Four years later, during the winter of 1889–90, the young Churchill, then a schoolboy at Harrow, listened spellbound to an address on the Imperial Federation of Wolseley's dreams. The speaker, Dr G.R. Parkin from Nova Scotia, foretold that one day, 'Nelson's signal [England expects that every man will do his duty] will be flashed, not along a line of ships, but along a line of embattled nations around the world.' These words, whose resonance was so close to that of his own rhetoric, stuck in Churchill's mind and he was able to recall them over sixty years after.[16] So too could another Harrovian listener, Leo Amery, who like Churchill was mesmerised by the 'big idea' of Imperial Federation. It held the key to the survival of Britain as a world power, and, like other late-Victorian imperial ideas, was breathtaking in its scope, which was perhaps why it appealed to youthful imaginations.

The idea of some kind of imperial unity was superficially attractive, especially to those disturbed by Britain's comparative decline as a world power. But practical attempts to facilitate closer relations between Britain and the dominions and the creation of a coordinated imperial defence policy ended in failure. A series of conferences of dominion prime ministers, held intermittently between 1887 and 1907, produced much talk but no results. There was an understandable suspicion that Britain was promoting imperial unity to further her own international interests, and dominion leaders were chary about committing their armed forces to British control. In Canada there were deep misgivings among the French-speaking population about becoming embroiled in a war with France, and in 1898, when such a war appeared likely, the Canadian government doubted whether *Canadien* militiamen could be persuaded to take part in the seizure of St Pierre and Miquelon islands.[17] Again, in 1899, French–Canadians were reluctant to support Britain in what they saw as a war of imperial aggression against the Boers.

Looming large over the British government's endeavours to secure imperial cooperation was the Irish Question. Before 1800, Ireland had had its own parliament, which was to a large extent the mouthpiece of the Protestant landowners. In 1801 this parliament was dissolved and thereafter Irish MPs went to Westminster. This arrangement was continually challenged by Irish nationalists, who grew stronger in numbers and determination as the franchise was extended to the majority of Gaelic, Catholic Irishmen. Militancy increased dramatically after 1870 with the foundation of the Irish Home Rule Party and the Irish issue was pushed into the forefront of British politics.

The Irish Question was debated on two levels. On one, it was a purely domestic matter concerned with the restoration of a measure of internal self-government to Ireland. On the other, it was an imperial issue of the greatest significance since it involved the future integrity of the empire. The enemies of Irish autonomy feared that it would fragment the United Kingdom and thereby wreck any chances of wider imperial union. Opposing Gladstone's first Home Rule Bill in May 1886, a Tory MP argued that if it was passed 'the colonies would not come to join such a federation if the United Kingdom was first broken up . . . [for] if we could not keep our own kith and kin together we could not be expected to keep our Colonies, which were at so great a distance from us, together.'[18] Gladstone, defending his measure, hoped that a self-governing Ireland would become a friendly and loyal dominion like Canada. This was wishful thinking; the legacy of hatred for England and the passionate anglophobia of nationalist rhetoric made it extremely unlikely that Anglo-Irish relations would ever be cordial. A semi-independent Ireland would always pose a danger in any future war, and one MP reminded the Commons how, in 1798, Irish nationalists had made common cause with France.'[19]

The threat to national security and possible harm to the empire convinced a substantial body of Liberal MPs, including Chamberlain, to defect and vote against the bill. Its successor, presented in the spring of 1893, passed the Commons but was thrown out by the Lords. It had been denounced by Chamberlain as 'the Bill for creating Little England', which would advertise irresolution to a jealous world:

All Europe is armed to the teeth, and the causes of dispute are very near the surface. Meanwhile, our interests are universal – our honour is involved in almost every land under the sun. Under such conditions the weak invite attack, and it is necessary for Britain to be strong.[20]

For some, like the poet Algernon Swinburne, the Union was one of those God-given advantages which had made Britain great:

> Three in one, but one in three
> God, who girt her with the sea,
> Bade our Commonweal to be:
> Nought, if not one.
> Through fraud and fear would sever
> The bond assured for ever,
> Their shameful strength shall never
> Undo what heaven has done.

Defence of the Union was fiercest among those, like Chamberlain, who favoured tighter links between Britain and the dominions. Although in political terms these appeared unobtainable during the 1890s, there were gratifying signs that loyalty to the crown was a powerful emotional force throughout the dominions. Its strength was publicly revealed during the 1897 Diamond Jubilee celebrations which witnessed not only dominion troops marching through London, but a cascade of congratulations from every corner of the empire. The temper of all was summed up by the address delivered by the Speaker of the Victoria parliament:

> At this moment there stand around her Throne representatives of every quarter of her world-wide Empire, all carrying messages of loyalty and goodwill, and accumulating the testimony that distance does not decrease patriotism. The Empire unites today in offering its homage and reverence to the illustrious Lady who for sixty years has been the worthy symbol and image of the power of a free nation.[21]

Two years later, when war between Britain and the Transvaal became unavoidable, such sentiment was translated into action. Australia and New Zealand immediately offered troops, as did Canada, despite considerable

misgivings among the *Canadien* community. The raising and departures of
the contingents were the cause for much celebration, and the mood of the
men who paraded through the streets and those who cheered them was
captured by a New Zealand poet:

> The signal had flash'd oe'r the water,
> The word that old England wants help;
> The Mother has cried to her daughter;
> The lion has roared to its whelp.
> Cast away any dread that appals ye,
> Any doubts to the sea winds toss —
> 'Tis the Old, Old Country that calls ye,
> Ye sons of the Southern Cross.

Those whose hearts were stirred by these and similar patriotic appeals
were mostly men and women who had never seen Britain for, by 1899,
nearly all Australians and New Zealanders were native-born. And yet they
felt a powerful emotional kinship with Britain which was nowhere better
summed up than by an Australian, Charles Bean, at the start of his account
of his country's participation in the First World War:

> The Australian spoke the same language, read the same books,
> loved the same sports, held the same ideas of honesty, of clean-
> liness, of individual liberty; his children learned at their
> mother's knee the same grand traditions of sea travel and old
> adventure, for he had as yet created few stories of his own.[22]

Just over 30,000 colonial troops fought in the Boer War and their activities were closely followed in the dominion newspapers, either as recorded
in letters home or in reports from war correspondents. Public interest in
the war and their countrymen's part in it was most intense in New Zealand
and Australia, which took the unusual step of issuing special postage stamps
to commemorate their contingents.

Military pomp and a pride in achievements on the battlefield were part
and parcel of nationalism everywhere in the late nineteenth and twentieth
centuries, and so it was both natural and inevitable that the Boer War gave
a fresh vigour to dominion patriotism. Participation in the war also contributed to a sense that the dominions had 'come of age', that is, had
reached a stage of maturity which entitled them to consider themselves

nations rather than colonies. Waving flags at parades and sending volunteers to fight the Boers was not merely an affirmation of youthful nationhood. Australia and New Zealand stood to lose from the extinction of British influence in South Africa, which would have led to a shift in the balance of power throughout the southern hemisphere.

Dominion help benefited Britain, both militarily and psychologically. Large numbers of tough, enthusiastic young men who had learned to ride and shoot in the outback were exactly what the British army needed in 1899, and in a world where Britain was conspicuously friendless, dominion support was a boost to national morale. None were happier than supporters of imperial federation, who believed their creed had been vindicated and looked forward to a post-war world in which the partnership formed on the battlefield would become permanent. As in 1885, the army's high command was quick to recognise the future value of colonial troops. In 1902, after hearing reports of an 'unfriendly spirit' being shown in some messes towards dominion officers, the adjutant-general rebuked those concerned. He warned them that, 'Imperial interests of the first magnitude depend on the reception given by British officers to those of the colonial brethren, now being introduced into our commissioned ranks.'[23]

Unlike the stand-offish regimental officers, he and his fellow staff officers were uncomfortably aware that in any new emergency Britain would have to depend heavily on dominion manpower to fill the ranks of its armies. Mass emigration, which showed no signs of diminishing, meant that by the beginning of the twentieth century 20 per cent of the empire's white population was living in the dominions.

10

Be Brave, Be Bold, Do Right!: The Edwardian Empire and the People

1902 ought to have been a year for hubristic celebration. It was not; imperial soldiers may have marched in step during the coronation procession of the new king, Edward VII, but the mood of the Imperial Conference was one of polite disharmony as dominion prime ministers rejected suggestions for closer links with Britain. Peace in South Africa gave no cause for jubilation. It had taken two exhausting years to overcome the Boers in a tedious campaign which had inspired no headlines, save ones which highlighted 'methods of barbarism'. The fighting over, a royal commission convened to hear evidence of how the war had been conducted. Much of it was a catalogue of mischance and muddle.

What was revealed to the commissioners on such matters as the lack of an army intelligence service, mismanaged hospitals and the rejection of thousands of young, working-class volunteers because of their physical debility appeared to confirm the fears of those who had been warning their countrymen of the dangers of national decline. Their jeremiads may have sounded ironic at a time of unparalleled imperial expansion but, as they were always pointing out, appearances were misleading. The empire may have grown, but it had also become infected with a malaise which, if untreated, would end with its dissolution. Extreme pessimists, such as Major-General Sir Robert Baden-Powell, the hero of Mafeking, imagined that Britain, like Rome, would be destroyed from within by a moral virus, which he believed was already spreading among the young.

There was also an external threat. Could Britain continue to survive as a global power under the pressure of challenges from Germany, the United States and Russia (now in the process of rapid industrialisation)? Nervous sidelong glances at the progress of those rivals revealed nations with greater populations and resources, and, in the case of the former two, economies that were outpacing Britain's in terms of productivity and growth. Social-Darwinism had intruded so far into the collective thought of the major powers that it was taken for granted that they now existed in a permanent state of acute competition. For this reason, periods of intense rivalry were commonly likened to races (the race for the Nile, or, after 1906, the Anglo-German naval race) which suggested a winning post, a prize and a string of also-rans. By this analogy, Britain had led the field for most of the previous century, but after 1900 seemed to be losing ground to stronger, healthier beasts.

The disturbing possibility that Britain might find itself among the also-rans prompted a bout of intense national soul-searching among politicians, economists, social commentators and journalists. Their diagnoses of national ills were usually accompanied by a quest for remedies that would revitalise the country, restore its self-confidence and reinforce its power abroad. Analysts of the right and left concluded that only radical nostrums had any hope of success. The old Liberal orthodoxies of free trade, *laissez faire* and the sovereignty of market forces had failed; indeed, had con-tributed to Britain's present misfortunes. Milner, who had returned in 1906 from his controversial period as high commissioner in South Africa determined to play a part in the rebirth of Britain and the empire, blamed the sad state of both on the 'old maidenly hands' of the Liberal leadership.

The Fabian socialist, Sydney Webb, believed that Liberal individualism had become obsolete. Writing in 1901, he insisted that, 'We have become aware, almost in a flash, that we are not merely individuals, but members of a community, nay citizens of the world.' The man in the street now appreciated that 'the good government of his city, the efficiency with which his nation is organised, and the influence which his Empire is able to exercise in the councils, and consequently in the commerce of nations' were vital for his and his childrens' survival and prosperity.[1] For Webb and imperialists on the right 'efficiency' became a talismanic word, holding the key to the restoration of national well-being and competitiveness.

The application of efficiency required strong government, willing to

plan ahead and intervene when necessary in all areas of national life to promote better education and state-funded pension and medical programmes.
'The building up of the nervous and muscular vitality of our race' was for
Webb 'the principal plank of any Imperial programme'.[2] A Liberal MP,
stating the case for child welfare and school meals in 1906, said that while,
in theory, it sounded like 'rank Socialism' it was in reality 'first rate
Imperialism', for the 'Empire cannot be built on rickety and flat-chested
citizens'.[3] Indeed it could not, and concern with high infant mortality rates
and the need to foster a sturdy 'imperial race' led to the first steps being
taken to provide widespread child care in the 1900s. What was in effect the
foundation of the welfare state was in many respects an imperial measure.
The district nurses and health visitors who instructed working-class mothers on how to bring up vigorous children were seen as serving the greater
good of the empire. Supporters of such activities argued that they had been
undertaken in Germany and Japan for some time.

The pursuit of efficiency in the name of empire demanded the discard-
ing of old shibboleths, breaking up vested interests and the abandonment
of systems which had become arthritic. 'Something businesslike' would
have to replace the 'smartness, gilt braid and gallantry' which had hitherto
characterised the army, insisted Leo Amery in 1900.[4] He was then *The
Times*'s correspondent in South Africa and so knew at first hand the shortcomings of the old army system. He was also a dedicated imperialist who
admired Milner, and became one of a knot of impatient young politicians
who were appalled by their elders' failure to grasp the imperial vision and
make it reality. Among his fellows was Max Aitken, a Canadian who held
a Tory seat in Lancashire and later became Lord Beaverbrook.

Imperial issues were now in the forefront of British political life. They
became the focus of a national debate in the spring of 1903 when
Chamberlain, inspired and invigorated by a tour of South Africa, launched
his tariff reform campaign. It was based upon the assumption that free trade
had failed disastrously and the British economy would only thrive again if
all foreign imports were taxed throughout the empire. Imperial products,
chiefly foodstuffs, would be admitted duty-free so creating an empire-wide
free trade system. The benefits were twofold; the imperial customs union
would pave the way for an imperial federation, and the revenues raised
would pay for the social reforms needed to create a robust imperial race.
'The ideals of national strength and imperial consolidation' were complementary to those of 'domestic and social progress', claimed Milner, a keen
tariff reformer. National greatness, he believed, rested ultimately on 'the

welfare and contentedness of the mass of the people' and he felt sure that working men took more pride in being members of the vast empire than their social superiors. But, he warned, patriotism could be 'choked . . . in the squalor and degradation of the slums of our great cities.'[5]

The sheer boldness of this dual programme for imperial unity and national regeneration was its political undoing. It proved too far-reaching and radical for most of Chamberlain's Conservative and Unionist colleagues, who split, with Churchill crossing the floor of the Commons to line up with the Liberals. The tariff debate was a godsend for the Liberals, who had spent the past eight years out of office and divided over policy, particularly towards the empire. Now they rallied behind the old battlecry of free trade and won the general election of January 1906 with a massive overall majority, their last this century. The Liberal victory owed much to their having frightened the working-class electorate into believing that the Conservatives would tax imported cereals and raise the price of bread. The most telling image of the election was a poster which showed a plump and substantial 'Free Trade' loaf alongside a miniature, bun-sized 'Tariff Reform' loaf.

Liberal vote-catching was not only aimed at the nation's stomach. Another imperial issue, the employment conditions of Chinese indentured labourers in South Africa, was invoked to stir the nation's conscience. What was by now an antique imperial expedient to provide cheap and abundant labour had been adopted as a stopgap measure to raise productivity in the gold mines. The scheme had Milner's blessing and he had, imprudently as it turned out, approved flogging as a means of imposing discipline on the Chinese. The cry of 'slavery' was immediately raised by Liberals, the Labour party and sundry Nonconformist clergy, and with some justification. British sexual morality was offended by the official banning of women from the mineworkers' compounds, a restriction which, it was alleged, would cause a mass outbreak of sodomy among the frustrated Chinese. This proved not to be the case as a government enquiry of 1906 discovered. Among the evidence were the tart remarks of the Medical Officer of Health for the Rand, in whose opinion there was, per head, more sodomy among the men of London than the Chinese in Johannesburg. Understandably, the report was never published.[6]

The affair of the Chinese coolies had aroused the passion of the Labour party, for which the 1906 general election had been a breakthrough. Labour politicians had been and would remain ambivalent in their attitudes towards the empire. On one hand, the middle-class intellectual Fabians such as Shaw and Sydney and Beatrice Webb considered the empire a national asset which, properly managed, could benefit all its subjects. On the other, Labour leaders whose origins were in the working class and whose ideology had its roots in mid-Victorian Nonconformity and Radicalism, were deeply apprehensive about an institution that was authoritarian in its nature and seemingly devoted to the world-wide extension of capitalism, often by force.

For this reason James Keir Hardie, a Scottish ex-miner who had become the Labour party's first MP, joined forces with left-wing Liberals to denounce the Boer War as capitalist aggression unleashed on a race of farmers, whom he likened to the now extinct, independent English yeomen. Like other Socialists, Keir Hardie was distressed by music-hall jingoism, which he believed was deliberately fomented by the bosses in the hope that working men, intoxicated by belligerent patriotism, might forget such knife-and-fork issues as wages and unemployment. This did not happen; the Labour party managed to increase its vote despite the clamour of the Jubilee and the street junketings during the early phases of the Boer War. More importantly, the party flourished in the face of a cheap popular press which, by 1910, had become for the most part Conservative and imperialist in outlook.

In determining its policy towards the empire, the Labour party was strongly influenced by parallels between its own struggles and those of contemporary embryonic democratic, nationalist and trade union movements in India, Egypt and South Africa. This consideration, a socialist faith in the brotherhood of man and an instinctive sympathy for the underdog made the Labour party the natural ally of what a later generation would call colonial freedom movements. Links were quickly established between the Labour leadership and nationalist politicians in India, where the anti-colonial opposition was strongest, Egypt and South Africa. Ramsay MacDonald, the future leader of the party, toured India and was dismayed by the racial aloofness of his countrymen and the lack of official energy in extending education for Indians.[7] Keir Hardie, who visited India in 1907, consorted with Bengali nationalists and was received by Hindus as a holy man, much to his secret satisfaction, for he was a vain man.[8]

Keir Hardie also had first-hand knowledge of South Africa, which he used to champion the blacks during the debate on the bill granting the country a federal constitution in 1909. The government's willingness to accommodate the Boers and disbar blacks from the franchise would, he predicted, sour relations between the races and reduce the blacks to a 'landless proletariat', forced to accept the lowest wages to keep alive.[9] In the same year, Keir Hardie lectured representatives of the Young Egypt party in Geneva and urged them to forge an alliance between students and fellahin. This accomplished, the Egyptians could proceed to press Britain for self-determination, but, as Keir Hardie insisted, in an orderly manner.[10]

The significance of these statements and the links between colonial liberation movements and what was, in the 1900s, still a small party lay in the future. Nonetheless, the educated élite who led the nascent nationalist movements in Asia, the Middle East and Africa believed that they would always receive a sympathetic hearing from the Labour leadership. In a letter of August 1917, which was intercepted by military intelligence, an Iraqi nationalist exile warned the Labour MP and member of the war cabinet, Arthur Henderson, that the government was mistaken in funding Hussain, sharif of Mecca, on the grounds that he was an untrustworthy reactionary. He added with premature and naïve optimism that he hoped Britain would withdraw from Iraq when the war was over.[11]

There was a wide gulf of attitude and temperament between the Labour party and the men who ran the empire and Conservative and Liberal imperialists at home. The Indian government smeared Keir Hardie as a firebrand and sedition-monger during his visit to the country, and Ramsay MacDonald wondered whether the empire's rulers would return home with their heads full of authoritarian ideas. This fear was not new; it had been expressed by Burke in the late eighteenth century and had been repeated intermittently by Liberals and Radicals in the next century who were disturbed by the fact that their countrymen, mostly from the upper classes, governed the colonies as autocrats. In his futuristic fantasy, *News from Nowhere* (1891), the Socialist William Morris described how a government faced with working-class unrest placed London under the control of one of the 'youngest and cleverest generals . . . who had won a certain sort of reputation in the disgraceful wars in which the country had long been engaged'. This thinly disguised Wolseley figure uses the weaponry of colonial warfare, machine-guns, to shoot down a crowd in Trafalgar Square.

Paradoxically, such an action would not have been beyond the real Wolseley, who was a host to Cromwellian phantoms. He once confided to his wife that he relished the coming of a time when 'the licence of democracy and socialism will be conquered by the sword, and succeeded by a cruel military despotism' under which Gladstone and his colleagues would be forced to polish officers' boots.[12] Admiral Lord Fisher was equally contemptuous of politicians, but his wry sense of humour prevented him from going as far as Wolseley. He did, however, once observe that his experience of politicians had convinced him that Divine Providence alone had enlarged and preserved the empire.[13]

Milner disdained party politics which he considered parochial, petty-minded and dangerously distractive for a country whose attention needed to be concentrated on the 'big' issues raised by the empire. He therefore deliberately chose the Lords as his platform for, like Coriolanus, he found the idea of directly canvassing the masses repugnant. Leo Amery thought imperial issues were too important to be bandied about the floor of the Commons, and hoped that in the future their discussion could be confined to a reconstituted House of Lords.[14] This body, swollen by peers from the dominions, would become an imperial legislature while the Commons concerned themselves with such mundane trivia as licensing laws and the disestablishment of the Welsh church.

Authoritarian imperialist sentiments were probably strongest among officers of both services. Just how strong was dramatically revealed by events in Ireland during the spring of 1914 after Herbert Asquith's government had been driven to contemplate measures for the enforcement of the Irish Home Rule Act. Necessity rather than conviction had forced the Liberals to introduce this measure in 1912 as a payment for Irish Nationalist support in the Commons, after their majority had been swept away by the two general elections of 1910. As in 1886 and 1893, Conservatives and Unionists denounced Irish self-government as a potentially lethal blow to imperial integrity. This time, however, the Lords could only postpone the bill's enactment, and so, having exhausted the customary forms of political opposition, its adversaries resorted to force. The Protestant majority in Northern Ireland screamed 'Home Rule! Home Rule!'; affirmed their wish to remain part of the British empire; formed a volunteer army and, early in 1914, began procuring rifles and machine-guns. Mainland Conservative and Unionist leaders applauded what they saw as a gallant defence of imperial solidarity.

Faced with a rebellion, the cabinet proposed at the end of March 1914 that troops from the Irish garrison (concentrated in the Catholic south of the island) might be used to guard arsenals, and prevent the Ulstermen from getting more weapons. The majority of officers involved promptly resigned; such a duty was against their consciences, as it was against those of officers on board the warships that had been ordered to take stations off Belfast. Senior officers openly sympathised with their subordinates' gesture, and a distraught cabinet was compelled to temporise. The outcome was a pledge that British soldiers would not be deployed to disarm the Ulster Volunteers, which was a victory for them and the officers.

What was called with discreet understatement the Curragh Incident (after the name of the camp where the first batch of resignations had occurred) was a testament to the depth and passion of imperial loyalty within the army. It was also revealing that those who approved the officers' actions believed that imperial considerations outweighed the traditional obedience of the military to the civil power. Imperialists on the right saw the moral issue as clear cut. One argued that the disaffected officers behaved as they did because they had realised that 'the Ulstermen are loyal subjects who refused to be placed under the heel of a faction which Mr Gladstone [before his conversion to Home Rule] asserted to be "marching through rapine to the dismemberment of the Empire." '[15] It was unthinkable that officers of an army which had by a hundred years of exertion and sacrifice enlarged and protected the empire, should have allowed themselves to become accomplices to what was widely seen as a betrayal of empire. They could not remain true to themselves if they made war against men who wished to remain part of the empire on behalf of those who wished to leave.

A private soldier, watching events at the Curragh from the sidelines, wondered why the officers of the 'aristocratic and plutocratic' army had previously shown not the slightest qualm about using force against those of their fellow countrymen who happened to be industrial workers on strike. This was the language of class politics, a recent phenomenon in British life which was a direct consequence of the growth of the Labour party and militant trade unionism. Class politics were wormwood to the Conservative and Liberal imperialists who saw them as undermining national unity and therefore weakening the empire. Out of a population of 45 million, 34 million were working class and it was therefore imperative that an antidote be found to the poison of class antagonism.

Chamberlain had hoped that his personal programme which melded dynamic imperialism and tariff reform would win over the working classes. Even the most traditionalist Conservatives were of the same mind. 'The greatest resource of the Empire is the British character,' proclaimed Lord Wylloughby de Broke, a right-wing Tory racing peer. But he admitted that the inner strengths of the Briton could only be sustained if everyone was allowed free access to what he described as 'the moral and material essentials of life'. Only then, no one could complain, 'The British Empire has done nothing for me.'[16] So long as there were large sections of society which felt no benefit from the empire, Britain could never obtain the national solidarity needed to guarantee its maintenance. Or, as Robert Blatchford, an ex-soldier who was both an imperialist and a Socialist, once observed, while the sun was said never to set on the British empire, there were city slums over which it had never risen.

The working classes had, therefore, to be made aware of the empire, taught to feel pride in it, understand how its existence was to their advantage, and most important of all, learn the special virtues that would be expected of them as its citizens. What today might be called raising imperial consciousness was a task undertaken by a collection of voluntary organisations founded and funded by the middle and upper classes. The lists of patrons and subscribers were roll calls of imperialists from all parties, former proconsuls and senior army and navy officers. Together they directed and paid for a formidable propaganda machine which operated throughout the years between the Boer and the First World Wars.

One of the largest and most influential of the bodies which broadcast the imperial message was the Primrose League. It had been established in 1883, was named after Disraeli's favourite flower, and claimed to be apolitical, although atheists and enemies of the empire were denied membership. In 1900 it had 1.5 million members, nearly all working class.[17] It promoted a robust imperial patriotism (one of its heroes was Gordon) through a mixture of entertainments and instruction, paying for lectures, lantern-slide shows, exhibitions and public rallies. A more forceful pressure group was the National Service League whose supporters campaigned across the country for compulsory military training for all schoolboys, and conscription. A living national hero, the aged but still sprightly Field Marshal Lord Roberts, frequently addressed its public meetings. The National Service League had accumulated 200,000 members by 1914, including some formerly attached to the Lads Drill Association with which it had merged in 1906.

The Lads Drill Association was the brainchild of Reginald Brabazon, Earl of Meath, an Anglo-Irish Tory who had dedicated his old age to spreading the gospel of empire to the young. His conversion to imperialism had occurred one winter's day in the 1850s when he had been a schoolboy at Eton. Wiping snow from his knees, he was upbraided by a schoolmaster, who used the occasion for an off-the-cuff sermon on imperial manliness:

Do you call yourselves British, boys? . . . Your fathers are the rulers of England, and your forefathers have made England what she is now. Do you imagine that if they had minded a little snow that Canada would have been added to the Empire, or if they had minded heat we should ever possess India or tropical Africa? Never let me see you shrink from heat or cold. You will have to maintain the Empire which they made.[18]

This harangue affected the young Meath deeply, and later he set about making sure that future generations would keep faith with their ancestors.

Homage to the imperial past and commitment to its future were the objects of Empire Day, which Meath wanted celebrated annually in schools throughout the empire on 24 May, Queen Victoria's birthday. Empire Day was commemorated first in 1902 and within four years was being observed in 6,000 schools. A parliamentary attempt to secure it official recognition failed in 1908, to the audible delight of Labour and Irish MPs, and Labour councils such as Battersea banned it from their schools as militaristic. Nevertheless, Empire Day increased in popularity, especially in south-eastern England and rural areas everywhere. In 1916 a wartime government, willing to do anything that would encourage popular patriotism, gave Empire Day official recognition.

Something of the flavour of an Edwardian Empire Day is conveyed by a pamphlet issued by the Empire Day League in 1912 with suggestions for uplifting entertainments. For older schoolchildren there was an abridged version of *Henry V* which centred on the scenes before, during and after Agincourt. Younger pupils were offered a simple pageant in which a procession of heroes, whose 'noble deeds' had contributed to the growth of the empire, paid homage to Britannia. Clive and Nelson rubbed shoulders with symbolic figures representing the army, navy and, an up-to-date touch, 'air power'. As each appeared, they were greeted with rehearsed cheers from the spectators – 'Hurrah to our brave soldiers!' and so on. In conclusion, Britannia made a short, inspiring speech: 'My Empire shall hold; and, like summer roses, perfume the world with freedom's gladsome fragrance. Be brave, be bold, do right!' In an alternative and equally colourful *tableau vivant* children dressed to represent the dominions and colonies paid their respects to their mother, Britannia. Recommended costume for South African blacks consisted of 'two fur rugs', 'strings of melon seeds' and an improvised assegai.[19]

The spectacles were a climax to a morning during which children had learned patriotic songs such as 'I'd like to be a soldier or a sailor', which was performed by girls, and memorised facts about the empire such as, 'They [the colonies] have helped to make our people the richest in the world'. Work and fun were not enough, and Meath emphasised that pupils should be given the rest of the day off. The young, he wrote, 'do not readily appreciate the importance of any event unless it brings a holiday in its train.'

Everyday lessons were constructed around imperial themes. The Prince and Princess of Wales's Indian tour of 1906 was an opportunity for elementary schoolchildren to learn about the subcontinent and the firm and fair way in which it was governed. Nationalist agitation, which had recently flared up in Bengal, was brushed aside with the statement, 'The British rule has brought peace . . . and the native police and soldiers are usually able to preserve order among a people who are naturally docile.'[20]

Public schoolboys continued to be bombarded with imperial propaganda, relentlessly delivered by headmasters who were invariably Anglican clerics of the muscular Christian persuasion. Themes of athletic prowess and warrior patriotism mingled in the rousing school songs which became so popular at this time. The sentiments of Harrow's '*Forty Years On*', which always brought tears to Churchill's eyes, were typical:

> *God gives us bases to guard or beleaguer,*
> *Games to play out in earnest or fun,*
> *Fights for the fearless and goals for the eager,*
> *Twenty and thirty and forty years on.*

Stiffened by such appeals and brought to a high pitch of fitness on the playing field, the public school man was ready to do his duty by the empire; but what of boys from other classes?

The question was asked continually in Edwardian Britain. The answers were often disquieting; in 1898 one commentator summed up working-class youth as 'stunted, narrow chested, easily wearied, yet voluble, excitable, with little ballast, stamina and endurance'.[21] Generalisations of this sort were confirmed by the cold statistics gathered by army doctors who examined would-be recruits, and the surveys undertaken in the urban slums by proto-sociologists like Seebohm Rowntree. The underfed, sickly sons of the industrial cities were evidence that Anglo-Saxon manhood was in decline. On one level, this fact was ammunition for social reformers of all persuasions, and on another, it provided the impetus for a body of determined imperialists to launch programmes for the regeneration of the masses. What was needed, claimed Baden-Powell, was the 'hardening of the nation' and the 'building up of self-reliant, energetic manhood' which would, in time, be able to populate and defend the empire.[22]

'Wishy-washy slackers' were Baden-Powell's target. A public celebrity, he used his considerable influence to awaken the nation's youth to its duty and prepare it for its fulfilment. In an appeal which echoed that of Meath's schoolmaster, he invoked the exploits of past heroes to shame their lethargic descendants:

> Your forefathers worked hard, fought hard, and died hard to make this empire for you. Don't let them look down from heaven, and see you loafing about with your hands in your pockets, doing nothing to keep it up.[23]

In December 1904 he exhorted the readers of *Union Jack* and the *Marvel* to learn how to drill and shoot. He concluded with an appeal for letters from captains of soccer and cricket XIs whose teams were keen to learn how to fight.[24]

Baden-Powell's ideas were translated into action in 1908 with the foundation of the Boy Scouts who, two years later, totalled 100,000. The scouting movement's philosophy was simple patriotism, and its activities, largely undertaken outdoors, were derived from Baden-Powell's textbook on fieldcraft and survival which was based on his experiences fighting the Ndebele in Rhodesia. Appropriately, Scouts wore a khaki uniform like that of one of Rhodes's troopers, complete with broad-brimmed bush hat and bandanna.

The Boy Scouts joined a number of other organisations dedicated to the proper diversion and instruction of youth. The well-established Boys Brigade drilled its largely working-class members with wooden rifles; dressed them in uniforms, which included the same pill-box hat that was then worn by soldiers; and instilled doctrines of Christian manliness and loyalty to crown and country. There were other, smaller bodies dedicated to the creation of upright and sturdy sons of empire, including the Anti-Smoking League and the League of St George. The latter campaigned against pornography and masturbation, which was also a source of anguish to Baden-Powell, who warned his scouts that, quite literally, it weakened the imperial seed, led to general debility and even madness.

The future mothers of the imperial breed received their own

indoctrination. The Church of England Girls' Friendly Society which, in 1913, had 200,000 members, was primarily concerned with giving moral guidance to young working-class women. As well as counselling deference, chastity and quietism, this society helped unmarried women to emigrate, and its leaflets contained a scattering of imperialist propaganda. 'I look on imperialism as a means of eradicating the selfishness of Socialism,' announced the Honourable Mrs Joyce, the society's emigration secretary, in 1913.[25] The Girl Guides, an offshoot of the scouting movement, adopted similar patriotic values. A leaflet issued for Guides in 1910 drew their attention to a role that they might have to play in defence of the empire:

> Girls! Imagine that a battle has taken place in and around your town or village . . . what are you going to do? Are you going to sit down and wring your hands and cry, or are you going to be plucky, and go and do something to help your fathers and brothers . . .?[26]

Just how far those on the receiving end of Edwardian patriotic and imperial propaganda were converted by it cannot be known. It contained, and this was recognised and regretted by those on the left, elements designed to smother class politics. There were also charges that the emphasis placed on such military values as obedience and duty fostered militarism, which was true up to a point. Admiration for the services had grown throughout the nineteenth century, but the British cult of the warrior hero had always laid great stress on his Christian faith which, as with Gordon, was the basis for his superior courage. The fighting man was respected not just because he was physically strong and brave, but because of that interior moral stamina which made him perform his duty.

Like his predecessor, the Edwardian soldier was essentially a bringer of civilisation. This was how he was depicted in newspaper reports of the small and rather unglamorous campaigns fought between 1902 and 1914 on various frontiers. The *Daily Mail,* now with a daily circulation of three quarters of a million, gave coverage to operations in Somaliland during 1902 and 1903, and the invasion of Tibet in 1903. In each case the old formula was adopted, with the empire's adversaries being represented as wild, brave and reckless savages engaged in a hopeless struggle against civilisation. Incidentally, in its reporting of the Somaliland war, the *Mail* astonishingly asserted that the Mad Mullah's near victory at Erigo in 1902 was certain proof of his clinical insanity.[27] Presumably only a lunatic could expect to defeat a British army!

The patrician high priests of imperialism, while they approved of attempts to widen the public's knowledge of the empire, had always been disdainful of the sudden upsurges of popular patriotism that had been triggered by victories in colonial wars. For the likes of Chamberlain and Milner, jingoism distracted the public from the more serious but less romantic aspects of empire, and was an uncomfortable reminder of the fickleness of public opinion. It was a drawback of democracy that the public at large was easily bored and could not be persuaded to concentrate on any issue for long. For this reason, such figures as Milner were anxious to convert to the imperial creed those who really mattered, the young men who would be the future rulers of Britain and the empire.

In South Africa, Milner had collected around himself a knot of young, zealous imperialists who had, between 1900 and 1906, worked with him towards the country's reconstruction. Known as the kindergarten, this band of talented Oxonians included the journalist and future novelist John Buchan, Philip Kerr and Lionel Curtis, all of whom would dedicate their lives to the promotion of imperialism. Their circle was joined by Leo Amery and formed the nucleus for the Round Table, a cross-party, imperial pressure group founded in 1910 and partly financed by the Rhodes Trust. The Round Table's object was to influence those who shaped public opinion in Britain and the empire by press articles, pamphlets, discussion groups and individual contacts.

An imperial federation was the Round Table's goal. Its members believed that Britain could not survive economically and remain a global power unless it became the dominant force within a closely bonded empire. They feared that this 'big' issue could easily get lost amid public debates over tariffs and the price of a loaf of bread. Just what the Round Table achieved is hard to judge, at least before 1914. Lionel Curtis, the Round Table's roving ambassador to the dominions was cordially welcomed by their leaders, but his message cut no ice with them. As in the colonial conferences, they identified manoeuvres to secure a formal imperial unity with the machinations of the British ruling class. There was also an understandable fear that if a federation was formed, the dominions would find themselves relegated to the role of passive junior partners.[28] So, while dominions were sincere in their profession of emotional attachment to Britain, they remained extremely lukewarm towards the forging of more tangible links.

By 1914 imperial union was as far off as ever. There had been greater progress in making the public and the working class in particular more aware of the empire. It is impossible to know how far the catchwords of those organisations which promoted various forms of patriotism and imperialism entered the national consciousness. Many who heard them became the rank and file of the mass volunteer army formed between 1914 and 1916 to fight on the Western Front. Then, as in the Boer War, the slogans of popular patriotism did not travel to the fighting line; the letters home written by working-class soldiers reflected little of the strident patriotism whipped up by the press and the recruiters or the lower key pre-war imperial propaganda. What they did reveal was an acute sense of duty, a determination to persevere and an intense loyalty to comrades and unit.

11

To Join the Khaki Line:
The Empire and the
Coming of War

Hints that a major war was imminent, even welcome, were implicit in much Edwardian imperial propaganda. Baden-Powell urged his Boy Scouts to 'Be Prepared', and in a pamphlet of 1911 the National Service League reminded the British 'lad' that he alone stood between 'his mother and sister, his sweetheart and his girlfriend' and the 'inconceivable infamy of alien invasion'. Any ethical or physical qualms which the young patriot might have had about taking up arms were swept aside by the unbelievably glib assertions that 'war is not murder, as some fancy, war is sacrifice – which is the soul of Christianity', and 'fighting and killing are not of the essence of it [war], but are accidents'.[1]

Speculation about the causes and likely course of a future war had become a well-established and highly popular literary genre by 1900. The next fourteen years saw a steady rise in the output of sensational, semi-fictional accounts of wars between Britain and one or more of the great powers. The demand for this sort of fantasy was in part a reflection of the prevailing national mood of uncertainty and in part fascination with the new technology, particularly aerial, which was currently being developed for military purposes. The scenarios for these imaginary wars changed significantly after 1900. William le Queux, a jobbing wordsmith who specialised in this kind of fiction, made France and Russia Britain's antagonists in his 1894 novel, *The Great War of 1897*, whereas Germany was the foe in his 1906 best-seller, *The Invasion of 1910*. This was serialised by the *Daily Mail*, whose owner, Lord Northcliffe, was a passionate

Germanophobe and always looking for an opportunity to awaken his countrymen to the peril across the North Sea. After a tour of Germany in which he visited its growing industrial cities, he remarked, 'Every one of these new factory chimneys is a gun pointed at England, and in many cases a very powerful one.'[2]

This sort of scare-mongering encouraged war-mongering. From 1906 onwards the country was convulsed by spasmodic bouts of spy mania, with rumours of an underground army of German secret agents and equally ridiculous reports of nocturnal Zeppelin flights over Yorkshire. Even the government got the jitters and introduced a badly prepared Official Secrets Act in 1912. Much of this agitation was orchestrated by the conscription lobby, which carefully exploited that intense, irrational fear of sudden invasion which had long been embedded in the national psyche. It had broken surface intermittently throughout the past century with invasion alarms and accompanying calls for national vigilance and rearmament. There was, however, an important difference between Victorian and early twentieth-century invasion scares which made the latter far more convincing; the growing German navy.

The 1898 German Naval Law and its successors outlined an ambitious programme of ship construction which, when completed in 1920, would provide Germany with a fleet of forty-five battleships and thirty-two cruisers. This projection had been revised by 1914 to give a total of sixty-one battleships by 1928. The inspiration for this enterprise was an American naval officer, Captain Alfred Mahan. His analyses of eighteenth- and early nineteenth-century British seapower convinced the Kaiser that if Germany, like Britain, possessed a large fleet, she could become a world power on the same scale and with equal, if not greater influence. At first, Wilhelm II had regarded the German navy as a necessary counterbalance to those of France and Russia, but it was soon apparent to him that it could be used as the servant of Germany's new *Weltpolitik*.[3] If, as he and his advisers wished, Germany was to acquire colonies and international power commensurate with its growing wealth, it would have to be prepared to challenge Britain on more-or-less equal terms.

This intention was conveyed in the belligerent preamble to the 1900 Navy Law which insisted that 'Germany must have a Fleet of such strength that a war, even against the mightiest naval Power would involve such risks as to threaten the supremacy of that Power.'[4] The German fleet might not be able to defeat the British, but it could inflict wounds that would prove mortal. There was even greater menace in the planned deployment of

Germany's new warships, for all but a handful were to be concentrated at Kiel and Wilhelmshaven. As one British naval commentator observed in 1905, the North Sea had become in effect an imperial frontier, and an extremely vulnerable one.

The creation of the German navy, its presence 400 miles from Britain's coastline, and the possibility that it might be used as a bludgeon to extort overseas concessions presented the government with three problems. The first two were practical: new ships had to be laid down to preserve the Royal Navy's advantage in numbers, and the existing fleet would have to be redistributed to provide squadrons for home defence. Calling home men-o'-war from overseas stations demanded a complete overhaul of Britain's relations with those powers against which they had hitherto been deployed, France and Russia. Rearmament and diplomacy therefore proceeded side by side in what became a search for world-wide security. The first phase of this new course in British policy opened with the Japanese alliance of 1902, which cleared the way for the reduction of the Far Eastern fleet.

The radical restructuring and modernising of the navy began in 1904 under the direction of the First Sea Lord, Admiral Lord Fisher. He was a pugnacious, effervescent sexagenarian, well aware of his intellectual superiority over his brother admirals and, unusually for his times, the possessor of a refreshing contempt for all forms of sport and organised games. Twice, in 1904 and 1908, Fisher proposed to remove the German threat once and for all by the ruthless stratagem that had been used in 1806 against the Danish fleet, and more recently by the Japanese against the Russians; a preemptive attack. 'My God, Fisher, you must be mad,' was Edward VII's reaction to the first suggestion, but it was aired in the press and caused consternation among German naval officers, who knew that their fleet could not have defended itself against such an assault.[5] It was not only the British who were jumpy about the 'bolt from the blue'.

Fisher's greatest contribution to the remaking of the Royal Navy was pushing through the design and building of a new type of battleship, HMS *Dreadnought*. *Dreadnought* took a record eleven months to construct, was completed in October 1906, and rendered all other battleships obsolete. It displaced 17,900 tons, mounted ten twelve-inch guns, and could steam at over twenty knots. Three more Dreadnought class battleships were laid down in 1906–7, along with two battlecruisers, HMS *Inflexible* and *Indomitable*. These were also novelties, faster than conventional battleships thanks to lighter armour-plating, but armed with eight twelve-inch guns.

Gatling unjammed: Jack Tars turn a machine gun on Egyptian rioters in the streets of Alexandria, 1882. *Author's own collection*

Civilising mission: a mocking look into the future with Kumasi (Ghana) transformed into a contemporary British suburb after its conquest in 1895. *Author's own collection*

Rhodesians rampant: British South Africa Company Police ride down Ndebele, 1896. Images such as this brought protests from anti-imperialists in Britain. *Author's own collection*

Dacoits rounded by mounted infantrymen, Burma, 1885. *British Library*

'Your new-caught, sullen peoples,
Half-devil and half-child'
Rudyard Kipling

Execution of dacoits, Burma, 1885. *British Library*

Servants of the Raj: Two of India's masters prepare to take exercise on horseback while a third takes tea. Servants surround them ready to attend to their every need, c.1880. *Barnaby's Picture Library*

Memsahibs going visiting: rickshaws convey three ladies on their social rounds, Ceylon, c.1925. *Topham Picture Source*

The King Emperor pots a tiger: George V relaxes after his Coronation Durbar in the manner of his Mughal predecessors, 1912. *Peter Newark's Historical Pictures*

Anglo-Saxon manhood: Imperial Yeomanry volunteers set off to look for Boers, South Africa, 1900. *Imperial War Museum*

England in India: the Mysore hunt complete with Indian whippers-in, 1923. *Topham Picture Source*

THE EMPIRE CHALLENGED

A Rolls Royce armoured car trundles down an Egyptian road as a member of the effendi class, distinguished by his European suit and fez, strolls contemptuously across its path and a peasant cowers beside a pile of stones abandoned by rioters, 1936. *Hulton Deutsch*

Black and Tans and Auxiliary police pass down an Irish street while women watch nervously from windows, 1920. *Imperial War Museum*

Sullen Arabs wait to be searched by British soldiers, Jerusalem, 1938. *Topham Picture Source*

The facade of power: The Viceroy and Vicereine of India (the Marquess and Marchioness of Reading) with equerries in gala dress, 1923. *Topham Picture Source*

The reality of power: Gandhi in customary peasant dress attends the Round Table conference in London, 1931. His appearance prompted Churchill's sneer about a 'half-naked faqir'. *Author's own collection*

These warships represented a revolution in naval architecture and gave a new, almost frenzied momentum to the race between Britain and Germany. In October 1906, as the original *Dreadnought* was beginning its trials, the German navy ordered its first 'Dreadnought', SMS *Westfalen*.

HMS *Dreadnought* was a two-edged sword. By relegating all earlier, conventional battleships to antique status, its launch had cut Britain's considerable lead over Germany in this class of warship. Nonetheless, *Dreadnought* and its immediate successors gave Britain a head start in what was a new contest with Germany; but the Germans possessed the will, technology, and most importantly the cash to narrow the gap. As German naval planners realised, the Anglo–German naval race was an economic marathon, rather like the American Star Wars project of the 1980s, in which victory would ultimately go to the power with the longest purse.[6]

Nearly every Dreadnought-class battleship and battlecruiser built between 1906 and 1914 was earmarked for service in the reconstituted Home and Channel fleets, which were now the empire's first line of defence. Since 1904 there had been a gradual redistribution of the fleet organised by Fisher, which included the scrapping of over 150 assorted gunboats and sloops, the small vessels which had hitherto policed Britain's official and unofficial empires. Large enough to overawe Chinese pirates or Arab slavers, they could play no useful part in a modern war, and the recent introduction of wireless now meant that the light cruisers, deployed on foreign stations, could be swiftly summoned to trouble spots. Reductions in the numbers of battleships attached to overseas squadrons was undertaken gradually and cautiously. The five serving in the Pacific were only withdrawn in June 1905, following the destruction of the Russian fleet at Tshushima and the renegotiation of the alliance with Japan in which each party pledged to assist the other in the event of attack by one rather than two powers. There was no such guarantee for British interests in the Mediterranean and so eight older battleships were retained there, supported after 1912 by two battlecruisers sent to shadow the German battlecruiser *Goeben*. The presence of these modern ships was needed in home waters, but it was thought that their withdrawal would have a disturbing effect in Egypt and India.[7] Nevertheless, between 1904 and 1910 Fisher had completely changed the disposition of Britain's navy: in 1896 there had been 74 ships stationed in home waters and 142 overseas, fourteen years later these totals were 480 and 83 respectively.

Such a sweeping change in the Royal Navy's deployment had been facilitated by the new course in Britain's foreign policy. In April 1904,

Britain agreed the *entente cordiale* with France, a collection of accommodations which ended twenty years of acrimony and sabre-rattling over colonial boundaries and spheres of influence. Most important in terms of imperial security was French recognition of Britain's position in Egypt, a concession paid for by Britain's acknowledgement of France's paramountcy in Morocco. This was put to the test in 1905 and 1911, when Britain stood by France in resisting German encroachments in this region.

It was less easy to come to a similar understanding with Russia, despite French encouragement. There was profound suspicion of Russian expansionism among British diplomats and strategists, and fears of a Russian attack on India were as strong as ever. This could have been forestalled had the Japanese been persuaded to lend troops for the defence of Afghanistan or diversionary operations in Persia, suggestions that were put to Japan's delegates during the renegotiation of the terms of the alliance in 1905. The response was disappointing since, while prepared to fight Russia in Manchuria and Siberia, the Japanese had no desire to defend Britain's empire.[8]

This rebuff drove Britain to open direct talks with Russia. The outcome was the Anglo-Russian Convention of August 1907, which terminated an eighty-year cold war in the Middle East and Asia. Russia promised to respect Indian integrity, and the two powers agreed to partition Persia into spheres of influence, Britain getting the south-eastern part of the country, which bordered on India, and the southern, which lay on the shores of the Persian Gulf. These terms had been extracted from Russia at a time when it was still recovering from its defeat by Japan and the subsequent revolution of 1905–6. By 1912, when a vast rearmament programme was in full swing and national confidence had been restored, there were clear indications that the Czar's ministers were reactivating old expansionist policies. There was evidence of fresh Russian interest in such sensitive areas as Tibet and Chinese Turkestan.[9] At the same time there was a recrudescence of Russian intrigue inside Persia which suggested that its government did not feel bound by the 1907 Convention.[10] Misgivings about Russia understandably remained strong in British official circles. A plan concocted in 1912 for the possible occupation of the Turkish province of Mesopotamia (Iraq) included a proposal to build a railway from Basra to Mosul which would make it easy to launch a counter-attack into the Caucasus if Russia made moves against India.[11]

Britain had done comparatively well from its *détentes* with France and Russia, even if Russian goodwill was brittle. Disentanglement from old disputes had left successive British governments free to adjust their overall strategy to meet the threat of the German fleet in the North Sea. This had been achieved without entering into any formal engagement binding the country to war if either France or Russia was attacked; indeed, as late as 1912 strategists could still seriously contemplate the possibilities of a war against the latter in certain circumstances. This view of future neutrality in a European conflict between the great powers was not taken by the War Office, which in January 1906 asked for and obtained cabinet permission to open covert discussion with the French general staff on future cooperation in the event of a war with Germany.

What turned out to be a momentous decision was taken by the new Liberal Prime Minister, Sir Henry Campbell-Bannerman, the Foreign Secretary, Sir Edward Grey, and the Minister for War, Richard Haldane. Knowledge of the Anglo-French military conversations, like that of Britain's atomic bomb programme forty years after, remained confined to an inner circle of ministers and the high-ranking officers involved. Only in 1912 was the whole cabinet informed of the by now well-advanced plan to send a 160,000-strong expeditionary force to the Franco-Belgian frontier if France was attacked by Germany.

One explanation for this secrecy was the fear that public opinion might react unfavourably to war plans devised by a government which continually declared that its principle foreign policy aim was the preservation of peace. Defenders of the arrangement could privately argue that helping France would preserve the balance of power on the continent, but the public might not be convinced that a diplomatic abstraction was worth dying for. For some time, ministers, diplomats, and senior army and naval officers had noticed that while the public could be raised to a pitch of clamorous indignation over bogus invasion and spy scares, it was bored by crises in such distant areas as the Balkans or Morocco. For some, this apathy appeared dangerous. In 1909, Captain David Beatty, later Admiral of the Fleet Lord Beatty, complained to his wife that 'the idle public are as blind in England, as they were in Russia before the Russo-Japanese war'.[12]

He was not entirely correct in his assessment. The Anglo-German naval race was one close-to-home issue which periodically aroused the interest of large sections of the public, thanks to the propaganda of the naval lobby and its attendant journalists. Keeping ahead in this contest was Liberal as well as Conservative policy and, when the former party came into power in January 1906, it accepted the target of four Dreadnoughts a year that had been set by its predecessor. By October 1907, Britain was managing to stay comfortably in the lead with seven Dreadnoughts and three battlecruisers commissioned or on the stocks, while Germany had still to complete its first batch of new battleships.[13] Nevertheless the government remained uneasy, and in 1908 the annual quota was raised to six Dreadnoughts. The following year, intelligence reports that Krupps were stepping up production of nickel were interpreted, wrongly as it turned out, as evidence of a rapid acceleration in German battleship construction. 'We want eight and we can't wait' chorused the naval lobby and despite anxieties about the cost, Asquith's cabinet caved in.

One of the new battlecruisers ordered in 1909, HMS *New Zealand*, was paid for by the New Zealand government, and Australia footed the bill for another, HMS *Australia*, which became the flagship of its new navy. These gestures represented a triumph for those British statesmen and diplomats who had for some years been attempting to persuade the dominion governments that it was in their interests to participate actively in the implementation of the new imperial grand strategy. It was assumed, at least by the British government, that measures undertaken to secure the defence of the homeland against the German navy were in the interests of all the dominions. Dominion politicians were not altogether convinced; Sir William Laurier, who was Prime Minister of Canada until 1911, believed that his country would remain inviolate from outside attack because of the Royal Navy and the Monroe Doctrine, by which the United States pledged itself to oppose any foreign intervention in any part of the Americas. It was therefore pointless for Canadians to reach into their pockets to subsidise defences they did not need.

Australia and New Zealand objected on other grounds. 'Germany is not a danger,' claimed Andrew Fisher, Australia's Prime Minister, on the eve of the 1909 imperial conference on defence, 'We have to look to the Pacific for a menace if there is any.'[14] For some time, Australians and New Zealanders had been nervously glancing northwards towards Japan. What they, and Canadians looking westwards, saw was 'a thousand million Asiatics . . . looking southward with hungry eyes'.[15] This frightening image of the restless masses of the Far East fanning out across the Pacific and eventually taking over the empty spaces of Australasia had become fixed in the consciousness of Australians and New Zealanders. It had impelled them to erect barriers against Indian, Chinese and Japanese immigration and made them deeply mistrustful of Britain's ally, Japan. It was defence of the 'White Australia' policy as much as defence of the empire as a whole which lay behind the 1903 and 1904 Defence Acts, which made all Australian males between eighteen and sixty liable for military service, and their successors of 1911 and 1912, which compelled all eighteen- to twenty-five-year-olds to undertake eight days of training every year. Likewise, Australia's decision to create its own navy in 1909 (which had an annual budget of over £2 million) was taken in the light of the imagined Japanese threat. New Zealand's introduction of compulsory military training in 1909 was similarly motivated.

Neither Australia nor New Zealand placed much trust in Britain's alliance with Japan, which to all intents and purposes placed the protection of British Pacific interests in the hands of the Imperial Japanese Navy. It was argued that in the event of Britain becoming embroiled in a war against Germany, Japan would snatch the opportunity to advance on Australasia and possibly British Columbia, which already had a Japanese immigrant community. It was, therefore, necessary for the British government to reassure Australia and New Zealand that by committing themselves to a grand strategy based upon the defence of Britain from the German navy, they were not leaving themselves vulnerable to Japan. At the same time, Britain could not abandon its alliance with Japan without seriously weakening its fleet in home waters.

Close and willing dominion cooperation was absolutely vital for Britain's grand strategy. If Britain found itself fighting an extended land war, it would have to rely heavily on dominion manpower since, by 1914, 20 million of the empire's 65-million-strong white population lived in Canada, South Africa, Australia, and New Zealand. For this reason alone Asquith's government had to calm whatever doubts the dominions entertained about their own safety and persuade them to integrate their armed forces with those of Britain. Technical, training and staff cooperation was supervised by the Imperial General Staff, set up in 1907, and in 1909 arrangements were made with the Admiralty to provide for the naval defence of the dominions. Here, Britain had to take account of Australia's and New Zealand's 'yellow peril' fantasies and provide units for a combined Pacific fleet. This was not enough, and so Sir Joseph Ward, the New Zealand Prime Minister, asked for and got private assurances of more substantial assistance 'in days to come (which I believe will come) when the Eastern races are a trouble to Australia and my own country, and when a great Power in the East, now happily attached to England . . . may be detached from it.'[16] The chance of such an emergency occurring was removed in 1911 when Britain renewed its alliance with Japan for a further ten years.

The 1911 conference on imperial defence witnessed the greatest breakthrough in the procuring of closer dominion participation in Britain's grand strategy. Sir Edward Grey held centre stage. In a compelling, eloquent speech, he broke with precedent and outlined Britain's present foreign policy and offered prognoses for the future. Britain would only involve itself in a European war if one of the powers adopted what he called a 'Napoleonic policy', that is establishing dominance over the entire continent by force or intimidation. In such an event, British seapower would be in jeopardy since the paramount state could confront Britain with the fleets of as many as five other countries. He concluded:

> So long as the maintenance of Sea Power and the maintenance
> and control of the sea communications is the underlying motive
> of our policy in Europe, it is obvious how that is a common
> interest between us at home and all the Dominions.[17]

Grey's audience agreed; without British seapower, the dominions would be unable to survive in their present state. It was for this reason imperative that they made common cause with Britain if the circumstances described by Grey came about.

Grey assured his listeners that Britain had no hidden understandings with any other power and the dominion representatives heard nothing whatsoever about the past five years of planning for the despatch of an expeditionary force to France. Nor would they hear anything in the future, for the dominion members on the Committee of Imperial Defence were specifically excluded from discussions of military and naval matters which did not concern the dominions.[18] Even if they were in the dark about Britain's tentative commitment to fight the Germans in northeastern France, the dominion leaders were now convinced that they would have to support Britain if and when she believed her seapower was threatened. As Grey had made clear, not to do so would imperil each dominion.

By making seapower the issue which would decide whether or not Britain entered a European conflict, Asquith's government had brought the dominions into line. Britain could, therefore, expect to be able to tap dominion sources of manpower which would be vital if the war was prolonged. Few present at the conference could have doubted that Germany would be the power whose 'Napoleonic' pretensions would precipitate a war. Taking breakfast with David Lloyd George the morning after Grey's address, Louis Botha, the Prime Minister of South Africa, announced that immediately the conflict began he would invade German South West Africa with 40,000 men.[19] Australia and New Zealand had already been urged to take swift action against German colonies in the Pacific once war started, although they probably needed little encouragement.

The 1911 Imperial Conference had been called against a background of deepening Anglo-German antipathy. The German navy remained the chief source of contention, but there were wider reasons for hostility. These concerned the question of what Germany would do next and were summed up in an article which appeared in the right-wing, imperialist journal *The Nineteenth Century and After* in 1912:

> Will a nation such as Germany, with the motive power supplied
> by a high birth-rate within it, and with every instinct of patri-
> otism alive in its heart, forgo willingly the prospect of national
> aggrandisement and the hope of territorial gain?[20]

The enlargement of the German empire and the extension of German political influence had lain at the centre of the policy of *Weltpolitik*, but, the Kaiser and his ministers claimed, this would not involve any infraction of Britain's official and unofficial empires. Rather, Germany demanded what it considered to be an equitable distribution of the spoils from those empires that seemed to be on the verge of dissolution: the Chinese, Turkish and Portuguese.

Britain was prepared to lend a cautiously sympathetic ear to German requests for alterations to the international *status quo*, although ministers and diplomats who were over-accommodating towards Germany ran the risk of public opprobrium. Nevertheless, a secret accord had been reached on the Portuguese colonies by 1913 and, after much wrangling, an agreement was made over the Berlin-Constantinople-Baghdad railway in 1914. Britain had originally been a partner in this enterprise, which was principally designed to open up the resources of the Tigris and Euphrates valleys, but withdrew in 1903 on the grounds that its share of the investment was too small. The line, later described by Curzon as a 'dagger thrust towards India', scared the government in Delhi. Its nerves were not soothed by an odd, off-the-cuff remark of the Kaiser's, made in 1907, that 'we should most assuredly want our armed men on a certain frontier not a very long

way from India'.[21] Such outbursts, a peculiar mixture of threat, braggado-
cio and silliness, came frequently from Wilhelm II's lips and did much to
increase international tension during this time.

Precautionary measures were quickly taken. In 1906 the Committee for
Imperial Defence had plans prepared for the occupation of Basra, which
included a proposal to populate southern Mesopotamia (Iraq) with Indian
immigrants.[22] A year later, the client sheik of Kuwait agreed to lease his
foreshore to Britain, which ruled out its use as the Persian Gulf terminus
of the Baghdad railway. The India and Foreign Offices also covertly cultivated the goodwill of Abd al Aziz Ibn Saud, the ruler of Najd, who, in the
process of extending his patrimony, occupied the coast between Kuwait
and Qatar in 1907. Conscious of the need to maintain the Persian Gulf as
a British lake, and also aware of the impropriety of openly backing a rebel
against the Turkish sultan, the Foreign Office simultaneously refused to
recognise Ibn Saud's independence and warned Turkey not to undertake
operations against him.[23]

Empire-building Arabian sheiks were the least of the Turkish government's worries. The 'Young Turk' revolution of 1908 had begun a period
of acute turmoil throughout the Ottoman dominions. Intensely nationalist, the Young Turks supported a far-reaching programme of modernisation throughout the Ottoman empire, which, when completed, would
make Turkey the Japan of the Near East. The European powers wanted it
to be the China, and interpreted the change of government as marking the
opening phase of Turkey's disintegration. Outlying Turkish provinces in
south-eastern Europe were successively snatched by Austria-Hungary and
the petty Balkan kingdoms. Italy, the Johnny-come-lately of imperial
powers, invaded Libya in 1911.

These assaults on Turkish integrity, together with the quickening tempo
of European, particularly French and German, commercial penetration of
the Ottoman empire (the German ambassador in Constantinople had
talked ominously of Turkey as 'Germany's Canada') encouraged local
nationalism. Soon after the 1908 revolution, a Turkish newspaper had
likened the great powers to 'scorpions, snakes and hyaenas preying upon
the land, so lost to all decency that they had been prepared in their lust to
export even the droppings of dogs'. The release of some, but not all of the
old régime's restraints on freedom of discussion stimulated political activity. Turks, Arabs and Kurds began to discover a sense of national identity.

Britain was not directly affected by these developments. The centre of
British influence in the Middle East had shifted from Constantinople to

Cairo. The security of British interests now depended on the Mediterranean fleet, the garrison in Egypt and the goodwill of France and Russia, rather than the friendship of the Sultan. British policy towards Turkey was constrained by the need to consider the special interests of her new partners. France was seeking a sphere of influence, possibly more in Syria, and Russia desperately needed a permanent guarantee of free passage through the Straits for the ships which carried her growing export trade, particularly in grain. There were also the peculiar requirements of the Indian government, which, in the event of a Turkish collapse, would want to safeguard its trade in the Persian Gulf and Mesopotamia, which was already being considered as a possible Indian colony.

Surrounded by rapacious powers and suffering an erosion of its territory, Turkey was anxious to obtain an arrangement which would protect it from further encroachments. When the reforming Committee of Union and Progress came to power in 1913, it approached Britain and then Russia and France for an alliance. Neither power would oblige; Britain could not compromise its relations with France and Russia, and the latter two had their sights set on more substantial gains at Turkey's expense. The crisis in July 1914 and the possibility that France, Russia and Great Britain would fight Germany drove a far from willing Turkish government into German arms. Only a German victory could save Turkey from partition by the *entente* powers. Ottoman enmity was reinforced by the peremptory seizure in August 1914 of two Turkish battleships then under construction in British yards, one having been funded by a public subscription.

There had been no 'scramble' for Turkey before 1914. Britain and Germany had been able to reach an accommodation over financial and political spheres of influence, although at that time there was no way of knowing whether the Germans would seek new arrangements once the Berlin-Constantinople-Baghdad railway had been completed. Germany was not yet satiated, nor had *Weltpolitik* run its course, as the German ambassador in London told Colonel John Seely, the Under-Secretary of State for War. 'Our people do not like your *status quo*,' argued the ambassador. 'It means that for all time you will have command of the whole of the sea and all the best places in the land. Our people cannot accept your *status quo*.' Nor could the British accept what was implicit in this statement and the more flamboyant outbursts periodically made by the Kaiser to the effect that at some time in the future Germany would demand radical changes in the world order. It was believed by a wide range of ministers (including Grey), diplomats, senior civil servants and commanders and journalists that these alterations would lead to a dilution of Britain's power.

That Germany had so far not been overreaching in its claims was largely attributed to the fact that, by 1912, Britain was clearly winning the naval race. The final score in 1914 was:

	Battleships/battlecruisers	Cruisers	Destroyers
Britain:	24	91	155
Germany:	16	41	88

As expected the cost had been heavy; the annual naval budget had jumped from £29.2 million in 1900 to £47.4 million in 1914. But it had been worth the strain, for Fisher, whose optimism matched his pugnacity, boasted in June 1911 that the Royal Navy 'at this moment could take on all the Navies of the World! Let 'em all come!'[24]

But when would they come, and why? The Balkan crisis of June–July 1914 aroused as little stir in Britain as its predecessors; even on 3 August, when Britain was on the eve of declaring war, Lady Beatty could report to her husband that, 'To see the crowds wandering round London you would not think anything is happening.'[25] The following day was a bank holiday and visitors to Lowestoft and Yarmouth seemed as indifferent to their country's predicament as the Londoners. A party of senior officers, summoned to the Suffolk coast after a false invasion alarm, were 'driven into' by four young lady golfers, one of whose shots nearly brought down a general. Furious, he called them over and asked, 'My dear young ladies, the Germans are expected to land this afternoon. Do you know what rape is? I advise you to head for home.'[26]

These sportswomen could be excused their ignorance of the events of the past six weeks and their climax early in August because they had not directly involved the interests of Britain or the empire. The assassination of Archduke Franz-Ferdinand and his wife in Sarajevo by Serbian terrorists had provoked a confrontation between Germany's ally, Austria-Hungary, and Serbia, which enjoyed Russian patronage. Germany was willing to back Austria-Hungary's demands which, despite Serbia's history of sponsorship of terrorism, appeared harsh. Russia, anxious to prove itself as the champion of all Slavs, backed its protégé in what was developing into a trial of strength with Austria. Everything hung on the attitudes of Germany and Russia. The Kaiser and his high command, frightened by the scale of recent Russian rearmament, had for some time been convinced that the sooner war came with Russia the better for Germany. Czar Nicholas II and his advisers were equally belligerent, and were driven by a deep-seated urge to prove that Russia was again a power to be reckoned with. The final week of July saw a rapid escalation of the dispute with the mobilisation of the Austro-Hungarian, Russian and German armies. With Russia beset by two assailants, France fulfilled its duty and ordered mobilisation.

So far Britain was under no threat. Grey, pestered by France for help, could only promise that the fleet would prevent any German seaborne attack on the French coast. He was an interventionist but, like others of similar mind within the cabinet, he knew that a declaration of war against Germany would require the backing of public opinion. There was, especially on the left, much hostility towards Russia, the most oppressive tyranny in Europe, and it could reasonably be argued that Serbia had brought its misfortunes on itself. What was needed, as in 1899, was a moral cause to unite the public. It was provided on 29 July when the German government demanded free passage through Belgium for its armies. Britain was one of the signatories to the treaty which guaranteed Belgian neutrality, and by upholding it could appear as the honourable defender of international good faith against a power which believed that might was right.

Belgium refused Germany's demand and was invaded on 2 August, giving the British cabinet the just cause it had been seeking. When, on 3 August, Grey outlined to the cabinet the reasons for intervention, one listener was surprised to hear nothing about immediate national and imperial interests.[27] Much could have been left unsaid: Germany's occupation of the Belgian coastline; the defeat of France; and a Carthaginian peace which might involve the surrender of its fleet and colonies would all endanger Britain and the empire. So too would neutrality, for it would transform France and Russia into enemies who between them had an infinitely greater capacity than Germany to harm Britain's overseas possessions. It was safer to have that mass of men and weaponry known as the Russian steamroller trundling towards Berlin rather than the Indian frontier.

Once it was clear that Germany would trample on Belgian neutrality, Britain declared war. The order for mobilisation was given at ten to four on 4 August; army officers playing tennis or cricket that sunny afternoon were notified by the waving of white handkerchiefs. Within a fortnight, the advance guard of the British Expeditionary Force was disembarking at the ports of northern France. They were warmly welcomed.

★★★

The Balkan crisis had excited as little concern in the dominions as it had in Britain. As the situation deteriorated and Europe's armies sprang to arms, the British government initiated the precautionary procedures agreed with its dominion partners and set down in the War Book. The governments of Canada, South Africa, Australia and New Zealand recognised that the crisis had come of which Grey had spoken three years before, and that Germany was that nation whose 'Napoleonic' ambitions in Europe now imperilled British seapower. 'If there is a war, you and I shall be in it,' asserted the Australian Prime Minister, Joseph Cooke, for, 'if the old country is at war, so are we.'[28] News that Canada's Prime Minister, Sir Robert Borden, had offered Britain his country's backing and 30,000 fighting men, prompted Australia to equal this number on 3 August.

The profoundly moving spirit of comradeship and carefree, jaunty patriotism which agitated the thousands of young men who rushed to recruiting stations in Britain during the late summer of 1914 was matched in the dominions. Many, perhaps the majority of young men welcomed the war as an adventure, but there was also a strong vein of patriotism running through the ranks of those who joined up. A nineteen-year-old Australian patriot wrote that he and his brothers-in-arms were preparing to uphold 'the traditions of the British race'; he was killed in action at Gallipoli. Another soldier of the new Australian and New Zealand Army Corps (ANZAC) expressed the same spirit in verse:

> The banners of England unfurled across the sea,
> Floating out upon the wind, were beckoning to me.
> Storm-rent and battle-torn, smoked stained and grey:
> The banners of England – and how could I stay!ic[29]

This sense of kinship and shared danger also inspired a Canadian soldier-poet:

> From Sydney to Esquimault, from the Lakes to Hudson Bay,
> Men who never saw you, Mother, those that left you yesterday,
> We have chucked the tools and ledgers, we have left the bench and mine,
> We are sailing east to Flanders to Join the khaki line.

> We are comng, wild and woolly,
> Hearts and hands are with you fully,
> Pledged to smash the Prussian bully,
> Five hundred thousand strong.[30]

A black soldier of the empire from Nyasaland struck another common chord. 'We joined the war because we were men,' he recalled many years afterwards.[31]

There was no choice for colonies such as Nyasaland and, for that matter, India which, as dependencies were bound to follow Britain into the war. The dominions fell into line in August 1914 because their leaders and people acknowledged a common peril and, bearing in mind what Grey had said three years before, realised that a German victory in Europe would be to Britain's and their own disadvantage. The flood of offers of men from the dominion governments which reached London within a few days of the declaration of war were a reassuring demonstration of imperial solidarity. So too was the response of thousands of young men who poured into the recruiting offices throughout the empire, although they, like their rulers, expected a short war.

PART FOUR

THE AGE OF IMPERIALISM IS ENDED
1914–45

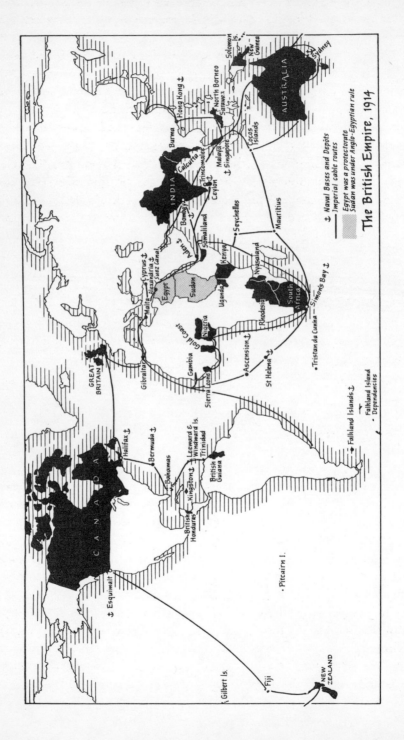

The British Empire, 1914

‡ Naval Bases and Depôts
—— Imperial cable routes

Egypt was a protectorate
Sudan was under Anglo-Egyptian rule

Falkland Island
· Dependencies

1

E is for Empire for which We Would Die: 1914–18

The resources of the empire made Britain the most formidable power engaged in the war. The empire covered a quarter of the earth's land surface and had a population of 425 million of whom 366 million were coloured, and of these, 316 million lived in India. This manpower was ruthlessly exploited to provide both fighting men and the host of labourers and carriers which supported the imperial armies on every front.

At the end of the war the total of imperial soldiers, sailors and airmen was 8.5 million. Of these, 5.7 million came from the United Kingdom (four-fifths from England), 1.4 million from India, 630,000 from Canada, 420,000 from Australia, 136,000 from South Africa, and 129,000 from New Zealand. This last figure was particularly impressive since it represented just over half the men eligible for service.[1] The African colonies produced 57,000 soldiers and an astonishing 932,000 porters and labourers, most for service in the German East African campaign.[2] There were a further 330,000 Egyptian labourers who worked in France and the Middle East, 43,000 black South Africans who undertook behind-the-lines chores in East Africa and northern France, and a specially recruited Chinese Labour Corps which was also employed in France. By 1918 there were nearly a third of a million Chinese, Africans and Egyptians in France alone. By undertaking the donkey work of total war, these men, like their counterparts on other fronts, released white men to replenish the firing line. The claim, based solely on a head count of servicemen, that Britain never fully utilised the empire's manpower is absurd; Nyasaland yielded

15,000 askaris and 200,000 labourers between 1914 and 1918, two-thirds of its adult male population.[3] The proportion of black soldiers could have been higher, but the Colonial Office was nervous about black men fighting white, and senior officers wrongly imagined that the negro lacked the steadiness and fortitude of the European.[4]

The war revealed in the starkest possible way the undercurrents of racial prejudice and tension which had long swirled and eddied just below the surface throughout the empire. Sir James Willcocks, who commanded Indian forces in France between October 1914 and September 1915, publicly praised the Indian fighting man as 'a first-class soldier and Nature's gentleman', but privately abhorred the thought of such men being tended by white nurses.[5] Lord Lugard was horrified by the idea of his wife being treated by a black doctor and, in 1918, a Colonial Office official was appalled by the possibility that West Indian convalescents in a Liverpool hospital were being looked after by English nurses.[6]

In March 1915, Maori troops in Egypt were ordered to undertake garrison duties in Malta rather than join their white colleagues in the attack on the Dardanelles, much to their disappointment.[7] It was axiomatic among senior commanders that imperial prestige in the Middle East was best upheld by white troops. This was not entirely racial prejudice; the sudden influx of Indian and black units into this region in June 1918 and the transfer to France of white soldiers fuelled rumours among the Egyptians that Britain was on the verge of defeat, and that the new arrivals were expendable men who would soon be swept aside by the Turks and Germans.[8] That the Egyptians should have thought along these lines says much about their experience of British racial attitudes.

These were apparent elsewhere in the Middle East army, which included British, dominion, Indian and colonial troops. Men from two Royal Fusiliers battalions, recruited from London's Jewish community, protested against being brigaded with the West Indians, who themselves were angry at being placed in hospital wards alongside Asian and African invalids 'who were ignorant of the English language and western customs'.[9] West Indians were further enraged by being ordered into foul railway carriages which Anzac soldiers had just refused to enter.[10]

This incident in 1918 was also an example of the notorious cussedness of Australian soldiers, which had become a constant headache for senior officers, long accustomed to the docility of the British Tommy. The Australian fighting man was an independent-minded creature whose first and often only attachment was to his immediate unit. Australian officers, although for the most part from middle-class backgrounds, had to spend some time in the ranks, and relations between them and their men were free and easy. Extending the spirit of 'mateship', one Australian officer shared his bottle of whisky with some British NCOs and found himself reprimanded by a British court martial, which interpreted his gesture as one likely to undermine discipline. Such a view of discipline, indeed the whole concept of hierarchy it was intended to uphold, was utterly incomprehensible to the Australian soldier. At first, Australians had been puzzled by the servile obedience shown to their officers by English soldiers (the Scots seemed far less passive), but their attitude later turned to one of contempt towards men who refused to stick up for themselves.[11]

British generals, Haig in particular, were disturbed by the possibility that the insubordinate spirit of the Australians might contaminate British personnel. It did not; in fact, there was an understandable jealousy felt by many British servicemen towards the 'fuckin' five bobbers', since Australians were paid five shillings (25p) a day as opposed to the one shilling allowed the British soldier.[12] In Egypt, and afterwards France, this extra cash was usually spent on drink and prostitutes, and there were protests in the Australian press about the exposure of the country's virtuous young manhood to the 'depravity' of the former country.[13] A near epidemic of venereal diseases among Anzac troops early in 1915 led to a riot in Cairo in which brothels were sacked and burned. Subsequent manifestations of Australian recalcitrance included two mutinies in France in 1918, and the destruction of the Arab village of Surafend and the killing of several of its inhabitants as retaliation for the murder of a New Zealander.

By contrast, the Indian professional soldier knew his duty and place in the scheme of things, or so his officers thought. The stress of war proved them wrong, for the fighting spirit of the two Indian divisions sent to France in the autumn of 1914 soon evaporated. Despite internal reforms of the past decade, the Indian army and its senior officers were physically and mentally unprepared to fight a modern, European war. A combination of cold, wet weather and extraordinarily heavy casualties (some units were reduced by half in a single action) suffered in battle led to a decay of morale which was reflected in a rash of self-inflicted wounds and malingering during the winter of 1914–15.[14] In May 1915, the censors of Indian soldiers' mail revealed that a large number were infected with 'despair of survival', and Haig feared that a mutiny was imminent.[15] The Indian government, which had vainly attempted to keep knowledge of its soldiers' discontent to itself, concurred, and in September the Indian contingent was pulled out of France for redeployment in Mesopotamia.

Mobilisation of the empire's manpower in 1914 had proceeded by slow stages, and according to no plan beyond the need to find dominion soldiers to replace imperial garrisons of British regulars, who were urgently needed in France. It was events there during the winter of 1914–15 which dictated the shape and direction of the empire's war effort. By the turn of the year the conflict in France had evolved into what is best described as an extended siege. Two increasingly well-protected lines of fortification, each many miles deep, stretched from the Channel to the Alps. For the next three and a half years, the Anglo-French and German armies attempted to fracture and penetrate their adversary's network of barbed wire, trenches and bunkers. At the same time, the opposing high commands endeavoured to discover a formula by which the innovations of modern warfare – machine-guns, high explosive shells, pinpoint bombardment, aircraft, poison gas, tanks, and wireless – could be brought together to deliver the knock-out blow. This task was made more difficult by simultaneous improvements in the techniques of defence.

The process of finding a way to end the deadlock in the West was painfully slow and bloody. It was marked by a sequence of mass offensives between 1915 and 1918 which consumed men by the hundred thousand and yielded relatively minor tactical gains. Haig, who took command of the British Expeditionary Force in December 1915, justified this strategy in terms of wearing down the German army to a point of moral and physical exhaustion. This was arguable. What was not was that the Allies would need a continual flow of fighting men to make good the losses which were the inevitable result of a war of attrition. To start with, and in the belief that the contest would be soon over, Britain and the dominions had relied on volunteers.

Conscription had long been regarded as inimical to those cherished notions of individual freedom which obtained in Britain and the dominions. Principles of this sort were luxuries in time of war, and as the flow of volunteers slackened the British government was forced to introduce conscription at the beginning of 1916. New Zealand followed suit in May, but in Australia, where the enlistment rate was falling, there was widespread resistance to compulsory service. The matter was twice put to the public in referendums in October 1916 and December 1917, and each time the vote was decisively against conscription. On each occasion there had been considerable opposition from Australians of Irish descent whose ancestral dislike for Britain had been sharpened by the condign measures employed after the 1916 Easter Rising in Dublin, and the British government's reluctance to allow Home Rule. Conscription also opened up racial divisions in Canada where French Canadians objected to conscription legislation passed in August 1917. Its enforcement during the winter and spring of 1917–18 provoked riots in Quebec. Fears of a similar rift between those of British ancestry who were wholeheartedly behind the war and the Afrikaners, of whom a minority were pro-German, inhibited the South African government from even considering conscription. The reactions to conscription of Australian Irish, *Canadiens* and Boers were a reminder that within the white dominions were communities whose collective historic memory made it impossible for them to have any natural affinity with Britain, or any emotional attachment to the idea of empire.

While the dominions had the final word as to whether or not conscription was adopted, overall control of the imperial war effort and allocation of imperial resources was the responsibility of the British war cabinet and high command. Both worked in harness if not harmony with their French counterparts, and were constrained by having to take into account their ally's needs. Domestic political intrigue and debate had not been suspended at the outbreak of war, rather they became more intense and bitter as it became clear that successive governments were failing to deliver victories. Asquith's Liberal war cabinet, to which the imperial hero Kitchener had been co-opted as Minister for War, was replaced by a coalition in April 1915. Asquith survived until December 1916, when he was unseated by a cabal of newspaper owners and politicians who believed that he lacked the energy and willpower needed to win the war. Lloyd George possessed both qualities, as well as charisma. He succeeded Asquith, heading a coalition which remained in power, often uncomfortably, for the next two years.

The entries and exits of ministries, ministers and for that matter generals and admirals, were the outward evidence of discord and divisions among those responsible for deciding strategy. By the beginning of 1915, two distinct views were emerging as to the nature of the war and how it might be won. On one hand there were the 'Westerners' who, with French backing, wanted a concentration of resources in France on the grounds that victory could only be achieved by the defeat of the German army there. On the other, there were the 'Easterners' who argued that the war in France had become a stalemate and, as the casualty lists were daily proving, attempts to gain a breakthrough just squandered lives. Instead, an attack should be made on Germany's allies, weaker vessels which would shatter easily, and whose destruction would undermine Germany.

Turkey was the first target of the Easterners. Forcing the Straits would bring down the Ottoman empire and open a passage to Russia, which was showing signs of extreme strain. Furthermore, and this made the enterprise highly attractive to imperialists such as Churchill and Kitchener, Britain could take a share of Turkish provinces. The 'scramble' for Turkey had, in fact, already started; in November 1914 an Indian expeditionary force had occupied Basra and was tentatively moving northwards, while the Russians had invaded eastern Anatolia. Diplomatic preparations for a post-war division of the spoils were in hand. By the end of the year, Russia had been allocated the Straits, and after much wrangling the Sykes–Picot agreement of May 1916 defined the boundaries of the British and French official and unofficial empires in Syria, the Lebanon, Palestine and Mesopotamia.

So, according to the Easterners, operations against Turkey would puncture Germany's 'soft underbelly'; might lead to a Balkan front against Austria-Hungary; and provide an opportunity to extend the empire. If, as seemed likely between 1915 and 1917, it was impossible to break the deadlock in France, then a negotiated peace with Germany would follow. Britain had, therefore, to acquire some bargaining counters and look to the future. Sir Mark Sykes, a Yorkshire MP with a specialist, first-hand knowledge of the Middle East, argued in 1916 that by tightening its grip on southern Mesopotamia Britain would be better placed to resist post-war Russian encroachments in the region. He, like many others, assumed that when the war ended the great powers would restart their former global jockeying for influence and territory.

The Easterners' arguments prevailed within the war cabinet and the result was the Dardanelles expedition in the spring of 1915. Its supporters not only claimed that it would knock Turkey out of the war, but it would be a spectacular affirmation of the military might of the British empire and France. This object lesson in imperial power quickly went awry. In all, 129,000 troops were landed, a third of them Anzacs, but Turkish resistance was dogged. The campaign dragged on into the autumn, and, when it was obvious that no breakthrough could be made, the war cabinet reluctantly approved a withdrawal.

The evacuation of the Gallipoli peninsula in December 1915 was a signal humiliation for the imperial powers, particularly Britain. The conventional imperial wisdom, expressed shortly after by a senior Indian army officer, held that, 'We owe our position to the fundamental and inherent superiority of the European as a fighting man over the Asiatic.'[16] But this no longer held true: a predominantly Turkish army had beaten a predominantly white one and proved that Europeans were not invincible. Gallipoli confirmed for the peoples of Asia and the Middle East the lesson of Russia's defeat at the hands of Japan ten years before; white armies were not unbeatable. Mustapha Kamal Pasha, who had masterminded the defence of the Dardanelles and is better known by his post-war name, Kamal Atatürk, became the focus for and leader of the Turkish national movement, and an example to other Middle Eastern nationalists. A further blow to European supremacy was delivered in April 1916, when an Anglo–Indian army was forced to surrender at Kut-al-Amhara on the Tigris.

The reverses at Gallipoli and Kut damaged British prestige. The last confirmed the unfitness for modern warfare of the Indian army, or at least its high command. The 'scramble' for Turkey was proving a far harder task than its earlier counterparts in Africa and China. In terms of winning the war, the Gallipoli and Mesopotamian campaigns were, as the Westerners had always insisted, sideshows which wasted manpower needed to fight the real war in France.

The Gallipoli campaign forms the background to John Buchan's thriller *Greenmantle*, published in October 1916. The plot revolves around an attempt by the Turko–German high command to enkindle a mass uprising among the Muslims of North Africa, the Sahara, the Middle East and India in the name of a messianic holy man. The fictional holy war is prevented in the nick of time, but the possibility of a real one was a source of unending anxiety for British and Indian governments throughout the war. In November 1914 the Turkish Sultan, speaking as khalifah (spiritual head of all Sunni Muslims), had declared a jihad against Britain, France and Russia. These powers were the merciless enemies of Islam; they had made war on Muslims for a hundred years, and had taken their lands from them in Africa, the Middle East, and Asia. Now Muslims could unite, fight back, and, in the name of their faith, take back what had been theirs.

A nightmare was coming true. Three years before, Lord Fisher had foretold that, 'The world has yet to learn what the Mohammedans can do if once their holy fervour seizes them.'[17] His apprehension was shared by those proconsuls who governed predominantly Muslim areas. The jihad had an enormous potential for mischief, especially in India, whose 57 million

Muslims were the main source of recruits for the army. Jihadic passion was strongest on the North-West Frontier, and sepoys from this region were always more likely to place faith before loyalty to the king emperor, and desert. A handful of Pathan deserters were known to be working with Turko-German intelligence during 1915 and 1916, and some may have returned to their homeland to foment uprisings against the British. Far more serious was a mutiny in November 1914, when men from the 130th Baluchis refused to fight against the Turks. There was a further, more violent mutiny in February 1915 by the 5th Native Light Infantry at Singapore during which the insurgents murdered European officers and civilians. In both instances the mutineers were rounded up, tried and the ringleaders publicly executed. An official enquiry after the Singapore affair revealed evidence of pan-Islamic subversion, and a widespread disquiet felt by many sepoys about reports of the heavy losses among Indian troops in France.

The Indian administration was severely shaken by these events and the prospect of further unrest. 'I want every white soldier in India I can get,' the Viceroy Lord Hardinge told Kitchener in March 1915.[18] His panic was contagious; in April 1916 the war cabinet earmarked two divisions then in Egypt for transfer to India the moment there were signs of a jihadic uprising or an Afghan invasion[19]. Two months later, Wingate was badgering London and Cairo for troops at the onset of Ali Dinar's revolt. Memories of the 1857 Mutiny in India and Mahdism in the Sudan were evergreen and contributed to the extreme jitteriness of officials, but their behaviour also suggests a deep-seated belief that Britain's authority in the Muslim world was brittle.

As it turned out these alarms were exaggerated. The ambitious and potentially dangerous programme of pan-Islamic subversion planned by the Turko-German secret service failed because of poor management, internal squabbles and overstretched lines of communication. The dreaded explosion of fanaticism, the mutinies apart, proved to be a series of damp squibs. The Libyan Sanusi attack on Egypt in 1915, Ali Dinar's revolt in the Sudan in 1916, and a string of rebellions in the French Sahara were all handled by local forces. The Sahara uprisings were partly suppressed by askaris of the Nigeria Regiment, loaned to the French in 1916–17, an interesting example of cooperation between the former imperial rivals.[20]

What helped dampen down Islamic fervour was the loyalty of those Muslim princes in India and Africa who owed their continued authority to Britain. The Aga Khan, the Sultan of Zanzibar and the emirs of northern Nigeria (who gave £188,000 to the British war chest) remained staunchly loyal and issued counter-jihadic appeals to their co-religionists which, among other things, argued that the khalifah's jihad was no more than a cunning German stratagem. The spiritual influence of Hussain, sharif of Mecca, also added desperately needed weight to Britain's propaganda campaign after June 1916, when he formally detached himself from the Ottoman empire and allied with Britain.

Hussain was the figurehead of what later became known as the Arab Revolt. What at first appeared an adroit imperial coup had been devised by a handful of dedicated Foreign and War Office officials and intelligence officers based on Cairo, of whom Captain, later Colonel T.E. Lawrence (Lawrence of Arabia) became the best known. By seducing Hussain, they had hoped to blunt the edge of the jihad and spark off a wholesale defection of Arabs from the Turkish to the Allied cause. Politically, the ultra-conservative head of the Hashemite family was an ideal partner, but Hussain's cause also attracted more radical Arab nationalists, who were looking ahead to post-war Arab nations arising from the wreckage of the Ottoman empire. The trouble was, and this became increasingly clear during 1917–18 as Arab forces guided by Lawrence moved northwards from the Hejaz, Britain and France had already staked out claims to lands which the Arabs hoped to have for themselves. Furthermore, the Indian government was laying plans for the post-war annexation of Mesopotamia, not only as a defensive measure, but as a colony which could be settled by Indian immigrants. By cultivating Arab nationalism, the London government was creating what Lord Hardinge prophetically described as 'a Frankenstein's monster'.[21]

Britain's ability to mount an attack on the Dardanelles, give seaborne assistance to the Arabs in the Red Sea and shift troops from India and the dominions to wherever they were needed, depended on command of the world's oceans. This had been achieved by the end of 1914. There had been one hiccough when a weak British squadron was all but destroyed by the German Far East squadron at Coronel, off the Chilean coast, in November. Within two months, prestige and local superiority had been restored at the battle of the Falkland Islands, where the German ships were defeated by a scratch force, including two battlecruisers, that had been hastily assembled and rushed from Britain.

The only large-scale fleet action was fought off Jutland at the end of May 1916, and concluded indecisively with the Germans returning to port after having inflicted heavier losses on the Grand Fleet. Nevertheless, the balance of seapower remained in Britain's favour. The Royal Navy was free to continue the tight blockade of Germany that had been established in August 1914. The German response, briefly tried in 1915, was unrestricted U-boat warfare, which was reintroduced on 1 February 1917. The Kaiser predicted Britain's doom and he was nearly right; the all-out attack on British and neutral shipping bound to and from British ports was intended to starve the country and overturn its economy within six months. Beatty, now commander-in-chief of the Grand Fleet, had guessed what was in store and, two days before the Germans opened their campaign, had gloomily summed up what would follow:

> France is becoming exhausted. Italy is becoming tired. Neither can keep their factories going owing to the shortages of coal, and we cannot keep the supply because our steamers are all being sunk. Our armies might advance and slay the Hun by thousands, but the real race is whether we shall strangle them with our blockade before they defeat us by wiping out our Merchant Marine.[22]

There were now two wars of attrition in progress, one at sea and the other on land, and the Allies were faring badly in each. In the former, the German submarines were getting the upper hand by April 1917, when it seemed that Britain's entire overseas trade was about to be paralysed. Disaster was averted at the last moment by the introduction of the convoy system in June, after Lloyd George had overruled the advice of those naval professionals who were certain the scheme could never work. Military professionals had got and continued to get their way in France, with results which brought final victory no nearer. British offensives on the Somme (July 1916), at Arras (April 1917) and Passchendaele (July 1917) and the French on the Aisne (April 1917) had failed to pierce the German line, and ended with the attackers suffering the heavier casualties. Moreover, the murderous battle of Aisne triggered widespread mutinies throughout the French army.

While the French will to fight on was beginning to crack, Russia's fell apart completely. Czarist autocracy disintegrated in February 1917, and the successor Provisional Government found it impossible to sustain the war effort. In November 1917 the Bolsheviks effortlessly snatched power and within six weeks signed armistices with Germany and Turkey. The United States's entry into the war in April 1917 had given comfort to the Allies, but at least a year was needed in which to recruit and equip American troops for service in France, where, it was believed, they would tip the balance. The Doughboys and the United States navy were welcomed by Britain, but not America's voice in the direction of the war. The private apprehensions of Britain's rulers were summed up by Robert Vansittart, a diplomat:

> The United States, still holier than we, still mulling over British Imperialism, George III and the Easter Rebellion in Dublin, slid into the Great War. We wondered whether the new belligerent's needs would interfere with ours.[23]

Seen from the bleak perspective of 1917 it appeared that the Allies might never beat the German army, whatever Haig and his acolytes said to the contrary. This conclusion, and its corollary, that the war would end with a negotiated settlement, permeated the minds of ministers and their advisers. If a treaty had to be arranged, it was assumed that it would be along the lines of the 1815 Vienna Settlement with a redistribution of territory and spheres of influence. It was therefore vital that when the fighting stopped, Britain was in a position to demand and get whatever was needed to safeguard and possibly extend her existing empire.

In many respects this view of British war aims was an extension of the Easterners' philosophy, and it had an obvious appeal to the knot of imperialists who dominated Lloyd George's inner war cabinet. The Prime Minister, who had once been a pro-Boer, anti-imperialist, was shifting his ground. In August 1918 he confessed his admiration for Disraeli and Chamberlain to an approving Leo Amery, although his knowledge of the empire was still hazy, since he once situated New Zealand somewhere to the west of Australia.[24] No doubt his ignorance of imperial geography was compensated for by the imperial experience of his close colleagues, Milner and Curzon. They were joined after March 1917 by dominion prime ministers or their representatives, who were allowed to attend war cabinet meetings from time to time. Of these newcomers, the most able and energetic was Lieutenant-General Jan Smuts, the South African War Minister. An Afrikaner, he was a Cambridge-educated lawyer who led a kommando during the Boer War and then became an imperialist convert and a strong supporter of the Anglo-South African connection. Like the rest of the war cabinet, Smuts was a recipient of weekly analyses of the world situation prepared by two strongminded imperialists, Leo Amery and Sir Mark Sykes.

'The defence and welfare of the British empire' was for Amery the paramount aim of his country's war policy. He had revealed how these objectives might be achieved in a memorandum of December 1916, which proposed that Britain allowed Germany to keep its colonies in return for untrammelled political control over a block of territory which stretched from the Red Sea to the Persian Gulf. 'Pure Germanism' was the response of Lord Robert Cecil, the Under-Secretary at the Foreign Office.[25] But in terms of future imperial security, Amery's political kite-flying made excellent sense. Within a few months Lloyd George had become committed to the post-war retention of Mesopotamia and Palestine, and in June he appointed General Sir Edmund Allenby to take command of the Egyptian Expeditionary Office with orders to capture Jerusalem by Christmas. The Prime Minister hoped that this victory would simultaneously embellish the reputation of his ministry and serve as an antidote to the war-weariness that was currently infecting many sections of British society.

Jerusalem fell according to schedule, and the official newsreel of Allenby's entry was distributed to cinemas throughout the empire as a morale booster. Lloyd George, speaking in the Commons debate before the Christmas recess, referred to the fall of Jerusalem and that of Baghdad a few months before in terms of old-style imperial conquest:

> I know there is a good deal said about sideshows. The British Empire owes a good deal to sideshows. During the Seven Years War, which was also a great European war . . . the events which are best remembered by every Englishman are not the great battles on the continent of Europe, but Plassey and the heights of Abraham.[26]

The implication of these references was clear: Britain had kept Canada and Bengal and would, therefore, retain Palestine and Mesopotamia after the war. Lloyd George's conversion to acquisitive imperialism must have pleased those high-ranking army officers who were forever worrying about safe, defensible frontiers. A swathe of Middle Eastern lands would create a vast corridor which would connect Egypt with India and serve as a shield against aggression from the north. The Great War's imperialists, like Cecil Rhodes, were thinking big. One, a staff officer with a long record of frontier service in Asia, believed that nothing like the advance of British armies had been seen in Mesopotamia and Palestine for nearly two thousand years. The natives, he believed, were impressed: 'the dogged perseverance of our race . . . had opened their eyes as no Europeans opened them since the days of the Roman Empire.[27]

What was to happen in Europe after this new *imperium* had been founded on the sands of the Middle East? Here matters were complicated by the attitude of President Woodrow Wilson and his fourteen points, which he presented to Congress in January 1918 as the Allies' war aims. His peace programme was concocted as a reply to the demands recently delivered to the Bolsheviks by Germany, which made it clear that the price of peace was German annexation of Russian territory. Wilson countered greed with idealism. His list of Allied conditions was a catalogue of impeccable rectitude and included pledges of post-war self-determination for the peoples of central and southern Europe, who had hitherto been under German or Austro-Hungarian rule. Article V tentatively extended this principle beyond Europe. Decisions as to the future of ex-German colonies and Ottoman provinces would be reached after balancing 'the interests of the populations concerned' with those of the imperial power claiming the territory in question. Wilson had been extremely hesitant about this proposal for fear of giving offence to Britain, but he persevered to find a form of words which, he hoped, would not distress America's ally.[28]

He did not succeed. Wilsonian high-mindedness had destroyed all hope of a peace along traditional European lines in which Britain would have bartered colonies for redrawn continental boundaries. This was a nuisance for Lloyd George and the government, but they had to put up with it as the price of American financial and material assistance. As Vansittart drily noted of Wilson's peace terms, 'Our ruling class did not relish the role of John Bull with a ring through his nose.' Nine months before the publication of Wilson's proposals, the former Conservative prime minister, Arthur Balfour, had warned the cabinet not to allow 'Central European Philanthropy' to stand in the way of the achievement of post-war imperial security.[29] The interests of Poles, Czechs, Rumanians and assorted Yugoslavs, who had done little or nothing to further the Allied cause, had to remain subordinate to those of Britain. Moreover, Australia and New Zealand, which had acquired Germany's Pacific islands, and South Africa, which had conquered South West Africa, refused to consider relinquishing them. Likewise, the British government was unwilling to surrender Togoland and the Cameroons, which had been overrun between 1914 and

1916, or German East Africa, which had been finally taken after a prolonged and arduous campaign in December 1917.

All speculation about peace was purely academic in January 1918. German forces, lately released from the Russian front, were being transferred to the West in preparation for a war-winning offensive which was expected to be of unprecedented ferocity. Those who had stayed behind were beginning to advance eastwards towards the Black Sea, while the newly formed Turkish 'Army of Islam' was preparing to push towards the Caspian Sea. No Russian troops worth the name were able to oppose them. As the year unfolded the Allied position seemed precarious everywhere save on the seas where the German submarine threat had been greatly reduced.

Three successive German offensives in France launched between March and July 1918 sliced through the Allied line, but on each occasion retreating forces were able to regroup and hold fresh defensive positions. The counter-offensives began in August and continued to the end of October. The German army lost ground and the will to fight on. The end came unexpectedly for the Allies, whose high command was preparing for operations in 1919 and a possible outright victory the following year. During the first week of November the disintegration of public order in Germany, the Kaiser's abdication and a mutiny by sailors of the High Seas fleet drove the government to ask for terms. The armistice, which was tantamount to a German surrender, took effect on 11 November. On other fronts it was the same story of hammer blows followed by a swift collapse. In the Middle East, Allenby's brilliant and fast-moving offensive shattered an outnumbered Turko-German army and Damascus was liberated by Australian cavalrymen on 30 September. Within a month, Aleppo and Antioch had fallen and the Turkish government had surrendered. Simultaneous Allied offensives in northern Italy and south-eastern Europe brought Austria-Hungary and Bulgaria to their knees.

The British empire had survived and won. Soon after Germany's capitulation, Curzon, in exultant mood, spoke of a future world in which the empire would be supreme:

> The British flag never flew over more powerful or united an empire than now; Britons never had better cause to look the world in the face; never did our voice count for more in the councils of the nations, or in determining the future destinies of mankind.[30]

Plenty of such hubristic stuff poured from the lips and pens of statesmen, politicians and journalists during the next few months. Much of it was justified, for the empire's subjects had made a titanic effort and paid a heavy price. The totals for dead and wounded were:

	Dead	Wounded
Great Britain:	702,000	1.67 million
India:	64,000	67,000
Australia:	59,300	152,000
Canada:	56,700	150,000
New Zealand:	16,700	41,300
South Africa:	7,000	12,000
Newfoundland:	1,200	2,200

Most of the casualties had been suffered in France where, in November 1918, there were just under two million British soldiers under arms, alongside 154,000 Canadians, 94,000 Australians and 25,000 New Zealanders. A further 306,000 imperial troops including 92,000 Indians and 20,000 Australians were deployed in Egypt, Palestine and Syria. There were 222,000 soldiers serving in Mesopotamia of whom 120,000 were Indian and 102,000 British. There were over a third of a million native labourers working on lines of communication throughout the Middle East.[31]

For the dominions, the experience of war had been a rite of passage to nationhood. Anzac Day, the anniversary of the landings at Gallipoli, became a national day of remembrance in Australia and New Zealand. Its emotional meaning and the part played by those who had died in the development of national consciousness were poignantly illustrated in a small ceremony re-enacted at school morning assemblies in New Zealand during the 1920s. A boy faced a portrait of George V, saluted and then announced: 'Our King inspires loyalty and devotion to our country and its laws because he rules by consent of the people. God Save the King!' The National Anthem was sung. Afterwards, a boy recited these lines:

> The Great War proved that thousands of New Zealanders thought our beautiful country worth dying for. Like them, we pledge ourselves to live and, if necessary, die for our country and for our comrades throughout the Empire . . .[32]

But had men died for the empire? Recruiting slogans and posters made much of the empire; a patriotic ABC for Canadian soldiers written in 1916 included the exhortation, 'E is the Empire for which we would die', and there were plenty of illustrations which showed the British lion roaring defiance with her cubs (the dominions) adding their yelps.[33] Keith Fallis, a missionary's son who at nineteen had enlisted in the Canadian army, believed that he, and presumably others, had been 'brainwashed' by pre-war imperial propaganda. 'I never questioned', he later recollected, 'that what we were doing was right and that the Germans were all wrong and that we were fighting to make the world safe for democracy.'[34] The front was no place for flag-waving since soldiers' minds were wholly concentrated on staying alive or recuperating from the trauma of battle. Working-class British soldiers in France were unmoved by the word 'empire', although some were stirred by it in the mistaken belief that it referred to the Empire Music Hall![35] During a war cabinet discussion of future imperial organisation in July 1918, the forthright Australian Labour Prime Minister, Billy Hughes, remarked that three-quarters of his countrymen then in France wanted nothing more to do with the empire.[36]

The black soldier's motive for fighting is not always easy to discern, for he seldom left any record of his experiences. When explanations of the war were offered them, they focussed on the possibility that the Germans would come and take their land. This was what recruits in Nyasaland heard in 1914.[37] A Nigerian who served as a porter during the 1916–18 Cameroons campaign was told 'that we were going to the great war to help keep the King's soldiers who were preventing the Germans coming to our country and burning it.'[38]

From the beginning of the war, there had been official misgivings about the mass recruitment of black soldiers. A Colonial Office official reminded the War Office in 1915 that:

> it must not be forgotten that a West African native trained to use of arms and filled with a new degree of self-confidence by successful encounters with forces armed and led by Europeans was not likely to be more amenable to discipline in peace time.[39]

The point was understood on the other side of the racial barrier. In South Africa, Solomon Plaatje also recognised the danger of black fighting white. 'The empire must uphold the principle that a coloured man must not raise his hand against a white man if there is to be any law and order in either

India, Africa, or any part of the Empire.[40] His fellow blacks were, quite deliberately, not being asked to kill white men but to do their chores, or, as George V told them when they arrived in France in July 1917: 'Without munitions of War my armies cannot fight; without food they cannot live. You are helping to send these things to them each day, and in so doing you are hurling your spears at the enemy.'[41] What his audience made of this speech is not known. Many had been astonished by meeting educated black men, apparently equal to whites, when they briefly disembarked at Freetown, Sierra Leone. They were also amazed by the sight of white men working on the docks at Liverpool and the free and easy ways of the women of the port.[42]

South Africa's blacks had left behind them a country where a black skin automatically relegated a man to the bottom of the social pile. West Indians came from a society where the black man enjoyed greater advantages; he was educated by missionaries and governed in a benevolent manner by a paternalist colonial administration. Despite their gallantry in the field during the Palestine campaign, West Indian volunteers, keen to serve Britain, endured racial slights which left them humiliated and angry. Their bitterness exploded in a mutiny at Taranto in December 1918. During a protest meeting one sergeant shouted out, 'The black man should have freedom and govern himself in the West Indies.' His views were applauded and some months after, Sir George Fiddes, the Permanent Under-Secretary at the Colonial Office, warned officials in the West Indies that the 'white class does not appreciate the altered tone of the black men'.[43]

Indian nationalists saw their country's war effort as a step along the path towards self-government. Their leader Mohandas Gandhi, who had served with a field ambulance unit in the Boer War and during the 1906 Zulu rebellion, offered his services again, but an attack of pleurisy prevented him from going to Mesopotamia. He accepted the Wilsonian vision of the war as one being waged on behalf of the 'weaker and minor nationalities' and, in June 1918, urged his followers to enlist. Nationalist volunteers, he told an audience in Bombay , would form 'a national army' of 'Home Rulers'. 'They would go to fight for the Empire; but they would so fight because they aspire to become partners in it.'[44]

No binding ideology held together the empire's fighting men. Imperial enthusiasts, mostly in Britain, who held up wartime cooperation as a shining example of how imperial unity could work and the basis for future cohesion were out of touch with reality. An emergency had drawn together Britain and the dominions who, in 1914, were reasonably alarmed by the repercussions of German domination of Europe. British and dominion soldiers fought well, but the latter, particularly Australians and Canadians, were appalled by the rigidity of Britain's social system which had been translated in its entirety into service life. Many were glad that they or their ancestors had emigrated. Black and brown men discovered new worlds; were exposed to new ideas; became conscious of their position within the empire; and returned home questioning some of its assumptions.

Nevertheless, the late-Victorian and Edwardian dream of the various parts of empire joining together to form one solid battleline had come true. What imperialists then and after failed to appreciate was that those who had been asked to make sacrifices might expect recompense. Furthermore, in what was its final surge of empire-building, Britain had used the war to conquer territories in the Middle East in alliance with Arab nationalism. In 1918 it remained to be seen how, if at all, acquisitive imperialism could be squared with the rights of Gandhi's 'weaker and minor nationalities' in whose interests Britain had ostensibly been fighting for the last eleven months of the war.

2

Clear Out or *Govern*: Troubles, mainly Irish, 1919–39

Two viruses afflicted the post-war world. One, Spanish influenza, attacked the body and the other, which no one could put a name to, infected the soul; they were equally devastating. While the origins of the second sickness were the subject of conjecture and debate, its symptoms were clear enough. Treatment seemed beyond the powers of statesmen, as Arthur Balfour, then acting Foreign Secretary, remarked in a letter to Sir Reginald Wingate, the high commissioner in Egypt, at the end of March 1919:

> The Egyptian unrest is doubtless part of a world movement which takes different forms in different places, but is plainly discernible on every continent and in every country. We are only at the beginning of our troubles and it is doubtful whether, and how far, the forces of an orderly civilisation are going to deal effectively with those of social and international disintegration.[1]

This was a bleak diagnosis from a man of seventy-one who had been brought up to have faith in the eventual triumph of human progress and those civilised forces which underpinned the old world order. At the end of what had been a distinguished political career, the urbane and cultivated minister looked out on a world full of mischief. Everywhere there was evidence of the disruptive energy of that protean force which appeared not only unstoppable, but threatened the existence of the empire.

In the past three months Balfour had witnessed the proclamation of an Irish republic by a band of Sinn Fein MPs, and the paralysis of Egypt by saboteurs and mobs clamouring for an end to British rule over their country. As Balfour had feared, matters soon got worse. During April and May, Gandhi's mass protest against the recent sedition laws triggered disorders on such a scale as to make some officials believe that India was on the verge of a second mutiny. There were anti-white riots in Trinidad, Jamaica and British Honduras; Kurds rebelled against the new British administration in Iraq; and in May 1920, the Arabs followed suit. In the same year there were anti-Jewish riots in Palestine and the spread of a guerrilla campaign by the Irish Republican Army (IRA).

Britain was not immune from the contagion. British and dominion troops mutinied and rioted against delays in demobilisation during the winter and spring of 1919. In June, a detachment of the Staffordshire Regiment refused to leave for service in India and the summer was marked by a series of police strikes.[2] Most alarming of all was an upsurge in trade union militancy which was reflected in a sequence of strikes throughout 1919 and 1920 that unnerved the government and stirred up fears that Britain was about to face a revolution along Russian lines.

Those of a conservative frame of mind like Balfour searched for a single guiding intelligence behind these repeated assaults on the established order. The Ulster Unionist leader, Sir Edward Carson, declared to the Commons in July 1920 his belief that there existed a 'conspiracy to drive the British out of India, and out of Egypt'.[3] Another Ulsterman of strong opinions, Field-Marshal Sir Henry Wilson, the Chief of the Imperial General Staff, was more specific. He listed the causes of national and imperial disaffection as: 'Sinn Feiners and Socialists at our own doors, Russian Bolsheviks, Turkish and Egyptian Nationalists and Indian seditionists'.[4] He did not say whether their activities were coordinated, but his intelligence department identified Russia as the ultimate source of all anti-British movements in the Middle East.[5] Sir Maurice Hankey, successively secretary to the Committee of Imperial Defence and to the war cabinet, blamed President Wilson's fourteen points which, by their promotion of nationalism and self-determination, 'struck at the roots of the British Empire'.[6]

The theory that all expressions of popular discontent in Britain and throughout the empire owed their origins to covert Communist agitation appealed to those on the right and in intelligence circles, and proved remarkably durable. Its persistence owed much to the anti-colonial rhetoric which poured out of Moscow after 1917, and Russia's offer of sanctuary and support to militant nationalists, particularly from India. Likewise, the Communist International (Comintern), founded in 1919 to propagate world-wide revolution, aimed to develop the revolutionary consciousness of all colonial peoples. This was, however, a secondary objective, for the Comintern's attention was principally focussed on the already organised industrial working classes of Europe and America, who were more susceptible to Communist propaganda than the politically unawakened peasantry of Asia and Africa.

Where they existed, colonial trade unions were a natural target for Comintern agents. British and Indian Communists were sent to India during the 1920s with orders to penetrate and convert local trade unionists. These agitators made little headway, thanks in large part to the counter-subversion measures adopted by the Indian Criminal Investigation Department.[7] Precautions against the infiltration of trade unions were taken in Egypt in 1920, when specially chosen native police officers were sent to England to undergo a course in 'anti-Bolshevist' surveillance techniques.[8] Elsewhere, colonial police departments kept an eye on local Communist parties. That established in Palestine in 1921 proved no danger to the state for, according to a police report, its subsequent history was 'little more than a dreary and uninspiring tale of doctrinal bickerings and fiercely waged disputes involving no more than a handful of obscure men and women in back rooms in Tel Aviv and Haifa'.[9]

Such details did nothing to allay the fears of British intelligence. In 1927, Field-Marshal Lord Milne, the Chief of Imperial General Staff, summed up an analysis of Communist activities in India with the observation that Soviet subversion was 'the gravest military menace which faces the British Empire today'.[10] This claim rested on reports that Soviet agents, drawing on experience gained in China, were preparing to subvert the Indian nationalist movement. What is striking about this information is what it reveals about the official mentality of the time: both Milne and his staff automatically assumed that the Indian national movement would easily succumb to Communist pressure and accept an ideology far different from that of most of its leadership and rank and file. More alarming was information which indicated that the Russian government was resuscitating Czarist expansionist policies in Afghanistan. During the brief Third Anglo-Afghan War of 1919, intelligence discovered that the Afghans were seeking Russian aircraft and pilots, and two years later Afghan aviators were being trained in Russia.[11] Old ghosts reappeared in the corridors of Delhi and plans for the defence of Afghanistan against a Russian invasion were brought out and updated.[12] Even in 1943, when Britain and Russia were allies, military intelligence was disturbed by accounts of Soviet agitators at work among the tribesmen of the North-West Frontier.[13]

The 'Red Menace' fitted neatly with the conspiracy theories which began to circulate in 1919 and provided a satisfying explanation for the plague of restlessness which was spreading through Britain and the empire. A coherent and terrifying pattern was imposed on this global phenomenon by the publication in 1919 of 'The Protocols of the Elders of Zion', which were given much prominence by the right-wing press, most notably the *Morning Post*. Fabricated by Russian anti-semites during the twilight of Czarist rule, this document outlined a plot hatched by Jews to secure world domination through subversion. The Russian Revolution and Communist agitation throughout the world were part of this plan, which had as one of its goals the overthrow of the British empire. Among the converts to this cock-eyed theory was Rear-Admiral Barry Domville, whose work for naval intelligence supported his conviction that the empire was endangered by a Judaeo-Masonic conspiracy masterminded by Moscow. The exposure of the Protocols as a forgery in 1920 did nothing to shake his faith nor that of other *fantasistes* who, from the mid-1920s onwards, joined various British fascist movements. All were pledged to defend the empire from its shadowy adversaries, who were invariably Jews or Communists or both.

The search for a common source for all the problems facing Britain and the empire was reflected in the thrillers of John Buchan and 'Sapper'. Both relied on their audience's willingness to accept a world in which secret intrigues flourished and a handful of determined men could seriously devise schemes to overthrow governments or destabilise whole societies. The villains were creatures of immense resource, utter amorality and were, almost to a man, aliens. Their machinations were always frustrated and the civilised order of things was preserved. That the readers of such fiction believed that the basic structure of their country and empire was so brittle suggests a flagging confidence in both.

It was arguable that the war had left the established order weakened and therefore vulnerable to the epidemic of protest and disorder that appeared in 1919. It was also politically convenient for defenders of that order to dismiss all assaults upon it as the products of a gigantic but ill-defined conspiracy. Doing so ruled out any suggestion that the assailants' grievances might be real or even justifiable.

Such attitudes, usually combined with an intense fear of Communism and its capacity to create mayhem everywhere, were prevalent among Britain's ruling class at this time. There was, therefore, a tendency, most common among soldiers, to classify dissidents of whatever complexion as either dupes or cunning men who manipulated the ingenuous and fundamentally decent masses to further their own ends. Such an explanation of the causes and manifestations of discontent often made it difficult for politicians and commanders to examine their sources dispassionately.

At the same time, conventional political wisdom made it very hard for Britain's rulers to comprehend the emotions which impelled their adversaries to extremes of stubbornness and, at times, violence. For most of the nineteenth century, and certainly during the lifetimes of the men who governed Britain in 1919, their countrymen had been learning to put their faith in reasoned debate between rational men as the best method of settling political differences. Given goodwill and flexibility, a solution could always be found to any problem. Contemplating the unquiet state of Ireland in May 1918, Walter Long, a Wiltshire squire and Unionist MP, expressed the faith of his generation and class in the processes of political dialectics. 'I feel', he wrote, 'that it cannot, must not, be beyond the power of statesmanship to avert the awful disasters with which we appear to be threatened.'[14]

Disaster had, in fact, already overtaken Ireland. Its Gaelic, Catholic majority no longer had any confidence in those essentially British ways of bringing about political accord. The failure of two Home Rule bills to be passed, and of a third to be implemented, convinced them that they could no longer rely upon the British parliament to provide them with what they wanted. Their salvation now lay in their own hands, and after 1914 many disappointed nationalists turned towards the Sinn Fein (Ourselves Alone) party, which called upon Irishmen and women to seize freedom for themselves even at the price of their own lives. Drawing heavily on the idealism of the Italian nationalist, Mazzini, Sinn Fein encouraged the Irish to discover their own sense of national identity which would give them the fixity of purpose and inner strength necessary for the inevitable struggle against Britain.

Sinn Fein gave an inspiring example of the sort of self-sacrifice that would be needed if Ireland was to free itself on Easter Day 1916, when its members attempted an armed coup in Dublin. It failed, and the leading

insurgents were court-martialled and shot at the orders of the local commander, General Maxwell, who had learned how to treat the empire's
enemies in the Sudan, and who justified his actions on the grounds that
traitors could expect no mercy in wartime.

The Easter Rising had been greeted with indifference by most
Irishmen, but the courage of the 'martyrs', and exasperation with an alien
government which showed scant interest in Irish opinion drove more and
more towards Sinn Fein. British influence over southern Ireland dissolved
slowly, unnoticed by a government whose attention was focussed on winning the war against Germany. Bit by bit, the administration in Dublin
Castle lost its grip over the remoter parts of the country and, when conscription was introduced in April 1918, it was thought prudent not to
enforce it, given the present humour of the Irish.

The test, both of public support for Sinn Fein and the authority of the
British government, was the general election of December 1918. Seventy-
six Sinn Fein MPs were returned (forty-seven were in gaol), together with
twenty-six Unionists, and six old-style Home Rule nationalists. The Sinn
Fein MPs gathered in Dublin in January 1919, formed the Dáil Eireann
and proclaimed Ireland a republic. There were now two governments in
Ireland, each claiming legality and denouncing its rival. One, under the
Viceroy, Field-Marshal Lord French, occupied Dublin Castle, and the
other, headed by President Eamon de Valera, was busy creating its own
administrative apparatus and a defence force, the IRA. With the confidence provided by this force, believed to number 100,000 volunteers, the
Dáil outlawed the Royal Irish Constabulary (RIC) and demanded the
immediate evacuation of all British troops.

The chief objective of Sinn Fein was to prove to the British government
that the authority of Dublin Castle had been superseded by that of the
Dáil, which was soon running a shadow administration. The first phase of
what soon came to be known as the 'Troubles' began during the early
summer of 1919, when the IRA launched a systematic campaign against
the RIC. The murder of policemen, lightning raids against police stations
and burning of police barracks were designed to intimidate and finally
destroy the principal instrument of Dublin Castle's control over Ireland. By
the end of the year, the police were in disarray and, most importantly, their
intelligence-gathering apparatus had fallen apart.

The British government had faced and overcome terrorist campaigns in
Ireland during the 1880s, and had coped with massive civilian unrest and
rebellion in 1798, the late 1820s, the 1840s and 1860s. There was, at least

from the perspective of Whitehall, no reason why the methods which had worked in the past, a mixture of political concession and coercion, would not prove successful again. Until midsummer 1919, the minds and energies of ministers were concentrated on the negotiations that preceded the signing of the Versailles Treaty. This accomplished, the cabinet turned to Ireland and the concoction of a political panacea which would cure its sickness, and keep it within Britain's orbit. While the remedy was being applied, every effort would be made to isolate and destroy Sinn Fein by force and resume the everyday government of Ireland.

For the next two years, the cabinet more or less accepted Lloyd George's comparison of the situation to that in the United States in 1861, when the southern states had seceded from the Union. Ireland was part of the United Kingdom and the empire and could never be detached. Nevertheless, the events there during the first half of 1919 indicated a degree of popular dissatisfaction that had to be remedied. It was taken for granted that Sinn Fein were a small group of fanatics whose power rested on terror alone, and that most Irishmen would welcome a compromise.

The cabinet had, in fact, mistaken the temper of the great majority of southern Irishmen. A further obstacle to a settlement was the widespread contempt for the Gaelic, Catholic Irish, which was the legacy of two hundred years of religious and political propaganda. The Irish were, in English eyes, a fickle, childlike race, unable to subdue their wilder passions. For generations, *Punch* cartoons had portrayed 'Paddy' as a wide-eyed, simian-featured clown brandishing his shillelagh and looking for a fight. This stereotype and all that it implied clouded ministerial judgements. Andrew Bonar Law, the Conservative leader, considered the Irish 'an inferior race' and Lloyd George once quipped, 'The Irish have no sense of humour, and that is why they make us laugh so much.'[15] As the terrorist campaign intensified in Ireland, British anger found an outlet in racial abuse. A letter which reminded readers of the *Saturday Review* how Britain had held Ireland in what was tantamount to slavery, provoked this outburst from a furious correspondent: 'Slaves have been made to work, and no one – not even Mr Ford, the great maker of motor-cars – has ever been able to make an Irishman work. The only thing the Irish have done consistently well throughout their history is murder; murder is the national pastime of the Irish.'[16]

The government thought that it would stop Irishmen killing each other and British soldiers by giving them a little of what they wanted. In December 1919, the cabinet approved the draft of an Irish Home Rule bill which was laid before the Commons the following spring and passed. It was a recipe designed to satisfy Gaelic nationalism, calm Ulster Protestants, and keep Ireland within the empire. First, Ireland was to be partitioned, since it was clear that the Protestant majority in Ulster, which had threatened to fight over the issue in 1886 and 1912, would never accept a government elected by all Irishmen. Ulster was still as defiant as ever. Ulstermen would never bend their knees to a Dublin government in which the levers of power would be operated by 'the hierarchy of the Roman Catholic Church', proclaimed the Unionist leader Carson. His listeners, all Orangemen assembled in Belfast on 12 July 1920 to celebrate the Protestant victory at the Boyne in 1690, cheered. They would, he claimed, only join hands with their Catholic countrymen if the latter chose to stay within 'the Empire [which has] spread civilisation . . . throughout vast regions'.

As it was, Irishmen would remain in the empire, at least if the British government got its way. Those in the south would have a parliament in Dublin and those in the north one in Belfast. Both assemblies would collect and spend taxes, but Ireland's foreign and defence affairs would remain Westminster's responsibility. Under the terms of the new Home Rule act, elections were scheduled for May 1921, by which time, it was hoped, the British army and the reinforced RIC would have beaten the IRA.

Sinn Fein rejected all that Lloyd George had to offer. Its supporters wished to part company with Britain and its empire for ever, and the concept of a divided Ireland was anathema to nationalists with a mystical belief in the essential oneness of their land. The republicans could afford to take an unbending line for they were gaining the upper hand in the war in which their adversaries were at a permanent disadvantage. The IRA fighting man wore no uniform and could not be identified; he slipped out of and into the crowd; and he moved among a people which, either through fear or out of sympathy, were prepared to harbour him or cover his tracks. He was also supported by another unseen army of men, women and youngsters who were his eyes and ears. They warned him of his enemy's movements and lied about his own, activities which sometimes cost them their homes, possessions and even lives.

Urban and rural guerrilla warfare was still a novelty in 1919. Its rules perplexed soldiers used to being able to recognise their opponents and led to a widespread feeling of impotent rage. This was expressed by General Sir Nevill Macready in his memoirs. 'The British Government never recognised the term 'guerrilla warfare,' he wrote. 'Had they done so the task of the soldier would have been infinitely easier.' He could, for instance, have shot every man found armed but not in uniform.[17] Macready had been appointed commander-in-chief in Ireland in April 1920. He was not a conventional imperial soldier, used to demonstrating the iron fist to rebellious natives, but an expert in civil-military relations whose experiences had been confined to industrial disputes and, during 1919, as, chief commissioner of police.

When Macready took up his duties it was obvious that the depleted and demoralised RIC could no longer withstand the IRA's guerrilla campaign without large-scale army assistance. Moreover, IRA terror tactics had reduced police recruitment so that the authorities had to look to the mainland for reinforcements and create what was, in effect, an alien *gendarmerie*. The result was the notorious Black and Tans of Irish nationalist mythology, ex-servicemen recruited in London, Glasgow and Birmingham, who appeared in Ireland in January 1920. Their improvised uniforms, a mixture of RIC dark green and army khaki, reminded somebody of a celebrated pack of Limerick foxhounds and got them their nickname. They were followed by the RIC Auxiliary Divisions ('Auxis'), also recruited outside Ireland. Both bodies quickly gained a reputation for hard drinking, promiscuous brutality and savage reprisals against a population which sheltered and sympathised with their enemies. The appearance of the Black and Tans and the Auxis marked the end of civilian policing over large areas of Ireland, where they were seen as a particularly undisciplined wing of an army of occupation.

By the summer of 1920, the pattern of the war had become established. IRA units, sometimes substantial flying columns, assembled, went into action, and then melted into the streets and countryside. They killed at random members of the security forces and anyone remotely associated with them, sometimes mistaking their targets. The IRA volunteer was a patriot, convinced that the moral rightness of his cause, a united republican Ireland, released him from obedience to normal codes of human behaviour. His enemies saw him as a cold-blooded murderer. Particularly horrific killings were answered by reprisals against a civilian population which was tainted with guilt by association. Most notorious of these spontaneous acts of revenge was after the IRA shot dead twelve British officers in their billets on 21 November 1920, alleging they were intelligence agents. That afternoon a detachment of Auxis fired into a crowd at a Dublin football ground, claiming they were answering IRA fire; twelve spectators were shot or crushed in the panic.

However regrettable, reprisals of all kinds were the unavoidable consequence of an army having to contain a guerrilla campaign without the
intelligence sources to detect their enemy. As the number of reprisals
increased, so did criticism of the government by the left-wing and liberal
press, which compared the behaviour of British forces in Ireland with
that of the Germans in occupied Belgium during the war. A gap was also
opening up between politicians and army commanders, who began to
argue that the imposition of martial law was the only way in which the
IRA could be beaten.

Sir Henry Wilson took a hard line. He wanted reprisals to be given full
official sanction, and the execution of all republican leaders.[18] In May
1920 he feared that Lloyd George had fallen victim to 'funk' because he
had temporised in his dealings with Irish trade unionists, who were then
hampering the movement of men and supplies. The circumstances
demanded ruthlessness, for what was at stake was the future of the empire,
which Wilson believed could be lost through a lack of prime ministerial
willpower.[19] Churchill was in broad agreement, equating concessions in
Ireland with those already made in Egypt, and believing that both would
contribute to a weakening of the empire.[20]

During the second half of 1920 ministers agonised over how far they
should go in the war against the IRA. Those in favour of a tough line
argued that it would signal the determination of Britain to hold on to its
empire. And yet, if the generals were given the free hand they sought, then
the politicians would loose control over events. Milner, the Colonial
Secretary, recalling his South African experience, saw no practical difficulties in enforcing martial law in Ireland, but he warned the cabinet that
it would place enormous power in the hands of junior officers.[21] Everyone
present knew that he had in mind not the conduct of subalterns, but that
of a relatively senior officer, Brigadier-General Reginald Dyer. In April
1919, Dyer had used martial law as the justification for opening fire on a
crowd of demonstrators in Amritsar, killing nearly 400. The shooting and
Dyer's subsequent régime of summary and condign punishments had provoked a political rumpus which had concluded with an acrimonious
Commons debate in July 1920. Nonetheless, Curzon saw no reason why
Ireland should be spared the traditional Indian methods such as inducing of
obedience, communal fines and the punitive disruption of everyday business life.[22]

The politicians gave ground, gradually. Macready was allowed to impose
martial law on four counties in December 1920 and a further four the

following month. Reinforcements, and additional motor transport for mobile patrols, encouraged him to predict victory by mid-1922. His optimism was dented by an upsurge in IRA activity during the spring of 1921, which ruled out elections in the south, still set for May. By early June, Macready's faith in coercion was waning.[23] And yet the internment by courts martial of 4,400 IRA suspects in six months, coordinated urban and rural sweeps and searches for arms and ammunition, were paying dividends. Looking back on this period, Michael Collins, the most brilliant and daring of the IRA's commanders, confessed, 'You had us dead beat. We could not have lasted another three weeks.' He was mistaken in his estimate of his adversary's strength; the British army had still not overcome many of its operational problems, not least the lack of a competent intelligence-gathering service. In fact, by early June, the two sides were facing deadlock.[24] It was broken by an appeal for negotiations made, at the cabinet's request, by George V when he opened the Belfast parliament on 23 June. A truce was agreed between Sinn Fein and the government on 12 July and Irish representatives arrived in London for talks three months later.

During the height of the fighting, Colonel Lawrence, who had commanded Arab nationalist guerrillas against the Turks, observed of Ireland, 'You can't make war upon rebellion.' On another occasion, he warned the government that the 'ordinary Englishman' did not desire and could not afford an empire which rested solely on armed force.[25] By June 1921, the cabinet had come to agree with him, grudgingly in the case of some ministers. Once it was clear that the IRA would do all in its considerable power to wreck the elections in the south, the only alternative was to declare the twenty-six counties a colony and administer them through a system of martial law. Macready doubted whether this policy would yield anything beyond a continuation of the war into the indefinite future.

The cabinet shrank from delivering the whole of southern Ireland into the hands of the generals. The past two years had seen a steady increase in protests by senior churchmen, Liberal and Labour MPs, the Trades Union Congress (which had demanded the evacuation of British troops during a special conference in June 1920) and journalists against what Asquith had described as the 'hellish policy' of repression and random revenge. It was alienating more and more Irish men and women and tarnishing Britain's moral reputation throughout the world.

There was much disquiet abroad about the turn of events in Ireland. De Valera had toured the United States during 1919 and early 1920, where he was treated as a nationalist hero on a level with Gandhi and Sun Yat-Sen.

He was most warmly received by Irish-American groups. These contributed $5 million in cash to help victims of the war, supplies of food and, clandestinely, arms, and they exerted political pressure on senators and representatives. This secured some anti-British resolutions, but nothing more. The new president, Warren G. Harding's isolationist credentials ruled out official intervention in what he regarded as a British problem and none of America's business.[26] Ireland was, however, the concern of the dominions, particularly Australia with its large Irish community. General Smuts foresaw that the methods being employed in Ireland would 'poison' relations between Britain and the dominions. In June 1921, he took time off from the Imperial Conference to visit Dublin, where, as a former enemy of Britain, he persuaded the Sinn Fein leaders to seek a compromise.[27] Britain, he told them, would never tolerate a republic, but would now accept a self-governing Ireland with dominion status.

Negotiations between Sinn Fein and the British government began in October and lasted for just under two months. What passed across the conference table and the treaty which was signed at the beginning of December have since been the source of considerable recrimination. Both sides regarded the truce as a breathing space and were ready to reopen hostilities. The IRA recruited 45,000 much-needed extra volunteers between July and December, and Lloyd George made it plain that he would restart and intensify the war if no agreement was forthcoming.[28] On 2 December, Churchill was reportedly 'full of threats of John Bull laying about with a big stick'. Four days later, when the treaty was about to be signed, he warned Collins, one of the Irish delegates, that the army was ready to resume operations in three days' time. [29] Bluster of this kind convinced many Irishmen then and later that the treaty had been squeezed out of their representatives by threats. It is more likely that Collins and his colleagues were the victims of a bluff; the principal reason why they had been invited to the negotiations was to forestall the extension of a war which was embarrassing the government, and which Macready believed was unwinnable.

Arguments about the circumstances in which the Anglo-Irish treaty was agreed were inevitable given its contents. Southern Ireland became a self-governing 'Free State' and a dominion. The treaty also recognised the detachment of Ulster and its Catholic minority from the Free State, and its status as a part of the United Kingdom, but with its own peculiar parliament. For those for whom the dream of Irish nationhood encompassed a single land, a hallowed historic entity, the border between the south and the north was a wound. It was an incision made for the sake of expediency, and its existence symbolised the ancient domination of Ireland by England. The nationalist movement, like Ireland, was split by the Treaty; although it was ratified in the Dáil by just seven votes, its opponents continued to fight it. The pragmatists fought and beat the idealists in a civil war that dragged on into 1923 and in which Collins was killed in a skirmish. The fighting spilled over the Ulster frontier, which anti-treaty forces attempted to redraw by force, provoking a vicious anti-Catholic backlash in Belfast.

The final victory went to de Valera and his followers. In 1937 he reframed the Irish constitution, making Eire a republic. This was not strikingly significant, although it mattered considerably to those whose nationalism had remained unsullied by the 1921 compromise. Ever since the 1931 Statute of Westminster, Ireland, like the other dominions, had enjoyed complete freedom in the management of all its external and internal affairs. This independence was asserted in September 1939 when de Valera declared Ireland neutral in Britain's war against Germany.

Opinion inside Britain was split over the Anglo-Irish Treaty and its implication for the empire's future. On one extreme, the *Spectator* had demanded that the Irish should be thrown out of the empire as they had shown themselves manifestly unfit to enjoy its enviable privileges.[30] The government could not afford to indulge in tantrums: strategic considerations alone (Irish bases had been invaluable during the recent campaign against the U-boat) required that southern Ireland remained a British satellite. And so it was on paper, and for this reason Curzon declared the treaty a victory for Britain, as did Lloyd George.[31]

Sir Henry Wilson and the diehards bitterly disagreed. By what he described as a 'cowardly surrender to the pistol', Britain had exchanged the substance of power for its shadow. The empire, he predicted, was now 'doomed'.[32] 'We must either clear out or *govern,*' Wilson insisted in May 1921, and when it became obvious that a pusillanimous cabinet had chosen the former course in Ireland, he resigned and got himself elected as a Unionist MP for an Ulster seat. Wilson, like many other senior officers, some ultra-Conservatives, and right-wing newspapermen, believed the empire ultimately rested on a narrow base. It would only survive so long as Britain possessed superior force and the will to apply it remorselessly whenever dissent broke surface. Politicians, whom Wilson despised, lacked this resolution because they were continually sidetracked by party considerations, the opinions of the press, and the need to further their own careers. Made distraught by the settlement in Ireland, which he believed would soon be repeated elsewhere, Wilson may have entertained fantasies of himself as the Caesarian saviour of the country and the empire, a British Mussolini or, more appositely, General Franco. He did not live to become Britain's man of destiny; in June 1922 he was assassinated outside his house in Eaton Square by two IRA gunmen, who were quickly captured (one had a wooden leg), tried and hanged.

Wilson was an embittered, perhaps slightly deranged military man whose outbursts would be echoed during the next forty years by those who believed that the empire had in some way been betrayed by indecisive or weak-willed politicians. In what was a long-drawn-out rearguard action, they argued repeatedly that strong men and firm measures would overcome the protests of the empire's discontented subjects who were, they always insisted, an unrepresentative minority of self-seeking troublemakers. But one knotty problem remained; if, as Wilson and those of like mind insisted, the empire had to be held together by force then how much force was the government entitled to use?

Gandhi, examining the implications of the Irish treaty, interpreted the circumstances which led to its agreement not as a failure of nerve, but as an assertion of traditional moral principles. 'It is not fear of losing more lives that has compelled a reluctant offer from England,' he wrote in December 1921, 'but it is the shame of any further imposition of agony upon a people that loves liberty above everything else.'[33] One who had felt this shame more deeply than some of his cabinet colleagues, the Liberal historian and president of the Board of Education, H.A.L. Fisher, later summed up the concessions offered to Ireland as 'achievements of the Liberal spirit'.[34] This spirit held the key to the empire's future, according to J.J. Jones, a Labour MP and former trade unionist. Shortly before the debate on the Anglo-Irish Treaty, he told the Commons, 'I believe the Empire will eventually be saved by self-determination. You cannot any longer keep the people in chains . . .'[35]

These statements had much in common with those made by opponents of the American War in the 1770s. More significantly, perhaps, they highlight the contradiction which lay at the heart of the twentieth-century British empire. It had been understood by Cleon, who, in the fifth century BC, had reminded the citizens of another imperial power, Athens, that 'a democracy is incapable of empire'. 'Your empire', he continued, 'is a despotism and your subjects disaffected conspirators, whose obedience is ensured not by your suicidal concessions, but by your own strength.' He concluded with a demand for the severest chastisement of rebels in terms of which Sir Henry Wilson would have approved. And yet Britain, like

Athens, was proud of its democracy and the freedoms enjoyed by its people, and from the seventeenth century onwards had exported its institutions and ideals to its colonies. Its empire was not and, despite growling on the right, would never be a military dictatorship.

What then would it become? In 1919 the empire had been given a new title, 'the British Empire and Commonwealth of Nations', a phrase first used by General Smuts. It was a felicitous choice of words which banished from the self-governing dominions that stigma of inferiority and subservience conveyed by membership of an empire. Invented by sixteenth-century political writers, 'Commonwealth' stood for a free community of equals with shared interests who worked together for the good of all. Emotional attachment to Britain and a common ruler, the British monarch, held together a Commonwealth whose states had undergone a similar evolutionary process, passing from dependent colonies to self governing nations. At every stage, this transformation had been made on Britain's terms, and on the assumption that Britain was legally entitled to give or withhold political rights to its subjects everywhere.

Between 1919 and 1922 the Irish had broken this pattern. They had called the tune and forced an extremely reluctant British government to dance to it. If the empire was a monolithic, essentially authoritarian structure then the Irish Revolution marked the beginning of its decline. If it was a living organism, continuously adapting itself to its environment, then the Irish troubles were no more than a chapter of unhappy accidents which would have little or no effect on the course of the empire's development.

3

Their Country's
Dignity:
Egypt, 1919–42

Field-Marshal Viscount Allenby, the commander-in-chief of the army that had finally overturned the Ottoman empire and made Britain the supreme power in the Middle East, was pessimistic about the future of the empire he had enlarged. He kept his doubts to himself, for he had been made high commissioner in Egypt in March 1919, an appointment which owed much to his well-known strength of character and iron will. But he lacked the inner conviction of other warrior proconsuls, for he was a man of broad intellectual horizons with a questioning mind. This enabled him to detect the historical forces that were beginning to gather momentum and would soon be ranged against the British empire. Talking with a close friend after dinner one evening early in 1920, he remarked that the empire would inevitably fall apart once more and more of its subjects became educated.[1] He was worried that what they learned would not provide them with the 'responsibility and integrity and leadership' which were essential for those who exercised power over others.

Events of the past eight months had made Allenby uncomfortably aware that pupils in Egypt's schools were learning to hate Britain and everything it stood for. One of them, Gamel Abdul Nasser, born in 1918, later recalled that 'when I was a little child every time I saw an aeroplane flying overhead, I used to shout: "O God Almighty, may a calamity overtake the English."'[2] Another future Egyptian leader, Anwar el-Sadat, born in 1921, remembered the bitter anglophobia of his father, whose hero was Kamal Atatürk, the Turkish nationalist leader who had successively overcome the

Italians, Greeks and the French, and then outwitted the British. In 1932 the young Sadat was excited by what he read in the newspapers about the life of Gandhi, then passing through Egypt on his way to argue India's case before the British government.[3]

And yet, paradoxically, the young nationalists shared with Allenby a sense that they too were resisting inexorable forces. Nasser, then a high-school student, recalled 'shouting himself hoarse' during anti-British demonstrations in 1935. 'But it was to no avail – our cries died into faint echoes that moved no mountains and blasted no rocks.' The empire seemed immovable, as it did to other young men who bellowed slogans, hurled stones and fought with police and soldiers. Moreover, as Egyptians had painfully discovered, the aeroplanes which periodically overflew their cities and towns could drop bombs.

Young men like Nasser and Sadat were among the thousands of Egyptians who regularly took to the streets between the wars to demand an end to British interference in the running of their country. Their protests were orchestrated by the Wafd, which was the largest political party in Egypt and, for Sadat and others like him, stood as 'a symbol of the struggle of the entire Egyptian people against the British'. For the British, the Wafd was a nuisance which might eventually go away. To speed its departure, they spied on its activities (without much success), arrested and exiled its leaders when it appeared to be getting too powerful and at other times tried to pretend it did not exist.

The Wafd had begun life peacefully enough. A few days after the end of the war, a delegation (wafd) of highly respectable Egyptian politicians approached the High Commissioner, Sir Reginald Wingate, and firmly but politely asked for an end to the British protectorate and the restoration of independence. Their leader, Said Zaghlul, a man once marked out by Lord Cromer for 'a career of great public usefulness', drew Wingate's attention to Britain's recent promises of self-determination for the Arabs, and suggested that the Egyptians, who were far better qualified to govern themselves, deserved the same treatment. He knew that the 'liberty-loving' British would be sympathetic and, to Wingate's alarm, indicated that Egypt was prepared to lay its case before President Wilson at the forthcoming Versailles conference.[4]

The High Commissioner treated the delegates firmly but did not dash their hopes to pieces. Egypt was suffering inflation and disruption on account of the war and a public reprimand might easily spark off popular unrest. Far away in London, Lord Curzon, the Foreign Secretary, was appalled by Wingate's conciliatory approach and ordered him home. A firm hand and not soft words were what was needed, and the Wafd had to be nipped in the bud before Egypt succumbed to the nationalist germ that was infecting India. In March 1919, at Curzon's instructions, local officials arrested Zaghlul and his companions and bundled them off to exile in Malta.

By taking the offensive Curzon had miscalculated the temper of the Egyptians. So too had the British administration in Cairo, and their error of judgement was less excusable since they might have been expected to have had some insight into the Egyptian mind. They did not; by and large, British civil servants kept their own company and stayed aloof from the Egyptian upper class, which they regarded with a mixture of amusement and disdain. A year before, a British official serving in the Sudan, had explained his colleagues' voluntary quarantine to Leo Amery:

> I am afraid our public school system, which discourages general intellectual curiosity and makes everyone flock together for certain stock games and amusements, undoubtedly acts as a great barrier between us and the educated class in a country like Egypt.[5]

There were a few exceptions to this rule. That most aesthetic and precious of colonial administrators, Sir Ronald Storrs, had once tried to instruct a Coptic colleague in the manly science of boxing, but on the whole the British stuck to their tennis and race meetings, and seldom ventured outside their clubs and Shepheard's Hotel. As Storrs noticed, few educated Egyptians ever bothered to learn English, but continued speaking French even after thirty-odd years of British domination.

There was also, and this became unpleasantly obvious as unrest increased, a widespread racial contempt for the Egyptians. At the onset of the troubles officials and soldiers had dismissed the hard core of nationalists as 'riff-raff', a gaggle of students, unemployed and unemployable intellectuals and rabble-rousers who had nothing better to do than idle away their hours in cafés plotting sedition.[6] During his discussions with Egyptians at the end of 1919, Milner was unfavourably struck by the 'vanity' of the effendiya class and described them and their supporters on the streets as 'all that is vocal' in the country, implying that they were a minority who spoke for no one but themselves.[7] Time spent arguing with clever Egyptians was wasted according to General Walter Congreve VC, commander-in-chief in Egypt after 1920. 'When you talk politics to an Easterner you may be sure you will get the worst of it, kick him and he loves and respects you.'[8]

Those who did the kicking agreed with the General. The troops who were called upon to restore order in 1919 relished the task, even though it held up their demobilisation. British, Indian and Anzac servicemen saw the 'Gyppo' as a devious creature who fleeced them whenever he could, and were therefore glad of a chance to get their own back during the suppression of the disorders which followed the exile of Zaghlul. The censors of soldiers' mail discovered a 'John-Bullish' attitude abroad and widespread 'anger and disgust' with the Egyptians.[9] This persisted after the 1919 uprising: Egyptians celebrating Allenby's concessions were waylaid and beaten up by British and Australian soldiers keen to uphold the empire's 'prestige', and during the 1920s the high commission had to handle a stream of complaints from Egyptians of all classes who had been manhandled or insulted by servicemen.[10] Racial contempt lay behind most of these incidents, although politically aware soldiers, who had sought a reason for the 1919 disturbances, blamed them on President Wilson's fourteen points.[11]

The Egyptian rebellion of March 1919 was a spontaneous protest against the high-handed treatment of the Wafd. There were riots in major cities and towns and a systematic attempt by strikes and sabotage to paralyse the country's rail, telephone and telegraph networks. The local commander, General Sir Edward Bulfin, responded swiftly with condign measures. Mobs were repeatedly fired on and on occasions bombed and strafed by aircraft, and suspected agitators were flogged or executed after summary courts martial. The murder of a number of British servicemen inflamed tempers, and for a time the high command felt that its men were out of control. At least 1,500 Egyptians died during eight weeks of fighting in a campaign whose ferocity bore comparison with the suppression of the Indian Mutiny.

At this stage Allenby appeared, a commander nicknamed 'The Bull' and from whom Curzon expected a display of bullishness which would bring the Egyptians to their senses. Again, the Marquess had miscalculated. Allenby was a pragmatist with enough imagination to appreciate that he could not rule Egypt by force for ever, especially as the men available to him were becoming mutinous because of postponed demobilisation. Egypt needed a civilian cabinet filled with Egyptian ministers who would cooperate with the high commissioner in the old manner. To bring this about,

Allenby offered an olive branch in the shape of an end to the banishment of the Wafd's leaders.

Allenby's concession began an elaborate political game between himself, his successors and the Wafd. For Britain, the stake was the future security of the Suez Canal, which was now sometimes called the Clapham Junction of the empire. During the early 1920s, British-registered ships accounted for between two-thirds and three-quarters of the tonnage of all the vessels that passed through the Canal. The strategic importance of the Canal became greater than ever after 1935, when Britain had to contend with the Far Eastern pretensions of Japan, and of Italy in the Mediterranean. If and when the Royal Navy had to concentrate against either power, it would have to use the Canal. The safety of the waterway rested on a British garrison and outlying detachments stationed near Cairo and Alexandria but, as Allenby realised, the Canal would be in permanent jeopardy if British forces were continually engaged in crushing Egyptian disorders.

Public opinion would not have tolerated a state of unending emergency in Egypt. Commenting on the need for a lasting Anglo-Egyptian agreement in 1920, the *Daily Mail* claimed:

> The British people never had much liking for holding down people in a perpetual state of 'unrest' . . . the best way to buttress the Empire for all time is to win the affection and trust of the peoples who have come under our charge.[12]

Much the same view was expressed in the Liberal *Manchester Guardian*, *Observer* and *Daily News,* although the *Morning Post* and *Daily Telegraph* echoed the opinions of right-wing Conservatives, who wanted the Egyptians brought down to earth with a bang by a further dose of martial law.

Force was applied periodically to the Egyptians. It had been in 1919 and was again during the political crises in 1924–5 and 1936, when British warships appeared off Alexandria and Port Said and British regiments paraded through Cairo. On both occasions, the British government was indirectly upholding the authority of the Egyptian crown, a valuable player in the game for control of his subjects. The Sultan Fuad (he assumed the title King in 1922) was a patriot after his own lights, and intensely anti-Wafd. This made him pro-British, insofar as he was always amenable to any manoeuvre that would hurt the Wafd. Once, in a state of rage, his words interrupted by a curious bark (the result of a throat wound he had suffered from an assassin's bullet), Fuad told Allenby that the Wafd's leaders were 'a crowd of revolutionaries and cads'.[13]

What galled Fuad was that the Wafd represented an alternative focus for national sentiment. Its leadership was drawn exclusively from the effendiya class of landowners and professional men, including the father of Boutros Boutros-Ghali, the present Secretary-General of the United Nations. Their wealth qualified them for seats in the Egyptian parliament and provided the wherewithal to finance the Wafd's organisation. Not surprisingly, the Wafd's social and economic policies were conservative, but its uncompromising nationalism won it support from trade unionists, students, schoolchildren and the fellahin, although, as British officials rightly guessed, the peasant vote was easily gained through coercion and bribery.[14] Throughout the 1920s and 1930s, the Wafd acted as if it possessed a monopoly of public opinion, and steadfastly refused to compromise its platform of complete independence from Britain. This intransigence was vital if the party was to hold together its various sections and resist pressure from more radical groups, such as the Muslim Brotherhood and Misr al-Fatah (Young Egypt) which emerged in the 1930s.

Outside the Wafd was a pool of Egyptian politicians who were willing to come to an accommodation with Britain and from whom King Fuad and successive high commissioners could choose ministers. Holding office wearing a British straitjacket was a hazardous job for there were, on the fringe of the Wafd, small cells of terrorists. They took melodramatic names such as the Black Revolver Gang or the Secret Sacrificers and murdered British officials, servicemen or Egyptians who worked with or for the high commission.

The first round in the game between Britain and the Wafd ended in 1922 when Allenby, exasperated by terrorism and Zaghlul's inflexibility, bullied Lloyd George into abandoning the protectorate. Churchill was furious with what he saw as a failure of nerve by Allenby, while Zaghlul and the Wafd leadership wanted further measures to give Egypt total freedom from British restrictions. Two years of bickering followed, in which Zaghlul was again exiled, and a new bone of contention emerged in 1924: ownership of the Sudan. Again Britain showed its muscle; the Labour government, anxious to show voters that it could be tough, refused even to consider a change in the Sudan's status.

The assassination of Sir Lee Stack, the Governor-General of the Sudan, in a Cairo street in November 1924, finally exhausted Allenby's patience. 'The Bull' went wild, accused Zaghlul and the Wafd of instigating the murders and demanded humiliating terms from Egypt, threatening among other things to take and shoot hostages if political violence continued. This was too much for the newly elected government of Stanley Baldwin, which recalled Allenby and replaced him with a dyed-in-the-wool imperialist of supposedly greater tact, Lord Lloyd.

Lloyd idealised British rule in Egypt. A romantic Tory, he imagined that the fellah was a stout-hearted, decent fellow who, at heart, knew the British were his true friends, but had been tricked by wily agitators. Much that was good had been achieved through Britain's supervision of Egypt's government; even today Egyptians use the expression 'the English path' to denote the way of proceeding fairly and honestly.[15] Lloyd feared, not without reason, that the form of government established in 1922 would bring back the graft and nepotism of pre-1882 days.[16] For this reason he was not a man for 'cutting losses', and refused to 'shelter behind the moral value which a policy of "self-determination" appeared superficially to possess'.[17] In 1929, the new Labour government sacked Lloyd, a man whose views seemed to belong to another age, and sent out a professional diplomat as high commissioner.

The game between Britain and the Wafd drifted into stalemate. Eight formal conferences had been held between 1919 and 1935 to settle the question of ultimate sovereignty in Egypt, without success. During the same period there had been twenty different governments, but the Wafd had not gone away. In 1935 it organised a fresh wave of popular demonstrations and strikes, which had to be taken more seriously than their predecessors because Britain's position in Egypt was now under an external threat. Mussolini's brutal consolidation of Italy's hold over Libya, his dreams of the Mediterranean as 'mare nostrum', and his recent ambitions in Abyssinia made it imperative that Britain resolved the Egyptian problem. If it failed to do so, and a crisis occurred between Britain and Italy, it would be impossible to withstand an attack from Libya and at the same time hold down Egypt. The Canal mattered more than prestige and the result was the Anglo-Egyptian Treaty of 1936. It was, given the history of the past seventeen years, a diplomatic triumph: Britain retained its garrison and air bases in Egypt, continued to enjoy naval facilities at Alexandria, and entered into an alliance with Egypt, which obtained full independence. The Cairo residency became the British embassy, and the high commissioner, Sir Miles Lampson, became Britain's first ambassador to Egypt since 1882.

The months which followed the outbreak of war in 1939 proved Egypt a lukewarm partner in Britain's struggle against the Axis powers. In September 1939 the Egyptian cabinet refused to declare war against Germany, but pledged that its country would stick to the terms of the treaty and 'render aid' to Britain. During the next few months Egypt was a benevolent neutral; diplomatic relations with Germany were broken off, Germans were interned and their property confiscated. Britain went ahead with the transformation of Egypt into a formidable base for the defence of the Canal and the entire Middle East.

The Egyptian government wobbled when Italy entered the war in June 1940, cutting formal relations, but procrastinating over the detention of the 60,000-strong Italian community in Egypt. Lampson suspected, with good reason, that Egypt's benevolent neutrality was a façade, and that King Faruq and many close to him were hoping for an Axis victory. Faruq had become king in 1936 and there was every reason to imagine that he might follow his father and tow the British line, for he had been trained as an officer at Sandhurst, where it was hoped he had absorbed British values. But 1936 was a bad year for kings; Faruq had inherited his father's distaste for the Wafd and his ambitions to become a focus for his people's national aspirations. The would-be patriot king was also a collector of pornography (he had one of the largest collections in the world), a womaniser and addicted to fast cars. His wartime behaviour revealed that his attachment to Britain was as brittle as his moral fibre. He, and many of his senior army officers and ministers, secretly believed that Britain was going to lose the war, an understandable view given the reverses suffered during 1940–41 in the Western Desert, Greece and Crete. Ordinary Egyptians were frightened about invasion and bombing raids (something which Cairo had suffered in 1917) and the upper classes found fascism and Naziism attractive creeds.[18]

At the beginning of the war, Lampson had had misgivings about Egyptian loyalty and, if necessary, had been prepared to revive the protectorate.[19] Throughout 1940 and 1941, he and the Foreign Office suppressed their suspicions about Faruq and pursued a policy of vigilant non-activity. They had an alternative government ready if Faruq began intriguing with the Germans or Italians. Ironically, Lampson believed that Britain's interests would be best served by the Wafd's leader, Mustafa al-Nahas, who, despite his party's traditional anti-British platform, was wholeheartedly pro-Allies.

By the end of 1941, the choice between the greater and the lesser evil, Faruq or the Wafd, was forced on Lampson. Faruq was swinging more and more towards the Axis and could no longer be trusted. Lampson decided the time had come either to bring him to heel or secure his abdication. During the night of 3–4 February 1942 a force of British, New Zealand and South African troops with bren-gun carriers secretly approached the Abdin Palace and surrounded it, while a number of tanks were driven to the Abdin Square. At nine in the morning Lampson entered the palace, presented the astonished Faruq with documents appointing al-Nahas prime minister, and demanded he signed it. Faruq complied with extreme reluctance, having, he claimed, protested strongly. He alleged that the paper he was handed was crumpled and grubby and an insult to his royal dignity. Later rumours circulated that a tank had been used to knock down the palace gates, and that two South African aides who had accompanied Lampson had brandished their revolvers at the indignant King.

Lampson had preserved the security of Egypt as a base for British operations. This end overrode all other considerations and he had been prepared to insist on Faruq's abdication if he had proved stubborn. But this display of force dismayed Egyptians, reminding them that they were still an impotent people with whom the British could do as they liked. 'What is to be done now that the catastrophe has befallen us?' asked Nasser, now a junior army officer. If only Egyptians existed who were willing to fight back, he argued, then 'Imperialism . . . would withdraw and recoil like a harlot.' Nevertheless, this demonstration of his people's continued abjectness, while unavenged at the time, had made a deep impact. 'That event had a new influence on the spirit and feeling of the army and ourselves,' Nasser remembered. 'Henceforward officers spoke not of corruption and pleasure, but of sacrifice and of their willingness to give up their lives to save their country's dignity.'[20]

4

———◆———

The Haughty Governess:
The Middle East,
1919–42

Five years before the outbreak of the First World War, the explorer Gertrude Bell began a Middle Eastern pilgrimage. She wanted to discover 'the Asiatic value of the great catchwords of revolution', and, after two years of wandering through Syria and Mesopotamia, concluded that 'fraternity and equality' were dangerous concepts in a region where different races and religions coexisted uneasily. A complete absence of what Miss Bell called 'the Anglo-Saxon acceptance of common responsibility in the problems which beset the state' among the people of the Middle East ruled out their future participation in any form of democracy.[1]

Variations on this theme were heard frequently after 1918, most commonly from those, like Miss Bell, who laid claim to an intimate knowledge of the Middle East. Colonel John Ward, a Labour MP and founder of a trade union for navvies, used his experience in the 1884–5 Sudan war to warn the Commons in 1922 that the imposition of European political ideas would prove 'poison and disaster' for all 'Oriental' people. It was preposterous to imagine 'that the poor Ryot [Indian farmer], the poor coolie in Colombo or any other port can be treated exactly the same as the educated working man in this country.'[2] A Liberal retorted that it was even more preposterous to assume that 'we have specific gifts from God to shape the destiny of Orientals'.[3]

The events of the past four years had shown that Lloyd George's government was filled with men who were convinced that they enjoyed the right, whether or not as a result of divine benevolence, to mould the future of the Middle East and its inhabitants. They exercised this right with the utmost rigour and an astounding disregard for reality. Through a mixture of big power diplomacy and force ruthlessly applied, the government implemented a policy of aggressive and acquisitive imperialism.

One of the mainsprings of this spasm of annexation and intimidation was the Foreign Secretary, Lord Curzon. He was then in his sixties and for the greater part of his career had fretted about the security of India. In November 1918 his worries seemed to be at an end; Turkey and Russia were prostrate, and Britain had over a third of a million fighting men distributed across the Middle East. Mesopotamia (Iraq), Syria and Palestine were occupied; there were 10,000 men in Persia protecting oil wells and upholding British interests on the southern shores of the Caspian; a flotilla of makeshift gunboats cruised on that sea; and to the east, in Trans-Caspia, small detachments of British and Indian troops garrisoned towns, guarded railway lines, and got into scrapes with local Bolsheviks. British warships dominated the Black Sea, and Constantinople was under British control.

This unprecedented concentration of British power gave Curzon a chance to fulfil his dream. Britain now had the wherewithal to create a secure corridor stretching from the Suez Canal to the borders of India and simultaneously form a buffer zone in central Asia, which would keep the Russians away from Persia and Afghanistan. The empire would be immeasurably strengthened if these swathes of territory stayed under Britain's direct control, since imperial communications would no longer be entirely dependent on the Suez Canal. Pioneer flights between Cairo and Bombay were undertaken early in 1919, and in November Sir Ross Smith flew a Vickers Vimy bomber from England to Australia via Egypt, India and Singapore. During the middle part of his journey he overflew southern Palestine, Iraq and Persia. In the next few years, plans were in hand for an overland motor route between Damascus and Baghdad.

Curzon's vision of the new Middle Eastern *imperium* soon turned into a nightmare. The vast army which straddled the region in November 1918 was made up of volunteers and conscripts, who had gone to war to beat Germany and Turkey and not, as they made abundantly clear, to found a new empire. During the first six months of 1919 these soldiers were sent home, their duty done, and replacements had to be found. Moreover, the British government had somehow to find extra manpower for commitments elsewhere; during 1919 and 1920 soldiers were needed to garrison the Rhineland, superintend the plebiscite in Silesia, stiffen anti-Bolshevik armies in Russia, police Ireland, defend the North-West

Frontier, and pacify large areas of northern India. Soldiers also had to be retained in Britain to meet the continual threats of large-scale industrial action by miners and railway workers. India, which was providing 180,000 men for Middle Eastern units, was also feeling the strain, and complained to London about the cost and the shortage of units for internal security. The dominions were asked to lend a hand, but only New Zealand agreed, the rest arguing that they had no direct interests in the Middle East save the Suez Canal, which was not threatened.[4]

Even if enough men could be found, the government did not have the money to pay them. The boom of 1919 burned itself out and was followed by a recession. Unemployment, which had been just under 3 per cent before the war, rocketed to 17 per cent by the end of 1921. A nation burdened with war debts faced a fall in revenue from taxation and a simultaneous increase in welfare payments. Retrenchment became an urgent necessity, and items such as the £30 million a year needed to underwrite Britain's presence in Persia were held up to close and critical scrutiny by the Treasury and tax-payers. Senior army officers, particularly the hard-pressed Sir Henry Wilson, became impatient with ministers who acted as if armies could be conjured out of a hat. His deputy, General Sir Philip Chetwode, bluntly remarked in August 1921 that 'the habit of interfering with other people's business, and of making what is euphoniously called "peace" is like "buggery"; once you take to it you cannot stop.'[5] Be that as it may, the government was already coming down to earth as it became embarrassingly obvious that its resources were being stretched to breaking point.

The penny packets of men in southern Russia were pulled out during 1920, which was just as well considering the weight of the Bolshevik offensive launched in the spring of that year. There was much grumbling about the damage inflicted on local British prestige, and there was more when the cabinet decided to evacuate units stationed in northern Persia in May 1920.[6] Curzon predicted, among other catastrophes, a Bolshevik revolution in Persia, echoing the view of the local commander, Major-General Sir Edmund Ironside, who believed the country was 'ripe for Communism' thanks to a 'thoroughly effete and rotten upper class'.[7]

In fact, Russia was in no position to interfere actively in the scramble for the Middle East, although the Communist government repeatedly denounced British imperialism and, in 1921, signed treaties of friendship with the nationalist governments of Turkey, Persia and Afghanistan. Resistance to British ambitions came from inside rather than outside the Middle East, and it was supported by a vocal and influential lobby in Britain. This group argued that the region could not be treated as Africa had been in the last century, as a backward area which could be partitioned and conquered without reference to the wishes of its people. Local nationalism, awakened during the last days of Ottoman rule, had become too strong a force to be pushed aside. Indeed, its present vigour and intensity were the direct result of wartime encouragement by Britain.

The trouble was that fostering Arab nationalism had been only one strand of Britain's wartime policy in the Middle East. The Sykes–Picot agreement of 1916 partitioned the area into future British and French spheres of influence, and the Balfour Declaration of November 1917 pledged a future Jewish 'homeland' in the British zone of Palestine. Matters were further confused as details of President Wilson's fourteen points began to circulate in the Middle East, making nonsense of the Sykes-Picot arrangements, which, incidentally, were well known to Arabs. It appeared that Britain and France might abandon their imperial ambitions, an impression which was confirmed in the closing days of the war when both governments announced their intention to apply Wilsonian principles to the former Ottoman empire. It was in this knowledge that the Kurds welcomed British and Indian soldiers as liberators in the autumn of 1918. Their leader Sheik Mahmud al-Barzani kept a copy of the Anglo-French pledge in an amulet as a talisman which would transform his people into a nation. Within six months he was busy setting up a Kurdish state in northern Iraq.

An independent Kurdistan, or for that matter self-government for anyone inside Iraq, was wormwood to Colonel Sir Arnold Wilson, the country's civil administrator. A former army boxing champion, who later in life seriously flirted with fascism, Wilson wanted Iraq as a dependency of India. It would be populated by Indian immigrants, of whom 'the stalwart Mohammedan cultivator' was the most desirable.[8] In May 1919, Sir Arnold ordered the destruction of the embryonic Kurdish state by a column of British and Indian troops. When Kurdish guerrillas proved too hard to catch, RAF officers asked Churchill, then Secretary for War, for poison gas. He agreed, but it was not used.[9] In less than a year, Britain had shed the mask of benevolence to reveal the snarling frown of the conqueror.

The metamorphosis had begun in December 1918 during private

horse-trading between the French President Clemenceau and Lloyd George. Britain took northern Iraq with its oil deposits, France got a quarter share in the company set up to exploit them, and a confirmation of its rights in Syria and the Lebanon. During the winter of 1918-19 French troops began to disembark at Beirut.

Disheartened Arab nationalists pinned their hopes on the Versailles peace conference and the conscience of President Wilson. Neither yielded much; the President prevaricated and, when confronted with Egyptian nationalists, told them that their dispute with Britain was none of his business. Syria and the Lebanon were to be given to France under a League of Nations mandate, and Palestine and Iraq to Britain. Mandate was a new word, which some thought a euphemism for old-style colonialism. The relationship between the mandatory power and its territory was the same as that of a guardian to a ward with the League of Nations Mandate Commission acting as a board of trustees. Their duty was to see that the nation which held the mandate governed in the best interests of its subjects, protected them from exploitation, and accelerated their moral, physical and political development. These arrangements were settled in May 1920 by the great powers at San Remo without heeding Middle Eastern opinion.

Arab nationalists put little faith in this brand of enlightened imperialism which reduced them to minors who could not survive without a substitute parent. The Emir Faisal, the Hashemite prince who had fought alongside the Allies in the mistaken belief that his reward would be the kingdom of Syria, returned there early in 1920 and proclaimed its independence. His gesture excited Arab nationalists in Jerusalem, some of whom were veterans of Faisal's army. There were riots in the city by Arabs who denounced the Balfour Declaration and attacked Jews and their property.[10]

What was, so to speak, a second Arab revolt spread to Iraq, following hard on the news of what had been agreed at San Remo. Throughout Ramadan (May) Shia and Sunni religious leaders joined forces with Hashemite agents and nationalists in a sequence of public protests against the continuation of British rule.[11] Riots turned into a revolution early in June, when a British political officer arrested a prominent nationalist sheik for alleged tax evasion. Wilson's fragile régime disintegrated swiftly, and a government strapped for cash and short of soldiers found itself dragged into a war.

Reinforcements were found after considerable exertion; in India, recently discharged Sikh soldiers were tempted back by 100-rupee (£16) bonuses.[12] By September the local commander, General Sir Aylmer Haldane, was beginning to get the upper hand, although he was still desperate enough to clamour for large supplies of poison gas.[13] It was not needed for, as he later admitted, air power had given his forces the edge whenever the going got tough. At the end of the year order had been restored by methods which did not bear too close examination. Viscount Peel, Under-Secretary at the War Ministry, was glad that the 'sentimentalists' at home had been so distracted by the brutalities of the Black and Tans in Ireland that they failed to notice what was happening in Iraq.[14]

The public, the press and the Commons did, however, notice that the government's policies in the Middle East were achieving nothing more than a colossal waste of money and lives. The Indian-style administration of Colonel Wilson was in ruins, and it was obvious that Iraqis did not want to be ruled by district officers who generally behaved like arrogant public-school prefects. It proved possible, largely through the employment of superior technology, for the French to crush the Arabs in Syria and the British to do likewise in Jerusalem and Iraq, but having done so, both powers faced an uphill struggle holding down their mandates. Moreover, it was impossible to square threats of using poison gas against tribesmen with the essentially humane and benevolent ideals behind the mandate system. The only answer lay in reaching an accommodation with the Arabs which would balance Britain's strategic needs with the aspirations of local nationalists.

This had been the line taken by T.E. Lawrence during 1920, when he had undertaken a press campaign in favour of Arab self-determination within the empire as an alternative to coercion. Might not the Iraqis become the first 'brown dominion'? he asked. The £40 million bill for the Iraq war convinced the government that he was right. Early in 1921 he joined the staff of Churchill, who had just taken over the Colonial Office with orders to negotiate a settlement in the mandates in which the security costs were kept to a minimum. The result was the Cairo Conference of March 1921. The wartime alliance between Britain and the Hashemite family was renewed; Faisal was given the throne of Iraq and his brother, Abdullah, that of a kingdom then known as Transjordan (Jordan) which consisted, as its name suggests, of land on the eastern bank of the River Jordan. Both kings would be advised by British officials to ensure that the terms of the mandate would be adhered to. Palestine would be the responsibility of the Colonial Office with internal security in the hands of a *gendarmerie* recruited from the now redundant Black and Tans and Auxis.

The peace of Iraq and Jordan would be kept by a novel system known as 'air control', which had the enthusiastic backing of Churchill, Lawrence, Leo Amery and Air-Marshal Lord Trenchard, the Chief of Air Staff. Aircraft had been used in pacification operations in the Sudan, on the North-West Frontier, and most recently in Somaliland. The final defeat of the Mad Mullah in 1920 had been achieved after the bombing of his strongholds in what the Colonial Office regarded as a model campaign. Its total cost was £70,000, which made it the cheapest imperial war ever, and did much to convince waverers that air control was the thriftiest way to police the empire's more unruly subjects.

The kings of Jordan and Iraq had at their disposal RAF bombers, supported by armoured car squadrons and detachments of locally-recruited levies under British officers. Any outbreak of truculence was handled by bombers, which first dropped warning leaflets, and then bombed property or livestock. The leaflets dropped on the Mullah's villages had been vivid, robust pronouncements ('the arm of the government is long . . . its officers fly like birds'), but afterwards their tone became almost apologetic. In December 1938, the inhabitants of Arsal Kot on the North-West Frontier were given nanny-like instructions as to what to do before the bombers appeared:

> You should . . . remove all persons to a place of safety outside the danger area and keep away until further notice is given to you. Government do not wish that your women and children should be harmed. . . . You are also warned that it is most dangerous to handle unexploded bombs.[15]

This last piece of advice often went unheeded; unexploded bombs were sometimes carried to military roads, placed in culverts and surrounded with brushwood, which was then ignited! In Iraq, delayed-action fuses were placed on bombs during operations in 1930–32 to prevent villagers creeping back to their houses under cover of darkness. During this campaign, leaflets were augmented by a loud-speaker system set up in a transport aircraft from which warnings were bellowed, a sensible measure in a country where less than one in ten of the population could read.[16]

Air control saved cash, but it generated a bitter debate between those who represented it as an efficient method of imposing order in wild and inaccessible districts, and those who represented it as a harsh and impersonal astringent. Champions of air control stressed its quickness. Whereas in the past a considerable time had elapsed between an act of defiance and its punishment, the chastising arm now moved swiftly. Every effort was made to prevent civilian deaths, and it was repeatedly pointed out that old-style punitive expeditions had always burned crops, killed livestock and demolished houses. Opponents of air control, often soldiers whose pride was hurt by being upstaged by the technicians of an upstart service, protested that it was inhumane. Colonel Francis Humphrys, an experienced North-West Frontier political officer who had also served as a pilot during the war, feared that air control would incense rather than pacify its victims:

> Much needless cruelty is necessarily inflicted, which in many cases will not cower the tribesmen, but implant in them undying hatred and a desire for revenge. The policy weakens the tribesman's faith in British fair play.[17]

There was certainly no sign of 'fair play', whatever that may have meant in terms of punishing tribesmen, during the early application of air control in Iraq. Within a few months of the Cairo Conference, Churchill was horrified by a report that described an air raid in which men, women and children had been machine-gunned as they fled from a village.[18] Care was taken to ensure that the public never learned about this incident, and it was understandably excluded from a lecture given by Air-Marshal Sir John Salmon in which he explained what had been achieved by air control in Iraq between 1921 and 1925. His talk ended on an optimistic note: thanks to air control 'a heterogeneous collection of wild and inarticulate tribes has emerged in an ordered system of representative government by the vote.'[19]

As well as bringing the semblance of political stability to Iraq, Salmon's aircraft had been decisive in the repulse of an admittedly half-hearted Turkish invasion of Mosul province during the winter of 1922–3. This attack was an uncomfortable reminder that Lloyd George's government had failed to neuter Turkey. During 1920 and 1921 every encouragement had been given to the French, Italians and Greeks to stake claims to parts of Asia Minor, but each power had been evicted by the armies of Atatürk. It was Britain's turn in the autumn of 1922, when the Turkish nationalist leader turned his attention to the British forces on the Asian shore of the Dardanelles. Despite some ministerial misgivings, the cabinet put on a bold face and announced its intention to remain in Turkey. Appeals for help from the dominions were rejected by all save New Zealand. At home, arguments about prestige cut no ice with the public or the press. The Conservatives deserted the coalition, Lloyd George fell from power, and, after a nail-biting confrontation at Chanak, British forces left Turkish soil.

The short era of bluster in the Middle East was over. Public disquiet, a scarcity of cash and a lack of fighting men had driven Britain to abandon belligerence in favour of compromise. From 1922 onwards, British power in the region rested on paper promises. An accord with Turkey was reached at Lausanne in February 1923, which gave Mosul to Iraq, although it was feared that Atatürk might break his word. In 1925 exigency plans were drawn up by which, if Mosul was invaded again, a seaborne force with aircraft-carriers would attack the Straits.[20] What was at stake in the dispute over Mosul was not Iraq's integrity, but oil.

Middle Eastern reserves of oil were not yet as great a factor in international affairs as they became after 1945. During the 1920s the United States and Mexico produced over four-fifths of the world's oil, although the greater part was for American domestic consumption. The demand was rising and even before 1914 preliminary exploration work was underway in Persia and Iraq. The Persian government had granted the Anglo-Persian Oil Company a concession covering half a million square miles which expired in 1961. Drilling began in 1909 and, three years after, work started on a massive refinery on Abadan Island. Output rose from 7.5 million barrels in 1919 to 57 million in 1934. In peacetime, the safety of the wells and the uninterrupted flow of the oil depended on the Persian government's goodwill and ability to maintain internal peace. Both were guaranteed by Reza Pahlevi, a former Cossack officer, who, with British approval, had managed a coup in 1920, and made himself Shah five years later. Supported by the army, Shah Reza was the ideal 'strong man' who would cooperate with foreign business interests. Iraq's Kirkuk oilfields were opened in 1927 and run by the Turkish Oil Company, which was financed by British, French and American capital. Its security and that of the supply pipeline which stretched to the Palestinian port of Haifa depended upon the Iraqi government.

Iraq and its oil remained firmly within Britain's unofficial empire. In 1930, Britain had relinquished its mandate and Iraq received what passed for independence. In fact, it remained a British satellite under the terms of an alliance signed the same year. Britain trained and equipped the Iraqi army, was promised extensive base and transport facilities in the event of war, and retained the RAF aerodrome and garrison at Habbaniya.

The Anglo-Iraqi Treaty was, like its Egyptian equivalent signed six years later, a focus for nationalist resentment. The two agreements and the bases they guaranteed were reminders that Britain was still the paramount power in the Middle East and that, ultimately, even those states with theoretic independence would not be permitted to act in ways which might harm British interests. Britain had not had everything its own way: insurrections in Egypt in 1919 and across the Middle East a year later had forced its government to reach an accommodation with local nationalism. But the events of this period had destroyed much, if not all of the faith which enlightened and politically conscious Arabs had had in Britain. Edward Atiyah, a Lebanese Christian and Anglophile, who had been educated at the British school at Alexandria and then at Oxford, remembered the bitterness felt by those who had once believed in British honour, integrity and sense of justice:

> The record of Anglo-French diplomacy during the War and immediately after it – the Sykes-Picot Agreement, the Balfour Declaration, the decisions of the San Remo Conference had shocked even the most loyal among them, and the disillusion had deepened as a result of personal contact and direct experience of Mandatory rule.[21]

What had also shaken Atiyah's admiration and respect for Britain was the crass behaviour of its representatives. He was dismayed by the aloofness of his British colleagues at Gordon College in Khartoum, where he was a teacher in the mid-1920s. When the governor-general visited the college, all the non-British staff were ordered to keep out of sight, a snub which deeply distressed Atiyah and converted him to a nationalism which had at its heart a loathing of Britain. Even so, he defended what Britain had achieved in the way of administrative reform and economic and educational regeneration, but he found it impossible to refute those Sudanese (they could equally well have been Egyptians or Arabs) who complained to him about the insults they had suffered from the British. 'Your friends are hopeless,' one claimed, 'they will never get rid of their racial arrogance; there is no chance of our ever becoming friends with them. They say they are taking us into partnership, treating us as equals, but it is all words. At heart they remain rulers, fond of domination, resentful of our claims to equality in practice.'[22]

Readers of T.E. Lawrence's *Seven Pillars of Wisdom* will be aware that he, in common with many of his countrymen, was distinctly cool towards

Arabs like Atiyah, who had absorbed a Western education, and as a consequence believed themselves the equals of Europeans. Lawrence preferred those Arabs who were untouched by outside influences and who continued to live in a traditional manner according to ancient values. The nomadic Beduin and the empty spaces they moved across had a special romantic appeal, as did their hierarchical social order and the dignified aristocracy who occupied its summit. The old, tribal world survived uncontaminated in that imperial backwater, the Persian Gulf. Here, undisturbed by the twentieth century, autocratic sheiks governed with British advisers at their sides and British subsidies in their treasuries. Britain's friendship still counted for something in this area; when Saudi tribesmen menaced the borders of Kuwait in 1929 two cruisers hove to and aircraft flew in from Iraq. The intruders quickly departed.

Following in Lawrence's footsteps, and often inspired by his portrayal of the Beduin and their way of life, came a generation of British officers, of whom the most celebrated were Colonel Frederick Peake and Glubb Pasha, successive commanders of the Jordanian Arab Legion. They established a rapport with the Arabs, relished the delights of remote, unpeopled places, and discreetly looked after Britain's interests in Jordan, Oman and the small sheikdoms of the Gulf.

Nurturing Arab goodwill became increasingly difficult after 1936. Britain's monopoly of power in the Middle East was coming under pressure as Italy made its bid to dominate the Mediterranean and extended its power in East Africa. The appearance of Mussolini and Hitler and their successive diplomatic engagements with Britain aroused enormous excitement in the Middle East:

> The masses in the Arab countries were dazzled by Hitler's might and repeatedly successful displays of force. Like the crowd that admires the hero of a cow-boy film they admired and applauded the German dictator. Simple, ignorant people, they saw Hitler as a glorified Tom Mix, avenging wrongs done to his country – the heroine in distress – after the last war, and they admired his prowess and success. They also derived a personal satisfaction from his success. It was humbling for England, and they liked to see England humbled. She had been the mistress of the world too long, the haughty governess of the Arab

countries. Her sons in their dealings with the Arabs had acquired a reputation for arrogance which made them unpopular.[23]

This may be exaggerated. What was important was that Mussolini's and Hitler's triumphs between 1936 and 1939 coincided with Britain's attempts to suppress the Arab Revolt in Palestine. It would be hard to overestimate the effect on Arab opinion of the events in Palestine; the rebellion and Britain's efforts to overcome it became the focus of Arab nationalist passions throughout the Middle East. Palestine symbolised Arab impotence and British indifference towards Arab sentiment; it was not surprising that the Arabs automatically considered Britain's international rivals as their friends.

The Palestinian imbroglio alternately baffled and exasperated successive British governments. As was so often the case when Britain found itself in charge of a racially and religiously divided province, the problem was how to balance the sensitivities and interests of one faction with those of the other. Under the terms of the Balfour Declaration, Britain had pledged itself to welcome Jewish immigrants into Palestine. It had, therefore, allied itself with the international Zionist movement which had been seeking a sanctuary for Europe's Jews. Zionism was a practical response to the state- and church-sponsored anti-semitism within the Russian empire and the rising number of pogroms there. There was also the insidious, less openly violent anti-semitism which flourished in outwardly more enlightened countries such as France and Austria. Quite simply, before 1914, large numbers of European Jews faced a precarious existence, unable to rely upon the normal protection afforded by the state to its subjects. Matters became worse during and after the war: between 1917 and 1922, there was a resurgence of pogroms in two areas where anti-semitism was most virulent, Poland and the Ukraine.

The Jewish predicament won the support of many humane and liberal-minded British statesmen such as Balfour, Churchill and Leo Amery, the latter two stalwart supporters of Zionism between the wars. But there were, from the moment that the Balfour Declaration was announced, deep misgivings among the Arabs. They naturally asked what would be the status of the Jewish refugees who entered Palestine, and how many would come.

T.E. Lawrence, who later converted to Zionism, shared Arab apprehensions and was worried about a mass influx of poorer, Eastern European

Jews, although he would have welcomed educated, middle-class American or British Jews, the sort he had known at Oxford.[24] His thoughts are interesting since they reflected the anti-semitism which had existed in Edwardian Britain, where the arrival of large numbers of working-class Jews from the Russian empire had led to an upsurge in hostility towards 'aliens'. Among the upper classes there were undercurrents of prejudice against Jews who had prospered in business, and there was a thread of thinly-veiled anti-semitism running through the works of the Catholic traditionalists, Hilaire Belloc and G.K. Chesterton. Alarmist speculation about links between Jews and Communists and the 'Protocols of Zion' hoax of 1919 fostered anti-semitism among those on the far right. In 1920, Colonel Richard Meinertzhagen, an ardent Zionist, was convinced that most of his brother officers serving in Palestine were tainted with anti-semitism, and therefore incapable of disinterested judgements in their dealings with Jews and Arabs.[25]

There was certainly some truth in this, but there were many men-on-the-spot and in Whitehall who believed that Arab rights were in danger and needed to be defended. Jewish colonists were well-financed and had the means to buy up large areas of land for their settlements, creating a class of landless labourers who were excluded from work in Jewish areas, where the owners preferred to employ men and women of their own race. Arabs began to compare Palestine to Algeria, where the French government had handed out the most fruitful land to French and Spanish colonists, and to Libya where, under Mussolini's colonisation policy, Italian settlers were edging out Arabs. Moreover, the Palestinian Arabs sensed that Zionists and their sympathisers had the ear of the British government.

Frustration and racial tension erupted in anti-Jewish demonstrations in 1920, 1921 and 1929, when nearly 900 Jewish settlers were killed or wounded. These outbreaks were a chilling reminder that the British government would eventually have to make a definite decision as to the final racial balance within Palestine. No one was prepared to grasp this nettle, for neither side in the dispute was open to compromise, since it was bound to involve a surrender of ideals and territory. The Arabs were resisting what they considered a usurpation of lands they had inhabited and tilled for centuries, and a future in which they might conceivably be an impoverished minority within a Jewish state. The Jewish colonists believed that they were the rightful inheritors of a land long ago bequeathed them by God, which they were using to its best advantage, and which offered a safe haven for Jews everywhere. Having, in 1922, made clear that the future of

Kenya would be decided in the interests of its indigenous races, rather than the white colonists, the British government thought it would be prudent to wait on events in Palestine. For a time it seemed that the problem might resolve itself naturally; between 1927 and 1932, the rate of Jewish immigration declined and, thanks to better medical treatment (a benefit of the Mandate), the Arab birth rate increased. At the beginning of 1933, there were 800,000 Arabs in Palestine and under 200,000 Jews.

At this stage, events in Europe radically changed the nature and scale of the Palestinian problem. There were about half a million Jews in Germany when Hitler manoeuvred himself into power in January 1933. During the next five years the Nazi authorities encouraged 150,000 to leave the country, even making arrangements with the Jewish Agency in Palestine to facilitate emigration there. At the same time, the numbers of Jews under Nazi rule increased with the annexation of Austria (1938) and Czechoslovakia (1938-9). Furthermore, the example of the Nazis encouraged anti-semitism in countries where the disease was already rife, and Jews found themselves persecuted in Poland, Hungary, Rumania and the Baltic states. There were, therefore, two mass exoduses of Jews from Europe. The first involved the flight of refugees from territory under Nazi government, of whom 57,000 went to the United States, 53,000 to Palestine and 50,000 to Britain. The second was undertaken by the Jews of Eastern Europe, including 74,000 who fled from Poland to Palestine. In all, 215,000 Jews reached Palestine in these six years, raising its total Jewish population to 475,000.[26]

Islam, in stark contrast to the Catholic and Orthodox churches, had traditionally shown toleration to Jews, but the prospect of a flood of Jewish immigration, and with it further transfers of land, provoked the Arab higher committee to seek restrictions on both and a timetable for Palestinian self-government. An equivocal response, together with economic distress, led to the Arab Revolt which began in April 1936. The uprising exposed the fragility of internal security within a region where, despite eighteen years of British rule, brigandage was still common and firearms were easily obtainable. As in southern Ireland in 1919, the local police force was unable to withstand a campaign of systematic ambushes, murders, sabotage of communications and a general strike. Efforts to restore the government's authority were feeble and fumbling. Nine thousand troops were drafted to Palestine in September 1936, but when they arrived their orders were hopelessly confused. On one hand, they were warned that 'All Arabs are your enemies', and on the other they were told to ensure that, 'Every effort was made to conciliate, to heal instead of wound afresh, and to restore order by pacific measures.'[27] This conundrum reflected irresolution at the top. In September the cabinet had sanctioned the bombing of villages used as bases by partisans, and early the next month sanctioned martial law .[28] General Sir Arthur Wauchope, the High Commissioner, refused to implement the first and thought the second unnecessary as it would impede progress towards a negotiated settlement, decisions for which he and the cabinet were later censured by the Mandates Commission.[29]

For the next three years, the army, navy and RAF waged an anti-guerrilla war during which large areas of the country, including Jerusalem and Nablus, passed temporarily into their enemies' control. At first it was hoped that a compromise might be achieved through a royal commission, that standard procedure by which British governments simultaneously avoided the necessity for an immediate political decision and allowed tensions to subside. The high-minded and well-meaning members of the Peel Commission collected evidence, sifted through it and, in September 1937, proposed partition and a reduced quota of Jewish immigrants. After some wavering, both sides rejected this solution.

By now the local difficulties in Palestine were becoming an international embarrassment for Britain. Haj Amin al-Hussaini, Grand Mufti of Jerusalem and the most trenchant Arab spokesman, fled into exile and began to persuade the independent rulers of neighbouring Arab states to exert pressure on Britain. His peregrinations and the flow of anti-British propaganda which poured from Palestinian Arabs and their supporters disturbed the Foreign Secretary, Sir Anthony Eden, and many of his officials who feared, with good reason, that continued equivocation and repression in Palestine might undermine British influence throughout the Arab world.

Growing Arab antipathy towards Britain was a bonus for Italy and Germany, and both began fishing in the troubled waters of Palestine. During 1938 and 1939, the propaganda agencies of these powers cynically broadcast allegations of British atrocities against Arabs. These stories, some of which were true, came from Arab sources outside Palestine, but at the beginning of 1939 British intelligence there was on the trail of two Nazi agents who had been collecting material which discredited British troops and, it was suspected, dispensing cash to Arab guerrillas.[30] There was evidence that Russia was recruiting agents from among the Arabs and had sent a handful to Moscow for training.[31] Despite counter-propaganda by the BBC's Foreign Service, British representatives in Arab states were obliged to ask the government to adopt milder measures in Palestine.[32]

The war of words would have been no more than an irritant had it not been for the international situation. Relations with Italy had deteriorated after its invasion of Abyssinia in 1935, the Sino–Japanese War had broken out in July 1937, and during 1938 Britain had discovered that it could only maintain a balance of power in Europe by making concessions to Germany, which served only to increase its strength and appetite for land. Whatever the circumstances or timing of a future collision with Japan or the Axis powers, Britain could no longer allow itself to be weakened by the Palestinian ulcer. In the event of war with Japan or Germany or Italy, Arab alienation and continued turbulence in a region which bordered on the Suez Canal would have been extremely dangerous.

After years of dithering, the government took swift and decisive action to pacify Palestine. In the months after the Munich agreement, reinforcements were hurried to Palestine, and operations there were intensified. By the early summer of 1939 a semblance of public order had been restored. In May, a White Paper was published outlining the province's political future: Britain would keep the mandate for the next five years, cut Jewish immigration to 25,000 a year, and prepare the ground for an independent state in which the Arabs would be a permanent majority. An attempt was made to divert Jewish refugees to other colonies, but with small success. The governor of Kenya thought a Jewish enclave would prove 'an undesirable feature', although he had no objections to the 'right type' of Jew (i.e. Austrian or German); the white settlers of Northern Rhodesia were very cool; and only British Guiana was encouraging.[33]

Strategic necessity had ended nearly twenty years of procrastination. Whatever its rights and wrongs, and nearly all Jews saw only wrongs, the 1938–9 military-political settlement revealed that in an emergency Britain could act with determination and ruthlessness. The same qualities were apparent in the early war years when it was clear that a considerable body of Arab opinion was hoping for an Axis victory as the Middle East's only means of escape from Britain's domination. In Iraq, where the repercussions of events in Palestine had been strongly felt, anti-British sentiment was strongest among the officer class. Britain's supervision of the Iraq army had not prevented those who passed through its military college from being taught to see themselves as an élite destined to be the liberators of their nation.[34] Political circumstances encouraged their daydreams; there had been no stability since Faisal's death in 1932 and for the next eight years transitory civilian governments were more or less the instruments of a cabal of colonels.

Although Iraq was technically allied to Britain, its government was grudging in the assistance it rendered to the British war effort, and, like Egypt's, hardly bothered to hide its sympathy for the Axis powers. In March 1940, the situation was such that the high command in Cairo prepared plans to occupy the Mosul oilfields as a precautionary measure, although no one had any idea where to find the necessary men.[35] Eight months later, deciphered German signals revealed that an overland attack on Iraq was being considered in Berlin. The German thrust through the Balkans and into Greece in the spring of 1941, and the likelihood that the Vichy authorities in Damascus would connive at German bases in Syria, forced Britain to intervene in Iraq. Two brigades of Indian troops were landed at Basra with orders to proceed to positions from where they could protect the northern oilfields.

This manoeuvre was completely within the terms of the Anglo-Iraqi treaty, but nationalists believed it was a prelude to an attack on Baghdad.[36] Rashid Ali, the prime minister who had seized power with army backing on 3 April, appealed directly for Axis help a fortnight later. The British were forewarned of his intrigues through intercepted German and Italian wireless messages, and forces in Palestine were ordered to enter Iraq.[37] An Iraqi attack on Habbaniya aerodrome was beaten off, and British motorised columns reached Baghdad by the middle of May. German and Italian aircraft, flown from Greece to Syria, arrived too late to influence the outcome of the six-week campaign in which 3,000 Iraqi troops were killed. Three thousand nationalist officers were subsequently purged from the army by a new, pro-British government under Nuri es-Said, who had fought alongside T.E. Lawrence twenty-five years earlier. Rashid Ali escaped and made his way to Berlin.

The *coup de main* against Iraq and the palace coup in Cairo nine months later were proof that, despite over twenty years of nationalist ferment, British power in the Middle East was still firm. Both were, however, exceptional measures, undertaken in the face of dire emergencies by a country fighting for its life. This was not how it looked to Egyptians and Arabs. Each display of force left a deep sense of bitterness and frustration because it had amply demonstrated the victims' powerlessness. Britain was still the dominant power in the region and would go to any lengths to get its way there.

5

A New Force and New Power: India 1919–42

The Indian empire had always been a heterogeneous organism. Its political map was a mosaic of princely states (there were over 500 in 1919) and provinces directly governed by British officials. These states covered two-fifths of the subcontinent and contained a quarter of its population. It would have been impossible to have drawn an exact racial or religious chart of India, although, as a general rule, Muslims were concentrated in the north-western regions and Bengal. They were a minority comprising a seventh of a population which stood at 280 million in 1940.

Racial and religious tolerance was scarce in India. The Ghurka soldiers who shot down demonstrators in Amritsar in 1919 later admitted that they had enjoyed killing people of the plains.[1] In 1923 intelligence sources revealed that Hindus had been secretly pleased by recent air raids on Pathan villages on the North-West Frontier.[2] An army inquiry of 1943 as to which soldiers were best suited for policing duties revealed that, 'The Sikh would at heart enjoy nothing more than hammering Muslims.'[3] There is no reason to disbelieve these statements, nor dismiss out of hand nationalist assertions that the British cynically exploited racial and religious antipathies in order to 'divide and rule'.

On the other hand, those diehards who wanted the raj to continue come what may, claimed that Britain alone could keep the peace and act as a dispassionate umpire, balancing the rights of one faith against the other. This argument was strengthened during the 1920s when sectarian disorders increased alarmingly. The most trivial incident could spark off massacre and looting: a street squabble between two schoolboys, one Hindu, the other Muslim, led to ten days of rioting and pillage in Dacca in 1929.[4] The leaders of the dominant Indian National Congress were horrified by such events, and sectarian malevolence in general. It was the greatest obstacle to national unity for it prevented Indians from thinking of themselves as Indians first and Muslims or Hindus second, and acting accordingly. Jawaharlal Nehru saw religion as India's greatest bane, believing that it fostered dogmatism and narrow-mindedness.[5] Educated at Harrow and Cambridge, he had travelled far from that world in which the public slaughter of a cow or lurid tales of the forcible conversion of Hindu maidens could drive a Hindu to such a pitch of fury that he would kill his Muslim neighbours and burn down their houses.

Most Indians, whatever their creed, were desperately poor, lived in villages, and made their living from the land. Gandhi who, from 1919, was the conscience of Congress, wished all Indians to remain a simple folk, and he encouraged them to cultivate the agrarian virtues which he believed would regenerate India. For this reason he spun cotton and spent much time persuading others to do so. He mistrusted the centralisation and industrialisation of the modern world, which he feared would erode all that was good in the traditional India. Gandhi also wanted to replace English as the language of education with Gujarati, and yet he and the upper echelons of his party had been taught in English (he was a Middle Temple barrister), and their political principles were essentially British.

In a sense the British-educated Congress élite were the product of the labours of those nineteenth-century idealists who had believed that education would emancipate India. A knowledge of Western philosophy and science would unlock the Indian mind and create a class of enlightened men, fit to run their own country. Education along British lines had spread throughout India, but unevenly. In Travancore (a princely state), 68 per cent of the population were literate, but there were other areas where the proportion was less than 20 per cent. A systematic attempt had been made to indoctrinate the sons of princes and business and professional men with the ideals of the British ruling classes through Indian public schools. These were reproductions of their British originals, and like them dedicated to the cultivation of 'character'. The old boys of these academies were uncannily like their British counterparts, according to an official report of 1942:

The product may be limited in its intellectual range, narrow in

its sympathies and arrogant in its assumptions, but at the same
time it displays a capacity to set up and abide by standards of
conduct and a readiness to accept responsibility.[6]

Government high schools fell short in this area, because unlike the Indian
public schools they did not devote the same amount of time to the playing of team games.

'Grinding grit into the Kashmiri' was how Cecil Tyndale-Briscoe,
headmaster of the Church Missionary school at Srinigar between 1890 and
1947 summed up his life's work. An energetic, singleminded, muscular
Christian and Cambridge rowing blue, he was abundantly qualified for the
task. Cricket, rugger, soccer and boxing (which he imagined was an antidote to the sodomy he feared was too common among Kashmiri
adolescents) were the backbone of his curriculum. Tyndale-Briscoe also
encouraged, with equal vigour, a sense of public duty. His boys formed a
fire brigade, learned to stand up for the weak and poor, were taught to
treat animals with kindness, and did their bit in helping relief work during
a cholera epidemic.[7] There were others like him scattered across India, not
only in schools, and on the whole what they did had a lasting value.

At university, Indian secondary-school pupils found themselves in surroundings where they were free to explore and discuss political ideas and
apply what they learned to contemporary India. For instance, those who
sat the University of Mysore's history examination in 1924 were asked,
'Democracy is a European invention and perhaps suited to the European
race and European culture. Examine this in the light of Indian History',
and, 'Comment on the change of name from Empire to Commonwealth –
how does this change affect Indians, Celanese and South Africans?'[8]
Burke's seminal speeches on American taxation were among the texts set
for English students at Calcutta in 1922.

Generations of young Indians were therefore absorbing a tradition of
political thought which emphasised the rights of the individual and the
limitations of the legal power of the state. Those who had learned to reason in the British way imagined themselves the intellectual equals of their
rulers, and naturally wished to be treated accordingly by the British. This
was not easy for men and women who had been conditioned to believe
themselves the representatives of a superior culture, and besides the educated élite of India was a very tiny segment of Indian society. Seen from
above, the advancement of Indians was an inexorable but very slow
process. Its completion, and with it the moment for self-government, was

still very distant, certainly a matter of many decades. The standard, administrative view on this subject was expressed in 1916 by General Sir Edmund Barrow, a senior military official whose Indian service had begun nearly forty years before:

> By bestowing liberty, justice and education in India we have done much to emancipate it from the shackles of caste and prejudice but it will take generations yet to reach the ideals of the philanthropists and philosophers and to satisfy the longings of an awakened India.[9]

After 1919 the pace of India's march towards self-rule quickened, gathering a momentum which simultaneously increased the impatience of nationalists and frightened conservatives in India and Britain. The engine for change had been the war. India had shown extraordinary steadfastness between 1914 and 1918, its people had resisted German-inspired subversion, provided 500,000 extra fighting men, and donated £100 million to the imperial war chest.[10] Effort on this scale deserved a generous response from Britain and, in August 1917, a grateful British government publicly committed itself to policies designed to set India along the road to 'responsible government' within the empire. Originally the promise had been for 'self government', but Curzon had objected.[11]

On one level this gesture, like the pledges given to the Arabs the following year, reflected the government's willingness to accept that the principles of self-determination were, in theory, not racially exclusive. On another, less obvious level, the declaration was an admission that the government of India needed a thorough overhaul. Edwin Montagu, whom Lloyd George appointed Secretary of State for India in 1917, had previously observed that, 'The government of India is too wooden, too iron, too inelastic, too antediluvian for the modern purposes we have.' What he had in mind was the inflexibility and poverty of imagination of the Indian bureaucracy as revealed by the inquiry into the Indian army's setbacks in Mesopotamia. The Indian army was all muscle and no brain, and in that condition could not be expected to uphold Britain's status as an Asian power.

Montagu visited India in 1918, making him the first Secretary of State who bothered to find out about the country at first hand. He combined with the new Viceroy, Lord Chelmsford, to produce a series of reforms which became law in March 1919. (Chelmsford was a rather unusual proconsul: the son of the luckless Zulu War general, he had served on the London County Council and then, like the hero of one of Belloc's cautionary tales, been sent out to govern New South Wales.) They intended to give the Indians their first taste of responsible government through the creation of eleven autonomous provinces in which such 'national building' activities as public health, education and agriculture would be managed by elected Indian ministers. Finance and public order were placed in the hands of ministers, British or Indian, chosen by the Viceroy.

Congress had wanted India to stride rather than inch cautiously towards self-government, and its members were therefore disappointed by the measure and detected a niggardly spirit behind it. Moreover, the announcement of the Montagu-Chelmsford reforms coincided with the introduction of the Rowlatt Acts, a sequence of laws devised to facilitate a clamp-down on subversion. This legislation symbolised all that was autocratic about the raj and so became a convenient focus for Congress agitation.

The struggle against the Rowlatt Acts was the first major contest between the raj and Congress. It also provided the testing ground for the principles of popular resistance which had been developed by Gandhi in his campaign for Indian rights in Natal twenty years before. Gandhi's weapon was satyagraha, which he variously translated as 'soul force' or 'love force'. As he explained to his followers during March 1919, they would harness metaphysics to political protest. Satyagraha was a spiritual state achieved by a man or woman which gave them the inner fortitude, patience and faith in God that were needed for passive resistance against an immoral authority. The degrees of physical suffering which the satyagraha acolyte endured would serve as a measure of his own integrity and that of his cause.[12] On the surface, satyagraha was a perfect instrument with which to challenge the raj. His target was the conscience of Britain. For generations the British people had assured themselves that they ruled India with the consent of its people, an assumption which meant that they could accept the idea of empire with a good conscience. If, as Gandhi intended, thousands, perhaps millions of Indians signified, in the gentlest possible way, that this was no longer so, then the ethical basis of the raj vanished.

As well as introducing his followers to the arcane mysteries of satyagraha, Gandhi proposed a nationwide hartal on 6 April as a protest against the Rowlatt Acts. This was a traditional public demonstration of mourning or disapproval during which all shops, businesses and schools were closed and public transport halted, leaving large numbers free to take to the streets and form processions. There was a body of sophisticated, middle-class Congress members who could grasp the essence of satyagraha and submit to the self-discipline it demanded. Most who joined the hartal appreciated neither. Marches became riots in which demonstrators fought with the police, attacked and murdered Europeans and plundered and set fire to property. Even Gandhi was appalled by the depth and passion of anti-British feeling which had been released and seemed beyond his control. [13]

The upheavals were most aggravated in the Punjab, where Sir Michael O'Dwyer was governor. He was a forthright, pugnacious Irishman who had a strong sense of justice and ruled with an iron hand. O'Dwyer had faced sedition during the war and got the better of it, and in April 1919 he was determined to do so again. The most destructive riots were in Amritsar, where Europeans had been slaughtered and where, for a time, the government had lost all control. Here arrived Brigadier-General Reginald Dyer with instructions to impose martial law and restore civil peace. He was not the ideal man for the job; over twenty years before, when at staff college, a brother officer had described him as a soldier 'happiest when crawling over a Burmese stockade with a revolver in his mouth' and, in 1919, a painful illness sharpened his natural belligerence.

When local Congress leaders defied his ban on public meetings, and after he had received an inflammatory leaflet predicting a mutiny by Indian soldiers, Dyer decided on a show of force. He led a small detachment into Amritsar where a demonstration was underway at the Jalianwala Bagh, and ordered his men to fire into the crowd. The carefully directed volleys lasted for ten minutes, killed 379 Indians and wounded hundreds more. Afterwards, Dyer regretted that he had been unable to use the machine-guns mounted on two armoured cars which he had brought into the city. In the next few days, he had real and suspect miscreants flogged, and ordered Indians to crawl on their bellies along a street where a woman missionary had been assaulted by rioters, and, incidentally, rescued by other Indians.

1919 was a turning point in the history of India and Amritsar was the pivot. On 18 April, five days after the shooting there, Gandhi called off the hartal. He had clearly lost control over his followers, although he blamed the turbulence on the police, claiming, with astonishing naïveté, that Indian crowds were 'the easiest in the world to disperse'.[14] His faith in satyagraha was still firm, and in June he declared that the hartal had revealed 'a new force and new power – a force that could prove irresistible under every conceivable circumstance provided that the truth was on our side.'[15] And so it seemed to be, for the Amritsar massacre proved that British rule in India ultimately rested upon force. This was confirmed in the minds of Gandhi and the Congress by the events which followed the pacification of the Punjab.

News of what exactly had happened in Amritsar spread slowly, and once its enormity had been recognised the government set up an inquiry under a Scottish jurist, Lord Hunter. Dyer's judgement was found wanting and he was effectively dismissed from the army, while O'Dwyer, who had ordered the bombing of rioters elsewhere in the Punjab, was exonerated. This verdict angered the British community in India, officers everywhere, and Conservatives in Britain who believed that the brigadier and the governor were heroes who had saved India from anarchy.

Dyer's British champions raised his case in parliament. His motives and actions were the subject of a vinegary debate in July 1920, in which right-wing Conservatives bayed for Montagu's blood. He was blamed for having been too soft on Indian sedition-mongers and too hard on an honourable man who had had the courage to deal firmly with them. Unperturbed, Montagu castigated Dyer for the 'racial humiliation' he had inflicted in Amritsar which violated the 'principles upon which our Indian empire had been built'. He proceeded, amid catcalls, to denounce the racialism of Dyer's allies:

*An Indian is a person who is tolerable so long as he obeys your orders, but if he thinks for himself, if once he takes advantage of the educational facilities which you have provided for him, if once he imbibes the ideas of individual liberty which are dear to the British people, why then you class him as an educated Indian and an agitator.[16]

Churchill weighed in, damning what had occurred in Amritsar as a 'monstrous event', and rejecting the suggestion that Dyer had somehow saved India on the grounds that British power there did not rest on naked force. The diehards responded, under the leadership of Sir William Joynson-Hicks, with charges that Dyer had been made a scapegoat for a government which had gone too far in its appeasement of a vociferous minority.

The government won in the division, but there was still plenty of fight left in the Dyer camp. The *Morning Post* opened a fund for him, and within a few weeks over £26,000 had been collected from donors, who included Kipling. Army officers were particularly sour about the treatment of a man who had done his duty as he saw fit, and then had been deserted by a government which should have loyally supported its servant.[17]

The repercussions of the Amritsar debate, as much as what had happened in the city, had a profound effect on Indian opinion. Gandhi and the Congress had hitherto proceeded in the belief that they could sway the collective moral conscience of Britain, but the debate over Dyer showed that no such thing existed. There was, as Montagu's speech proved, a body of liberal-minded opinion which held that educated Indians deserved to be treated as rational creatures and were fit to exercise the freedoms cherished in Britain, but there was another section of British public opinion which claimed that Indians were intrinsically incapable of responsibility. Consider a *Spectator* editorial of December 1919, which argued that British rule in India was an 'absolute necessity' since the raj protected Hindus and Muslims from themselves. If the British departed, India would fall into the hands of 'the Brahminical caste' and slide into anarchy. 'We Anglo-Saxons like to rule ourselves,' the piece concluded. 'Why assume that our desire is not shared by men of darker complexion? The answer is to be found in the Oriental temperament and Oriental History.'[18] Both disqualified Indians from self-government then and for many years to come, if not ever.

Sir Michael O'Dwyer, who campaigned for Dyer until the latter's death in 1927, and then against any concessions towards Indian self-rule, repeatedly alleged that Indians were helplessly addicted to graft. Furthermore, Congress was merely a mouthpiece for a small clique of grasping and ambitious men who wanted only power. 'The fact is,' wrote O'Dwyer, 'as everyone, British or Indian, who understands the east will, if honest, admit, that 99 per cent of the people do not care a brass farthing for the "forms of government" about which Congress lawyers were always arguing. This was one of the tacks adopted by Churchill who, from 1930, led a Conservative rearguard in a parliamentary struggle against measures leading towards responsible government in India. Even when prime minister he could not mask his contempt for Congress. It was, he told the Commons in September 1942, 'a political organisation built round a party machine and sustained by manufacturing and financial interests' which was 'opposed by all Muslims and the millions of Indians who were subjects of the princes'.[19]

His statement shocked Labour MPs. Aneurin Bevan asked whether the Prime Minister's 'silly language' was endorsed by the Labour members of the coalition. Churchill said it was, and dismissed his questioner as 'a merchant of discourtesy'. He may well have been right on the second point, but was mistaken about the first. Ever since the beginning of the century, the Labour party had extended friendship, sympathy and encouragement to the Congress party. There were close links between such intellectuals as Nehru and Krishna Menon and their opposite numbers within the Labour party, based to a large extent on shared radical and reformist traditions stretching back into the previous century.

For most people in Britain and India, Congress meant Gandhi. It would be as hard to overestimate his influence over events in India after 1919 as it is to strip away the layers of sentimental adulation that have been applied to him by his various hagiographers. He was an international figure who captured headlines and the imaginations of his countrymen, as well as those of nationalists engaged in struggles against Western imperialism outside India. His charisma was remarkable, although there were times when his humility seemed close to inverted arrogance. He was also capable of the most breathtaking humbug, as in June 1942, when he wrote that, 'Nazi power has arisen as a nemesis to punish Britain for her sins of exploitation and enslavement of the Asiatic and African races.'[20]

Gandhi's most impressive achievement was to stamp his ideals of nonviolence on the Congress party, even though, as he admitted to an Australian journalist in April 1942, the mass of Indians seemed unable to appreciate what satyagraha required.[21] This had been obvious ever since the 1919 disturbances. There was a vast, unbridgeable gulf between the pacific ideals of Gandhi and the behaviour of his followers on the streets. When he opened his civil disobedience campaign at Bardoli in November 1921, there were riots in which 53 died and 400 were wounded. He was, as on all such occasions, shocked, and postponed a return visit to the town, which did not prevent further disorders there in February 1922. This pattern was repeated whenever he launched a campaign of passive defiance or non-cooperation.

From 1920, Gandhi's aim had been swaraj, complete self-government and independence, which were one part of a vast programme for the moral regeneration of the Indian people. During the 1920s, he spent much time and energy in trying to convert the Indian middle-class Congress members to cotton-spinning and with it the discovery of their true roots in the countryside. His insistence on a revolution within the individual soul rather than one within society as a whole did not satisfy many Congress members. Nehru, for one, could not subscribe to his master's reverence for poverty, which the younger man hoped to eliminate. Nor was it practical to disregard what had occurred within India during the past two hundred years and embrace the Gandhian ideal of small, self-sufficient rural communities. And yet the force of Gandhi's spirituality was so great that the radical wing of Congress acquiesced to his authority and guidance. While Gandhi's obstinacy exasperated the British, his leadership of the Indian national movement gave them many advantages. He restrained the firebrands and turned the party away from the paths of Communism and armed revolution. His influence, as much as police surveillance, ensured that in 1942 the Indian Communist party had only 5,000 members.

The struggle for swaraj was slow and convoluted. Congress sought to extract concession, through a sequence of peaceful acts of defiance and non-cooperation, which invariably ended in bloodshed. The British government attempted to keep the initiative through offering compromises, but dodged the issue of when and how full independence might be achieved. From 1929 everything hinged on the phrase 'dominion status' which had been hesitantly offered to India. As understood by all involved, dominion status would give India the same political freedom and detachment from Britain as was enjoyed by, say, Canada. But what if India took the path of another dominion whose people's ties with Britain were, to say the least, extremely tenuous – Ireland? For India to follow such a course was unthinkable for it would have knocked away the chief prop of British power in Asia and the Middle East.

Whatever settlement was reached, Britain could never permit India the right to neutrality implicit in dominion status. To have done so in the international situation of the mid-1930s would have been suicidal. It was, however, possible to extend the participation of Indians in government without engaging head-on the knotty question of dominion status. The 1935 Government of India Act created an Indian federation embracing the British-ruled provinces and the princely states in which careful provision was made for the representation of the non-Hindu minorities. Elections for the provincial governments were held in 1937, and Congress secured a dominant position in each.

Congress's electoral success was to have been expected. It had about a million members across India, and a country-wide organisation which gave it its muscle and an advantage over all other parties. For this reason, it had always asserted that it was the voice of India. And yet, even in the periods of intensive public protests in 1919 and 1930–34, it had never come close to toppling the raj or even proving beyond doubt that India was ungovernable. There were no more Amritsars, but the authorities somehow managed to keep the upper hand through mass arrests of leading party activists, including Gandhi, and disorders were held in check by the police with army help. When matters appeared on the verge of getting out of control, as they did during the 1930 disturbances in Peshawar, armoured cars and aircraft were deployed. Such astringent measures were exceptional; there were 200,000 police in India in the 1930s, and they were well paid and their morale remained high. With a loyal police force, the backing of an army which numbered 194,000 in 1939, and a considerable degree of determination among its officials, the raj was able to hang on without too much strain on its resources.

And yet, while the raj still appeared formidable, especially from the perspective of the streets of Peshawar or anywhere else in India during the 1930s, its future was no longer certain. All three British political parties had acquiesced to the gradual introduction of self-government since 1919, despite the outcry on the right of the Conservatives. There was a general understanding that, in principle, a limit now existed to the life of the raj, although no one had yet drawn up the timetable for its extinction. Congress accepted, grudgingly, the 1935 Act. but only as a milestone on a road which led to unconditional swaraj in the near future.

It had been assumed during the early stages of the campaign for Indian independence that the state which would emerge would encompass all the territory then under British rule. This seemed reasonable during the early 1920s, when an accord existed between the overwhelmingly Hindu Congress and Muslim organisations. This was a result of an upsurge in anti-British feeling among Muslims everywhere, after it had become known that Britain was intending to force the Turkish sultan to renounce his spiritual title as Khalifah (successor) to the Prophet. From the British standpoint this measure was an insurance against future jihads, but from the Muslim it was an affront to Islam. Indian Muslims therefore joined with Congress during the disturbances of 1919, and for the next five years there were a series of pan-Islamic uprisings on the North-West Frontier.

Muslim militancy subsided after 1924. Henceforward there was a steady growth of Muslim apprehension about the power of Congress, and the position of Islam within an Indian state in which Hindus were paramount. Clashes between Muslims and Hindus increased in scale and ferocity; the refusal of Muslim shopkeepers to join a hartal in Calcutta in February 1930 lead to a riot in which between four and five hundred died. This resurgence of Muslim consciousness directly threatened Congress, since hitherto its political strength had rested upon its claim to be the authentic voice of the entire population, and its programme for complete independence had emphasised the ability of all Indians to live in harmony.

The historic memory of India's Muslims, who had been the country's masters during the Mughal period, gave an added edge to existing religious antipathies. When Dr Muhammad Jinnah, President of the Muslim League, proceeded through Karachi in October 1938, he was followed by a three-mile-long procession of supporters, a parade which had marked similarities to the public shows held by the Mughal emperors.[22]

By this date, the Muslim League had become the focus for Muslim aspirations and the guardian of their political interests. It may have exaggerated its grass-roots support, but by the end of 1943 the League was claiming to speak for all of India's Muslims. The British, following that well-established imperial rule of doing business with those who appeared to possess power, accepted the League's credentials. These had been considerably enhanced by the results of the 1937 elections, which revealed that Muslims were fast losing confidence in Congress.[23] More and more Muslims were alienated by Congress's attempts to secure a monopoly of power within the provincial governments and its agrarian reforms, which hurt Muslim landowners. Conscious of its value to the British as a counterweight to Congress, the Muslim League began to nudge its way towards a final settlement of India that would involve partition and the establishment of a Muslim state, Pakistan.

The idea of Pakistan had begun to circulate in Muslim intellectual circles in the mid-1930s. There was much subsequent debate as to how and when a division of India became unavoidable, and even more as to whether it was desirable. What mattered was that in August 1940 the Muslim League publicly committed itself to the formation of Pakistan, and during the next three years it transformed itself into a mass political organisation dedicated to that end. At the heart of its ideology was the old battle cry 'Islam is in danger', and there were distinctive jihadic undertones running through its propaganda. Among the League's repertoire of popular songs in 1941–2 was '*Moo mein kalma, hath mein talwar, larke lenge ham Pakistan*' ('With a Quranic verse on the lips and a sword in hand, we shall fight for Pakistan').[24]

On 3 September 1939 the Viceroy, Lord Linlithgow, announced on the wireless that India was at war with Germany. He was perfectly entitled to do so under an amendment to the Government of India Act which had been rushed through parliament the previous April.[25] Congress was stunned by the declaration of war, and protested that a Scottish aristocrat had no right of any kind to drag the Indian people into a war on Britain's behalf. Yet while the Viceroy's action symbolised India's continued subservience to Britain's will, Congress members were also acutely aware that Britain was fighting against political systems which most found repugnant. During the past four years, Congress had taken a left-wing stance on foreign policy, opposing the appeasement of Hitler and Mussolini and British neutrality during the Spanish Civil War.

Divisions over what, if any, part it ought to play in India's struggle against Naziism and fascism contrasted with Congress's determination to use the war as a chance to squeeze concessions from Britain. On the extreme left, Chandra Subhas Bose, leader of the Forward Bloc inside Congress, favoured a course similar to that taken by Sinn Fein in 1916; all-out rebellion. He had been elected Congress president in 1938, but was manoeuvred out by Gandhi. At the end of 1941 he fled to Berlin, by way of Kabul, and offered his services to Hitler who, much to Bose's dismay, turned out to be an admirer of the raj.

The years between 1939 and 1941 were relatively calm. Gandhi neither said nor did anything that might have disrupted the war effort, but continued to press for complete independence. The wrangling between Congress and the government over constitutional quiddities proceeded with little reference to the momentous events which were occurring outside India, or to the mobilisation of its manpower and resources which was gathering pace.

The Japanese entry into the war in December 1941, their capture of Singapore in February 1942, and the subsequent swift advance through Burma the following month brought the war to India's borders by April. Burma, which had been officially separated from India in 1935, had its own nationalist movement, which was quick to throw in its lot with the Japanese. Military intelligence reported droves of Burmese peasants, policemen and students coming forward to assist the invaders. 'No difficulty was experienced in obtaining volunteers to join willingly without payment in order to free their country.'[26]

Even before the Japanese army had exposed the fragility of Britain's power in Asia, Linlithgow was full of pessimism. Late in January, he had written candidly and bleakly to the cabinet:

India and Burma have no natural association with the Empire, from which they are alien by race, history and religion, and for which as such neither of them have any natural affection, and both are in the Empire because they are conquered countries which had been brought there by force, kept there by our controls, and which hitherto it has suited to remain under our protection.[27]

For these reasons, the army's intelligence department kept a close surveillance over Indian troops and examined their letters for traces of dissatisfaction, restlessness and political agitation. Sixty per cent of the Indian officers serving in Malaya during 1941–2 had strong nationalist sympathies and looked forward to an independent India at the end of the war. And yet they were continually reminded of their separateness from the empire when they were refused entry into the clubs of that most starchy and conceited of all British colonial societies, the Malayan planter and business community. One Indian officer remarked that he and his brothers-in-arms 'have been sent all the way from India to defend these —— Europeans' and he was damned if he was going to 'lift a little finger to do it if and when the time came.'[28] A Celanese artilleryman, hanged for mutiny in 1942, said at his trial that his anti-British feelings had first come to the surface after he had suffered racial insults in Malaya.

Somehow brown men had to be persuaded to die for a white man's empire. One way in which this could be done was by breaking the deadlock over India's future, and in March 1942 Sir Stafford Cripps, a left-wing Labour minister with lofty principles, was sent to India to reach an accord with Congress. He failed, despite United States intervention, largely because neither he nor the war cabinet could accept Congress's demands for immediate participation in all areas of government, particularly defence.

It was now Gandhi's turn to seize the initiative. At the end of April he wrote that if Britain immediately withdrew from India, the Japanese would not attack. India's enemy was British, not Japanese imperialism, and United States military assistance then pouring into India would mean 'American rule added to British'.[29] He had never seen the Japanese as liberators, but he imagined that if their army invaded India they could be overcome by satyagraha![30] The British certainly could, he believed, and in July he called upon his followers to mobilise for a massive 'Quit India' campaign.

Even though Congress was disunited over the new campaign, it could not have come at a worse time for the British. Preparations were in hand for the defence of the North-West Frontier against a possible German advance from the Caspian, and there was a recrudescence of unrest in this area, led by Mirza Ali Khan (the Faqir of Ipi), an old-style messianic Muslim holy man who had been directing Pathan resistance for the past seven years. On the North-East Frontier a Japanese attack was expected, which might be combined with a seaborne invasion of south-eastern India or Ceylon. In the light of the breakdown of talks between the government and Congress, the Joint Planning Staff in Delhi placed little faith in the Indian will to resist.[31] Nevertheless, those responsible for the wartime defence of India had taken into account the likelihood of internal unrest and had made careful provisions for it, including a violent confrontation with Congress.[32] Moreover, the emergency law which had empowered the Viceroy to declare war also gave him the means to take whatever measures were needed to safeguard India's war effort.

The 'Quit India' campaign was launched during the second week of August and took the form of a mass effort to paralyse the country, with systematic attempts to sever rail and telegraph communications. The areas worst affected were Madras, Bihar and the United Provinces, where rail links between Calcutta, Delhi and Bombay were imperilled, and British servicemen were attacked and murdered by rioters. The Muslim League, which had been solid in its support for the war, stood aloof. Hindu students filled out many of the mobs, which were egged on by local Congress politicians. The government was ready for the emergency and acted with the utmost rigour: Gandhi and hundreds of Congress leaders were arrested and interned; the press was censored; fifty-seven brigades of Indian and British troops were diverted from training camps to support the police; urban mobs were fired upon and, at Lithlingow's orders, aircraft were permitted to strafe rioters tearing up railway lines.[33] In Bombay, demonstrators were beaten with a rattan cane, a punishment which, Leo Amery told the Commons, had a 'high deterrent value . . . to the hooligan type of offender'.[34] As in all previous political disorders, the temporary breakdown of order on the streets gave badmashes and petty criminals the chance to make mischief and plunder.

Order was restored within six weeks. At the beginning of September, the official and therefore lowest estimate of deaths was 300. Despite fears that the unrest was a cover for pro-Japanese fifth columnists, there was no evidence of collusion between Congress and Japan. Once again, the raj had emerged from a prolonged period of civil disturbance as strong as ever, although those within and outside India could be excused for believing

that its underlying authority rested on armed force. Gandhi and Congress
had been temporarily discredited by the 'Quit India' upheavals, particularly
in the United States which, during the first six months of 1942, had been
applying pressure to Britain to come to a solid agreement with Congress.

The raj had survived the strains of three years of war, and for the next
two, India would remain a safe base for Allied forces in south-east Asia. No
constitutional settlement had yet been reached which satisfied Indian
nationalists and their rulers. By the end of 1942 it was clear that when such
an arrangement was finally thrashed out, the final word would rest with the
Indians and not their masters. Indian politics no longer revolved around the
question of how long the raj would last, but how it was to be dismantled
and what would replace it.

6

For the Benefit
of Everyone:
Concepts of Empire,
1919–39

The First World War had dealt a mortal blow to jingoism, although its death throes continued for a further forty or so years. The belligerent patriotism of pre-1914 Britain, which had been stirred to fever pitch during the war, had a hollow ring after 1918, when a stunned nation contemplated the mass slaughter, and asked whether it had been really worthwhile. Britain had emerged victorious, but its people shrank from having to face, let alone engage in, another European war. The experience of the Western Front and the new public mood made it impossible to resuscitate the late-Victorian and Edwardian jingoistic imperialism, which had shouted defiance at the world and urged men and women to sacrifice themselves for the empire. This strident brand of patriotism had certainly intoxicated the public in the years before the war and, some argued, had done much to make war acceptable and its losses bearable.

Not only was the old imperialism discredited and out of fashion, but its champions were revealed to have had feet of clay. The wartime strategic and tactical decisions taken by those imperial warriors who held high command came under critical scrutiny, and were found wanting. Haig, who had sincerely imagined himself destined by God to save the British empire in its time of extreme peril, was toppled from his pedestal. Yesterday's heroes and prophets became today's figures of ridicule. In his

Eminent Victorians (1918), Lytton Strachey poked fun at, among others, Gordon of Khartoum. Collectively and in unflattering form, the living old guard of empire were embodied in the stout figure of Colonel Blimp, a walrus-moustached retired officer with diehard Tory views, created in 1934 by the Australian cartoonist, David Low.

There were plenty of Blimps around between the wars, and they had much to say about such matters as holding on to India but, wisely, the Conservative party distanced itself from them and their opinions. The Conservatives no longer chose to beat the imperial drum, preferring instead to court the electorate through policies of low taxation, the extension of earlier welfare legislation, and home-ownership.[1] The mixture worked; the Conservatives were in power throughout most of this period, and dominated the Lloyd George coalition and the 1931–5 national government. On the whole, imperial issues were pushed into the background by more pressing matters such as the economy and the quest for international security. When they were the subject for debate, party leaders went to considerable lengths to secure a crossbench consensus. All parties were consulted on the Montagu-Chelmsford proposals for India; Stanley Baldwin concurred with MacDonald's Indian policy despite backbench Conservative growls; and the 1935 Government of India Act received all-party support.

Many Conservatives were infuriated by these developments. In February 1931, Churchill expressed outrage at the sight of 'Mr Gandhi, a seditious Middle Temple lawyer, now posing as a faqir of a type well known in the East, striding half-naked up the steps of the Viceregal palace, while he is still organising and conducting a campaign of civil disobedience, to parley on equal terms with the representative of the King-Emperor.' This and subsequent protests against the extension of self-government in India struck a chord with many Conservatives, and up to sixty MPs were willing to back Churchill in his campaign to reverse official policy. His efforts were to no avail, but they were reminders that, then and later, there was a vociferous minority on the right of the Conservative party for whom the empire was impartible and could somehow be maintained indefinitely.

History could not support this view of empire. It had always been protean, undergoing frequent alterations in its composition and purpose. Public perceptions of the empire also changed. Addressing the Commons during a debate on the colonies in 1938, Ernest Evans, a Liberal MP, contrasted the popular view of the empire in his youth with that of the present day. Born in 1885, his boyhood had been a time 'when the idea of Empire in the minds of the people was associated with the spirit and practice of flag-waving'. Now, the temper of the country was very different: there was a deeper knowledge of the empire, regret for some of the exploits of the past, and a sincere desire to develop the colonies for the benefit of everyone.[2]

This selfless view of Britain's duty towards its subjects was not new. It owed much to those late eighteenth- and nineteenth-century evangelical and liberal idealists, who had believed that it was Britain's mission to uplift, morally and physically, ignorant and backward races. To some extent, this vision of an essentially benevolent empire had been lost sight of during the aggressive expansion of the 1880s and 1890s, when empire-building had been a competitive activity in which economic and strategic advantages were the prizes. And yet, even when the jingoes roared the loudest, imperialism had not shed its moral principles. They continued to flourish, although their application was confined to the white dominions which enjoyed the freedoms of the mother country and, ultimately, achieved home rule.

The post-war world was more receptive to this traditional concept of empire as an agency for regeneration and progress. Unselfish, paternalist imperialism had been revived by the League of Nations when it introduced the mandate system in 1920. Britain received former German East Africa, renamed Tanganyika, the Cameroons, Iraq, and Palestine, while New Zealand and Australia shared Germany's Pacific colonies. Each nation solemnly promised to devote itself to 'the well being and development of colonial races' that had been placed under its charge. How these aims were being fulfilled throughout the empire was explained by William Ormsby-Gore, the Colonial Secretary, in a BBC broadcast in May 1937. His department was responsible for forty crown colonies and mandated territories with a combined population of 55 million. Their future depended upon their people mastering what he called 'the art and practice of civilised administration' through instruction and example. In time, 'a native Civil Service completely and finally responsible for administration' would emerge and step into the shoes of its British predecessor. This was both inevitable and welcome for, as Orsmby-Gore concluded, 'even the best and most enlightened external rule is in the long run no satisfactory substitute for self-government in accordance with the traditions and local characteristics of one's own people.'[3]

The quality of British colonial administration was the source of justifiable pride. 'The peoples of the colonies are not merely content to be His Majesty's subjects,' boasted Malcolm MacDonald, Colonial Secretary from 1938 to 1940, 'they are positively happy to be his Majesty's subjects.'[4] This was how they appeared in the popular press. In April 1939, readers of *Picture Post* saw photographs of keen Indian schoolboys clustered round a blackboard in an open-air school. A month later the magazine showed pictures of chiefs from the Cameroons being taught how to govern justly, alongside a text that contrasted the humane enlightenment of the present British administration with that of Germany, which had ruled the colony before 1916.[5]

The chiefs' lessons were part of what MacDonald had called 'an evolutionary process' that was underway throughout the colonial empire. Official policy towards Africans was: '"to teach them and to encourage them always to be able to stand on their own feet". That love of ours of freedom not only for ourselves but for others, inspires policy right through the Colonial Empire.' Turning this principle into action would take time, and he added pointedly that Nigeria, then one of the most advanced colonies, was 'not ripe for self-government'.[6] In the words of one contemporary commentator on imperial affairs, 'In relation to the European the African is still a schoolboy.'[7] This was, at least, a marginal improvement on the childlike ignorance and wilfulness which had characterised him fifty years before.

When the black and brown races of the empire moved forwards, it was tacitly assumed they were also moving upwards. Mankind's progress towards civilisation was still seen as the steady ascent of a mountain. Europeans had climbed most rapidly and were now close to the summit, if not astride it, while other races had not passed the foothills. This perception of the nature of human progress, together with the recent theories of social Darwinism, gave Europeans a powerful sense of racial superiority. While they may have adapted well to their environments, the peoples of Asia, Africa and Australasia manifestly lacked the scientific and technical skills which had propelled Europeans forward and, during the nineteenth century, made them masters of most of the world. By contrast, so-called backward or primitive peoples had been held back by an irrational attachment to absurd, even dangerous shibboleths. Hence the references, still common in the inter-war years, to Hindu practices as a brake on India's advancement.

The taboos and observances of African animists were commonly represented, particularly by missionaries, as obstacles to moral and physical improvement. For those at its centre, the heart of darkness often appeared impossible to illuminate. In 1921, a Kenyan missionary lamented the power which pagan beliefs still exercised over the minds of young natives. 'A girl', he wrote, 'is a chattel under the care of her heathen mother whose ideas of sex and relaxation appear unspeakably vile in the light of Christian teaching.'[8] Just what he had in mind was described by a Kenyan magistrate who witnessed a female circumcision ceremony in 1944. Afterwards he wrote, 'The whole business was fanatical and diabolical and left me wondering whether we were getting anywhere with the Africans.'[9] Such experiences convinced even the most liberal-minded that the redemption of Africa was a sisyphean undertaking which would require many decades to accomplish.

Popular travel literature emphasised either the backwardness of Britain's colonial subjects or the quaintness of their customs and dress. An account of a journey through Nigeria in 1925, dedicated to shooting its wildlife, contained this revealing aside: 'Here is manhood fully attained in respect to physical development, but possessing a mind still in the process of evolution, cognition being present to a limited degree.' The author considered this state of affairs as the consequence either of 'laziness' or 'incomplete brain development'.[10] More usually, writers about Africa and Australasia concentrated on the exotic and, through a combination of condescending prose and glamorous photographs, portrayed the tropical empire as a sort of human menagerie inhabited by creatures who wore picturesque clothes or sometimes none at all. Material of this sort appeared regularly in the *Illustrated London News* and *The Sphere*, often in connection with a royal tour which made newsworthy an otherwise obscure colonial backwater.

Popular anthropology of this kind was one of the mainstays of the American *National Geographic Magazine*, which produced features on Britain's remoter colonies. These articles were lavishly illustrated and accompanied by texts that were largely anecdotal and written in a chatty journalistic style. In between accounts of tussles between the authors' motor cars and rhinoceroses, the native population appeared, usually smiling and in their gala finery. Their qualities were described in a patronising manner and their place in the scheme of things was clearly defined: 'The Baganda are a pleasant and courteous people, and quick to emulate the white man in clothing and ways of living. They train easily, whether as domestic servants, scouts, or seamstresses.'[11]

Another familiar stereotype of the period was the comic black man of the stage and humorous magazines. He appeared frequently during the late 1930s in the *Punch* cartoons of Charles Grave, which were usually set against a West African background. These burlesques relied upon the appearance of the characters, who often wore travesties of European dress, and their pidgin dialect. In one, a stevedore working on a dockside encounters a rather swell-looking African in an ill-fitting white suit, battered homburg and wing collar, who is wearing sunglasses. The caption reads: 'Why you wear dem dark glasses? Is der somethin' wrong wid yo' eyes?' 'No; but dey go wed me face.'[12]

Images like this and the portrayals of native peoples in more serious books and magazines were indirect reminders that there was still a racial hierarchy within the empire. Those at the bottom of the pile were there because of a variety of shortcomings, mainly moral. They were, however, free to elevate themselves if they dropped values and customs abhorrent to their rulers and accepted their guidance. And yet when they took this course they were liable to ridicule and could not expect automatically to achieve equality with the white man and enter his society.

Was the effort worth it? Thomas Birley, the Bishop of Zanzibar, whose diocese extended across Tanganyika, wondered in 1920 whether a black man was ultimately the loser when he attempted to transform himself into a 'base imitation' of the white. 'Becoming conscious of what Europeans despise in them', negroes 'seek to "camouflage" themselves by feeble imitations of the "higher race"'.[13] Those whose outlook was being changed through a Western education were also perplexed by what was happening to them, particularly their alienation from their roots. In 1916, the *Lagos Daily Record* suggested that educated Nigerians might learn something from the recent history of Japan, a nation that had absorbed much from Europe, but which had not jettisoned its indigenous religion, ethical codes and styles of dress.[14] Such an appeal was understandable once black men began to find themselves frozen out of the company of whites who, in terms of accomplishment, might be considered their equals.

The West Indian writer C.L.R. James thought they should, and explained why in a talk broadcast by the BBC in May 1933. It was the centenary of the abolition of slavery, and James, the descendant of slaves, described how his family had advanced itself through education. Listeners were reminded that the West Indian cricket XI that had toured Britain in 1931 contained teachers, businessmen, a cashier and a sanitary inspector, who represented the growing middle class of the islands. And yet the whites still argued that blacks were unready for self-government. West Indian loyalty to the empire was very strong, as had been proved in the First World War and would be again in the Second, but, James argued, 'People who are governed from abroad often feel that they are considered in some way inferior, backward or immature, and that many of us resent.'[15]

According to James, the West Indies's future lay in the hands of its young men, who were then going to Britain to study. Some would have experienced a frosty welcome. None, whatever their qualifications, would have been allowed to study at St Mary's Hospital, London, since its dean, Churchill's doctor Lord Moran, had an aversion against all blacks.[16] Black men were also debarred from enrolment at the Royal Academy of Dramatic Art.[17] These were outstanding examples of what was then called the 'colour bar', a lattice fence of individual prejudices which excluded black and brown people from lodgings, hotels and places of public entertainment, notably dance halls, across Britain.

The depth and violence of British racism had been revealed in the Liverpool and Cardiff race riots of June 1919. Both cities possessed unusually large black populations made up of seafarers, and recent arrivals who had come seeking wartime work on the docks and in factories. The experience of Irish and Jewish immigrants during the previous century had shown that tension was always worst in areas where they had congregated in great numbers, and where the struggle to find work was always intense. These circumstances applied in Liverpool and Cardiff as discharged servicemen entered the labour market, and they added to racial antipathy.

In Liverpool, where the black population was estimated at about 5,000 a coloured men's boarding house was attacked by a 2,000-strong mob. Many blacks fled in terror to the protection of Toxteth police station; one was arrested carrying an iron bar and a banner inscribed 'Down with the White Race', and others pleaded that they were British subjects and therefore entitled to justice. In Cardiff, where there was a community of negroes, Arabs and Somalis, the trouble started with a brawl between groups of black and white men close by the Labour Exchange. This led to a large-scale riot during which gangs rampaged through what the locals called the Nigger Town district, close to the docks. Mobs stormed black people's homes, and some owners defended themselves with revolvers. An Irishman and a negro were killed. Reports of these disorders mentioned that very considerable animus was shown against black men who had married white women.

This revelation aroused Ralph Williams, a former administrator in

Bechuanaland, to a pitch of fury. He wrote to *The Times* and asserted that 'intimate association between black or coloured men and white women is a thing of horror' to every white man in the tropics.[18] Sexual anxieties and jealousies were close to the heart of British, and for that matter American racism. For centuries, negroes were believed to possess a peculiar sexual energy, part animal and part on account of that legend which endowed them with larger penises than white men. No such sexual envy or accompanying animosity was directed towards the men of the Far East or the Maoris, who were thought not to measure up to Europeans, which may explain New Zealand's fine record of racial harmony.[19] Unease about the black man's alleged sexual powers lay behind the laws in those parts of southern Africa that had been colonised by Europeans, such as South Africa's 1927 Immorality Act, which forbade casual sex between the races. British actors who travelled to South Africa for the making of the film *Zulu* in 1962 were lectured on the country's sexual interdictions, which prompted Sir Stanley Baker to remark that several hundred Zulu women extras represented at least a thousand years in prison. Mixed marriages were allowed in South Africa until 1949, but those who contracted them faced ostracism and, for white women, the contempt of their own race. In 1915, when the Rajah of Pudukota married Miss Molly Fink, an Australian girl, he faced the combined disapproval of Austen Chamberlain, the Secretary of State for India, George V and Queen Mary, and forfeited any chance of ever being presented at court.[20] Interestingly, at this time thirty out of forty-eight American states banned mixed marriages.

It was axiomatic that the life and virtue of a white woman were sacrosanct throughout the empire, at least as far as the natives were concerned. The murder of a British woman and the abduction of her daughter by Pathans on the North-West Frontier in 1923 convinced one senior officer that Indians no longer respected British power.[21] Convention did not extend the same protection to black and brown women. 'Europe embraces the African woman, and calls the African man "a damned nigger",' was how Bishop Birley of Zanzibar described the distinction.[22] It was also evident in that contemporary practice by which it was permissible for respectable publishers to illustrate books with photographs of bare-bosomed, scantily-clad African and Australasian women, but not near-naked white women. Needless to say, unclad black men were always coyly posed.

To a large extent, the colour bar was a barrier against sexual contact and was welcomed as such. 'What a packet of trouble there would be if susceptible English youths went dancing every night with pretty and lady-like Malay, Chinese and Indian girls, and there are plenty of them about,' an anxious mother informed a London local newspaper in 1943.[23] Such prejudice was not confined to uneducated whites or the Blimpish right; it transcended all class boundaries and political affinities. While middle-class radicals and socialists usually found it easy to mix with their Indian or African counterparts, they could easily succumb to racial intolerance. Beatrice Webb was appalled by the habits of the Chinese during her visit to their country in 1911, and she left convinced that homosexuality, drugs and quack medicines were evidence of a moral decay which was irreversible.[24] In general, the Labour party had always stood out against all forms of racial discrimination, but when, in 1948, Seretse Khama, the heir to the Bangwato chieftaincy in Bechuanaland, chose to marry Ruth Williams, a white clerk, Labour ministers placed expediency before principle. Bowing to pressure from South Africa, and fears of adverse reactions from the Bangwato, the government barred Seretse Khama from his inheritance. Patrick Gordon Walker, then Secretary for Commonwealth Relations, wanted to ban all such marriages.[25] There was, however, a freemasonry among aristocrats which enabled Malayan sultans and Indian rajahs to move freely among the British upper classes. By one of those bewildering convolutions of British social and racial etiquette, the Nawab of Pataudi travelled as a 'gentleman', that is an amateur, with the English cricket team which toured Australia during the winter of 1932–3. Before and after matches, he shared changing-rooms with other gentlemen, apart from the professionals or 'players', a ritual which was all the more bizarre since it was performed in a country which excluded all coloured immigrants.

The colour bar was a canker within the empire. It had been experienced, in varying degrees, by black and brown soldiers during the First World War, and had shaken their faith in the empire as a community of equals. The colour of a man's skin determined whether or not he could settle in Australia, vote in British Columbia, and circumscribed his every activity in South Africa. The British too were tainted. When Sir Hugh Knatchbull-Hugessen became ambassador to Persia in 1934, he discovered that, 'There was a feeling that we had not yet divested ourselves of the "nineteenth-century complex" and were not disposed to treat the Persians as equals.'[26] Egyptians, Arabs and Indians shared this sentiment, and detected that behind successive British governments' stonewalling over increased self-determination for their countries lay a fundamental belief that the non-white races suffered from some inbred incapacity to manage their own affairs. By contrast, political maturity was more easily and quickly attained by white men. For the impatient and the disappointed, the Commonwealth was a white man's club as racially exclusive as those of Singapore, Nairobi or, for that matter, the Hammersmith Palais de Dance.

7

————•—

The Bond of One Spirit: The Public Face of Empire, 1919–39

The colour bar was making itself felt during a period when tremendous efforts were being made to promote Commonwealth and imperial unity. The revolution in communications, which gathered pace after 1919, enhanced the prospects for a more closely bonded empire. Long-distance air travel and wireless had the potential to liberate the empire from the fetters of its geography. Aviation was immediately recognised as a cord which could bind together territories scattered at random across the globe. After his epic twenty-day flight from London to Australia at the end of 1919, Sir Ross Smith believed that he had helped 'bind closer the outposts of the Empire through the trails of the skies'. Another pathfinder, Mrs J.A. Mollinson, told a BBC audience in 1932 that the purpose of her latest flight from London to the Cape by way of West Africa had been to 'keep together in friendship and good fellowship all the scattered parts of our Empire'.[1]

The government's response to the challenge of imperial flight was fumbling and unimaginative. At the end of the war, Britain possessed the world's largest aircraft industry which, in mid-1918, was producing 4,000 machines a month, and a pool of trained pilots.[2] Within months of the war ending, the most skilled and daring were making ambitious pioneer flights; Alcock and Brown crossed the Atlantic in May, Sir Ross Smith reached Australia by way of Iraq, India and Malaya, and in May 1920 two South Africans flew from Cairo to Cape Town. These achievements aroused tremendous public excitement, but the government's approach to imperial civil aviation was timid. Deference to *laissez faire* and free market principles

· 438 ·

made ministers and civil servants extremely reluctant to invest public funds in air transport at a time when the government was short of money. There were plenty of ideas, like that for a West African air service, but each fell victim to official lassitude. Only in December 1923, and after pressure had been exerted by the 1921 Imperial Conference, did the government decide to take civil aviation seriously.

The result was Imperial Airways which had a share capital of £1 million, a government subsidy of a further £1 million spread over ten years, and a monopoly of imperial and continental routes. It was a case of too little and too late for Britain's aircraft industry, which was now being overtaken by its German, French and American competitors.[3] Far greater imagination and enterprise was shown by the Australians; the Queensland and Northern Territories Air Service (QANTAS) had been founded in 1920, linking the dispersed settlements of the outback, and in 1925 it began regular flights from Brisbane to Singapore. Imperial Airways inaugurated its services to Cairo and Karachi in the same year, against the background of a row with the Egyptian government, which objected to the British company's monopoly. In January 1932, thirteen years after the first preliminary reconnaissance, regular flights began between London and Cape Town via Paris, Brindisi, Alexandria, Cairo and Khartoum. They were heavily subsidised by the governments of the colonies along the flight path, Britain and South Africa, who together pledged over £1 million for five years.[4]

After an experiment with airships, which ended disastrously in 1929 when the R101 crashed on its maiden flight to India, the Air Ministry turned to aircraft for all imperial services. Since all long-distance flights had to be staggered and harbours, rivers and lakes were the most convenient staging-posts, flying boats were adopted for most imperial routes. The result was the development of Short 23, known as the Empire Flying Boat, which came into operation in 1938 and carried eighteen passengers. By then, Imperial Airways was offering an extensive service: there were seven flights a week from England to Egypt, four to India, three to East Africa, and two respectively to East Africa, Singapore, Hong Kong and Australia. Superficially, this appeared an impressive total, but it might have been greater had it not been for the lack of official vision in the immediate post-war years.

Wireless, like flight, had owed its rapid technical development to wartime needs. It was soon converted to civilian uses and was identified as a device which would strengthen imperial links and promote a sense of common identity among the empire's subjects. 'Contact with civilisation' was how an officer serving on the North-West Frontier described the faint signals from the BBC's Daventry transmitter which he picked up in 1927. Wireless was spreading quickly throughout the dominions; in 1929 there were 299,000 licensed receivers in Australia, 216,000 in Canada, 41,000 in New Zealand, and 16,800 in South Africa. Ceylon had its own station by 1925, but progress in India was slow and haphazard. By 1935, there were transmitters at Bombay and Calcutta, and a programme was in hand to distribute radios to rural villages.

In time, even the most far-flung colonies were able to pick up BBC longwave broadcasts, and local stations proliferated. In 1941 there were 385 wireless receivers in North Borneo among a population of 300,000, who were served by two local stations.[5] Their output seems to have had little appeal to the Chinese community, which preferred to listen to popular music programmes from Saigon and Manila. Radio could and did expose the empire's subjects to other cultures and ideas, not all of them conducive to imperial harmony.

The greatest value of wireless lay in its power to draw people together. It was therefore the ideal device to enkindle a sense of community among the disparate races of the empire; to strengthen the ties of kinship between Britain and the dominions; and, most important of all, to focus the loyalty of all the empire's subjects on the figure who symbolised imperial unity, the monarch. It was therefore appropriate that on Christmas Day 1933 members of the extended imperial family heard the gruff, fatherly voice of George V speaking from Sandringham. In the first royal Christmas message, the King thanked his subjects for their loyalty, pledged them his continued service, and sent them the season's good wishes. This brief, simple and warm address had been preceded by an hour-long programme made up of short pieces contrived to convey a sense of familial closeness among the peoples of the empire. There were short live broadcasts from Canadian, Australian and New Zealand towns and cities, Gibraltar, and a ship lying off Port Said.

George V's 1933 broadcast was an imperial *coup de théâtre*. The airwaves had united the empire in a wonderful and moving manner, and a technically more ambitious programme was prepared for Christmas Day 1934. Again, the themes were kinship and harmony, but the rich diversity of the empire's people was also explored. A handful were invited to speak about themselves and their daily lives. So, during the prelude to the King's address, listeners heard, among other things, songs sung by native 'boys' on a Cape vineyard, an officer speaking from an outpost on the Khyber Pass, and a few words from a life-saver on Bondi Beach, Sydney. There was an endearing candour about some of the performances. A Tasmanian fisherman drily announced, 'There ain't much difference being a fisherman here and a fisherman anywhere else. It's mostly pretty cold and pretty wet.' An old Cotswold shepherd remarked, impromptu, that he had a brother in New Zealand who, if he was listening, might take the trouble to write home. At three in the afternoon, the King spoke and praised that 'bond of one spirit' which held all his scattered subjects together.

The wireless was also helping the people of the empire to find out about each other. The BBC, then guided by the high-minded principles of Sir John Reith, its director-general, gave time to fifteen-minute talks by experts on different aspects of the empire, past, present and future. Controversial issues were not side-stepped or glossed over; in 1930, the archaeologist Louis Leakey drew on his Kenyan experience to warn that if officials continued to govern Africa 'in ignorance of native custom' they ran the risk of accumulated resentment breaking into unrest.[6]

These broadcasts were reminders of the continual need to inform the public about the empire, what it stood for, and how its existence benefited them. These matters were all touched upon in various ways by the cinema, then enjoying its golden age. Films were the greatest source of public entertainment between the wars: there were 3,000 picture houses in Britain in 1926, a total that had risen to 5,000 by 1940, the year in which 1,000 million tickets were sold.

The cinema therefore offered an unprecedented opportunity to spread the imperial message to the masses. Attention had been drawn to the persuasive power of films during the 1926 and 1930 Imperial Conferences, which called for the expansion of the empire's film industry, and the encouragement of films that upheld imperial virtues. After the earlier conference, Sir Philip Cunliffe-Lister, the president of the Board of Trade, admitted the political value of films that 'unconsciously influence the ideas and outlook of British people of all races' which was why they ought to become the 'universal means through which national ideas can be spread'. More forceful in tone was General Sir Granville de Laune Ryrie, a sexagenarian veteran of the Boer War and Australian high commissioner in London. He demanded that all the empire's children should 'be marched to the cinema in the morning to see wholesome British films depicting what is going on in the Empire.'[7] Such uplifting stuff would be a welcome antidote to the deluge of sensational, violent and often openly sexual material which poured from the Hollywood studios. Nine out of ten of the films shown in Britain came from America, and the stiffer elements in society saw them as a source of moral contamination.

The government did what it could to contain this pollution. It also insisted that every film which portrayed the empire or its servants showed both in a flattering light. Defending the celluloid integrity of the empire was the duty of the British Board of Film Censors, founded in 1912, and armed with a list of taboo subjects and scenarios. In theory independent, the Board was always willing to yield to government pressure and did so regularly. In 1925 it refused a licence to D.W. Griffith's *America* because it showed British soldiers behaving badly during the American War of Independence.

Sexual or potentially sexual relations between black or coloured men and white women were among the prohibited subjects appended to the Board's catalogue of the forbidden in 1928. This ban was invoked in 1933 on Frank Capra's *The Bitter Tea of General Yen*, in which an American girl falls in love with a Chinese warlord. Other new interdictions included 'British possessions represented as lawless sinks of iniquity' and 'White men in a state of degradation amidst Far Eastern and Native surroundings'.[8] Protection was extended on characters from soldiers to colonial officials whose screen conduct had always to be irreproachable.

There was, in fact, little to fear from Hollywood's version of the empire. In its widest sense, Britain's empire, like America's Wild West, was just a fruitful source of adventure stories. Hollywood's *Lives of the Bengal Lancers* (1934) was, like other American 'imperial' epics, a straightforward tale of derring-do with occasional statements about duty to the king emperor from officers keeping his peace. The villains were Pathans, but they might as well have been Apaches, and not long after the film's storyline was adapted for a Wild West film. What Hollywood wanted was an exotic background and a dramatic scenario, and attempts at verisimilitude were, therefore, desultory or ludicrous. *Storm over India* (1939) made Kabul the capital of Burma and showed an amazing ignorance of the British army, solecisms which enraged Colonel John Hanna, a former artilleryman who undertook much of the Board's script vetting. Technical blunders apart, there was little in Hollywood's picture of the empire to upset official sensibilities. Films like *Lives of the Bengal Lancers* or *Gunga Din* (1939) probably did little to influence public opinion beyond complementing older, Hentyesque images of resourceful and gallant men serving their country on distant frontiers.

British-made imperial films were always more than entertainment. They deliberately presented the empire as a virtuous and benevolent institution, guarded and served by brave, dedicated men of the highest probity. This was what the censors demanded, but it also represented the private sentiments of two of the most gifted contemporary British film-makers, Michael Balcon and Alexander Korda. Each was intensely patriotic and had advised Baldwin on Conservative political films.[9]

The government acknowledged the value of their work and helped smooth Korda's path during the location filming of *The Drum* (1938) and *The Four Feathers* (1939). The Indian army provided troops for the battle scenes in the former, and the Sudanese authorities loaned Korda 4,000 askaris and the East Surrey Regiment for the spectacular re-enactment of the battle of Omdurman which marked the climax of *The Four Feathers*. The Sudanese government also assisted in the procurement of large numbers of Hadanduwa warriors (Fuzzy-Wuzzies), who added a striking and authentic touch to the battle sequences. According to a puff for the film which appeared in *Picture Post*, it was difficult to persuade these proud men to 'die'. One asked, 'Why should I die? I fought in the real battle of Omdurman and did not die!' He was eventually persuaded that there was no shame in a screen death and complied.[10]

The message of Korda's and Balcon's imperial films was unambiguous. The latter's *Rhodes of Africa* (1935) and *Clive of India* (1936) were complimentary biographies from which their subjects emerged as far-sighted visionaries, stripped of their historical duplicity and avarice. Sanders, the district officer hero of Korda's *Sanders of the River*, is both a dreamer and a practical man who gives his life for the redemption of Africa. He is the firm but just ruler of a stretch of river who commands by force of character. As he tells the riverine chiefs, his king's law will bring them and their people peace and prosperity. The empire is a force for human progress, and this is appreciated by Chief Bosambo (Paul Robeson), who idolises Sanders and shares his hopes for the future. The African past of animist superstition and internecine war is symbolised by King Mofobula, a grotesque figure attended by witchdoctors and addicted to slave-raiding. When Sanders goes on leave, rumours spread of his death and the King's peace crumbles. The old barbaric Africa reasserts itself, but Sanders returns in the nick of time and Mofobula is overthrown and killed. The new Africa moves forward, guided by Sanders's strong hands, and Bosambo, now a paramount chief, promises that his son will go to the government college for chiefs' sons, where he will learn those principles by which Sanders lives and rules.

The clash between imperial enlightenment and tribal obscurantism is the theme of *The Drum*. The setting is the contemporary North-West Frontier of India where an upright British Resident (Roger Livesey) confronts a devious khan (Raymond Massey) set on fomenting a jihad against the raj with the help of modern weapons smuggled from Russia. The conspiracy is exposed by the Resident, aided by the young rajah (Sabu) who, like Bosambo, learns to respect the individual courage of the empire's servants and their code of values. One of these is self-sacrifice. Before visiting the khan, the Resident rejects pleas to stay safely within his fort with the argument that if he is murdered, which seems highly likely, then his death, like that of Gordon, will further the advance of civilisation.

The Drum and *Sanders of the River* blended adventure yarn with imperial homily. Filmgoers went home with a satisfying belief that their empire represented stability and equity, and was managed by brave, right-minded men who knew what was best for the natives. When the time came for Bosambo's son and the young rajah to take responsibility for their people, their models would be men like Sanders who had taught them to love justice and truth. Indian audiences reacted differently; when *The Drum* was screened in Madras and Bombay, they poured out of picture houses and protested in the streets against a film which struck them as crass imperial propaganda. It was quickly withdrawn from circulation.

In retrospect, it is hard to imagine why this advertisement for benevolent imperialism was ever shown in India. In 1938, the Marquess of Zetland, Secretary of State for India, forestalled the making of *The Relief of Lucknow*, which he believed would inflame local passions. His intervention was discussed during a Commons debate on censorship towards the end of the year, when the Labour MP Emmanuel Shinwell mischievously suggested that the government might consider a blanket ban on all references to the Indian Mutiny in the interests of imperial harmony.[11] On a graver note, there were allegations that the government had tampered with newsreels of events before, during and after the recent Munich crisis.

The newsreel and the documentary film were ingenuously believed to be records of fact. Ever since 1903, when the North Borneo Company sponsored a short film about its colony, there had been a steady stream of didactic, imperial documentaries. Many were commercially inspired, like a Cadbury's promotional film of 1913 which traced the progress of the cocoa bean from a Gold Coast plantation to the chocolate factory at Bournville. As part of the wider promotion of imperial wares, the Empire Marketing Board formed a film unit in 1933 which produced *Song of*

Ceylon and *Cargo from Jamaica*. These improving and earnest films, like those from the General Post Office and Imperial Airways film units, were loaned free of charge to schools and youth groups. Convincing this audience of the value of empire was very low on the Treasury's priorities, and the Empire Marketing Board's film unit soon fell victim to official cheeseparing. Colonial Office officials were secretly rather pleased since they considered the whole business of public relations and 'selling' the empire to be vulgar.[12]

The empire was 'sold' to the public in an unprecedented and unashamed manner by the British Empire Exhibition held at Wembley during 1924 and 1925. It was a splendid show in which the exotic and progressive aspects of the empire were carefully interwoven. The exhibition's various pavilions and 'palaces' were spread across a two-hundred-acre site and were connected by streets with such names as Dominion Way and Atlantic Slope, which had been chosen by Kipling. The total cost of the show was £2.2 million, half of which was provided by a government keen to foster imperial trade. At the official opening of the exhibition in April 1924, the Prince of Wales promised his father, George V, 'a complete and vivid representation of your Empire' and an advertisement to the world 'that the most powerful agency of civilisation had its heart set upon peaceful actions and the good of mankind'. In reply, the King extolled 'the spirit of free and tolerant cooperation which had inspired peoples of different races, creeds, institutions and ways of thought to unite in a single Commonwealth.'

Twenty-seven million people visited the exhibition. They came away with an impression of a thriving, forward-looking and diverse empire, and memories of glimpses of how some of its more picturesque inhabitants lived. There were huge palaces of art and industry built in the most up-to-date material, concrete. The Australian and Canadian pavilions were in a restrained neo-Georgian style, an elaborately fretted mock pagoda represented Burma, and minarets Malaya. Most awe-inspiring of all was the reproduction of the great fortified gateway of Kano, complete with crenellations, at the entrance of the Nigerian exhibition. These buildings were inhabited: visitors stared at richly robed and bejewelled Asante princes guarded by native policemen in a tarbooshes, and Malay women spinning by a lakeside. West Africans accosted passers-by and offered them medallions inscribed 'Drink More Cocoa', for the show was also a massive trade fair.

It was, however, the glamorous rather than the commercial that captivated most visitors. 'Dusky figures flit about the spot for all the world as if
one was actually in Africa, instead of a few miles from Charing Cross,'
enthused one journalist. For all his excitement, he found walking from one
pavilion to another rather tiring, and suggested that Zulu rickshaw boys
might be provided for the footsore.[13] Some blacks felt patronised. The
Union of Students of Black Descent felt that their kinsmen were demeaned
by being stared at like exhibits in a raree show, and were insulted by references to African sorcery and cannibalism in the exhibition's guidebook.[14]

George V and his eldest son were closely identified with the exhibition
and its objectives. Their exchange at the opening ceremony was a carefully
crafted public statement of the humane and progressive ideals of an empire
whose subjects were bound together by mutual goodwill and respect. These
were appropriate sentiments, for the monarch had always been a symbol of
imperial unity, a totemic figure who commanded affection and loyalty.
Abstract bonds had to be strengthened, and so the monarch, or more usually his or her immediate kin, had periodically to reveal themselves to the
distant peoples of the empire. This almost mystical concept was charmingly
put into words by a Maori bishop, when he hailed the Duke of Gloucester
during his tour of New Zealand in 1934: 'Welcome O son, in whose face
we see your royal father, mother and eldest brother, whose Royal and
princely footsteps trod the broad billowy waves of Tangaroa . . .'[15]

It is unlikely that Indians had recognised much of his august mother in
the bearing of the Prince of Wales during his tour of their country in
1877. He traversed the subcontinent, shot tigers, and hobnobbed with
rajahs and senior administrators and officers in what was the first official
royal tour of the empire. His son, George V, made what was the most magnificent in 1912, when he and Queen Mary, wearing their crowns and
coronation robes, received the homage of the Indian princes at a huge durbar held at Delhi.

There was less accent on pseudo-Mughal pageantry and pomp during
the post-war royal tours undertaken by the Prince of Wales. The future
Edward VIII was sent off on his travels by Lloyd George, who saw the royal
peregrinations as an exercise in political showmanship that would entrance
the dominions and make their rulers more tractable. 'The appearance of the
popular Prince of Wales might do more to calm the discord than half a
dozen solemn Imperial Conferences.'[16] Up to a point the Prime Minister
was right. The young prince was a decent, affable fellow whose good
looks, youthfulness and unstuffy manner made a favourable impression

throughout the empire. He had been well prepared for his duties; Churchill coached him in the art of public oratory, and Lord Stamfordham, the King's secretary, lectured him on the seriousness of his new responsibilities. 'The Throne is the pivot upon which the Empire will more than hinge,' he intoned. 'Its strength and stability will depend entirely on its occupant.'[17]

With this admonition hanging over him, the Prince embarked for Canada in August 1919. During the next nine years, he successively visited the West Indies, New Zealand, Australia, India, Canada again (in 1923 and 1927), the Gambia, the Gold Coast, Nigeria, South Africa, Kenya and Uganda. He was fêted everywhere, and received local worthies, inspected guards of honour, opened public buildings and made the appropriate speeches with a cheerful enthusiasm that must at times have been hard to sustain. There were also those concerts of native music and displays of dancing which became commonplace features of all royal tours, and were popular with newsreel cameramen. When he ascended the throne in January 1936, Edward VIII knew more about the empire and its people than any of his predecessors. As Lloyd George had predicted, he had won hearts and had done what he could to ease ethnic and political tensions in Canada and South Africa. Given to occasional radical outbursts at home, the prince revealed himself a reactionary abroad, observing that Indians were unfit to govern themselves and openly sympathising with the white settlers in Kenya.[18]

It would be impossible to calculate what contribution these and other royal tours made to imperial cohesion. Documentaries like *50,000 Miles with the Prince of Wales* (1925) and newsreels of his and other imperial progresses showed images of diverse peoples cheering and waving flags, united in loyalty to the crown and, by inference, the empire. It was all very reassuring, as were newspaper reports of facile and emollient speeches of welcome and thanks, which emphasised allegiance and affection on one side and paternal devotion on the other. No chance was missed to reiterate the common values upon which the Commonwealth and empire were based. They lay at the heart of the valedictory message sent to the Prince by Billy Hughes, the Labour prime minister of Australia: 'The Australian people see in you all that our glorious Empire stands for, that deathless spirit of liberty, of progress, that distinguishes it from all other Empires, ancient or modern . . .'

A new token of the bond between the crown and the empire was the issue of special postage stamps by each dominion and colony to celebrate George V's Silver Jubilee in 1935. The colonial issues shared a standard, dignified design which showed the King and Windsor Castle. A further mass issue marked the coronation of George VI in May 1937. By the uniformity of their designs, these royal stamps reflected the unity of the empire, and, incidentally, boosted the collection of other imperial issues, especially among the young.

Imperial stamps had recently undergone a change in appearance thanks to Sir Ronald Storrs. As governor of Cyprus, he ordered an issue of handsome pictorial stamps in 1928 to commemorate fifty years of British rule and provide 'that publicity which the colony so sorely needed'.[19] It was a brilliant idea; the Cyprus Treasury received a much-needed £20,000 from sales to philatelists, which may have encouraged other colonies to follow suit. In 1933 Sierra Leone issued a set of stamps to celebrate the centenary of the abolition of slavery with designs showing local scenes and, as an acknowledgement of benevolent imperialism, a hospital. Within a few years, every colony had abandoned the old utilitarian stamps that had just shown the monarch's head, and replaced them with pictorial issues. These illustrated aspects of each colony's distinctive peoples, culture, economic progress, landscape, transport and natural history. The iconography of imperial postage stamps embraced native huts, canoes, palm trees, tobacco plantations, frigate birds, crocodiles, railway bridges and harbours. Colourful and well-executed, these tiny vignettes of colonial life proved immensely popular with collectors and added considerably to the public's knowledge of the empire.

Stamps were probably collected by Richmal Crompton's William and members of his gang of Outlaws, as they were by boys and girls throughout the country at a time when the mature still urged the young to fill their spare time with 'useful', that is to say, improving occupations. When encaged in the classroom, the Outlaws endured history lessons crammed with facts about how the empire had been created, a form of indoctrination which failed in the case of William, who was convinced that the horrors of Calcutta's 'Black Hole' had occurred in Blackpool. During geography, he and his fellows would have peered at and handled the empire's products, neatly laid out in partitioned boxes, which were distributed to schools by the Empire Marketing Board. Birthdays and Christmas were marked by gifts of informative and entertaining 'Empire' annuals, one for boys and one for girls. In each, there was a mixture of adventure stories set against an imperial background and informative articles on such topics as Scouting in Fiji.

The empire had now become part of the ritual of British life. Families gathered round the wireless after Christmas dinner to hear the King speak. The seasons were marked by the comings and goings of various cricket and rugby union teams to and from the dominions. Two predominantly English and middle-class games had, from the mid-nineteenth century, gained a considerable following in various parts of the empire. By the 1920s, South Africans considered rugby union to be their national game, and it had also made great headway in Australia and New Zealand and, by a process of sub-colonisation, to Fiji and Western Samoa. Cricket had taken hold in South Africa, Australia, New Zealand, India and the West Indies. From the last quarter of the nineteenth century, a pattern had been established by which dominion teams toured England during the summer, and in the winter English teams travelled to the dominions. These contests attracted enormous public attention, particularly the intermittent, hard-fought contests between English and Australian cricketers for the Ashes. National pride was deeply involved; when an English XI embarked for Australia and New Zealand in September 1932, the *Spectator* solemnly announced that they left 'as Sir John Jellicoe sailed in August 1914, for the North Sea, freighted with the prayers and hopes and anxieties of the whole English people'.[20]

This comparison of sport and war was unintentionally prophetic. During the third test match at Adelaide in January 1933, Harold Larwood, a Yorkshire fast bowler, delivered a devastating sequence of 'express' balls at the Australian batsmen's leg sides. Several Australians were struck on the body and two retired hurt. The 35,000-strong crowd exploded with rage and hurled abuse at the English team. The spectators' surly mood was shared by the Australian Board of Control which sent a telegram to the MCC (Marylebone Cricket Club) accusing the English team of unsports-manlike, aggressive tactics. If they were not immediately abandoned, it would 'upset friendly relations between England and Australia'. The MCC could not understand what the fuss was about, and there were hints in the British press that it was a case of sour grapes, since the English had at last found an answer to Australia's formidable batsmen. In its reply, the MCC stuck by what was being called 'bodyline' bowling and implied that Australian batsmen lacked manliness. As the cricket correspondent of the *Sphere* noted, 'Cricket may be a "nasty rough game", but let's go on play-ing it without the sob stuff.'[21]

Tempers eventually cooled down. Larwood continued to bowl 'body-line' balls, England won the Ashes, and the *Spectator* hoped the ruckus would not jeopardise future test matches, which were a 'bond of union . . .

between two sensible and friendly partners in the Commonwealth'.[22] Those outside the arcane world of cricket were amazed that large numbers of Australians and Englishmen could become obsessed with and over-heated by such a trivial matter during the weeks when Hitler took control over Germany and Franklin Roosevelt was sworn in as President of the United States. Whatever else it may have been, the bodyline brouhaha was an occasion when the affairs of the empire, albeit very minor ones, were at the centre of national consciousness.

On the whole, the British public was more familiar with the empire than it had been in any previous period. This is not to say that whenever people gathered in pubs, railway carriages or on the football terraces they fell to talking about the empire. At a time when the ordinary people of Britain were more concerned with knife-and-fork issues such as jobs, the means test and the prospects for industrial revival, such recondite matters as Indian constitutional reform or native policy in Kenya could hardly have been expected to stimulate much public interest. Nonetheless, through the wireless, cinema and lessons in school, more and more people were aware of the empire's existence. They were also, and this was most important, conscious of the empire as a valuable asset of which the British people could feel proud. Its public face was always a benevolent one, and its sub-jects appeared to be contented and glad to be British. The collective imperial image projected on the cinema screen or brought into people's homes by the annual royal broadcast was reassuring and, so to speak, exor-cised any feelings of guilt about oppression and exploitation.

At the time, the public knew that the empire was changing for it was, after all, a force for human progress. No one knew how long the present era of transition would last or in what form the empire would emerge. Neville Chamberlain, who became prime minister in 1937, imagined that India would only achieve full independence by 1980 at the earliest. Churchill thought in similar terms and, in 1937, wrote to the Viceroy, 'I want to see the British Empire preserved for a few more generations in its strength and splendour. Only the most prodigious exertions of British genius will achieve this result.' The strength and splendour of the empire were there for all to see as they watched newsreels of battleships steaming into Cape Town or Sydney harbours, conveying royal princes to their adoring subjects. But was the empire permanent? Probably not, but its pos-session was very comforting in a world which, after 1935, had suddenly become mutable and dangerous.

8

No Good Blustering: The Limits of Imperial Power, 1919–36

In 1924, Adolph Hitler called Britain 'the greatest world power on earth' and wrote, part in envy, part in awe of 'British world hegemony'.[1] His verdict, reached in a cell in a Bavarian prison and set down in *Mein Kampf*, was correct in all but one detail; Britain was the *only* global power in 1924. The pre-war European powers were in disarray: Russia was still recovering from seven years of civil war; France had been debilitated and was at the onset of an extended period of political instability; Germany had been gelded and truncated by the Versailles Treaty; and the Austro-Hungarian empire had been transformed into a patchwork of petty states. The United States, since 1890 the richest power in the world, had voluntarily isolated itself from the affairs of Europe and refused to divert its wealth into the warships, aircraft and armies needed for great power status. It continued to dominate its own backyard, Latin America, in much the same way as Japan, the only industrialised state in Asia, did the Far East. Britain alone had territories and interests everywhere and the means to safeguard them.

The backbone of Britain's power was its empire. 'Count the Empire as one, and we need call no other nation master,' trumpeted the *Morning Post* in May 1919.[2] No one, within or beyond Britain, would have questioned this statement, whose truth had been so recently demonstrated by the empire's contribution to the British war effort. The empire had given Britain more than men and war materials, it was the essential ingredient in British prestige. 'Prestige is what makes Great Britain a great power,' an American analyst observed at the outbreak of the Second World War.[3] He

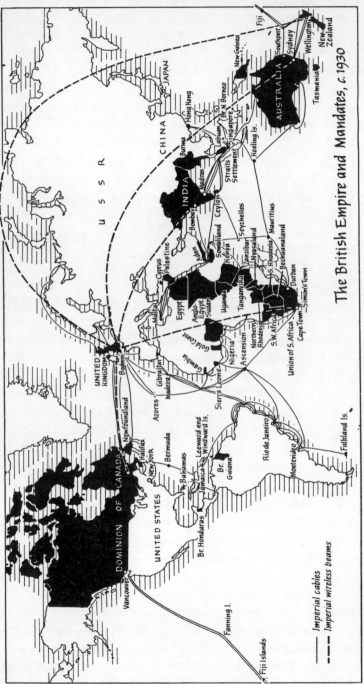

The British Empire and Mandates, c. 1930

Imperial cables
Imperial wireless beams

did not show precisely how this abstraction worked to Britain's advantage in international affairs, but then neither did those British statesmen, commanders and diplomats who invoked the word 'prestige' whenever crucial decisions had to be made.

Prestige counted most at a local level, particularly among those races in the Middle and Far East who had grown up in a world in which Britain was accustomed to getting its own way. Everyone knew what to expect; if the lion's path was crossed, it roared, bared its teeth and, when this was not enough, pounced. Prestige always carried with it the threat of force and so, ultimately, it was inseparable from the ability of Britain to square up to its enemies and beat them. Early in 1942, the reaction of Pathans on the North-West Frontier to the news that Singapore had fallen to the Japanese was 'one of disdain that so grave a reverse should have been suffered at the hands of such foes'.[4] Hitler agreed with them, and wondered if the world had grossly overestimated Britain's prestige during the past twenty years.[5]

Others were not taken aback by this turn of events. In 1934, a Japanese staff officer, reflecting the thoughts of many of his countrymen, stated that, 'The British empire is already an old man.'[6] His counterparts in American military and naval staff colleges were being encouraged to think in the same way.[7] Some inside Britain also concurred. The feebleness of Britain's response to affronts suffered by her subjects at the hands of Japanese troops in Tientsin in June 1939 dismayed Admiral Lord Chatfield, the First Sea Lord. Such incidents, he wrote, 'would have made a Georgian or Victorian statesman issue violent ultimatums'.[8] So they would, had the offending nation been unable to defend itself; but this point, well understood by former practitioners of gunboat diplomacy, was seldom appreciated either by subsequent statesmen or historians.

John Bull was still alive and kicking in those regions where no one was likely to kick back. An Egyptian looking at the line of battleships and cruisers anchored off Alexandria in 1936, while his government haggled over the terms of a new treaty with Britain, would have been in no doubt of this. Nor would the Chinese. In 1928 there were 11,000 British and Indian troops scattered across northern China, guarding British property and investments against the depredations of local warlords.[9] Gunboats still chugged up and down the Yangtze River and handed out condign retribution if British subjects were abused. There was more than a spark of Palmerstonian bravado in Sir Anthony Eden, the Foreign Secretary, who, in September 1937, proposed to sink the Spanish cruiser, *Canarias* if the Nationalists and their allies persisted in attacks on British shipping. In the end, there was no need for retaliation as the dispute was settled by diplomacy.

There was no question that the Mediterranean fleet could have knocked out a Spanish cruiser without difficulty. What mattered was whether the British government had the nerve to act so drastically. Hitler, whose yard-stick for a nation's political vitality was its willingness to act ruthlessly in its own interests, felt sure in 1924 that Britain's rulers still possessed the reso-lution necessary to preserve their empire. Various Indians, Egyptians and Arabs would have ruefully concurred. Later historians were far less certain. Those who have become engaged in tracing the path of Britain's decline as a global, imperial power have come to regard the inter-war years as a period during which Britain found it harder than ever to uphold its inter-national pretensions.

One possible explanation has been offered to explain this phenomenon. The thesis, advanced by Correlli Barnett, alleges that Britain's governors were psychologically unfitted to make the sort of decisions that were imperative if the country was to survive as a world power. The fault lay with their moral outlook, which was the product of ideas implanted in them by the public schools and universities of late-Victorian and Edwardian Britain.[10] That blend of evangelical Christianity, chivalric virtues, a sense of fair play, and a faith in man's ability to solve his problems through reason produced a breed of rulers who were mentally unprepared to face up to, let alone outwit, Hitler, Mussolini and Hirohito's generals and admirals.

Americans recognised few signs of mildness, moderation and a desire to conciliate among British ministers, diplomats and strategists. A 1931 State Department analysis of Britain's future detected a strong urge to recover lost ground and restore the country to the eminence it had enjoyed in the last century. The methods to be employed included 'a reversion to the Palmerstonian "damn your eyes" tradition in diplomacy'.[11] The first con-sultations between British and American staff officers in 1941 left the latter with the impression that they were dealing with an artful, grasping and hard-headed crew. After the conference at Argentia Bay in August, one American officer commented, 'One point which stood out in the British Papers was adherence to the long-established policy of directly organising other peoples to do the fighting necessary to sustain a mighty empire.'[12] From the President down, Americans knew that their partners could never be trusted. 'It was always the same with the British,' Roosevelt observed, 'they are always foxy and you have to be the same with them.' What also struck Americans was the chasm which separated Britain's public image and private conduct in international affairs. It was paradoxical that, in the words of one American minister, 'the British do not know how to play cricket'.[13]

Clearly, the Christian gentlemen who ruled Britain never behaved as if the Queensberry rules could be freely applied to all human activities, nor had their schooling neglected Machiavelli. Even those unaware of his texts would have learned something of his stratagems for survival from the everyday life of their public schools. Whatever these institutions professed in terms of providing moral and spiritual enlightenment, they were microcosms of the outside world, and, like it, were inhabited by the cunning, the vicious and the dishonest. For this reason alone, the men who emerged from public schools could never have been ignorant of the nasty side of human nature nor how to contend with it. As Americans discovered during the war, the British ruling class was a match for anyone when it came to underhand political sparring.

British power did not decline because its governors lived in a world of make-believe in which foreigners, even dictators, were all fundamentally decent chaps who played with a straight bat. Neville Chamberlain may have faced the newsreel cameras after Munich and attested to Hitler's trustworthiness, but he never for a moment imagined that a man whom, on first acquaintance, he had characterised as 'the commonest little dog' could ever act like an English gentleman.[14]

Yet Britain's behaviour before and during the Munich crisis was widely seen as evidence that the country's power had diminished. As will be explained later, the policy of appeasement was devised to assist the preservation of the empire when external circumstances had severely reduced Britain's scope for manoeuvre. Even so, and with hindsight, it is still possible to argue that for some years before Munich, and certainly after, British prestige had become a façade that masked a structure which was becoming more and more rickety. What had happened was that Britain's reputation as a global power had somehow outlived its actual strength in terms of wealth and economic capacity.

Photographs of derelict factories, idle cranes standing over empty shipyards, and disconsolate, jobless men at street corners are still the most familiar images of the British economy of the 1930s. They portray human as well as economic tragedy, and are supported by the statistics. Within two years of the Wall Street stockmarket crash of 1929, unemployment had soared to over 3 million, just over 20 per cent of the nation's workforce. The already vulnerable and decaying staple industries were hardest hit;

unemployment in ship-building and repair touched 62 per cent in 1932, and there were mass lay-offs from the textile mills, coal mines, iron and steel foundries and heavy engineering works, which were all concentrated in South Wales, the North and Scotland. During 1932 nearly half the national budget was dispersed in welfare payments, chiefly to the families of men without work. Recovery was gradual and patchy. Unemployment fell to 11 per cent by 1939, but the older industries remained in the doldrums. After 1937 the demand for housing in the South East and the Midlands, together with that for armaments, had triggered a limited revival whose effects were most marked in the growth of domestic demand for such 'new' products as radios, motor cars and refrigerators. But, as in the previous decade, expansion in modern industries was insufficient to take up the slack created by the terminal decay of the older.

Britain had endured and, up to a point, been able to come to terms with stagnation before 1914 largely because of its invisible earnings. Much foreign investment had been disposed of for ready cash during the war, and it was not replaced. The international demand for outside capital fell after 1918, and what there was tended to be met by American banks. Between the wars, corporate and private British investors were cautious, particularly after 1930, when there was an understandably nervous mood abroad. Low-risk, secure government stock, unit trusts, and building societies were therefore highly popular.

There had been, especially on the left, demands for government-directed investment policies as a means to redress both short and long-term economic deliquescence. The government preferred old nostrums, and so thrift, balancing the budget, and *laissez faire* were the order of the day during the Slump. Free trade, however, was killed off. Imperial preference was resuscitated by the 1931 national government, not as a visionary measure to bind together the empire, but as a desperate device to secure raw materials and cheap food, and to keep some outlets for industrial goods in a rapidly shrinking world market. The result was a series of agreements made during and after the 1932 Ottawa conference. Suggestions that Britain and the dominions might cooperate in Keynesian joint-investment schemes were pooh-poohed by the British government. A further economic link between Britain and the empire was the creation of the sterling block which was intended to defend the value of the pound when it, like the rest of the world's currencies, was sliding about helplessly. All dominion and colonial reserves were to be in pounds, and the exchange value of their individual currencies was pegged against the pound.

Government policies staved off disaster, but the economy remained frail. In 1937, there was a trade deficit of £302 million, which was reduced to £70 million by invisible earnings. By comparison, the force-fed, state-controlled economies of the dictatorships seemed to have pulled through the Slump rather more successfully than Britain's in terms of their share in the world's manufacturing output.

	Percentage of world's manufacturing			
	1929	*1932*	*1937*	*1938*
United States:	43.3	31.8	35.1	28.7
Russia:	5.0	11.5	14.1	17.6
Germany:	11.1	10.6	11.4	13.2
Britain:	9.4	10.9	9.4	9.2
France:	6.6	6.9	4.5	4.5
Japan:	2.5	3.5	3.5	3.8
Italy:	3.3	3.1	2.7	2.9

The peculiar circumstances of the global depression apart, Britain's position was weaker than these statistics suggest. Throughout this period British governments, always hesitantly interventionist, left too much to the market, as the immediate post-war decay of aircraft manufacture showed. At the same time, British exporters neglected such entrepreneurial techniques as selling, packaging and advertising. In 1921, virtually no British businessman was showing interest in the fast expanding Malayan market.[15] In the aftermath of the wartime rubber boom, Malaya imported goods worth nearly £100 million a year, of which Britain supplied a sixteenth. The default was most noticeable in the export of modern commodities. Nearly all Malaya's cars came from America, and the West African haulier bought Ford rather than Austin trucks for, in 1926, only 139 of the 2,400 lorries in the Gold Coast were British-made.[16] It was worse with the older export staples; 93 per cent of the cotton goods sold in East Africa in 1938 came from Japanese mills.[17] Moreover, capital for new imperial enterprises, like the copper mines of Northern Rhodesia or the oil wells of the Persian Gulf, was largely American.

Malayans drove Oldsmobiles, Ford wagons trundled along the streets of Accra, Kikuyu women wore cotton spun in Osaka, and New York financiers put up cash for mines in what had been Cecil Rhodes's backyard. As much as the locked factory gates in Rochdale or the closed shipyard on Clydeside, these were indicators of Britain's persistently poor economic performance. Did it then automatically follow that Britain's prestige was a sham and her power in terminal decay? Superficially, the answer would appear to be yes, but with qualifications. One measurement of international power was a nation's ability to channel its surplus wealth into weaponry. Here, Britain's record was still good: in 1938, Britain produced 7,940 aircraft, Russia 10,382 (many of poor quality), Germany 8,295, Japan 4,467, France 3,163, and the US 2,195. But Britain's survival in a world war would not only depend on her ability to produce armaments, she would have to find the wherewithal to purchase commodities abroad on a scale equal at least to that of the First World War. The decrease in value of overseas investments and a trade balance permanently in the red rendered such an undertaking extremely difficult. Britain's prestige may still have been high and its armed strength formidable by any standard, but, in the event of an emergency, the government would have to be sparing when it came to signing cheques. This fact of life considerably reduced Britain's freedom of action and made ministers, diplomats and strategists tread warily. As a diplomat, Sir Alexander Cadogan, told a sailor, Admiral Lord Chatfield, during the China crisis of 1937, it was 'No good blustering unless we are sure we can carry out our threats.'[18]

Before 1935 Britain's rulers did not expect to have to repeat the Herculean effort of 1914 to 1918. They had done everything in their power to construct and operate a system for international stability and peace based upon the League of Nations and a sheaf of non-aggression pacts, signed during the 1920s. What became known as collective security was not only a guarantee of a new international order in which war was outlawed, it created a world in which the empire would be protected and allowed to flourish. For this reason, as much as an idealistic faith in universal brotherhood, British statesmen tailored their policies to the principles of the League.

For a time, the League generated enough optimism to convince many of its supporters that a new millennium was imminent. Blind faith in the League was most pronounced between 1933 and 1936 when, ironically, collective security was on the verge of collapse. Almost in desperation, large sections of the public, mostly middle-class, succumbed to pacifism, and in various ways pledged themselves never to fight 'for King and Country'. This mood slowly vanished once it was obvious that no one in Berlin, Rome or Tokyo took any notice of self-indulgent moralising and peace ballots. Nonetheless, the government, while largely unmoved by the pacifist lobby, had to proceed carefully for fear of being branded as war-mongering.

Nor could Britain ignore the views of the dominions. They had joined the League as independent states and were wholeheartedly committed to collective security. When Britain had appealed for dominion assistance during the 1922 Chanak confrontation, Australia had pointedly suggested that it was a matter for the League's arbitration. A few months later, Stanley Bruce, who had represented Australia at the League, warned Britain that, 'We cannot submit blindly to any policy which may involve us in a war.'[19] Similar caveats came from South Africa, Canada and the Australian Labour party during the European crisis of August and September 1938. Even when collective security lay in ruins, Britain could no longer take for granted unqualified dominion support for its European policies.

The mainstay of collective security was international disarmament. Between 1920 and 1932, successive British governments had calculated their defence budgets on the understanding that there would be no general European war within ten years. A new balance of power was engineered in the Far East early in 1922, after Britain had refused to renew the alliance with Japan, largely in deference to the United States and Australia, neither of which had ever been happy with the arrangement. At the same time, restraints were imposed on the sizes of the great powers' fleets by the Washington Naval Treaty. Battleships were still the measurement of seapower, and so comparative naval strengths were fixed according to the following proportional scale:

	Battleships
Great Britain and the United States:	5
Japan:	3
France and Italy:	1.66

Similar ratios were allocated for cruisers, aircraft carriers and destroyers in 1930, although, oddly, no restrictions were placed on submarines.

Always touchy about real or imaginary racial snubs, the Japanese chafed at an agreement which consigned them to an inferior position, and were bitter about what they saw as Britain's rejection of them in favour of the Americans. There was disquiet too in the Admiralty about arrangements which effectively left the Imperial Japanese Navy sole master of the China Sea and the western Pacific. In 1919, Admiral Jellicoe had returned from Australia and New Zealand full of foreboding. He foresaw, with uncanny exactness, the 1941–2 'nanshinron' of the Japanese navy, army and air force, a relentless thrust southwards through south east Asia, Malaya, the

Dutch East Indies and the islands of the western Pacific. His colleague Beatty, now First Sea Lord, was also apprehensive about the scope of Japan's ambitions.

As Lord Salisbury had once wisely remarked, endless poring over maps was a dangerous activity. In his time, imperial strategists had been making everyone's flesh creep with scary tales about the grand masterplans of the empire's enemies, which had in the end come to nothing. Alarmist forecasts about Japanese expansionism were therefore greeted with scepticism in some quarters. Churchill and many others were certain that the Japanese were mentally and physically incapable of carrying through a campaign of conquest on the scale predicted by the scaremongers. Racial contempt for the Japanese was found at every level in the British and American governments throughout the 1920s and 1930s.[20] What had happened during the Russo-Japanese War had been forgotten; public men preferred to hark back beyond to the days when Asian armies had been swiftly and totally overwhelmed by smaller numbers of Europeans. This fatal purblindness was summed up by the observation made in 1934 by the British naval attaché in Tokyo. The Japanese, he told the Admiralty, have 'peculiarly slow brains'.[21]

The British may have felt racially superior to the Japanese, but they were not inclined to take chances with their former allies. In June 1921, the cabinet tempered its faith in collective security, and agreed in principle to the construction of a massive naval base on Singapore island, which was intended to tilt the delicate balance of power in the Far East in Britain's favour.

This proved to be one of the most significant decisions in the empire's history. It was also possibly the most ill-considered. The strategic thinking behind Singapore belonged to the eighteenth century. The base was designed as a modern Gibraltar, a reinforced concrete stronghold bristling with big guns commanding the passage between the Indian and Pacific oceans. In theory, it was intended to function as Gibraltar had done during the French wars, as the means of sustaining British seapower in distant waters. If the Japanese behaved as Jellicoe imagined they might, and advanced southwards, their path would be blocked by Singapore. In the meantime, a British battlefleet would assemble in home waters and set out to relieve the base. Even allowing for operational mischances such as bad weather and the Suez Canal being out of action, it was estimated that the relief force could reach Singapore within seventy days. On arrival, it would raise the siege, refuel, and then engage the Japanese navy. This was how

Gibraltar and British seapower in the Mediterranean had been saved at the end of the American war.

With a great deal of luck, this strategy might just have worked again if Singapore had been adequate for the task. It was not, thanks to Treasury economies. The total bill for the installations was £16.5 million with a further £9 million for the fuel oil that was to be stored at the base. This was all the Admiralty dared asked for from a Treasury short of cash and obsessed by thrift.[22] As a result, the dockyard facilities were too small for a fleet needed to take on the Japanese with any hope of winning. Nonetheless, construction started in 1923 and continued for the next fourteen years. During this time, the Australians and New Zealanders, for whom Singapore was the first and only line of defence, became increasingly uneasy about its usefulness and the viability of the strategy of which it was the keystone. Their disbelief was shared by senior naval officers serving in the Far East.[23]

In the event of a collision with Japan, Britain's actual muscle in the Far East consisted of an aircraft carrier, a handful of cruisers and a pack of destroyers, an unfinished base of doubtful efficiency nearly 3,000 miles from Tokyo, and a deterrent force 10,000 miles away on the other side of the world. In these circumstances, it was not surprising that British governments persevered with efforts to restore the old accord with Japan. As late as November 1934, Britain still believed that an Anglo-Japanese non-aggression pact was possible, even if it involved conceding Japan greater influence in China. The Japanese were not interested, and at the end of the year they withdrew from discussions on naval disarmament. 'Japan can no longer submit to the ratio system,' announced Rear-Admiral Yamamoto Isoroku, who would later mastermind the attack on Pearl Harbor. The invidious naval limitation treaties were due to expire at the end of 1936, and in January 1934 the Japanese government gave notice that after that date it would feel free to build as many warships as it needed.

Japan's belligerence was the result of its government slipping into the hands of a cabal of senior officers who upheld the ancient warrior codes of the samurai and preached modern, aggressive imperialism. They manipulated the *fainéant*, weathercock Emperor Hirohito, and promised national economic salvation through a mixture of conquest and autarky. Japan could protect itself from the world recession, acquire raw materials and markets, and feed its growing population through a programme designed to make China its economic dependency. Between 1929 and 1932 Japan overran Manchuria, acquiring its minerals and a springboard for future incursions southwards into China.

The balance of power in the Far East was now swinging against Britain. The Admiralty hoped it might be corrected by additional men-o'-war in the region, but, in 1934, the country could not afford such a gesture. The national government had been elected in 1931 because it was pledged to careful housekeeping and a balanced budget. Neville Chamberlain, the Chancellor of the Exchequer, therefore kept a tight hold on the purse strings, believing in the current wisdom that Britain's economic strength would prove its most powerful weapon in any future war. Imperialist blood ran in Chamberlain's veins: his father, Joseph, had made the empire his creed and had staked his career on it. The son was also an imperialist; he was convinced that the British empire was an unequalled force for good throughout the world and its maintenance took precedence over all other considerations, even his deep personal commitment to international peace.

During the first half of 1934, Chamberlain and his colleagues were faced with the problem of how to balance the nation's books and simultaneously safeguard its empire in a world which was about to revert to the law of the jungle. In February, a stark memorandum from the new Defence Requirements Committee identified Japan as posing an immediate danger to the empire, but predicted that in the long term Germany was the adversary most to be feared. Chamberlain had been among the first to interpret recent Japanese aggression, its departure from the League, and Hitler's coming to power as tokens of the impending collapse of collective security. Britain, had, therefore, to direct cash into rearmament, and, for Chamberlain, the first priority was home defence, particularly the enlargement of the RAF.

This was a traditional and proven response to an old problem. For the past two hundred years, governments had recognised that the empire's survival rested ultimately on the strength of its home base. As Chancellor, and the most forceful member of the cabinet, Chamberlain threw his weight behind a rearmament programme which channelled the bulk of available funds into projects for the defence of Britain rather than the overseas empire. His argument was unanswerable:

> . . . if we had to enter upon such a struggle [against Germany] with a hostile Japan in the East, if we had to contemplate the division of our forces so as to protect our Far Eastern interests while prosecuting a war in Europe, then it would be evident

that not only would India, Hong Kong, and Australia be in dire peril, but that we ourselves would stand in far greater danger of destruction by a fully armed and organised Germany.

This was the old strategic dilemma. How could Britain defend both its mainland and its empire in a global war? There was, however, a new and frightening dimension to the arithmetic of dispersing ships and men. In 1934 a European war would involve the extensive use of aerial bombardment by both sides. London had suffered extensive air raids during 1917–18, and the RAF had been preparing for a similar offensive against Berlin. Subsequent developments in aircraft design and chemical weapons meant that, in the event of war, Britain would be attacked again on a far greater scale. Prognoses about the extent of casualties and damage were uniformly chilling, with predictions of mass deaths and the possible dissolution of civil order in the larger cities. A glimpse of what might happen was provided during the Spanish Civil War when the Nationalist air force bombed Granollers, Barcelona and Guernica during 1937 and 1938. There was also the grim prospect of a repeat performance of the last war, for conventional military wisdom insisted that Britain would again contribute a mass army to the European battlefield.

These prospects and the recent upsurge in popular pacifism placed the government in a quandary. One way out was to jettison the League and the ideals of collective security and return to the old give-and-take power diplomacy of the pre-1914 era. This course was bound to offend a large and clamorous section of the public, especially on the left, which retained a faith in the League and was certain that rearmament increased the chances of war.

The effectiveness of the League was tested in 1935 in an episode which incidentally exposed the fragility of the empire's defences. Shortly before he had come to power in 1922, Mussolini had asserted that 'the Fascist ethos demanded the avenging of Adowa', and by the end of 1934 he was preparing for a showdown with Abyssinia. A border incident was the pretext for a quarrel which Haile Selassie, the Abyssinian emperor, referred to the League of Nations. By July 1935 it was clear that Italy would disregard the League's injunctions against aggression, which left no alternative to the imposition of economic sanctions. A naval blockade would have to be imposed on Italy, which Britain, as a League member, would be obliged to support with warships. France was unready and lukewarm, and the Mediterranean fleet needed eight weeks in which to be ready for action.

In anticipation of sanctions, reinforcements were hurried to the Mediterranean from the home fleet and the China, Pacific, American and West Indian stations.

This exercise had made the Admiralty twitchy for it was clear that Japanese planners would draw the obvious conclusion, which was that if Britain was forced to fight Italy for mastery of the Mediterranean, there would be no ships to spare for Far Eastern waters. 'The cable of Imperial Defence was stretched bar taut,' remarked Chatfield; 'Italy was the gnat whose weight could snap it.'[24] Worse still, the Suez Canal was now endangered since Italy had increased its Libyan garrison from 20,000 to 50,000, ten times the number of British troops in Egypt. Chatfield's observation has enormous significance even though he was by nature inclined to pessimism and, some thought, rather too willing to raise potential snags whenever a course of action was proposed. His predecessors at the Admiralty had faced similar difficulties, most notably in 1779 and 1797–8. But then there had been some lucky breaks and, above all, a willingness to gamble, a quality which was notoriously absent in Britain's leaders during the 1930s. Even if it had been present, it was very unlikely that the voters to whom they answered would have tolerated daring and risky policies which might easily have led to war.

Unlike their eighteenth- and early nineteenth-century counterparts, Britain's rulers were now circumscribed by the morality of collective security and the opinions of a mass electorate flirting with pacifism. Both ruled out a Copenhagen-style pre-emptive strike against the Italian navy which, at a stroke, would have saved the empire and blocked further aggression by Mussolini and Hitler. The temper of the times as much as the temperament of the country's rulers meant that the empire's strategic weakness was lamely accepted as a fact of life, and policies would be devised accordingly. Imperial decline was now underway.

With Britain effectively in check, Italy invaded Abyssinia in October. Six weeks after, the League announced a feeble programme of sanctions which, amazingly, gave the aggressor access to the Suez Canal and all the oil its war machine needed. As their ships entered Port Said, Italian sailors jeered at their British counterparts and some got knocked about in bars for their impudence. Britain had abdicated its control over the Mediterranean, and in December Sir Samuel Hoare, the Foreign Secretary, and his opposite number Pierre Laval (the future traitor) concocted a hugger-mugger deal which offered Italy two-thirds of Abyssinia as a placebo. There was a howl of rage from the left and the peace groups, who saw the bargain as a negation of all the League had represented and a return to the pre-1914 style of diplomacy in which the great powers bartered other peoples' countries. In Britain the indignation was so great that Hoare had to resign.

In March 1936, while Britain and France were still agonising over what, if anything, could be done to restrain Italy, Hitler reoccupied the Rhineland. Two months later, the Italian army marched into Addis Ababa. Within less than nine months, Italy had torn up the covenant of the League, and Germany had repudiated the Versailles territorial settlement. There were many in Britain, most notably Chamberlain, who, while dismayed, found themselves arguing that national interests were not imperilled. Germany had a moral right to its historic boundaries, and Italy had extended its empire by the annexation of a ramshackle, semi-barbaric state. Less than twenty years before, a lobby of Kenyan settlers had urged Britain to seize Abyssinia, 'a wonderful country in which you can grow two crops of everything'. 'Including dragon's teeth,' a Colonial Office official drolly minuted.

Chamberlain, his imperial thinking rooted in his father's age, was prepared to sanction a new partition of Africa if, like the old, it would help bring stability to Europe. A month before the Italians completed their conquest of Abyssinia, he wrote:

> I don't believe myself that we could purchase peace and a lasting settlement by handing over Tanganyika to the Germans, but if I did I would not hesitate for a moment to do so. It would be of more value to them than it is to us.

The empire's African subjects were appalled by what they saw as British dithering and impotence over Abyssinia. Nigerian nationalists interpreted Britain's behaviour as evidence of waning power. Elsewhere, black nationalists contrasted Britain's readiness to send troops to protect the Jews in Palestine with its callous abandonment of the Abyssinians to bombs and mustard gas. Subsequent public discussion of a possible redistribution of Britain's African colonies as part of a bargain with Germany further alarmed and angered black nationalists. Their persons and lands were still regarded as pawns in an international chess game, to be sacrificed when necessity demanded. Britain's credentials as a generous, benignant imperial power had been ripped to flinders.

The events of 1935–6 had greatly tarnished British prestige. The reinforcement of the Mediterranean fleet and the accompanying hostile noises about sanctions had turned Italy, a friend for the past seventy-five years, into an enemy, and demonstrated to Japan that the moment Britain became embroiled in a European conflict, her Far Eastern dependencies were defenceless.

9

We Shall Come to No Good: The Empire Goes to War, 1937–9

Neville Chamberlain became prime minister in May 1937. It was an office he had coveted for years, for he was vain, ambitious and relished the exercise of power. He also had a mission: Chamberlain believed that he alone could rescue Britain and its empire from the predicament they were now in, and possibly avert a European war. In many ways he was an unlikely national saviour, for he had made his reputation as a social reformer, knew little about diplomacy, and was thin-skinned, which was why he liked to surround himself with yes-men. He had none of the charisma of, say, Pitt or Lloyd George, and little presence. Once, when things were not going his way, Anthony Eden cruelly likened him to 'a turkey who has missed his Christmas'.[1]

Chamberlain was not helped by his prejudices. He had 'an almost instinctive contempt for the Americans and what amounted to a hatred of the Russians'.[2] A newcomer to the world of international negotiations, he assumed that they would be of a kind with which he was familiar, that between English bosses and workers.[3] This did not promise well, for the comparison took for granted a parity of goodwill and a joint willingness to reach an equitable compromise. But Chamberlain was persistent, confident of his abilities and unshakeable in his belief that he was acting in the best interests of Britain and its empire.

These were best served, he imagined, by a return to the old-fashioned way of conducting foreign policy, that is through give-and-take bargaining between powers. Those who agreed with him, and those who did not, called it appeasement. Appeasement had played a prominent part in Britain's relations with other nations throughout the eighteenth and nineteenth centuries. Then, Britain had encouraged transfers of territory which reduced tension in Europe and maintained a balance of power. To this end, Britain had been willing to evacuate Malta in 1802, surrender captured Dutch and French colonies in 1814–15, and at the same time permit Austria to govern much of northern Italy, and Russia Poland. Such arrangements left Britain free to devote her attention and resources to what really mattered, her overseas empire and interests. Both were in jeopardy in 1937, and could be saved only if a measure of stability was restored to Europe.

Appeasement offended consciences everywhere. Its end result was that the inhabitants of small, weak nations were forced to accept unwelcome rulers, and this blatantly violated those principles of self-determination that the League had stood for. Appeasement also meant an end to collective security and the revival of old-style, cynical power-broking. And not a moment too soon thought some on the right: 'What we require is to divest our diplomacy of cant, metaphysics, and the jargon of collective security, and to begin talking to Mussolini in terms of *Realpolitik*.' Only then, could Britain 'preserve the peace and protect our vital Imperial interests'.[4]

The left were horrified by this reversion to old methods and the jettisoning of the noble idealism which the League embodied. Then and after, Chamberlain's political enemies branded him as the arch-appeaser, the most culpable of the so-called 'Guilty Men' of left-wing mythology. The legend (a distillation of contemporary journalism, post-war historiography and Comintern propaganda) depicted appeasement as the instrument of capitalism. Abyssinia, the Spanish Republicans and Czechoslovakia were successively thrown to the Fascist wolves because they were the beasts which would eventually devour Russia, and with it Communism.

The Conservative government was the handmaiden of capitalism and its preservation was the sole object of Chamberlain's foreign policy. According to the Left Book Club's *The Road to War* (1937), the appeasement of Japan over Manchuria and China was being undertaken for sinister motives:

> It was literally unthinkable to our propertied classes that they should incur the slightest risk of war, or even of loss of trade

and investments, for a result that would most certainly include a social revolution in Japan! Hence the violently pro-Japanese feeling manifested in the City, by most of the Government press, and by a powerful section of the Conservative Party.[5]

Appeasement was therefore a device to frustrate the aspirations of the Japanese working class and, so the conspiratorial school of commentators believed, the masses everywhere. Such paranoid stuff had a wide circulation and many converts, including the Australian Labour party which suspected that Chamberlain was pro-fascist.[6]

Those who made the policies of appeasement did not think in terms of the struggle between ideologies, but of national survival. 'We shall come to no good, and I don't see how we're to defend our interests here, in the Med or in the F[ar] E[ast]. Most Depressing,' were Alexander Cadogan's thoughts on how matters stood in 1937.[7] Chamberlain did see a way out through short-term appeasement and long-term rearmament. As the latter gathered momentum, the need for appeasement would disappear, for the greatest threat to Britain's security, Hitler, would shrink from further aggression. But Hitler could only be deterred if he was isolated, and so Chamberlain needed to resuscitate cordial relations with Italy. Once Hitler was neutralised and Mussolini friendly, Britain could turn its attentions towards the Far East and Japan.

Chamberlain's quest for a stable Europe was accompanied by the acceleration of Britain's rearmament programme. Traditional, imperial strategic priorities were adhered to in a way that would have won the approval of any eighteenth- or nineteenth-century statesman, and as it turned out they held the key to the nation's deliverance in 1940. Home defence came first, with the RAF receiving the biggest share of the budget. The money was split between defence (Hurricane and Spitfire fighters and RADAR) and medium and long-range bombers for offensives against the industrial heartlands of Germany. Progress was impressive; by September 1939, when the programme still had three years to run, the RAF mustered 608 fighters and 536 bombers ready for action, 2,000 aircraft in reserve, and a further 425 deployed in the Middle East, India and Malaya.

These totals were, however, only superficially reassuring. Throughout the past five years, British policy-making had been pervaded by fears about the size and offensive capability of the Luftwaffe. Both were consistently overrated; at the outbreak of war it was officially calculated that Germany possessed over 2,000 bombers, whereas in fact it had 1,180 and 366 dive-bombers. One incubus spawned another. The government felt certain that the moment war was declared, if not before, the bulk of Hitler's airforce would be used for a sustained aerial bombardment of British cities. Hence the hurried construction of shelters, rehearsals of air-raid drill, distribution of gas masks, and the emptying of 50,000 London hospital beds in readiness for casualties during the Czech crisis in September 1938. These chilling preparations for a holocaust gave international crises a peculiar horror, and explain the heartfelt sense of national relief the moment it was known that Chamberlain had returned from Munich with a formula for peace.

Britain's second and third strategic priorities were the protection of the world's seaways and the defence of the empire; again, a policy which would have recommended itself to earlier statesmen. For practical and emotional reasons, Chamberlain was opposed to the despatch of a second massive expeditionary force to the Franco-Belgian frontier. The promise of such an army would discourage the French from extending the Maginot Line from the southern border of Belgium to the Channel coast, and would commit Britain to another extended, bloody war of attrition in Flanders. As a result, the army was pushed to the back of the queue for cash. It was, therefore, ill-equipped for a European war when, in February 1939, Chamberlain reluctantly consented to sending an expeditionary force to those same fields where another had nearly bled to death between 1914 and 1918.

Since October 1935, British military intelligence had been closely following developments in the German army. Most important of these were the creation of Panzer divisions and the novel theories of close cooperation between tanks and aircraft known as *Blitzkrieg*. If, as seemed very likely, the Wehrmacht was embarking on a new type of mobile warfare, the British army was not ready to counter it.[8] Britain lagged behind in the tank race; a lack of funds slowed down the formation of armoured divisions, and none was ready for deployment during the battle for France in May 1940. The demand for anti-aircraft batteries meant that there were serious shortages in artillery of other kinds, including anti-tank guns, which were not expected to be remedied before 1942.

Britain's authority at the conference tables of Europe and its military muscle depended ultimately on support from the empire. This had never been more vital for, in 1931, the total white population of Britain and the

Commonwealth had stood at 67 million, of whom 19 million lived in the dominions. As in the period before 1914, Britain needed the assurance that, in the event of war, the dominion governments would fall into line and deliver their quotas of fighting men, ships and aircraft.

It was again imperative to take the dominion governments into Britain's confidence and explain to them the aims of its foreign policy and outline possible wartime strategy. A Commonwealth conference, the first for six years, was called at the beginning of 1937, and at the centre of its proceedings was an assessment of Britain's present and future position, compiled by the chiefs of staff. At its heart lay the inescapable fact that Britain's defeat in a continental war 'would destroy the whole structure of the Commonwealth, which in its present state could not long exist without the political, financial and military strength of the United Kingdom.'[9] As Sir Edward Grey had made clear over twenty years before, without Britain the dominions were isolated and unable to fend for themselves. This being so, and Germany the hypothetical enemy, Britain would commit itself to the defence of the Low Countries and France and would expect dominion assistance.

Outside Europe, Indian troops would be deployed in the Middle East and Egypt if Italy threw in its lot with Germany. Singapore remained the key to the defence of the Far East and Australasia in the by now very likely event that Japan would attempt to acquire forcibly raw materials in Borneo, the western Pacific and the Dutch East Indies, the latter now designated 'a major British interest'. Singapore was still beyond the range of Japan's land-based bombers, but if this immunity disappeared, Britain would shift additional squadrons to Malaya from the Middle East, relying on the South African airforce to replace them. This arrangement proved inadequate since the RAF was understrength in the Middle East, and by the spring of 1939 it was under pressure to transfer aircraft from India to Singapore in the event of an emergency. Breaking point had been reached. As Sir Cyril Newall, the chief of air staff, observed, fewer aircraft in India would force the government there to adopt a less aggressive stance on the North-West Frontier, which would of course diminish British prestige.[10]

The question of how to defend Singapore was naturally the concern of the Australian and New Zealand delegates to the conference. They were assured that the promised relief armada would sail and would pass unhindered through the Mediterranean and Suez.[11] The Australian Prime Minister, Joseph Lyons, was not satisfied, and proposed either a *rapprochement* with Japan or a Pacific defence pact that would include the one power which possessed the means to withstand Japanese aggression swiftly, the United States. This suggestion was squashed by Anthony Eden, the Foreign Secretary, for its acceptance would have been tantamount to an admission that Britain could no longer defend its empire unaided.[12] Undercurrents of doubt about Singapore's impregnability remained, and there were darker suspicions that once Britain had become entangled in a European war circumstances would force it to abandon Singapore, and with it Australasia.

These fears were partly confirmed when Britain dragged its heels in providing aircraft for Australia's rearmament programme. Potential allies in the Mediterranean came first on British aircraft manufacturers' list of priorities; orders from Rumania, Greece and Turkey took precedence over those for the Royal Australian Air Force (RAAF) between 1937 and 1939.[13] In exasperation, Lyons turned to the American suppliers, Lockheeds, and ordered fifty Hudson bombers in 1938. The following year, American-made engines had to be fitted to Beaufort fighter-bombers, recently delivered from Britain.[14] Henceforward, the United States and not Britain would be Australia's main arsenal; the old rule by which the dominions only used British or locally made equipment was quietly dropped.

Local problems and doubts about Britain's ability to solve them were beginning to nudge Australia towards America's orbit. Internal politics and an unsentimental view of its own, rather than the empire's interests, dictated Canada's foreign policy. Ever since the Chanak crisis in 1922, Canada had made it clear that its parliament alone would decide whether or not it went to war. Canada could afford to take an independent line since it enjoyed the immeasurable advantage of closeness to the United States, which, following the Monroe Doctrine, could reasonably be expected to take care of Canada's only vulnerable region, its Pacific seaboard. Inside Canada, the racial mix ruled out unquestioning attachment to Britain and the Commonwealth. Its 11-million population was split three ways; just over half were of British stock, a quarter French, and the rest Red Indians and the descendants of central and eastern European immigrants. Imperial loyalty remained solid in some sections of the English-speaking community, but there was an equally sturdy and growing sense of a purely Canadian identity. In 1925, prospective immigrants were warned: 'Don't forget that a Canadian-born Britisher is just as good as an English-born one, and that he won't be patronised.'[15]

The assay of Commonwealth fidelity or, one might say, biddableness came during the autumn of 1938. The issue was Hitler's claim to the Sudetenland, that region of Czechoslovakia whose inhabitants were predominantly German. Chamberlain, harking back to his father's time, likened the Sudeten Germans to the Transvaal's Uitlanders, a people also stranded in a foreign land whose affinities were elsewhere.[16] He reconciled himself to the eventual merging of Sudetenland with the Reich, which he agreed with Hitler during a personal meeting at Berchtesgaden in mid-September. What Chamberlain and a majority of the British public could not stomach was Hitler's next demand, for an immediate military occupation of the disputed Czech territory. Suddenly, and much to Chamberlain's distress, the question had changed to one of war or peace; would Britain and France resist a German invasion of Czechoslovakia?

British public opinion was divided and the dominions shrank from committing themselves. For the Australian government, 'almost any alternative is preferable to involvement in a war with Germany in the event of the latter forcibly intervening in Czechoslovakia.'[17] Anti-war sentiment was even more marked in Canada, where violent racial clashes were expected if the matter came to a parliamentary debate.[18] Mackenzie King, the Prime Minister, therefore trod warily, privately admitting his sympathy for Britain, but publicly opposing a war over Czechoslovakia.[19] The South African government, conscious that Afrikaner nationalist opinion was against a war, also signalled its unwillingness to fight for the Czechs.[20] Ireland had already served notice of its neutrality. It was Chanak all over again, and yet, on the eve of his last-minute attempt to avert a war, Chamberlain spoke to the nation as if he headed a united empire: 'However much we may sympathise with a small nation confronted by a big and powerful neighbour, we cannot in all circumstances undertake to involve the whole British empire in a war simply on her account.'

The truth was that Britain had not convinced the dominions that the integrity of Czechoslovakia was worth fighting for. Chamberlain flew to Munich at the end of September full of uncertainty. If his talks with Hitler broke down and war followed, he could not rely upon a Canadian expeditionary force to materialise or Anzacs to rush to the defence of the Suez Canal. Furthermore, France was wobbling; most of the battlefleet was refitting; and Britain's rearmament programme still had a long way to go. Czechoslovakia had to be left to its fate and Chamberlain went home with Hitler's promise that all remaining Anglo–German differences would be amicably resolved. It was 'peace in our time' he announced, echoing Disraeli's words in 1878 when he returned from the Congress of Berlin.

The choice of words was unintentionally apt, for Chamberlain, like Disraeli, was accused of following a course dictated by expediency rather than morality. The British public was undoubtedly relieved by the peaceful resolution of the crisis, even though it had been an exercise in buying time and was seen as such. Pragmatism had triumphed at Munich, as it had in 1877–8 when Disraeli had resisted the pressure of the high-minded, who had insisted that Britain had a moral duty to support those Balkan nationalists who were struggling for freedom, rather than to back Turkey. Sixty years after, there was a similar wave of protest from a coalition, embracing right and left and including Churchill, which saw the crisis in purely moral terms with Czechoslovakia as the hapless victim of injustice. Predictably, this group bitterly denounced Munich as a cowardly and cynical sell-out. But, Chamberlain's supporters argued, Britain could not seriously contemplate entering a European war over a region where she had no interests when she was being threatened in areas where she had many, all of them vital. It was a view expressed by a young correspondent to the *Spectator*, who argued that 'my generation . . . is not prepared to fight for the integrity of various territories in Central and Eastern Europe which contain big and discontented minorities.' It would, he claimed, fight for India, the dominions, the colonies and France.[21]

Imperial security had been uppermost in Chamberlain's mind when he had gone to Munich. 'If only we could get on with Germany, I would not care a rap for Musso,' he had once remarked.[22] Ever since he had become prime minister and virtually taken over the direction of foreign policy, Chamberlain had endeavoured to reach an understanding with Mussolini that would preserve Britain's strategic position in the Mediterranean. There was an urgency about Chamberlain's overtures to Italy which owed much to the service chiefs' unrealistic assessments of the strength and capabilities of its army and navy.[23] The result was the ironically named 'gentlemen's agreements' of 1938 by which Britain, and later Australia and Canada, recognised Italy's occupation of Abyssinia, and Italy promised to accept the *status quo* in the Mediterranean.

These accords reflected Chamberlain's utter failure to comprehend the nature of Italian fascism and the personality of its leader. Neither could tolerate the *status quo* in any form; fascism was about continual, often frenzied action and radically transforming the existing order of things. This perpetual political motion included imperial expansion and Mussolini constantly bragged about the new Roman empire which he would create. At the close of 1938, well-rehearsed fascist deputies, heartened by Hitler's acquisition of the Sudetenland, demanded Corsica, Tunisia, and France's colony of Djibouti at the foot of the Red Sea. Early in the new year, Mussolini threw down the gage to Britain in a belligerent speech to his ministers:

> Italy is washed by the waters of the Mediterranean. Her links with the rest of the world are through the Suez Canal, an artificial channel which could easily be blocked, even by accident, and through the Straits of Gibraltar, commanded by the guns of Britain. Italy therefore has no free access to the oceans; she is actually a prisoner in the Mediterranean, and as her population grows and she becomes more powerful, the more she suffers in her prison. The bars of that prison are Corsica, Tunisia, Malta and Cyprus, and its guards are Gibraltar and Cyprus.[24]

At some date in the future Italy would break free from this gaol, an escape which would inevitably lead to war with Britain and France. In the meantime and in spite of official protests, Radio Bari broadcast anti-British propaganda to the Arabs and Egyptians, and the Italian consul in Kabul offered covert help to the tribesmen of the North-West Frontier.[25] In private, Mussolini described Britain as a decrepit, weary nation which, in the fascist nature of things, would inevitably have to give way to a youthful and virile imperial power.

This judgement was also being reached in different parts of the empire, where British moral reputation and prestige had been tarnished by the Italian agreements and Munich. After Eden's resignation as Foreign Secretary early in 1938 in protest against Chamberlain's policies, the *Gold Coast Spectator* predicted that, 'Eden may come back as a Premier of Great Britain, and early too; a terror to dictators, and a bulwark against attacks upon the traditional character of all Britons and the liberty of Britain.' In November 1938, Sierra Leone nationalists declared that by acknowledging Italian sovereignty over Abyssinia, Britain had stepped down from 'the pedestal of Justice and Equity'.[26]

For the rest of the world, Munich had been an object lesson in British impotence. In October 1938, the *Economist* gloomily noted a sudden increase in contempt for British power:

> From Palestine it is reported that the new boldness and aggressiveness of the Arabs is due to their belief that they can

negotiate with the British Empire as equals. In the Far East, the Japanese descent on Southern China, which, if it does not actually invade Hong Kong is designed to ruin its trade, is ascribed to Japanese confidence that the Western powers need not be seriously considered.[27]

Sir Alexander Cadogan was of similar mind; he feared that Japan's assault on China and indifference towards British commercial interests there were a signal to the rest of Asia that Britain now counted for less and less in the world. Chamberlain may have staved off a war that Britain and a disunited Commonwealth were unready to fight, but the hidden price of appeasement had been high. Serious damage had been inflicted on Britain's moral and political standing within the empire and throughout the world.

After Munich, Hitler continued to order the pace and course of events, and their direction was towards war. There was no ambiguity in the unending rant of a man who believed with all his heart that, 'War is eternal and everywhere. There is no beginning and no peace treaty.' He was Napoleon reborn, a megalomaniac who could never be trusted and was prepared to risk everything to get what he wanted. His nature and the compass of his ambitions were now fully understood by many members of the government and the great majority of the British public. There was, however, a band of appeasers silly enough to imagine that Hitler could still somehow be bought off. At the beginning of 1939, one of the more abject went so far as to argue that Germany's old African colonies should be returned, a shameful stratagem which even Chamberlain had abandoned.[28] It is of more than passing interest that he, and others who ought to have known better, ever contemplated the transfer of colonies which had enjoyed twenty years of humane British rule to a régime that was now a byword for brutality.

Chamberlain's confidence in his policy refused to wilt in the face of reality. Much to his irritation, the Foreign Office was prepared to abandon wishful thinking about the dictators' honesty. At the end of January 1939, it warned the Australian government that intelligence sources indicated that Hitler was now poised to undertake fresh 'foreign adventures' in eastern Europe, possibly with an eye to the occupation of the Ukraine. Alternatively, and this was a reminder to the Australians how much their fate was tied to Britain's, he might overrun Holland and afterwards deliver the Dutch East Indies to Japan.[29] At the same time, fears persisted that Hitler might suddenly order a pre–emptive aerial strike against Britain.

In the event, Czechoslovakia was Hitler's next target. On 15 March his army occupied the rump of that country. The jackal followed the lion, and on 7 April Mussolini invaded Albania. Chamberlain was stunned; he had been hoodwinked and took the dictators' actions as a personal affront. 'Musso has behaved to me like a sneak and a cad,' he complained to his sister.[30] Reluctantly, after much agonising, and under intense parliamentary and public pressure, he reversed the course of British foreign policy. On the last day of March, he pledged Poland every support if Germany threat-ened its independence. If Britain went to war, it would be in response to Hitler's aggression. Chamberlain was never a wholehearted convert to a policy which, in effect, dared Hitler to begin a war. He kept his blind faith in the possibility that further compromises might be contrived which would postpone a general European conflict until Britain was strong enough to deter Hitler. This was a forlorn hope from a statesman whose nostrums had manifestly failed and whose authority was consequently diminished. Having played the leading part in British diplomacy since May 1937, Chamberlain slipped into the sidelines during the late spring and summer of 1939 when Britain was busy seeking allies, most notably the Soviet Union.

Commonwealth solidarity was now vital, but the dominions remained nervous about following Britain into a European war. According to Smuts, there was 'no enthusiasm' for Poland in South Africa, even at the end of August when its invasion seemed imminent.[31] Canada had refused to add its name to the Anglo-French guarantee of Polish integrity, although Mackenzie King promised he would recommend his parliament to declare war if Britain was directly attacked. A spiritualist, King did try to invoke occult powers in an effort to penetrate Hitler's mind, but without success. He was luckier during a visit to London in 1942, when he made contact with Florence Nightingale (who advised him about his health), Anne Boleyn and Queen Victoria during a séance. [32]

Australia was in a quandary: her government had to choose between delivering a blank cheque to Britain to be cashed on a European battlefield or consolidating resources to deal with a peril closer to home, Japan. Conservatives favoured the former course. 'Either we go forward,' argued Sir Earle Page, leader of the Country Party, 'with the rest of the Empire, secure and prosperous, because of the Empire's strength or we are to turn aside upon some lonely road . . . never to be free from the menace of covetous peoples.'[33] John Curtin, the Labour party leader, was unconvinced by this classic imperial argument. 'Australia First!' was his party's slogan, which in practical terms meant devoting all the country's wealth and manpower to defence, in particular the reinforcement of the RAAF.[34]

Behind this debate lay anxieties about British strategy in the Far East. The start of the Sino-Japanese war in 1937, and early Japanese successes, had driven Australia and New Zealand to rearm rapidly. Both dominions became more and more frantic in their demands for reassurances that Singapore would be relieved come what may. On the eve of his pledge to Poland, Chamberlain personally affirmed that, 'in the event of war with Germany and Italy, should Japan join in against us it would still be His Majesty's Government's full intention to despatch a fleet to Singapore.'[35] His message disturbed Australians and New Zealanders, for it failed to answer the question that mattered most to them; how many ships were to be sent? Chamberlain's subsequent refusal to send a battlefleet to the Far East as a demonstration of power, on the grounds that its departure might tempt Mussolini to precipitate action in the Mediterranean, confirmed the unspoken fear that in the event of a war, European fronts would always have first call on Britain's resources.[36] With this in mind, the new Australian prime minister, Robert Menzies, broadcast to his people at the end of April that when war came they would fight alongside Britain, but, as things then stood, 'not on European battlefields, but defending our own shores'.

Even so, Australia still needed the Royal Navy's battleships and aircraft carriers. When this matter was raised in June by the Australian high commissioner in London, H. A. Bruce, he found Admiral Chatfield, the new coordinator of defence, hard to pin down on just how many battleships would be available for the relief of Singapore. He was told that, despite recent clashes over British interests in China, Britain expected Japan to keep out of a general war. In which case, the destruction of the Italian navy would have priority.[37]

The strategy of which Singapore had been the lynchpin had been overtaken by events which left it in disarray. In February, the Japanese had seized Hainan Island, 250 miles south of Hong Kong, and a month later occupied the Spratly Islands, 650 miles to the north-east of Singapore. Taking these developments into account, Anglo-French staff planners concluded in June that Singapore was no longer the Gibraltar of the Far East. Its future security would depend upon a network of airfields across the Malay Peninsula which would have to be defended by infantry and anti-aircraft batteries.[38]

For the first time since the American War, Britain clearly lacked the wherewithal to defend its empire adequately. The safety of Britain's possessions in the Indian and Pacific oceans depended upon a battlefleet based at Alexandria, which had to stay there as long as the Italian navy could put to sea. Menzies foresaw disaster, and, in September, pleaded with Chamberlain to persuade the French to release Tunis and Djibouti and so keep Mussolini quiet.[39] He seemed to have learned nothing from the lessons of the past eighteen months, which had proved beyond doubt that limited concessions merely whetted the dictators' appetites for bigger prizes.

The urgent demands of Australia's security had taken High Commissioner Bruce to the United States, the country which now held the key to the Pacific. He had questioned President Roosevelt as to how America might react if a Japanese battlefleet steamed south across the Equator, and was told, 'You need not worry.'[40] In Britain, Churchill had already concluded that the preservation of Britain's Far Eastern and Pacific territories rested in the hands of the United States. At the outbreak of war, Smuts expressed the hope that America, which now held 'the last resources of our human causes' would soon intervene.[41]

The United States and Britain were not natural partners, despite a common language and attachment to democratic principles. Their relations after 1919 had been polite, frosty and tinged with mutual suspicion. Chamberlain, disheartened by the United States's unwillingness to make common cause with Britain over China, believed that Americans were unreliable in all things. State Department policy-makers were always on their guard against becoming ensnared in the schemes of a power whose rulers were imagined to be exceptionally self-seeking and devious.[42] There was, however, a deeply-felt Anglo-American concern for international stability, but no way was found to translate this into joint action.

The largest stumbling block to Anglo-American cooperation was trade. Since the 1932 Ottawa Conference, Britain had stuck to the protectionist policy of imperial preference, which was wormwood to Cordell Hull, Roosevelt's Secretary of State. Hull was a passionate believer in international free trade and he channelled his considerable energies into the negotiation of what he called (he spoke with a lisp) a 'wecipwocal twade agweement pwogam to weduce tawiffs'.[43] Britain with its imperial trading block, and Japan, Germany and Italy, whose economic policies were based on autarky, were not interested for fear that they might be overwhelmed by American competition.

A further impediment to an Anglo-American partnership was the isolationist tradition which had been strengthened by memories of the United States's involvement in the First World War. 'Any question of intervention in Europe was always connected with enormous loss' by American public opinion, reported H.A. Bruce after his visit in 1939. As Roosevelt appreciated, Americans needed to be educated about Europe, and myths about its cynical power-broking diplomacy dispelled. This was far from easy in the wake of Britain's recognition of Italy's dominion in Abyssinia and the partition of Czechoslovakia.

Furthermore, there existed in America a widespread distrust of colonial powers, which tended to be directed against Britain since its empire was the one most familiar to Americans. Roosevelt was not immune from this anti-imperialism; when, during 1941, the Japanese took over Indo-China, he remarked, 'Anything must be better than to live under French colonial rule.'[44] On the other hand, naval and military men regarded the British empire as a source of international stability and therefore not to be tampered with.

These sources of misunderstanding, together with the American peoples' unwillingness to get involved in the chaotic and dangerous affairs of distant countries, rendered an Anglo-American understanding impossible before 1939. Ideological enmity and hesitant diplomacy ruled out the inclusion of Russia in the Anglo-French front. Hitler also needed the Soviet Union, although he was no more frightened of its power in the summer of 1939 than he was two years later when he attacked Russia. What he did need was a cooperative, neutral Soviet Union, which would leave him free to deal with Britain and France and allow him access to Russian raw materials. He got both in the German–Soviet Pact at the end of August. The way across Poland was now open and the German army launched its invasion on 1 September.

Britain declared war on 3 September with a BBC broadcast by Chamberlain in which he harped on about the personal slights he had suffered from the man he had trusted. More inspiring, perhaps, was the legendary cable which arrived in London from the West Indies: 'Don't worry; Barbados is with you.' So too were the rest of the colonies which, of course, had no choice, and India, where, as has been seen, the Viceroy's declaration of war upset the Congress party.

Australia had followed events in Europe closely, despite having had some difficulty in extracting secret documents from the British government. On

25 August, Menzies had broadcast to the people, reminding them that, 'We in Australia are involved, because the destruction or defeat of Great Britain would be the destruction and defeat of the British Empire, and leave us with a precarious tenure of our own independence.' The same arguments had prevailed in 1914 and again swung Australia and New Zealand behind Britain.

In South Africa the ruling United party (formed in 1934 to reconcile Boers and British) favoured benevolent neutrality. When this was put to the parliament, eighty members voted against and sixty-seven for, forcing the Prime Minister, General Hertzog, to resign on 5 September. His deputy, Smuts, took power after the governor-general had rejected a call for a general election, and South Africa entered the war. Boer extremists were bitter; many openly sympathised with Naziism and one, the future architect of apartheid, Dr Malan, proclaimed that, 'The Union of South Africa has sunk to the level of a vassal state of Europe.' Fears that French Canadians would strenuously oppose the war quickly evaporated. Mackenzie King gave notice of his emotional support for Britain in a broadcast on 3 September, and seven days after sought parliamentary approval for a declaration of war, which was accepted without a division. Maurice Duplessis, the Quebec Nationalist leader, dissolved his province's assembly and called a general election in October. It proved a damp squib; pro-war candidates took sixty-eight of the eighty-six seats.

The Commonwealth and empire went to war in the first week of September, but its unity had by no means been unquestioning or instantaneous. There was none of the emotional, patriotic shenanigans of August 1914; rather the mood of the public was sober and businesslike. A hard task lay ahead, and those about to get down to it rolled up their sleeves rather than unrolling and waving flags. They were about to fight the 'People's War', and, when it was over the people, not only in Britain but throughout the empire, would expect a reward for their toil.

10

Finest Hour:
The Empire at War,
1939–41

In a talk entitled 'What the Empire Means for Us', broadcast in October 1940, the Colonial Secretary, Lord Lloyd, warned his audience that the Axis 'gangsters' wanted to get their hands on the 'glittering prizes' of Britain's colonies. But they would not be easily taken; a West African chieftain had lately written to the Colonial Office describing how he had disinterred an ancient flintlock musket for use against the king's enemies. The old warrior added: 'In the day of rejoicing such as Coronation, my country is representing in London, so why not now Europe is at agony, my country must share it also. Being a poor man I can only bring my service.'[1] It was a touching statement of loyalty, which must have struck a chord with most listeners in a country that was desperately fighting for its life, and where Home Guard volunteers drilled with antique shotguns.

The past year had witnessed the 'phoney war', that interlude of watchful inertia between the collapse of Poland and Hitler's lightning attack in the West. During May and June 1940 the Wehrmacht and Luftwaffe had swept through Belgium, Holland, Denmark and Norway. Seeing which way the wind was blowing, Mussolini had declared war on 11 June. Four days after, the French government opened negotiations which ended with its unconditional surrender on the 18th. Britain's position was now extremely perilous. For the first time since 1806 it lacked allies and faced a Europe whose manpower and industry were at the disposal of a tyrant intent on the destruction of Britain and the eventual dispersal of its empire. During the earlier crisis the imperial base had been relatively safe, thanks to an unbeaten and superior battlefleet, but in the summer of 1940 Britain was vulnerable to aerial attack and a cross-Channel invasion. The situation seemed hopeless, and in Washington General George C. Marshall, the US Chief of Staff, and many others predicted that Britain would be knocked out of the war within six weeks.[2]

What followed was the British people's 'finest hour'. The phrase was Churchill's and part of a stirring call to arms delivered on 18 June, just over a month after he had become prime minister: 'Let us therefore be braced to our duties, and so bear ourselves that, if the British Empire and its Commonwealth last for a thousand years, men will say: "This was their finest hour."' Among the listeners may have been the Geordie workman, overheard in a pub describing Churchill as one of 'them pig-sticking buggers from India' who had at last found the fight he had been looking for throughout his career. Nevertheless, the speaker was prepared to get stuck in with him.

As the Tynesider and everyone else knew, Churchill's long military and political career had been bound up with the empire. In 1897 he had fought Pathans on the North-West Frontier; a year later he had charged with the 21st Lancers at Omdurman; and then he had waged war against the Boers, who briefly held him prisoner. The imperial *beau sabreur* became the imperial statesman, and Churchill twice occupied the Colonial Office, first as a Liberal under Asquith and later under Lloyd George.

Churchill's imperialism was complex and at times contradictory. On a broad level, he never wavered in his belief that the empire gave Britain its international power and authority, and imperial government bestowed peace and prosperity on peoples who could not achieve either unaided. In this he was, as Lord Moran, his physician and chronicler of his indiscretions, observed, a child of his age. 'It is when he talks of India or China that you remember he is a Victorian,' Moran noted in 1943. Churchill thought in terms of a carefully graded racial hierarchy, once remarking, 'When you learn to think of a race as inferior beings it is difficult to get rid of that way of thinking; when I was a subaltern the Indian did not seem to me equal to the white man.'[3] In fact, his racial attitudes were not as simple as this, for he swung between extremes of harshness and humanity when it came to the treatment of the empire's subjects. In 1903 he praised the Tibetans for defending their native soil against Curzon's invading army; sixteen years later he approved the use of poison gas against Kurds and Pathans who were doing the same thing; and in 1921 he accused Dyer of callousness at Amritsar. Churchill the Victorian liberal was a staunch champion of Zionism, and had wanted to improve the lot of the Egyptian fellahin, but not the Kikuyu, for he supported Kenya's white settlers.

On India his views were fixed and fearsome. When, in 1921, an Indian delegation from Kenya attempted to explain how they had helped develop the colony, they were put down with the remark, 'You would not have invented the railway let alone constructed it.'[4] His subsequent outbursts on Indian self-government had been so intemperate that Eden wondered whether they might disqualify him from ever becoming prime minister.

In June 1940 the empire which Churchill so vigorously upheld was fighting for its existence against what seemed overwhelming odds. He ignored these, and declared that he would wage war with the utmost energy, resolution and, when necessary, ruthlessness. His willingness to persevere come what may made him the equal of the two Pitts and Lloyd George at his best. Churchill's rhetoric, like Henry V's at Harfleur and Agincourt, set the tone of Britain's war. His words summoned up the blood and stiffened the sinews of men and women in factories and mines, on farms and battlefields. He could also provide that 'little touch of Harry in the night' which enkindled hope and courage. General Lord Ismay recalled how, when Churchill toured Bristol in 1941 after an air raid, he entered a rest centre where an old woman, whose house and possessions had been destroyed, sat weeping disconsolately. When the Prime Minister appeared, 'she took her handkerchief from her eyes and waved it wildly shouting, "Hooray, hooray."'

What Churchill said and did created a sense of national unity and purpose which was unprecedented and will probably never be revived. There was, and is for those who are its beneficiaries, something deeply moving about that spirit of 1940. Its lustre will certainly survive the smears applied recently by writers who either dislike its collectivist overtones or are impelled by an urge to whittle away every source of national pride.[5]

Churchill guided the country through the twelve months between the surrender of France and Hitler's invasion of the Soviet Union on 22 June 1941, during which time Britain and its empire alone defied the Axis powers. Throughout this year and for the next four, Churchill spoke and acted as if the empire would outlast the war and continue unchanged thereafter. There was, therefore, an extraordinary paradox in the fact that his greatest stroke of genius was the recognition that Britain's survival depended ultimately on America, a nation whose rulers and citizens were instinctively hostile towards the British empire.

Not that this mattered greatly in the summer of 1940, when American arms and equipment were desperately needed. As well as the products of American industry, Churchill wanted the goodwill of the United States. Even if America did not fight, and Churchill thought that it would eventually, its moral backing counted for much with those already engaged in the struggle and in the world at large. America's moral support as well as its weaponry was an assurance that even if Britain could not win single-handed, it could not be beaten.

America took time to swing behind Britain. During June and July 1940 senior officials and commanders favoured conserving America's resources rather than delivering them to a nation which appeared to be on the verge of defeat. Two months of prevarication followed Churchill's request for fifty redundant destroyers in return for bases in the West Indies. The deal was finally agreed at the beginning of August after American opinion had faced up to the possible consequences of a Europe dominated by Hitler and Mussolini. There were well-founded fears that the Axis powers might join forces with the ultra-rightwing régimes in the Argentine and Uruguay and foment an anti-American movement among the five million or so South and Central Americans of German, Italian and Japanese descent.[6] This prospect also disturbed the British government which, from 1942 to 1944, kept an infantry battalion on the Falklands to forestall a landing by German, Japanese or Argentine forces.[7]

By the late autumn of 1940, when the chances of a successful German invasion had diminished, Roosevelt and his advisers were at last certain that Britain was now America's first line of defence. The result was that America became what Britain had been during the Revolutionary and Napoleonic wars, part banker and part armourer, providing the wherewithal for others to make war. There were problems, particularly when the President had to convince the Senate and House of Representatives to pour taxpayers' dollars into Britain's war effort. From the beginning of 1941, it was painfully clear that the British government could no longer pay for its requirements. Hitherto, Britain had settled its American bills by borrowing from the deposits of sterling block countries (including India and the colonies), liquidating overseas holdings and selling off gold and dollar reserves. All these assets were soon exhausted and, by June 1941, Britain's gold and cash reserves had fallen to $150 million and bankruptcy appeared imminent.

Britain's financial collapse was prevented by the Lend Lease Act which was passed by Congress in February, after the legislators had been shown that Britain had done everything it could to raise the cash needed for its war effort. Lend Lease gave Britain sufficient credit to purchase whatever it required in return for a pledge to repay the debt when the war was over. Similar arrangements were extended to the dominions. In August 1945 the final account was:

	Munitions	Other Goods
	(Millions of dollars)	
United Kingdom:	8,648	7,442
India:	1,422	768
Australia:	899	483
New Zealand:	144	95
South Africa:	194	67
Colonies:	325	194

The full total of Britain's, the Commonwealth's and the empire's debts was $30,073 million. Not surprisingly, when Lend Lease was first discussed nervous spirits, including Leo Amery and some Foreign Office officials, were horrified by an emergency measure that would inevitably transform Britain from a major creditor nation to one of the world's biggest debtors.[8]

And yet without the sinews of war provided by Lend Lease Britain could not have kept up the struggle. Since the fall of France, Churchill had pursued a strategy with three broad aims which were essentially those followed during the Napoleonic Wars: the defence of the home base; keeping open the sea lanes, especially those across the North Atlantic by which the country was victualled and supplied; and the preservation of supremacy in the Mediterranean and Middle East.

The first objective had been achieved on 12 October 1940 when Hitler postponed Operation Sealion, the invasion of Britain. During the previous ten weeks the RAF had retained control over the skies over Britain and the Channel, and destroyed 600 German aircraft. The Battle of Britain had been a close-run thing, particularly during the first fortnight of September when the pool of trained pilots sank to a dangerously low level. There were, however, more than enough aircraft; during 1940 British factories turned out 15,049 machines compared to Germany's 10,826 and Italy's 3,257. Britain stayed ahead in this vital area, producing over 20,000 aeroplanes during 1941 while the combined total for Germany and Italy was 15,000.

Hitler finally abandoned the invasion of Britain in January 1941. For the past four months he and his strategists had devoted nearly all their attention and energies to the forthcoming attack on Russia, which was to be the first stage in the fulfilment of the ambition closest to Hitler's heart, the creation of a vast Nazi empire in the east. The defeat of Britain was of secondary importance and would, he believed, inevitably follow that of Russia. In the meantime, German forces waged a war of attrition against British towns and cities, which were regularly bombed. Simultaneously, an increasing U-boat fleet harried Britain's maritime supply lines. This last offensive suffered a considerable setback in June 1941, when British codebreakers cracked the Enigma cipher used for signals between the submarines and Admiral von Dönitz's Paris headquarters. The first phase of the Battle of the Atlantic therefore went Britain's way, until February 1942, when the Germans revised their code and discovered how to read that used by the Royal Navy for Atlantic operations.

During the winter of 1940–41, British signals intelligence had alerted the government to the possibility of a German spring offensive that would thrust through the Balkans and then possibly roll on towards Syria (then ruled by adherents of the neo-fascist Vichy government which had been set up in France in June 1940), Palestine and the Iraqi oilfields. This thrust would, it was assumed, coincide with an Italian advance into Egypt.

It was imperative that Britain retained command of the Mediterranean so that the Middle East would not be isolated. Naval supremacy was preserved by a sequence of Nelsonian blows. The first was delivered against the powerful French fleet that had taken refuge at Mers-el-Kébir, near Oran. Its commander, Admiral François Darlan, was convinced that Britain faced defeat and there were sound reasons for thinking that he might offer his ships to the Vichy government or Italy. Disregarding the advice of the cabinet and senior staff officers, Churchill ordered the bombardment of the French warships on 3 July.[9] At a stroke he had saved the balance of naval power in the Mediterranean, even though the heavy loss of life generated considerable acrimony.

Italy's naval pretensions were quickly exploded. In November 1940 three Italian battleships were sunk in Taranto harbour by torpedoes fired from carrier-borne aircraft, an operation which aroused considerable interest in Japan. Clever use of deciphered signals enabled a superior force to intercept an Italian squadron off Cape Matapan and sink three cruisers in March 1941.

On land, Italy fared equally badly. Neither its army nor airforce were adequately trained or equipped, and Mussolini's bombast failed to fire the hearts of his fighting men. After two feeble offensives against Kenya and

Somaliland, Italian forces in East Africa were overwhelmed, and Abyssinia was liberated early in 1941 by British, Indian, African and South African units. Prisoners were abundant and lavishly decorated, which puzzled West African troops who 'found it difficult to understand how an enemy who has put up so little fight could be so bedecked with medals'. [10] News of the victories in East Africa was enthusiastically received in the Gold Coast, where memories of Abyssinia's recent trouncing were still fresh. A black poet celebrated the reversal of fortune:

> Run, you Italians,
> Leave your ill-gotten conquests;
> Fly on the wings of defeat,
> For where Britain stands
> Your craven armies scatter. [11]

Italian armies were also in full retreat in North Africa where, by February 1941, Libya was within Britain's grasp. Following his strategy of wearing down Britain, Hitler committed German troops to this dissolving front and, in April, launched an attack on Greece which was in part intended to cover the southern flank of the invasion of Russia, and in part a means of keeping up the pressure on Britain in the Middle East. Churchill ordered one British and one Anzac division to Greece in what turned out to be a quixotic gesture, although he had dreamed of another Thermopylae in which the Australians and New Zealanders would throw back the Panzers. [12] It was the British who were thrown back, first from Greece and then Crete. Further south, General Irwin Rommel's Panzer corps expelled the British from Libya, encircled Tobruk, and had reached the Egyptian frontier by May. There were two compensations: German subversion in Iraq was thwarted (see page 411) and a mixed force of British, dominion and Free French units overthrew the collaborationist government in Syria.

Events in the Far East and Russia during the second half of 1941 made it absolutely vital that, with American support, Britain held on to every inch of ground in the Middle East. Since September 1939, British policymakers had been tormented by one question: for how long would the Japanese restrain from seizing the South-East Asian regions they openly coveted? At first, they had proceeded by stealth, putting pressure on the Vichy administration in Saigon, which proved malleable, and the Netherlands government in the Dutch East Indies, which did not. The result was that in July 1941 Indo-China was under virtual Japanese occupation and an airfield was under construction near Tonkin, bringing the whole of Malaya within range of the Imperial Japanese Air Force.

Britain and Australia had temporised. In July 1940, the British closed Burma Road, the major supply route for the Chinese Nationalist army of General Chiang Kai-Shek, and Australia continued to export cereals to Japan, allowing it generous credit.[13] As for the defence of the area, Churchill pinned all his hopes on Roosevelt being able to handle what he called 'the Japanese dog' in the Pacific. But the United States Pacific fleet, based at Hawaii since May 1940, could provide little protection for Malaya or the Indian ocean, a point stressed during a conference of senior British, American, Dutch and Australian commanders held at Singapore in April 1941. Furthermore, in the absence of a formal alliance, there was no certainty that Congress would accept an attack on British and Dutch colonies as a reason to declare war on Japan, which was tantamount to 'sending American boys to support tottering colonial empires'. Roosevelt finally relented and planned to announce America's commitment to British and Dutch territories on 10 December.

The twists and turns of relations between Japan, the United States and Britain were followed in Australia and New Zealand with a mixture of anger and anxiety. As the war in Europe proceeded, Menzies's government became increasingly panicky about Australia's defences and whether earlier British pledges would be honoured. He had visited Britain in February 1941 to press the war cabinet for dominion representation in decision-making, and returned convinced that Churchill was too rash and high handed to be trusted with grand strategy. Menzies was a conceited man and host to many phantoms; he fancied himself as a Commonwealth statesman equal in stature to Smuts, and entertained absurd daydreams of himself as Churchill's replacement.[14]

Menzies's meddlesomeness would not have mattered greatly had it not been for the despatch of Anzac forces to Greece and Crete. 'Cold-blooded murder' was how one Australian Labour MP described campaigns in which over 6,000 Anzacs had died. Ugly memories were dredged up of Gallipoli, for which Churchill had traditionally been blamed in Australia as well as Britain. Forthright to the point of tactlessness, the Labour leader, Curtin, resurrected charges that Britain was indifferent to Australia's safety. In June, he demanded that Britain 'Scrap the African Empire' and close the Suez Canal, a measure which could hardly have assisted Australia.[15] General Sir Thomas Blamey, the Australian commander in the Middle East, also weighed in with a call for his men to be withdrawn from what he considered the futile defence of Tobruk.[16] Blamey also put his finger on an official habit of mind, exhibited by Churchill, which rankled with his countrymen: 'There was a curious element in the British make-up which led them to look on the dominions as appendages of Britain.'[17] The row spluttered on for the next few months, and became known about in Japan, where it prompted the headline, 'British Empire Crumbling to Pieces'.[18]

Although subsequently exaggerated, this squabble was an indication of how desperate Australians had become. Their mood was sensed by the State Department, which, in April 1941, ordered a powerful squadron of warships to undertake a cruise to Fiji, New Zealand and Australia, in the hope that it would, in the words of the United States navy's official history, 'hearten our Antipodean friends, who felt forgotten and virtually abandoned by Mother England'.[19]

Churchill too was anxious to dispel this mood of resentful isolation. In October, he promised Menzies's successor, Curtin, that the battleship *Prince of Wales*, the battlecruiser *Repulse* and the aircraft carrier *Indomitable* would be immediately sent to Far Eastern waters. Australia and New Zealand had originally hoped for more, but there were only two capital ships to spare. It was a gesture of reassurance, but the aircraft carrier broke down, leaving the two capital ships to operate in a region where the enemy enjoyed air superiority.

Two warships could not obscure the frailty of imperial defences in the Far East. Duff Cooper, who visited Malaya in August and was appointed Minister for Far Eastern Affairs, reported to Churchill two months later that the colony's defences were ramshackle. Many senior civil and military officials were insouciant about the dangers facing them, and the seventy-two-year-old governor of the Straits Settlements, Sir Shenton Thomas, was a dithering blunderer who needed to be sacked.[20] It was Thomas who, when war broke out, refused to evacuate white women and children from a war zone for fear of upsetting Malay and Chinese opinion; perhaps the only time in the empire's history that 'women and children last' was an official command. Cooper's impression of dud officials and a general lassitude at the top was confirmed by New Zealand airmen who arrived in Malaya during 1941. They were astounded by the languid atmosphere; there was a half holiday every Wednesday, Sundays were off, and flight training was confined to seven hours a day. 'To the New Zealanders, imbued with the vital need for haste in reaching operational efficiency, it seemed that far too much valuable time was wasted.'[21] The local high command was untroubled since it believed that Japanese air crews and machines were both of poor quality.[22] An American journalist described Singapore as 'the City of Blimps', which got him expelled by the authorities. Racial hubris infected the Blimps and their wives, and their arrogance towards Indians spawned 'a good deal of bitterness' among the men who came to defend their pampered existence.[23]

What still remains astonishing in the light of the catastrophe which overtook Malaya is the ostrich-like outlook of those responsible for its safety. A joint-service assessment, compiled in October 1940, concluded that 'our ability to hold Malaya beyond the immediate vicinity of Singapore in the face of a determined attack is very problematical. Moreover, in the event of a successful invasion, the survival of Singapore for more than a short period is very improbable.'[24] Nevertheless, a strong sense of racial superiority comforted everyone involved, including Churchill, who once rated the Japanese 'the Wops [slang for Italians] of the East'; it was felt that they lacked the nerve, the wherewithal and the organisational skills to launch a successful invasion of British and Dutch possessions.[25] Even if they did attack, the local strength of the combined United States, British, Dutch and Australian navies more than matched the Japanese fleet, even though the former was far stronger in aircraft carriers. At the end of November, Churchill was assured by an intelligence assessment of the Far Eastern situation that the Japanese would stay out of the war until the spring, and then their first target would be a soft one, Siam.[26]

The Japanese government did not behave as predicted. By early autumn, the new prime minister General Hideki Tojo and his cabinet had decided to attack British, Dutch and American colonies in the Far East if, as was likely, the three nations refused to lift an oil embargo imposed on Japan after the occupation of Indo-China. The oil blockade hurt, but what really swayed the Japanese ministers was the possibility that Germany would beat Russia and Britain during the following year, thereby making it easier for Japan to retain the former British, French and Dutch colonies which could fall into its hands. Tojo and his colleagues also naïvely imagined that, in time, America would accept the new imperial *status quo* in Asia.

Japan's war plans were audacious and ambitious. On 7 December, carrier-borne aircraft attacked the United States navy's anchorage at Pearl Harbor, knocking out several battleships and temporarily swinging the Pacific balance of naval power in Japan's favour. Between 8 and 17 December, seaborne forces landed on the coasts of Siam (which immediately surrendered), Malaya, Borneo, Sarawak, the Philippines, Guam and

Wake Island. Conventional naval wisdom had hitherto ruled out the possibility of Japan undertaking so many operations simultaneously, and surprise was all but total.[27] After the war, mischievous allegations were made that Churchill had been informed by signals intelligence of the movement and destination of the Pearl Harbor force, but refused to alert Roosevelt so as to make certain America's entry into the war. This is a *canard*; signals picked up by the Hong Kong listening post were believed, probably rightly, to be from a Japanese flotilla heading through the South China Sea for Malaya, not from the Pearl Harbor armada.[28]

Britain's Far Eastern empire fell with a swiftness which both astonished and dismayed everyone. Singapore's uselessness as a base was demonstrated by air raids by bombers based in Indo-China on 8 December. Two days later, bombers flying from Saigon sank the *Repulse* and *Prince of Wales*, while RAF, RAAF and RNZAF aircraft were busy trying to stem the Japanese advance from the three bridgeheads they had established on the eastern shores of Malaya. On land, the Japanese advanced through the jungle with a deadly efficiency, and their aircraft systematically destroyed British airfields, nearly all of which were sited in the north of the colony. After three days of an unequal aerial contest, the local RAF commander warned that his forces could only last out for a fortnight.[29] By the end of the month, British, dominion and Indian ground troops were in full retreat towards Singapore, having fought gallantly against an enemy their commanders had so grossly underrated.

Hong Kong capitulated on Christmas Day. Its position had been precarious since the outbreak of the Sino-Japanese war four years before. At the end of 1940 there had been a serious mutiny by Sikh artillerymen in the garrison, who, it appeared, had been subverted by Japanese propaganda.[30] White troops were needed to defend a white man's empire so, during 1941, Canadian infantry were sent to the colony at Britain's request. They were to all intents and purposes a forlorn hope, and after the war the local commander, Major-General Christopher Maltby, accused them of indiscipline and cowardice during the closing stages of the siege.[31]

There were similar recriminations after the defences of Malaya had crumpled. General Sir Archibald Wavell, commander-in-chief in South-East Asia, blamed Australian soldiers, alleging that they had run away from the front in disorder, pillaging, raping and even murdering as they went. The local Australian commander, Major-General Gordon Bennett, castigated the lacklustre leadership of British officers chosen by what he called 'the "old school tie" method of selection'.[32] Not that this aptly-named general was particularly well-qualified to pronounce on leadership since he was 'a rasping, bitter man who fell out with everyone including his own staff'.[33] Once it was clear that Singapore was about to fall, he set about finding himself a ship to escape in, claiming that he wanted to tell Australia what had happened. Obviously he had never heard of the Jacobite ballad 'Johnny Cope', in which General Cope 'ran with the news of his own defeat' after the battle of Prestonpans. Bennett's, Maltby's and Wavell's allegations were hotly denied by survivors of the campaign. Whatever the exact truth, there was and still is something distasteful about beaten generals making scapegoats of their men; when armies fall apart it is invariably from the top downwards.

The record of the civilian and military leaders in Malaya supports this dictum. Penang with its valuable port and stores intact was surrendered on 15 December. Indian soldiers who took part in the retreat afterwards complained of insufficient ammunition, orders which denied them the chance to make a stand, the absence of air cover, erratic delivery of rations, and a host of operational mischances which could have been avoided.[34] Nothing like this troubled the Japanese, who shattered the myths cherished by British, and for that matter American, commanders by revealing themselves as hardy, resourceful and well-trained fighting men. After a duel with a Japanese submarine in January 1942, an officer on board the destroyer *Jupiter* remarked of his adversaries, 'they showed guts and fighting spirit, to say the least, that took us by surprise.'[35] There were many surprises for Allied servicemen in the Far East during December 1941, and there were more to come.

While imperial troops were being forced back through the jungles of Malaya, and Singapore, the keystone of the empire's defences in the Far East, stood in increasing jeopardy, Churchill's mood swung between despair and exhilaration. The latter predominated; on 11 December 1941 Germany and Italy declared war on America and spared Roosevelt the awkward necessity of having to seek Congress's approval for entering the European conflict. With the United States now a full combatant, Churchill felt sure that the Allies (soon to be known as the 'United Nations') would eventually win the war on all fronts, although there was no way of knowing how long this would take.

The Prime Minister and his chiefs of staff were unwavering in their belief that, despite the recent setbacks in the Far East and the Pacific, Britain's primary objective was still the defeat of Germany. Japan would have to wait and British prestige and territories in Asia would have to be sacrificed, although for a short time hope was placed on the Allies being able to hold a defensive line stretching from Burma southwards through Singapore and the Dutch East Indies to the northern coast of Australia.

Beating Germany and sustaining a defensive front in the Far East required Britain to keep control of the Mediterranean and the Middle East. Both were under growing German pressure. At the beginning of winter, the German Army Group South had penetrated southern Russia as far as Rostov and, British intelligence believed, would push into the Caucasus at the onset of spring. If this advance succeeded, Germany would be well placed to intervene directly in Iraq and Iran (where Axis fifth columnists were already making mischief) at the same time as Rommel's forces renewed the assault on Egypt. Axis attempts to disrupt supply lines through the Mediterranean were being stepped up, and there were fears that Germany would seek Spanish assistance for an attack on Gibraltar.

More than the Suez Canal was now at stake, for during 1941 the Middle East had become the focus of an aerial lifeline. Aircraft, supplied under Lend Lease, were being ferried across the Caribbean to Trinidad, and from there south to Natal on the eastern coast of Brazil for the transatlantic flight to a new airfield at Takoradi in the Gold Coast. The machines then flew overland to Khartoum for the final leg of their journey to aerodromes in Egypt. At first only long-range bombers could make the journey, but at the beginning of December the United States approached Britain to build a transit airfield for medium-range machines on Ascension Island.[36] The Far Eastern conflict added to the importance of this route, for machines could be flown on from Egypt to India. In the spring of 1942, and in response to a shortage of fighters, some were carried by the carrier USS *Ranger* to a point 125 miles off the coast of West Africa and then flown to Accra on the first stage of an aerial marathon that would take them to India.[37]

Aircraft using this route were serviced by RAF and USAAF personnel, and Pan American airlines, turning a wartime emergency to profit, used the ferry service to break into the imperial air transport market. They established a civil route between Accra and Khartoum, and gained permission for the conversion of the Ascension base into a civil aerodrome after the war.[38]

If this route was fractured, the defence of India and the Far East, as well as that of the Middle East and Mediterranean would be gravely imperilled. Faced with what might turn out to be a double-pronged German assault on the Middle East during 1942, Churchill sailed to America on

15 December prepared to convince Roosevelt that the only viable Allied strategy had to be one in which Germany was overcome first. In reaching this conclusion, he and his advisers had to face the bitter fact that, for the time being, imperial interests in Asia would have to be abandoned, although Churchill hoped that those defending them would fight stubbornly. Their efforts would, however, turn out to be futile if Germany was allowed to establish itself in the Middle East, and thereby secure the means to cooperate directly with Japanese forces which, by the turn of the year, were beginning to advance westwards through Burma to the borders of India. By sacrificing one part of the empire, Churchill hoped that he might ultimately secure all of it.

Allied grand strategy for 1942 was hammered out by Churchill, Roosevelt and their advisers during the last two weeks of December. They agreed to the principle of Germany first, then Japan. First would come the expulsion of German and Italian forces from North Africa, and then USAAF and RAF bombers would begin the systematic pounding of Germany, using British airfields. No longer able to defend itself, the British empire in the Far East would pass under American protection; GIs were to be rushed to Australia and, if the Philippines fell, the remnants of its garrison would be shipped to Singapore, if it was still tenable.

11

Steadfast Comrades: The Stresses of War

1942 was a bleak year for the British empire. On 15 February, the 130,000- strong garrison of Singapore yielded to a smaller Japanese army. Four days later, the war reached Australia; Darwin suffered a devastating air raid while a panic-stricken government in Canberra prepared for invasion. Burma was overrun, with Rangoon falling on 1 March and Mandalay on 1 May. The Andaman Islands were captured on 23 March, and during the first fortnight of April a Japanese armada cruised at will in the Bay of Bengal. Calcutta and Colombo suffered air attacks and two British cruisers were sunk. A weak Allied squadron was overwhelmed in the Battle of the Java Sea at the end of February, and within two months Japanese forces had conquered the Dutch East Indies, the Philippines, much of New Guinea and a string of British island colonies in the south-western Pacific. In the meantime, Japanese strategists were planning the seizure of Fiji and long-range operations in the Indian Ocean.

Despite sybilline voices which had foretold disasters on this scale, these reverses stunned Britain and the rest of the empire. What was happening in the Far East and Pacific triggered a spasm of national introspection, accompanied by much hand-wringing, in which searching questions were asked about the nature of the empire and its future. There was also plenty of angry name-calling as everyone directly and indirectly responsible for the reverses excused themselves and incriminated others.

Australia saw itself as the chief victim. After the fall of Singapore ('Australia's Maginot Line'), the *Sydney Morning Herald* announced that,

'The Empire is suffering from a series of disasters which are shaking it to its foundations,' and concluded, 'we do not seem to be muddling through as much as muddling along.' Speaking as he usually did, from the shoulder, Curtin alternately blamed Britain for his country's predicament and appealed to the United States to rescue it. His charges of betrayal incensed Churchill, who was also accused by H.V. Evatt, the Minister for External Affairs, of succumbing to partisan prejudice in his treatment of Australia. The Prime Minister, he claimed, 'seems to have a deep hatred of Labour governments and a resentment of independent judgement which makes it impossible for us to work with him.'[1] The mood of near hysteria which seemed to grip the Australian government so worried Major-General Lewis Brereton, USAAF commander in the Far East, that he suggested the imposition of 'strong centralised control of Australian politics under American influence'.[2]

New Zealanders were prepared to take their blows on the chin. Reacting to the news of Singapore's surrender, New Zealand's prime minister, Peter Fraser, proclaimed, 'We will not wince and will not indulge in unhelpful, carping criticism of those who have the higher direction of the war effort.' In Britain many, including Churchill, contrasted Australia's tantrums with the stoicism of the British people when they had been faced with danger. Oliver Harvey noted in his diary:

> The Curtin government have screamed for help from the Americans, making it clear that they think us broken reeds. I'm afraid it is the 'good life' in Australia which has made them soft and narrow. Not so the New Zealanders, however, who have been models of restraint, dignity and helpfulness.[3]

Curtin responded to this criticism in a broadcast made to the British people in May 1944 in which he reminded his listeners that Australians were suffering as much as if not more than they were in terms of rationing and shortages.[4]

Australia's strident appeals during the first three months of 1942 were cries of desperation rather than a declaration of independence. And yet it was plain to everyone that Britain was unable to defend the extremities of its empire unaided. Nor was any help available from other dominions. An attempt to by-pass Britain and appeal directly to Canada for armaments was snubbed. The Canadian minister of munitions bluntly informed the Australian government that, 'If Britain tells us to send our supplies to the

Middle East, we send them to the Middle East, if she tells us to send them to Australia, we send them to Australia.'[5] America stepped in to become the arsenal for Australia and New Zealand: between January and June 1942 the RAAF and RNZAF received 54 aircraft from Britain and 230 from the United States, the bulk of Britain's spare machines being rushed to India.[6] At the same time, 50,000 GIs were drafted to defend Australia at Churchill's request, although he believed, correctly as it turned out, that the Japanese invasion would never materialise.[7]

Relations between Britain and Australia took a severe battering at the beginning of 1942 and, although they improved once the threat of Japanese landings receded, sour memories lingered. They surfaced in 1991–2 when the republican Australian prime minister, Paul Keating, repeated allegations that Churchill had left Australia in the lurch so as to concentrate on the war in the Middle East. This charge, like those levelled in 1941–2, was a simplification which failed to take into account the precariousness of Britain's position in Egypt and on the north-eastern frontier of India. It was, and clearly still is hard for Australians to stomach the fact that in its direst moment their country was low down the list of British strategic priorities.

Britain's lost colonies, if not its prestige, were eventually restored through the efforts of the United States which, at the beginning of 1942, had taken over the main burden of imperial defence. It was American warships which defeated the Japanese navy in engagements at the Coral Sea and Midway in May and June. The latter victory swung the balance of seapower in the Pacific in the Allies' favour and halted Japanese expansion. By August, American and Australian forces had counter-attacked and begun the long, grinding process of ejecting the Japanese from the south-western Pacific. The defence of India and the reconquest of Burma in 1942–5 was conducted by imperial forces, but here, as on all other fronts, American-made aircraft and armaments were vital.

The baleful events in the Far East caused consternation in Britain. The country was already in the middle of a period of intensely critical self-examination as plans were being framed for post-war reconstruction. There was an overwhelming sense that whatever else happened there could never be a return to the pre-war world with its inefficiencies, social inequality and economic drifting. The new Britain would be a nation which cultivated social harmony and devoted a substantial portion of its wealth and energies to the regeneration of industry, full employment and providing a fair and generous system of education and welfare for all. How this last might be achieved was set out in the famous Beveridge report, which was issued in December 1942, and widely welcomed as a goal worth fighting for. The country was going to change for the better; but what of its empire?

The empire's past, present and future came suddenly under public scrutiny during the weeks after the fall of Singapore. The shock of a capitulation which effectively shattered Britain's admittedly fragile pretensions as a global, imperial power was followed by a series of disconcerting revelations about the character of the empire. A frank and devastating analysis of the background to the surrender written by *The Times*'s Far Eastern correspondent was published on 18 February. It argued that the 'easy-going routine of colonial administration' had sapped the will of officials who had shown themselves devoid of the 'dynamism' and 'aggression' now evident in other areas of public life. 'The government had no roots in the life of the people,' the writer concluded, and his point was expanded in an editorial which condemned the Malayan administration for the 'lack of touch between the local Government and the vast Asiatic population, whose attitude, with the honourable exception of the Chinese, was passive, timorous and apathetic.'

Official censorship prevented the publication of details of defections to the Japanese by Malays, disheartened Indian troops and Burmese. Nonetheless, parliamentary critics of the government contrasted the indifference of the natives of Malaya with the fierceness with which the Filipinos were fighting for their American masters, who had promised the Philippines self-government after the war.[8] According to the *Economist*, Britain's subjects in the Far East had lost faith in the empire and the Allied cause.[9] Defending his former colleagues, Captain Leonard Gammans, a Unionist MP and sometime district officer in Malaya, detected a collapse in national self-confidence. 'We cannot expect Asiatics and Africans to believe in us as a colonial Power unless we believe in ourselves,' he argued. What was needed was new life to be injected into the old imperial ideals of 'common citizenship and trusteeship and vision'.[10]

In broad terms, the débâcle in Malaya was yet another example of the failure of the old order and its servants. The figure of Colonel Blimp soon entered the debate. He had come to symbolise the ossified thinking, complacency and obscurantism which were now seen as the outstanding features of the 'Old Gang', that band of men who, according to left-wing mytholoy, had guided the country so maladroitly between the wars. The routine analysis of servicemen's mail undertaken to measure morale revealed that in the wake of the disasters in the Far East there had been an increase in complaints about Blimps in high places.[11] A.L. Rowse, a distinguished Oxford historian, used the columns of *The Times* to speculate on how far the empire's recent misfortunes stemmed from that dogma fostered in public schools, which elevated character over cleverness. It was the latter quality which had marked the men who had built the empire in the time of Elizabeth I, Anne and the two Pitts.[12] On the same day, the government announced rigorous testing of all army lieutenant-colonels over the age of forty-five, presumably to weed out Blimps.

There was also a hunt for Blimps in the Commons. The government was savaged over the blunderer who had permitted Penang to be abandoned without a fight, making a gift to the Japanese of its stocks of rubber.[13] Here was a Blimp to be punctured along with many others, who were imagined enjoying a privileged life in other corners of the empire. 'The majority of British officials live in a by-gone world,' alleged Major James Milner, a Labour MP. 'At this very moment they will be dining in short coats and all the rest of the palaver, in Calcutta, only a few miles away from the front line.'[14] He was very close to the mark. In Burma, the acerbic American General 'Vinegar' Joe Stilwell was peeved by his meetings with the 'bored and supercilious limies' who ran the empire and commanded its troops. One easily recognisable specimen tried his patience, and he noted in his diary: 'Monocled ass at lunch: "One does enjoy a cawktail doesn't one? It's so seldom one gets a chawnce. In my case I hardly have time for a glahss of bee-ah."'[15] The condescending, off-hand manner of men of this stamp, and there were plenty of them, galled Americans, who were now beginning to encounter them elsewhere in the empire, and in the higher ranks of the armed services and the government. General Dwight D. Eisenhower, then in charge of strategic planning in the Far East, was irritated by the 'stiff-necked' response of Wavell after he had been offered Chinese troops to help shore up the crumbling front in Burma.[16] All too often, Americans were left with the impression that Britain's ruling class lacked the inner drive and energy to wage, let alone win, a modern war.

There were some in America and Britain who were wondering whether the class which still largely had the governance of the empire deserved to retain its power. 'There must be no place after the world for special privileges, either for individuals or nations,' Roosevelt had proclaimed in November 1941. His countrymen tended to agree, as did a substantial body of opinion in Britain, mostly on the left and centre. So too, but to a lesser degree, did the government, whose propaganda continually exhorted everyone to work together and share the burdens of war equally. An egalitarian and democratic spirit was abroad, and was often forcefully expressed in servicemen's letters, which contained plenty of grumbling about 'stand-offish' officers and the amorphous, but all-too-recognisable, 'they' and 'them' who exercised authority.

Within the empire the social hierarchy was unshaken by the war. Servicemen attached to the units which reoccupied Malaya in the summer of 1945 were hurt by the snobbery of those they had liberated, the planters and their wives, who, like the Bourbons, appeared to have remembered everything and learnt nothing.[17] This was not surprising; throughout most of the empire's existence the élite which managed the colonies had been drawn almost exclusively from the upper and upper-middle classes. Men in senior positions during the war had been recruited from public school alumni, who had passed through Oxford or Cambridge and shown themselves more adept on the playing field than in the examination hall. Character counted for much; when interviewing potential district officers, Sir Ralph Furse made a point of looking for such telltale signs of an interior weakness as 'a languid handshake'.[18] Before 1914, and probably after, a 'social test' was applied, and the candidate who offered his interrogator a Virginia rather than a Turkish cigarette was automatically scratched for what was then a social solecism.[19]

The tone of the empire was therefore aristocratic and conservative. It may be judged by the reactions of the group of Indian officials and their wives to the news of Labour's general election victory at the end of July 1945, which they heard while homeward-bound in a liner passing through the Mediterranean. There were anxious remarks about whether pensions, public schools and coal royalties were in jeopardy, and then a discussion as to who would replace Leo Amery as Secretary of State for India:

> Amery is out, but who is in? This is a favourite point of speculation. The Colonel – I think he's a boxwallah but that's what everyone calls him – has got hold of a rumour that it's this Palme Dutt [a Communist MP of Indian and Swedish descent] fellow. Good God, they might at least choose Britishers to run the blasted country, not niggers.[20]

Social and racial arrogance went hand in hand, and both were capable of injuring the empire. So thought Margery Perham, an exceptionally well-informed and percipient commentator on colonial affairs who, until the events of February 1942, had unreservedly endorsed current paternalist imperial ideals. In two articles which appeared in *The Times* in March, she asked and answered the uncomfortable question as to how the Kenyans would behave if a Japanese task force hove to off Mombasa. They might, she feared, act like the Malays, for British rule in Kenya had failed to kindle any deep sense of loyalty or common purpose among its different races. The root of the trouble was that the diligent and hard-working British officials who governed the colony, once their daily tasks had been completed, would withdraw to their houses and clubs and each other's company. This voluntary detachment did not win men's hearts, and left the rulers 'insulated' from that growing minority of educated blacks who would, in time, succeed them.[21]

Miss Perham had struck a raw nerve. The war in the Far East, which in the spring of 1942 showed every sign that it would soon extend to the Indian Ocean, was a racial conflict. Japanese propaganda hailed the fall of Singapore, Hong Kong and Manila as triumphs for the peoples of Asia and milestones on the road to their liberation from white rule. Australian POWs were forced to sweep the streets of Singapore as a token that the old racial order had been overturned; white civilian and military prisoners were systematically humiliated and maltreated in what the victims interpreted as a form of racial revenge; and some were wantonly murdered, like the twenty-two administrators, missionaries and wireless operators killed in the Gilbert Islands in October 1942.[22]

Japan's call for a race war reached many ears. 'I have heard Natives saying, "Why fight against Japan? We are oppressed by the whites and we shall not fare worse under the Japanese," ' Smuts wrote after inspecting a newly raised contingent of black troops. 'But', he consoled himself, 'I am sure the great majority are still loyal in their conservative way.'[23] Many Indians, Malays and Burmese were not. In what still remains a shadowy episode in the war (thanks to the furtiveness of Britain's official secrecy regulations) large bodies of Indian, Ghurka and Tamil troops defected to the Japanese and formed the Indian National Army (INA), a nationalist force dedicated to the overthrow of the raj. The full numbers are not known; in 1944, military intelligence believed the INA contained 35,000, and a year after it was estimated that 20,000 Indian troops had gone over to the Japanese, two out of every seven captured.[24]

In the summer of 1945, when the Indian army had the wretched task of sifting through the survivors of the INA, its intelligence staff identified a hard core of 7,600 who had actively assisted the Japanese, and in some cases committed horrendous war crimes which deserved punishment.[25] The rest were for the main part decent soldiers disorientated by the chaotic retreats in Malaya and Burma during the winter and spring of 1941–2, or prisoners who collaborated to get better rations and treatment. In this category were many who had been genuinely shocked by the defeats inflicted on Britain and had lost confidence in their old rulers.

Among the convinced nationalists who saw themselves as India's future liberators was Captain Garbaksh Singh Dhillon, a sadist who tortured and murdered Indian and Chinese prisoners in Changi gaol, Singapore.[26] There were other fanatics, like those members of the Rani of Jhansi's women's regiment who were defiant under interrogation and devoted to Chandra Subhas Bose, the former Congress politician who had fled to Germany in 1941.[27] After broadcasting propaganda from Berlin, in which he denounced democracy and pilloried Britain as 'the impeccable foe to progress and evolution', Bose travelled by submarine to Tokyo, where he arrived in June 1943.[28] Assuming the title 'Netaji' (leader) of the INA, Bose threw himself into its reorganisation. He was a mesmeric speaker, and the Indian government recognised him as a formidable adversary.[29]

The INA was part of a wider, Japanese-supervised organisation for nationalist subversion in India and anti-European propaganda throughout Asia. It included the Swaraj Young Men's Training School in Rangoon, which specialised in sabotage and guerrilla warfare, and an academy in Penang which trained Malay, Chinese and Siamese propagandists.[30] INA soldiers were told that once they and the Japanese penetrated Bengal, there would be a mass anti-British uprising.[31] In the meantime, trained saboteurs and partisans were landed from submarines, but nearly all were intercepted. By the end of October, forty-two Japanese Inspired Fifth Columnists (JIFs) had been rounded up by intelligence.[32] On the battlefield, the INA proved a disappointment to its masters and desertions back to the British were frequent.

The government in India took the INA very seriously, fearing that its propaganda might entice front-line troops to surrender, and that its agents might foment sedition in areas already convulsed by Congress agitation. There was, therefore, close intelligence surveillance of Indian units and the inspection of troops' mail for signs of discontent.[33] Counter-propaganda programmes were concocted, although their authors were warned to proceed gingerly when presenting such controversial issues as post-war 'social development' in Britain, which might provoke Indian soldiers to ask why such measures were not introduced in their country.[34] Post-war Asian politics were a minefield which British propagandists did all they could to avoid beyond pointing out that a Japanese victory would dash all hopes of Indian self-government. American propaganda was not so inhibited; in 1944 its message to the Burmese was that an Allied victory would 'bring Burma peace and freedom'. The Colonial Office protested at this promise of independence, but was overruled by the Foreign Office, which wanted to keep on the best of terms with the United States.[35]

British propagandists were on safer ground with the Josh (literally 'zeal') programme for the Indian army, which was designed to encourage a cheerful, positive spirit among the troops. A dose of Josh may have inspired a Punjabi soldier serving on the frontier with Burma, who, on hearing a Japanese wireless announcement that Bose and the INA would be in Delhi within ten days, remarked, 'Not if they go by train they won't.' In the end, neither Bose nor the INA made much impact on the outcome of the Far Eastern war, although both were seen as having an unlimited potential to create trouble inside India. Bose died in an air crash at the end of the war, much to the relief of the Indian government, which feared that his former followers might be a source of violent upheavals when they returned home.[36]

Among the troops fighting in Burma during 1944 were 30,000 askaris from East and West Africa, and, like their Indian comrades, they had their correspondence and conversations monitored for signs of political restlessness.[37] Although the War Office had allowed the issuing of commissions to men of mixed race in October 1939, black troops continued to be commanded by white officers.[38] In the case of the Gold Coast askaris, white officers were imported from the settlers of Southern Rhodesia.[39]

While the war loosened the social hierarchy in Britain, its racial counterpart in Africa and the West Indies remained as rigid as ever. The Colonial Office went to considerable lengths to ensure that its black subjects were cocooned from any outside influences that might upset them or make them unhappy with their lot. Contact between British blacks and negro American servicemen was officially seen as a potent source of discontent and disruption. Well-dressed and well-paid black American GIs turned the heads of poorer Bermudan blacks and so, under Colonial Office pressure, the former were withdrawn. Black servicemen stationed in Liberia were banned from taking leave in nearby British African colonies, again for fear that their self-confidence and prosperity might cause unrest.[40]

The 2,000 black soldiers, all relegated to labour duties under the United States army segregation rules, who arrived in Trinidad in 1941, caused a great stir. They had money to spend on drink and women, causing an anonymous calypso writer to lament: 'I was living with a decent and contented wife/Until the soldiers came and broke up my life.'[41] The governor of Trinidad was also disturbed by this irruption into his colony, but for different reasons. He saw the American negroes as envoys of the black militant and Back-to-Africa movements which were gaining ground in their homeland. Neither was welcome in Trinidad, with its recent history of strikes by black workers, and in 1943 the American government obligingly replaced the negroes with Puerto Ricans.

This episode revealed the peculiar ambiguity of Anglo-American thinking about race. While the United States authorities were more than willing to cooperate with the Colonial Office in providing a quarantine for the empire's blacks, many American politicians and pressmen continually sounded off about these same people being oppressed and exploited by their rulers. But the moral force of these attacks was blunted by America's shocking racial record. Racial inequality was a way of life in the United States; throughout the war there were many, frequently bloody, race riots involving opposing bodies of white and black servicemen, including one on a USAAF base in Britain.[42] Echoing the emotions which might have agitated members of the INA, an American negro soldier destined for the Pacific front was alleged to have asked for the following epitaph: 'Here lies a black man, killed fighting a yellow man for the protection of a white man.'[43]

British wartime propaganda found no difficulty in combating such cynicism, at least when it came to explaining why Germany had to be beaten. A particularly venomous passage from *Mein Kampf* was widely circulated among the African colonies to remind black men what Hitler thought of their kind: 'It is an act of criminal insanity to train a being who is semi-ape till you pretend he has turned into a lawyer.' Since 1939, the colonial section of the Ministry of Information had been busy outlining Britain's war aims throughout the empire through films, lectures, exhibitions, leaflets and street theatre. A Nazi victory would destroy the empire, which was its subjects' only hope of justice and advancement. As in India, official propagandists had to be careful that their material did not boomerang; excessive vilification of the Germans was avoided for fear of a backlash against the white race in general, and references to a war being waged for freedom and democracy were deliberately circumspect.[44] On the other hand, the colonial empire's subjects were reminded that after the war they would be treated as partners rather than dependencies.

Hitler provided an excellent bogey-man. In this form, he appeared in a splendid Hausa song, 'Hitler bata kasa', which loses none of its vigour in translation:

> The English have a remedy for hopeless mischievousness;
> Hitler brings treachery and mischief to everyone.
> The English have a remedy for Hitler of Germany,
> Hitler has no Father and is a dog (bastard)
> He has no money and no home and is a thief.
> The English have a remedy for Hitler of Germany.[45]

A Gold Coast lyricist invoked the theme of imperial unity in a traditional-style battle song, written for women and chanted to the accompaniment of war drums:

> Let the women of Britain's Empire
> Sing praises and their warriors inspire
> Steadfast comrades who stand ready to die for liberty.
> Sons of the Dominions and India
> And far-flung islands of the seven seas,
> Sons of the Motherland,
> England the Motherland,
> Sing out, women of the Empire.[46]

Modern persuasive techniques were employed in North Borneo during 1941. A touring exhibition showed enlarged and, given the Japanese threat, reassuring photographs of British battleships and aircraft carriers. Reports of the war's progress were circulated in English and Malay with a note to householders: 'Please give the Malay news sheet to your orderly or boy.' There were public lectures on such topics as 'Flying in Borneo' and 'Lend for Victory', and a screening of the inspirational film *Nurse Cavell*, in which the heroine defies the Germans in 1914 and is executed for her courage.[47]

In contrast with the Japanese, the Germans and Italians made no attempt to enlist the support of the empire's subjects: understandably, since Naziism and fascism were both racist creeds. There was, however, a concerted effort to win over Arab opinion by exploiting the recent upheavals in

Palestine. Britain and America were portrayed as the accomplices of the Jews and, *ipso facto*, the enemies of Arabs everywhere. After Allied victories in Egypt and North Africa, Radio Tunis claimed in December 1942 that, '*Les Anglo-Américains champions rétribués des Juifs, veuillent faire du Maroc et de l'Algérie une seconde Palestine.*'[48]

Britain's programme of propaganda not only extolled the justice of the Allies' cause, it exhorted men and women at every level and in every part of the empire to do their 'bit' for the war effort. As in the First World War, all the resources of the dominions and colonies were mobilised for war. Raising and training fighting men and women was still immensely important, and the full totals for the entire war were:

Great Britain:	4,650,000	
Australia:	570,000	
Canada:	770,000	
India:	1,789,000	
New Zealand:	97,000	
East African colonies:	225,000	(plus 30,000 pioneers)
West African colonies:	150,000	(plus 16,000 pioneers)[49]

These figures represent the sum of all men and women in the services and ignore the fact that, at various stages of the war, there were partial demobilisations. The South African 1st Division returned home after the liberation of Abyssinia, and, the Japanese having been evicted from New Guinea, Australian and New Zealand servicemen were released for industry during 1943 and 1944. Nonetheless, Australia had 365,000 men and women under arms in 1945, four-fifths of them volunteers. Canada faced the same manpower problems it had in the First World War; by 1943 the number of volunteers for overseas service was dwindling and conscription was introduced the following year, although the pressed men were sent for garrison duties in the West Indies rather than to the fronts in France and Italy.

The African record was particularly impressive. At the beginning of 1943, Nyasaland had contributed 20,000 men to the King's African Rifles, and a further 103,000 were undertaking war work, most in the Northern Rhodesian copper mines. This represented over a third of the adult male population.[50] By this date, the colonial authorities were running into difficulties finding men, especially labourers for work on the airfields and bases in Egypt and North Africa. As in the last war, there was pressure from the high command for black men to release white for the fighting line, and it intensified during 1943 and early 1944 as forces were being concentrated for the D-Day landings in France.[51]

In July 1943, the Kenyan government reported that it had reached the limit, and, with 67,000 men already in the army, could find no more.[52] In general, 'portering' was unpopular throughout East Africa despite the government's 'careful propaganda', which proved ineffective in the face of folk memory. 'Hardships and losses of the last campaign are vividly recalled and the feeling we broke faith still lingers,' the governor of Uganda informed Whitehall.[53] Both he and his counterpart in Tanganyika were dismayed by the lack of volunteers of suitable physique and stamina, and the latter feared that he might be driven to compel men to come forward.[54] Somehow, the quotas were met by the colonial governments but, as they pointed out, at the cost of taking men away from the production of war matériel.[55]

A balance between men and women in uniform and those in overalls producing food and munitions was vital. 'This is not a war of men but a war of highly specialised machines,' Churchill told Mackenzie King in August 1941.[56] Outside Canada, the empire's potential for the manufacture of sophisticated weaponry was small, leaving dominions and colonies in the southern hemisphere almost entirely dependent on Britain and the United States. There was, however, an attempt in July 1940, to rationalise the production and distribution of war materials in this region after a conference of the governments concerned in Delhi.

As a result, there was a degree of specialisation and cooperation. Australia, which possessed an advanced machine-tool industry, began producing light machine-guns, twenty-four pounders and anti-aircraft guns in August 1941, some of which were shipped to Britain until early 1942. South Africa's metallurgical industries were responsible for aircraft hangars and collapsible bridges, but was initially hampered by a lack of technicians for more complex work.[57] New Zealand manufactured wireless sets, and the tropical colonies contributed raw materials with Ceylon swiftly raising its rubber output after the loss of Malaya.

This crash programme filled some gaps, but the final statistics for the imperial industrial effort reflect the concentration of manufacturing capacity within the empire:

	Aircraft	Tanks	Anti-Aircraft Guns	Tracked Vehicles	Machine-Guns
Canada:	15,957	5,678	4,286	33,987	251,925
Australia:	3,181	57	768	5,501	30,992
New Zealand:	Nil	Nil	Nil	1,210	Nil
India:	Nil	Nil	Nil	Nil	6,991

These figures do not include the armoured cars and mortars made in South Africa and rifles and ammunition manufactured in India.

A substantial part of the final bill for equipment, commodities and services provided by the empire was footed by Britain. At the outbreak of war, all Indian and colonial sterling reserves held in London were effectively frozen by being declared non-convertible. They were subsequently commandeered for the British war effort, and thereafter colonial imports were paid for by credit, treasury bills. The result was that Britain's debt to its colonies rose from £150 million in 1939 to £454 million in 1945. India benefited from this arrangement for, under the 1940 Defence Expenditure Agreement, Britain promised to meet all the expenses of Indian troops deployed outside the subcontinent. India, which had owed Britain £350 million in 1939, was itself owed £1,200 million when the war ended.

Britain faced other, less tangible reckonings in 1945. During the war, Churchill had banned a poster which showed a child with rickets playing in a dank and gloomy yard, with walls inscribed 'Disease' and 'Neglect', and the caption, 'Your Britain For It Was'.[58] Other approved and less trenchant propaganda conveyed the same message; the people's war would be the prelude to an era of national regeneration in which ignorance, poverty, shoddy housing, unemployment and sickness would be eliminated by a benevolent state. How this would come about had been the subject of countless lectures, discussions and debates organised by the services' educational staff which, in five years, had produced fighting men less deferential, more politically radical and aware of the world than their predecessors in 1918. They contributed, though not decisively as is commonly believed, to Labour's victory in July 1945, and were by and large excited by the prospects it brought. Among troops stationed in India and the Far East, the army censors discovered 'a widespread feeling that they [Labour] would produce some new and magic methods of solving the problems of reconstruction'.[59]

Coloured soldiers also expected a brighter future. According to Arthur Creech Jones, Labour's expert on colonial matters, black servicemen shared the aspirations of their British comrades.[60] In October 1945, a survey of Indian soldiers revealed that after the war they wanted, in order of preference: a comfortable home, a pension, a loving wife, children, an understanding of how to take precautions against malaria, one or two cows, schools, a maternity and general hospital, a gun for shooting game and a horse.[61]

For many Indian soldiers the experience of service on the Italian front in 1944–5 had been a revelation of the extent of their country's backwardness, and had left them with a strong urge to return home and put matters right. Knowledge appeared to be the key to national salvation, and some sepoys demanded a national education system that promoted the teaching of technical subjects. One observed: 'People of the West are far advanced in Art, Culture and Social Reform. In every respect India stands last. The main cause is too many castes, and our people will never unite together to do anything.'[62]

The war had also encouraged African soldiers to examine themselves and the world outside their villages. 'The African is feeling his feet and is looking round with different eyes,' wrote the novelist Gerald Hanley, who commanded East African askaris in Burma. After witnessing the poverty of India, the soldiers' respect for the Indians had dissolved. Most significantly, the African was acquiring new tastes: 'If a man learns to smoke, eat tinned food and to read newspapers, he will generally wish to continue satisfying these appetites and he will need to earn money to do so.' One casualty of this revolution was the old African culture. Asked why the men did not sing traditional songs, a Rhodesian askari replied, 'Why should we sing such stuff any longer? We have newspapers and ideas like Europeans. This music belongs to the old men and times that are gone.'[63] But old loyalty remained strong; Hanley's soldiers were untouched by the political radicalism of Africa's small educated élite. 'The feeling for "Kingi Georgi" among the askaris', Hanley asserted, 'is not just a "bwana's" sundowner story, but a real thing . . . they regard him as the King of all the British and treat him accordingly.'[64]

12

The Defence of
Archaic Privilege:
The Empire Restored,
1942–5

Just over a year after the end of the war, Willie Gallacher, the Communist MP for West Fife, declared to the Commons that, 'The British Empire [is] handed over to the American pawnbroker – our only hope.' To prove his point and taunt the Conservatives, he then quoted a remark Churchill had made to Roosevelt in August 1941, 'Without America, the Empire cannot stand.'[1] Like all maverick MPs, Gallacher had a knack of bluntly expressing home truths which other politicians preferred to ignore or evade.

Since 1941, Britain had been mortgaged to the United States. As the war had progressed, it became clear that the loss of financial independence had reduced the government's freedom of choice when it came to making decisions about the empire's future. American opinion could not be disregarded because American fighting men were bearing the brunt of the war against Japan. Victories in the Pacific between 1942 and 1945 were making it possible for Britain to regain its Far Eastern colonies. For large numbers of Americans this was not a worthy cause; many asked why American manhood should be sacrificed in order that Britain could continue to lord it over Malays and Burmese.

Emotional anti–imperialism was endemic in America. The general line was that all empires, including the British, were parasitic tyrannies which were fast becoming obsolete. 'The age of empires is dead,' proclaimed the

Under-Secretary of State, Sumner Welles. For him and millions of Americans the war was a crusade for democracy and human rights throughout the world. Dynamic historical forces were gathering momentum which would create a new world order in which no country could expect the right to rule others without their consent. The man on the sidewalk concurred; opinion polls taken in 1942 and 1945 suggested that 56 per cent of Americans believed that the British empire was in some way 'oppressive'.[2]

This response was predictable given the American press's treatment of Britain's empire. 'The British game never varies,' alleged the *Chicago Tribune* in April 1945 in a typical attack. 'What Britain has she will hold. What other nations obtain Britain will share.' Evidence of this rapacity, and the chicanery that invariably accompanied it, was the speed with which British officials took up the reins of power after American troops had liberated the Solomon Islands. America was in the throes of building a new, fairer world in which there was no place for district officers laying down the law, and the *Tribune* demanded an international debate on the future of all territories 'where native populations have been long oppressed'.[3] Ironically, and unknown to the *Tribune*'s high-minded editor, the newly-returned British administrators had been protesting at the recent use of USAAF aircraft in bombing raids on the villages of pro-Japanese Solomon Islanders.[4]

Behind visceral anti-imperialism lay that schoolroom version of the American War of Independence in which liberty-loving colonists rose up against the arrogant and despotic George III and his brutal redcoats. It was no accident that British apologists for the empire were often branded as 'Tories', the term of abuse which had been applied to loyalists in 1776. At a more sophisticated political level, there was a strong feeling that the protectionist empire and the sterling block were major barriers to the creation of open free markets throughout the world, to which the United States government was committed.

The British were also devious and, whatever might be said in public, their principal war aim was always the preservation of their empire and world power. Major-General Patrick Hurley, a former Oklahoma cowboy proud of his quickness on the draw, made it his business to sniff out British perfidy and alert the State Department. In 1942 he was in Persia where, he claimed, the British were siphoning off Lend Lease materials to further their imperial ambitions, which also involved a hugger-mugger deal with the Russians. Two years later, when he was serving in the Far East, Hurley accused Britain, France and the Netherlands of making secret preparations to repossess their old colonies despite the promises made by the Allies in the Atlantic Charter.[5] Hurley's was an extreme case of anti-British paranoia, but his sentiments were not exceptional; there were occasions when Roosevelt inveighed against British duplicity and greed.

Hurley and other American anti-imperialists set the greatest store by the Atlantic Charter. It was an idealistic statement of Anglo-American war objectives, which had been agreed between Churchill and Roosevelt in August 1941. For many, perhaps the majority, of those who read it, the Atlantic Charter was a blueprint for a new and just world order. Taken literally, it appeared to undermine the moral base for all empires. The President and the Prime Minister had pledged themselves to uphold 'the rights of all peoples to choose the form of government under which they live; and they wish to see sovereign rights and self-government restored to those who have been forcibly deprived of them.'

Churchill disliked this phraseology which, taken at face value, challenged Britain's right to rule her colonies. On reflection, he satisfied himself that in the case of those colonies in Japanese hands the 'sovereign rights' concerned were those of Britain and not the indigenous inhabitants. Churchill also conveniently assumed that the rest of the colonial empire was exempt from the Atlantic Charter. His deputy, the Labour leader Clement Attlee, thought otherwise and, like many within Britain and the empire, believed the Charter had universal application. The Colonial Office adopted a grudging, middle-of-the-road position, indicating that in the 'far distant future' some colonies might achieve dominion status. Others never would; strategic considerations demanded that Britain held on perpetually to Gibraltar, Malta, Cyprus and Aden, and for various other reasons could not relinquish control over the Gambia, Borneo, Malaya, Hong Kong, Bermuda, Fiji, the Falkland Islands and British Honduras (Belize).[6] Those responsible for war propaganda in the colonies were instructed to stay as mute as possible about the Charter and its implications.[7]

One way to sidestep the moral dilemma created by the Atlantic Charter was to persuade the Americans that the empire's subjects were not down-trodden and exploited. From 1941 onwards, the government went to considerable lengths to educate American politicians and opinion-makers, a process which continued for the next twenty years. The message was always the same: British colonial government was unselfish, humane, just and always conducted in the best interests of people who would be lost

without it. The star wartime apologist was Lord Hailey, a former administrator in India with a deep understanding of African affairs, who
embodied everything that was good and honourable in a colonial mandarin. After hearing this Olympian figure expound the virtues of British
rule to a group of American intellectuals, a Colonial Office official sourly
commented, 'What a stupid tragedy it would be to take the management
of great affairs from men like Hailey and give them to the boys with
thick-lensed glasses, long hair, and longer words nasally intoned.'[8]

Behind these remarks lay a half-hidden welter of anti-American prejudices. Proud of their own rectitude, the British, then and later, were
sensitive to moral criticism from Americans. Pre-war hostility towards
America and its people had been restricted to the upper and upper-middle
classes, according to George Orwell. These feelings were, he believed,
based upon distrust of the United States's expanding commercial power
and its peoples' egalitarian outlook. By contrast, the working class had
been entranced by American films and popular music and impressed by
American living standards.[9] As the war proceeded British attitudes fell
into line, as the presence of large numbers of American servicemen made
itself felt. They were commonly seen as 'over-paid, over-sexed and over
here', although Orwell oddly blamed the new, resentful anti-Americanism
on the fact that all United States personnel were middle class, and therefore unlikely to get on well with the British working class.

It was upper-class Englishmen who dealt with Americans at the highest levels, an experience that many found trying. John Maynard Keynes,
who negotiated wartime financial deals, found the American accent discordant and called it 'Cherokee' English.[10] Harold Macmillan's patrician
sensibilities were bruised by American manners, speech and verbosity.
How Americans may have felt about him and his kind can be guessed from
his revealing observation that traditional British snobbery disappeared
overseas, and was replaced 'by the bond of contempt for and antipathy to
foreigners'.[11]

One persistent source of resentment was American allegations about the
mistreatment of colonial races. The British were quick to counter-attack,
launching their offensive in an area where America was vulnerable, domestic racism. The socialite commentator Nancy Cunard, appealing in 1942
for legislation to outlaw the colour bar, claimed that whereas the British
displayed 'unthinking prejudice' towards blacks, Americans showed 'rabid
hatred'.[12] A visit to Monroe, Georgia, where four negroes had been
lynched in 1946, provoked the left-wing Labour MP Tom Driberg to

boast that such barbarism would never have occurred within the colonies or in Britain, where there was 'no racial discrimination or practically none'.[13] This was not entirely true; but segregation and lynchings in the South and race riots everywhere made American sermons about colonial oppression sound like humbug. This point was made obliquely by Gandhi in a personal message to Roosevelt in 1942, and was not well received.[14]

The roots and history of Anglo-American bickering have been exhaustively studied, and sometimes the results give the impression that relations between the Allies were an unending and unedifying dog fight. This was not so, thanks in large part to the characters of Churchill and Roosevelt. Not always smooth, their association rested on a warm personal friendship, mutual admiration and a remarkable degree of candour on both sides. A further strong bond was the common determination to beat Hitler, even though, during 1942 and 1943, American commanders suspected Britain of having cold feet when it came to getting to grips with the German army in Western Europe.

When it came to prosecuting the war, more percipient Americans detected two Britains, strangely at odds with each other. In April 1942, the columnist Walter Lippmann told Keynes that there existed in America 'a strong feeling that Britain east of Suez is quite different from Britain at home, that the war in Europe is a war of liberation and the war in Asia is the defence of archaic privilege.'[15] Up to a point, Lippmann was right, although when he was writing the 'archaic privilege' of the old colonial order was withering. It had been physically overturned in shameful circumstances when Singapore fell, and its ethical foundations were being eroded by public criticism in Britain and the United States.

British public opinion, as much as American anti-imperialism, made it impossible for the British government to put the clock back. Henceforward, the empire's rulers knew that for the colonies to survive in the post-war world they would have to jettison the maxim 'Nanny knows best', and instead listen and respond to the aspirations of their subjects. The point was made by Lord Hailey in the *Spectator* on 17 March 1942, in which he discussed the difficulties of restoring imperial government in the Far East. Early in 1945 Lord Lugard, then in his eighty-eighth year, looked benignly on the new spirit abroad in the world. A new age was imminent and it would be Britain's duty to extend to the colonies those fundamental freedoms for which the war was being fought. It was now the moment for the colonies to begin their apprenticeship for home rule.[16]

It says much about the shift in attitudes during the war that a veteran of

Queen Victoria's imperial campaigns and the architect of indirect rule should embrace ideas whose practical application was bound to bring about the dissolution of the colonial empire. And yet Lugard's conversion is not altogether surprising, given the nature of the empire. It had undergone many changes during his lifetime, and if an imperial philosophy existed, it was that the empire was an evolving organism. By 1945, there was a consensus as to the direction the empire should take: the colonies would slowly be transformed into self-governing dominions, wherever such a change was viable. The Labour party had already pledged itself to Indian home rule, and promised the same to the colonies, with the caveat that they needed to remain under British control 'for a long time to come'.[17] The Labour minister Herbert Morrison put it more bluntly; premature independence for the colonies would be a folly equivalent to delivering 'a latch key, a bank account and a shot-gun' to a ten-year-old child.[18]

Imperial propaganda was adjusted to the new mood in Britain, taking on a defensive, sometimes apologetic air. 'To many people nowadays the word "Empire" has a nasty sound. It reminds them of Nazi ideas of a master-race ruling others,' ran an advisory pamphlet issued by the Directorate of Army Education in April 1944.[19] Teaching soldiers about the empire and the vital part it would play in the post-war world had been one of the tasks of army instructors since the end of 1941.[20] Classes were to be reminded that to be a part of the empire was to be 'a member of a great powerful world-wide family instead of the citizen of a small, weak country'. At the same time, lecturers were encouraged to demolish the myth that most natives were ineducable, and extol their talents such as craftsmanship and a sense of rhythm. Colonial peoples were now partners with Britain, which safeguarded them against exploitation by 'ruthless private enterprise', and helped them towards prosperity and independence. The way forward was explained in a simple sketch which showed a matchstick figure of a native with a huge bundle on his head walking towards a grass hut, which contained two women and no furniture. Opposite was a bungalow with a bed and a chest of drawers, and outside the same native was cycling with his bundle on the back of his bike.[21]

Benevolent imperialism had come of age. Like Britain, the empire was moving into a new and better era in which the well-being of its subjects was of paramount importance. The empire had become very worthy, and was stripped of its old glamour. Nevertheless, it was essential that Britain presented its empire in a way which showed that there was a place for humane imperialism in the millenniumal world which, it was hoped, would emerge after the war.

Not only did Britain have to convince the United States that its empire was a force for good, it had to secure American assistance for the defence of India and the recovery of its colonies in the Far East. Both were secondary war aims and far beyond Britain's capabilities. Allied resources and strategy in the region were in the hands of South-East Asia Command (SEAC), set up in the summer of 1943, and quickly nicknamed 'Save England's Asiatic Colonies' by cynical Americans. SEAC also had the task of reviving Britain's almost moribund prestige in the area, and Churchill was anxious that it should have a British commander-in-chief.

His choice was eccentric and controversial. Vice-Admiral Louis Mountbatten was forty-three in 1943, had a fine fighting record, and had been promoted at a pace which would have raised eyebrows in the eighteenth century. He was the younger son of a German princeling who was, like most of his kind, a member of Queen Victoria's distended family, and had made himself an impressive career in the Royal Navy. The son was vain, ambitious, and hard-working, although his attention to his duties never quite wiped out his reputation as a playboy. For Churchill, Mountbatten was the ideal figurehead for what was essentially an imperial campaign. Years before, Churchill had developed a deep admiration for T.E. Lawrence, whom he and many others regarded as a true hero of empire, perhaps the last. His death in 1935 had dismayed Churchill, who deeply regretted the loss of a talent which would have been invaluable in another war. Churchill was, therefore, always on the look-out for another Lawrence. He was captivated, but not for long, by Orde Wingate, who commanded behind-the-lines units (Chindits) in Burma.[22] His choice finally fell on Mountbatten who, if he did not possess Lawrence's intellect and imagination, had his gallantry, good looks, assiduity and flair for showmanship.

The United States government approved Mountbatten's appointment, for he appeared less starchy and more 'democratic' than the run-of-the-mill British general or admiral.[23] Older, more experienced men, who had been by-passed, were disgruntled, even though Mountbatten faced an uphill struggle in Asia, against not only the Japanese but the Americans. All SEAC's offensive operations required American sanction. The situation was candidly summed up by General Sir Henry Pownall, Mountbatten's chief of staff, in April 1944: 'The Americans have got us by the short hairs . . . We can't do anything in this theatre, amphibious or otherwise, without material assistance from them . . . So if they don't approve they don't provide.'[24] It was the same in the Mediterranean in 1943–4, when the American high command was extremely reluctant to send landing craft and warplanes to the Italian front, which was considered of secondary importance to the Pacific.

In SEAC's area, the United States set its highest hopes on Chiang Kai-Shek's nationalist army, followers of a loftier cause than the restoration of British, French and Dutch colonies. Moreover, American post-war plans envisaged China as the major regional power in the Far East, and assumed that it would take on major peacekeeping responsibilities. Until his replacement in October 1944, Chiang's chief of staff was the anglophobe, anti-imperialist Stilwell, who, while civil in public, was contemptuous of the British in private. Mountbatten was at various times reviled as 'the Glamour Boy', 'an amateur', 'a fatuous ass', 'childish Louis, publicity crazy' and a 'pisspot'. His countrymen were 'bastardly hypocrites [who] do their best to cut our throats on all occasions. The pig fuckers.'[25]

Stilwell's expletives were a vivid reminder of American misgivings about Britain's wartime goals. In the Far East these were contrary to Allied ideals; by no stretch of the imagination, and in spite of the brutality of Japanese rule, could the retaking of Burma and Malaya be depicted as liberation. Both were repossessed by their former owner, Britain.

In December 1943 Roosevelt announced that he intended to have Indo-China administered by an international commission rather than let it remain in French hands. It was harder to extend such an arrangement to Britain's former colonies, since Churchill was adamantine whenever the subject of the post-war empire was raised. With strong, all-party backing he and his successor, Attlee, stonewalled at the Yalta and Potsdam conferences when discussions moved towards some form of international control for Europe's colonies. Americans were also disturbed by Britain's policy in Greece where, during 1944–5, British troops supported the anti-Communist faction, in what resembled a Palmerstonian bid to secure total control over the eastern Mediterranean. As the tide of war turned during 1944, it seemed that Britain, so lately the champion of democracy and freedom, had metamorphosed into the hungry imperial lion of a past age, wanting the biggest share of whatever was available.

Shortages of the wherewithal to wage war slowed down the lion in the

Far East. India had finally been made secure by the battles of Kohima and Imphal in March and June 1944. Eight months before, Churchill had pressed for Operation Culverin, a landing on Sumatra, which would provide a base for an attack on Singapore. It was abandoned because Churchill's attention had been taken up by another chimerical scheme, the expulsion of the Germans from the Dodecanese Islands, which, he imagined, would propel Turkey into the war as an ally. This was overruled by the Americans, who rightly wanted all spare forces concentrated on the imminent invasion of France. European fronts continued to enjoy precedence over the Far East; in October 1944 Mountbatten was told that no forces could be spared for a seaborne assault on Rangoon.

It was only in February 1945 that permission was given for an advance on Rangoon. This was to be followed by large-scale seaborne landings on the Siamese and Malaya coasts between June 1945 and March 1946, code-named Roger, Zipper and Mailfist. (There is a peculiar poetry about the titles given to Second World War operations; their origins and originators deserve a close study.)

As it was, Zipper and Mailfist turned out to be bloodless enterprises. Overstretched everywhere since the middle of 1942, Japan had been fighting and losing a defensive war. The Imperial Japanese Navy had lost both its preponderance and initiative at Midway and, despite considerable effort, failed to recover either in the next two years. By the winter of 1944–5, American forces had secured the Ryukyu Islands, Iwo Jima and Okinawa, and by the spring mass raids against Japanese cities by the USAAF's B-29 bombers were underway. In June 1945, less than a month after Germany's defeat, a detailed plan for invasion of Japan had been prepared. Thirteen or fourteen United States divisions were to attack Kyushu in November 1945, and a further twenty-five, with a Commonwealth contingent, would land on Honshu in March 1946, coinciding with the final push in Malaya. Hitherto, Britain had played virtually no part in the Pacific war, but once the defeat of Germany was imminent, Churchill fulfilled his pledge to Australia and began to move ships to join the USN. By the summer of 1945 nearly a hundred British and Commonwealth men-o'-war were operating in Japanese waters.

Neither the ships nor the elaborate plans for landings on the Japanese mainland and Malaya were needed. On 6 August an atomic bomb was exploded over Hiroshima, followed by another over Nagasaki three days later. These blows, combined with Russia's declaration of war, forced the Japanese government to surrender unconditionally on 15 August. The way was now open for Britain to take back its colonies, and incidentally assist the French and the Dutch to regain theirs. Rangoon had fallen in the spring, and on 9 September British and Indian forces went ashore in Malaya. Three days later Singapore was recaptured without a fight. As the Japanese generals proffered their swords, they struck Mountbatten as resembling 'a bunch of gorillas, with great baggy breeches and knuckles almost trailing to the ground'. Lee Kuan Yew, the future prime minister of Singapore, thought the 'final humiliation of these little warriors' was 'one of the greatest moments of the history of South East Asia'.[26] Was it one of the greatest moments in the empire's history? Probably not, for the British had come back into Malaya on the coat tails of the Americans. Nonetheless, British rule was infinitely preferable to Japanese, and the army was warmly welcomed, although one journalist was dismayed to notice how a 'blundering and stuffy' administration encouraged the recrudescence of 'all the petty snobbery of second-rate Singapore'.[27] There was nothing stuffy about the soldiers of the liberating army; they dressed untidily and were slack in saluting superiors, much to Mountbatten's annoyance.[28] It was, perhaps, their way of saying goodbye to all that, for the war was over.

The British empire had survived the war without loss of territory, although damage to prestige, sustained since Munich, was impossible to calculate. The human cost of victory had been far less than in 1918; casualties were:

	Dead	Missing	Wounded
Great Britain:	233,042	57,472	275,975
Canada:	36,018	2,866	53,073
Australia:	21,415	6,519	37,477
New Zealand:	9,844	2,201	19,253
South Africa:	6,417	1,980	13,773
India:	23,295	12,264	62,064
Colonies:	6,741	14,811	6,773

Economic losses were far heavier than in 1918 for, as Chamberlain had foretold, the war effort ate up Britain's reserves. Britain had been stripped of two-thirds of her pre-war export trade and a quarter of her stored wealth. In December 1945 she had to obtain a $375,000 million loan at 2 per cent from the United States in return for a pledge that a year after the sums had been transferred the pound would become freely convertible. This would hamper an economic recovery based on exports, but the American government cancelled $20,000 million of Lend Lease obligations.

So, in 1945, Britain had emerged from war a debtor nation with an empire, (still the largest in the world) and clinging to old pretensions of global power. But when Churchill had met Stalin and Roosevelt at Yalta, one observer had likened the trio to the Roman triumvirs who held power after Julius Caesar's death. Stalin and Churchill were the titans, Octavius and Mark Antony, while Churchill, for all his rhetoric, was the all-but-forgotten Lepidus. Russia and America had become, through their industrial and armed strength, 'superpowers', leaving Britain to occupy a humbler position. The United States was for the moment the mightier of the two superpowers; she held two-thirds of the world's gold reserves, aerial and naval supremacy and, most importantly, the technology to produce atomic bombs. Her industrial and banking systems were undamaged by war, and she was to all intents and purposes enjoying the same international pre-eminence as Britain had in 1815.

The empire alone qualified Britain to project itself as a global power. Its future in a world dominated by two states which, for various economic and political reasons, were inimical to territorial as opposed to ideological or economic empires, was far from certain. Furthermore the new Labour government had, since 1938, promised to give India self-government, and was determined to honour this pledge. Independence was also the destination of the larger colonies, although no one was prepared to say how long the journey would take. In terms of political logic, if such an abstraction exists, Britain had now committed itself to the eventual dissolution of its overseas empire and therefore its world power. Of course, the new pattern of thinking about the empire was not seen as a suicide note; it was assumed that old colonies would become new dominions whose association with Britain would somehow preserve her as a force to be reckoned with in the world.

PART FIVE

THE SETTING SUN
1945–93

1

The Colonialists are
on the Rampage:
The Empire in the
Post-war World

The history of what turned out to be the final decades of the British empire was largely determined by the course of the Cold War. It began in the winter of 1944–5, when British and American strategists began to get the jitters about the extent and purpose of the formidable build-up of Soviet military strength in eastern and central Europe. It ended in December 1988, when Mikhail Gorbachev announced the imminent dismantling of Russia's European war machine. In some respects the Cold War was like its predecessor, known less menacingly as the Great Game, which had been played between Britain and Russia in central Asia throughout the nineteenth century. It was a contest of nerve, diplomatic manoeuvre, arms races, intelligence gathering and subversion in which each side was continually nervous about the other's intentions and capability for making mischief. Here the similarities end, for more was at stake in the Cold War. Antagonists in both camps regularly predicted that their goal was a world dominated by either Communism or capitalism. Furthermore. from August 1949, when the Soviet Union tested its first atomic bomb there was always a chance that a severe crisis might lead to a nuclear war.

The Cold War was not started deliberately nor, in its early stages, was anyone clear as to how long it might last or what course it would take. What was clear to those in Washington and London with responsibility for forward planning was that by the end of the war Russia would possess a vast unofficial empire in eastern Europe. Fears that it might extend it by proxy, using the expanding European Communist parties, were confirmed with the outbreak of the Greek Civil War in December 1944. Four months after, Macmillan described Stalin as 'a sort of Napoleon', a conclusion already reached by American strategists who, from May 1944, felt that Britain could not resist post-war Russian encroachments in western Europe without the United States's assistance.[1]

British apprehension about Russia's future behaviour was focussed on threats to the empire, and they assumed a disturbing substance during the first half of 1946, when Russia demanded bases in Libya and the Dardanelles, and refused to evacuate northern Persia. Soviet attacks on British policy in the Mediterranean, India, Persia and the Dutch East Indies during the first United Nations meeting in February 1946 convinced the Foreign Secretary, Ernest Bevin, that Russia 'is intent on the destruction of the British Empire'. The same view was taken by American military planners, who were now regarding the empire as a valuable asset in what might develop into a protracted global confrontation.[2]

Anglo-American solidarity was now as vital as ever it had been during the war. The point was vividly emphasised by Churchill in his celebrated 'Iron Curtain' speech, delivered with President Harry Truman's warm endorsement at Fulton, Missouri, in February 1946. America's need of Britain as an ally against a malevolent Russia helped soften Washington's attitude towards the empire. There had been signs of a change of heart during the winter of 1944-5, after Roosevelt had relaxed his objections towards France's repossession of Indo-China. There were substantial Communist, anti-Japanese resistance movements there (Ho Chi-Minh's Viet Minh) and in Malaya. Both had a vast potential for subversion, and it was, therefore, politically prudent to allow the re-occupation of both colonies by their former rulers. Decolonisation would follow, but the process was best left to Britain and France, who would deal with the local Communists before handing over power to more tractable groups. The first skirmishes of the Cold War were fought around Saigon during the winter and spring of 1945-6, when Anglo-Indian forces secured the city in readiness for the disembarkation of an army from France. Japanese POWs were re-armed and took part enthusiastically in the operations against the Viet Minh partisans.[3] General Douglas MacArthur was incensed by the cynical employment of old enemies against old friends; obviously he had still to grasp the new pattern of loyalties and alignments which was emerging throughout the world.

The Cold War was an unwelcome distraction for the Labour government, not least because it acted as a brake on national recovery since sparse resources had to be channelled into rearmament. Labour had won the 1945 election with a visionary programme; its manifesto, *Let us Face the Future,* was a masterplan for a social and economic revolution designed to create a new Jerusalem. A bountiful state took responsibility for welfare and education, and the economy was to be revitalised through a mixture of public ownership, regulation by Whitehall and private enterprise. The philosophy which underlay this policy dominated British politics until the early 1980s, when Margaret Thatcher started a new and as yet unfinished revolution based upon the values of an unrestricted free market. Her adherents, like Labour's supporters in 1945, were Utopians, believing that they had discovered a perfect system which would bring universal content and prosperity.

The empire had been a peripheral issue during the 1945 general election. Labour did affirm that it would give self-government to India, but when George Orwell raised the issue at the hustings, he and it were politely ignored.[4] Used to hearing sympathetic noises from Labour politicians, mostly on the left of the party, West African students in Britain threw themselves into the campaign in the hope that a Labour victory would bring nearer their countries' independence. They were disappointed, and within a few years were finding it impossible to tell the difference between Labour and Conservative colonial policies.[5]

This was unfair but understandable. Having set its heart on a new Jerusalem in Britain, Labour was busy setting up smaller Jerusalems in the colonies. This was the principal aim of Labour's colonial policy which, in practice, differed little from old-style benevolent imperialism. Social justice mattered as much if not more than eventual self-government. 'There is in Kenya a civilisation of the dominant race, supported by cheap labour, and that kind of society is intolerable,' announced Creech Jones, although as Colonial Secretary from 1946 onwards he did little to change matters.[6] He did, however, frighten white settlers in Africa and they were relieved when the Conservatives won the October 1951 general election.[7]

The guidelines for Labour's colonial policies had been drawn just before and during the war. Social and economic regeneration took precedence over schemes for self-government, although the two were ultimately complementary. The problem was that Britain's tropical colonies were impoverished and backward. A commission of enquiry which had toured the West Indies shortly before the war uncovered a stagnant backwater: illegitimacy rates were between 60 and 70 per cent, venereal diseases were spreading and malaria was endemic. One in fifteen of the population of Dominica (notable for its cultivation of limes and colourful postage stamps) was infected by yaws, and the average annual income was £15. The remedy for such economic and physical debilitation was the Colonial Development Acts of 1940 and 1945, which offered grants and loans for road and bridge building, clinics, schools and hospitals and waterworks. An efficient infrastructure would, it was argued, prepare the way for economic self-sufficiency. It was axiomatic that the colonies could only govern themselves if they had the means to support themselves. Between 1946 and 1951, £40.5 million was distributed for improvements, but during the same period the Treasury insisted that £250 million earned by the colonies from their export trade was deposited in London to bolster Britain's sterling reserves.[8] It was a crazy situation; the colonies made do on a shoestring of government hand-outs while their real wealth remained idle in London.

Treasury intransigence was compounded by Colonial Office folly. Grandiose, state-funded plans for the mass production of eggs in the Gambia and groundnuts in Tanganyika came to expensive grief through slipshod preparation and mismanagement. The latter consumed £40 million, for which the Tanganyikans gained 11,000 acres of tillable land, three cattle ranches and a tobacco plantation. Another government-financed venture, the Colonial Development Board, also foundered with no advantage to the colonies and great loss to the taxpayer. Two strands in Labour's thinking contributed to these disasters. The first was the dogma that private investment in the colonies equalled exploitation, whilst enterprises underwritten by the state did not. Secondly, there was a feeling that carefully planned development of colonial production, particularly of foodstuffs, would save much needed dollars. Britain could import comestibles without using up precious dollar reserves, and colonial exports would augment them. In the end nobody benefited, and in the colonies there was a feeling that their economies were being manipulated solely to enrich Britain. This was true up to a point, but defenders of the government's colonial enterprises argued that they would in time enrich the colonies involved.

Business misadventures in Africa coincided with a sequence of domestic and international crises. In 1948 the Cold War entered a new and dangerous phase with the Russian annexation of Czechoslovakia, the blockade of Berlin and the start of the Communist guerrilla campaign in

Malaya. Britain and the empire were already committed to supporting the United States, which, by the Truman Doctrine of March 1947, was now pledged to resist further Soviet expansion, whether in the form of direct aggression or conspiracy. A year later, Marshall Aid began to flow into western Europe to succour economies and populations which, if unassisted, could fall to Communism.

The iron economic and military realities of the post-1945 world relegated Britain to the position of America's junior partner. After a meeting with President Truman in January 1952, Evelyn Shuckburgh observed, 'It was impossible not to be conscious that we were playing second fiddle.'[9] Filling a supporting role did not come easily to the servants of a nation which had grown accustomed to being at the centre of the stage. They continued to think and act as if they were the policy-makers and agents of a great power. The most striking evidence of their attitude was the decision to proceed with the manufacture of an atomic bomb.

After the termination of close Anglo-American cooperation in nuclear research at the end of 1945, the government went ahead with the construction of plant for the extraction of plutonium at Windscale on the Cumberland coast, which was judiciously renamed Sellafield after a nearly disastrous accident in 1957. In the meantime, the Air Ministry was mapping out a network of strategic air-routes, criss-crossing the empire and linking twenty-seven airfields built to take extra-heavy bombers.[10] On paper, it appeared as impressive as its Victorian counterpart, the worldwide chain of naval bases and coaling stations. One projected aerodrome, at Karachi, was among those earmarked by the Joint Technical Warfare Committee for atom-bomb raids on sixty-seven Russian cities in an exigency plan devised in April 1946.[11] The boffins had jumped the gun, for the cabinet had yet to approve the programme for making the bombs.

Permission was granted the following October by Attlee, a small cabal of senior ministers and their technocrat advisers. The Prime Minister was worried whether at some future date the United States might revert to its customary isolationism, leaving Britain alone to face the Red army. Ernest Bevin, the Foreign Secretary, was sore about the condescending attitude of his American counterpart, and was determined to get the weaponry which would qualify him and his successors to speak as representatives of a great world power.[12] The atom bomb had become the mid-twentieth century equivalent of a fleet of Dreadnoughts; the symbol of a global power's determination to hold on to its status.

Blunt in his speech and John Bullish in his demeanour, Bevin never doubted that he was the foreign minister of a world power, and acted accordingly. The former trade union leader's common sense, robust opinions and pugnacity were judged sound by military men and diplomats.[13] A portrait of George III hung over his desk, and there were times when he appeared animated by the spirit of Palmerston, whom he admired.[14] Bevin's chief task was to cooperate with the United States in the fabrication of a barrier of mutually dependent states in Europe, the Middle East and Asia, strong enough to withstand Russia. The first link, the North Atlantic Treaty Organisation (NATO) was in place by 1949, guaranteeing the security of Western Europe.

Both American and British strategists identified the Middle East as a region ripe for Soviet subversion and penetration. Its Cold War significance was twofold. From the end of 1947, America's war plans depended on Middle Eastern bases for an atomic strike against the industrial heartlands of the Don basin.[15] Secondly, the Middle East's oilfields were taking up the spiralling demand for oil; by 1950–1, and after a period of rapid development, they were producing 70 per cent of the West's requirements. Britain had traditionally been the dominant power in this region, and during the late 1940s America was prepared to underpin this arrangement for the time being for no other reason than necessity. In 1949–50, the Pentagon's gurus estimated that, in the event of a global war, no American forces could be spared for the Middle East for at least two years, and so British and Commonwealth troops, ships and aircraft would have to hold the line.

Whether they could undertake such a responsibility was open to question. During 1946 Attlee had been disturbed by the costs of Britain's presence in the Mediterranean and the Middle East, and he had contemplated a large-scale withdrawal. He was dissuaded by Bevin, who argued that the Russians would take over once Britain had departed. The chiefs of staff threw their weight behind the Foreign Secretary, threatening resignation in the event of any evacuation. Early in January 1947 Attlee caved in.[16] Within a year, his government was forced to cut off aid to Greece and Turkey, and pull its forces out of Palestine. The trouble was that Britain could no longer afford a champagne-style foreign policy on a beer income, which was what the country had been reduced to by 1947. Two years afterwards, in the wake of a currency crisis and devaluation, the defence budget had to be cut by £700 million a year.

Men were as hard to find as money. At the end of the war, there had been 200,000 British and Indian forces stationed throughout the Middle

East. About half that number was considered a bare minimum (the Suez Canal Zone garrison was 80,000 in 1948) and that old standby, the Indian army, had disappeared in August 1947, when India and Pakistan became independent. Strapped for manpower, the government vainly tried to hire Pakistani troops.[17] Another, more fruitful attempt to compensate for the loss of the Indian army was domestic conscription, something which once would have been considered unthinkable in peacetime. The National Service Act of 1947 corralled all eighteen-year-olds for eighteen months of military service, a period which was extended to two years in 1949 at the onset of the Korean War.

An Indian barracks could be replaced by an African one. In December 1949, Attlee requested the Colonial Office and his chiefs of staff to explore the possibilities of raising a mass army from the African colonies. Their report took a year to draft, was pessimistic in tone, and reflected the prejudices of its compilers as much as the realities of the situation. It was calculated that Africa might yield 400,000 men, but of dubious quality. The black infantryman was poor value for money since he took longer to train, and could never attain the same level of 'operational efficiency' as his white counterpart. The African was also judged incapable of undertaking technical duties in the navy or RAF. Lastly, the deployment of black servicemen in the Mediterranean and Middle East might stir up a racial and political hornets' nest, and they would have to be kept isolated from South African units.[18] A black substitute for the Indian army remained a might-have-been of imperial history.

The dominions were indisposed to take a share of Britain's Cold War burden. An appeal for combined defence planning had met a lukewarm reception at the 1946 Commonwealth conference. Henceforward, attempts to hammer out a common and mutually supportive security policy were hampered by the presence of India and Ceylon, which then declared themselves neutral in the struggle between Russia and the West. Both dominions' delegates were excluded from discussions on global strategy at the 1948 conference, and from the revelations of Britain's Middle East plans in that of 1951.

The response of the white dominions for requests for specific assistance were mixed and disheartening. During the 1948 conference, Australia's Labour government made it plain that whilst it was anti-Communist, it had no desire to become an accomplice to the repression of popular nationalist movements, a line also taken by India. The burden of raising domestic living standards was the excuse given in October 1948 for not sending Australian formations to help fight the Communists in Malaya. The Communist victory in China in 1949 and the start of the Korean War radically changed Australia's outlook. Menzies, elected in December 1949, offered ground troops for service in Malaya. They were declined, although a squadron of Lincoln bombers was accepted. 'Australian troops are splendid fighters,' observed a Foreign Office official, 'but they tend to give trouble when they are not fighting.'[19] Given that the Malayan campaign was based upon the winning of Malay and Chinese hearts and minds, it would perhaps have been unwise to introduce soldiers with a historic reputation for treating native populations roughly.

The emergence of a Communist threat in the Far East between 1948 and 1950 naturally distressed Australia and New Zealand, although both were soon calmed by the 1950 ANZUS pact, which placed the defence of the Pacific under an American umbrella. This guarantee of local security would, it was hoped in Whitehall, persuade the two dominions to commit forces to the Middle East. They were needed more than ever in 1951, with the Persian oil crisis and the rapid deterioration of Anglo-Egyptian relations. The response was tepid. New Zealand and Southern Rhodesia were willing to lend a hand, with the former offering a squadron of the new Vampire jet fighters.[20] In the event of a war, Australia and New Zealand promised in December 1951 to earmark a 27,000-strong force for Malta and Cyprus, but its despatch would ultimately depend on conditions in the Far East.[21] Memories of having been left in the lurch in 1942 were obviously still strong in the Antipodes. Canada had nothing to offer, for its armed forces were entirely committed to NATO.

South Africa's position was equivocal. The anti-Communist credentials of the extreme right-wing Afrikaner Nationalist party, elected to power in 1948, were flawless, and it wanted American military aid. It was willing to offer Britain aircraft for the defence of the Middle East in an emergency. Nothing more was forthcoming, despite British arguments that Russia's way into Africa would be through Egypt. The War Office had hoped for an armoured brigade at least, on the grounds that South Africans were temperamentally suited to mobile warfare. 'They are "trekkers" by nature, and they get easily browned off if they are called upon to carry out the rather more steady and perhaps dull role of infantrymen,' commented one British general.[22] In 1953 Churchill's government tried to tempt the grandsons of the 1899 kommandos to come north with an offer of the Simonstown naval base in exchange for help in the Middle East, but was unsuccessful.[23]

It was left to Britain to man the thinly-stretched Cold War battleline in the Middle East, backed by a pocketful of promises of aid from the white dominions once the shooting started. Dominion units were not included in the exigency plans drawn up for a *coup de main* in Egypt in 1951, or a similar enterprise against Persia the same year.[24] And yet, when Sir Anthony Eden heard the first news of Nasser's nationalisation of the Suez Canal in 1956, he took for granted the services of the New Zealand cruiser *Royalist*, then in the Mediterranean.[25]

Between 1945 and 1951, the Labour government had engaged in the Cold War with all the resolution and, at times, bravado that might have been expected of a virile world power. Its conduct of foreign affairs contrasted strikingly with the tergiversation and nervelessness of the Conservatives in the years immediately before the war. Attlee's ministers acted as they did because they believed that it was right to parry Russian expansionism, and they were prepared to overlook the vast costs incurred. These soared after the start of the Korean War and, it could be argued, seriously impeded the economic recovery which had been gathering pace since 1949.

Throughout this period, Britain behaved as if it was an imperial power with global interests, even though the effort was back-breaking without the Indian army. Between 1949 and 1953, the Labour government and its Conservative successor imagined that the African empire might prove a substitute for India as a provider of men and material to sustain British pretensions.

Above all, there was the new, multi-racial Commonwealth, in which both Labour and the Conservatives made a substantial political and emotional investment. The dividends then and after were scanty. Two non-white dominions, India and Ceylon, refused to become Britain's allies in the Cold War; Burma left the Commonwealth in 1948, having become a republic, and was followed by Ireland, also now a republic, in 1949. India adopted a republican constitution in the same year but, after some legal acrobatics, remained a member of a Commonwealth whose nominal head was King George VI. The reason for permitting this anomaly was the fear that India, once outside the Commonwealth, might easily slide into the Communist block. Pakistan joined the anti-Soviet Baghdad Pact in 1955, not as a favour to Britain, but as a result of having been seduced by America, which had come courting with a gift of military aid worth $25 million dollars. The white dominions had been indifferent to calls to defend the old imperial lifeline through the Mediterranean and across the

Middle East. It now mattered less than ever; the safety of Australia and New Zealand was in American hands, as it had been effectively since 1942, and Canada was solely concerned with the Atlantic and Western Europe.

In a sense the Commonwealth was becoming a surrogate empire. Indeed, when plans for colonial self-government finally matured, it was assumed in London that the former colonies would automatically join the Commonwealth. Whether this body would endow Britain with the same authority, armed strength and prestige it had enjoyed when it ruled a territorial empire and the dominions did whatever London decreed was open to question. And yet, few in mid-twentieth-century Britain chose to examine the nature and function of the Commonwealth too critically. A BBC talk, delivered after the end of the Commonwealth foreign ministers' conference at Colombo in January 1950, suggested that the Commonwealth might be dismissed as a 'sentimental, disintegrating club for Blimps'. Then, having said that the Commonwealth lacked both a unified voice on foreign affairs and material strength, the speaker turned a summersault and announced that it 'has brought us close to the One World idea'.[26] If this was the case, the sceptical listener might have wondered why two members, India and Pakistan, were at daggers drawn over Kashmir, and a third, South Africa, in the midst of constructing apartheid, a social order based upon the supremacy of the white race.

As Britain entered the second half of the twentieth century it began to fall victim to the politics of illusion. In 1950 the Labour and Conservative parties had convinced themselves that the Commonwealth was something that should be cherished and was beyond criticism. It was simultaneously advertised to the world as a shining example of international cooperation and evidence of Britain's continuing status as a world power. This was make-believe on the part of politicians who had failed to come to terms with Britain's relative decline, and still hoped that the country might somehow manage to stand apart from its overmighty patron, the United States, and a Europe which, by the early 1950s, was taking its first steps towards economic unity. The illusion of power was better than none at all, and Commonwealth leaders were willing accessories in the charade. It offered them the chance to attend high-level conferences and be treated with a reverence their standing and calibre might otherwise not have commanded.

★

The increasing use of the word 'Commonwealth' to encompass the colonies as well as the dominions coincided with a sustained Communist propaganda campaign in which 'colonialism' was equated with the 'slavery' and 'exploitation' of coloured races by the capitalist powers. Whatever their political complexion, colonial protest movements were grouped together as part of a world-wide struggle against rapacious imperialism. At the end of 1948, *Pravda* reported how in French and British West Africa, the 'names of Lenin and Stalin were very well known even in forests and [the] smallest villages,' where people clubbed together to buy wireless sets so they could listen to Radio Moscow.[27] Strikers in the Gold Coast in 1948 were inspired by the example of Communist partisans in Indo-China and Indonesia [the former Dutch East Indies], where the Dutch were the pawns of 'the monopolists of Wall Street' who were ready to engorge themselves on the country's wealth. According to *Trud* of 19 August 1948, these bloodsuckers in harness with the City of London, were encouraging the destruction of the Malayan nationalist movement (i.e. Communist party) so as to get their hands on the country's raw materials.[28]

The tentacles of the global capitalist conspiracy reached into Africa. According to the veteran West Indian journalist George Padmore, editor of the London-based *Negro Worker*, Britain and America were about to swallow up its resources. Padmore regularly contributed Marxist articles to the *Gold Coast Observer*. During 1948–9, he accused the 'Trade Union Boss' Bevin of carrying out Tory policies in Palestine, and speculated as to whether African troops would be used alongside 'headhunters and blood hounds' in the anti-Communist war in Malaya.[29]

Colonial campaigns were a godsend for Communist copywriters. In November 1952, *Zyčič Warzawy* published a photograph of Mau Mau suspects with the caption: 'Here are two members of the "Mau Mau" organisation, manacled like slaves . . . They fought to liberate Kenya from the imperialist yoke, and for this they were regarded as bandits.' Under the headline 'The Colonisers are on the Rampage', *Komosol Pravda* of 30 June 1953 gave details of operations against the Mau Mau. 'The soldiers and police are cruelly persecuting the Negro population of this country. News of the mass murders of Negroes arrives each week from Kenya.' Among the reports cited was one from the British Communist newspaper, the *Daily Worker*, which proclaimed that, 'Terror reigns in Kenya which can be compared in brutality with only the occupation régime introduced by Nazi SS units.'[30]

Two things emerge from this welter of crude polemic. The first is the remarkable degree of press freedom which existed in Britain's colonies. It was in part the result of the application of domestic liberal principles, and in part an acknowledgement of the fact that outspoken journalism was unlikely to upset the colonial apple cart. The ability of a partisan press to make mischief was limited by the absence of mass political parties, or trade unions. In West Africa, where there were more newspapers and readers than elsewhere in the tropical empire, these conditions changed, slowly before the war and rapidly after. Nonetheless, the Colonial Office and its local officials felt strong enough to let matters stand. Had they wished to do otherwise, there would have been repercussions in Britain where, traditionally, state censorship of newspapers was considered intolerable in peacetime.

External Communist propaganda produced by Russia, its satellites, and later China, presented colonial unrest everywhere as part of a single, global struggle between the haves and have-nots, and pledged Communist support to the latter. The fear of Russian and Chinese-sponsored mass revolution in what today is called the Third World scared Washington and London. Whether or not the alarm was in proportion to the actual threat is irrelevant. What mattered was that from 1948 onwards both the British and American governments were extremely jumpy about subversion, not least because they were aware that in many colonies the social and economic conditions were perfect for Communist agitation. Whatever their actual root cause, strikes and political demonstrations were regularly diagnosed as symptoms of underground Communist activity.

At the end of 1947, the Colonial Office asked all colonial governments to report evidence of Soviet propaganda in their local press.[31] None was uncovered in Northern Rhodesia, the Gambia, the Seychelles, Bermuda or the Bahamas. From Nigeria came evidence of some academic interest in Marxism and the presence of Communist literature, but no organised party. Cypriot newspapers had contained Communist articles, including one which predicted a surge in American imperial expansion, and there was an abundance of Communist material in the Gold Coast newspapers. This was disturbing, given the high level of political and trade union activity in the colony, and an unexpected outbreak of rioting in Accra in February 1948. Investigations into this outbreak, and others in Singapore and Kenya, added to official jumpiness for they revealed a chilling lack of popular support for the colonial authorities.[32]

There was, inevitably, an intelligence trawl for evidence of Soviet intrigue in disaffected areas and among African nationalists. Particular attention was given to African students in Britain and politicians who visited the country. For over fifty years, both groups had gravitated towards left-wing circles, including the British Communist party. MI5 reported in 1953 that two prominent Kenyan dissidents had made contact with British Communists, who were 'apparently afraid to take them much into their confidence'.[33] African visitors were more warmly received and fêted by those left-wing Labour MPs, such as Fenner Brockway, who, in Barbara Castle's words, had a 'consuming interest' in all colonial freedom movements.[34] Liaisons of this kind worried the Colonial Office which, in a 1951 memorandum on the welfare of colonial students, suggested that the provision of 'healthy social interests and good living conditions' might prove an antidote to Communist influences. It was noted that the Conservatives had begun to court African students, who were by now being regarded as the future leaders of their countries.[35]

In Africa, evidence of organised Soviet subversion was fragmentary. The 1952 Kenyan emergency produced a shoal of intelligence red herrings, and one suspected Soviet agent, Mrs M.A. Rahman, the wife of an Indian diplomat who had just joined the Indian high commission in Nairobi.[36] Both she and her husband were carefully watched, but nothing concrete emerged to link either them or Russian intelligence to unrest in Kenya and central Africa.[37]

The intelligence offensive against what proved to be some somewhat exaggerated Communist infiltration of anti-colonialist movements was matched by official counter-propaganda. Here the United States was keen to lend a hand, and in 1950 the State Department proposed a joint programme of publicity suitable for colonies, using wireless broadcasts in native languages. The Colonial Office was cool. It foresaw 'political problems' if Africans were employed by the 'Voice of America' in New York, and was unhappy about scarce dollars being spent on imports of American wireless sets into the colonies. Most significantly, there were fears about American control over the content of the broadcasts.[38] The Colonial Office placed its faith in existing colonial broadcasting stations, and the sale of 'saucepan specials', receivers made by Pye and destined for African listeners. These sets cost £5 each and were, therefore, affordable. In Northern Rhodesia, where the average weekly wage was about one pound, the 'saucepan specials' were an immediate success, with a thousand being sold monthly during 1951.[39] It was estimated that each receiver attracted an audience of ten, and there were plenty of appreciative letters to the radio station at Lusaka. One read, 'These wireless sets are ours. Please try to make use of them if we are to be a civilised nation.'[40]

The prospect of the colonies becoming a Cold War ideological battlefield had a profound effect on policy towards self-government. During 1947, senior Colonial Office officials had been compiling detailed plans for the slow, systematic and piecemeal transfer of power within the colonies. It would be an evolutionary process, beginning with elected local councils, and proceeding as it were upwards, towards a national parliamentary government with powers over the colony's internal affairs. With a fully-fledged parliamentary democracy, the colony would be ready for independence. Nothing was to be rushed; it was calculated that it would take at least twenty, probably thirty years for native populations to learn the ways of democracy and, most importantly, to create a body of responsible and trustworthy native politicians.

This tidy, pragmatic and above all realistic programme was suddenly jettisoned in 1948. The immediate cause was the panic which beset the Colonial Office after the Accra riots in February, whose roots were economic distress rather than impatience with the pace of political change. Nonetheless, an official investigation recommended a swift constitutional change, promoting Africans to the Gold Coast's Executive Council. The further opening of government at all levels was proposed by a second report, compiled in 1949 by a commission of Africans under an African judge.[41] The British government accepted both reports, and the process of evolution was effectively compressed into a few years, for elections were held in 1950. In February 1952, Kwame Nkrumah, leader of the majority Convention People's party, became Leader of Government Business and, a year later, Prime Minister.

Why did the government take fright in 1948? The Gold Coast administration had been taken unawares by the disturbances, and its reaction was ham-fisted. There was no guidance from above as to how to handle riots, and it was only in 1955 that the Colonial Office attempted to devise a common policy on riot control. The preliminary enquiry yielded a fascinating variety of techniques; under the 1948 regulations for the St Vincent police, the issue of blank cartridges was forbidden, as was firing over the heads of rioters since 'this may give confidence to the daring and guilty'.[42] Whatever the circumstances, shooting rioters, as occurred in Accra, looked bad in the press, and from 1945 the government had found it impossible to keep details of colonial unrest from the newspapers.[43]

The British government was always sensitive about the use of force, especially firearms, to quell colonial tumults because it was a denial of what the empire stood for. In theory and popular imagination, British rule had always rested on the goodwill and collaboration of the governed, not coercion. The latter had to be applied in certain situations, but as a final resort and sparingly. Officials and soldiers whose job it was to keep order were also aware of an ill-defined but strong public hostility to the application of the iron fist. It was described by an NCO in Simon Raven's *Sound the Retreat* (1974) which was set in India in 1946:

> 'Doesn't matter,' said Cruxtable with sombre relish; 'as things are nowadays, these bloody wogs only have to open their mouths and dribble, and everyone in the world's on their side against us. No one wants to know the truth of it. They're just for the wogs and against us — and so are half our own people, come to that.'

Variously expressed, the same complaint was heard many times during the final years of the empire.

Rather than ruthlessly crush dissent, the British government chose to embrace and, so to speak, smother it. By accelerating the Gold Coast's passage to self-government, Britain imagined it had rescued the colony from possible Communist subversion and won the goodwill and gratitude of local political leaders. The conditions of the Cold War had wiped out the chances of a leisurely, measured progress from colonial tutelage to responsible government. Henceforward, British policy would concentrate on the cultivation of the most influential native politicians, who could be trusted to take over the reins of government in the empire's successor states. It was an answer to the problems of decolonisation which dismayed many, who foretold that it would create as many problems as it solved.

Echoing the doubts of those proconsuls who had been uneasy about India's advance towards home rule, the veteran Colonial Office mandarin, Sir Ralph Furse, wondered whether the government had been listening to the right voices:

> It is, and always has been, extremely difficult for a European to discover what Africans are really thinking. On the whole the primitives cannot now help us very much, though an old and very poor man in the bush district of Barotseland may have come as near the mark as most when he told Lord Monckton's Commission that 'he wished to remain under the gracious

protection of the blanket of King George V. The African political intelligentsia are not a very safe guide. Like other politicians
they mostly have axes to grind, and several, from having been
educated abroad, are to some extent *déraciné* . . . Because
African crowds shout slogans at the behest of such leaders it
does not follow that they understand what the slogans mean.[44]

There were still in the late-1940s large areas of the empire without any
political consciousness and largely untouched by the outside world. Old
patterns of life continued as did old hierarchies. A sportsman visiting
Darfur in the southern Sudan in 1949 encountered a local chief who was
'a tremendous old fellow with jutting beard, red robes, gold trappings and
a 5-foot whip hanging from his wrists, eleven sons and daughters
uncounted. Behind him rode an escort of 60 men in, of all things, chain
mail.' Old men could recall the days before British rule when Ali Dinar
was sultan, although none could remember what he looked like for 'we
were never allowed to look above the knees'.[45] The British had governed
Darfur for just over thirty years. Further south, in northern Uganda, colonial government was roughly the same age and still not firmly in place, for
in the Karanoja district cattle-rustling continued intermittently throughout
the 1940s.[46]

As late as November 1957, patrols of the King's African Rifles tramped
through remote districts of Kenya to remind Suk and Turkana tribesmen
of the retribution in store for lawbreakers. Demonstrations of rifle and
Bren gun fire were mounted for parties of tribesmen and after one, which
included the explosion of phosphorus grenades, a district commissioner
remarked, 'I believe the lesson has sunk in.'[47] Nothing much seemed to
have changed in fifty years. Aerial policing continued in the hinterland of
Aden where sixty-six tons of bombs and 247 rockets were needed to punish caravan raiders and stop an inter-tribal war in 1947.[48] That same year
a revival of tribal feuding left several hundred dead and wounded in
Somaliland, a protectorate where British rule had only been fully installed
in 1920.[49]

Colonial authority was also fragile in another volatile outpost, the
Solomon Islands. After the end of the Japanese occupation, a substantial
body of natives had virtually declared independence, and bound themselves
together under what was called the 'Marching Rule'. This was in part a
cargo cult, whose devotees expected the arrival of huge ships bringing
lavish gifts from a world power. Under the Marching Rule, men and

women lived in disciplined communities and shared everyday tasks. The movement's Communist undertones worried local officials who, after attempts at conciliation, were driven to use force in August 1947. A visit from a submarine in June did not impress the dissidents, and so the aircraft carrier *Glory* and the destroyer *Contest* were sent for. Their cruise through the islands, and the appearance of fifty native constables with rifles and fixed bayonets (borrowed from the New Guinea force) brought about the downfall of the Marching Rule. Its dénouement resembled an Ealing comedy film. The policemen, some of whom were members of the Rule, played a game of soccer with the natives, winning 4–3, and afterwards there was a Fijian feast and a cocktail party for naval officers and officials.[50] It took a further two years for the government to feel secure enough to reimpose the island poll tax, the islands' main source of revenue.

It is worth remembering that at the moment when Britain was making arrangements which would lead to the liquidation of the empire, there were still areas which had been under effective colonial rule for less than a man's lifetime, and there were others where imperial authority was precarious and shallow-rooted. Even under Labour, old hierarchies stayed the same; there were, in 1949, ten lavatories on the railway station at el Qantara in the Suez Canal Zone, labelled as follows:

Officers European
Officers Asiatic
Officers Coloured
Warrant Officers and Sergeants European
Warrant Officers and Sergeants Asiatic
Warrant Officers and Sergeants Coloured
Other Ranks European
Other Ranks Asiatic
Other Ranks Coloured
ATS [Auxiliary Territorial Service – i.e. women][51]

———•———

2

Friendly Relations: India and the Liquidation of Empire, 1945–7

In 1945, the gravediggers of empire commenced work. No government before or after 1945 ever took a conscious decision to dissolve the empire, but equally none was prepared to embark on an alternative course, its preservation come what may. The ministers, diplomats, soldiers and civil servants who found themselves responsible for devising and carrying out the policies of imperial disengagement did not imagine that they were parties to a funeral. Rather, they saw themselves as midwives, facilitating the births of new nations which were emerging from the imperial womb. The conventional, bipartisan wisdom which held sway for the next twenty-five years insisted the infant states would grow up within the extended family of the new, multi-racial Commonwealth, whose members shared a maternal affection for Britain, its democratic system and traditional respect for individual freedom. Never was an empire dismantled with such a sense of hope for the future.

There were circumstances in which Britain was willing to forgo an orderly retreat from empire and dig its heels in, but they were exceptional. Britain was engaged in the Cold War, and so no colony could be allowed to pass under Communist control after independence. So, while committed to future Malayan self-determination, Britain was prepared in 1948 to fight an extended campaign (euphemistically called an 'emergency' to avoid charges of colonial oppression) against local Communist guerrillas. Nor could the government allow a colony to dissolve into chaos, and for this reason operations were undertaken against the Mau Mau in Kenya between 1952 and 1954; another 'emergency'.

None of Britain's rearguard colonial wars matched the ferocity and length of those waged by the French in Indo-China and Algeria, and the Portuguese in Angola and Moçambique. British politicians needed to look no further than events in North America in the 1770s or, more pertinently, in southern Ireland after 1918 to identify the pitfalls that lay in wait for those who wanted to cling to empire at any cost. The Irish campaign also illustrated the fact there was a point beyond which the public was unwilling to tolerate armed coercion. This was understandable since a constant theme of modern imperial propaganda had been the goodwill which existed between the empire's rulers and its subjects.

Furthermore, for the first time in its history, the entire British people was directly involved in the defence of the empire. Between 1947 and 1960, its outposts and trouble spots were manned and policed by peacetime conscripts, national servicemen. Professional fighting men played their part, but the casualty rolls of imperial conflicts now included sons and sweethearts who were not under arms by choice.

The public was also made more intimately aware of imperial campaigns and the issues behind them through the novelty of the television set, which was rapidly entering homes from 1950 onwards. The government quickly appreciated that, carefully handled, the medium could be manipulated to show colonial conflicts in a favourable light. At the end of 1957, the ITV Christmas Day show 'Christmas in Cyprus' concentrated on the festivities of soldiers, including national servicemen, who were there dealing with another 'emergency'. The script was vetted by the army and Colonial Office, and both warmly endorsed 'natural unrehearsed shots of soldiers assisting Cypriot civilians etc.; particularly women and children in the streets'. The programme opened on a positive note with the announcement, 'Cyprus is part of the British Commonwealth,' and continued with the assertion that British troops were only there to help its people.[1] Those viewers whose wits had not been dulled by seasonal indulgence may have wondered, if this was so, why were Cypriots shooting at soldiers? Others no doubt settled down and watched troops giving a party for Cypriot children.

'Emergencies' of the sort experienced in Cyprus were relatively rare. The British empire did not dissolve like the French, Portuguese, and for that matter the Russian, in tears and blood. In India and the colonies an alternative way was devised, which involved an orderly and cordial withdrawal, and the assumption of power by a government which had been elected. At its best, from Britain's standpoint, this arrangement was accomplished with a minimum of fuss, and wherever possible the retention of strategic bases, behind-the-scenes political influence and commercial advantages. What had to be avoided at all costs was a helter-skelter retreat which left behind a political vacuum, or worse, chaos.

Mastering the arcane diplomatic art of colonial disengagement took time, and to begin with its practitioners were moving in the dark and learning as they went. With little else to guide them, they turned, in British fashion, to the past and adopted the old empire-builders' rule, which was to find someone with legal authority, such as a chief or rajah, and do business with him. Now, the empire's demolition men had to cultivate and work in harness with the new power-brokers, local politicians. The leaders of various parties and national movements were assumed to speak for the majority of the people. Whether or not they did, these tribunes found themselves treated as spokesmen for nations and the eventual successors to the imperial administration. There were certain rituals; at some stage local political leaders would find themselves in collision with the colonial authorities and were consequently locked up in prison. In time, and with their nationalist credentials enhanced by their detention, they were discharged to take their places at their gaolers' conference tables. This pattern had been established during the 1930s and 1940s when Indian Congress leaders, including Gandhi, were incarcerated: Nkrumah, Jomo Kenyatta and Dr Hastings Banda followed, in the Gold Coast, Kenya and Nyasaland respectively.

On the one hand, those responsible for surrendering power wanted above all to deliver it to someone who could exercise it effectively and preserve order. On the other, Britain was publicly pledged to confer on its colonies parliamentary government and a legal system designed to protect individual freedoms. This transfer of institutions had been easily undertaken in the white dominions, for their inhabitants were already steeped in British political tradition. But in India and the colonies there was a very different political culture. Organised political activity in the Western manner had begun very recently (the Indian National Congress had been founded in 1885, the African in 1912) and, from its beginnings, had revolved around a single issue: the termination of foreign rule. This overriding objective determined the evolution of political life and its

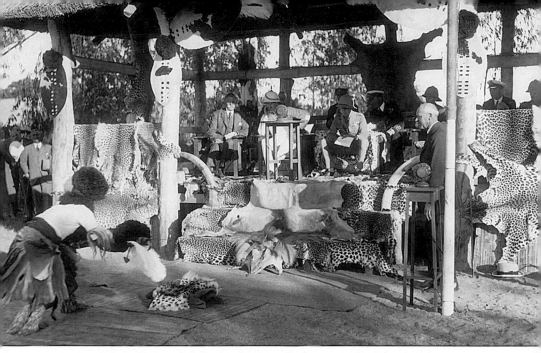

Africa honours the Prince of Wales: the future Edward VIII sits surrounded by all the panoply of a paramount chief, South Africa, 1925.
Hulton Deutsch

Imperial images: colonial postage stamps of the 1930s and 1940s celebrate royal occasions and advertise the wealth and natural history of the empire.
Author's own collection

A discordant rhythm: a scene from *The Drum* in which the young rajah beats a tattoo to warn the British of ambush. This film was so blatantly pro-raj that its screening caused riots in India in 1939. *Popperfoto Collection*

Stiff-upper lip: a scene from the film of Noël Coward's *Cavalcade* in which Diana Wynyard sheds a womanly tear as her husband Clive Brook leaves to fight the Boers. Films such as this advertised manly, imperial virtues during the 1930s. *Author's own collection*

The avenging arm of empire: RAF bombers fly over Egypt in 1936, a sight which enraged, among others, the young Nasser. *Author's own collection*

The forlorn hope of a crumbling empire: the battleship *Prince of Wales* arrives at Singapore in December 1941. Within a few days it and the *Repulse* will be sunk by Japanese aircraft. *Imperial War Museum*

Asia for the Asiatics: Burmese hail Japanese infantrymen as liberators, 1942. Cheers soon turned to tears as the Burmese discovered their new rulers were infinitely harsher than the British. *Imperial War Museum*

Conquerors conquered: Japanese guards from the infamous Changi prison prostrate themselves before a British officer, Singapore, 1945. *Popperfoto Collection*

Quitting India: Indian rioters send packing a distinctly Churchillian British Tommy. This was a Japanese propagandist's pipe dream; the 1942 'Quit India' movement and Bose's Indian National Army frightened the raj but could not overthrow it. *Peter Newark's Military Pictures*

Commonwealth cooperation: the Canadian cruiser *Uganda* [centre] is fuelled from a Royal Navy tanker as an Australian destroyer comes alongside with mail off the Japanese coast in the summer of 1945; soon after most of the crew of the *Uganda* demanded to be demobilised on the grounds that they had enlisted only to fight Germany. *Imperial War Museum*

The Rivals: Colonel Nasser and Sir Anthony Eden in 1954; each believed that his country should dominate the Middle East. *Popperfoto Collection*

EDEN'S BLUNDER

Left-wing worthies, including Tony Benn (seated with pipe, fourth from left),
wait their turn to speak in a Trafalgar Square anti-Suez rally, November 1956.
Topham Picture Source

The audience responds: these demonstrators belonged to a well-established
radical, anti-imperialist tradition which stretched back over a hundred years. For
them, like Cobden and Bright, empire equalled war and oppression of the weak
by the strong. *Popperfoto Collection*

Uhuru: the Union Jack comes down in Nairobi and Kenya achieves independence, 1963. *Topham Picture Source*

Pomp in reduced circumstances: H.M. the Queen and Prince Philip visit Fiji. As the empire became the Commonwealth, royal tours became more and more common, serving to replace physical ties with emotional bonds. *Foreign and Commonwealth Office*

domination by tightly-organised parties, which had to be big enough to engage a powerful and equally monolithic government. Circumstances had, therefore, discouraged a diversity of parties or the growth of two or three of more or less equal popular appeal as had occurred in Britain and the dominions. The one-party state had its genesis in the history of Indian and colonial struggles for independence.

Imperial demography hindered decolonisation. No one concerned with drawing the empire's frontiers had ever imagined that he was setting the boundaries for a future self-governing independent state. Antipathetic racial, tribal and religious groups had often been corralled together willy-nilly. When the depth of ethnic, tribal and sectarian antagonism became apparent, it was argued that they could be contained by a firm, even-handed imperial administration backed by police and soldiers. So it was that in India, Ceylon, Burma and elsewhere Britain became the protector of various minorities who were shielded from the ill-will of their neighbours. Old prejudices were not, however, eliminated by the fear of imperial punishment; they remained, as it were, frozen. The makers of new governments had to find ways to provide for the continued safety of vulnerable minorities even if this meant the dilution of the democratic ideal.

None of these hurdles along the path towards colonial self-determination was insurmountable, given time and the forebearance of everyone involved. Neither was readily available. Once decolonisation was underway, it gathered a momentum of its own which made it impossible for the assortment of proconsuls, civil servants and constitutional lawyers who devised new governments to pause. Impatient local politicians and their followers interpreted delays as evidence of cold feet, and so procrastination, whatever its cause, could easily provoke the kind of popular disturbances which Britain was desperate to avoid. Disposing of an empire was hard and dispiriting work; Attlee publicly described Mountbatten's labours in India as truly heroic. Not everyone concurred; Harold Nicolson noted in his diary: '. . . . it is curious that we should regard as a hero the man who liquidates the Empire which other heroes such as Clive, Warren Hastings and Napier won for us. Very odd indeed.'[2]

At the time (June 1947) Indian independence was a few weeks off, and its achievement was being hailed as a triumph. A simultaneous and less well-known essay in imperial disengagement was being undertaken in Burma, and served as a perfect example of what could go wrong. His reluctant service as a policeman in Burma had convinced Orwell of the evils of colonialism, which was understandable since British rule was disliked by many sections of Burmese society. Political and racial divisions and the brittleness of imperial loyalties were exposed when the Japanese invaded in 1942. The Burmese inclined towards their conquerors while the inland hill tribes, the Karens and the Kachins, supported Britain, which had protected them from their lowland neighbours.

The most prominent Burmese nationalist, Thakin Aung San, the general-secretary of Our Burma League, had defected to Japan in 1940, returned, and was installed by his patrons as head of the Burma National Army. In August 1943, Japan declared Burma independent, but Aung San, a consummate opportunist, abandoned his old friends and threw himself and his followers behind the British in March 1945, when it was clear that they would expel the Japanese.

There was no clear blueprint for a post-war Burma beyond the promise that it would eventually achieve independence within the Commonwealth. The reinstated governor, Sir Reginald Dorman-Smith, proposed a six- or seven-year period of reconstruction and the British government set aside £84 million for the task. Ultimate authority lay with Mountbatten as commander-in-chief of SEAC, and he suspected Dorman-Smith and his staff were Blimps who would hold up independence.[3] He preferred to reach an accord with the man who seemed to have popular support, Aung San. This was unavoidable expediency, for Mountbatten could not spare white troops to police Burma, and was chary about testing the obedience of his Indian soldiers in a showdown with Burmese nationalists.

Mountbatten's instinct appeared sound at first. Aung San's Anti-Fascist People's Freedom League gained an overwhelming majority in the April 1946 election, but the result was deceptive. The polls had been boycotted by three other parties, and the Karens refused to take the twenty-four seats allocated to them as a minority, choosing instead to press for a separate state. Even though the country was on the verge of fragmentation, Mountbatten pressed on in the belief that the Burmese would have to settle their own problems. Through backstairs string-pulling, he engineered Dorman-Smith's dismissal in August.[4] What followed was exactly the anarchy which cautious men had feared: in July 1947 Aung San and six other ministers were shot dead by a gang of political rivals who, in Al Capone style, burst into the cabinet room with sub-machine guns, and there was a widespread upsurge in dacoity. Notwithstanding these indications of a breakdown in order, full independence was attained in January 1948.

Within twelve months Burma had declared itself a republic and left the Commonwealth, and there were rebellions by Communist and Karen separatists. Whether or not these events were an indictment of British rule in Burma, they were an inauspicious prelude to the dissolution of the empire.

India's progress to self-government was a compelling drama with a convoluted plot that unfolded at two levels. On the upper, British and Indian statesmen, politicians, lawyers and administrators sat in rooms in Delhi and, when it became too stifling, Simla, and endeavoured to construct an apparatus of government that would satisfy the whole of India. They were participants in a race against time for, on the lower level, and in the cities, towns and countryside, hundreds of thousands of Indians were beginning to turn against and kill each other. As the violence spread and the casualties multiplied, onlookers feared the onset of a civil war which the principal actors were powerless to stop.

The chief British actor was Attlee, who towards the end of his life believed that he would be best remembered for what he had done to facilitate the transfer of power in India. He saw it as a moral duty, to which he and his party had long been pledged, and, for he was a pragmatist, an advantage to Britain. The Treasury would no longer have to dispense money to maintain a British garrison in the subcontinent and, if Britain got the terms it desired, commerce with India would continue to flourish. Attlee also appreciated that a peaceful exchange of power and a stable India would add to British prestige and serve as a bulwark against Communism in Asia. He and his chiefs of staff also wanted India within the Commonwealth, and if possible as an ally which would continue to host British bases. Attlee's mandate to Mountbatten, delivered in February 1947, instructed the Viceroy to secure 'the closest and most friendly relations between India and the UK. A feature of this relationship should be a military treaty.'[5] By this time, Attlee had conceded that the subcontinent would be split between India and Pakistan, which he had not wanted, for it was not in Britain's interests. A divided India was a weakened India, and the western segment of its most vulnerable portion, Pakistan, faced Afghanistan and beyond it Russia. In terms of the Cold War, the partition of India was a setback.

Mountbatten, whom Attlee had chosen to accelerate and superintend the final handing over of power, was the last in a sequence of officials and ministers sent to negotiate with the Indian leadership. His predecessor as viceroy had been Field-Marshal Wavell who, faced with mounting disorder during 1946, despaired, and was ultimately removed by Attlee for his pessimism. This had owed much to the failure of Attlee's three-man cabinet mission, which had arrived in India at the end of March 1946 with instructions to arrange a constitution which would keep India intact and offend as few of its people as possible. Cripps, the mission's head, was a left-wing idealist in tune with Indian aspirations, who knew what to expect from his last series of negotiations in 1942 and, according to Bevin, was too pro-Congress. Lord Pethick ('Pathetic')-Lawrence was a frail old-Etonian Labour veteran of seventy-four, who had also been chosen for his experience of Indian affairs. The third member of the mission, A.V. Alexander was a Co-op-sponsored MP with a good record in office, and, like many working-class Labour ministers, was a bit of a sentimental imperialist. This was not surprising, for he and others of his generation, like Bevin, had grown to manhood when jingoism was rampant.

Opposite the cabinet mission were the figures whom Wavell called 'the great tribunes of the Indian people', Nehru and the Congress leadership. Their aim was to replace the raj by Congress, and they spoke and acted as if it was the mirror of the whole Indian nation, which, according to Gandhi, was indivisible. There was also Dr Jinnah, who thought that it was not, and spoke for the subcontinent's 92 million Muslims. Wavell disliked Jinnah, whom he believed a megalomaniac; suspected Gandhi of malevolence towards the British, but respected Nehru as a truly 'great man'.[6]

While the architects of India's future deliberated, the people became increasingly restless. During the winter of 1945–6, the government's decision to prosecute a handful of prominent former INA men for treason, and in some instances war crimes, was bitterly opposed by Congress. In September 1945 Congress had resolved that the thousands of INA soldiers could be 'of the greatest service in the heavy work of building up a new and free India'.[7] In the next few months they were lionised as heroes by Congress and those imprisoned or awaiting trial received the aura of martyrdom. In January 1946, an outraged *Hindustan Times* alleged that twenty-five INA prisoners had been bayoneted for singing the Congress anthem 'Jai Hind' (Long Live India), but an official investigation revealed that they had merely been 'prodded' in the buttocks.[8] These men's case had been taken up by Gandhi, whose attitude towards the ex-INA men was characteristically ambivalent. 'Though I can have nothing in common with any defence by force of arms,' he wrote, 'I am never blind to the valour of patriotism often displayed by persons in arms, as seems to be the case here.'[9] He did not say whether his definition of patriotism embraced the two million Indians who had fought for rather than against Britain.

As matters stood at the beginning of 1946, Indian security rested on the Indian army and the British garrison. Among the latter were many men who were unenthusiastic about defending the raj and anxious to get home. During the summer of 1945 army censors uncovered many complaints about an 'absence of purpose' in the letters of soldiers serving in Asia, and those in India believed that a shorter spell of overseas duty and swift demobilisation were 'inalienable rights'.[10] Just over a year later morale in India was drooping and complaints about slow demobilisation were rising.[11] Disaffection was greatest and most vocal among RAF personnel in India; during 1946 there were mutinous demonstrations at a dozen bases.[12] This was disturbing, since the commander-in-chief in India, Auchinleck, had considered resurrecting the precedents of 1919 and 1942 and using aircraft if popular disorders got out of hand.[13]

Of far greater concern was the erosion of the morale of the Indian servicemen. This was spectacularly demonstrated by the four-day mutiny by 7,000 ratings of the Royal Indian Navy (a quarter of its strength) at the end of February 1946. The trouble began aboard the frigate *Talwar*, whose commanding officer, Commander F.W. King frequently addressed his men as 'black buggers', 'coolie bastards' and 'jungli Indians'. Given the tension in India, such loutish provocation was bound to provoke a violent backlash and an incident involving King triggered a mutiny which swiftly spread to other RIN ships in Bombay. Using their wireless transmitters, the Bombay mutineers alerted the crews of vessels in Calcutta and Madras who joined the revolt.[14] Congress and Muslim League flags were hoisted over the Bombay flotilla and attempts to suppress the mutiny led to serious rioting on shore. The restoration of order by British and Mahratha troops left 223 dead and over 1,000 wounded.[15]

Attempts by the sailors to enlist the Mahrathas failed, and after the appearance of the cruiser *Glasgow* and the buzzing of the rebellious ships by Mosquito bombers, the mutiny collapsed. Both the government in Delhi and Congress were stunned by the mutiny which seemed to suggest that the authority of both might be on the verge of disintegration. Many British official files on the mutiny and its aftermath are still inexplicably closed, but local intelligence sources suspected that Communist agitators had been at work in the Bombay docks.[16] Since December 1945, military intelligence had been nervous about Russian agents exploiting the situation in India, and a careful watch was kept for evidence of Communist subversion.[17]

The RIN mutiny was followed by more outbreaks of unrest, including so-called strikes by Royal Indian Air Force (RIAF) men, a mutiny by seventy-five signallers at Allahabad, and a walkout by 300 policemen in Delhi.[18] There was also a steady trickle of desertions to the Indonesian nationalists by Indian troops serving in Sumatra. Congress had condemned these operations and demanded that the government stopped using Indian soldiers as mercenaries of imperialism.[19] By the end of March, military intelligence considered all army ancillary units, the RIN and the RIAF as still 'suspect', and was apprehensive about the Indian army's future loyalty, for 'only day to day estimates of its steadiness' could be made.[20] With such gloomy reading on his desk, it was not surprising that Wavell wrote to King George VI that India was now beset by a 'general sense of insecurity and restlessness'.[21] In June, the defence committee of the cabinet concluded that no evacuation of India could be allowed if the Indian army's constancy was in doubt. In this event, five divisions of British troops would be required to keep order in India, although their deployment would pose a heavy strain on commitments elsewhere.[22]

What was surprising about the unrest among Indian servicemen was the absence of hostility to Britain. In the final days of the raj, relations between the British and Indians were better than they had been for the past thirty years, or so Auchinleck believed.[23] This cordiality may have owed much, if not everything, to the fact that every Indian knew the British were about to leave. But there was still no timetable for their departure nor, more importantly, a form of government for independent India. In midsummer 1946 the cabinet mission recommended an elaborate constitution with a federal government for the whole country and, below it, two layers of local and provincial assemblies, which were designed both to satisfy and safeguard minorities. At first both Congress and the Muslim League acquiesced to this formula, but mutual suspicion proved too deep-rooted, and the two sides were soon squabbling over minutiae and the balance of communal representation. The upshot was Jinnah's determination to go it alone and demand an independent Pakistan.

Jinnah called a Muslim hartal in Calcutta on 16 August. Four days of religious riots followed in which 4,000 were killed and 10,000 wounded. The British general whose Anglo-Indian forces restored order thought the slaughter many times worse than the Somme. News of what was happening in Calcutta sparked off massacres in Bombay where 1,000 died and over 13,000 were wounded. In Bihar, where the allegiance of the local police was wobbling, Hindus murdered 150 Muslim refugees in

November. Here and elsewhere, the victims of religious frenzy were poor and humble; some months later a British journalist observed that few of their bodies were ever claimed from the police morgues.[24]

As the religious massacres proliferated, India appeared to be moving inexorably towards a civil war. After visiting Calcutta, Wavell concluded that the game was up, and drew up exigency plans for the evacuation of all British civilians and servicemen. Their safety was paramount, and if necessary they would depart before any political settlement, and certainly before the onset of the bloodbath which Wavell expected.

Wavell's scheme was political disaster for India, Britain and the Labour party. Attlee was determined to prevent it, and in December Wavell was removed. He was succeeded as viceroy by Mountbatten, Attlee's choice and a brilliant one in terms of *Realpolitik*. Attlee had been impressed by his conduct in Burma (that country's descent into anarchy was not yet underway); he was a member of the royal family; and his nephew, Philip, was about to marry Princess Elizabeth. At a time when the royal family was held in almost pious awe, Mountbatten was more immune to public criticism than other comparable figures in public life. Most importantly, he saw eye-to-eye with Attlee on what had to be done in India and the speed with which it had to be accomplished. His brief gave him some leeway in negotiation, but Attlee always remained the master and the Viceroy his servant. There was close contact between Downing Street and Delhi; Mountbatten was recalled to London at a crucial moment in May, and himself suggested that Attlee went to India to deal personally with matters concerning partition.

Mountbatten arrived in India at the end of March 1947. He threw himself into his tasks with immense zeal and energy, using every ounce of his charm to persuade and cajole India's tribunes, although he was brusque with Jinnah to the point of rudeness. He was assisted by his wife, Edwina, who had an engaging manner and a cocktail-party vivacity which captivated Nehru, now prime minister in an interim government and the voice of Congress. The Mountbattens at Viceregal House were a refreshing change from the staid Wavells; the Field-Marshal was a scholarly, contemplative and shy figure, and Lady Mountbatten once remarked that Viscountess Wavell dressed like her maid.[25] Whatever else they did, the Mountbattens ensured that, at the top level at least, the final act in the drama of India's independence was played out with panache.

The new viceroy's most important duty was to stick as closely as possible to the revised timetable for self-government that had been set by

Attlee. Previously, power was to have been handed over in June 1948, but in the light of the gradual disintegration of public order the date was brought forward to 15 August 1947. The new schedule was revealed by Mountbatten at a press conference on 4 June and was received with a mixture of delight, amazement and, in some quarters, foreboding. Soon after, he issued his officials with a 'tear-off calendar indicating the days left for the partition' as if the event was the last day of a public-school term.[26] The divorce of Hindu and Muslim India had been a political reality since the December 1945 and March 1946 local and provincial elections, in which Hindu Congress candidates had secured 90 per cent of the votes in the predominantly non-Muslim regions, and Muslims had come out on top in their areas. No number of intricate political checks and balances could have prevented the polarisation of India and preserved it as a single polity. This was reluctantly recognised by Congress, and during May a plan for partition was agreed by Mountbatten and the Indian leadership, and subsequently rubber-stamped by the cabinet in London.

Winding up the raj was a relatively easy business which had been quietly underway for the past twenty years. By 1946, more than half the 1,026 senior officials of the Indian civil service were Indians, and the total of native Indian army officers had risen from 1,000 in 1939 to 15,750 in 1946. Old traditions of discipline and comradeship made it possible to break down the multi-racial and religious units of the Indian army, separate them, and apportion officers and men to the new forces of India and Pakistan. This minor triumph was achieved with a minimum of fuss and considerable goodwill, thanks to the patient wisdom of Auchinleck, who predicted that his men would find it easy to shift their loyalties from the king emperor to their new communities. For one Subadar-Major, the whole thing was an expression of British genius. During the parade to mark Pakistan's independence, he remarked to a British officer, 'Ah, Sahib, the British have been very cunning. We Muslims have our Pakistan; the Hindus have their Hindustan; and the British soldiers will be able to go home.' Sadly, it was not that simple. Not far away, Hindu and Sikh troops sulked and refused to join the march past for Jinnah.[27]

Their recalcitrance was understandable given the events which had occurred in the three months before independence. It would have been beyond the wit of any man to have created boundaries which would have satisfied everyone; there were bound to be communities who found themselves on the 'wrong' side of the frontier and felt isolated, outnumbered and frightened.

Fear was greatest in the Punjab, home to a substantial portion of India's five-and-a-half million Sikhs (one in six of the province's population), which was to be split between India and Pakistan. The Sikhs rejected Muslim domination and answered Jinnah's newly-coined slogan *Pakistan Zindabad!* (Long Live Pakistan) with *Pakistan Murdabad!* (Death to Pakistan). By late spring, the Punjab was wracked by massacres, counter-massacres, looting and arson. Their heritage of Muslim persecution and their historic reaction to it gave the Sikhs a peculiar resilience, and a powerful urge to seek revenge. An indication of their sufferings and present temper may be found in a leaflet circulating at the beginning of April 1947:

> Thousands of Sikh and Hindu women have been murdered; *Keshas* [long tresses] and beards of hundreds have been chopped off and an effort has been made to convert them to Islam; hundreds of women have been abducted. Whole villages have been burnt up . . . Rest assured, as it is only a small specimen of Pakistan and more terrible incidents are yet to come. But Khalsaji [warriors], we are Sikhs of that Guru who having had his four children slaughtered said, 'What if four have fallen? Thousands will survive.' We have to fight this tyrannical Pakistan . . .[28]

A British civil servant, Sir Cyril Radcliffe, drew the line which bisected the Punjab. It was a thankless task whose consequences haunted him until his death. What he and others had decided was kept in Mountbatten's safe for publication *after* Independence Day, when the whole affair would no longer be Britain's responsibility. There had been leaks about the future of the Chittagong region which had sparked off a minor row, and this was enough to convince Mountbatten that secrecy was best.

His primary duty was to the British government; he had already stated that British forces would be evacuated as quickly as possible, which ruled them out as an impartial police force during the enforcement of partition, and he had an overriding wish to see that power was handed over with decorum. The shows (there was one in Delhi and another in Karachi) came first.[29] The official ceremonies passed off smoothly; the declaration of the partition award, made the following day, did not.

The massive bloodletting which occurred across northern India after partition is well known. Perhaps half a million died, although no one has ever calculated the exact numbers killed. The details were reported by newspapermen, most notably Louis Heren of *The Times*. He and others heard the grisly catalogue of past outrages which were the murder gangs' justification for their crimes. In August, Sikhs and Hindus were killing Punjabi Muslims in revenge for the massacre of their co-religionists in Rawalpindi the previous March. This holocaust was vengeance for the slaughter of Muslims by Hindus in Bihar five months before, and, in turn, this was retaliation for the bloodbath in Calcutta in August 1946.[30] British and Indian officers who watched and, where they could, attempted to stop the slaughter, told Heren it was 'a thousand times more horrible than anything we saw in the war'. One eyewitness description of events in Lahore (Pakistan) in mid-August, a soldier's, may stand for many others:

> Corpses lay in the gutter. Nearby a posse of Muslim police chatted unconcerned. A British Major (a sapper) had also arrived. He and his driver were collecting the bodies. Some were dead. Some were dying. All were horribly mutilated. They were Sikhs. Their long hair and beards were matted with blood. An old man, not so bad as the rest, asked me where we were taking them. 'To hospital,' I replied; adding to hearten him, 'You're not going to die.'
> 'I shall,' he said, 'if there is a Muslim doctor.'[31]

There is no simple answer to the question whether all this could have been avoided. Mountbatten's reactions showed him at his most shallow; back in England in November he tried to minimise the scale of the disaster, and claimed that it had surprised him.[32] But there had been a steady build-up of violence since August 1946 and military intelligence knew that it would worsen. Aware of this, Auchinleck had wanted to keep British troops behind after independence, but had been overridden by Mountbatten.[33] And yet, if such a course had been followed, British servicemen would have become embroiled in a struggle from which it might have been very hard to extricate them. Major-General T.W. Rees's short-lived and undermanned Punjab Frontier Force accomplished wonders, but this is not to say that larger detachments would have enjoyed the same success.

Senior military men in India, including Auchinleck, were critical of Mountbatten, whose Toad-of-Toad-Hall exhibitionism irritated a caste which traditionally prized reticence and self-effacement. Lieutenant-General Sir Reginald Savory, Adjutant-General of the Indian army, accused him of having 'tried to make it appear to India and the world and to ourselves that we were committing a noble deed'.[34] This charge confuses Mountbatten's self-publicity with government policy; he was always Attlee's agent, carrying out the will of the cabinet and parliament. He thought he had done the job rather well, and said so so often that it was easy to forget this fact.

What he had accomplished was essentially a pragmatic measure which was, as Attlee appreciated, a sensible reaction to historic forces which had been gathering momentum for thirty years. The raj could not be maintained by force, for its end was wished by the great mass of the Indian people, and there is no reason to believe that the British would have been willing to see it prolonged at the cost of an interminable war of repression. Even if it had been contemplated, such a policy would have played havoc with Britain's commitments elsewhere. These were stretched to breaking point and, in 1946, the government was worried about the consequences for industry of having 18.6 per cent of the country's manpower in the services. The choice facing Attlee was graphically portrayed in a *Daily Herald* cartoon of 24 May 1946. Two saloons labelled 'Labour Government' and 'Dominions' surge forward along a road, while a jalopy inscribed 'Jingo' plunges over a cliff, its blimpish driver and passenger calling out, 'Come On! This Way!' There were some on the right who muttered about a failure of 'nerve' in India and elsewhere in the empire, but nerve without muscle could not have saved the raj or the colonies.

The loss of India was felt most keenly by the men and women who had served there and devoted their lives to its people's welfare. Many old servants of the raj were bitterly dismayed by the unseemly haste of the transfer of power and its baleful consequences. But those who had connections with the raj represented a narrow section of British society. In June 1946 there had been 44,537 civilians and 10,837 service wives and children in India, together with the garrison and Indian army officers. They were the last representatives of a British population which, since the days of Clive, had been transient. Men and women came to India, performed the duties they had been sent to undertake, and then returned home. Even so, the rearguard of 1947 and previous exiles found it extremely hard to accept the emotional break with a country and a people which they had come to love and to which they had given so much of their lives. Forty-five years later, newspaper announcements of various Indian reunion dinners, usually regimental, in London clubs are a testament to their sense of comradeship and nostalgia for the raj.

The strategic and psychological consequences of the loss of India were enormous but their effect was, at first, limited. Mountbatten had not clinched a military alliance with either India or Pakistan, although both elected to enter the Commonwealth. Ceylon was more accommodating and agreed to allow Britain use of its bases, so Britain could maintain its old, dominant position in the Indian Ocean. This was small consolation for control over India. A pantheon of statesmen from Disraeli to Bevin had convinced themselves and the country that ownership of India was the key to Britain's greatness. Take away India, Curzon had warned, and Britain would become a second-rate power.

Strategists from Wellington to Attlee's chiefs-of-staff agreed, and the latter feared that Britain's future as a world power would be in jeopardy without India's reserve of manpower, which had proved so vital in two world wars and sundry smaller imperial campaigns throughout the Middle East, East Africa and the Far East. Within a year of Indian independence, a senior officer was calling for the creation of an Anglo-African army on the lines of the Indian:

> If British units were mingled with East African units on a similar but miniature model of the recent Army in India, their standard of efficiency and pleasure in soldiering could rise to unprecedented heights. The British ranks of the African units could be filled by the cream of those attracted by the life and people.[35]

As has been seen, Attlee was eventually attracted by this idea, But mass standing armies were expensive to maintain in peacetime. Since mid-1946, British strategic planners had been concentrating on a cheaper source of strength that was more relevant to Cold War needs; long-range bombers and atomic bombs. As a source of power and prestige, the Indian army had become an anachronism, although its loss would be felt in the so-called 'bush-fire' campaigns of the Far and Middle East during the 1950s and early 1960s.

These were the years during which the British public found itself slowly coming to terms with the delayed trauma of imperial decline. The slowness of the reaction owed much to the fact that the Commonwealth had served as an invaluable shock-absorber in the years immediately after 1947.

It had helped salve pride hurt by the loss of territory and prestige, and appeared to offer compensation for both. It gave Britain a special moral status at a time when France was fighting two bloody colonial wars. For those whose political opinions were primarily determined by ethical considerations, it embodied all the old idealism of benevolent imperialism without any of the guilt associated with alien rule. Reporting with approval the 1956 Young Commonwealth conference, the *Observer* referred to the 'moral benefits' which delegates felt they had acquired during discussions on such matters as literacy campaigns.[36] It was all very earnest, and heartwarming for those of the left and centre who had never quite lost their pre-war faith in international cooperation.

After 1950, the virtues and value of the Commonwealth became part of that centrist British political consensus which accepted unquestioningly the virtues of the mixed economy and the welfare state. Senior Labour and Conservative politicians were committed to perpetuation of the Commonwealth, and publicly proclaimed it as a manifestation of Britain's residual influence in the world. It was, according to one defender, 'a logical outcome of our own development', the heir-general, as it were, of the empire and, in moral terms, infinitely preferable.[37] The conventional, bipartisan wisdom was expressed by Queen Elizabeth II during her visit to one of its newest members, Ghana, in November 1961. She defined the body of which she was head as: 'A group of equals, a family of like-minded peoples whatever their differences of religion, political systems, circumstances and races, all eager to work together for the peace, freedom and prosperity of mankind.'[38] What was needed for the Commonwealth to flourish was an act of 'faith' by all its members. This must have been an extremely difficult speech to deliver, and harder still to believe in, for her host, Dr Nkrumah, was currently arresting and locking up opposition politicians.

The tough lessons of the past fourteen years had dented this rosy and optimistic view of the Commonwealth. There were a handful of dissidents unprepared to make the leap of faith necessary for belief in the Commonwealth. In 1956, the year when Britain's global pretensions were tested to breaking point, a few isolated voices were prepared to ask searching questions about the practical value of the Commonwealth in an increasingly unfriendly world. In a mordant analysis, written shortly after the June 1956 Commonwealth prime ministers' conference, the veteran diplomat Lord Vansittart argued that apart from the old white dominions the Commonwealth gave no advantage to Britain.[39] South African apartheid made a mockery of claims that the Commonwealth stood for racial equality; Pakistan was a republic, but at least lined up with the West against Communism, while India and Ceylon, who had just evicted Britain from her bases, were obstructive Cold War waverers. The conference's communiqué was full of 'colourless platitude' and the Commonwealth was, in Menzies's words, 'just a scattered group of nations, unattached but friendly'.

At the other end of the political spectrum, the *New Statesman* was equally dismissive. The Commonwealth was 'entirely formless' for it lacked 'any basis of unity', being without even rudimentary machinery for political, economic or military cooperation.[40] Britain might congratulate itself on the largely peaceful metamorphosis of empire into Commonwealth, and draw some moral satisfaction from it as a glowing example of goodwill between nations, but it was not a makeweight for the power and prestige of empire. Nevertheless, it helped protect the British people from suddenly coming face to face with the fact that after 1947 their country's power was dwindling. With hindsight, it is possible to see that the Commonwealth enabled Britain to accept the loss of India without too much heartache. Strange to say, the Labour government which had engineered the liquidation of the Indian empire continued to act as if Britain was still a formidable global power. It was left to the Conservatives, inheritors of this hubris, to come to terms with reality.

3

The World as It Is: Middle Eastern Misadventures, 1945–56

'We have to make a policy on the assumption that there is not an Indian army to send to Basra,' argued Labour MP Richard Crossman. He was defending his party from charges of irresolution during a debate on the Middle East in July 1951. According to the Conservatives, the past six years had witnessed the sacrifice of British interests in an area where previously they had been upheld with the utmost vigour. And yet, during the same period, Attlee's government had been channelling large sums into the development of a British atomic bomb, possession of which would uphold Britain's claim that it still was a world power.

It was easier for Labour to acquire the sinews of power than it was to exercise it. In 1945, Attlee inherited all the pre-war problems of the Middle East: the worsening Arab-Jewish conflict; the simmering resentment of the Egyptians against alien domination; and the widespread feeling that Britain was the greatest hindrance to Arab national aspirations and unity. Labour was instinctively sympathetic to liberation movements; it was an internationalist, progressive party which thought itself in harmony with the trends of the modern world. The Conservatives were locked into the past and hosts to atavistic concepts of racial superiority and thinly disguised xenophobia. During a debate in which the subject of the Burmese came up, the volatile George Wigg shouted at the Tory benches, 'The

Honourable Gentleman and his friends think they are all "wogs". Indeed, the Right Honourable Member for Woodford [Churchill] thinks that the "wogs" begin at Calais.'

High principles and ideals of international brotherhood were not always compatible with the pursuit of British interests, particularly in the Middle East and under the conditions imposed by the Cold War. The government had constantly to heed the demands made by its partner, the United States. During 1946, Pentagon and Whitehall strategists began to plot the course of a hypothetical war against Russia and both concluded that control of the Middle East was vital for victory. If the Soviet Union was to be beaten, a substantial part of its war machine would have to be destroyed by atomic bombs. Nuclear attacks on Russia's industrial heartlands required bases relatively close to its borders. So, in the summer of 1946, Britain secretly agreed to allow B-29 bombers to fly nuclear sorties from airfields in East Anglia and Egypt.[1] The latter were crucial, for they made possible a concentrated nuclear assault on the oilfields, refineries and industrial centres of the Caucasus and Don basin. With these levelled, Russia's capacity to wage a war in western Europe would be severely curtailed. Atomic weapons alone would redress the imbalance between Russia's massive ground forces and the West's.

Working from this premise, Pentagon experts revised and amended their plans during the next few years. The 1947 and 1948 versions, with the innocuous codenames 'Broiler' and 'Speedway', gave the USAAF fifteen days in which to deploy their bombers and their atomic payloads on the runways of the Canal Zone airfields.[2] Local defence, indeed that of the entire Middle East, was entrusted to British and Commonwealth forces.[3] The scale of the offensive against Russia's 'soft underbelly' increased as America's stock of atomic bombs rose from fifty in 1948 to three hundred in 1950. In 1949, plan 'Dropshot', outlining a war scenario for 1957, proposed an attack on southern Russia by ninety-five bombers flying from Egypt.[4] Like its predecessors, this warplan took for granted that Britain would still be in control of the Canal Zone.

Egyptian airfields were also an essential part of the RAF's nuclear programme. This had its genesis in 1946, when the chiefs-of-staff, particularly Air-Marshal Lord Tedder and Field-Marshal Montgomery, persuaded an initially lukewarm Attlee that it was imperative for Britain to maintain its old predominance in the Mediterranean and Middle East.[5] Their argument was simple: Britain would remain a first-rate, global power and enjoy a measure of independence from the United States if it acquired atomic bombs and the means to deliver them against the Soviet Union. In the event of war, a substantial part of Britain's nuclear strike force would fly from the Canal Zone towards southern Russia. During the next six years, Britain implemented an ambitious nuclear programme. Work went ahead on the development of the long-range, jet-powered V-bombers and the first, the Valiant, was operational by 1955. Three years before, Britain's first atomic bomb was tested off Monte Bello island on the north-west coast of Australia.

According to Britain's warplan 'Trojan' of 1952 (codenames became more belligerent as the Cold War intensified), the Monte Bello bomb's successors would be dropped on Russia and, if the sums had been added up correctly, could reduce Russia's industrial capacity by 30–40 per cent.[6] By the beginning of 1956, major changes had been made to targeting policy. A large-scale Russian land and air offensive was expected in the Middle East against eastern Turkey and the Iraqi and Persian oilfields. Given a three-week warning before the outbreak of hostilities, Britain would be in a position to mount a counter-attack which would include nuclear sorties against concentrations of Soviet forces, their airfields and lines of communication.[7]

None of these prognoses assumed that a nuclear exchange would bring outright victory to either side. Although crippled, the antagonists would, it was believed, still retain the will and some of the wherewithal to fight on with conventional weaponry. In this situation, Britain would have to defend the world's sealanes which provided it with access to food and oil. Data gathered from the Monte Bello test was used to discover the possible effects of a nuclear attack on a large port, Liverpool, and this study was extended to the Suez Canal. The boffins were remarkably confident that both Liverpool and Port Said could be restored to a semblance of working order within four months. The problems of contamination could be overcome and, if a Russian atomic bomb exploded over the Suez Canal, it was estimated that earth-moving equipment operated by a 'rotation of men' could open a navigable passage within several months.[8] This astonishing information, presented in a report of July 1956, assumed that sufficient men and machinery would be on hand for what would have proved an extremely hazardous enterprise for those whose job it was to shovel sand.

The Canal Zone became a vital integer in the sombre arithmetic of nuclear war. If such a conflict was winnable, and the strategists who drew up the various warplans believed it was, then Anglo-American control of the Middle East had to be maintained. Even without schemes for launching potentially war-winning nuclear attacks against southern Russia, the region would have had to be kept within the western camp and defended for the sake of its oil. The Second World War had seen the transformation of the world pattern of oil consumption. By 1951, the Middle East was providing 70 per cent of the West's oil, and all its reserves for the future were thought to be concentrated in Saudi Arabia and the Persian Gulf.

Oil and airfields had replaced the defence of India as Britain's reason for paramountcy in the Middle East. In a sense, the old strategic and geopolitical catchwords of Disraeli and Curzon still held true. They were heard frequently during the late 1940s and early 1950s, largely from the Conservative benches and in the committee rooms of the War Office, Admiralty and Air Ministry. But had Britain kept its old nerve and was it, when faced with difficulties, prepared to act boldly? On paper at least, Britain was as formidable a power in the region in 1945 as it had been twenty or so years before when the young Nasser had cursed the RAF biplanes that flew over his house. In 1945, Jordan, Iraq, Iran and the sheikdoms of the Persian Gulf were still in Britain's thrall. So too was Egypt, the sullen host to the vast Suez Canal Zone complex of barracks, storehouses and airfields which straddled the Canal. This strip, 120 miles long by 30 wide, was the largest military base in the world, and the pivot of British power in the Middle East and Africa. Radiating from the Canal Zone was a web of satellite garrisons, aerodromes and naval bases in Malta, Cyprus, Haifa, the ex-Italian colony of Libya (which Russia had briefly coveted), Jordan, Iraq, Aden and the Persian Gulf.

These scarlet specks on the War Office's map offered little comfort to Bevin. He was aware of a new, uncompromising and anti-British mood abroad in the Middle East, and it was being encouraged by what was widely seen as Britain's retirement in the face of Indian nationalism. Britain could be undone and, on the first day of 1947, he warned Attlee of troubles ahead. 'You cannot read the telegrams from Egypt and the Middle East nowadays without realising that not only is India going, but Malaya, Ceylon, and the Far East are going with it, with a tremendous repercussion in the African territories.'[9] Five months later, as Britain faced another financial crisis, Bevin candidly admitted to some of his staff that he would have 'to bluff his way through' in handling the Middle East's affairs.[10]

These were presently in an appalling mess. Since the end of 1944, British forces had been vainly attempting to contain the Jewish revolt in Palestine. It was a guerrilla campaign of assassination and sabotage waged by partisans as elusive, intrepid and ruthless as the IRA. Like the Irish campaign, the Palestinian one earned Britain opprobrium abroad, particularly in America, and used up scarce treasure. The lack of funds was now dictating policy. Paupers did not make convincing dissemblers, and at the beginning of the year Bevin had had to withdraw subventions from the anti-Communist governments of Turkey and Greece, which were subsequently rescued by American subsidies. At the end of September 1947, the cabinet washed its hands of the embarrassing and costly Palestinian imbroglio. One hundred thousand servicemen had not broken the cycle of terror and counter-terror, and the province was clearly ungovernable. Britain surrendered its mandate to the United Nations with a promise of evacuation by May 1948.

This announcement was tantamount to a victory for the Jewish partisans, who were quickly embroiled in a civil war with the Palestinians. During the next eight months, the United Nations tried unsuccessfully to arrange a partition of the country between two races who were each set on the other's extinction. It was bad enough that Britain had had to scurry out of a protectorate which it had ruled for barely thirty years, but worse followed. The last days of the mandate witnessed the massacre of 240 Arabs, including women and children, by a Jewish unit at Deir Yassim. This incident helped trigger a mass exodus of Palestinians and, by 1949, 720,000 refugees had fled either to Gaza or Jordan. Their legal statelessness and bleak camps were a reproach to Britain, and a reminder to the Arab world of her impotence and perfidy. After 1948, Britain and the infant state of Israel became symbols of alien domination and Arab powerlessness. It was left to the United States to offer the refugees financial assistance and, where possible, attempt their resettlement.

Whatever post-war official spokesmen said to the contrary about Britain's future good intentions in the Middle East, it had not shaken off its pre-war reputation for high-handedness and Machiavellian intrigue. Lawrence of Arabia may have been a hero in his own country, but for the Arabs he was just the first in a line of imperialist tricksters who had coveted their resources and land. 'The British position in the whole area is hopeless. They are hated and distrusted almost everywhere,' concluded a *Time* survey which appeared at the beginning of 1952. A fortnight after, the magazine noted the 'old game of baiting the British' was being played with relish in Egypt and Persia; it could have added that the players were feeling more confident than ever of eventual victory.[11]

In April 1951, Dr Mohammed Mussadiq's Nationalist party had won the

Iran

general election in Persia, or Iran as it now called itself, having plucked a name of antique glory from the history books. The frail, elderly Mussadiq had come to power on a programme of anglophobia and national regeneration. He captivated the masses by the power of his eloquence, sometimes fainting in mid-flow, physically overcome by the emotion of his rhetoric. He saw himself as his country's saviour, once telling an audience in New York that Iran in 1951 was doing what America had done in 1776: freeing itself from an arbitrary and rapacious overlord. In January 1952, the general assembly of the United Nations heard an extended recital of Britain's misdeeds in Iran, Mussadiq's favourite theme. The embarrassed British representative, Sir Gladwyn Jebb, pooh-poohed this catalogue of iniquities as 'the profitless and indeed sterile interpretation of past events', and asked Mussadiq to look towards the future.

No amount of bland requests to forget and presumably forgive the past could expiate Britain's guilt in the eyes of Iranian, or for that matter Arab and Egyptian, nationalists. Memories were long and bitter; Mussadiq was old enough to recall Indian troops marching through his country during the First World War, unequal treaties, governments which rose or fell according to the whims of bureaucrats in London or Delhi, and, in 1942, the return of British forces. Iranians, like other peoples of the Middle East, had had their destinies decided for them; now, Mussadiq believed, they were about to make their own history. It was futile to explain to him and those who cheered his speeches that Britain had changed, and that it was now ready to help them in the development of their country as friendly partner, or that British companies were progressive and philanthropic employers. They may have been, but they were also the beneficiaries of past injustices, and this was how they appeared to Mussadiq and millions of other Iranians.

In May 1951, Mussadiq kept faith with those who had voted for him by nationalising the Anglo-Iranian Oil Company's assets. This firm was a symbol of Iranian subservience and British power, a leech which had been sucking Iran's life blood, leaving its people poor and hungry. The riches generated by the oil company had been unevenly distributed; in the year before nationalisation, Iran received £9 million in royalties, a million more than the Inland Revenue took from the company's profits. In purely commercial terms, the Anglo-Iranian Oil Company might have saved some of its profits by adopting a 50-50 deal, which its American counterparts had recently made with Iraq and Saudi Arabia, although this would have been painful, and not to the liking of the company's chairman and presumably his stockholders. As the crisis unfolded and details of Anglo-Iranian's record became known, there was much muted criticism of its past selfishness in the corridors of Whitehall.[12] But in public, ministers and the press presented the company as a model of commercial generosity.

More than Anglo-Iranian's contractual rights were at stake. Iranian oil provided 31 per cent of Europe's imports, and 85 per cent of the fuel used by the Royal Navy. Moreover, and this animated everyone on the right and quite a few on the left, Musaddiq had snapped his fingers at Britain, setting an example which, given the present temper of the whole area, might be followed elsewhere. 'Once upon a time Asiatics would be cowed by a show of force,' announced the *Economist*, echoing Conservatives who thought that this still ought to be the case. The trouble was that nowadays Iran would protest to the general assembly of the United Nations about British aggression, and win support from Middle Eastern, Asian and Latin American countries, and, of course, the Communist bloc.[13] Nonetheless, Bevin's successor and fellow devotee of Palmerston, Herbert Morrison, ordered the cruiser *Mauritius* to heave to off Abadan Island. In the meantime, staff officers gathered and produced two aptly-named exigency plans, 'Buccaneer' and 'Midget', one for armed intervention, the other for the evacuation of the 4,500 British technicians who ran the refinery. If they left, the installations would quickly fall into desuetude for the Iranians lacked the expertise to operate them. Like silly children who meddled with what they could not understand, the Iranians would learn a lesson. As the *Economist* disdainfully explained: 'Nationalisation is a mid-century fashion. Even though it is demonstrably unprofitable, nationalists will want to try it.'[14]

There were plenty who thought a sharp rap on the knuckles was a better way of bringing the Iranians to their senses and Britain's heel. This might prove harder than first imagined, for the Admiralty was having trouble finding the ships required for 'Buccaneer' since the navy was heavily committed to the Korean War.[15] In the Commons, the Conservatives were restless and wanted blood. Churchill opened the Iran debate on 20 July by taunting Morrison for his cockneyfied pronunciation of 'Euphrates'. He then bemoaned the loss of India and chided the government for its faintheartedness throughout the Middle East. Britain had only 'to be pressed sufficiently by one method or another,' for it meekly to forfeit its rights and interests.[16]

Brigadier Anthony Head followed up the attack with the charge that there had been too much 'Socialism' injected into Britain's foreign policy, with the result that the Middle East's masses had been pandered to, while Britain's prestige languished. The view from the bar of Shepheard's Hotel was delivered by Julian Amery, who had taken on board some of his father's paternalist imperialism. According to the younger Amery, Britain had misjudged the true feelings of the man in the bazaar, for an Egyptian had once told him: 'Independence good for pasha, bad for fellah. British rule good for fellah, bad for pasha.'[17] Alas for those of Amery's mind, fewer and fewer fellahin or their counterparts appeared to regard Britain as their even-handed protector. Attlee closed the debate with a pertinent history lesson, referring back to a previous war waged for the rights of British shareholders: 'In Egypt I see they are remembering the bombardment of Alexandria. That kind of thing could be done in the Nineteenth Century: it cannot be done now, we are working under an entirely different code.'[18]

Churchill had been eight when the guns had roared off Alexandria in 1882, and he wanted their thunder to resound in the Persian Gulf. As he later remarked, had he been prime minister 'a splutter of musketry' would have been heard and felt by the Iranians.[19] Attlee chose 'Midget' rather than 'Buccaneer'. The latter would have dangerously stretched manpower, and an invasion of Iran could easily have driven Mussadiq to appeal to the Soviet Union for help. This was the view of the American Secretary of State, Dean Acheson, who thought that whether invited or not, the Russians would snatch at any chance to slip back into northern Persia, their old stamping ground from which they had been evicted with some difficulty five years before.

Attlee had no wish to turn Iran into a Cold War cockpit. Moreover he had, in December 1950, flown to Washington to persuade Truman to dis-avow General MacArthur's proposal to use an atomic bomb against Chinese forces in Korea. A soft line on Iran was a diplomatic *quid quo pro*. On 27 September, Mussadiq took control over the Abadan refinery and its staff departed. 'We have lost prestige on an unprecedented scale,' com-plained the *Spectator*, ruefully adding that had a *coup de main* been delivered, the Communist and Arab worlds would have seen the subsequent contest as 'a simple battle between a top-dog and an under-dog'.[20] There was, however, some consolation for those fire-eaters who would have relished the sound of *Mauritius*'s guns being fired in anger; on 25 October the Conservatives won the general election with a small majority.

A few weeks after the evacuation of Abadan Island, Acheson stung Evelyn Shuckburgh with the remark, 'You must live in the world as it is.'[21] The events in Iran during the past few months had provided a glimpse into the future. Britain could no longer expect to do business either with deferential sheiks, grateful for a sackful of sovereigns, or conservative and compliant politicians in frock coats and tarbooshes, who could be scared by threats of battleships if they stepped out of line. Now Britain faced populists who ranted about imperialism. Mussadiq was a man in the new mould; he wore green pyjamas when he received Sir Francis Shepherd, the ambassador in Tehran. This insult, together with his habit of swooning in public, convinced Shepherd that the Iranian was mad, a diagnosis which was accepted in Whitehall and by the British press.

There was another, equally distressful implication behind Acheson's observation. Throughout the Iranian crisis, the British government had had to seek American advice and sometimes received it unasked. Much of it had come from George McGhee, a former oil geologist who had served for three years as the State Department's roving emissary in the Middle East. A former Rhodes Scholar at Oxford, McGhee shared his benefactor's belief in 'the white man's burden', and was therefore more sympathetic to Britain's present predicament than many other American diplomats. Nevertheless, he was wrongly suspected of being hand-in-glove with American oil interests, and a Treasury official warned Morrison that McGhee's youth, Texan upbringing and Irish ancestry made him a man whose judgement might be unsound when it came to British interests.[22]

Anglo-American tensions were as strong as ever they had been during the war, and took a turn for the worse with the appointment as Secretary of State of John Foster Dulles in 1953. Like President Coolidge, another Puritan who achieved high office, Dulles had the demeanour of one who had been 'weaned on a pickle', and his anti-Communist fervour was only matched in intensity by his loathing for imperialism. The British ambassador in Washington, Sir Roger Makins, described the latter as a 'deep seated feeling about colonialism, which is common to so many Americans, occasionally welling up inside Foster like lava from a dormant volcano'.

What lay behind these eruptions was the fear that the United States could become tainted by the vices of its partner in the Middle East. If America was to hold its own in the Cold War, it could not afford to become too closely associated with a declining power which, as public reaction to the Iranian crisis proved, tended to see the world from the bridge of a cruiser or the turret of an armoured car. Vice-President Richard Nixon recognised the danger when he toured Asia during the spring of 1953. He returned to Washington convinced that 'three centuries of European colonialism [were] on their deathbed'. America would have to distance itself from those powers which were still clinging to their fief-doms. In a revealing and, given the subsequent course of American involvement in South-East Asia, ironic passage in his memoirs, Nixon wrote of his attempts to woo the nationalists:

> Many people in these countries knew America only as an immensely powerful nation that both Communist propaganda *and European snobbery* [my italics] had painted as crass and rapacious. I reassured them that we were not a colonial power, nor did we approve of the lingering colonialism of our European allies.[23]

American policy towards the Middle East and Asia was already changing direction. Since 1947, the United States had been cultivating Turkey, which joined NATO in 1951 and offered the USAAF airfields under its own control for nuclear strikes against Russia.[24] A British proposal to have the Turkish army placed under Britain's Middle East command was rejected by the Americans during a planning conference in Istanbul in 1951.[25] Henceforward, the aim of America's policy was to cajole rather than coerce independent Middle Eastern states into the West's camp. Any action which might be interpreted as an attempt to uphold or further British supremacy would rebound against the United States. Cooperation with Britain was expedient, but outright cohabitation would discredit America and lose friends.

American incursions into a region where Britain had hitherto enjoyed a monopoly of power were resented and, at first, resisted. Towards the end of the war Ibn Saud of Saudi Arabia (and his oil deposits) had been lured into America's orbit by a $25 million loan and a payment of $10 million for the lease of an airfield at Dharan. This was poaching in Britain's coverts, and in 1943 the India Office banned the establishment of an American consulate in Bahrain.[26] Within ten years, the interlopers were unstoppable, because when necessary they could sign large cheques, a luxury denied post-war Britain. By 1960 the United States had distributed $2,702 million to Middle Eastern states.

While usurping Britain's position in the area, America felt obliged to restrain its ally. After the Iranian crisis, State Department diplomats acted as mediators between Britain and Mussadiq and, during the exchanges, found him as fickle as his antagonists were stubborn. The British government's obduracy may have been based on its faith in a novel form of gunboat diplomacy. During 1952 MI6 was busy fomenting a plot to overthrow Mussadiq with the help of Iranian dissidents. This exercise in subversion was known as Operation Boot, and among those drawn in was Kermit Roosevelt, the grandson of President Theodore Roosevelt and a Central Intelligence Agency (CIA) employee with Middle East responsibilities.

Early in 1953, the new Eisenhower administration took over 'Boot' which was renamed 'Ajax'. American Cold War warriors were haunted by the 'loss' of Czechoslovakia to a Russian *coup d'état* in March 1948 and that of China a year after. Iran was seen as vulnerable to Soviet-inspired sedition and Mussadiq had revealed himself as too volatile to make a steadfast ally. The upshot was the implementation of 'Ajax' under Kermit Roosevelt's vigorous direction. In August 1953, an uprising in Tehran was financed and stage managed by CIA agents with some British help. Mussadiq was toppled and replaced by the exiled Shah Mohammed Reza Pahlevi, the son of the former Cossack officer whom Britain had assisted to the Peacock Throne thirty years before. Iran had been snatched for the West, and Shah Mohammed Reza served his American patrons faithfully until 1979. He was, in turn, overthrown by the Ayatollah Khomeini, who had written of the events of 1953 that Iran had been 'the slave of Britain one day, of America the next'.[27] This was just the invidious comparison which the American policy-makers were striving to avoid. Sir Anthony Eden, the new Foreign Secretary, while satisfied with the result of 'Ajax', was 'jealous' of what had been an American triumph.[28]

While on his way to lay Iran's case before the United Nations in November 1951, Mussadiq had briefly stopped over in Cairo. His welcome was ecstatic, there were anti-British riots, and he joined with the Egyptian prime minister, Mustafa al-Nahas, to declare that 'a united Iran and Egypt will together demolish British imperialism'.

Al-Nahas had been chipping away at the foundations of British power since January 1950, when the Wafd had come to power with over half the popular vote. Its platform was the same as it had been during the 1920s and 1930s: an end to the British military presence in Egypt and the restoration of Egyptian sovereignty over the Sudan. The disastrous 1948-9 war against Israel had given Egypt a further grievance against Britain, which was accused of having prevented the Egyptian armed forces from acquiring modern weapons. As far as Britain was concerned, Egypt counted for a bagatelle, and had been equipped with what Bevin once called 'junk'. [29]

It was the Canal Zone base which remained the chief source of contention. Its barbed wire, concrete and tarmac symbolised Egypt's subservience to a foreign power, which believed it had the inalienable right to interfere in Egyptian affairs whenever it chose, and had done so as recently as 1942. Furthermore, for those who shaped his destiny, the Egyptian remained a lower form of life. During conversations with senior British diplomats and commanders in 1950, George McGhee detected the 'traditional condescension' towards the Egyptians, who were commonly spoken of as 'Gippies'.[30] Contempt was matched by malevolence; another American emissary reported at the end of 1951 that, 'The hatred against them [the British] is general and intense. It is shared by everyone in the country.'[31]

McGhee and his colleagues came and went from Egypt as part of an intensive diplomatic effort contrived to prevent it from sliding towards Russia. But attempts to persuade al-Nahas and the rest of the Egyptian cabinet foundered because they insisted that British imperialism, not Communism, was Egypt's real enemy. Americans tended to sympathise, but they could not ignore the strategic importance of the Canal Zone and its airfields, still earmarked for the nuclear offensive against Russia. The 1936 Anglo-Egyptian treaty had permitted a garrison of 10,000, but by 1950 the base was home to 38,000 British servicemen, including 8,000 infantry from Mauritius who acted as guards, and contained stores worth £270 million. Ideally, from the American standpoint, the British should have withdrawn, leaving the facilities intact and ready to be put on a war footing at the first hint of an international crisis, a solution which the chiefs-of-staff would have tolerated. Anglo-Egyptian discord might then cease, and Egypt could be invited to join America in an anti-Soviet regional defence pact.[31] Negotiations over these points dragged on from the middle of 1950 until the autumn of 1951 in an atmosphere of increasing frustration and acrimony.

On 8 October 1951, al-Nahas unilaterally revoked the 1936 Treaty, theoretically terminating British occupation of the Canal Zone. His sense of timing was acute and provocative; the last British technician had left Abadan Island four days before, and the British general election campaign had been underway for three days. Within a few weeks, the 70,000-strong Egyptian labour force had left the Canal Zone, and a campaign of terrorism began with covert government backing. The new prime minister, Churchill, was beside himself with rage. In the middle of discussions about Egypt on 15 December, he rose from his chair and advanced on Eden with clenched fists. He growled, 'Tell them [the Egyptians] if we have any more of their cheek we will set the Jews on them and drive them into the gutter from which they should never have emerged.'[32] He then sat down and warmly recalled his visits to Cairo in the days when the Egyptians had understood their place in the scheme of things.

Churchillian fury was being translated into a plan to restore the old order in Egypt. By the end of December, Whitehall's strategists had concocted Operation Rodeo, a repeat performance of the 1882 occupation of Egypt. Forces from the Canal Zone, reinforced by units from Malta, Libya and Cyprus, were to occupy Cairo, the Nile delta and Alexandria, the last being taken by an assault from the sea. Ground troops and aircraft could be mustered within thirty-six hours, warships within seventy-two, and the coup's main objectives could be achieved within a day.[33]

In the meantime, the Canal Zone had been placed under military government, which involved disarming all the Egyptian police within its perimeter. On 25 January 1952, an auxiliary detachment at Ismailia refused to give up their guns, barricaded themselves inside their station and were evicted only after a siege in which fifty were killed and a hundred wounded. At last the 'splutter of musketry' had been heard, and the 'about-time-they-were-taught-a-lesson' Conservatives were cock-a-hoop. Their oracle, the *Daily Express*, proclaimed that Britain was now 'making a mighty affirmation of its Imperial Destiny'.[34] The Egyptians answered with an equally bloody affirmation of their destiny; within three days, Cairene mobs had stormed the citadels of their overlords and burned down the Turf Club, Shepheard's Hotel and various British commercial premises, murdering those of their occupants whom they caught.

The Canal Zone was now embattled and could no longer be counted upon in an emergency. Like the British garrison, Egypt's old ruling class also had their backs to the wall. King Faruq sacked al-Nahas and his ministry immediately after the riots, and was himself deposed in July 1952 by a knot of army officers led by General Mohammed Naguib. The stout monarch shuffled off to continue his sybaritic existence in various Mediterranean resorts. Egypt's new governors were soldiers who, following the tradition of Urabi Pasha, regarded themselves as the nation's saviours, ordained to lead it, advance its honour and defend its integrity. They were idealists who wanted a social revolution, and their creed was a blend of Islamic ethics, pan-Arabism and socialism.

British reaction to the July revolution was fumbling. The embassy had no forewarning of trouble, and the ambassador was on holiday. Five days after the coup, the chargé d'affaires suggested that Britain could reverse the course of events 'by a clear show of determination and by an immediate show of force at the appropriate moment'.[35] The ghosts of Cromer, Milner and Allenby would have applauded.

The CIA was better informed. It had got wind of the plot against Faruq, but it was unperturbed, having long recognised the need for radical social change inside Egypt. Moreover, the Americans had good reason to believe that the revolutionaries, of whom Colonel Nasser was the most dynamic, might align with the West if carefully handled. Britain remained the chief obstacle to such an understanding. Soon after he had taken over the State Department, Dulles described Britain's presence on Egyptian soil as the 'psychological block' which prevented Egypt from joining an anti-Soviet pact.[36] Furthermore, the Canal Zone had now become a strategic white elephant. Incidents during the past two years had revealed how vulnerable it was to sabotage by disaffected Egyptians, and recent advances in thermonuclear weapons (America exploded its first hydrogen bomb in March 1954) dictated that in future bases would have to be smaller and dispersed. As it was, the USAAF's airfields in Turkey were now operational, making their British-run, Egyptian counterparts redundant.

There was, therefore, no purpose in Britain's continuing to dig its heels in. The 1936 Anglo-Egyptian treaty expired in 1956, and in July 1954 arrangements were agreed for a piecemeal evacuation of the base over the next two years. There was a settlement too of the old dispute over the Sudan, where Britain had made an astute alliance with local nationalists who were averse to any restoration of Egyptian sovereignty. On 1 January 1956 the Sudan became independent.

Some years ago I was told by one who had been among the last British servicemen to leave the Canal Zone that as his boat drew away from the Port Said quayside, an Egyptian youth raised his robe and passed water onto the soldiers below. One looked up, and took a shot at him. Whether or not this story is true, it was in a way oddly symbolic of the past thirty or so years of Britain's presence in Egypt.

4

---•-•---

Kick Their Backsides:
The Suez War and
Beyond

The re-ordering of Britain's relations with Egypt was another achieve-ment for Sir Anthony Eden, the Foreign Secretary, adding to his reputation as a consummate diplomat. He had a strong faith in his own abilities and was highly ambitious, but seemed destined to serve as second-in-command to more forceful figures. He had been such to Chamberlain, who had insisted on conducting crucial negotiations in person, a habit which Churchill also adopted, much to Eden's chagrin. He was the Prime Minister's heir-apparent, but grew increasingly impatient as the old man soldiered on, ignoring two strokes. Eden did not hide his frustration, once describing his chief as 'gaga'. He finally got the succession in April 1955 when Churchill resigned, and with it the chance to usher in a new and glittering era for Britain in the Middle East.

Dulles and the clever men in the State Department may have written off Britain as a loser in the region, but Eden was certain that its prestige could be restored and enhanced. After all, Britain was still master of bases in Malta, Libya, Cyprus, Aden, the Persian Gulf and Iraq, whose Hashemite king, Faisal II, like his cousin Hussain of Jordan, was Britain's friend. Building on these foundations, Eden believed that he could, with American cooperation, construct an anti-Soviet alliance as solid as NATO, which would strengthen Britain's strategic position in the Middle East and serve as a barrier guarding its oilfields.

Between March and October 1955, Turkey, Iraq, Iran and Pakistan had been induced to join the Baghdad Pact. Britain kept its Iraqi airfields, and promised to provide the muscle needed to throw back a conventional Russian offensive. It included the armoured brigade now dispersed across the Middle East, Commonwealth reinforcements, and a reserve of nuclear weapons which would redress any imbalance in numbers.[1]

The Baghdad Pact was wormwood to Nasser, Egypt's prime minister and from 1956 its president. He reviled the agreement as a thinly disguised attempt by Britain to reassert its old supremacy and split the Arab world. He responded with a campaign of virulent radio propaganda beamed across the Middle East and North Africa, addressed to the masses and designed to discredit Britain and its stooges. Nasser's message was simple and compelling: Egypt was the spearhead of revolutionary nationalism and he, a modern Saladin, was ordained to unite all Arab peoples and destroy their enemies. For millions of Arabs who read or listened to his words he became an almost messianic figure, a liberator who would free them from a past in which they had been divided and subservient.

Radio Cairo's rant and the figure behind it awakened unpleasant memories. For Eden, Nasser was Mussolini reincarnate. Like the Italian, he was both a contemptible 'cad' and a megalomaniac, whose sole aim was to install himself as 'a Caesar from the Gulf to the Atlantic'.[2] Macmillan, like Eden an opponent of appeasement, concurred, and reckoned Nasser was 'an Asiatic Mussolini'.[3]

These intuitive comparisons offer an important clue as to Eden's subsequent behaviour. He and those who shared his alarm convinced themselves that they were engaged in a trial of strength with an autocrat as fissile, unpredictable and ruthless as Mussolini. If Nasser was the man Eden took him to be, and the events of the late 1930s were about to repeat themselves, then temporising would be suicidal. To offer concessions to Nasser would encourage him to up the stakes, raise his stature in the eyes of the Arab world, and further depress Britain's.

At the end of 1955, Eden and his advisers believed they had identified the carrier of a virus which could infect the entire Middle East, but they had no remedy. Whatever this might turn out to be, it could not be applied without American approval and possibly assistance. This would only be forthcoming if Nasser aligned Egypt with Russia, by when it might be too late. MI6 agents in Cairo discovered that he was inclining more and more towards the Soviet Union, and this was confirmed by his decision in September to acquire arms from Czechoslovakia.[4] Signs that Egypt and its partner, Syria, were beginning to edge towards the Soviet

Union raised the possibility that they, and maybe other friendly Middle Eastern states, might soon be 'lost' to the West.

During the winter of 1955–6, the government faced a mounting pile of reports which together suggested that Britain had lost the initiative in the Middle East, and was about to part with what remained of its influence. Jordan, hitherto a steadfast ally, appeared to be on the verge of succumbing to Nasser's propaganda and subversion. On 1 March, King Hussain dismissed General Glubb, the commander of the Arab Legion, who had long been vilified by Radio Cairo as the power behind the throne and a cunning agent of British imperialism. A further blow followed a few days after, when the Foreign Secretary Selwyn Lloyd was hooted and pelted by an anti-British mob during a visit to another supposedly friendly outpost, Bahrain.

'We are in a mess,' Eden admitted on 3 March, adding; 'we are at our best in a mess.' Panic and fury were also very much in evidence in the next few days. The chiefs-of-staff imagined that Jordan's desertion was imminent, which would deprive Britain of an uncontested flight path to its Iraqi bases. Selwyn Lloyd's misadventures in Bahrain angered Eden and his colleagues, who wanted to put some troops ashore 'to show that we are alive and kicking'.[5] The trouble was that there was as yet no one to kick. By the end of the month, rage had given way to resolution, or so it appeared from a remark made to a CIA agent by George Kennedy Young, the director of MI6. 'Britain', alleged Young, 'is now prepared to fight its last battle . . . no matter what the cost, we will win.'[6]

This prediction was and still is mysterious. Young may have been referring to Operation Straggle, an Anglo-American plot contrived to strip Nasser of an ally through the overthrow of President Shukri al-Quwatli of Syria, whose country would then be brought under the aegis of friendly Iraq.[7] A conspiracy which involved local dissidents was uncovered in Damascus at the very end of October, but whether or not Britain was its instigator remains unclear since the relevant files remain closed. At the time, Egyptian Intelligence believed that the CIA had something afoot in Syria, and that a British brigade, then in Cyprus, was being held in readiness for use against Syria.[8]

And yet Young's words suggest that the British government had something more fearsome up its sleeve than a repetition in Damascus of the sort of coup that had unseated Mussadiq two years before. Young may have had in mind Operation Cordage, a response to MI6 reports of an impending Israeli attack on Britain's ally, Jordan. 'Cordage' included the destruction of the Israeli air force, commando raids and a naval blockade, which would have added up to an awesome demonstration of might, as well as an earnest of Britain's determination to take care of its friends in the Middle East.[9]

A third and tantalising possibility was that cabinet was preparing to apply *force majeure* against Egypt in the near future. The mood of ministers at the beginning of March had been uncannily like that of Liberal MPs during the first phase of the 1882 Egyptian crisis when, in their indignation, they had wanted nothing more than to kill someone.[10] Nasser was the obvious target, and, according to the former MI6 agent Peter Wright, schemes were in hand to have him killed.[11] The CIA had been informed of this at the end of February, and Egyptian authorities believed that at least three British assassins and one German were sent to Cairo, but all lost their nerve.[12] Details of another clandestine British operation were revealed early in September, after the arrest of a number of Egyptians who had been instructed to foment disorders in major cities.[13] It was assumed by the Egyptian government that an outbreak of rioting might have been used by the British as an excuse for armed intervention as it had been in 1882.

Together, these fragments of information suggest that from March 1956 the government was determined to engineer a showdown with Nasser. Just how this might have been achieved will remain obscure until all the official papers are released. What is known strongly suggests that British intelligence had been ordered to contrive a situation akin to that of 1882, when the Egyptian government had lost control and internal disorder was getting out of hand. Such circumstances were, of course, an excellent pretext for armed intervention and the installation of a puppet administration, which was what Eden wanted.

However it was approached, the overthrow of Nasser was an extremely hazardous enterprise. But Eden was prepared to accept the risk, and there was some comfort in the fact that something along the same lines, although on a smaller scale, had been successful in Iran. That Nasser would have to be removed was beyond question if Britain was to preserve its prestige and friends in the Middle East. For Eden, and to some extent Macmillan, the contest became a personal vendetta and, to judge from the plans to assassinate Nasser, was pursued as such.

Politically, Eden had been on shaky ground since the beginning of the year, when sections of his party and the *Daily Telegraph* had been demanding what was called 'firm government'. Complaints on this score may in part explain the outburst of anger during March, and the subsequent urge to 'do something' about Nasser. He was also a scapegoat for the unavenged humiliations suffered in Iran and Egypt over the past six years. In a sense the loss of what was to a large extent Britain's unofficial empire in the Middle East seems to have rankled more than the departure from India. At least Britain had parted company from India with dignity and a sense of achievement, whereas the abandonment of old spheres of influence in Iran and Egypt had been retreats in the face of insults and brickbats. National pride had been bruised; Britain's ability to dominate the Middle East had traditionally been a measure of its standing in the world. Now it was being hustled out, humbled, and forced to comply with the wishes of the United States, which seemed poised to usurp its old position.

It is impossible to read through the newspapers for the first half of 1956 without sensing that Britain felt itself at bay, and at the mercy of anyone, anywhere, with a grievance against it. Headlines announced the random murders of servicemen and sometimes their wives by EOKA (*Ethniki Organosis Kyprion Aghoniston*: 'National Organisation of Cypriot Fighters'), who wanted *Enosis*, union with Greece. There were also reports of riots in Aden in May, when a junior minister was mobbed by crowds calling for independence. And there was always Nasser, denouncing Britain and intriguing against it. Britain appeared powerless and on the run, something which was galling and inexplicable to generations who had grown up in a world in which no one had defied Britain with impunity, certainly not Egypt. Those who lived through this period may judge for themselves, but a great deal of what was said and written during and after the Suez crisis gives a strong impression that Britain was suffering from the delayed shock of imperial disengagement and its concomitant, relative impotence in world affairs.

As before the First World War, when there had been similar qualms about the country's future as a first-rate power, Britain's authority in the world was imagined to be inseparable from the national moral tone. This seemed to be taking a turn for the worse during the early 1950s. Horror comics, juke boxes, jive, rock and roll and teddy boys all appeared as milestones along a downhill track which led to the total corruption of the young, and with it the final stage of national decline.[14] All these seductive innovations came from the United States, the power which was supplanting Britain in the world, and this no doubt added a note of stridency to the clamour of various editors, Conservative MPs, churchmen, magistrates and judges who saw themselves as keepers of Britain's old values. Discussing the matter with friends, including Mrs Robert Makins, the wife of a diplomat and 'Evelyn Home' (the *Woman's Own* agony aunt), Evelyn

Shuckburgh concluded that Britain had become 'bloodless and effete'.[15]

Nasser thought likewise, and during the first half of 1956 he set Egypt on a collision course with Britain. It would end with a trial of strength between the two countries, which, Nasser believed, would result in a new balance of power in the Middle East favourable to Egypt. First, he undertook an extended tour of non-aligned states in Asia to establish his credentials as a leader of the anti-imperialist, neutral block. He also showed that he was his own man by recognising Communist China and receiving Russian emissaries in Cairo.

Inside Egypt, his attentions were occupied by the projected Aswan high dam and the future of the Suez Canal Company, in which foreign investors still had a 49 per cent holding. On the surface, the question of which powers would underwrite the building of the dam and the nationalisation of the Canal have always appeared connected. On 19 July, Dulles bluntly informed Egypt that no American loan would be forthcoming for the dam, and as a tit-for-tat Nasser took over the Canal seven days later. In fact he had been contemplating sequestering the Canal company and its assets for some time. From the start he had known that such a gesture would be a gamble, but he estimated that the odds were in his favour. America would be distracted by the campaign for the presidential election at the beginning of November, France had its hands tied by the Algerian war, and only Britain might take action.

Egyptian intelligence was therefore instructed to assess Britain's readiness. Using sources inside EOKA and Maltese trade unionists, Nasser discovered that no immediate response was possible, and that at least eight weeks were needed for Britain to mobilise for an invasion of Egypt.[16] Everything would therefore depend on Eden's grit, and Nasser, on the strength of a single meeting two years before, took him to be a man who would mask interior weakness by public bravado. He would plump for a war. Even so, the chances of a fight would progressively diminish as time went by; Nasser calculated that they were 90 per cent before 10 August and would then plummet to 20 per cent by the second half of October.[17] Israel was not included in his reckonings.

Eden was sitting at dinner in Downing Street with King Faisal II of Iraq and his prime minister, Nuri es-Said, a steadfast friend of Britain, when news of the canal's nationalisation was first received. Nuri urged a tough line with Nasser, telling Eden, 'You must hit him hard and you must hit him now.' Eden retired to spend the rest of the evening on the arithmetic of war, which he thought was two or three weeks away.[18]

The Prime Minister and the inner knot of six ministers who advised him on Egypt had two ambitious objectives. Nasser had to be tumbled from power and a government set up in Egypt that would acknowledge British paramountcy in the rest of the Middle East.

The Canal would be placed under international control to forestall any future threat to Britain's and Europe's oil supplies. At a stroke, British prestige would be restored and the Baghdad Pact preserved. The overriding question was, what sort of stroke would be needed?

Two plans of action were adopted. On one hand, Britain rallied international support for a diplomatic offensive which might force Nasser to disgorge the canal. On the other, it prepared for war, summoning up reservists on 2 August. They were needed to implement Operation Musketeer, which emerged in its final form by mid-September. Anglo-French forces would deliver an aerial bombardment of Egyptian strategic targets (including Radio Cairo), undertake a landing at Port Said, and seize the Canal. Having defeated Egypt and presumably overthrown Nasser, three or four divisions would garrison the country until a suitable government could be found. The cabinet expected that there might be a brief interim period in which British administrators would assist in the governance of Egypt.

Such a far-reaching and, given the climate of British and world opinion in 1956, daring reassertion of unofficial empire needed substantial backing at home and abroad. From the start, Britain had the wholehearted support of France, whose animus towards Nasser stemmed from his help to the Algerian nationalists. The Commonwealth was equivocal: India, Pakistan and Canada came down firmly against any use of force, South Africa was neutral, Australia and New Zealand were hesitantly loyal, and only the fragile Central African Federation (Nyasaland and Southern and Northern Rhodesia) said it would stick by Britain come what may. Both New Zealand and Australia urged caution and warned Britain not to act precipitately or without American approval. It was Chanak and the Munich crisis all over again.

Inside Britain, opinion was split. Eden, Macmillan and Alec Douglas-Home were the most hawkish ministers, beyond whom was an outer circle of waverers including R.A Butler (an instinctive temporiser who had been willing to do a deal with Hitler as late as the summer of 1940), Edward Heath and Iain Macleod. What worried these men, and for that matter the Labour leader Hugh Gaitskell and many members of his party, was the government's procrastination. To judge by the tenor of the

Commons debates during the early days of the crisis, Eden might have got away with a swift retaliatory grabbing back of the Canal. But it was beyond the capacity of the army, navy and air force to mount such a surgical operation. The result was a policy which thrust in two opposite directions; Britain and France were openly and ponderously preparing for war at the same time as actively encouraging an international settlement by negotiation. Lord Killearn, who as Sir Miles Lampson had had first-hand experience of delivering a bolt from the blue against the Egyptians, saw the delay as fatal. 'To allow ourselves to be drawn into a welter of committees and conferences', he wrote, 'was to permit the aggressor to get away with his crime.'[19]

There were, of course, plenty of old warhorses who sniffed blood and believed that the time had at last arrived for a few hard thumps delivered in the old manner. Brigadier M. F. Farquharson-Roberts, addressing an old soldiers' reunion in Derby, was fed up with the government's pussy-footing. 'Politicians don't know Orientals like we do,' he thundered, 'they don't know that the only way to deal with them is to kick their backsides.'[20] The splendid fox-hunting Labour MP Reginald Paget angrily asked, 'How much and for how long have we given to Egypt and got kicked in the teeth for it?'[21] Inaction was an advertisement of British powerlessness. 'If Nasser gets away with it,' claimed Macmillan, 'we are done for.'[22] The Egyptian dictator was no more than 'a weak bombastic troublemaker', who could and should be squashed, argued Captain Charles Waterhouse, a trenchant spokesman for the Blimpish faction inside the Conservatives.[23] Denis Healey derided them as 'dinosaurs' and 'teddy boys', but the *New Statesmen* described them more elegantly in a profile of Waterhouse: 'His period is *Daily Mail* 1920, the time when Imperial Britain could give short, sharp orders to the foreigner abroad and the working classes at home.'[24]

Warlike noises resounding through Westminster alarmed Eisenhower, then running for a second term, and Dulles. The latter told Macmillan that Britain was making too much fuss about Nasser, rating him 'a much more important figure than he is'. Both the Secretary of State and the President insisted that Britain held back from war and sought, alongside the United States, to reach a settlement through negotiation.[25]

Despite a sequence of conferences and exchanges between leaders, there was no sign of any agreement by 15 September, the date originally set for the attack on Egypt, and, interestingly, within the eight weeks Nasser had set for Britain's mobilisation. The cabinet was now in the grip of its war machine and its immutable timetable. The weather ruled out operations after 21 November, and the service chiefs insisted that 31 October was the final date when they could be commenced with a fair chance of success. At the beginning of October, there were murmurs of discontent among some of the 20,000 reservists who had been kicking their heels for over two months, and were anxious to get back to families and jobs. Manpower had been causing snags from 31 July, when the cabinet had agreed that to make up numbers the lower age limit for front-line national servicemen should be reduced from its Korean-War level, nineteen, to eighteen-and-a-half. Even so, the navy carped about a shortage of trained signallers, disrupted training programmes, and the depletion of the home and Mediterranean fleets. Shortages of ratings meant that the six-inch gun cruisers could fire only two of their four turrets and two, the Jamaica and Glasgow, were unable to defend themselves against attack by modern aircraft.[26]

Time seemed to be running in Nasser's favour and against Eden. Unable to gain a favourable solution through diplomacy, he faced either a decision to attack or a climb-down. A gallup poll in August showed that 59 per cent of the country backed his mixture of firmness and apparent diplomatic flexibility but, by the middle of September, this total fell to 49 per cent. There were fresh difficulties at the beginning of October, when there were indications that after the recent upsurge in cross-border raids, an exasperated Israel might attack Jordan, forcing Britain to come to the rescue of its ally. On 11 October, the Israeli government was officially warned that Britain would defend Jordan.[27] Three days after, United Nations discussions of the Canal question reached an *impasse*, when Russia employed its Security Council veto.

For some weeks the French had been courting the Israelis, who they believed could help find a way out of the diplomatic deadlock. It was a simple stratagem, so much so that it convinced no one at the time, although the exact details of the hugger-mugger deal were not known until twenty years after. Israel attacked Egypt and its forces advanced through Sinai, thereby providing Britain and France with a pretext to seize the Canal on the grounds that they were protecting it, as well as separating the combatants. Eden jumped at what was a last-moment chance to avoid a humiliating climb-down, and on 17 October Canberra heavy bombers were on their way to airfields in Cyprus. Six days after, Selwyn Lloyd flew to Paris, where he was closeted with Guy Mollet, the French prime minister, his Israeli counterpart, David Ben Gurion, and General

Moshe Dayan in a secret hideaway in the suburb of Sèvres. The outcome was the secret Treaty of Sèvres, of which no copy seems to have survived, but whose outlines were made absolutely clear by the events of 29-30 October.[28]

There were two Suez wars in November 1956. The first was fought by British, French, Israeli and Egyptian forces in the Sinai peninsula, Port Said and along the banks of the Suez Canal. The second was fought in the Commons chamber, newspaper columns and everywhere where people gathered in Britain, and concerned whether or not the British government had acted wisely and honestly.

The first war ran according to the Sèvres schedule and took Nasser by surprise for he had never expected Israel to intrude itself into the Canal dispute. Indeed, after September had passed, he had picked up from American sources information which led him to think Egypt would not be attacked. Both Eisenhower and Dulles claimed astonishment as well, which is hard to understand given that an American U-2 spy plane (flown by Gary Powers who was later shot down over Russia) had criss-crossed the eastern Mediterranean and Middle East on 27 September, and its cameras could not have missed the Anglo-French build-up of troops and warships on Cyprus.[29] Of course this could have been taken as evidence of sabre-rattling, but British ministers thought they detected nothing in Dulles's utterances which indicated that America would object too vigorously to armed intervention in Egypt. It was thought, wrongly as it turned out, that Dulles's main concern was that the outbreak of fighting should not coincide with polling day in America, 6 November. Custom and courtesy had dictated that Commonwealth governments were party to British policy, but after the Sèvres agreement the flow of information ceased.

The Suez War started on time, with the Israeli irruption into Sinai on 29 October. The following day, as Israeli troops and armour sliced through the dazed Egyptian army, Britain and France issued an ultimatum, giving both sides twelve hours in which to stop fighting. This was ignored, and on 1 November Canberra bombers began high-level attacks on Egyptian strategic targets and cities, while airborne and amphibious units prepared for the landings at Port Said. The next day, the United States (backed by Australia among others) supported a United Nations motion for an immediate ceasefire by all the belligerents. Britain and France were thrown into a panic. They bargained for time, insisting that they would only agree to an armistice if United Nations forces took control of the Canal, and at the same time hurried forward the deadline for the invasion.

Following a new schedule, the first paratroopers landed on 5 November and the amphibious forces were ashore on the 6th. In the meantime, there had been two further United Nations calls for a truce and, with their forces in possession of Port Said and a twenty-three-mile-long section of the canal, the British and French governments complied on the evening of 6 November. In purely military terms, the operation was a shining success; Egyptian losses had been over a thousand and Anglo-French under a hundred. 'It was all like a bloody good exercise,' a colonel told one journalist, 'a lot of fun and very interesting.'[30]

The other Suez War also had its moments. Eden's moves between 30 October and 6 November were a catalyst for a political rumpus which convulsed the entire nation. Inside the Commons, government statements on Egypt were a signal for uproar; fists were shaken and catcalls exchanged. The Conservatives were 'fascists' and 'murderers' (this from the sturdy Mrs Bessie Braddock) and Labour were 'cowards', who had stabbed their country in the back. The press took up the cudgels, mostly for the government, and there were two mass demonstrations, one outside the Commons, the other in Trafalgar Square, where Aneurin Bevan denounced Eden. Eastbourne Methodists marched through the streets and were abused as 'dirty Nasserites' by onlookers, who took the view, common enough at the time, that those who condemned Eden were the allies of Nasser and, *ipso facto*, all but traitors.

There were also many sharp exchanges wherever people congregated and talked. I recollect that in my school, in a predominantly middle-class Conservative area, those who did not take an outrageously gung-ho line were shouted down, sometimes receiving a knock in the process. Conservative MPs believed that the working class was behind the government and angry with Labour for its lack of patriotism. One, with a southern constituency, commented revealingly: 'I have lost my middle-class followers, but this has been at least balanced by backing from working-class electors who normally vote Socialist and who favour a strong line on Suez.'[31]

And yet the overwhelmingly middle-class readership of the *Observer* was disturbed by its editorial of 4 November which alleged: 'Never since 1783 has Great Britain made herself so universally disliked.' The country was now in an 'isolated moral position', having re-asserted its old belligerent imperialism and discarded the internationalism which had guided its foreign policy since 1945. During the following week, the editor received 866 letters defending the government (including 500 cancelled subscriptions) and 302 supporting the government.[32]

The Suez debate of November 1956 was like others which had flared up over the past hundred years, for in essence it was concerned with the nature of Britain's relations with the rest of the world. In one corner were the raptors who saw the world as a field of ceaseless conflict in which the strongest and most determined survived by a mixture of cunning, ruthlessness and muscle. They believed in imperialism as a reflection of the natural order, and considered expediency and the pursuit of one's country's interests the only principles upon which to base foreign policy. In the past, the raptors had cheered victorious generals and admirals home from the wars, as well as Palmerston, Disraeli, Joseph Chamberlain and Churchill; now Eden was their hero. In the other corner were the columbines. They dreamed of a harmonious world in which strife was eliminated through cooperation between countries, and they disliked imperialism as the coercion of the weak by the strong, but tolerated modern forms of benevolent colonialism. Pacifist by inclination, progressive in politics, the doves believed that Britain's special place in the world derived solely from its moral values. In the past, the columbines had upheld Cobden, Bright, Gladstone and the League of Nations.

Since the war, the columbines had become more and more optimistic about a world which seemed to be moving in the right direction. Imperialism was in retreat, the United Nations was flourishing despite the Cold War, and Britain seemed to be shedding its old domineering ways. Now all this had been changed by Eden. Worse still, the invasion of Egypt had coincided with the final stages of the suppression of the Hungarian uprising by the Soviet army. How could moral outrage at this barbarity be expressed, when the thuggish Russian leader, Nikita Kruschev, could turn round and accuse Britain and France of bullying Egypt?

This loss of the moral high ground was felt most keenly in the United States whose public exposure of Soviet brutality was diminished by its allies' behaviour in Egypt. When the world should have been concentrating its wrath on Russia, some of the fury was diverted to Britain and France. Even old friends joined in; 3 November was 'Hate Britain' day in Pakistan, and the Australian Labour leader, Evatt, denounced Eden's 'naked aggression'.

In Britain the raptors, who above all had always counted themselves as realists, were having some nasty shocks. Having agreed to an armistice, the government insisted that Anglo-French units in Egypt should remain, and form part of the United Nations force which would eventually take over the Canal. America stuck out for unconditional evacuation and a brief, one-sided test of wills followed, which brutally exposed Britain's financial weakness.

In the early days of the crisis, foreign and dominion holders of sterling were extremely jumpy, especially Middle Eastern governments which feared that their assets would be frozen like Egypt's if they stepped the wrong way. During August £129 million was withdrawn from sterling accounts. The haemorrhage ceased in September, but began again in October when £85 million was removed as the situation worsened. The crash came after Egypt was invaded and £279 million (including India's deposits of £150 million) was lost by conversion into gold and dollars. By the end of November Britain's reserves had dropped to £1,965 million, and it seemed possible that the pound's days as a major international currency were numbered. In desperation, Macmillan appealed to the International Monetary Fund for a $560 million loan. The American government refused his request, relenting only when Britain agreed to pull all its forces out of Egypt. On 10 December, Macmillan heard that $1,300 million had been placed at Britain's disposal to help shore up sterling. By January 1957 the value of the pound against the dollar returned to its pre-crisis level.

Britain had been undone because of what Macmillan called the 'inherent weakness of our post-war economy'. This was true up to a point. The disastrous runs on the pound in 1931, 1947 and 1949 were the direct consequences of chronic malfunctions within the economy. That of 1956 was triggered by political fears that Britain would overreach itself and become entangled in a Middle Eastern war which it could not afford.

Even before Macmillan had gone begging to Washington, realists within his party were coming to terms at last with the world as it was. According to Angus Maude MP, the outcome of the Suez War left Britain with no choice but 'to admit to the world that we are now an American satellite'. Subservience to the United States was, in some ways, harder to swallow than the knowledge that the days of ruling the roost in the Middle East were finally over.

Unofficial empire, as it would have been understood when Wolseley overthrew Urabi Pasha, did not disappear immediately the last British serviceman embarked from Port Said. In February 1957, RAF bombers strafed Yemeni artillery positions on the Aden border in retaliation for recent shelling. Given the present climate of international opinion, punitive bombing of targets in the Yemen was forbidden.[33] Soon after, British aircraft were in action again in Oman, helping protect its sultan against his more progressive subjects. Shortly after the 1958 palace revolution which toppled over British client, King Faisal II of Iraq, troops were rushed to Jordan to save his cousin, King Hussain from the same fate. An Iraqi annexation of Kuwait was forestalled in 1961 by the arrival of British units. By Suez standards, all these were small-scale operations, justified by treaty obligations and undertaken with America's blessing.

Oil and the Cold War meant that there was work for small, often highly-specialised British detachments in southern Arabia. Having lost the centre of its old Middle Eastern sphere of influence, Britain had withdrawn to the periphery where there were nervous Arab autocrats who needed protection from the twentieth-century and its ideas. There was plenty of scope for G. A. Henty-style skirmishes on bare hillsides, camping out under the stars like Lawrence of Arabia, and commanding bands of irregular tribesmen who accepted the old hierarchies and had never heard of Nasser. The modern, and, as it turned out, the last practitioners of old-fashioned imperial soldiering once showed their native levies the film *Zulu*. As expected, it stirred up their fighting spirit and several fired at the charging Zulus on the screen.

Operations in southern Arabia were undertaken for Sultan Taimir bin-Said of Oman, a mediaeval despot who, fortunately for his embarrassed British sponsors, was deposed in 1970 and packed off to exile in the Dorchester Hotel. His son, Qabus, began a programme of reform, using his principality's oil revenues, and limited modernisation. Unlike Africa or India, Arabia and the Gulf had never felt the weight of Britain's 'civilising' mission, and so local rulers were allowed to maintain old customs, which would have been abandoned elsewhere at the insistence of British residents. Slavery was not officially abolished until 1949 in Kuwait and 1952 in Qatar. It was still common in the antique sheikdoms of the Aden protectorate in the early-1950s and in Oman until 1970. Whether or not rulers in these states and Saudi Arabia meant what they said when they proclaimed an end of slavery and slave trading is still a matter of great contention. Large numbers of Asians, particularly Filipinos, are imported into this region as labourers and domestic workers under conditions which Victorian philanthropists and consuls would have called slavery.

In the post-Suez, Cold War years, Britain needed as many friends as it could get in the Middle East and therefore could not afford to take a high moral line with those it had. Between 1965 and 1975, British forces helped preserve the Omani monarchy against Marxist partisans, and, until 1967, attempted to hold on to Aden and its hinterland. After various political stratagems designed to preserve the local and loyal sheiks, and a guerrilla war in and around the port, the government gave up a base which was now strategically redundant. As the last detachments left, a band played 'Fings Ain't What They Used to Be'. After a brief internecine war between the partisan factions the People's Republic of South Yemen was declared. It did not join the Commonwealth.

5

The Old Red, White and Blue: Reactions to a Dying Empire

The wrangling over the rights and wrongs of Suez gradually ceased once the British army had withdrawn from Port Said. The event passed into history, where its significance was plain: it had been a very prominent signpost which simultaneously indicated a turning point, warned against reckless driving, advised giving way to more powerful vehicles, and announced that from now on the way was all downhill. In other words, Britain had at last to say goodbye to the days when it had been free to do what it liked anywhere in the world. It had come unstuck, and now was the moment to allow the more powerful American car to overtake and speed ahead. Decline in power and status were a fact of life which Britain would have to get used to.

As well as coming to terms with the reduction of their country's international power and standing, the British people also had to face the disappearance of its territorial empire. In the thirteen years following Suez, nearly all the African, Far Eastern and West Indian colonies received their independence and became part of an enlarged Commonwealth. The trauma, both in Britain and the colonies, was remarkably mild. Outsiders were astonished, the more so since the Algerian war brought about the downfall of the Fourth Republic in 1958, a large-scale mutiny by the French army in 1961, tumults in Paris, and a spate of terrorist outrages undertaken by the Algerian settlers movement, the OAS (Organisation Armée Secrète) during 1961–2. Portugal's farewell to empire was equally turbulent and bloody: between 1960 and 1976 135,000 Portuguese troops were deployed against nationalist partisans in Moçambique and Angola. There were also repercussions at home with a revolution which overthrew the right-wing régime of President Caetano in April 1974. Within a month of Belgium granting independence to the Congo (Zaïre) in June 1960, the new state had disintegrated into anarchy and civil war with massacres of white settlers.

Britain was spared such upheavals; it carefully avoided being dragged into futile wars; its soldiers did not mutiny in protest against decolonisation; and the white settlers of Kenya and Southern Rhodesia did not explode plastic bombs in London streets. In February 1963, an anglophile American sociologist attributed the comparative orderliness of the dissolution of empire to the evolution of enlightened national spirit:

> [The] progressive moral transformation which was expressed in the willingness to renounce the empire has been manifested in the unwillingness to continue with the *ancien régime*. Respect for the rights of Indians and Africans is of a piece with the aspirations to improve the quality of life, the level of taste, to cultivate the whole capacities of the whole population, to make society more just, more efficient and more humane.[1]

This was very satisfying, but not altogether surprising. For at least thirty years, politicians of both parties had repeatedly promised that the colonies were on course for independence, although they were evasive about precisely how and when it would be obtained. The officially-inspired public perception of the empire made it virtually impossible for any government to justify extended wars of repression fought to maintain British rule perpetually. When they proved unavoidable, as in Malaya, elaborate efforts were made to present the conflict in such a way as to reassure the public that Britain had the best interests of its subjects at heart. In the middle of the campaign, against the Malayan Communist partisans, the local commander-in-chief, Field-Marshal Sir Gerald Templer, explained his purpose to Vice-President Nixon:

> What I am trying to do is convince all the native leaders and the native troops that this is *their* war, that they are fighting for

their independence, and once the guerrillas are defeated it will be *their* country and *their* decision to make as to whether they desire to remain within the British Commonwealth.[2]

It was perhaps fortunate that the state of television technology ruled out on-the-spot coverage of Britain's final colonial campaigns. The British public did not share the disturbing experience of the American, which, from the mid-1960s, watched Viet Nam operations as they happened. What was shown stunned America, adding immeasurably to the scope and passion of anti-war protests. Ten years before, the British government had sensed television's potential for swaying public opinion, and camera crews who visited war zones were carefully monitored. Distressing scenes, which might be interpreted as brutality, were excised. After the filming of a BBC documentary on Cyprus in 1958, the governor, Sir Hugh Foot, warned the Colonial Office censors to look out for any sequences which showed villages being cordoned by troops and their inhabitants spread-eagled against walls. Textual revisions were imposed: the opening lines 'As a crown colony Cyprus jogged along until a few years ago' were amended to 'As a crown colony Cyprus went quietly along until a few years ago'. Presumably 'jogging' summoned up the image of a casual, unconcerned administration. Throughout the rest of the script 'terrorists' (EOKA) replaced 'the enemy'.[3]

The Cold War ruled out handing over power to Communists, although even Conservative ministries were content to make terms with nationalists of a pinkish complexion, as most were. Decolonisation policies were, by and large, bipartisan with Labour tending to favour speeding up the process. The Conservatives had to be more cautious because of right-wing elements in the party which mistrusted nationalists, or were sympathetic towards the white settler communities in East and Central Africa. This group found natural allies among former colonial civil servants who were unhappy about policies which paid too much heed to nationalists and too little to tribal rulers. According to Sir Mervyn Wheatley, an ex-governor of a Sudanese province, only 'experienced administrators' could really get inside the heads of 'unsophisticated tribesmen' and discover what they really wanted.[4]

The behaviour of colonial politicians aroused misgivings and ridicule in equal parts among those of the outer fringes of the right. In 1950, the veteran Tory spokesman on colonial policy, Captain Gammans, was outraged by the substitution of Nkrumah's name for God's in the Lord's Prayer, and for Christ's in *Hymns Ancient and Modern*, as they were read and sung in the Gold Coast.[5] Peter Simple, the *Daily Telegraph's* mordant right-wing columnist, constantly mocked the rum aspects of Africa's nascent democracy. 'Spells, witch-doctors and the use of fetishes' in the 1956 Gold Coast elections caused him great amusement.[6] Mirth of another kind was provided by the League of Empire Loyalists, founded in 1954 to defend the empire. Its upper echelons included a bevy of retired high-ranking officers of blimpish frame of mind, who were apoplectic about the decay of everything they had held dear. The nostalgic fantasies of upper- and upper-middle-class men and women who had talked about and thought on England as they sipped gin on colonial verandahs must have been often rudely and swiftly dispelled when they returned home. High blood pressure and enlarged spleens were not, therefore, surprising, and the League catered for both.

Its programme looked back to a golden age when Britannia had ruled the waves and the world, and was largely negative. It was against Asian and African nationalism, coloured immigration, the United Nations, the present-day Conservative party, Harold Macmillan, Jews, and the United States, but favoured apartheid and getting back the empire. The League saw its tasks as shaking the country out of its liberal complacency, and most of its energies were spent on a series of stunts designed to publicise its causes and embarrass its adversaries. In 1958, League activists disrupted the Conservative conference, and got knocked about, and, in July 1962, interrupted a dinner given by Macmillan for the United Nations Secretary-General, U Thant. Like other fringe right- and left-wing groups, the League was extremely friable, and in time its few hundred members drifted off to embrace other outlandish and hopeless causes. Its farcical exploits achieved no more than a few headlines.

Harold Macmillan was a constant target for the League, as he is for its mental offspring, the young fogeys of 1990s journalism. Prime minister from January 1957 until October 1963, he considered himself patrician, a believer in 'one-nation' paternalist Conservatism, and, on matters relating to the empire and his country's place in the world, a pragmatic realist. During his term of office the following colonies and protectorates received independence: Gold Coast (Ghana), Malaya (joining with North Borneo [Sabah] and Sarawak to make Malaysia in 1963), Cyprus, Nigeria, Somaliland (with Italian Somaliland as Somalia), Sierra Leone, Jamaica, Tanganyika, Uganda, Kenya and the Gambia. Plans were also in hand for the independence of Northern Rhodesia (Zambia) and Nyasaland

(Malawi) and the creation of the West Indian federation. Attlee apart, no other prime minister was responsible for such a sweeping programme of decolonisation.

Right wingers shuddered. One, a Colonial Office bureaucrat, could not understand why the Conservatives had given way so easily on this issue:

> We could have stood up to the Americans. And we could have stood up to the Russians. And we could have stood up to the Labour Party. What we couldn't stand up to was the Labour Party *and* the left wing of the Conservative Party.[7]

Interestingly, he failed to mention facing up to local nationalists. What he and many others, especially white settlers in Africa, failed to comprehend was that since Disraeli, Conservatism had always been a flexible and opportunistic creed, free from the shackles of dogma which hampered its rivals. Tories no longer beat the imperial drum because its resonance no longer attracted votes, if it ever did. Following a course first set by Baldwin, the Conservatives lured the electorate with promises of prosperity and home-ownership. Imperial sentiments still crept into election manifestos, but as platitudes. The party's 1950 manifesto. *This Is the Road*, spoke of 'fortifying every link with the nations of our Empire and Commonwealth', and that of October 1952, *We Shall Win Through*, proudly announced that, 'The British Empire and Commonwealth is the supreme achievement of the British people.' Solid patriotic stuff, but not a clarion call to hold on to the colonies come what may.

There was a knot of right-wing MPs who, together with the *Daily Express*, and to a lesser degree the *Daily Telegraph*, made jingoistic noises and deprecated the speed with which the empire was relinquished. But Macmillan offered compensations to these disgruntled souls by an ambitious foreign and military policy designed to keep Britain in the front rank of world powers.

As early as August 1955, it had been painfully obvious that Britain could no longer afford to spend 10 per cent of its gross national product on defence. It was then proposed to reduce the number of servicemen from 835,000 to 700,000 over the following three years. Suez intervened to play havoc with the Treasury's arithmetic, but in January 1957 Duncan Sandys, the new Minister for Defence, began concocting plans for a far-reaching overhaul of strategy and expenditure. He worked from three propositions: defence was eating up cash which Britain could not afford; the Suez war had exposed the inability of Britain's conventional forces to react quickly to a crisis, and in any case such adventures were a thing of the past; and it was now vital to have an independent nuclear force with a capability to strike at Russia. Like Labour in 1946, the Conservatives did not trust the United States to support Britain in every emergency, an apprehension which was justified by its conduct during the Suez war.

Translated into strategy these premises produced a white paper in May 1957 which horrified the service establishment. The army, navy and air force were to be pruned to 375,000 men by 1962, and thereafter national security would rest upon a stock of thermo-nuclear weapons and missile systems to deliver them. The old naval stations in the South Atlantic, North America and the West Indies would be abolished, and forces east of Suez drastically reduced. Henceforward, Britain would simply not have the manpower to wage a large-scale colonial campaign, even if it discovered the political will. In 1959, national service was phased out, to despairing groans from the old guard who imagined that decadence and disorder among the young would now increase at a faster pace than ever.

Sandys's 'new look' armed forces were greeted with a mixture of rage and sulkiness by the defence chiefs. At one stage in the debate with the cabinet, they revived the idea of finding extra men from the African colonies, which assumed, interestingly, that these territories would remain under British control for many years to come.[8] In the end, the service heads gave way and accepted the recall of legions, and with it the rolling up of that map which marked out, in fading ink, the old areas of Britain's unofficial empire. Token forces would remain in Aden and the Far East until the late 1960s, when another government strapped for money, Labour this time, called it a day. As was so often the case with late twentieth-century cheeseparing, schemes for retrenchment made little impression on the budget; in 1963 the total cost of defence was £1,721 million, about a tenth of the gross national product.

In May 1957, while ministers, generals, admirals and air marshals haggled over who should have what, Britain's first thermo-nuclear bomb was exploded at Christmas Island in the western Pacific. Three more were detonated before November, and the government sanctioned the development of a long-range missile, Blue Streak. At the same time, Macmillan busied himself in restoring the old friendship with the United States, imagining, like his predecessors and successors, that the 'special relationship' would add a peculiar lustre to Britain's position in the world. In 1957 Britain agreed to play host to American Thor rocket silos, and, in

1960, to allow USN Polaris-equipped nuclear submarines to use the Holy Loch base on the Clyde. Two years after, Macmillan persuaded President John F. Kennedy to give Britain Polaris missiles; the Blue Streak project having been abandoned as too expensive. The possession of an independent arsenal of hydrogen bombs and rockets kept Britain, and later France, within the great power league. It also provided a valuable electoral bonus for the Conservative party; Labour was split over nuclear weapons with a sizeable CND (Campaign for Nuclear Disarmament) faction demanding their renunciation. For a time during the early 1960s, Labour paradoxically found itself arguing for a non-nuclear Britain with old-style overseas commitments with conventional forces.

So, under Macmillan's adroit guidance, Britain shed imperial burdens but stayed a great power, theoretically capable of resisting nuclear intimidation by the Soviet Union, so long as America delivered the appropriate gadgetry. On the surface at least, imperial decline had not gone hand-in-hand with a complete loss of standing in the world, and the Conservative right wing could feel satisfied. Voters at large were more concerned with domestic knife-and-fork issues, and here Macmillan made the Conservatives the party of prosperity – and, his enemies would later allege, inflation.

The late 1950s saw rising living standards throughout the country. 'The luxuries of the rich have become the necessities of the poor,' claimed Macmillan, who made it clear that they would get them thanks to his party's economic policies. His part-patronising, part-exultant phrase, 'You've never had it so good', had the ring of truth and was a vote-catcher. What had happened at Suez and the likelihood that the empire would disappear did not unduly trouble the voters, nor were their consciences upset by Labour's charges of oppression in Nyasaland and the brutal treatment meted out to Mau Mau internees at Hola detention camp. In the 1955 general election the Conservative share of the popular vote had been 49.7 per cent (its highest ever since the war), and, in October 1959 it was 49.3 per cent, giving Macmillan a comfortable victory.

Although it would be hard to quantify exactly, it appears that the mass of British voters were largely indifferent to the loss of colonies whose names were probably best known by stamp collectors. No party had consciously adopted imperialism as part of its ideology. National self-respect had not been diminished by the slow disengagement from empire; rather it had been enhanced, since the process had been undertaken in the name of a higher morality and was being accomplished without excessive bloodshed or recriminations. Sidelong glances at how France and Portugal were managing served as a salutary reminder of the results of a policy of clinging on at all costs.

There were small groups who regretted the passing of empire, but while sometimes clamorous, they carried little political clout. Few outside some London clubs and service messes were agitated by the knowledge that Britain could no longer lay down the law throughout the Middle East, or that white settlers in East and Central Africa were about to face a future ruled by black men. The settler lobby did, however, have tentacles which stretched into right-wing Conservative circles, and so Macmillan had to tread carefully over African policy if only to secure his base inside the party. One imperial diehard and ally of the settlers, the Marquess of Salisbury, resigned in March 1957 in protest at the return from exile of the Cypriot nationalist leader, Archbishop Makarios. The Marquess was not missed, the party did not fall into disarray, and the Archbishop became Cyprus's first president in 1960, having agreed to allow Britain a base on the island, and thereafter he dutifully attended Commonwealth conferences.

No jobs were lost, factories closed or investment opportunities frustrated as a result of the loss of the colonies. Britain's exports to Commonwealth countries grew fitfully: in 1958 they totalled £1,240 million, in 1962 £1,193 million, and in 1969, £1,419 million. By contrast, exports to the countries of the European Economic Community (EEC) were increasing, standing at £2,634 million in 1969, although Britain had to wait a further four years for full membership. Inside the Commonwealth, patterns of trade were changing rapidly with members seeking new markets and sources of raw materials outside the group. Canada's exports to the United States rose from £329 million in 1958 to £534 million in 1962. The new states which had replaced the old colonies did not automatically give Britain special trading advantages. In Africa only the Gambia and Malawi (ex-Nyasaland) were offering British importers preferential terms in 1967, together with South Africa which had left the Commonwealth six years before.

This is not the place to trace the long, arduous and often exasperating route by which Britain found its way into the EEC. The first steps were taken in 1957, and in a sense were an admission that Britain was looking for a new role in the world. Imperial and global power would be exchanged for the next best equivalent, the leadership of Western Europe. This was understood by General Charles de Gaulle, who in 1958 had become president of a country which, like Britain, was losing its former international power as well as its overseas empire. He too wanted compensation for lost *gloire*, and was therefore unwilling to tolerate the presence of what he once called two cockerels in the European hen roost. As a consequence, Britain's advance into Europe was more painful in terms of national pride than its retirement from empire.

In some quarters, Britain's approach to Europe seemed circumspect and half-hearted. The explanation lay in an unwillingness to make a clean break with the past and acknowledge that the Commonwealth, like the empire, was a dead letter. 'A Conservative' writing in *The Times* in April 1964 attempted to brush away the cobwebs by accusing his party and the country of having fallen the victims to 'self-deception . . . on a grand scale' in their appreciation of where real power lay in the modern world. The Commonwealth was 'undefined and undefinable' and three of its leaders, Nehru, Nkrumah and Makarios, were parasites: 'They give nothing: they get any advantage that may be going.' As for the residual and soon-to-be-redundant bases in Aden and across the Indian Ocean, they were 'positions enabling us to reach places where we do not need to go'.[9] West Germany and Japan flourished without bases and a Commonwealth, and so, presumably, could Britain whose economy now lagged behind both. This hard-nosed realism was too much for the author's fellow Conservatives, who rallied behind the Commonwealth in the newspaper's correspondence columns.

At the same time as Britain was shedding its empire it shed many of its inhibitions. In 1960 gambling was legalised and the crown lost its case against the publication of D.H. Lawrence's *Lady Chatterley's Lover*; in 1965 official censorship of the theatre was ended; in 1967 homosexual acts and abortion became legal; and in 1969 divorce became easier to obtain. Britain appeared suddenly to have relaxed and the old imperial capital, London, became a byword for novelty, stylishness and, like the 1960s as a whole, sexual permissiveness. Nothing was more revealing of the collapse of the old order and its codes than long-haired pop stars and their imitators cavorting in jeans and that revered symbol of empire, the British army's scarlet jacket. This fashion, like others of the period, came and went quickly, but not before there had been some surly comments from the old brigade. Worse followed as another sacred imperial totem, the Union Jack, found its way on to everything from knickers to shopping bags.

This impiety towards the past and its icons was one of many manifestations of the profound change which British society was undergoing. What amounted to a revolution in the ways in which the British people behaved, thought and regarded themselves had begun in the early 1950s. At first, its pace was slow and uneven, and no one could then have foretold either its future tempo or what its end might be. That this transformation coincided with the break-up of empire is important for two reasons. First, it encompassed a radical assault on traditional values and attitudes, many of which were closely associated with the empire and those who had made and ruled it. If their ideals were bogus, then perhaps the institution itself was rotten throughout. Second, as the pace of change quickened and the public, particularly the young, found themselves with more money to spend on diversions, it mattered little that Britain was a declining power. In any case, there were plenty of iconoclasts around to expose the hollowness of past glories.

The first catchword of the revolution in Britain's habits and morals was 'anger', the common bond which united a handful of young 1950s writers whose reaction to the world about them was a mixture of boredom, impatience and rage. For them, mid-twentieth-century Britain was a stagnant society in which every form of human activity and emotion was stifled by an all-enveloping, self-satisfied, philistine conservatism. Respect for the past blighted the present and reduced progress to a snail's pace.

Discontent was felt most keenly by the young and they, together with some of their elders, responded warmly to writers who articulated their own frustrations. Each new battering of the old order and its shibboleths won over new rebels, many of whom were already embracing those other subversive novelties of the time, American rock 'n' roll, jazz and their burgeoning, home-grown variations. But in that seminal text of the period, John Osborne's *Look Back in Anger*, the major protagonist, Jimmy Porter, laments the lack of causes to take up. He is revealingly described as a man who 'thinks he's still in the middle of the French Revolution . . . He doesn't know where he is or where he's going.' Without palaces and châteaux to storm, Porter and his fellows lashed out at the values and totems of the *ancien régime*. The empire was one. It was both an offshoot and an expression of the social deference and conservatism they despised. Moreover, it had been created and was now run by representatives of that class whose monopoly of power was the principal cause of the country's present mental arthritis.

A glancing blow was struck against that mainstay of imperial ideology, the innate moral stamina and resourcefulness of the British race, by William Golding's *Lord of the Flies* (1954). Golding's party of schoolboys stranded on a tropical island do not, in the manner of Robinson Crusoe, hold on to their old standards and master their environment. Rather, they regress to primitive 'savagery', and are transformed into those imaginary South Sea islanders who might have been encountered by some young shipwrecked adventurers in a Victorian schoolroom yarn. This parable about the thinness of civilised values soon became a set text in schools, a pessimistic, mid-twentieth-century answer to R.M. Ballantyne's *Coral Island*.

A real imperial superhero, Lawrence of Arabia, was assailed by an angry old man, Richard Aldington, in 1955. His biography exposed Lawrence as a fraud who lied to the Arabs, his friends and himself. His mendacity and self-pity therefore qualified him as a hero 'appropriate . . . for his class and epoch'. Establishment defenders of Lawrence, his class and the achievement of his epoch denounced Aldington as a cad, and proceeded to discredit him in ways which were extremely caddish. Their stridency strongly suggested that more than one man's reputation was at stake: by vilifying Lawrence, Aldington had called into question what he had stood for and the values of a country that still honoured his memory.[10] It is unlikely that Aldington's tirade would have had the same impact or response had it appeared after Suez.

The Suez war and the survival of the archaic patriotism which had made it possible are themes of John Osborne's *The Entertainer*, first staged in April 1957. The play combined a lament for the old music hall and a jeer at working- and lower-middle-class jingoism. The entertainer of the title, Archie Rice (played by Laurence Olivier), is a broken-down but jaunty comedian, who laces his patter with sentimental songs. His views, like his act, belong to the age when music-hall audiences had roared out the chorus of 'Soldiers of the Queen'. Rice also has a line in similar ditties:

> *The Army, the Navy and the Air Force,*
> *Are all we need to make the blighters see*
> *It still belongs to you, the old red, white and blue.*
>
> *Those bits of red still on the map*
> *We won't give up without a scrap.*

In the Suez 'scrap' Archie's son, Mick, is killed, leaving his father devastated. The play ends with Rice going through his routine which opens with a burst of rock'n roll and is performed in front of a thin gauze screen behind which sits Britannia, unclad save for a brass helmet. Osborne's empire, like Rice, is tawdry and on its last legs.

Another 'angry' playwright, John Arden, used an episode in the war against EOKA as the basis for *Sergeant Musgrave's Dance*, which appeared in October 1959. Its setting is the 1870s, but references to 'terrorists' and 'state of emergency' indicate that the scenario is modern in all save the costumes. Four deserters, carrying with them the skeleton of a comrade, turn up in his home town which, like contemporary Britain, is wracked by industrial strife. The dead soldier had been shot in the back by a guerrilla, and his death had been the occasion of a mass round-up of suspects in which thirty-eight civilians were killed. Armed with a stolen Gatling gun, Musgrave is intent on taking a bizarre revenge on the townsfolk who, indirectly, sent the lad to his death in the name of empire.

The play's moralising belongs to the mid-twentieth century. Musgrave speaks of having just returned from 'a colonial war that is a war of sin and unjust blood', and calls the empire's enemies 'patriots'. A parson-magistrate intones about Britain's special 'responsibilities' – 'They are world wide. They are noble. They are the responsibilities of a first-rate power.' The words might have been Eden's. Arden's empire is a source of corruption, particularly of the working class who end up having to do its dirty work and dying for it.

Much in *Sergeant Musgrave's Dance* belongs to the old, anti-imperialist traditions of the radical left. Although Arden and other *avant-garde* dramatists of the late 1950s and early 1960s hoped to command a working-class audience, those who watched their plays largely came from the middle class. Nonetheless, in the next two decades their works and their ideas entered secondary school classrooms via examination syllabuses. Television formed the staple of working-class entertainment, slowly edging out the cinema.

Imperial problems were aired in topical programmes such as 'Tonight' and 'Panorama', which often contained on-the-spot footage and interviews. This type of programme made the government uneasy, and at least once it attempted to assert editorial control over coverage of a sensitive colonial issue. At the beginning of March 1959, the governor of Nyasaland declared a state of emergency in his colony, allegedly to forestall an uprising and attacks on Europeans. Desperate to dispel the idea that Britain was 'striking against African nationalism', the Colonial Office asked the BBC's chairman, Lord Hill, for assistance. It was, the bureaucrats argued, 'better to choose one's own ground rather than participate in a programme which must be "balanced" either by a needling questioner or some opposition spokesman.' In other words the Colonial Secretary, Alan Lennox-Boyd, was either to deliver a self-justificatory monologue or else be interviewed from a prepared script. Lord Hill spurned this clumsy attempt to smother open discussion, and Lennox-Boyd was given the same treatment as any other minister whose policies were contentious.[11] He put his case in the normal way on 'Panorama', and, the next evening, James Callaghan expressed Labour's view on the matter in 'Tonight'.

One explosive aspect of the Nyasaland affair had been the shooting dead of twenty demonstrators at Nkata Bay. An incident of the same kind, loosely based on the Amritsar massacre of 1919, but set in the present day, was the subject of the television play *Conflict at Kalanadi* screened by the BBC in January 1961. It concerns an uprising in a fictional British possession in the Middle East which gets out of hand because of a shilly-shallying official. The local army commander steps in, declares martial law, and his troops fire into rioting crowds, killing and wounding 700. Additional dramatic tension and political debate are provided by the officer's daughter, just down from Oxford with a head full of fashionable, left-wing anti-colonialism. In the end the officer is dismissed after an official investigation. Serving the empire in the 1960s was a tough business and soldiers who did what they saw as their duty could expect no mercy.

Such fictional excursions into imperial and post-imperial conflicts were uncommon. Where the empire was concerned both the BBC and the independent companies preferred to stick to the safer ground of factual documentaries. After the shooting of sixty-seven blacks at Sharpeville near Johannesburg in March 1960, ITV took the bold step of cancelling the immensely popular 'Double Your Money' and replacing it with 'Divided Union', an hour-long report on South Africa. Soon after, ITV's 'This Week' paid for the recently released Nyasaland political leader, Dr Hastings Banda, to be flown to London for a live interview on the programme, much to the anger of the *Daily Express*, which would rather not have had his views broadcast. At the end of the year, Granada offered a documentary on the Boer War as a part explanation of the present conflict in South Africa. It was called, strangely in the light of some of its incidents, 'The Polite War'.

For the first time in the history of the empire, the British public were brought face to face with its realities. Moreover, at a crucial stage in African decolonisation, all involved were able to address the country directly. It is tempting to speculate on the course of imperial history had this facility been available eighty or a hundred years before.

Post-war film-makers continued to use imperial plots and backgrounds. There were, however, significant changes in tone and approach which suggest that the outlook of audiences had altered during the past twenty years. Out went district officers extolling the virtues of British colonial government, and thankful natives no longer blessed the king emperor. Even stiff upper lips were allowed to quiver occasionally. Nevertheless, the glamour and the action remained.

North-West Frontier (1959) is in many respects a run-of-the-mill tale of derring-do set in Edwardian India. But it contains modern undercurrents: there are religious massacres, racial intolerance and hints of nascent nationalism. A British officer (Kenneth More) rescues a boy rajah and, after a thrilling train chase, brings him to safety. Unlike his counterpart in *The Drum*, the prince admits that gratitude and shared perils will not make him the friend of Britain. As he grows older, he will be taught to mistrust the British; the forces of history are turning against the raj.

There is plenty of dramatic action in the visually stunning *Lawrence of Arabia*, (1962) but the hero is tormented by self-doubt, there is a suggestion of his homosexuality, and the script makes it clear that Britain is double-crossing the Arabs. *Zulu* is perhaps the most spectacular and accomplished of all imperial films. It tells the story of a 'glorious' episode of imperial history, the defence of Rorke's Drift during the Zulu War, but its theme is the grit shown by ordinary men in extraordinary circumstances. The battle is stripped of its romance, and the audience watches the collision between brave men, black and white, who are thrown against each other for reasons neither attempt to understand. The mood is fatalistic: 'We are here because there's no one else,' comments the colour sergeant. He fights, like everyone else, to save the lives of his comrades. No one mentions queen or country.

Winding up the empire was the subject of the taut and prophetic *Guns at Batasi* (1964) in which Richard Attenborough played a stiff-necked warrant officer training African troops on the eve of their country's independence. A visiting Labour MP (Flora Robson), the patroness of a local black politician she had known when he had been at university in England, suspects that the NCO is at heart a racist and imperialist. He is, in fact, an unsentimental realist. He tells her: 'Our good is as good as their good, and their bad is as bad as our bad.' The atmosphere is sombre with hints of corruption and future military intervention in politics. Its pessimism was justified, for in 1966 an army coup unseated President Nkrumah of Ghana, Britain's first African colony to receive independence.

The passing of empire witnessed assaults on its moral justification and mythology. Charlton Heston, who played General Gordon in what was the last spectacular imperial epic, *Khartoum* (1966), realised this was the end of the road for films of this genre. 'The middle of the twentieth century is not much of a time for heroes,' he told a BBC interviewer in 1969. 'It seems that society's interests are focussed on victims rather than heroes.'[12] It was now the time for the underdogs of empire to have their say.

Imperial history from below had its début in 1964 with the first production of Peter Shaffer's splendid and moving *Royal Hunt of the Sun*. The play tells the story of Pissaro's conquest of the Inca kingdom of Peru in the sixteenth century, the overthrow and murder of its ruler, and the subjection of its people to Spanish greed and Catholic bigotry. An entire culture is systematically and pitilessly uprooted in the name of a higher civilisation. That this had occurred in South America was irrelevant, for events there were repeated throughout the world during the next two hundred and fifty years.

There was nothing new in the equation of imperialism with the exploitation of the weak by the strong. What was novel was the suggestion that not only were helpless people plundered, but their societies and cultures were torn apart in the process. As the British empire disappeared, one of its most cherished assumptions came under attack. The so-called superior civilisation which it had offered its subjects was nothing of the sort, and certainly not a justification for the wholesale destruction of other systems. Britain should feel guilt rather than pride for its imperial past. In November 1967, Dennis Potter, the left-wing, iconoclastic television playwright summed up the new orthodoxy: 'Perhaps the noblest task of the popular historian should be to make us ashamed of our forefathers . . . now that the hilarious residue of the White Man's Burden has been chased out of the reading books of schoolboys.'[13]

It was relatively easy for the post-imperial guilt complex to penetrate the public consciousness during the late 1960s. The image of empire, as daily projected in the television news, was one of iron-fisted coercion in Viet Nam, Moçambique, Angola, South Africa and, from 1972 onwards, Southern Rhodesia. The news from those countries where the Union Jack had been recently hauled down was also bleak and bloody. In 1966, the year of a Commonwealth conference in Lagos, there was a military coup in Nigeria and another in Ghana. 1967 saw the beginning of a three-year civil war in Nigeria and a new wave of military take-overs in Ghana and Sierra Leone. There were military coups in the Sudan in 1969, and two years later the preposterous General Idi Amin seized power in Uganda and began a reign of terror. For its former subjects, the inheritance of empire appeared to be political corruption, a succession of praetorian governments and internecine warfare. Not surprisingly, touring companies of British actors found African audiences very responsive to *Macbeth*, *Julius Caesar* and *Richard III*, all of which mirrored political life in their countries. It was natural in the successor states, and in some quarters in Britain, to blame these woes on the empire.

Faced with what appeared to be the failure of its imperial mission, Britain was also undergoing a re-evaluation of the principles which had formerly guided its rulers and empire. From the mid-1950s, social anthropologists had been busy analysing what was called 'the establishment'. They uncovered and closely examined the world and values of an exclusive network which extended through London's clubland, politics, the higher civil service, the colleges of Oxford and Cambridge, the boardrooms of banks and large companies, the bench of bishops, the judiciary and the commanders of the armed services. Public school and Oxbridge education formed a common bond and had helped to mould a common humane, cautious, conservative outlook. Britain's rulers were also the empire's rulers. The establishment saw the exercise of power as a right, and its members had relished governing India and the empire since they had been able to do so without being unduly trammelled by expressions of the popular will.[14]

Those who scrutinised the establishment were also its critics. The general argument ran that those who had discreetly but firmly pulled the strings for so long were to a great extent responsible for national decline and stagnation. They were also capable of colossal blunders. 'After Suez we can no longer have . . . confidence in this government's sanity,' observed one establishment analyst, himself a former Tory MP.[15] The same could have been said, and was, somewhat less harshly, after the fall of Singapore. The difference was that in the mid 1950s everything seemed to be going wrong for Britain abroad. All that the establishment seemed able to do was either reach for old remedies, like Eden, or stand back in bewilderment. From the military wing of the establishment, Glubb Pasha complained: 'While British citizens discuss . . . noble plans for the betterment of the human race a great part of the world is convinced that Britain is greedy, reactionary and intent only on exploiting other nations.'[16]

Misunderstood abroad, Britain's establishment was coming under fire at home, and seemed unable to find the confidence to defend itself. The television programme 'That Was the Week that Was' and the satirical magazine *Private Eye*, both of which appeared in 1961, lampooned public figures with a contemptuous abandon that had not been seen since the eighteenth century. In 1963, the Profumo scandal inflicted a further blow on the establishment by revealing that some of its members enjoyed eighteenth-century-style sexual lives. Ridicule of the establishment, hints of its moral bankruptcy, together with a pervasive feeling that it had somehow failed the country, contributed to Harold Wilson's general election victory in October 1964. On the hustings, Labour alternately berated the stuffy old guard and promised a dazzling era of social and economic regeneration.

Assaults on the establishment and its values gathered pace. Aristocratic blockheads in high command were assailed in the musical *Oh What a Lovely War* (1964) and the film *The Charge of the Light Brigade* (1967). This last is particularly instructive, for a film of the same name, starring Errol Flynn, had appeared thirty years earlier; a wildly unhistorical yarn, full of dashing heroism, which linked a British cavalry regiment's exploits in India with the famous charge. The new version, better on historical verisimilitude, turns into a bitter indictment of the bloodthirsty, dim-witted, bigoted and immoral officer class who hold command solely because of their blue blood.

The same class and its atavistic values were savaged in Lindsay Anderson's *If* . . . of 1969, which also delivered a few well-aimed side-swipes at the lingering ideals of empire. Set in a contemporary public school, the film takes the title of Kipling's best-known poem, that lodestar which had guided past generations of public-school men as they went forth to take charge of the destinies of others. Despite the headmaster's faith in leadership 'in the modern world', his school is a tyranny, run by sadistic prefects known as 'whips' who occasionally speak about 'duty' and service to country in the manner of G.A. Henty heroes. Their antagonists, three school 'rebels', are a modern Stalky and Co., but unlike their past equivalents they do not employ their energy and ingenuity in empire-building. They identify with the destroyers of empire, one of whom, a black guerrilla, appears on a poster in their study.[17]

The film's climax involves the threesome, augmented by the girl lover of one and the boy lover of another, staging an uprising on commemoration day. The main speech is delivered by a moustachioed, well-medalled general who could have stepped from a 1930s imperial movie. He mouths the clichés of that time:

> It's a very sad thing. But today it is fashionable in Britain to belittle tradition. The old order that made our nation a living force are for the most part scorned by modern psychiatrists, priests, pundits of all sorts . . . Never mind the sneers of the cynics. Let us be true to honour . . . duty . . . national pride.

The rebels, armed with machine-guns and grenades, attack, and a cleric and the general organise resistance. Prominent among those fighting back is a middle-aged woman who speaks with the South African or Rhodesian twang.

In *If . . .* the empire and the values of its architects are part of a broader target, an inwardly cankered establishment. By the time the film first appeared on the screens, the physical empire had dissolved, for Harold Wilson had continued his predecessor's policy of disengagement. So in a sense the film is tilting at windmills; boys from this school will not end up as district officers in Somaliland or in command of frontier posts, even though the school's emphasis on team games and cadet training suggests otherwise. And yet these young men, the establishment they are destined to join and the country which it dominates, are, according to *If . . .* still in the grip of outmoded patterns of thought which can only be swept away by violence.

The phenomenon of social, political and intellectual dissent of which *If* was an extreme example formed a backdrop to the last days of empire. The same period saw the arrival in power of a generation of parvenus who had climbed the lifelines offered by the 1944 Education Act and had no immediate interest in the preservation of the old order. They did not all reject its view of Britain and the world; grammar school boy Harold Wilson spoke about Britain as a 'world power' in much the same way as Etonian Curzon had, and he was right in so far as the country possessed a formidable nuclear arsenal.

Hydrogen bombs, Polaris rockets, nuclear-power submarines (the first appropriately named *Dreadnought*) kept Britain among the first rank of powers, and were some compensation for an empire that was slipping away piecemeal. As it passed away, late nineteenth-century anti-imperialism, padded out with currently fashionable Marxism, became campus and classroom orthodoxy. All overseas empires were extensions of capitalism, which oppressed and exploited their subjects pitilessly. The children and grandchildren of those who had been taught to feel pride in the empire, now learned to be ashamed of it. Britain had been demeaned and corrupted by its empire, and whether true or not, this knowledge may have made its loss more bearable.

6

———•———

Uhuru:
Tying up Loose Ends,
1959–80

'Britain's not bloody well going to make us live under a bunch of fuck-ing black monkeys. Look at South Africa, that's how to fix them.' This outburst was overheard in a bar in Salisbury, Southern Rhodesia during the spring of 1963, and the speaker was a first-generation Scottish immigrant.[1] Africa was changing, but the Rhodesian mind remained fixed in that uncomplicated past when Rhodes's columns criss-crossed the country and the answer to the native problem had been the Maxim gun. Another relic from that age, the Marquess of Salisbury, had told the House of Lords in March 1961: 'I may speak as a moaner and a croaker, I shall not speak as a cynic; for no one believes in the British mission in Africa more passion-ately than I do.' He went on to explain that giving self-government to black people and ignoring the wishes of white was not part of that mission. His wallet may have lain close to his heart since he was a director of the British South Africa Company, but he was very touchy whenever this mat-ter was raised, insisting it had no influence whatsoever on his judgement.[2]

For the man in the bar and the Marquess, Africa was taking a turn for the worse, and its present mutability threatened the descendants of those white men and women who had settled there over the past seventy years. At the same time, there was a strong body of opinion in Britain, embrac-ing the Labour party and the liberal wing of the Conservative, which saw this period as a new dawn for Africa. It is hard nowadays to comprehend the optimism which attended the gradual granting of independence to Britain's African colonies during the early 1960s. Independence day

ceremonies were conducted with a remarkable degree of goodwill in a car-
nival atmosphere. Royalty stood by as flags went down and up, and
speeches were made in which Britain wished the infant nation every good
fortune. The paraphernalia of the post–colonial order was reassuring: there
were secret ballots, and elected assemblies with maces, and wigged and
gowned speakers. African judges, who had learned their law at London's
inns of court and wore robes of scarlet and ermine, presided over replicas
of English assize courts. Democracy and the rule of law seemed firmly in
place. Britain could feel satisfied that it had guided its subjects wisely and
that they were setting off along the right road.

This euphoria was premature and probably naïve. For the Sudan,
Ghana, Sierra Leone, Nigeria, and Uganda the post-independence path
variously led to the overthrow of democracy, a sequence of praetorian
coups, military dictatorships, corruption and chronic economic instability.
This was all grist to the mill of those, like Salisbury, who had doubted the
African's ability to manage his own affairs unaided, and naturally were
quick to say 'we told you so'. Others, disappointed by what seemed the
failure of a noble experiment, argued that Africa's woes were a direct
result of the imperial era. State boundaries drawn for the convenience of
bureaucrats or at the whim of representatives of the great powers created
tribal mixtures that were bound to fail. Moreover, the colonial era had witnessed the dislocation of old local social and economic orders, and it was
foolish to imagine that colonial government, which had seldom lasted for
more than a man's lifetime, could have created a powerful sense of national
coherence and identity. In any case, this had never been its primary
purpose.

It was certainly true that at least until 1948 the British government
imagined that the time would not be ripe for independence until the last
quarter of the century. In any event, the timetable would have to be staggered according to the political sophistication of the natives and the
experience of those who would take over the reins of government. But
expediency had intervened when events in the Gold Coast made it clear
that if the brake was applied violence might follow. Even so, this colony
had had longer experience than others in democracy. Since 1894, ratepayers had been able to vote for half the membership of village and town
councils, but it was a right which few chose to exercise. In 1922 only 46
of the 1,117 registered electors in Accra turned out on polling day and
none of the 717 in Sekondi bothered to appear at all.

Political activity increased throughout West Africa between the wars, and was most intense among the Western-educated élite. Aspirants to leadership tended to learn about politics among émigré student organisations during periods of prolonged exile in Britain or the United States. Nkrumah spent ten years at American universities, and a further two studying law in London before returning home in 1947. Kenyatta was out of Kenya between 1931 and 1946, studying and taking various jobs in England, including one as an extra in *Sanders of the River*. Banda read medicine in various American colleges between 1927 and 1937, and from 1939 until 1953 was a general practitioner in England. He spent the next four years in Ghana, where he learned the mechanics of party organisation and how to mobilise public opinion. What was most striking about these political apprenticeships was that administrative experience was confined to running the party machine. Alongside professional politicians there were men who had worked in harness with British officials in the various provincial councils that had been designed as kindergartens for future rulers. Nigeria's Benjamin Azikwe (ten years lecturing in American universities) had a record of serving in local administration from 1944 onwards, and Tom Mboya (Ruskin College, Oxford) served in Kenyan trade unions and local government in the decade before independence.

These men were prominent in a growing class of professional politicians with whom the British administration could collaborate. Old allies from among Africa's old ruling class were discreetly put on one side, a change which some resented. 'Right thinking people', complained a Yoruba chief, 'are beginning to feel that the arrogance of the British administrator is preferable to the exploitation of our national leaders.'[3] His apprehension was understandable, for Africa's politicians were beginning to see themselves as governments-in-waiting and, as deadlines for independence came closer, were treated as such by colonial bureaucrats and British ministers.

In tone and behaviour, African politics closely resembled those of pre-independence India, and Egypt during its struggle against Britain. African political movements tended to focus on a single charismatic figure, the leader of a monolithic, well-disciplined party which claimed to speak for the entire nation. The chants and responses of the mission churches were adapted to create a nationalist liturgy, which would be recited at mass political rallies. From Kenya came:

'Uhuru!' [Freedom]
'Uhuru!'
'Uhuru na umoga!' [Freedom is unity]

'Uhuru na KANU!' [Freedom is the Kenyan African National
    Union]
'Uhuru na KANU!'
'Uhuru na Kenyatta!' [Freedom is Kenyatta]
'Uhuru na Kenyatta!'

These forms of mass persuasion were needed to give Africans a sense of
power and confidence in themselves. Tom Mboya recalled how in 1952 his
father and tribal elders had advised him to steer clear of politics: 'We can
never compete with the European. After all, he has aeroplanes, he flies
about while we walk on foot. He has cars and guns.'[4] And yet within five
years Ghana had gained independence, and for a time became the powerhouse for African nationalism. In 1958 Accra was host to the first
All-African Peoples Conference which called for the liberation of the
whole continent from imperial rule.

For the British government it was not a question of whether the African
empire would be dissolved, but when and how. The process had been relatively easy in Ghana, and afterwards with the other West African colonies
for they had wholly black populations. In East and Central Africa the situation was complicated by the presence of white settlers, largely of British
stock, who looked upon themselves as the economic backbone of their
colonies and had grown accustomed to lording it over the blacks. In
Southern Rhodesia the whites had had a measure of self-government
since 1923, but in Kenya the Colonial Office had deliberately blocked any
attempt by the colonists to acquire political paramountcy.

Any residual belief that the white settlers in Kenya might go it alone was
shattered by the Mau Mau uprising which started in 1952. It was a peasant *jacquerie*, confined to the Kikuyu, and randomly directed against all
things European. Mau Mau was a cabalistic union whose members were
bound together by oaths, sworn to the accompaniment of horrific sexual
rituals. Most of Mau Mau's victims were Kikuyu who were suspected of
collaboration with the colonial authorities. These reacted by declaring a
state of emergency, and by December 1953 over 150,000 Mau Mau suspects were in detention centres, 12,000 had been convicted of membership
and 150 hanged. The war was savage and one-sided; between November
1952 and April 1953, 430 prisoners had been shot dead while attempting
to escape, and there were cases of others being tortured.[5]

Mau Mau had brought about a civil war among the Kikuyu, the majority of whom sided with the British, who held all the trump cards. Their

enemies possessed few firearms and were nowhere near strong enough to engage the colonial forces on equal terms. Very few settlers were killed by the Mau Mau, but its psychological effect was enormous, reminding them of their smallness in numbers and isolation. Mau Mau was the ultimate white man's nightmare whose ingredients were images of a dark, impenetrable Africa of witchcraft and fear of sudden attack by crazed tribesmen armed with pangas and spears. But Kenya's whites, after some nail-biting moments, were able to sleep in peace thanks to British-trained askaris (who did the brunt of the police work), regular soldiers, national servicemen, and aircraft. By 1956, all but a handful of guerrillas had been tracked down, and the rest were either dead or incarcerated in camps, where they underwent a form of brainwashing designed to release them from the magic of their oaths.

For all its nihilism, Mau Mau briefly caught the imagination of other Africans. 'We want Mau Mau here; we want to kill Europeans because we are tired of them,' shouted one African at a political meeting at Lusaka, Northern Rhodesia, in April 1953.[6] The police intelligence officer who took down his words also noted that Harry Nkumbula (London School of Economics, 1946–50), the president of the Northern Rhodesia African National Congress, urged his listeners to wage war with words.

The struggle in Northern Rhodesia was against the Central African Federation. This hybrid had been foisted on the Labour government in 1951 by tidy-minded Colonial Office officials, who believed that it would solve the future economic and political problems of Southern Rhodesia, Northern Rhodesia and Nyasaland. It was a shotgun marriage which forced cohabitation between two crown colonies, with tiny white minorities, and white-dominated Southern Rhodesia. At its birth in 1953, the proportion of white to black in the Central African Federation was 1 to 66. Most of the former lived in Southern Rhodesia where there were 220,000 to 3.5 million Africans. Blacks had no faith whatsoever in the new state, which they believed was a device to extinguish their political rights and drag them into the orbit of Southern Rhodesia.

Just what this might entail was spelled out in the 1950 version of Southern Rhodesia's handbook for British immigrants. Only skilled men were wanted, 'Because of our African population, and the fact that Africans do the unskilled and bulk of the semi-skilled work.' A good life was promised, especially for women: 'On the whole, the lot of the Rhodesian housewife is much more pleasant than that of her sisters in England.' Black servants were plentiful, but the newcomer had to bear in mind 'that the average Native servant is of childlike simplicity' and prone to pilfering, so firmness was vital.[7]

Segregation was enforced rigorously everywhere. Visiting the country in 1955 to advise on its broadcasting system, Sir Hugh Greene encountered Sir Godfrey Huggins, then the Federation's prime minister, who told him that white and black MPs were forbidden to dine together in Parliament House. Nothing had changed since the time of Rhodes and Jameson. A factory manager told Greene that:

> I had a friend from Northern Rhodesia down here the other day who said what a relief it was to see a really good flogging again. He told me: 'You know up in Northern Rhodesia, if you raise your hand against one of these chaps, he drags you off to the police station.'[8]

That year, a white man who had flogged to death one of his servants was given a year in gaol and ordered to pay his victim's family £100 compensation. An African found guilty of stealing sixteen shirts also got a year's imprisonment.[9] It was, therefore, not really surprising that the Colonial Office found it hard to whip up enthusiasm for the Federation among blacks in Northern Rhodesia and Nyasaland.

Opposition to federation was most vehement in Nyasaland where, from July 1958, the newly-returned Dr Banda had taken over as president-general of the African National Congress. The governor, Sir Robert Armitage, toed the official line over the Federation, and was scared by Banda's trenchancy and the support he was gathering. In what turned out to be a ham-fisted attempt to force a show-down, Armitage declared a state of emergency in Nyasaland on 18 February 1959, using the discovery of an alleged Mau Mau-style conspiracy to massacre the colony's 8,000 whites as an excuse. Plot or no plot, and the evidence is far from certain, Armitage had secured a chance to uncover the real strength of the anti-Federation movement and silence it.[10] The suspension of normal legal rights and judicial processes allowed for dawn raids, arrests and internment. Banda was seized and bundled off to Gwelo gaol in Northern Rhodesia and troops were rushed in from Northern Rhodesia and Tanganyika to handle the inevitable protest demonstrations. Within four weeks the death toll had risen to fifty-two.[11]

Armitage's action had embarrassed the government at a time when it was facing criticism for the deaths of Mau Mau detainees in Hola Camp in

Kenya. As has been seen, the Colonial Secretary, Lennox-Boyd, was anxious to forestall television criticism of the state of emergency, and there were charges in the Commons that the Nyasaland authorities had tried to censor journalists reporting on conditions there.[12] Resisting pressure from Southern Rhodesia, where the Nyasaland clamp-down had been welcomed, Macmillan ordered a senior judge and sometime Tory candidate, Lord Devlin, to chair a commission of inquiry into the causes of the emergency.

Devlin's report appeared at midsummer and made disturbing reading. Armitage had blundered, Banda was exonerated, and Nyasaland was described as 'a police state'. Macmillan was furious and claimed that the judge had acted out of ancestral and personal spite. He was Irish ('no doubt with that Fenian blood that makes Irishmen anti-Government on principle'), a lapsed Catholic with a Jesuit brother (in fact a missionary in Northern Rhodesia), and was getting his own back for not having been appointed Lord Chief Justice.[13] The cabinet rejected Devlin and hurriedly drew up a counterblast, allegedly penned by Armitage, which was published on the same day as the judge's report.

Together, the reports on the killings at Hola Camp and the blunders in Nyasaland were an indictment of a colonial policy which had lost direction and moral basis. Enoch Powell, a former government minister, took his colleagues to task on the last score in a speech which repeated the classic argument that imperial authority could never exist in an ethical vacuum, or in defiance of its subjects' wishes. It was indefensible to say: 'We will have African standards in Africa, Asian standards in Asia and perhaps British standards here.' He continued:

> All Government, all influence of man upon man, rests on opinion. What we do in Africa, where we still govern and we no longer govern, depends upon the opinion which is entertained of the way in which Englishmen act. We cannot, we dare not, in Africa of all places, fall below our own highest standards in the acceptance of responsibility.[14]

To this invocation of traditional benevolent imperialism was added a warning from the Opposition front bench, delivered by Aneurin Bevan, to the effect that Britain could not allow its national life to be poisoned in the way that France's had been by African conflict. Central Africa might yet prove Britain's Algeria.[15]

Macmillan was determined that this should not happen. In the wake of the Nyasaland débâcle, he had decided to send a commission under Sir Walter Monckton, a silver-tongued lawyer and skilled arbitrator, to investigate opinion throughout Central Africa. This was wormwood to the Federation's new prime minister, Sir Roy Welensky, a former railwayman and prize-fighter, who had never pulled his punches. In 1957 he had ominously remarked that he had never believed 'that the Rhodesians have less guts than the American Colonists had'. His predecessor Huggins (now Lord Malvern) had issued a similar threat. Speaking of Rhodesia's army, he observed: 'I hope we shall not have to use them as the North American Colonies had to use theirs, because we are dealing with a stupid Government in the United Kingdom'.[16] Macmillan took this bluster very seriously, and imagined that if Labour was returned to office in the imminent general election, Southern Rhodesia might rebel.

In August, Macmillan had counselled Monckton to do all in his power to create a multi-racial state in Central Africa. Failure would turn the region, and Kenya as well, into 'a maelstrom of trouble into which all of us will be sucked'. He added that white supremacy was foredoomed, but hoped that something might be accomplished to accommodate the white settlers, who were vital for the continent.[17] The alternative was another extended and unwinnable conflict of the sort which was then being fought in Algeria. British treasure and British blood would never be expended to defend white supremacy in East and Central Africa.

His standing within the Conservative party enhanced by his sweeping victory in October, Macmillan was free to embark on a radical African policy. His chosen instrument was the forty-six-year-old Iain Macleod, a talented, sharp-witted and sometimes acerbic liberal Conservative who was temperamentally suited to carry out what were at heart paternalist colonial policies. He had what the Prime Minister called 'the worst job of all' with the prospect of bloodshed if he failed. After a year in office, Macleod justified his actions to his party conference on the grounds that they were an extension to Africa of the 'one nation' principles of Disraeli. Black and white would have to be drawn together in the same way as the rich and the poor of Victorian Britain.

Procuring compromise and cooperation were not easy, but Macleod had a flair for chairing conferences and considerable patience. He was also willing to stick his neck out: one of his first acts was to end the state of emergency in Kenya; in April 1960 he restored normal government to Nyasaland and, two months later, had Banda released in spite of howls of anger from Armitage and Welensky. Macleod was publicly announcing that he was the friend of African nationalism, although common sense demanded an end to the Nyasaland emergency which had become a heavy burden on the colony's limited resources. In 1939 the total bill for policing had been £22,000; in 1960, it was £1 million, a sixth of the entire colonial budget.[18]

Macleod's greatest achievement lay in the revision of the schedules for independence and overseeing the peaceful dismemberment of the Central African Federation. Preparing for the transfer of power was not a glamorous task for it involved drawing up draft constitutions and discussing them at conferences, activities which did not make headlines or win public acclaim. Macleod's work was acknowledged, at least by Africans, for 'Iain' became a popular Christian name in Uganda and Nyasaland, where, after independence a thoroughfare in Blantyre was named 'Macleod Street'.[19] This was some reward for labours which ended with Tanganyikan independence in 1961, Ugandan in 1962, and Kenyan in 1963, and in the same year the dissolution of the Central African Federation. The next year Nyasaland became independent as Malawi, and Northern Rhodesia as Zambia.

Macmillan had been the guiding force behind these changes. He had always judged the empire in empirical rather than emotional terms, asking what economic or strategic value colonies possessed for Britain.[20] It was as a pragmatist that he made his celebrated tour of sub-Saharan Africa at the beginning of 1960. He was rowed ashore at Accra like Sanders of the River, and in Nigeria he found a successor to that fictional district officer in the sagacious figure of Sir James Robertson, the colony's governor-general. Robertson told Macmillan that, while Nigerians might need twenty-five years in which to prepare themselves for self-government, it was wiser to let them have it immediately. Delay would turn those intelligent men who were now being trained for leadership into rebels and 'violence, bitterness and hatred' would follow. The choice was between instant Uhuru and twenty years of repression.[21]

In South Africa, it was Macmillan's turn to deliver a homily, designed to be heeded by whites throughout the continent. It was delivered to the South African parliament in Cape Town and opened with a history lesson: 'Ever since the break-up of the Roman Empire one of the constant facts of political life in Europe has been the emergence of independent nations.' This process was now underway throughout Africa, and, during his passage through the continent, Macmillan had been struck by its inexorability:

> The wind of change is blowing through this continent, and, whether we like it or not, this growth of national consciousness is a political fact. We must all accept it is a fact, and our national policies must take account of it.

The South African MPs politely applauded, but it took thirty years for the import of Macmillan's words to sink in.

For white settlers in Britain's African colonies Macmillan and Macleod were a pair of Judases whose words and actions added up to a form of treason. 'We've been thoroughly betrayed by a lousy British government,' complained one Kenyan farmer in 1962. 'We'll throw in our allegiance with somebody who's not always prepared to pull the bloody flag down.' He had first come to the country in 1938, secured a 999-year lease on his crown land farm, and had been officially encouraged to see himself as part-squire part-schoolmaster when dealing with the blacks: 'I'm not a missionary, I hate the sight of the bastards. But I came here to farm, and look after these fellows. They look up to you as their mother and father; they come to you with their trials and tribulations.'[22] Now, Kenya's future prime minister and president, Kenyatta, was saying that any white Kenyan who still wanted 'to be called "Bwana" should pack up and go'. This form of address, and the deference it implied, mattered greatly to some; Kenya's white population fell from 60,000 in 1959 to 41,000 in 1965.

Sir Michael Blundell, the leader of Kenya's moderate whites, explained this exodus in terms of psychology. Post-1945 immigrants were, he thought: 'the kind that couldn't adapt to a Labour government. And if they couldn't adapt to a Labour government, how the hell could they hope to adapt to Africa?'[23] If egalitarian Britain became unbearable, the middle and upper-middle classes could take refuge in Africa where the old values still obtained and servants were freely available. The Duke of Montrose found Southern Rhodesia a welcome change from a Britain which he believed to be afflicted with a terminal moral cancer, whose symptoms he outlined in a memorable speech to the House of Lords in March 1961. There was, he asserted: 'A great sickness in England . . . Immorality is made to appear innocent: literature which our fathers banned [*Lady Chatterley's Lover*] we set free for people to read . . . the trouble is not only in Africa; the trouble is here too . . .' To escape infection, the Duke was prepared to rough it in the bush: 'I never thought, as a boy, that I should see my father helping to wash up dishes, but I did before he died. He did not complain, and neither shall I complain if I have to do the same in Africa.'

These ramblings formed part of a concerted attack on Macmillan's new African policy which was led by another feudal dinosaur at war with evolution, the Marquess of Salisbury. He blamed Macleod: 'He has been too clever by half. He has adapted, especially in his relationship to the white communities of Africa, a most unhappy and wrong approach.' The result was that the whites, by implication a none-too-clever group, believed they had been replaced by black politicians as Britain's partners in Africa.[24] Ninety Conservative MPs shared the Marquess's misgivings and signed a motion of protest against what Macleod was doing. The dissidents included most of the right wing of the party, including Captain Waterhouse (who was chairman of Tanganyika concessions) and, interestingly, a scattering of Ulster Unionists. The latter, presumably, found it easy to identify with white settlers south of the Zambesi.

The revolt over African policy was a damp squib which spluttered harmlessly. The cause of the white minorities did not stir up the same passion in Britain as it did in France, and to have split the Tory party over a minor imperial issue would have been suicidal folly. Nonetheless, Macleod's liberalism may have helped lose him the chance of gaining the party leadership after Macmillan's resignation in October 1963. An indirect but grateful beneficiary was Harold Wilson, who had rated Macleod the man most to be feared in the upper ranks of the Conservatives.

The evidence heard by the Monckton Commission sealed the fate of the Central African Federation. It was universally detested by blacks throughout Nyasaland and Northern Rhodesia and was, therefore, unenforceable. Its obsequies were conducted by Macleod's successor, R.A. Butler, at a conference at the Victoria Falls in the summer of 1963. Northern Rhodesia and Nyasaland proceeded on separate paths to independence, while Southern Rhodesia sulkily prepared to go it alone. A new party, the Rhodesia Front, made the running on a white supremacy ticket.

Between 1963 and 1980 successive British governments were tormented by the Rhodesian ulcer. It was a source of international embarrassment, the cause of interminable rows inside the Commonwealth, and a distraction from more pressing domestic and European matters. It was the last and least welcome legacy of empire and, as the Commonwealth and United Nations made repeatedly clear, it could only be cured by Britain.

With the disintegration of the Central African Federation, the Rhodesian whites were overwhelmed by a feeling that Britain had deserted them, and that henceforward they would have to shape their own destiny.

This was independence under the 1961 Constitution which perpetuated white paramountcy. As Ian Smith, the Rhodesian Front leader, was fond of saying, there would be no black majority rule in his or his childrens' lifetimes. He was forty-five when he became prime minister in 1964. Smith was an unlikely man to take on the empire, for he saw himself and his countrymen as embodiments of all those old, manly imperial virtues which would have been applauded by G.A. Henty. No scholar (in later life he seemed unable to distinguish between 'actual' and 'factual'), Smith was, like most Rhodesian men, sports mad, excelling in rugger, cricket and tennis. A Hurricane pilot during the war, his political hero was Churchill, a man, he always believed, who would never have abandoned Rhodesia to the blacks. As a negotiator, Smith was stubborn and cunning by starts. As a politician he was plain-spoken and, according to his lights, intensely patriotic. His following among the white community was enormous; in the May 1965 elections his Rhodesia Front won all the fifty seats reserved for whites.

This election provided the popular imprimatur for UDI (Unilateral Declaration of Independence) which was announced on 11 November. It had been preceded by desperate last-minute negotiations between Smith and Harold Wilson, who had flown to Salisbury. The British Prime Minister insisted, as did his successors, that the British parliament alone had the legal right to grant Rhodesia its independence, and then only when blacks as well as whites had the vote. The talks broke down and Wilson returned after what had been a highly disagreeable mission. During a dinner he had to endure the oafish clowning of the Duke of Montrose who told blue jokes and performed a belly dance.[25] Sadly, this aristocrat appears to have succumbed to the creeping degeneracy he had denounced in the Lords four years ago.

On his homecoming, Wilson publicly announced that in the event of UDI Britain would not employ force to bring Rhodesia back to its obedience. It was an immensely controversial statement which gave heart to Smith who, with good reason, was worried that his own army and air force would shrink from fighting the British. Wilson was unaware of his anxieties; what he did know was that the Rhodesian forces were well-equipped and trained, and that Britain's service chiefs were nervous about engaging them with extended lines of communication. Moreover, it would take time to establish a secure base in Zambia. Even if logistical problems were overcome, there was no popular enthusiasm for the war, although the Archbishop of Canterbury and Jo Grimond, the Liberal leader, were making loud belligerent noises. Opinion polls suggested that they were out of touch with public opinion, which was against a Rhodesian war. This was comforting for Wilson, who was not a warrior by nature and feared that precipitate action might lead to a second Suez, or worse, a British Viet Nam. Rhodesia, he announced, would be overcome by economic sanctions.

Britain lost the war of attrition against Rhodesia. The rebel state flourished and confidence soared. Between 1967 and 1973, 39,000 immigrants arrived to share its prosperity. According to the BBC's local correspondent, 'most of them . . . are in Rhodesia for the good life, and there's no doubt that they are getting it.'[26] Negotiations continued fitfully. Wilson and Smith met twice, first in December 1966 on board the cruiser *Tiger*, and again in October 1968 on board its sister ship *Fearless*. Both meetings ended in deadlock over majority rule. During the first encounter, the naval officers' feelings had been 'Good Old Smithy, bloody old Wilson'. They changed their tune after intimate contact with the Rhodesians who revealed themselves 'rude, racist and even nigger-bashing in their conversations in the mess'.[27]

Those Rhodesian qualities which some found repellent, attracted others, especially on the outer right wing of the Conservative party. One such, Harold Soref MP, claimed that: 'Rhodesia represents Britain in its halcyon days: patriotic, self-reliant, self-supporting, with law and order and a healthy society. Rhodesia is as Britain was at its best.'[28] This other Eden was sometimes known as 'Basingstoke-in-the-Bush', a parody of a pre-war middle-class suburb transported across the Equator, complete with its tennis and golf clubs, and populated by aggressively hearty men in shorts, blazers and cravats, who talked of nothing but sport, and women who knew their place. So too did the black man. Soon after UDI, a former recruit to the Rhodesian police told a journalist that he had been taught that the African 'is muck to be kicked down and kept there'.[29]

Inevitably Africans fought back. Black nationalist movements had been banned and their leaders were either under arrest or in exile. The armed struggle began slowly after UDI and only began to gather momentum by 1972. The pattern of the war was familiar: raids and assassinations by guerrillas, called the 'boys in the bush', designed to wear down the enemy's will. There were two main partisan armies: Joshua Nkomo's Zimbabwe People's Revolutionary Army (ZIPRA) and Robert Mugabe's Zimbabwe African National Union (ZANU). The guerrillas knew their trade, they were armed with modern Soviet weaponry, including rockets, and were

trained in extensive base camps in Zambia and, from 1975 in
Moçambique.

The anti-guerrilla war was a corrosive, inconclusive struggle which ate
up Rhodesia's manpower and treasure. By 1979, 47 per cent of Rhodesia's
revenues were consumed by the war effort, and the government was being
forced to mobilise more and more black men to fill the gaps in its army. At
the same time, its adversaries seemed to be getting stronger; in September
1978 the guerrillas used a Sam 7 heat-seeking missile to shoot down a
Viscount airliner on an internal flight, and another was similarly destroyed
in February 1979. Rhodesians began to feel that victory was beyond their
grasp and voted with their feet. Between 1977 and 1980, 48,000 whites,
a fifth of the European community emigrated.

The truth was, as it had been in Kenya and the Portuguese colonies, that
the settlers could not sustain their position without the military power of
the mother country. Moreover, by the late-1970s the technical gap
between the equipment of the Rhodesian forces and their opponents was
narrowing. The destruction of the two airliners had been dramatic proof
of this. A similar lesson would be learned more painfully by the Soviet
Union during the early 1980s, when it embarked on an imperial war of
coercion in that former graveyard of British armies, Afghanistan.

By the beginning of 1978, Smith and the Rhodesia Front had to choose
between fighting on and possibly losing a war of attrition, or a salvage
operation which would involve considerable concessions to the blacks.
They decided on the latter and entered into an alliance with three relatively moderate African parties, Bishop Abel Muzorewa's United African
National Council, Ndabaningi Sithole's African National Council, and
Chief Chirau's Zimbabwe United People's Organisation. The upshot was
the 'internal settlement', which created a constitution that increased black
representation. In April 1979, Bishop Muzorewa became prime minister of
the cumbersomely-named Zimbabwe-Rhodesia. A month later, the
Conservatives under Mrs Margaret Thatcher won a general election, raising hopes in Rhodesia that a settlement with Britain was imminent.

The Rhodesian imbroglio was one of many intractable problems
bequeathed Mrs Thatcher by her predecessors. She was determined to act
decisively and swiftly and, at the same time, demonstrate how fumbling
past governments had been. At the Lusaka Commonwealth conference in
the summer she insisted that Britain alone would unravel the Rhodesian
knot. The answer lay in bringing the country back under a British government, which would supervise an election in which all political parties,

including those of Mugabe and Nkomo (who had boycotted the April poll) would compete. The Commonwealth ministers, who had no alternatives, acquiesced. Zimbabwe–Rhodesia, war-weary and still without the international recognition it craved, also agreed.

Representatives of all factions, including Ian Smith (who had been allowed immunity from a prosecution for treason), assembled in London in the autumn. The Lancaster Gate conference chaired by the Foreign Secretary, Lord Carrington, finally lanced the Rhodesian ulcer. The country passed back to Britain's jurisdiction and its new governor, Lord Soames, with a small contingent of troops and advisers, oversaw the surrender and disarming of the guerrillas and a general election. It was won by Mugabe who became prime minister in a coalition government in which his Zimbabwe African National Union shared power with Nkomo's Zimbabwe African People's Union. Mr Smith held one of the twenty seats reserved for whites in the new Zimbabwe assembly. One of its first acts was to pull down a statue of Cecil Rhodes.

7

Unfinished Business

While Zimbabweans were plucking down Rhodes from his plinth, the British were trying to forget about him and the rest of their imperial past. All that now remained of it were a few scarlet pinpricks on the globe: Gibraltar, Ascension, St Helena, Tristan da Cunha, the Falklands and their scattered, snowbound dependencies, Pitcairn Island (home to the descendants of the *Bounty* mutineers and their Tahitian brides), Hong Kong, Bermuda, the Cayman Islands and Montserrat. Few people knew where they were, let alone how and why they had been first obtained. They were an imperial legacy and their inhabitants' welfare was and is Britain's responsibility.

The possession of these outposts was largely irrelevant to a nation which entered the 1980s in search of a new, post-imperial identity. It proved hard to find. For the past fourteen years Britain has been a wavering and luke-warm European power, forever wary of its partners' motives, and, at the same time, a zealous client of America.

The Commonwealth remained and today has forty-nine members, rep-resenting a quarter of the world's population. Its size is a reflection of the empire at its height and a reminder of Britain's impact on the world. The history of North America, most of Africa, India, the Middle and Far East has been shaped by Britain and in many of these regions English is still the language of the law, commerce, government and education. And yet, inexplicably, Britain's part in the transformation of the world is gradually being excluded from the history syllabuses of its schools. A generation will grow up whose knowledge of the empire, how it grew, and what it did for its subjects and for Britain will be drawn from fiction and films.

As a political force in the world, the Commonwealth's achievements have been severely limited. Throughout the 1970s and 1980s its regular heads of government meetings have been stormy with Britain's prime ministers having to endure Pecksniffian harangues about its handling of the Rhodesian crisis, and, more recently, its alleged half-heartedness in backing economic sanctions against South Africa. Mrs Thatcher found these occasions bothersome and did not always hide her feelings. Once, during the 1985 Nassau conference, she rounded on a Ugandan delegate after he had lectured her on racial discrimination, and reminded him of his country's shameful expulsion of its Asian population. Afro-Asian states are always touchy whenever attention is drawn to their racism. Moreover, sermons on human rights from leaders of those Commonwealth states which lock up dissidents or smother political debate sounded like humbug.

By contrast, the Commonwealth functions more smoothly and effectively at the middle and lower levels. Exchanges of ideas and cooperation in such practical areas as education, medicine, agriculture and technology provide an invaluable bridge between its rich and poor members. The sundry good works sponsored by its agencies provide vital assistance for developing nations and, in a way, are a fulfilment of the old ideals of benevolent imperialism. One feels that Joseph Chamberlain would have warmly approved of Canadian vets working to improve Kenyan cattle stocks or young men and women from Britain teaching English in Indian schools. He, and all those of similar mind, would have enjoyed seeing African, Asian and Chinese names among the lists of graduates from British universities and those attaining British professional qualifications in law and accountancy. What Edmund Burke once called the 'small platoons' of individuals with common interests and working together are strong and active throughout the Commonwealth. What they are achieving explains why two former Portuguese colonies, Angola and Moçambique, have recently applied to join it.

Royal tours of Commonwealth countries continue. These progresses generate much goodwill and provide plenty of excitement and fun for all involved, as well as occasional entertaining ruckuses over protocol. Queen Elizabeth II is known to have a strong affection for the Commonwealth and she undertakes her duties towards its members with charm and dignity. Her and her family's peregrinations have a deeper significance: they provide a sense of historic continuity for the former subjects of the empire and their descendants. They may, at times, regret their imperial past, but feel unable to turn their back on it and their former mentor. The Queen represents that shared past, and that she can return to her father's colonies as a welcomed and fêted guest may say something about the nature of imperial rule and how it was ended.

The Conservative governments which have ruled Britain since 1979 have not been noted for their strong sense of history. Indeed, Mrs Thatcher and those ideologically close to her have an instinctive dislike of arguments which appeal to past traditions, particularly of their own party. There is no room in the universal free market for sentimentality about days gone by, or public institutions whose survival has, in part, depended on a reverence for the ways things have always been done. Three of the latter, the Commonwealth Office, the British Council and the BBC World Service have suffered cuts in their budgets. These lacerations have been made in the name of economy and despite arguments that each of these public services has helped to win hearts, minds and friends throughout the world. Britain's international reputation as a moral and cultural force cannot be easily measured in terms of profit and loss.

The prevailing philosophy among Mrs Thatcher's and John Major's supporters has been that the empire, the Commonwealth and all that went with them in the way of obligations belong to the past. And yet unlooked for events in the Falkland Islands in 1982 and the approaching termination of the ninety-nine-year lease of Hong Kong have made it impossible for either prime minister to escape from history. The Argentinian invasion of the Falkland Islands on 1–2 April 1982 was a bolt from the blue. Critics of the war which followed have claimed that the withdrawal of a British warship from the South Atlantic encouraged the Argentinian junta, and that intelligence assessments of its intentions were hopelessly mistaken. Be that as it may, there is also evidence to suggest that the clique of senior officers who ran the Argentine acted precipitately, and that the assault on the islands was mounted at less than twenty-four hours' notice.

Britain reacted with a mixture of astonishment and fury. For Mrs Thatcher the issue was stark and one of principle:

> The Falkland Islands and their dependencies must remain British territory. No aggression and no invasion can alter that simple fact. It is the Government's objective to see that the Islands are freed from occupation and returned to British administration at the earliest moment . . . The people of the

Falkland Islands, like the people of the United Kingdom are an
island race . . . they are few in number, but they have the right
to live in peace, to choose their own way of life and to deter-
mine their own allegiance. This way of life is British: their
allegiance is to the crown.

The Falklands, although a colony, were an extension of Britain. Michael
Foot, the Labour leader, reminded the Commons that the Argentinian
junta was a collection of military thugs whose hands were stained with the
blood of their countrymen. The Falkland Islanders should be delivered
from their tyranny for they had a right to live in association with Britain
and 'we have a moral duty, and a political duty, and every other kind of
duty to ensure that that is sustained.' The mood of the Commons was
angry and in favour of war; Julian Amery spoke for many on both sides
when he referred to 'a stain on Britain's honour'.

So Britain embarked on its last imperial war to redeem its honour and
recapture what had always been seen as one of the least of its colonies. It
was ironic that many of the warships which steamed to the South Atlantic
had been earmarked for the scrapyard by defence cuts proposed the year
before by the Defence Secretary, John Nott. Alternately petulant and
lugubrious, Nott appeared regularly on television with one of his civil servants, chosen it seemed for his funereal voice, to explain the daily course
of the war. At the same time, a squad of military experts offered their inter-
pretations of war as well as unsolicited advice. These armchair strategists
were a substitute for first-hand footage of the fighting, which could not be
transmitted directly.

The outcome of the war depended upon the cooperation of the United
States which was confronted with a war between a major and a minor
Cold War ally. President Reagan plumped for Britain, despite pleas that
such a choice would jeopardise relations with other South American states.
During the campaign, United States weaponry and intelligence was placed
at Britain's disposal.

Once it was underway, American newscasters called the war 'the Empire
strikes back'. Inside Britain, there was a strong, and at times unpleasantly
strident feeling that a country that had for so long patiently endured
knocks throughout the world was at last hitting back. A spirit of jingoism
of Boer War vintage pervaded the popular press and reached its highest
peak with the *Sun* headline 'Gotcha', which appeared over a photograph
of the waterlogged Argentinian cruiser *General Belgrano*. The sinking of this

formidable warship was one of the most controversial episodes in the war. Orders to intercept and destroy it had been given after signals intelligence revealed that it was about to engage the British task force.

Those who were, in principle, opposed to the war claimed that the torpedoes which holed the *Belgrano* ended all chances of a negotiated peace, although there was very little evidence to suggest that the Argentinian junta was on the verge of a *volte face*. What upset the left more than the fate of the *Belgrano* was the way in which the war revealed the depth and intensity of residual, aggressive John-Bullish patriotism. It seemed strongest among sections of the working class; a few days after the invasion of the Falkland Islands, a body of skinheads gathered outside a recruiting office in the Midlands, demanded rifles, and were angry when told that they would need to be trained. Old, belligerent, imperial emotions had not been dispelled by the disappearance of empire, and they surfaced again during the 1991 war against Iraq. It might also be said that they are frequently heard, seen and felt whenever English soccer teams play abroad. A sizeable body of young working-class men now regard an away match in Europe as a chance to create mayhem, and they seem unstoppable. There is much official hand-wringing, in which Dr Johnson's observation about what is called insolence in the masses in time of peace being called courage in time of war, is conveniently forgotten. Whatever else it may have done to the national character, the loss of empire and world power has not made the British less aggressive.

The reconquest of the Falklands at the end of May was a triumph for the stamina and courage of Britain's fighting men, and a tribute to the resolution of Mrs Thatcher. It also gave a fresh lustre to national pride which had become tarnished after years of retreat from empire, economic debility and internal industrial strife. Overnight, Britain had been transformed from a passive nation, an international has-been to which things happened, into a power to be reckoned with. What was, in effect, Britain's last imperial war, fought in unforeseen and extraordinary circumstances, reversed a string of humiliations going back to Suez. It also enhanced the reputation of Mrs Thatcher, now the 'Iron Lady', and helped her win a second term of office in 1983.

Disengagement from Hong Kong has occasioned no flag-waving. Most of the mainland colony had been leased from China in 1898 and Hong Kong island had been acquired as a result of the 1839–42 Opium War. The colony's existence since 1949 has depended on the tolerance of the People's Republic of China which, as heir-general of the Manchus, acquired the right to reoccupy what its predecessor had granted away. For these reasons, successive British governments had not treated Hong Kong like other parts of the empire and its people were not prepared for self-government in the 1950s and 1960s. The official line with the Hong Kong Chinese was Louis Phillippe's dictum '*enrichissez-vous*', and the colony prospered, becoming, by the 1980s, one of the leading commercial and banking centres of the Far East. As the rest of China began to share in the Pacific boom and, tentatively, to embrace capitalism, it appeared that when the time came for it to resume control over Hong Kong, it would treat it gently as a valuable asset.

This may have been wishful thinking, designed to assuage the fears of the people of Hong Kong and make the task of the British government easier. From 1984 onwards it had been willing to allow limited representative government in Hong Kong, and had pledged that democratic institutions would survive the transfer of power. The terms of this had been agreed by 1989, but the mass shootings of pro-democracy dissidents in Tiananmen Square, Peking were a brutal reminder that China was an authoritarian state. The British government faced a quandary: on one hand it knew that China possessed a *force majeure* which it could not match, and, on the other, it was under pressure from Hong Kong to speed up the process of democratisation. But to follow this course would provoke China and so the future of Hong Kong became a struggle between expediency and principle.

The new governor, a former Conservative minister, Chris Patten, appointed in 1992, adopted a traditional paternalist line, insisting that, 'Our responsibilities to Hong Kong's citizens come first.' He pressed ahead with the introduction of reforms for elections in 1994 in the teeth of opposition from China, which, in December 1993, withdrew from discussions of the issue. The solution is presently far from clear, nor can it be certain that China's ageing ruling élite will be in place for much longer.

The issue of Hong Kong's future is about more than the last act of imperial disengagement. Governor Patten and his supporters have put forward classic imperial arguments involving a duty towards Britain's subjects. Their adversaries claim that such moral responsibilities are a luxury which modern Britain cannot afford. Career diplomats, who have spent their lives dealing with China, believe that muted sycophancy is the best approach to Peking, which, if offended, might harm British trade or worse.

In the past fourteen years, variations on the view that commercial considerations are always paramount have carried great weight within

Thatcherite circles in the Conservative party. While making much of herself as a global champion of democracy, Mrs Thatcher has not shrunk from currying favour with autocrats, most notably King Fahd of Saudi Arabia and the sheiks of the Persian Gulf, all of whom are customers for British-made weaponry. What might be called the policy of guns before principles led her government to grovel to the Saudis in 1982 after they made a fuss about a television film, *Death of a Princess*. By contrast, Mrs Thatcher dealt sharply with a loyal ally, the gallant and humane King Hussain of Jordan, when he chose to tread cautiously after his powerful neighbour, Iraq, invaded Kuwait in 1990. The moral imperative which lay behind the Falklands War did not extend into other areas of foreign policy.

Another moral issue emerged during the debates over the future of Hong Kong. This was the question of whether large numbers of Hong Kong Chinese should be admitted to Britain. The 1948 British Nationality Act had extended British citizenship to subjects in all the colonies. As it passed through the Commons, the steamer *Empire Windrush* docked at Tilbury and four-hundred West Indian immigrants came ashore. Like the English, Scots and Irish who had crossed the Atlantic in the seventeenth and eighteenth centuries, they had left poverty behind them and come in search of prosperity.

The years which saw the dissolution of the empire witnessed the last of the great migrations it had made possible. From 1948 onwards large numbers of West Indians, Indians and Pakistanis and smaller numbers of West Africans, Maltese and Cypriots settled in Britain. The flow of immigrants gathered pace in the late 1950s and early 1960s and continued after two acts of 1962 and 1968 which were designed to restrict it. This is not the place to discuss the consequences of this shift of populations for Britain, which, by the 1970s had become a multi-racial society, even though the bulk of the new arrivals had settled in London, the Midlands and the decayed industrial towns of northern England. Reactions to this demographic change have been mixed and often, as they had been towards the Irish in the nineteenth century, violent. Old imperial attitudes played their part in determining how the immigrants were received. Imperial ideas of racial superiority led to condescension or even contempt, but at the same time benevolent imperial paternalism dictated that blacks and Asians should be treated decently and fairly. How the immigrants, their children and grandchildren fare will depend ultimately on the moral sense and flexibility of the British people.

The story of the rise and yet-to-be-completed fall of the British empire suggests that they once had both qualities in abundance, as well as <u>ruthlessness</u> and <u>rapacity</u>. A superficial glance at Britain's imperial past can lead to the conclusion that the last two were always in the forefront, but this is misleading. <u>Britain's empire was a moral force and one for the good.</u> The last word should lie with Nelson <u>Mandela</u>, recalling his schooldays in Natal in the 1920s:

> You must remember I was brought up in a British school, and at the time Britain was the home of everything that was best in the world. I have not discarded the influence which Britain and British history and culture exercised on us. We regarded it as the capital of the world and visiting the place therefore had this excitement because I was visiting the country that was my pride . . . You must also remember that Britain is the home of parliamentary democracy and, as people fighting against a form of tyranny in this country, we look upon Britain to take an active interest to support us in our fight against apartheid.

Few empires have equipped their subjects with the intellectual wherewithal to overthrow their rulers. None has been survived by so much affection and moral respect.

Bibliography

Abbreviations

AHR	*American Historical Review*
AHS	*Australian Historical Studies*
AJ	*Asiatic Journal*
AJPH	*Australian Journal of Politics and History*
BIHR	*Bulletin of the Institute of Historical Research*
CHR	*Canadian History Review*
CSP	*Calendars of State Papers*
EHR	*English Historical Review*
EcHR	*Economic History Review*
HJ	*Historical Journal*
HMC	Historic Manuscripts Commission
IHR	*Irish Historical Review*
IHS	*Irish Historical Studies*
Int. HR	*International History Review*
IJMES	*International Journal of Middle East Studies*
IOL	India Office Library
IWM	Imperial War Museum
JAH	*Journal of African History*
JCH	*Journal of Canadian History*
JCont.H	*Journal of Contemporary History*
JICH	*Journal of Imperial and Commonwealth History*
JMAS	*Journal of Modern African Studies*
JMH	*Journal of Modern History*
JRAHS	*Journal of the Royal Australian Historical Society*
JRCAS	*Journal of the Royal Central Asian Society*
JSAHR	*Journal of the Society for Army Historical Research*
JSH	*Journal of Social History*
JTH	*Journal of Transport History*
LHC	Liddell Hart Centre
MES	*Middle East Studies*
MM	*Mariner's Mirror*
NAM	National Army Museum
NLS	National Library of Scotland
NZJH	*New Zealand Journal of History*
PP	*Past and Present*

PRO   Public Record Office
RHL   Rhodes House Library
RUSI   *Royal United Services Institute Journal*
SRO   Scottish Record Office
WMQ   *William and Mary Quarterly*
WS   *War and Society*

Sources

Unpublished

India Office Library

Letters and Papers Military and Political

Imperial War Museum

Papers of Air-Marshal Sir Harold Lydford

Liddell Hart Centre for Military Archives

Papers of Brigadier-General Sir James Edmonds

National Army Museum:
Anon (Private of 5th Dragoon Guards and 11th Light Dragoons), Memoirs
Brigadier-General Sir Archibald Eden, Diary
Lieutenant William Fleming, 45th Regiment, Letters
Private John Mitchell, 58th Regiment, Memoirs
Surgeon Pine, Diary
Private J.C. Rose, 2nd Rifle Brigade, Papers and Diary
Major Stockwell, Diary and Papers

National Library of Scotland:
Papers of General Sir George Brown
Colin Campbell, 'Voyage of the Unicorn'
Papers of Admiral Sir Alexander Cochrane
Papers of Admiral Charles Graham
Papers and Diary of Field-Marshal Lord Haig
Papers of Major Alexander Murray
Papers of George Murray
Letters of Charles Cochrane, 4th Regiment (in Stuart-Stevenson Papers)
Papers of the Marquess of Tweeddale

Public Record Office:
Admiralty: Adm 1; Adm 53; Adm 116; Adm 123; Adm 125
Air Ministry: Air 5; Air 8; Air 9; Air 20; Air 24
Colonial Office: CO 23; CO 123; CO 201; CO 227; CO 318; CO 773; CO 856; CO 874; CO 968; CO 1015; CO 1027; CO 1037
Home Office: HO 51
Foreign Office: FO 141; FO 195; FO 371; FO 406; FO 413; FO 848
War Office: WO 1; WO 3; WO 32; WO 33; WO 86; WO 90; WO 92; WO 95; WO 208; WO 216

Rhodes House Library, Oxford

Papers of Captain Abadie

Scottish Record Office:
Clerk of Penycuik Papers
Dalrymple Papers
Dundonald Papers (Sudan Diary and Letters of Captain Lord Cochrane)
Logan Hume Papers
Lord Loch Papers
Lieutenant Colin MacKenzie, Letters
Lieutenant Stewart Mackenzie, Letters
Captain John Peebles, 42nd Regiment, Diary
General Robertson, Letters and Papers

Published

Magazines and Newspapers:

Africa; The Anti-Jacobin; Asiatic Journal; Blackwoods Magazine; British and Foreign Review; Coburn's United Service Magazine; Contemporary Review; Daily Express; Daily Graphic; Daily Herald; Daily Mail; Daily Telegraph; Edinburgh Review; Foreign Affairs; Fortnightly Review; The Graphic; Harpers; Illustrated London News; Imperial Commerce and Affairs; The Independent; Journal of the Royal Africa Society; The Listener; London Magazine; Manchester Guardian; Morning Post; National Geographic Magazine; National Review; New Statesman; Nineteenth Century; Nineteenth Century and After; The Observer; Picture Post; Private Eye; Quarterly Review; Review of Politics; Round Table; Saturday Review; Spectator; Sphere; Standard; Sun; Sunday Times; Time; The Times.

Articles and Books (all published in London unless stated otherwise):

D. Acheson, *Present at the Creation: My Years at the State Department* (1970).
C.A. Ageron, 'Les Populations du Mahgreb face à la Propagande Allemande', *Revue d'histoire de la Deuxième Guerre Mondiale*, 114 (1979).
R.G. Albion, 'The Timber Problem of the Royal Navy', *MM*, 38 (1952).
M. Alston (Mrs Conyers Alston), 'Women and the Overseas Empire', *National Review*, 79 (1917).
R.D. Altick, *The Shows of London* (Cambridge, Mass., 1978).
R. von Albertini and A. Wirz, *European Colonial Rule: the Impact of the West on India, South East Asia and Africa*, trans. O.G. Williamson (Oxford, 1982).
R.J. Aldrich, 'Conspiracy or Confusion? Churchill and Roosevelt and Pearl Harbour', *Intelligence and National Security*, 7 (1992).
L.S. Amery, *My Political Life, I: England before the Storm, 1896–1914* (1953).
_____, *The Leo Amery Diaries, I: 1896–1929*, ed. J. Barnes and D. Nicholson (1980).
E. Ames, *An ABC for Baby Patriots* (1898).
K.R. Andrews, *Elizabethan Privateering: English Privateering during the Spanish War, 1585–1603* (Cambridge, 1964).
Anon, Review of R. Perceval, *An Account of the Island of Ceylon, Edinburgh Review*, 2 (1803).
Anon, *A Concise History of the English Colony in New South Wales from the Landing of Governor Philip in January 1788 to May 1803* (1804).

Anon, *Review of A. von Humbolt, Tableaux Physiques des Régions Equatoriales, Edinburgh Review,* 16 (1810).

Anon, 'Transactions of the Missionary Society in the South Sea Islands', *Quarterly Review,* 2 (1811).

Anon, *Slavery No Oppression, or Some New Arguments and Opinions Against The Idea of Africa Liberty,* (n.d. *c.* 1815–20).

Anon, 'Emigration to the Cape of Good Hope', *Blackwoods Magazine,* 15 (1819).

Anon, (A Field Officer of Cavalry) (Digby Macworth) *The Diary of a Tour through Southern India, Egypt and Palestine in the Years 1821 and 1822* (1823).

Anon, 'A Convict's Recollections', *London Magazine,* 2 (1825).

Anon, 'The Invasion of India', *Blackwoods Magazine,* 22 (1827).

Anon, (Madras Officer) *A Sketch and Review of Military Service in India* (Glasgow, 1833).

Anon, (Citizen of Edinburgh) *Journal of an Excursion to the United States and Canada in the Year 1834: With Hints to Emigrants &c.,* (Edinburgh, 1835).

Anon, 'The Battle of Chillianwalla', *Colburn's United Service Magazine* (1850 Pt.3).

Anon, (9176 IY) (P. Sturrock) *The Fifes in South Africa: Being the History of the Fife and Forfar Yeomanry in the South African War, 1900–1901* (Cupar, Fife, 1903).

Anon, 'The British and the German Fleets', *Fortnightly Review,* New Series, 77 (1905).

Anon, 'The Native and the Settler and the Administration in British East Africa', *Contemporary Review,* 118 (1920).

Anon, *The Road to War* (Left Book Club, 1937).

Annual Report for the Gold Coast for the Year 1946 (1947).

J.C. Appleby, 'An Association for the West Indies? English Plans for a West India Company', *JICH,* 15 (1987).

M. Archer, *India and British Portraiture* (1979).

S.K.B. Asante, *Pan-African Protest: West Africa and the Italo-Ethiopian Crisis, 1934–1941* (1977).

B. Ash, *The Lost Dictator: A Biography of Field-Marshal Sir Henry Wilson* (1961).

C. Atkinson, *The Emigrants Guide to New Brunswick, British North America* (Berwick-on-Tweed, 1842).

E. Atiyah, *An Arab Tells His Own Story: A Study in Loyalties* (1946).

R. Attwood, *The Hessians: Mercenaries from Hessen-Kassell in the American Revolution* (Cambridge, 1980).

B. Bailyn, *The Peopling of British North America: An Introduction* (1986).

B. Bailyn and B. de Wolfe, *Voyages to the West* (1986).

The Endeavour Journal of Joseph Banks, ed. J.C. Beaglehole (2 vols, 1962).

J.P. Barber, 'The Karamoja District of Uganda', *JAH,* 3 (1962).

J. Barker, 'The Diary of Lieutenant John Barker, November 1774 to May 1776', *JSAHR,* 7 (1928).

C. Barnett, *The Collapse of British Power* (Gloucester, 1984 ed.).

Real Old Tory Politics: The Political Diaries of Sir Robert Sanders, Lord Bayford, ed. J. Ramsden (1984).

C.E.W. Bean, *Official History of Australia in the War of 1914–1918,* 1 and 2 (Sydney, 1938 and 1940).

The Beatty Papers, I (1902–1918), ed. B.Mcl. Rauft (Navy Records Society, 1989).

H. McD. Beccles, 'A riotous unruly lot: Irish Indentured Servants and Freemen in the English West Indies, 1644–1714', *WMQ* 47 (1990).

H.R. Beddoes, *Report on the Military Operations in Ashanti, 1900* (1901).

G. Bell, *From Amurath to Amurath* (1910).

C. Beresford, *The Memoirs of Lord Charles Beresford* (2 vols, 1914).

C. Berger, *Broadsides and Bayonets: The Propaganda War of the American Revolution* (Philadelphia 1961).

H. Bindloss, *In Niger Country* (1897).

J. Binney, *The Legacy of Guilt: A Life of Thomas Kendall* (1968).

M.B. Bishku, *The British Empire and the Question of Egypt's Future, 1919–1922* (Ann Arbor, 1988).

J. Black, 'Anglo-Spanish Naval Relations in the Eighteenth Century and the Anglo-Spanish Naval Race', *MM*, 77 (1991).

J. Black and P. Woodfine ed., *The British Navy and the Use of Naval Power in the Eighteenth Century* (Leicester, 1988).

R. Blake and W.R. Louis, ed., *Churchill* (Oxford, 1988).

W. Bligh, *A Voyage to the South Seas Undertaken by the Command of His Majesty for the Purpose of Conveying the Bread-Fruit Tree to the West Indies in His Majesty's Ship the Bounty* (1792).

W.S. Blunt, *Secret History of the English Occupation of Egypt* (New York, 1967 ed.).

Boscawen's Letters to his Wife, 1755–1756, ed. P.K. Kemp, in *Naval Miscellany 4* (Navy Record Society, 1952).

G. Bourchier, *Eight Months Campaign against the Bengal Sepoy Army during the Mutiny of 1857* (1858).

F. Bourne, 'Rorke's Drift' ('I was there'), *Listener*, 30 December 1936.

John Bowle, *The Imperial Achievement: The Rise and Transformation of the British Empire* (1974).

T. Bowrey, *A Geographical Account of the Countries around the Bay of Bengal, 1669–1679* (Hakluyt Society, 1905).

A. Boyle, *Trenchard: Man of Vision* (1962).

H.J. Brands, 'The Cairo-Teheran Connection in Anglo-American Rivalry in the Middle East', *Int. HR*, 11 (1989).

Lord Brassey, 'The Diamond Jubilee in Victoria', *Nineteenth Century*, 42 (1897).

J.S. Bratton, R.A. Cave, B. Gregory, H.J. Holder and M. Pickering, *Acts of Supremacy: The British Empire and the Stage, 1790–1930* (Manchester, 1991).

H.H. Breen, *St Lucia: Historical and Statistical Description*, (1844).

British Parliamentary Papers: Industrial Revolution, I (Trade) (Shannon, 1968).

British Parliamentary Papers: Colonies I (Report of the Select Committee on Ceylon and British Guiana (Shannon, 1968).

The British Way (Directorate of Army Education, 1944).

C. Brooke, *Ten Years in Sarawak* (2 vols, 1856).

J. Brown, *An Estimate of the Manners and Principles of the Times* (1757).

N.J. Brown, *Peasants Against the State: The Political Activity of the Egyptian Peasantry, 1882–1952* (Ann Arbor, 1988).

W.H. Brown, *On the South African Frontier* (Bulawayo, 1970 ed.).

R. Buchanan, 'The Voice of the Hooligan', *Contemporary Review*, 76 (1899).

R.N. Buckley, 'The Destruction of the British Army in the West Indies, 1793–1815: A Medical History, *JSAHR*, 56 (1978).

J. Burchett, *Memoirs of Transactions at Sea during the War with France beginning 1688 and ending in 1700* (1703).

The Correspondence of Edmund Burke, V (Oxford, 1965).

W. L. Burn, *The Age of Equipoise* (1968 ed.).

B.C. Busch, *Britain, India and the Arabs* (Berkeley, Calif., 1971).

J. Butler, 'The German Factor in Anglo-Transvaal Relations', in ed. Gifford and Louis, *Britain and Germany in Africa.*

The Diaries of Sir Alexander Cadogan, 1938–1945, ed. D. Dilks (1971).

P.J. Cain and A.G. Hopkins, 'The Political Economy of British Expansion Overseas', 1750–1914 *Ec.HR*, 33 (1980).

Calendars of State Papers, America and the West Indies, 1574–1738 (44 volumes, 1860–1969).

R.M. Calhoun, *The Loyalists in Revolutionary America, 1760–1781* (New York, 1965).

C.E. Callwell, *Field-Marshal Sir Henry Wilson, his Life and Diaries* (2 vols, 1927).

Canada Today (1927).

L.G. Carr and L.S. Walsh, 'The Planter's Wife: The Experience of White Women in Seventeenth Century Maryland', *WMQ,* 24 (1977).

A. Cassells, 'Deux Empires face à face: La chimère d'un rapprochement anglo-italien (1936–1940)', *Guerres Mondiales et Conflits Contemporains 161* (January 1991).

B. Castle, *Fighting All the Way* (1993).

D. Caute, *Under the Sun: The Death of White Rhodesia* (1983).

J. Chamberlain, 'A Bill for the Weakening of Britain', *Nineteenth Century 33* (1893).

M. E. Chamberlain, 'The Alexandria Massacre of 11 June 1882 and the British Occupation of Egypt', *MES,* 13 (1977).

George Chapman, Ben Jonson and John Marston, *Eastwood Ho,* ed. R.W. Fossen (Manchester, 1979).

J. Charmley, *Lord Lloyd and the Decline of Empire* (1987).

Chambers Information for the People (1842).

N. Chauduri, *Clive of India* (1975).

E. Childers, *In the Ranks of the CIV* (1901).

I. Clark and N.J. Wheeler, *The Origins of British Nuclear Strategy, 1945–1955* (Oxford 1989).

The American Revolution: Sir Henry Clinton's Narrative of his Campaigns, 1775–1782, ed. W.B. Willcox (Yale, 1954).

W.L. Clowes, *The Royal Navy from Ancient Times* (7 vols, 1897–1903).

A.J. Cobham, *My Flight to the Cape and Back* (1926).

S.A. Cohen, 'A Still Stranger Aspect of Suez: British Operational Plans to Attack Israel', *Int.HR,* 10 (1988).

S. Cohen, 'Mesopotamia and British Strategy, 1903–1914', *IJMES,* 9 (1978).

(Lt. Collins) *A Concise History of the English Colony of New South Wales* (1803).

R.O. Collins, *Shadows in the Grass: Britain and the Southern Sudan, 1918–1956* (1983).

Congress Responsibility for the Disturbances (New Delhi, 1943).

S. Constantine, ed. *Emigrants and Empire: British Settlement in the Dominions Between the Wars* (Manchester, 1990).

Constitutional Relations between Britain and India: The Transfer of Power, 1942–1947. ed. N. Mansergh and E.W.E. Lamby (12 vols, 1970–1987).

S. Conway, 'British Army Officers and the American War of Independence', *WMQ,* 41 (1984).

_____, 'The Recruitment of Criminals into the British Army', *BIHR,* 58 (1985).

D. Cooper, *Old Men Forget* (1953).

The Cornwallis Correspondence, ed. J. Ross (3 vols, 1859).

The Letters and Prose Writings of William Cowper, 1750–1781, ed. J. King and C. Ryskamp (Oxford, 1979).

N.F.R. Crafts, 'Industrial Revolution in England and France: Some thoughts on the Question, "Why was England First?"', *Ec.HR*, 30 (1977).

Lord Cranworth, *Profit and Sport in British East Africa* (1919).

The Crawford Papers: The Journal of David Lindsay, Twenty-Seventh Earl of Campbell and Tenth Earl of Balcarres, ed. J. Vincent (Manchester, 1984).

D. Cressy, 'A New New Letter from America: Newfoundland in 1610', *MM*, 72 (1986).

_____, *Coming Over: Migration and Communication between England and New England in the Seventeenth Century* (Cambridge, 1987).

Lord Cromer, *England in Egypt* (2 vols, 1908).

F. Crouzet, 'The Sources of England's Wealth: Some French Views on the Eighteenth Century', in ed. P.L. Cottrell and D.H. Aldcroft, *Shipping, Trade and Commerce* (Leicester, 1981).

N. Cunard, 'On Colour Bar', *Life and Letters*, 32 (1942).

H. Cunningham, 'The Language of Patriotism, 1750–1914, *History Workshop* 12 (1981).

H.G. Dalton, *The History of British Guiana* (2 vols, 1855).

M.W. Daly, *Empire on the Nile: The Anglo-Egyptian Sudan, 1898–1934* (Cambridge, 1986).

J. Darwin, 'The Central African Emergency, 1959', *JICH*, 21 (1993).

A. Davin, 'Imperialism and Motherhood', *History Workshop*, 5 (1978).

K.G. Davis, *The North Atlantic World in the Seventeenth Century* (Oxford, 1974).

R. Davis, *The Rise of the English Shipping Industry in the Seventeenth and Eighteenth Centuries* (1962).

D. Day, 'Anzacs on the Run: The View from Whitehall, 1941–1942', *JICH*, 14 (1986).

De Latocnaye, *Promenade autour de la Grande Bretagne* (Edinburgh, 1795).

Lord Denman, *A Letter from Lord Denman to Lord Brougham on the Final Extinction of the Slave Trade* (1848).

A. Desmond and J. Moore, *Darwin* (1992 ed.).

Development and Welfare in the West Indies, 1940–1942 (1943).

D.R. Devereux, 'Britain, the Commonwealth and the Defence of the Middle East, 1948–1956', *JCont. H*, 24 (1989).

H.T. Dickinson, 'Popular Conservatism, Militant Loyalism, 1789–1815', in ed. H.T. Dickinson, *Britain and the French Revolution* (1989).

O.S. Djan, 'Drums and Victory: Africa's Roll Call to the Empire, *Journal of the Royal African Society*, 42 (1942).

F.D. Djang, *The Diplomatic Relations between China and Germany since 1899* (Shanghai, 1936).

Documents Concerning English Voyages to the Spanish Main, 1569–1580, ed. I.A. Wright (Hakluyt Society, 1932).

Documents of the American Revolution, 1770–1783 (21 vols, Shannon, 1972–81).

Documents of British Foreign Policy, 1919–1939, ed. W.N. Medlicott, D. Dakin and G. Bennett, 2nd Series, 18 (1980).

Documents of Australian Foreign Policy, 1937–1949, ed. R.G. Neale, P.G. Edwards and H. Kenoway (6 vols, Canberra, 1975–1983).

D. Dodds, M. Giles, I. Orr-Ewing, M. Ross, P. Wall, *A Presence East of Suez* (1969).

H.J. Dooley, 'Great Britain's "Last Battle" in the Middle East: Notes on Cabinet Planning during the Suez Crisis, 1956', *Int.HR*, 11 (1989).

Captain Doveton, 'The Company's Troops', *AJ* 3rd Series, I (1843).

_____, 'The Bangalore Conspiracy of 1832', *AJ* 3rd Series, II (1844).

A. Draper, *The Amritsar Massacre: Twilight of the Raj* (1985 ed.).

H.T.B. Drew, *The War Effort in New Zealand* (vol. 4 of the Official History, Auckland, 1923).

T. Eddy and D. Shreuder, *The Rise of Colonial Nationalism* (Sydney, 1988).

G. Edmondson, *A Narratine of Personal Adventures at Banda and elsewhere during the rebellion of 1857* (1858).

H. Edwardes, *A Year on the Punjab Frontier, 1848–49* (2 vols, 1851).

P. Edwards, 'The Australian Commitment to the Malayan Emergency, 1948–1950', *AHS*, 22 (1987).

C.C. Eldridge, ed. *British Imperialism in the Nineteenth Century* (1984).

The Papers of Dwight David Eisenhower: The War Years, 1, ed. A.D. Chandler, S.E. Ambrose, J.P. Hobbs, E.A. Thompson and E.F. Smith (Baltimore, 1970).

Empire Day Book (1912).

K. Feiling, *The Life of Neville Chamberlain* (1946).

J.R. Ferris, 'The Greatest Power on Earth: Great Britain in the 1920s', *JInt. H*, 13 (1991).

J.M. Fewster, 'Prize-Money and the British Expeditionary Force to the West Indies of 1793', *JICH*, 12 (1983).

D.K. Fieldhouse, 'The Labour Government and the Empire Commonwealth', in ed. R. Ovendale, *The Foreign Policy of the British Labour Government*.

H. Finber, *Rival Empires of Trade in the Orient, 1600–1800* (Minneapolis, 1976).

First, Second and Third Reports for the Select Committee on Emigration from the United Kingdom (Shannon, 1977).

D.H. Fischer, *Albion's Seed: Four British Folkways in America* (Oxford, 1989).

H.A.L. Fisher, 'Mr Lloyd George's Foreign Policy, 1918–1922', *Foreign Affairs* 1 (September, 1922).

N. Fisher, *Iain Macleod* (1973).

R. Fisher and H. Johnston ed., *Captain Cook and his Times* (Seattle, 1979).

A.C. Flick, *Loyalism in New York during the American Revolution* (New York, 1901).

G.E. Fox, *British Admirals and Chinese Pirates, 1823–1869* (1940).

The Papers of Benjamin Franklin, 17 (Yale, 1978).

D. Fraser, *Impressions: Nigeria 1925* (1926).

C.J. French, 'Productivity in Atlantic Shipping Industry', *JIDH*, 17 (1987).

A.L. Friedberg, *Change, Assessment and Adaptation: Britain and the Experience of Relative Decline, 1895–1905* (Ann Arbor, 1987).

A. Frost, 'New Geographic Perspectives and the Emergence of the Romantic Imagination', in ed. Fisher and Johnston, *Captain Cook and his Times*.

I.W. Fuchser, *Neville Chamberlain and Appeasement: A Study in the Politics of History* (Ann Arbor, 1982).

J. Fuller, *Troop Morale and Popular Culture in British and Dominion Armies* (Oxford, 1990).

F. Furedi, 'Creating a Breathing Space: The Political Management of Colonial Emergencies', *JICH*, 21 (1993).

R. Furse, *Acuparius: Recollections of a Recruiting Officer* (Oxford, 1962).

J.S. Galbraith, 'British War Aims in World War I: A Commentary on Statesmanship', *JICH*, 13 (1984).
The Collected Works of Mahatma Gandhi, (82 volumes, Delhi, 1958–80).
N.G. Garson, 'South Africa and World War I', *JICH*, 8 (1979).
D.B. Gaspar, 'The Antigua Conspiracy of 1736: A Case Study in the Origin of Collective Resistance', WMQ, 35 (1978).
P. Gifford and W.R. Louis ed., *Britain and Germany in Africa*, (Yale, 1967).
_____, *France and Britain in Africa*, (Yale, 1971).
P. Gifford and T.C. Westell, 'African Education in a Colonial Context: French and British Styles', in ed. Gifford and Louis, *France and Britain in Africa*.
M. Gilbert, *Winston S. Churchill* (6 volumes, 1966–1983).
D. Gillison, *Royal Australian Air Force, 1939–1942*, (Australia in the War of 1939–1945, Series 3, I) (Canberra, 1962).
W.E. Gladstone, *Speeches in Scotland* (3 volumes, Edinburgh, 1879–80).
J. Goldberg, 'The Origins of British-Saudi Relations: The Anglo-Saudi Treaty Revisited', *HJ*, 28 (1985).
H. Goldwin, *The Empire: A Series of Letters* (1862).
J. Gooch, 'Hidden in the Rock: American Military Perception of Great Britain, 1919–1940', in ed. L. Freedman, P. Hayes and R. O'Neill, *Essays in Honour of Sir Michael Howard* (Oxford, 1992).
S. Gopal, *British Policy in India* (Cambridge, 1965).
D.C. Gordon, *The Dominion Partnership and Imperial Defence, 1870–1914* (Baltimore, 1965).
B.M. Gough, *The Royal Navy and the Northeast Coast of North America, 1810–1914: A Study in British Maritime Supremacy* (Vancouver, 1971).
R.J. Goven, 'British Legerdemain at the 1911 Imperial Conference: The Dominions, Defense Planning, and the Renewal of the Anglo-Japanese Alliance', *JMH*, 52 (1980).
B.I. Grainger, *Political Satire in the American Revolution, 1763–1783* (Ithaca, NY, 1960).
M. Green, *Dreams of Adventure, Deeds of Empire* (1980).
J. Greenhut, 'The Imperial Reserve: The Indian Corps on the Western Front, 1914–1915', *JICH*, 12 (1983).
L.D. Gregg, 'Shipmasters in Early Barbados', *MM*, 77 (1991).
W. Gregory, 'Egypt in the Soudan', *Nineteenth Century*, 17 (1885).
The Grenville Papers, ed. W.J. Smith (7 volumes, 1852).
P. Griffiths, *To Guard My People: The History of the Indian Police* (1971).
I.D. Gruber, *The Howe Brothers and the American Revolution* (Williamsburg, Va., 1972).
J.J. Gurney, *A Winter in the West Indies* (1840).
J. Guy, 'A Note on Firearms in the Zulu Kingdom with special reference to the Anglo-Zulu War, 1879', *JAH*, 12 (1971).
_____, *The Destruction of the Zulu Kingdom* (1979).

D. Haglund, 'George C. Marshall', *JCont.H*, 15 (1988).
A Handbook of the Anglo-Egyptian Sudan, 1922 (Naval Staff Intelligence Division, 1922).
J.S. Handler and R.S. Corruccini, 'Plantation Slave Life in Barbados: A Physical Anthropological Approach', *JIDH*, 14 (1983).
S. Hamid, *Disastrous Twilight: A Personal Record of the Partition of India* (1986).

Lord Hankey, *The Supreme Command* (2 vols, 1961).

G. Hanley, 'Bantu in Burma', *Spectator*, 19 January 1945.

_____, 'Resettling the West African', *Army Quarterly*, 52 (1946).

J.C. Hansard, *The Parliamentary History of England from the Earliest Period to the Year 1803* (36 volumes, 1806–1820).

Hansard's Parliamentary Debates

F. Harcourt, 'Disraeli and Imperialism, 1866–1868: A Question of Timing', *HJ*, 23 (1980).

J.D. Hargreaves, *Decolonisation in Africa* (1988).

J.H. Harris, 'Back to Slavery?' *Contemporary Review*, 120 (1921).

J.P. Harris, 'British Military Intelligence and the Rise of German Mechanical Forces, 1929–1940', *Intelligence and National Security*, 6, ii (1991).

B. Harrison, 'For Church, Queen and Family: The Girls Friendly Society, 1874–1920', *PP*, 61 (November 1973).

R. Hart, *Slaves who Abolished Slavery*, II (Blacks in Rebellion) (Kingston, Jamaica, 1955).

The Political Diaries of Oliver Harvey, 1937–1940, ed. J. Harvey (1970).

The Wartime Diaries of Oliver Harvey, 1937–1940, ed. J. Harvey (1978).

B. Hasluck, *The Government and the People 1939–1941* (Australia in the War of 1939–1945, Series 4, I) (Canberra, 1956 ed.).

R.G. Haycock, 'The "Myth" of Imperial Defence: Australian and Canadian Bilateral Military Cooperation, 1942', *WS* 2,i (1984).

S. Heap, 'The Development of Motor Transport in the Gold Coast, 1900–1939', *JTH*, 11 (1990).

R. Heber, *Narrative of a Journey through the Upper Provinces of India* (2 vols, 1849).

M.H. Heikal, *Cutting the Lion's Tail: Suez Through Egyptian Eyes* (1986).

M.A. Henniker, 'Early Days in Pakistan', *RUSI*, 93 (1948).

P. Hennessy, *Never Again* (1993 ed.).

A. Hilgruber, 'England's Place in Hitler's Plans for World Domination', *JCont.H*, 9 (1974).

ed. F. Hinsley and others, *History of the Second World War: British Intelligence in the Second World War* (5 vols, 1979–86).

HMC, *Reports on the Manuscripts of Reginald Rawdon Hastings Esquire* vols III (1903) and IV (1947).

HMC, *Reports on the Manuscripts of Mrs Stopford-Sackville* (2 vols, 1904–10).

HMC, *Reports on the Manuscripts of Earl Bathurst preserved at Cirencester Park* (1923).

The History and Proceedings of the House of Commons from the Restoration to the Present Day (14 vols, 1742–44).

The History of the Bermudas or Summer Islands, ed. J.H. le Froy (Hakluyt Society, 1882).

E.J. Hobsbawn, *The Age of Empire* (1986).

C. Hollis, 'Chamberlain's Policy', *Review of Politics*, 1 (1939).

P.M. Holt, *The Mahdist State in the Sudan*, 1881–1898 (Oxford, 1958).

H.D. Hooper, *Leading Strings: National Development and Missionary Education in Kenya Colony* (1921).

A.G. Hopkins, 'The Victorians and Africa: A Reconsideration of the Occupation of Egypt', *JAH*, 27 (1986).

D. Hopwood, *Tales of Empire: The British and the Middle East, 1880–1952* (1989).

A. Horne, *Macmillan, 1884–1956* (1988).

_____, *Macmillan, 1957–1986* (1989).

S. Hornstein, *The Deployment of the Navy in Peacetime, 1674–1688* (Leiden, 1986).
House of Commons Sessional Papers of the Eighteenth Century, (George III: Quebec and New South Wales, 1791–1792) ed. Lambert (Wilmington, Delaware, 1975).
I.C.Y. Hsü, *The Rise of Modern China* (Oxford, 1990 ed.).
Hudson's Bay Company, Letters Outward, 1688–1969, Hudson's Bay Company Record Society, 20 (1957).
Hudson's Bay Miscellany, 1670–1870, Hudson's Bay Company Record Society, 30 (1975).
R. Hyam, 'Empire and Sexual Opportunity', *JICH*, 15 (1985).
_____, 'The Political Consequences of Seretse Khama: Britain, the Bangwato and South Africa', *HJ*, 29 (1986).
_____, *Empire and Sexuality* (Manchester, 1990).

Lord Ironside ed., *High Road to Command: The Diaries of Major-General Sir Edmund Ironside, 1920–1922* (1972).
R. Isaacs, *The Transformation of Virginia, 1740–1790* (Chapel Hill, North Carolina, 1982).

C.L.R. James, 'A Century of Freedom', *The Listener*, 31 May 1933.
L. James, *Mutiny* (1985).
_____, *Imperial Rearguard* (1988).
_____, *The Golden Warrior: The Life and Legend of Lawrence of Arabia* (1990).
_____, *Imperial Warrior: The Life and Times of Field-Marshall Lord Allenby* (1993).
S.V. James, *Colonial Rhode Island: A History* (New York, 1975).
A. Jayal, 'Towards the Baghdad Pact: South Asia and the Middle East Defence in the Cold War, 1947–1955', *Int. HR*, 11 (1989).
K. Jeffrey, *The British Army and the Crisis of Empire* (Manchester, 1984).
E.H. Jenkins, *A History of the French Navy* (1973).
D.W. Jones, *War and Economy in the Age of William III and Marlborough* (Oxford, 1988).
T. Jones, *Whitehall Diaries* III (Ireland, 1918–1925), ed K. Middlemas (1971).
D.H Johnson, 'The Death of General Gordon: A Victorian Myth', *JICH*, 10 (1982).
H.J.M. Johnston, *British Emigration Policy, 1815– 1830* (Oxford, 1972).
W.D. Jordan, *White Over Black: American Attitudes to the Negro, 1580–1812* (Williamsburg, North Carolina, 1968).

R. Kaplan, 'The Hidden Hand: British Intelligence Operations during the American Revolution', *WMQ*, 47 (1990).
J.W. Kaye, *Lives of the Indian Officers* (2 vols, 1867).
J.E. Kendall, *The Colonial and Imperial Conferences, 1887–1911* (1987).
P. Kennedy, *The Rise and Fall of British Naval Mastery* (1976).
_____, *The Rise of Anglo-German Antagonism, 1860–1914* (1982 ed.).
_____, *The Rise and Fall of the Great Powers* (1988).
L. Kennet, *French Forces in America, 1780–1763* (Westport, Conn., 1977).
M. Kent ed., *The Great Powers and the End of the Ottoman Empire* (1984).
Imam Khomeini, *Islam in Revolution* (Berkeley, Calif., 1981).
I. Klein, 'British Intervention in the Persian Revolution, 1905–1908', *HJ* 15 (1972).
H. Knatchbull-Hugessen, *Diplomat in Peace and War* (1949).
D. Killingray, 'Repercussions of World War I in the Gold Coast', *JAH*, 19 (1978).

_____, 'Ex-Servicemen in the Gold Coast', *JMAS*, 21 (1983).

_____, 'A Swift Agent of Colonial Government: Air Power in British Colonial Africa', *JAH*, 25 (1984).

_____, 'Labour Exploitation for Military Campaigns in British Colonial Africa, 1870–1945, *JCont.H*, 24 (1989).

R.J. King, 'Ports of Shelter, and Refreshment . . . Botany Bay and Norfolk Island in British Military Strategy, 1786–1808', *AHS*, 22 (1986).

K.O. Kupperman, 'The Puzzle of the American Climate in the Early Colonial Period', *AHR*, 87 (1982).

_____, 'Fear of Hot Climates in the Anglo-American Colonial Experience', *WMQ*, 41 (1984).

M. Lake, 'Identifying the Masculine Context', AHS, 22 (1986).

I.K. Lambi, *The Navy and German Power Politics* (1984).

J.D. Lang, *A Historical and Statistical Account of New South Wales* (2 vols, 1834).

S.M. Lawler, 'Ireland from Truce to Treaty: War or Peace? July to October 1921', *IHS* 22 (1980–81).

T.E. Lawrence, *Letters*, ed. D. Garnett (1938).

F.H. Lawson, 'The Iranian Crisis of 1945–1946 and the Spiral Model of International Conflict', *IJMES*, 21 (1989).

_____, *Fur: A Study in English Mercantilism, 1700–1775* (Toronto, 1943).

League of Nations: Permanent Mandates Commission Minutes (vols 1–4, Geneva, 1921–23).

D.E. Leach, *The Northern Colonial Frontier, 1607–1763* (New York, 1966).

M.P. Leffler, *A Preponderance of Power: National Security and the Truman Administration in the Cold War* (Stamford, 1992).

J.D. Legge, *Britain in Fiji* (1958).

J. Lemisch, 'Jack Tar in the Streets: Merchant Seamen in the Politics of Revolutionary America', *WMQ*, 25 (1968).

M.G. Lewis, *Journal of a West India Proprietor, 1815–1817*, ed. C.M. Wilson (1929).

D. Livingstone, *A Popular Account of Missionary Travels and Researches in Southern Africa* (1861).

Lord Lloyd, *Egypt Since Cromer* (2 vols, 1934).

S. Lloyd, *Suez, 1956* (1980 ed.).

W.R. Louis, *Imperialism at Bay, 1941–1945: The United States and the Decolonisation of the British Empire* (Oxford, 1977).

_____, *The British Empire in the Middle East* (Oxford, 1984).

C.R. Low, *The Life and Correspondence of Field-Marshal Sir George Pollock* (1873).

D.A. Low ed., *Congress and the Raj: Facets of the Indian Struggle, 1917–1947* (1977).

P.L. Lovejoy and J.S. Hagendorm, 'Revolutionary Mahdism and Resistance to Colonial Rule in the Sokoto Caliphate, 1905–06, *JAH*, 31 (1990).

F.D. Lugard, *The Rise of our East African Empire* (2 vols, 1893).

R.H. MacDonald, 'Reproducing the Middle-Class Boy: From Purity to Patriotism in the Boys' Magazines, 1892–1914', *JCont.H*, 24 (1989).

J.M. Mackenzie, *Propaganda and Empire: The Manipulation of British Public Opinion, 1880–1960* (Manchester, 1984).

H. Macmillan, *War Diaries: The Mediterranean Diaries, 1943–1945* (1984).

N. Macready, *Memoirs of an Active Life* (2 vols, 1927).

The Life and Correspondence of Sir John Malcolm, ed. J.W. Kaye (2 vols, 1856).

N. Malcolm, 'On Service in Uganda', *Blackwoods Magazine* 166 (November 1899).

E.P. Malone, 'The New Zealand Journal and the Imperial Ideology', *NZJH*, 7 (1973).

J. Mangan, *The Games Ethic and Imperialism* (1986).

M. Mann, *China, 1860* (1989).

G.J. Marcus, *A Naval History of England, 1: The Formative Years* (1961).

ed. A.J. Marder, *Fear God and Dread Nought: The Correspondence of Admiral of the Fleet Lord Fisher of Kilverstone*, II: *The Years of Power, 1904–1914* (1956).

A.J. Marder, *From the Dardanelles to Oran: Studies in the Royal Navy in War and Peace* (Oxford, 1974).

_____, *Old Friends, New Enemies: The Royal Navy and the Imperial Japanese Navy, Strategic Illusions, 1936–1941* (Oxford, 1981).

_____, M. Jacobson and J. Horsfield, *Old Friends and New Enemies: The Royal Navy and the Imperial Japanese Navy, The Pacific War, 1942–1945* (Oxford, 1991).

P.J. Marshall, 'British Expansion in India in the Eighteenth Century: A History Revision', *History*, 60 (1975).

G. Martin, 'The Influence of Racial Attitudes on British Policy towards India during the First World War', *JCont.H*, 24 (1989).

N. Martin, 'A Different Kind of Courage: The French Military and the Canadian Irregular Soldiers during the Seven Years War', *JCH*, 70 (1986).

A.H. Mason, *Expeditions against the Black Mountain Tribes* (Simla, 1899).

_____, *Expedition against the Hasanzai and Azakai Tribes of the Black Mountain, 1891* (Simla, 1894).

H.L. Maw, *Memoir of the Early Operations of the Burmese War* (1832).

T. Mboya, *Freedom and After* (1963).

R. Matthew Bray, 'Fighting as an Ally: The English-Canadian Patriotic Response to the Great War', *CHR*, 61 (1980).

L. McCardell, *Ill-Starred General: Braddock of the Coldstream Guards* (Pittsburgh, 1958).

J.M. McCarthy, 'Australia and Imperial Defence: Cooperation and Conflict, 1918–1939', *AJPH*, 17 (1971).

R.L. McCormack, 'Imperial Mission: The Air Route to Cape Town, 1918–1932', *JCont.H*, 9 (1974).

_____, 'Missed Opportunities: Winston Churchill and the Air Ministry in Africa', *Int.HR*, 11 (1989).

J. McCracken, 'Coercion and Control in Nyasaland: Aspects of the History of the Colonial Police Force', *JAH*, 27 (1986).

G. McGhee, *Envoy to the Middle World* (New York, 1983).

W.D. McIntyre, *The Imperial Frontier in the Tropics, 1865–1875* (1967).

B.T.C. McKercher, 'Our Most Dangerous Enemy: Great Britain's Pre-eminence in the 1930s', *Int.HR*, 13 (1991).

J.R. McNeil, *Atlantic Empires of France and Spain: Louisbourg and Havana* (1985).

R. Meinertzhagen, *Kenya Diary* (1957).

The Life and Correspondence of Charles, Lord Metcalfe, ed. J.W. Kaye (1854).

K.A. Miller, *Emigrants and Exiles: Ireland and the Irish Exodus to North America* (Oxford, 1985).

Lord Milner, *England and Egypt* (2 vols, 1892).

Lord Milner, *The Nation and the Empire: being a collection of Speeches and Addresses* (1913).

A.F. Mockler-Ferryman, *Up the Niger: Narrative of Major Claude Macdonald's Mission to the Niger and Benue Rivers* (1892).

The Naval Tracts of Sir William Monson, ed. M. Oppenheim (2 vols, Navy Records Society, 1902).

J. Montgomery, *The West Indies* (1809).

M. de Moraes Ruehsen, 'Operation "Ajax" Revisited', *MES*, 29 (1993).

Lord Moran, *Winston Churchill: The Struggle for Survival, 1940–1965* (1968 ed.).

K.O. Morgan, *Keir Hardie, Radical and Socialist* (1975).

S.E. Morison, *The Rising Sun in the Pacific 1931–April 1942* (History of United States Naval Operations in World War II, vol 3) (Oxford, 1948).

J. Morris, *Pax Britannica* (1968).

_____, *At Heaven's Command: An Imperial Progress* (1973).

_____, *Farewell the Trumpets* (1978).

R. Morris, *The Royal Dockyards during the Revolutionary and Napoleonic Wars* (Leicester, 1983).

L. Morsy, 'The Military Clauses of the Anglo-Egyptian Treaty of Friendship and Alliance, 1936', *IJMES*, 16 (1984).

_____, 'Britain's Wartime Policy in Egypt, 1940–42', *MES*, 25 (1989).

_____, 'The Role of the United States in the Anglo-Egyptian Agreements of 1956', *MES*, 29 (1993).

W.M. Mumford, 'Education and Social Adjustment of the Primitive People of Africa to European Culture', *Africa*, 2 (1929).

T. Mun, *England's Benefit and Advantage by Foreign Trade* (1698 ed.).

M.H. Murfett, 'Living in the Past: A Critical Re-examination of the Singapore Naval Strategy, 1918–1941', *WS*, 11, i (1993).

R. Murphy, 'Walter Long and the Making of the Government of Ireland Act', *IHS*, 25 (1986–87).

G.C. Nammack, *Fraud, Politics and the Dispossession of the Indians: The Iroquois Land Frontier in the Colonial Period* (Norman, Oklahoma, 1969).

W.P.F. Napier, *The Conquest of Scinde* (1846).

A.G. Nasser, *The Philosophy of Revolution* (Cairo, n.d.).

Naval Documents of the American Revolution, I, ed. W.B. Clark (Washington, DC, 1964).

M.S. Navias, 'Terminating Conscription? The British National Service Controversy, 1955–56', *JCont.H*, 24 (1989).

_____, *Nuclear Weapons and British Strategic Planning* (Oxford, 1991).

H. Neatby, 'C.J.W. Smith, an Eighteenth-Century Whig Imperialist', *CHR*, 27 (1947).

C.W. Newbury and A.S. Kanya-Forstner, 'French Policy and the Origins of the Scramble for West Africa', *JAH*, 10 (1969).

H. Nicolson, *Letters and Diaries, 1945–1961*, ed. N. Nicolson (1968).

R. Nixon, *The Memoirs of Richard M. Nixon* (New York, 1990 ed.).

K. Nkrumah, *The Autobiography of Kwame Nkrumah* (1957).

D. Norman ed., *Nehru: The First Sixty Years* (2 volumes, 1965).

D. Norris, 'Caspian Naval Expedition, 1918–1919', *JRCAS*, 10 (1923).

B.B. O'Brian, 'Empire v. National Interests in Australian-British Relations during the 1930s', *AHS*, 22 (1986–89).

P.K. O'Brian, 'Public Finance and the War with France', in ed. Dickinson, *Britain and the French Revolution*.

J. Ochterlony, *The Chinese War* (1844).

M. O'Dwyer, *India as I Knew It* (1926 ed.).
Official History of Operations in Somaliland, 1901–1904 (2 vols, 1907).
Oh Canada: A Medley of Stories, Verses, Pictures and Music Contributed by Members of the Canadian Expeditionary Force (1916).
The Old World and the New Society (Labour Party, 1942).
R. Oliver, 'The Two Miss Perhams', *JICH*, 19 (1991).
Orderly Books of the Fourth New York Regiment, 1778–1780 and the Second New York Regiment, 1780–1783 (Albany, NY, 1932).
R. Orme, *A History of the Military Transactions of the British Nation in Indostan from the Year MDCCXLV* (2 vols, 1763).
G. Orwell, *Collected Essays, Journalism and Letters of George Orwell*, III, *As I Please, 1943–1945*, ed. S. Orwell and I. Angus (1968).
R. Ovendale ed., *The Foreign Policy of the British Labour Governments, 1945–1951* (Leicester, 1984).

M. Page, 'The War of *Thangata*: Nyasaland in the East African Campaign, 1914–1918', *JAH*, 19 (1978).
T. Pakenham, *The Scramble for Africa* (1991).
A. Palmer, 'Black American Soldiers in Trinidad, 1942–44: Wartime Politics in a Colonial Society', *JICH*, 14 (1986).
R. Pares, *A West India Fortune* (1950).
M Pawson and D. Bussett, *Port Royal, Jamaica* (Oxford, 1975).
R.H. Pearce, *Savagism and Civilisation: A Study of the Indian and the American Mind* (Baltimore, 1977).
G. Pearson, *Hooligan: A History of Respectable Fears* (1983).
J.B. Peires, '"Soft" Believers and "Hard" Unbelievers in Xhosa Cattle-Killing', *JAH*, 27 (1986).
M. Perham, *Lugard: The Years of Adventure, 1858–1898* (1956).
F.W. Perry, *The Commonwealth Armies: Manpower and Organisation in two World Wars* (Manchester, 1988).
M. Peters, *Pitt and Popularity: The Prime Minister and London Opinion during the Seven Years War* (Oxford, 1980).
J.M. Phillips, *Jamaica: its Past and Present* (1843).
T. Phillips, 'The New Africa: The Need for New Forms of Government', *Nineteenth Century and After*, 182 (1937).
J.W. Pickersill, *The Mackenzie King Record*, I (1939–1944) (Chicago, 1960).
B. Pimlott, *Harold Wilson* (1992).
D.C.M. Platt, 'Economic Factors and British Policy during the "New Imperialism"', *PP*, 32 (1968).
W. Platt, 'East African Forces in the War and their Future', *RUSI*, 93 (1948).
A.W. Pollock, 'The Government and the Army', *Fortnightly Review*, New Series, 95 (January–June, 1914).
C. Ponting, *1940: Myth and Reality* (1990).
A. Porter, 'The South African War (1899–1902): Context and Motive Reconsidered', *JAH*, 31 (1990).
P. Porter, 'The Exotic as Erotic: Captain Cook in Tahiti', in ed. G.S. Rousseau and R. Porter, *Exoticism in the Enlightenment*.
B. Prasad, *Defence of India: Policy and Plans* (Cawnpore, 1965) (Official History of the Indian Armed Forces in the Second World War, 1939–1945).
N. Pronay and D.W. Spring ed., *Propaganda, Politics and Film, 1918–1945* (1982).

N. Pronay, 'The Political Censorship of Films in Britain before the War', in ed. Pronay and Spring, *Propaganda, Politics and Film, 1918–1945*.
V. Purcell, *The Boxer Uprising: A Background Study* (Cambridge, 1963).

A. Al-Qazzaz, 'The Iraqi-British War of 1941', *IJMES*, 7 (1976).
D.B. Quinault, 'Churchill and Australia: The Military Relationship, 1899–1945, *WS*, 6 (1988).
D.B. Quinn, 'James I and the Beginnings of Empire', *JICH*, 2 (1974).

Sir Walter Raleigh, *The Discovery of the Large, Rich and Beautiful Empire of Guiana*, ed. R.H. Schomberg (Hakluyt Society, 1848).
D. Read ed., *The Great War and Canadian Society* (Toronto, 1978).
The Records of the Virginia Company of London, ed. S.M. Kingsbury (3 vols, Washington DC, 1933).
Report of the Select Committee on Ceylon and British Guiana (1849).
Report of the Jamaica Royal Commission, 1866 (1866).
J. Richards, *The Age of the Dream Palace: Cinema and Society in Britain, 1930–1939* (1984).
J. Richards and A. Aldgate, *Best of British: Cinema and Society 1930–1970* (Oxford, 1983).
G. Rizvi, *Linlithgow and India: A Study of British Policy and the Political Impasse in India*, 1936–1943 (1978).
W.R. Rock, *Chamberlain and Roosevelt: British Foreign Policy and the United States, 1937–1940* (Columbia, Ohio, 1988).
Lord Ronaldshay, *The Life of Lord Curzon* (3 vols, 1928).
N.A.M. Rodger, *The Wooden World: An Anatomy of the Georgian Navy* (1986).
S. Roskill, *Naval Policy Between the Wars* (2 vols, 1976).
J.H.S. Ross, *Royal New Zealand Air Force* (Official History of New Zealand in the Second World War) (Auckland, 1955).
P.T. Ross, *A Yeoman's Letters* (Hastings, 1901).
R.I. Rotberg, 'Resistance and Rebellion in British Nyasaland and German East Africa, 1888–1915', in ed. Gifford and Louis, *Britain and Germany in Africa*.
G.S. Rousseau and R. Porter, *Exoticism in the Enlightenment* (Manchester, 1988).
T. Royle, *The Last Days of the Raj* (1989).
D. Rule, *The Pursuit of Progress: A Study of the Intellectual Development of Romesh Chander Dutt, 1848–1888* (Calcutta, 1977).
S. Runciman, *The White Rajahs: A History of Sarawak from 1841 to 1946* (Cambridge, 1960).

B. Sacks, *J. Ramsay MacDonald in Thought and Action* (Albuquerque, 1952).
A. Al-Sadat, *In Search of an Identity: An Autobiography* (1978).
P.M. Sales, 'W.H. Hughes and the Chanak Crisis of 1922', *AJPH* 17 (1971).
J. Salmon, 'The Air Force in Iraq', *RUSI*, 70 (1925).
S. Sandber, 'Homefront Battlefront: Racial Disturbances in the Zone of the Interior, 1941–1945', *WS, 11, ii (1993)*.
G.N. Sanderton, 'The Origins and Significance of the Anglo-French Confrontation at Fashoda, 1898', in ed. Gifford and Louis, *Britain and France in Africa*.
J.E. Seely, *Adventures* (1930).
The Crisis of British Power: The Imperial and Naval Papers of the Second Earl of Selbourne, 1885–1910, ed. D.G. Boyne (1990).

F. Selous, *Sunshine and Storm in Rhodesia* (1896).

Y. Shaffy, 'Unconcern at Dawn, Surprise at Sunset: Egyptian Intelligence Appreciation before the Sinai Campaign, 1956', *Intelligence and National Security*, 5 (1990).

J. Sherer, *The Gold-Finder in Australia: How he went, how he fared and how he made his Fortune* (1853).

R.B. Sheridan, 'The Jamaica Slave Insurrection Scare of 1776 and the American Revolution', *Journal of Negro History*, 3 (1978).

E. Shuckburgh, *Descent to Suez: Diaries, 1951–1956* (1986).

L. Simon, *Journal of a Tour and Residence in Great Britain during the years 1810 and 1811* (2 vols, Edinburgh, 1815).

G. Smith, *The Empire: A Series of Letters Published in 'The Daily News', 1862, 1863* (1863).

R. Smith, *14,000 Miles Through the Air* (1922).

R. Smith, 'Britain's African Colonies and British Propaganda during the Second World War', *JICH*, 14 (1985).

Historic Memoirs from 12 July 1776 to 25 July 1778 of William Smith, ed. W.H.W. Sabine (New York, 1958).

T. Smollett, *Continuation of the Complete History of England* (5 vols, 1763–67).

The Letters of Tobias Smollett, ed. L.M. Knapp (Oxford, 1970).

Selections from the Papers of Jan Smuts, ed. J. v. der Poel, 6 (Cambridge, 1973).

D. Sonden, 'Rogues, Whores and Vagabonds? Indentured Servant Emigrants to North America and the Case of Mid-Eighteenth-Century Bristol', *JSH*, 3 (1978).

D. Spadadora, *The Idea of Progress in Eighteenth-Century Britain* (Yale, 1990).

E.M. Spiers, *The Army and Society, 1815–1914* (1980).

D. Spinney, *Rodney* (1969).

——, 'Rodney and the Saintes: A Re-assessment', *MM*, 68 (1982).

J.O. Springhall, 'Lord Meath, Youth and Empire', *JCont.H*, 5 (1970).

——, 'Baden-Powell and the Scout Movement before 1920: Citizen Training and Soldiers of the Future', *EHR*, 102 (1987).

Statistics of the Military Effort of the British Empire during the Great War, 1914–1920 (1922).

A.G. Steel and R.H. Lyttleton, *Cricket* (Badminton Library, 1888).

R. Stephens, *Nasser: A Political Biography* (1971).

H. Stewart, *The New Zealand Divisions, 1916–1919* (Auckland, 1921).

E. Stirling, *Some Considerations of the Political State of the Intermediate Countries between Persia and India* (1835).

E. Stokes, *The English Utilitarians and India* (Oxford, 1959).

——, *The Peasant Armed: The Indian Revolt of 1857* (Oxford, 1986).

A. Summers, 'Militarism in Britain before the Great War', *History Workshop*, 2 (1976).

——, 'Scouts, Guides, and VADs: A note in reply to Allen Warren', *EHR*, 102 (1987).

R. Swinhoe, *Narrative of the North China Campaign of 1860* (1861).

D. Syrett, 'The Methodology of British Amphibious Operations during the Seven Years and American Wars', *MM*, 58 (1972).

Viscount Templewood (Sir Samuel Hoare), *Empire of the Air: The Advent of the Air Age, 1922–1929* (1957).

J.J. Terry, *The Wafd, 1919–1952* (1982).

G. Thayer, *The British Political Fringe* (1965).

J. Thomson, *Through Masai Land* (1885).

M. Thomson, 'A Year Round in Northern Nigeria', *Blackwoods Magazine*, 175 (May 1909).

C. Thorne, *Allies of a Kind: The United States, Britain and the War against Japan* (Oxford, 1978 ed.).

R.L. Tignor, 'Decolonisation and Business: The Case of Egypt', *JMH*, 59 (1987).

H. Tinker, 'India in the First World War and After', *JCont.H*, 4 (1968).

M.E. Townsend, *The Rise and Fall of Germany's Colonial Empire, 1884–1914* (New York, 1966).

N. Townsend, 'Moulding Minds: The School Paper in Queensland, 1905 to 1920', *JRAHS*, 75 (1989–90).

C. Townshend, *The British Campaign in Ireland, 1919–1921: The Developments of Political and Military Policies* (Oxford, 1975).

_____, 'Martial Law: Legal and Administrative Problems of Civil Emergencies in Britain and the Empire', *HJ*, 25 (1982).

_____, 'The Defence of Palestine: Insurrection and Public Security, 1936–1939', *EHR*, 103 (1988).

N. Tracy, 'British Assessments of French and Spanish Naval Reconstruction', *MM*, 61 (1975).

_____, *Navies, Deterrence and American Independence: British Seapower in the 1760s and 1770s* (Vancouver, 1988).

B.G. Trigger, 'Early Native American Response to European Contact: Romantic versus Rationalistic Interpretation', *Journal of American History*, 77 (1990–91).

A. Trotter, *Britain and East Asia, 1933–1937* (Cambridge, 1975).

J.S. Tucker ed., *Memoirs of Admiral the Right Honourable, the Earl of St Vincent* (2 vols, 1844).

J. Turner, *British Politics and the Great War: Coalition and Conflict, 1915–1918* (1992).

G. Vancouver, *A Voyage of Discovery to the North Pacific Ocean and Round the World, 1791–1795*, ed. W. Kaye Lamb (Hakluyt Society, 4 vols, 1984).

C. Van Onselen, 'The 1912 Wankie Colliery Strike', *JAH*, 15 (1974).

R. Vansittart, *The Mist Procession: The Autobiography of Lord Vansittart* (1958).

The Narrative of General Venables, ed. C.H. Firth (Camden Society, 1900).

A. Vinogradov, 'The 1920 Revolt in Iraq Reconsidered: the role of Tribes and National Politics', *IJMES*, 3 (1972).

M. Volodarsky, 'Persia's Foreign Policy between the two Herat Crises', *MES*, 21 (1985).

F.B. Vrooman, 'The Imperial Idea: From the Point of View of Vancouver', *Nineteenth Century and After*, 73 (1913).

F. Waite, *The New Zealanders at Gallipoli* (Official History of New Zealand's Effort in the War) (Auckland, 1921).

A.J, Ward, *Ireland in Anglo-American Relations*, 1899–1922 (1969).

F.R. Ward, *British West Indian Slavery: The Process of Amelioration* (Oxford, 1989).

A. Warren, 'Sir Robert Baden-Powell, the Scout Movement and Citizen Training in Britain, 1900–1920', *EHR*, 101 (1986).

B. Wasserstein, *Britain and the Jews of Europe, 1939–1945* (Oxford, 1979).

F. Watson, 'India Returned', *Life and Letters*, 49 (1946).

D. Cameron Watt, 'Britain, the United States and the Opening of the Cold War', in ed. Ovendale, *The Foreign Policy of the British Labour Governments, 1945–1951*.

I. Watts, *The Psalms and Hymns of the Reverend Isaac Watts, DD* ed. E. Williams (Doncaster, 1805).

Lord Wavell, *The Viceroy's Journal* (1973).

S.S. Webb, 'William Blathwayt, Imperial Fixer: From Popish Plot to Glorious Revolution', *WMQ*, 25 (1968).

——, 'Army and Empire: English Garrison Government in Britain and the Americas, 1569 to 1763', *WMQ*, 34 (1977).

S. Webb, 'Lord Rosebery's Escape from Houndsditch', *Nineteenth Century and After*, 50 (1901).

D. Wellesley, *Sir George Goldie: Founder of Nigeria* (1934).

We Shall Win Through (Conservative Party, 1952).

J. Wells, *Stewart of Lovedale: The Life of James Stewart* (1901).

West India Colonies and Mauritius: Immigration, I: British Guiana, Jamaica and Trinidad (House of Commons Papers, 1859).

A. Carton de Wiart, *Happy Odyssey* (1950).

G.R. Wilkinson, 'Soldiers by Instinct and Training: The *Daily Mail* and the Image of the Warrior, 1899–1914', *Newspaper and Periodical Society*, 8 (1992).

B.P. Willan, 'The South African Native Labour Contingent', *JAH*, 19 (1978).

H. Williamson, *Donkey Boy* (1962).

B. Wilson, *The Life and Letters of James Wolfe* (1909).

K.M. Wilson, *Empire and Conflict: Studies in British Foreign Policy from the 1880s to the First World War* (1987).

——, 'The Anglo-Japanese Alliance of August 1905 and the Defending of India: A Case of the Worst Scenario', *JICH*, 21 (1993).

The Papers of Woodrow Wilson 45 (1917–1918) (Princeton, NJ, 1984).

J.M. Winter, 'The Webbs and the Non-White World: a Case of Socialist Racism', *JCont.H*, 9 (1974).

L.B. Wright, *Religion and Empire: The Alliance between Piety and Commerce in English Expansion, 1558–1625* (Chapel Hill, North Carolina, 1943).

P. Wright, *Spycatcher* (New York, 1987).

H.F. Wyatt, 'The Cause of National Insecurity', *Nineteenth Century and After*, 71 (1912).

Lord Wylloughby de Broke, 'National Toryism', *National Review*, 59 (1912).

A.C. Yate, 'Britain's Buffer States in the East', *JRCAS*, 5 (1918).

P.J. Yearwood, 'Great Britain and the Repartition of Africa', *JICH*, 18 (1990).

G. Younghusband, *Forty Years a Soldier* (1923).

P. Ziegler, *Mountbatten* (1985).

——, *King Edward VIII: The Official Biography* (1990).

Notes

Part One: Excellent Opportunities: 1600–89

1: My New-Found Land: North America

1 Andrews, 39, 81–2.
2 *The Historye of the Bermudas or Somers Islands*, 35–6.
3 Kupperman, 'Fear of Hot Climates &c.', *WMQ*, 41, 218.
4 Monson, 2, 289.
5 *CSP, America and the West Indies, 1574–1660*, 25.
6 Sondem, 'Rogues, Whores &c.', *JSH*, 3, *passim*.
7 Raleigh, 115.

2: Baubles for the Souls of Men: The West and East Indies

1 *Documents Concerning English Voyages to the Spanish Main*, 120–21, 127–8.
2 Kupperman, 'The Puzzle of the American Climate &c.', *AHR*, 87, 1266.
3 Buckley, 'The Destruction of the British Army &c.', *JSAHR*, 56. *passim*.
4 Venables, 42, 7.
5 Beckles, 'A "riotous and unruly lot" &c.', *WMQ*, 47, 519–21.
6 HMC, *Stuart*, III, 304–5.
7 *CSP, America and the West Indies, 1661–1668*, 167.
8 *Ibid., 1681–1685*, 25.
9 Phillips, 363.
10 F.R. Ward, 26–7.
11 Handler and Corruccini, *JIDH*, 14, *passim*.
12 Bowrey, 3, 5, 11.

3: The Necessary Union of Plantations: Crown and Colonies

1 Gregg, 'Shipmasters &c.', *MM*, 77, 107.
2 Hornstein, 19–21.
3 Venables, 109.
4 *CSP, America and the West Indies, 1661–1668*, 281–2.
5 *Ibid.*, 22–3.
6 *Ibid., 1675–1676*, 498.
7 *Ibid.*, 476–7.
8 *Ibid., 1689–1693*, 110.
9 *Ibid., 1700*, 217.
10 PRO, CO 23/23, 28.

4: Dispositions of Providence: The Colonists

1 M. Green, 81.
2 Jordan, 65.
3 *CSP, America and the West Indies, 1675–1676*, 526.
4 Fischer, 229.
5 Carr and Walsh, 'The Planter's Wife &c.', *WMQ*, 34,543.
6 Cressy, *Coming Over*, 71.
7 *Ibid.*, 117.
8 *Ibid.*, 97.
9 *CSP, America and the West Indies, 1661–1668*, 145.
10 Isaacs, 39–40.
11 *CSP, America and the West Indies, 1689–1692*, 666–73, 732–4.
12 *Ibid.*, 316; Hart, 2, 21.
13 Jordan, 109–10.
14 Gaspar, 'The Antigua Conspiracy &c.', *WMQ*, 35, 322.
15 N.L.S., Colin Campbell, 'The Voyage of the Unicorn', 29 September 1698.
16 *CSF, America and the West Indies, 1675–1676*, 205.
17 Mun, 3.
18 *Hudson's Bay Miscellany, 1670–1870, passim.*
19 *Hudson's Bay Company, Letters Outward, 1638–1696*, 131.

Part Two: Persist and Conquer, 1689–1815

1: Rule of the Main: The Making of British Seapower, 1689–1748

1 Crouzet, 'The Sources of England's Wealth &c.', in ed. Cottrell and Aldcroft, *Shipping, Trade and Commerce*, 71.
2 *PRO*, Adm 1/3962, I, 149.
3 McNeill, 167.
4 Burdett, 305, 320–21.
5 Marcus, I, 220–21.
6 *The History of the House of Commons from the Restoration to the Present Time*, 12, 15.
7 *Ibid.*, 65.
8 SRO, Clerk of Penicuik, GD 18/4181.
9 *The History of the Proceedings of the Third Parliament of King George II held in the Years 1741 and 1742*, 2, 304.

2: Tis to Glory we Steer: Gains and Losses, 1749–83

1 Rodger, chapter V, *passim*.
2 Lemisch, 'Jack Tar in Streets &c.,' *WMQ*, 25, 383.
3 Rodger, 85–7.
4 Boscawen, 205.
5 T. Hansard, *The Parliamentary History of England from the Earliest Period to the Year 1803*, 15, 1266–7.
6 Jenkins, 125–7.
7 PRO, Adm 1/54.
8 Smollett, *Continuation of the Complete History of England*, II, 115.
9 Smollett, *Letters*, 87.

10 Spadafora, 220.
11 *Gentleman's Magazine,* 29, 585.
12 *Ibid,* 587.
13 J. Brown, 35–6, 62, 74, 88–9.
14 Watts, No. 454.
15 Smollett, *Continuation of the Complete History of England,* I, 480.
16 PRO, Adm 1/3946, 157, 193; Tracy, 12 ff.
17 PRO, Adm 1/3836, 63, 108–9, 188.
18 Tracy, 29.
19 PRO, Adm 1/3966, 1, 140–41, 186–7, 266, 296–8.
20 SRO, Logan Hume, GD1/384.
21 Spinney, 'Rodney and the Saints &c.', *MM,* 68, 381–2, 338.
22 Clowes, 3, 467.

3: *The Empire of America: Settlement and War, 1689–1775*

1 Nammack, xv.
2 *Ibid.,* 43.
3 Leach, 146–7.
4 *Documents of the American Revolution,* 7, 91.
5 M.G. Lawson, *passim.*
6 *Northcliffe Collection,* 73.
7 McCardell, 161.
8 Syrett, 'The Methodology of British Operations &c.', *MM,* 68, *passim.*
9 B. Wilson, 353.
10 HMC, *Stopford-Sackville,* II, 226.
11 N. Martin, 'A Different Kind of Courage &c.', *CHR,* 70, 58.
12 B. Wilson, 379–80.
13 HMC, *Stopford-Sackville,* II, 264.
14 *Northcliffe Collection,* 81.
15 Bailyn and De Wolfe, 53.
16 *Ibid.,* 41.
17 R.M. Brown, 6–7.
18 Nammack, 89–90.

4: *The Descendants of Britons: North America Rebels, 1765–75*

1 PRO, CO 227/2, 3d.
2 NLS, Stuart Stevenson, Ms 5375, 31d; Berger, 55.
3 SRO, Peebles Diary, GD 21/492/3, 15.
4 SRO, Robertson Papers, GD 172/2599, 26.
5 *Documents of the American Revolution,* 9, 75.
6 *Papers of Benjamin Franklin,* 17, 268–9.
7 SRO, Peebles Diary, GD, 21/492/3, 14.
8 Isaacs, 162.
9 Flick, 9.
10 *Documents of the American Revolution,* 9, 107.
11 *Ibid.,* 2, 50.
12 *Ibid.,* 9, 60.
13 Grainger, 67.
14 *Naval Documents of the American Revolution,* 1, 27.

5: The World Turned Upside Down: The American War of Independence, 1775–83

1 *Documents of the American Revolution*, 9, 60.
2 Cowper, 569–70.
3 *Naval Documents of the American Revolution*, 1, 125.
4 *Documents of the American Revolution*, 9, 65.
5 NLS, Stuart Stevenson, Ms 5375, 31d.
6 Clinton, 569.
7 Conway, 'British Army Officers &c.', *WMQ*, 41, 375.
8 Barker, 'The Diary of Lieutenant John Barker', *JSAHR*, 7, 101.
9 SRO, Peebles Diary, GD 21/492/11, 6.
10 Conway, 'The Recruitment of Criminals &c.', *BIHR*, 58, 380–81.
11 Attwood, 233, 238.
12 HMC, *Hastings*, III, 167, 169.
13 SRO, Peebles Diary, GD 21/492/3, 12.
14 Clinton, 56.
15 Berger, 27.
16 NLS, Stuart Stevenson, Ms 5375, 30–30d.
17 Kaplan, 'The Hidden War &c.', *WMQ*, 47, 122–3.
18 W. Smith, 39.
19 Clinton, 62, note 7.
20 Gruber, 233, 238–9.
21 SRO, Robertson, GD 172/2599, 52.
22 Berger, 91.
23 *Ibid.*, 100–1.
24 SRO, Peebles Diary, GD 21/492, 4, 9.

6: The Terror of Our Arms: Conquest and Trade in India, 1689–1815

1 SRO, Dalrymple, GD 110/1021, 4.
2 Stokes, *The Peasant and the Raj*, 26.
3 Orme, I, 265.
4 Chauduri, 232.
5 *Ibid.*, 97.
6 SRO, Seaforth, GD 46/17/4, 512.
7 NAM, Memoirs of a Dragoon, 60–61, 65.
8 Blakiston, 1, 229–30.
9 Malcolm, I, 51, note, 208, 259.
10 SRO, Seaforth, GD 46/17/4, 434–9, 448, 532.
11 Malcolm, I, 8.
12 PRO, Adm 2/5119.
13 Altick, 299–300.
14 NLS, Tweeddale, Ms 14558, 18d.
15 Metcalfe, I, 54.
16 NLS, Stuart, Ms 8252, 63.
17 PRO, WO 3/610, 163–4.
18 *AJ*, 1, (1816), 66.
19 Kaye, I, 93.
20 *AJ*, 1 (1816), 145–6.
21 Kaye, I, 29.

22 Malcolm, I, 23.
23 *Ibid.*, 269.
24 PRO, WO 1/902, 174.
25 Doveton, 'Companies Troops &c.', *AJ,* New Series, 1 (1843), 651.
26 PRO, WO 1/343, 56, 71–5.

7: *The Desert of Waters: The Pacific and Australasia*

1 Vancouver, I, 34.
2 Gough, 2n.
3 Vancouver, I, 44.
4 Bligh, 6–7.
5 R. Porter, in ed. R. Porter, *Exoticism and Enlightenment,* 126–7.
6 *Quarterly Review,* 2 (1811), 52.
7 *Ibid.,* 33.
8 Anon, 'Review of R. Perceval &c.', *Edinburgh Review,* 3, 31.
9 Lang, I, 119.
10 *House of Commons Select Papers of the Eighteenth Century . . . Quebec and New South Wales, 1791–1792,* 119.
11 PRO, CO 201/11, 11–12.
12 Lieutenant Collins, xi–xiii.
13 Anon, 'A Convict's Recollections', *London Magazine,* 2, 51.
14 PRO, CO 201/11, 9–10.
15 *Ibid.,* 49, 105.
16 *Ibid.,* 9–10.
17 Anon, *A Concise History of the English Colony in New South Wales,* xvi.
18 PRO, WO 92/1, 13; CO 201/11, 11.
19 Lang, 1, 119.

8: *Wealth and Victory: The Struggle against France, 1793 1815*

1 *Anti-Jacobin,* 9 April 1798.
2 P.K. O'Brien, in ed. Dickinson, *Britain and the French Revolution, passim.*
3 T. Hansard, *The Parliamentary History of England from the Earliest Time to the Year 1803,* 35, 1073–4.
4 *Anti-Jacobin,* 25 May 1798.
5 Dalton, 247.
6 Buckley, 'The Destruction of the British Army &c.', *JSAHR,* 56, *passim.*
7 PRO, CO 318/31, 141, 152, 153.
8 PRO, Adm 1/265.
9 NLS, Cochrane, Ms 2315, 21–2.
10 PRO, Adm 54/1.
11 PRO, Adm 1/4366.
12 PRO, Adm 1/3994.
13 HMC, *Bathurst,* 672.
14 De Latocnaye, 100–101, 112, 166, 311.
15 Dickinson, in ed. Dickinson, *Britain and the French Revolution, passim.*
16 *Anti-Jacobin,* 1 January 1798.
17 Simond, I, 21.
18 *Blackwoods Magazine,* 6 (February 1820), 578.
19 NAM, Memoirs of a Dragoon, 90.
20 Denman, 39.

Part Three: Wider Still and Wider: 1815–1914

1: Power and Greatness: Commerce, Seapower and Strategy, 1815–70

1 Desmond and Moore, 176–7.
2 Livingstone, 293.
3 NAM, Pine, 18 July 1844; August, no date.
4 Cam and Hopkins, 'The Political Economy &c.', *Ec.HR*, 33, 476.
5 PRO, Adm 1/221, 579.
6 HMC, *Bathurst*, 535–6.
7 Bartlett, 261–2.
8 PRO, Adm 1/5603.
9 PRO, Adm 1/5548; FO 406/8, 152.
10 PRO, Adm 127/58.
11 PRO, Adm 125/43.
12 *Hansard,* 3rd Series, 111, 301.
13 *Ibid.,* 144, 1823–4, 1830.
14 PRO, Adm 53/10269; Clowes, 6, 235–7, 239–43.
15 PRO, Adm 123/10.
16 G Smith, ix.
17 Bartlett, 23.
18 *British and Foreign Review,* 1 (July–October 1835), 102–3.
19 Anon, *India, Great Britain and Russia,* 48.
20 Maw, 106.
21 Anon, 'The Invasion of India', *Blackwoods Magazine,* 22 (September 1827) *passim.*

2: We are Going as Civilisers: Empire and Public Opinion, 1815–80

1 *Sun,* 2 January 1847.
2 *Standard,* 2 June 1840.
3 Denman, 24.
4 Livingstone, 256–7.
5 Bratton, Cave, Gregory, Holder and Pickering, 131.
6 Heber, I, 33.
7 Anon, *Slavery No Oppression,* 20.
8 *Anti-Jacobin,* 26 (January 1807), 26, 29.
9 *Barbados Report &c..,* 17.
10 HMC, *Bathurst,* 549–50.
11 Anon, *Slavery No Oppression,* 17.
12 Gurney, 61, 184.
13 *British Parliamentary Papers, Colonies General,* 1, 14–15, 75.
14 *West India Colonies and Mauritius &c.,* 21, 309.
15 Binney, 5.
16 *Blackwoods,* 6 (October 1819), 80–81.
17 Wells, 145.
18 PRO, Adm 1/6491.
19 Brooke, II, 323.
20 Altick, 283.
21 Wells, 158–9.
22 *The Standard,* 10 January 1840; 24 March 1840.
23 *Illustrated London News,* 13 March 1852.

24 Burn, 84.
25 *National Review,* (January 1858), 17.
26 *Report of the Jamaica Royal Commission,* 1122.
27 *Quarterly Review,* 120, (July 1866), 257, 259.
28 Guy, *The Destruction of the Zulu Kingdom,* 62.
29 *The Witness,* 18 January 1865.

3: The Mission of Our Race: Britain and the 'New Imperialism', 1880–1902

1 PRO, Adm 123/10.
2 Platt, 'Economic Factors &c.,' *PP,* 39, 131.
3 Williamson, *Donkey Boy,* 46–7, 48.
4 A. Porter, 'The South African War &c.', JAH, 31, 41.
5 MacDonald, 'Reproducing the Middle-Class Boy &c.', *JCont.H,* 24, 528.
6 *Saturday Review,* 82 (12 December 1896).
7 *Ibid.*
8 MacDonald, 'Reproducing the Middle-Class Boy &c.', *JCont.H,* 24, 526.
9 Henty, *With Buller in Natal,* 12, 15, 33.
10 Childers, 19.
11 *Practical Teacher,* 16 (June 1896).
12 *Daily Graphic,* 7 October 1898.
13 Friedberg, 273, 275.
14 *Ibid.,* 403.
15 Buchanan, 'The Voice of the Hooligan', *Contemporary Review,* 76,775–6.

4: The Miracle of the World: India, 1815–1905

1 Bratton, Cave, Gregory, Holder and Pickering, 170.
2 Gopal, 224.
3 *Ibid.,* 225.
4 ed. Eldridge, 76, 80.
5 Edwardes, I, 723.
6 Stokes, *English Utilitarians and India,* 54.
7 *Ibid.,* 46.
8 *Edinburgh Review,* 217 (January 1858), 46.
9 *National Review,* 16 (January 1858), 20.
10 Heber, 1, 165.
11 Griffiths, 167–71.
12 *AJ,* 1, (February 1816), 113.
13 Heber, 1, 235.
14 Kaye, *Lives of the Indian Officers,* I, 414, note; Hyam, 'Empire and Sexuality &c.', *JICH,* 14, 38, 52.
15 *Ibid.,* 52.
16 *AJ,* 23, (May-August 1837), 134.
17 NLS, Sir George Brown, Ms 2845, 17.
18 NLS, James Grant, Ms 17904, 7.
19 Napier, 307–8.
20 NLS, Sir George Brown, Ms 2845, 67.
21 'The Battle of Chillianwala', *Colburn's United Service Magazine,* 3, (1850), 1.
22 Maw, 70–71.

23 Doveton, 'The Bangalore Conspiracy', *AJ,* 3rd Series, 2 (1844), 631–3; NLS, Tweeddale, Ms 145558, 3, 13, 15–15d, 18d.
24 Stokes, *The Peasant Armed,* 229.
25 Bourchier, 95.
26 Wolseley, 1, 420.
27 Edmondson, 3.
28 Rule, 22.
29 O'Dwyer, 12.
30 Younghusband, 5.
31 Willcocks, 72.
32 Mason, *Expedition against the Hansanzai and Asakai Tribes,* 20.
33 IOL, Letters and Papers Political Military, 17/13/64.

5: They Little Know Our Strength: The Far East and the Pacific

1 *Chamber's Information for the People,* No. 25 (1842), 398–9.
2 Ochterlony, 99, 398.
3 NAM, Pine, 26 August 1841.
4 *Ibid.,* 5 June 1842.
5 PRO, Adm 125/145.
6 Moyes was actually Scottish (Mann, 73–4).
7 Swinhoe, 193.
8 *Hansard,* 4th Series, 79, 46.
9 PRO, Adm 125/146, 3–9.
10 PRO, Adm 1/7459.
11 M.E. Townsend, *The Rise and Fall of Germany's Colonial Empire,* 197, 266.
12 PRO, Adm 1/7549.
13 PRO, CO 856/1 (Reports for 1921, 1922 and 1932).

6: A Great English-Speaking Country: South Africa

1 PRO, WO 1/343, 57.
2 Marder, *From Dreadnought to Scapa Flow,* 41.
3 PRO, WO 33/37, 2.
4 PRO, WO, 33/46.
5 NLS, Sir George Brown, Ms 2846, 17d, 159.
6 *Ibid.,* 19d.
7 NAM, Fleming, 14–15, 31.
8 Peires, 'Soft Believers &c.', *JAH,* 27, 445.
9 PRO, WO 32/8329–31.
10 Guy, 'A Note on Firearms &c.', *JAH,* 12, 560–63.
11 Guy, *The Destruction of the Zulu Kingdom,* 47.
12 Bourne, *Listener,* 30 December 1935.
13 Guy, *The Destruction of the Zulu Kingdom,* 57.
14 Killingray, 'Labour Exploitation &c.', *JCont.H,* 24, 488.
15 PRO, WO 33/256.
16 Selbourne, 75.
17 I am indebted to Dr John Mackenzie for this detail.
18 *Saturday Review,* 29 August 1896.
19 Selous, 20.
20 NAM, Rose, 4 August 1896.

21 *Hansard,* 4th Series, 39, 1174–5, 1518; 40, 1137–8; 41, 1326–7.
22 Rotberg, 'Resistance and Rebellion &c.', in ed. Giffard and W.R. Louis, *Britain and Germany in Africa,* 673.
23 Von Albertini, 467.
24 W.H. Brown, *On the South African Frontier,* 420.
25 Von Albertini, 469.
26 PRO, DPP 1/2, 681 ff.; SRO, Loch, GD 268/576/15, 4–5.
27 *Ibid.,* 6.
28 Selbourne, 78.
29 R. Porter, 'The South African War &c.', *JAH,* 31, 43.
30 Anon (P. Sturrock), 25.
31 Ross, 180–81.

7: *That Heroic Soul: The Struggle for the Nile*

1 A.G. Hopkins, 'The Victorians and Africa &c.', *JAH,* 27, 384.
2 *Hansard,* 3rd Series, 272, 178.
3 Lord Cromer, *Modern Egypt;* Lord Milner, *England in Egypt.*
4 Gregory, 'Egypt and the Sudan', *Nineteenth Century,* 17, 425–6, 428.
5 W.S. Blunt, *Secret History of the English Occupation of Egypt.*
6 PRO, WO 32/6383.
7 Holt, 80–81.
8 SRO, Dundonald, GD 233/130, 8.
9 *Ibid.*
10 Beresford, II, 271.
11 Johnson, 'The Death of General Gordon &c.', *JAH,* 10, 294–5.
12 Sanderson, 'Anglo-French Confrontation at Fashoda, 1898', in ed. Giffard and W.R. Louis, *France, Britain and Africa,* 309.
13 *Ibid.,* 309.
14 Daly, 1.
15 I am indebted to Samuel Clayton, whose father, Sir Gilbert Clayton, was present at Omdurman and the capture of Khartoum.
16 Daly, 3–4.
17 *Hansard,* 4th Series, 66, 385–7, 393, 396, 398.
18 Daly, 8.
19 *Ibid.,* 183, 184.
20 *Ibid.,* 130.
21 Collins, 139.
22 Daly, 132–3.
23 PRO, Air 20/680.
24 Collins, 134.

8: *The Greatest Blessing that Africa has known: East and West Africa*

1 N. Malcolm, 'On Service in Uganda', *Blackwoods Magazine,* 161, 633, 643.
2 Lugard, I, 72, 74.
3 PRO, WO 106/342.
4 Lugard, I, 32–4.
5 Meinertzhagen, 9–10, 179.
6 Lugard, I, 293–4.
7 Mockler-Ferryman, 13, 18, 27–8; Bindloss, 197.

8 Mockler-Ferryman, 3–4.
9 Lugard, II, 651.
10 Mumford, 'Education and Social Adjustment &c.', *Africa*, 2, 148.
11 Meinertzhagen, 32.
12 J. Thompson, 574.
13 Lugard, I, 285.
14 Van Onselen, 'The 1912 Wankie Colliery Strike &c.', *JAH*, 15, 276–7.
15 PRO, Adm 1/8404/450.
16 Cranworth, 240.
17 *Ibid.*, 35, 115.
18 *Ibid.*, 4, 7–8.
19 Duder, 'Settler response &c.', *JICH*, 17, *passim*.
20 W.R. Thompson, 'A Year round &c.', *Blackwoods Magazine*, 175, 649.
21 NAM, Eden, 23.
22 Perham, I, 493–4.
23 *Ibid.*, 680.
24 Willcocks, 101–4.
25 RHL, Abadie, 8.
26 PRO, WO 32/7620.
27 Beddoes, 138–42.
28 RHL, Abadie, 7–8.
29 NAM, Eden, 34.
30 Lovejoy and Hagendorm, 'Revolutionary Mahdism &c.', *JAH*, 31, *passim*.
31 Mockler-Ferryman, 12.

9: Ye Sons of the Southern Cross: The White Dominions

1 J. Mackenzie, 160–61.
2 Atkinson, 5.
3 *First, Second and Third Reports of the Select Committee on Emigration*, 130.
4 PRO, Adm 1/6788.
5 Anon, *Journal of an Excursion to the United States &c.'*, 13.
6 Eddy and Shreuder, 230–31.
7 NAM, Pine, 15 May, 1845.
8 NAM, Mitchell, 13.
9 N. Townsend, 'Moulding Minds &c.', *JRAHS*, 148.
10 Scherer, 10, 350–51.
11 N. Townsend, 'Moulding Minds &c.', *JRAHS*, 155.
12 Bean, I,3–4, 6–7.
13 Steel and Lyttleton, 226–7.
14 Gordon, 187–8.
15 SRO, Loch, GD 268/459, 10–13.
16 Amery, *My Political Life*, I, 37.
17 Gordon, 123.
18 *Hansard*, 3rd Series, 305, 635.
19 *Ibid.*, 1207.
20 Chamberlain, 'A Bill for Weakening Britain', *Nineteenth Century*, 33, 547.
21 Brassey, 'The Diamond Jubilee &c.', *Nineteenth Century*, 42, 3.
22 Bean, I, 3.
23 PRO, WO 108/104.

10: Be Brave, Be Bold, Do Right!: The Edwardian Empire and the People

1 S. Webb, 'Lord Rosebery's Escape &c.', *Nineteenth Century and After*, 50, 369.
2 *Ibid.*, 382.
3 Davin, 'Imperialism and Motherhood', *History Workshop*, 5, 13, 17.
4 Amery, *Diaries*, I, 33.
5 Milner, *Nation and Empire*, 352, 353–4.
6 Hyam, *Empire and Sexuality*, 99–100.
7 Sacks, 399–400.
8 K.O. Morgan, 191.
9 *Hansard*, 5th Series, 9, 992, 998, 1571, 1607, 1622.
10 K.O. Morgan, 198.
11 PRO, WO 106/1417, 9.
12 Spiers, 227.
13 Marder, *Fear God and Dread Nought*, 17.
14 Amery, *Diaries*, I, 35.
15 Pollock, 'The Government and the Army', *Fortnightly Review*, New Series, 95, 789.
16 Wylloughby de Broke, 'National Toryism', *National Review*, 59, 98.
17 J. Mackenzie, 150.
18 Springhall, 'Lord Meath &c.', *JCont.H*, 5, 98.
19 *Empire Day Book*, *passim*.
20 *Practical Teacher*, January 1906.
21 Pearson, 71.
22 *Ibid.*, 56, 70.
23 *Ibid.*, 113–14.
24 Springhall, 'Baden Powell &c.', *EHR*, 939.
25 Harrison, 'For Church &c.', *PP*, 61, 176.
26 Summers, 'Scouts, Guides &c.', *EHR*, 102, 946.
27 Cunningham, 'Soldiers by Instinct', *Journal of the Newspaper and Periodic Society*, 8, 19, 23.
28 Eddy and Shreuder, 47.

11: To Join the Khaki Line: The Empire and the Coming of War

1 Summers, 'Militarism in Britain &c.', *History Workshop*, 2, 120–21.
2 Kennedy, *The Rise of Anglo-German Antagonism*, 376.
3 Lambi, 34, 146.
4 Anon, 'The British and German Fleets', *Fortnightly Review*, New Series, 77, 20.
5 Marder, *Fear God and Dread Nought*, 20; Lambi, 148.
6 *Ibid.*
7 Beatty, 98.
8 K.M. Wilson, 'The Anglo-Japanese Alliance &c.', *JICH*, 21, *passim*.
9 K.M. Wilson, *Empire and Continent*, 153, 155–60.
10 Klein, 'British Intervention in the Persian Revolution', *JMH*, 15, 731, 733, 736.
11 Cohen, 'Mesopotamia &c.', *IJMES*, 9, 173.
12 Beatty, 29.
13 Marder, *Fear God and Dread Nought*, 140.
14 Gowen, 'British Legerdemain &c.', *JMH*, 52, 389 note.
15 Vrooman, 'The Imperial Ideal &c.', *Nineteenth Century and After*, 73, 504.
16 Gowen, 'British Legerdemain &c.', *JMH*, 52, 390–91.

17 Hankey, I, 128–9.
18 *Ibid.*, 132.
19 *Ibid.*, 129.
20 Wyatt, 'The Cause of National Insecurity', *Nineteenth Century and After*, 71, 800.
21 Cohen, 'Mesopotamia &c.', *IJMES*, 9, 176.
22 *Ibid.*, 129.
23 Goldberg, 'The Origins of British–Saudi Relations &c.', *HJ*, 28, 697–8.
24 Marder, *Fear God and Dread Nought*, 375.
25 Beatty, 104.
26 LHC, Edmonds III/8, 8–9.
27 K.M. Wilson, *Empire and Continent*, 149.
28 Bean, I, 16–17.
29 *Ibid.*, 18–19.
30 *Oh Canada: a Medley of Verse*, 48, 62.
31 Page, 'The War of *Thangata* &c.', *JAH*, 19, 88.

Part Four: The Age of Imperialism is Ended: 1914–45

1: E is for Empire for which We Would Die: 1914–18

1 Drew, 13.
2 Killingray, 'Labour Exploitation &c.', *JCont.H.* 24, 485.
3 Page, 'The War of *Thangata* &c.', *JAH*, 19, 94–5.
4 Killingray, 'Repercussions of World War I &c.', *JAH*, 19, 49.
5 Willcocks, 300; G. Martin, 'The Influence of Racial Attitudes &c.', *JICH*, 14, 93.
6 Osuntokun, 97; PRO, CO 318/350.
7 Waite, 62.
8 PRO, WO 33/946, 9762.
9 PRO, WO 33/960, 9961; CO 123/296.
10 *Ibid.*
11 Fuller, 50–51, 161, 167.
12 *Ibid.*, 76.
13 PRO, FO 141/466/1429, I.
14 Greenhut, 'The Imperial Reserve &c.', *JICH*, 14, 106.
15 NLS, Haig, 5 May 1915.
16 G. Martin, 'The Influence of Racial Attitudes &c.', *JICH*, 14, 106.
17 Marder, *Fear God and Dreadnought*, 389.
18 PRO, WO 30/57/69.
19 PRO, Cab 42/11.
20 Osuntokun, 152–3.
21 Busch, 80.
22 Beatty, 393.
23 Vansittart, 168.
24 Amery, *Diaries*, I, 229.
25 *Ibid.*, 134.
26 *Hansard*, 5th Series, 100, 2211.
27 Yate, 'Britain's Buffer States &c.', *JRCAS*, 5, 13.
28 W. Wilson, *Collected Papers*, 45, 552.

29 Amery, *Diaries*, I, 147.
30 Ronaldshay, III, 199.
31 *Statistics of the Military Effort of the British Empire &c.'*, 61–3, 237, 474–8.
32 Malone, 'The New Zealand School Journal &c.', *NZJH*, 7, 22.
33 *Oh Canada: a Medley of Verse*, 62.
34 Read, 98.
35 Fuller, 36.
36 Amery, *Diaries*, I, 229.
37 Page, 'The War of *Thangata* &c.', *JAH*, 19, 78–9.
38 Killingray, 'Labour Exploitation &c.', *JCont.H*. 24, 484.
39 Osuntokun, 45.
40 Willan, 'The South African Labour Contingent &c.', *JAH*, 19, 63–4.
41 L. James, *Mutiny &c.*, 253.
42 Willan, 'The South African Labour Contingent &c.', *JAH* 19, 78–9.
43 PRO, CO 318/350.
44 Gandhi, 14, 428–9.

2: *Clear Out or* Govern: *Troubles, mainly Irish, 1919–39*

 1 PRO, FO 848/2, Balfour to Wingate, 26 March 1919.
 2 *Times*, 16 June 1919.
 3 *Hansard*, 5th Series, 131, 1718.
 4 Jeffery, 161.
 5 PRO, WO 33/699, 9.
 6 Jeffery, 161.
 7 Griffiths, 352–3.
 8 Lockman, 'British Policy towards Egyptian &c.', *IJMES*, 20,276.
 9 PRO, CO 537/1735, 9.
10 PRO, WO 33/5916.
11 PRO, Air 2/125, B11395; WO 33/5916.
12 PRO, Air 8/104, D.1.36.
13 PRO, WO 106/3793, 162Λ.
14 Murphy, 'Walter Long &c.', *IHR*, 25, 95.
15 Jones, *Whitehall Diaries*, III, 49–50; *Crawford Papers*, 422.
16 *Saturday Review*, 28 May 1921.
17 Macready, II, 426, 434.
18 Ash, 257–8, 268.
19 Calwell, II, 241.
20 Jones, *Whitehall Diaries*, III, 61.
21 *Ibid.*, 42.
22 Jeffery, 86.
23 Jones, *Whitehall Diaries*, III, 77.
24 Townshend, *British Campaign &c.*, 186–93.
25 Lawrence, *Letters &c.*, 308, 322.
26 Ward, *Ireland in Anglo-Irish Relations &c.*, 252–4.
27 Jones, *Whitehall Diaries*, III, 74-5.
28 Lawler, 'Ireland from Truce to Treaty &c.', *IHS*, 12, 53–4, 57–8.
29 Gilbert, *Churchill*, IV, (Companion volume, Part 3), 1681, 1685.
30 *Spectator*, 8 October 1928.
31 Jeffery, 93

32 *Ibid.,* 76.
33 Gandhi, 21, 17.
34 Fisher, *Foreign Affairs,* 1, iii, 84.
35 *Hansard,* 5th Series, 150, 144.

3: Their Country's Dignity: Egypt, 1919–42

1 James, *Imperial Warrior,* 203.
2 Stephens, 29.
3 Sadat, 23.
4 PRO, FO 848/2.
5 Amery, *Diaries,* 1, 207.
6 Eg: PRO, FO 371/3714, 53, 98; WO 95/4372, June 1919, Appendix C1.
7 Bishku, 58; PRO, FO 848/5, 77.
8 James, *Imperial Warrior,* 208.
9 PRO, FO 141/825/1132, 14, 16, 52, 65; WO 33/981, 11045; WO 154/164.
10 PRO, FO 141/825/1132, *passim.*
11 PRO, WO 33/981, 11043.
12 *Daily Mail,* 24 August 1920.
13 PRO, FO 141/502/17490, 23A.
14 Brown, *Peasants Against the State &c.,* 239–40.
15 Lloyd, II, 23–4.
16 Charmley, 153.
17 Lloyd, II, 5.
18 Morsy, 'Wartime Policy in Egypt &c.', *MES,* 25, 68, 82.
19 *Ibid.,* 64.
20 Nasser, 13–14.

4: The Haughty Governess: The Middle East, 1919–42

1 Bell, 3–4, 5, 7.
2 *Hansard,* 5th Series, 150, 79–80.
3 *Ibid.,* 97.
4 Jeffery, 60.
5 *Ibid.,* 36.
6 Sykes, 'Persia and the Great War &c.', *JRCAS,* 9, 187.
7 Jeffery, 143; Ironside, 153.
8 A. Wilson, 'Revolt in the Desert', *JRCAS,* 14, 151.
9 PRO, WO 32/1584.
10 PRO, WO 32/9614.
11 Vinogradoff, 'The 1920 Revolt &c.', *IJMES,* 3, 134–6.
12 PRO, WO 95/5214 (15th Sikhs).
13 PRO, WO 32/5191.
14 Jeffery, 153.
15 PRO, Air 8/529.
16 PRO, Air 5/1292, Operational Summaries, 1932.
17 PRO, Air 8/46, Report 5.
18 Boyle, *Trenchard,* 389–90.
19 Salmon, 'The Air Force in Iraq', *RUSI,* 70,497.
20 PRO, Adm 116/3190.
21 Atiyah, 152.

22 *Ibid.*, 175.
23 *Ibid.*, 198–9.
24 James, *Golden Warrior*, 232.
25 PRO, WO 32/9614, 22.
26 Wasserstein, 8–12.
27 'Service Problems in Palestine', *RUSI*, 81, 804.
28 PRO, CO 733/315/6, 16; WO 32/9618.
29 PRO, CO 733/315/6, 8; Townshend, 'The Defence of Palestine &c.', *EHR*, 103, 919.
30 PRO, WO 106/1594C.
31 PRO, CO 537/1735, 10.
32 PRO, WO 106/1594C; *Hansard*, 5th Series, 349, 897.
33 Wasserstein, 28.
34 Al-Qazzaz, 'The Iraqi War &c.', *IJMES*, 7, 594.
35 PRO, Air 9/146.
36 Al-Qazzaz, *op. cit.*, 595.
37 Hinsley, 1, 409–10; 574.

5: A New Force and New Power: India, 1919–42

1 Draper, 90–91.
2 PRO, Air 8/46, Report 5, 9.
3 PRO, WO 208/774.
4 Griffiths, 302–3.
5 Norman, I, 118.
6 *The Indian Public School*, viii, 34.
7 Mangan, 179–91.
8 *University of Mysore: The Calendar for the Year 1925–1926*, 87–8.
9 G. Martin, 'The Influence of Racial Attitudes &c.', *JICH*, 14, 106.
10 Jeffery, 3–4.
11 Tinker, 'India and the First World War &c.', *JCont.H*, 3, 89.
12 Gandhi, 15, 130–31, 136, 145, 157.
13 *Ibid.*, 221, 234.
14 *Ibid.*, 185.
15 *Ibid.*, 16, 375.
16 *Hansard.*, 5th Series, 131, 1710.
17 Ash, 268.
18 *Spectator*, 20 December 1919.
19 *Hansard*, 5th Series, 383, 302–5.
20 Gandhi, 76, 50.
21 *Ibid.*, 3.
22 Talbot, 'The Role of the Crowd &c.', *JICH*, 21, 313–14.
23 Rizvi, 25–26, 122.
24 *Ibid.*, 125.
25 *Ibid.*, 131; Prasad, 48.
26 PRO, WO 106/3723, 125.
27 *Constitutional Relations &c.*, 1, 49.
28 PRO, WO 208/819A.
29 Gandhi, 76, 49.
30 *Ibid.*, 49–50.

31 Prasad, 169–70.
32 *Ibid.*, 167.
33 *Congress Responsibility &c.*, 23, 27–28, 32; PRO, WO 106/3721; WO 208/761A.
34 *Hansard*, 5th Series, 383, 295–6.

6: *For the Benefit of Everyone: Concepts of Empire, 1919–39*

1 Pugh, 'Popular Conservatism &c.', *JBS*, 27, 274, 280.
2 *Hansard*, 5th Series, 342, 1226–7.
3 *Listener*, 2 June 1937.
4 *Hansard*, 5th Series, 342, 1243, 1247.
5 *Picture Post*, 29 April and 27 May 1939.
6 *Hansard*, 5th Series, 342, 1247.
7 Philips, 'The New Africa', *Nineteenth Century and After*, 22, 587.
8 Hooper, 41.
9 Hyams, *Empire and Sexuality*, 199.
10 Fraser, *Impressions: Nigeria 1925*, 114.
11 Marston, 'Lands Something New', *National Geographic Magazine*, 71, (January 1937), 125.
12 *Punch*, 3 January 1934.
13 Birley, 'Africa and the Blight of Commercialism', *Nineteenth Century and After*, 87, 1083–4.
14 Osuntokun, 76, 87.
15 *Listener*, 31 May 1933.
16 PRO, CO 537/1224, 6, 4.
17 *Ibid.*
18 *Times*, 14 June 1919.
19 Hyams, *Empire and Sexuality*, 205.
20 G. Martin, 'The Influence of Racial Attitudes &c.', *JICH*, 14, 103.
21 PRO, Air 8/46 Report 5, 9.
22 Birley, 'Africa and the Blight of Commercialism', *Nineteenth Century and After*, 87, 1085.
23 Quoted in *New Statesman*, 2 October 1943.
24 J.M. Winter, 'The Webbs &c.', *JCont.H*, 9, 183–4.
25 Hyams, 'The Political Consequences of Seretse Khama &c.', *HJ*, 29, 927.
26 Knatchbull-Hugessen, 82.

7: *The Bond of One Spirit: The Public Face of Empire, 1919–39*

1 Ross Smith, 136; *Listener*, 28 December 1932.
2 R. McCormack, 'Missed Opportunities &c.', *IHR*, 11, 210.
3 *Ibid.*, 223.
4 R. McCormack, 'Imperial Mission &c.', *JCH*, 9, 95.
5 PRO, CO 874/1097, 67.
6 *Listener*, 20 October 1930.
7 Richards, *The Age of the Dream Palace*, 134, 135.
8 Pronay, 'The Political Censorship of Films &c.', in ed. Pronay and Spring, *Propaganda, Politics and Film*, 106, 137–8.
9 *Ibid.*, 136.
10 *Picture Post*, 8 April 1939.
11 *Hansard*, 5th Series, 342, 1271, 1306–7.

12 R. Smith, 'Britain's African Colonies &c.' *JICH*, 15, 65.
13 *Spectator*, 26 April 1924.
14 Mackenzie, 111.
15 *Times*, 24 December 1934.
16 Ziegler, *Edward VIII*, 113–14.
17 *Ibid.*, 113.
18 *Ibid.*, 137, 139, 191.
19 Storrs, 488.
20 *Spectator*, 10 September 1932.
21 *Sphere*, 28 January 1933.
22 *Spectator*, 27 January 1933.

8: No Good Blustering: The Limits of Imperial Power, 1919–36

1 Hitler, *Mein Kampf*, 563.
2 *Morning Post*, 24 May 1919.
3 Grattan, 'The Future of the British Empire, *Harpers*, 179, 489.
4 PRO, WO 106/3793, 43A, 48A.
5 Hitler, *Table Talk*, 435–6.
6 Ferris, 'The Greatest Power on Earth &c.', *IHR*, 13, 743–4.
7 Gooch, 'Hidden in the Rock &c.', in ed. Freedman, Hayes and Gooch, *War Strategy &c.*, 162–3.
8 Marder, *Old Friends and New Enemies*, 55.
9 PRO, WO 106/106.
10 Barnett, *The Collapse of British Power, passim*.
11 McKercher, 'Our Most Dangerous Enemy &c.', *IHR*, 13, 755.
12 Gooch, 'Hidden in the Rock &c.', *op. cit.*, 155.
13 Thorne, 98–9.
14 Cooper, *Old Men Forget*, 229.
15 *Imperial Commerce and Affairs*, 2 February 1921.
16 Heap, 'The Development of Motor Transport &c.', *JTH*, 2, 31–2.
17 Hargreaves, 93–4.
18 Cadogan, 15.
19 Sales, 'W.H. Hughes and the Chanak Crisis &c.', *AJPH*, 17, 405.
20 Thorne, 4–7.
21 *Ibid.*, 4.
22 Murfett, 'Living in the Past &c.', WS, 11, 80–81.
23 *Ibid.*, 85.
24 Marder, *From Dardanelles to Oran*, 84n.

9: We Shall Come to No Good: The Empire Goes to War, 1937–9

1 Harvey, *Diplomatic Diaries*, 289.
2 Cadogan, 53.
3 *Ibid.*
4 *Morning Post*, 25 May 1936.
5 *The Road to War*, 15.
6 Hasluck, 88–9.
7 Cadogan, 15.
8 J.P. Harris, 'British Military Intelligence &c.', *Intelligence and National Security*, 6, 413–14.

 9 *Documents in British Foreign Policy, 1919–1939,* 2nd Series, 18, 968.
10 PRO, Air 8/529.
11 *Documents in British Foreign Policy, 1919–1939,* 2nd Series, 18, 982.
12 McCarthy, 'Australia and Imperial Defence &c.', *AJPH,* 17,20.
13 *Ibid.,* 24, 29–30; Gillison, 51.
14 *Ibid.,* 71.
15 *Canada Today,* 65–6.
16 Fuchser, 203.
17 *Documents on Australian Foreign Policy,* 1, 430.
18 *Ibid.,* 464.
19 Pickersgill, 12.
20 Cadogan. 92; Roskill, II 442–3; Cooper, *Old Men Forget,* 239.
21 *Spectator,* 30 September 1938.
22 Feiling, 329.
23 *Ibid.,* 297; Cooper, *Old Men Forget,* 239.
24 Cassells, 'Deux empires &c.', *Guerres Mondiales et Conflits Contemporains,* 161, 83–4.
25 See, Hauner, 'One Man Against Empire &c.', *JCont.H,* 16, *passim.*
26 Asante, 129, 173.
27 *Economist,* 15 October 1938.
28 I.E. Hollis, 'Chamberlain's Policy', *Review of Politics,* I (1939); see also Fuchser, 202, 226–8.
29 *Documents on Australian Foreign Policy,* 2, 20–21.
30 Fuchser, 354.
31 Smuts, VI, 181.
32 G. Martin, 'Mackenzie King &c.', *British Journal of Canadian Studies,* 4, *passim.*
33 Hasluck, 85.
34 *Documents on Australian Foreign Policy,* 2, 432.
35 *Ibid.,* 75, 175.
36 *Ibid.,* 83–84, 94, 99, 143, 151.
37 *Ibid.,* 153; Murfett, 'Living in the Past &c.', *WS,* 11, 91.
38 Roskill, II, 437.
39 *Documents on Australian Foreign Policy,* 2, 257.
40 *Ibid.,* 143,
41 Smuts, VI, 190.
42 Rock, 17.
43 Acheson, 10.
44 W.R. Louis, *Imperialism at Bay,* 27.

10: Finest Hour: The Empire at War, 1939–41

 1 *Listener,* 31 October 1940.
 2 Haglund, 'George C. Marshall &c.', *JCont.H,* 15, 746–7.
 3 Moran, 395.
 4 Hyam, 'Churchill and the British Empire', in ed. Blake and Louis, *Churchill,* 175.
 5 E.g. Barnett, *The Audit of War,* and Ponting, *1940: Myth and Reality.*
 6 Haglund, 'George C. Marshall &c.', *JCont.H,* 14, 747–51.
 7 PRO, CO 537/1879, 46.
 8 Harvey, *Wartime Diaries,* 90.
 9 Marder, *From Dardanelles to Oran,* 222–3.

10 *Journal of the Royal African Society,* 41, 21.
11 Ojan, 'Drums and Victory &c.', *Journal of the Royal African Society,* 41, 31.
12 D. Day, 'Anzacs on the Run &c.', *JICH,* 14, 188.
13 *Documents on Australian Foreign Policy,* 5, 10.
14 See D. Day, *Menzies and Churchill at War.*
15 D. Day, 'Anzacs on the Run &c.', *JICH,* 14, 189; Hasluck, 357–8.
16 Thorne, 63.
17 Hasluck, 347.
18 *Ibid.,* 346.
19 Morison, 1, 54–5.
20 *Independent,* 26 January 1993.
21 Ross, *Royal New Zealand Air Force,* 81–2.
22 *Ibid.,* 23.
23 PRO, WO 208/819A.
24 Gillison, I, 143.
25 Aldrich, 'Conspiracy and Confusion &c.', *IJNS,* 7, 340.
26 Hinsley, Thomas, Ransom and Knight, 2 76–7.
27 Morison, 1, 167.
28 Aldrich, 'Conspiracy and Confusion &c.', *IJNS,* 7, 340.
29 Gillison, 1, 220.
30 PRO, CO 968/13/3, 9, 42.
31 *Sunday Times,* 31 January 1993.
32 Thorne, 203.
33 I am indebted to David Elder for this observation.
34 PRO, WO 208/819A.
35 Marder, Jacobson, Horsfield, *Old Friends and New Enemies,* 2, 14.
36 PRO, Air 8/629.
37 Eisenhower, 1, 252.
38 PRO, Air 8/629; *Annual Report for the Gold Coast for the Year 1946,* 113.

11: Steadfast Comrades: The Stresses of War

1 *Documents on Australian Foreign Policy,* 5,559.
2 Eisenhower, 1, 78.
3 Harvey, *Wartime Diaries,* 111.
4 *Listener,* 1 June 1944.
5 Haycock, 'The Myth &c.', *WS,* 2, i, 73.
6 PRO, Air 8/374, 3, 9: Air 8/675, 6, 57.
7 Quinault, 'Churchill, Australia &c.', *WS,* 6, ii, 57.
8 *Hansard,* 5th Series, 377, 98, 621; *Economist,* 7 March 1942.
9 *Economist,* 28 February 1942.
10 *Times,* 23 February 1942.
11 PRO WO 32/1577Z, 16A.
12 *Times,* 27 February 1942.
13 *Hansard,* 5th Series, 377, 198, 550.
14 *Ibid.,* 378, 171.
15 Thorne, 97.
16 Eisenhower, 1, 85, 115.
17 PRO, WO 32/15772, 74A.
18 Furse, 230–31.

19 Storrs, 199.
20 F. Watson, 'India Returned', *Life and Letters,* 49, 12–13.
21 *Times,* 13–14 March 1942.
22 PRO, CO 537/4005, 9.
23 Smuts, 6, 366–7.
24 PRO, WO 208/803; *Constitutional Relations &c.,* 6, 50–51.
25 *Ibid.*
26 PRO, WO 208/804A.
27 PRO, WO 208/761A (Intelligence Report, 31 August 1945).
28 PRO, WO 208/804A.
29 *Constitutional Relations &c.,* 5, 1284–5.
30 PRO, WO 208/803, 105A.
31 *Constitutional Relations &c.,* 5, 1128.
32 PRO, WO 208/803, 82A; WO 208/819A.
33 *Ibid.*
34 PRO, WO 208/804A (Guidance Notes on Psychological Warfare Directed to Indians in Japanese Occupied Territories).
35 PRO, CO 537/3735, 10.
36 *Constitutional Relations &c.,* 6, 50–51, 273, 319.
37 Killingray, 'Ex-Servicemen in the Gold Coast &c.', *JMAS,* 21, 527–8.
38 PRO, CO 537/1224, 6.
39 *Annual Report for the Gold Coast for the Year 1946,* 111.
40 Eisenhower, 1, 208–9; Killingray, 'Ex-Servicemen in the Gold Coast &c.', *JMAS,* 21, 525.
41 A. Palmer, 'Black American Soldiers &c.', *JICH,* 14, 205.
42 Sandler, 'Home Front Battlefield &c.', *WS,* 11, 1,103–5, 110.
43 Thorne, 275.
44 R. Smith, 'Britain's African Colonies &c.', *JICH,* 14, 73–4.
45 *Ibid.,* 78, 81–2.
46 Djan, 'Drums and Victory &c.', *Journal of the Royal African Society,* 41, 31.
47 PRO, CO 874/1097, 67.
48 Ageron, 'Les Populations du Maghreb &c.', *Revue de l'Histoire de la Deuxième Guerre Mondiale,* 114, 31.
49 Perry, 227; PRO, CO 537/1879, 31, 35.
50 PRO, CO 968/3/15, 5.
51 *Ibid.,* 28.
52 *Ibid.,* 8.
53 *Ibid.,* 89, 99.
54 *Ibid.,* 89.
55 *Ibid.,* 5, 50.
56 Pickersgill, 238.
57 Hall, Wagley and Scott, 455.
58 Summerfield, 'Education and Politics &c.', *International Review of Social History,* 26, 144.
59 PRO, WO 32/15772, 74A.
60 *Hansard,* 5th Series, 395, 1903.
61 PRO, WO 208/761A (Fortnightly Security Review, 12 October 1945).
62 *Ibid.*
63 Hanley, 'Resettling the East African', *Army Quarterly,* 52, i, 125–8.
64 Hanley, 'Bantu in Burma', *Spectator,* 19 January 1945.

12: The Defence of Archaic Privilege: The Empire Restored, 1942–5

1 *Hansard,* 5th Series, 430, 337.
2 Thorne, 209, 592–3.
3 *Ibid.,* 593.
4 PRO, CO 968/10/3, 1, 5, 12.
5 Acheson, 133–4; Thorne, 593–4.
6 W.R. Louis, *Imperialism at Bay,* 126.
7 R. Smith, 'Britain's African Colonies &c.', *JICH,* 14, 74, 76.
8 W.R. Louis, *Imperialism at Bay,* 13.
9 Orwell, 58–9.
10 Thorne, 97.
11 Macmillan, 325.
12 Cunard, 'On Colour Bar', *Life and Letters,* 32, 172.
13 *Hansard,* 5th Series, 430, 430, 364.
14 Thorne, 238.
15 *Ibid.,* 149.
16 *Times,* 10 January 1945.
17 *The Old War and New Society,* 21.
18 W.R. Louis, *Imperialism at Bay,* 14.
19 *The British Way and Purpose,* 461.
20 Summerfield, 'Education and Politics &c.', *International Review of Social History,* 26, 137.
21 *The British Way and Purpose,* 495.
22 Moran, 124.
23 Ziegler, *Mountbatten,* 169–70, 221.
24 Thorne, 450.
25 *Ibid.,* 337.
26 Ziegler, *Mountbatten,* 303–4.
27 *World Affairs,* June 1946, 22–4.
28 PRO, WO 203/4460, 8 January 1946.

Part Five: The Setting Sun, 1945–93

1: The Colonialists are on the Rampage: The Empire in the Post-war World

1 Macmillan, 721; Cameron Watt, 'Britain, the United States &c.', in ed. Ovendale, *The Foreign Policy of the British Labour Governments &c.,* 50–53; Leffler, 47.
2 Leffler, 61, 92, 183, 236.
3 James, *Imperial Rearguard,* 135.
4 Orwell, 397.
5 Nkrumah, 57–8.
6 *Hansard,* 5th Series, 395, 1907.
7 PRO, CO 1015/463, Report, November 1951.
8 Fieldhouse, 'The Labour Government and the Empire Commonwealth', in ed. Ovendale, *op. cit.,* 98.
9 Shuckburgh, 32.
10 PRO, CO 537/1288, 18.
11 Hennessey, 262–3.

12 *Ibid.,* 267–9.
13 E.g. Carton de Wiart, 173; Wavell, 130–31; Cadogan, 776.
14 Acheson, 270–71.
15 Leffler, 238.
16 Hennessey, 271–2.
17 Jayal, 'Towards the Baghdad Pact &c.', *Int.HR,* 9, 416.
18 PRO, CO 537/5324, 2, 25.
19 P. Edwards, 'The Australian Commitment &c.', *HS,* 22, 610.
20 Devereaux, 'Britain and the Commonwealth &c.', *JICH,* 24, 340–41; PRO, Air 8/1459, 2–3, 7–8, 28–30.
21 Devereaux, 'Britain and the Commonwealth &c.', *JICH,* 24, 338.
22 PRO, WO 216/724.
23 Devereaux, 'Britain and the Commonwealth &c.', *JICH,* 24, 341.
24 PRO, WO 216/799; Adm 1/27285.
25 Dooley, 'Great Britain's Last Battle &c.', *Int. HR,* 11, 493.
26 *Listener,* 26 January 1950.
27 PRO, CO 537/5120.
28 PRO, CO 537/3333, 12.
29 PRO, CO 537/5120.
30 PRO, CO 822/461, 31, 68.
31 PRO, CO 537/5120.
32 Furedi, 'Creating a Breathing Space &c.', *JICH,* 21, 93, 98–9.
33 PRO, CO 822/461, 29.
34 Castle, 259.
35 PRO, CO 537/7618, 1, 2, 5.
36 PRO, CO 822/461, 29, 94.
37 *Ibid.,* 90; CO 1015/463, Report, February 1953.
38 PRO, CO 537/7542, 1, 7.
39 *Ibid.,* 4.
40 *Listener,* 6 July 1950.
41 Fieldhouse, 'The Labour Government and the Empire Commonwealth', in ed. Ovendale, *The Foreign Policy of the British Labour Governments &c.,* 110–13.
42 PRO, CO 1037/80.
43 Furedi, 'Creating a Breathing Space &c.', *JICH,* 21, 98.
44 Furse, 306.
45 *Country Life,* 12 August 1949.
46 J.P. Barker, 'The Karamojo District &c.', *JAH,* 3, 123–4.
47 NAM, Stockwell Papers, 1, 6–26.
48 IWM, Lydford Papers, Box 6.
49 *Ibid.,* Box 7.
50 PRO, CO 587/7417, 45–6; CO 537/2449, 50; CO 537/2450, 24, 32, 42.
51 *Time,* 7 December 1949.

2: *Friendly Relations: India and the Liquidation of Empire, 1945–7*

1 PRO, CO 1027/317, 27.
2 Nicolson, 24.
3 Thorne, 611.
4 *Ibid.,* 684–5; Ziegler, *Mountbatten,* 323.
5 Moore, 223.

6 Wavell, 437, 439.
7 *Constitutional Relations*, 6, 273.
8 Gandhi, 72, 378.
9 *Ibid.*, 438–9.
10 PRO, WO 32/15772, 74A.
11 *Ibid.*, 104A.
12 *Hansard*, 5th Series, 430, 1581–2.
13 PRO, WO 208/761A.
14 I owe these details to John Hailwood.
15 PRO, 208/761A (Intelligence Summary 25 March 1946).
16 *Ibid.*, (Situation Report 8 March 1946).
17 *Ibid.*, (Intelligence Summary December 1945).
18 *Ibid.*, telegram GHQ to cabinet, 3 April 1946.
19 *Ibid.*, (Intelligence Summary December 1945).
20 *Ibid.*, (Intelligence Report 25 March 1946).
21 *Constitutional Relations*, 6, 1233.
22 *Ibid.*, 7, 926.
23 *Ibid.*, 8, 75.
24 *Times*, 11 July 1947.
25 Hamid, 172.
26 *Ibid.*, 179.
27 Henniker, 'Early Days of Pakistan', *RUSI*, 93, 117.
28 Hamid, 158–9.
29 Ziegler, *Mountbatten*, 418–19, 422.
30 *Times*, 25 August 1947.
31 Henniker, 'Early Days of Pakistan', *RUSI*, 93, 118.
32 Ziegler, *Mountbatten*, 432–3; Hamid, 297.
33 *Ibid.*, 435.
34 *Ibid.*, 297.
35 W. Platt, 'East African Forces &c.', *RUSI*, 93, 410.
36 *Observer*, 8 July 1956.
37 *Ibid.*, 24 June 1956.
38 *Daily Telegraph*, 11 November 1961.
39 *Daily Telegraph*, 10 July 1956.
40 *New Statesman*, 30 June 1956.

3: The World as It Is: Middle Eastern Misadventures, 1945–56

1 Clark and Wheeler, 116, 120; Leffler, 77, 113, 225.
2 Leffler, 238, 286.
3 Leffler, 238.
4 Clark and Wheeler, 124.
5 Hennessey, 262.
6 Clark and Wheeler, 153.
7 Navias, *Nuclear Weapons &c.*, 41–3.
8 PRO, Adm 1/26927.
9 *Constitutional Relations*, 9, 432.
10 W.R. Louis, *The British Empire and the Middle East*, 13.
11 *Time*, 7, and 21 January 1952.
12 McGhee, 342.

13 *Economist,* 30 June 1951.
14 *Ibid.,* 23 June 1951.
15 PRO, Adm 1/27285.
16 *Hansard,* 5th Series, 491, 978.
17 *Ibid.,* 1020.
18 *Ibid.,* 1178.
19 Brands, 'The Cairo-Teheran Connection &c.', *IHR,* 11, 440–1.
20 *Spectator,* 5 October 1951.
21 Shuckburgh, 27.
22 McGhee, 339.
23 Nixon, 134.
24 Leffler, 124–5, 239, 288–9.
25 McGhee, 270.
26 Lawson, 'The Iranian Crisis &c.', *IJMES,* 21, 309–10.
27 Khomeini, 214.
28 Shuckburgh, 105.
29 W.R. Louis, *The British Empire and the Middle East,* 586.
30 McGhee, 371.
31 Leffler, 477.
32 Shuckburgh, 29.
33 PRO, WO 216/799.
34 Mason, 'The Decisive Volley &c.', *JICH,* 19, 50.
35 Heikal, 29–30.
36 Leffler, 484–5; Brands, 'The Cairo-Teheran Connection &c.', *IJMES,* 21, 446.

4: Kick Their Backsides: The Suez War and Beyond

 1 Navias, *Nuclear Weapons and British Strategic Planning,* 42–3, 46.
 2 Shuckburgh, 318–19, 329.
 3 Horne, *Macmillan 1894–1956,* 395.
 4 Shuckburgh, 327, 341.
 5 *Ibid.,* 344.
 6 Dooley, 'Great Britain's Last Battle &c.', *Int.HR,* 11, 490–91.
 7 *Ibid.,* 491; *Times,* 1 January 1987.
 8 Heikal, 187, 191.
 9 Cohen, 'A Still Stranger Aspect &c.', *Int.HR,* 10, *passim.*
10 See page 271.
11 Wright, *Spycatcher,* 84–5.
12 Heikal, 154n., 215n.
13 *Ibid.,* 153 note 3.
14 Pearson, 19–20.
15 Shuckburgh, 163.
16 Shaffy, 'Unconcerned at Dawn &c.', *Intelligence and National Security,* 5, 10–11, 49.
17 *Ibid.,* 30.
18 Dooley, 'Great Britain's Last Battle &c.', *Int.HR,* 11, 493.
19 *Daily Telegraph,* 6 November 1956.
20 *New Statesman,* 15 December 1956.
21 *Hansard,* 5th Series, 559, 1631.
22 Horne, *Macmillan, 1894–1956,* 393.

23 *Hansard*, 5th Series, 559, 1618.
24 *Ibid.*, 1626; *New Statesman*, 17 November 1956.
25 Dooley, 'Great Britain's Last Battle &c.', *Int.HR*, 11, 504–6.
26 PRO, Adm 1/26826.
27 Cohen, 'A Still Stranger Aspect &c.', *Int.HR*, 10, 261.
28 S. Lloyd, *Suez*, 170–94.
29 Shaffy, 'Unconcerned at Dawn &c.', *Intelligence and National Security*, 5, 41, 56.
30 *Time*, 17 November, 1956.
31 *Spectator*, 9 November 1956.
32 *Observer*, 4 and 11 November 1956.
33 PRO, CO 1015/202, 1.

5: The Old Red, White, and Blue: Reactions to a Dying Empire

 1 *Sunday Times Magazine*, 24 February 1963.
 2 Nixon, 134.
 3 PRO, CO 1027/317, 40, 43.
 4 *Daily Telegraph*, 24 August 1956
 5 *Hansard*, 5th Series, 478, 2766.
 6 *Daily Telegraph*, 17 July 1956.
 7 Oliver, 'The Two Miss Perhams &c.', *JICH*, 19, 26.
 8 Navias, 'Terminating National Conscription &c.', *JCont.H*, 24, 202.
 9 *Times*, 2 April 1964.
10 I am indebted to Professor Fred Crawford for these details of the Lawrence-Aldington affair.
11 PRO, CO 1027/177, 1–3, 14–16.
12 *Listener*, 30 October 1969.
13 *Daily Telegraph*, 23 November 1967
14 H. Thomas, *The Establishment*, 10–11, 19.
15 *Ibid.*, 187.
16 *Daily Telegraph*, 5 July 1956.
17 Richards and Aldgate, 158.

6: Uhuru: Tying up Loose Ends, 1959–80

 1 *New Statesman*, 10 May 1963.
 2 *Hansard*, 5th Series (House of Lords), 229, 305, 431.
 3 *New Statesman*, 10 May 1952.
 4 Mboya, 64.
 5 PRO, CO 822/474, 20.
 6 PRO, CO 1015/463 (Report April 1953).
 7 *Southern Rhodesia: Facts and Figures &c.*, 1, 13.
 8 *Listener*, 31 July 1969.
 9 *New Statesman*, 30 January 1956.
10 Darwin, 'The Central African Emergency &c.', *JICH*, 21, 223–4.
11 *Hansard*, 5th Series, 602, 1506.
12 *Ibid.*, 1509–10.
13 Horne, *Macmillan, 1957–1986*, 181.
14 *Hansard*, 5th Series, 610, 237.
15 *Ibid.*, 422–3.

16 *Ibid.*, 426.
17 Horne, *Macmillan, 1957–1986*, 181–2.
18 McCracken, 'Coercion and Control &c.', *JAH*, 27,141.
19 Fisher, *Iain Macleod*, 160, 163.
20 Horne, *Macmillan, 1957–1986*, 187–8.
21 *Ibid.*
22 *Sunday Times Magazine,* 3 June 1962.
23 Caute, 88.
24 *Hansard,* 5th Series, 229, (House of Lords), 401, 409–10.
25 Pimlott, 270.
26 *Listener,* 5 December 1968.
27 Pimlott, 451.
28 Caute, 90.
29 *Sun,* 15 November 1965.

Index

Countries have been indexed under the name by which they were known at the time, with references to alternative names. Page numbers in *italics* refer to the maps.

· *Index·*